The Palestine Yearbook of International Law, Volume 20 (2017)

The Palestine Yearbook of International Law

Editor-in-Chief

Ardi Imseis

Consulting Editor

Anis F. Kassim

Assistant Editors

Reem Al-Botmeh
Ata R. Hindi

Editorial Board

Anis F. Kassim Ardi Imseis
Camille Mansour Mu'ein Barghouthi
Ata R. Hindi Reem Al-Botmeh

Advisory Board

Georges M. Abi-Saab Awn Al-Khasawneh
Ahmed Abouelwafa Mahmoud Mubarak
Abdallah Alashaal Mohammad K. Al-Musa
Badriya Al-Awadhi Anis M. Al-Qasem
Mohammed Bedjaoui Muhammad M. Al-Saleh
Salah Dabbagh Moufid M. Shehab
Riad Daoudi Muhammad Y. Olwan
Nabil Elaraby Muhammad Aziz Shukri

VOLUME 20

The titles published in this series are listed at *brill.com/pyil*

The Palestine Yearbook of International Law, Volume 20 (2017)

Edited by

Ardi Imseis

BRILL
NIJHOFF

LEIDEN | BOSTON

The *Palestine Yearbook of International Law* is published in cooperation with the Birzeit University Institute of Law, under whose auspices it is edited. Established in 1993, the Institute of Law is research based and aims to contribute to the modernization of Palestinian legal structures both at the academic and professional levels.

All e-mail correspondence concerning the Yearbook should be sent to the Editor-in-Chief at: iol.pyil@birzeit.edu. Posted correspondence may be sent to: Attn: *Palestine Yearbook of International Law*, BZU Institute of Law. P.O. Box 14, Birzeit. Palestine. Telecommunication may be directed to the Institute of Law, at: Tel: (972) (2) 298-2009; Fax: (972) (2) 298-2137.

Typeface for the Latin, Greek, and Cyrillic scripts: "Brill". See and download: brill.com/brill-typeface.

ISSN 1386-1972
E-ISSN 2211-6141 (e-book)
ISBN 978-90-04-38652-5 (hardback)

Copyright 2019 by Koninklijke Brill NV, Leiden, The Netherlands.
Koninklijke Brill NV incorporates the imprints Brill, Brill Hes & De Graaf, Brill Nijhoff, Brill Rodopi, Brill Sense, Hotei Publishing, mentis Verlag, Verlag Ferdinand Schöningh and Wilhelm Fink Verlag.
All rights reserved. No part of this publication may be reproduced, translated, stored in a retrieval system, or transmitted in any form or by any means, electronic, mechanical, photocopying, recording or otherwise, without prior written permission from the publisher.
Authorization to photocopy items for internal or personal use is granted by Koninklijke Brill NV provided that the appropriate fees are paid directly to The Copyright Clearance Center, 222 Rosewood Drive, Suite 910, Danvers, MA 01923, USA. Fees are subject to change.

This book is printed on acid-free paper and produced in a sustainable manner.

Contents

PART 1
Articles

Palestinian Refugees in South East Asia: New Frontiers of a 70-year Exile   3
   Francesca Albanese

Continuing or Settled? Prosecution of Israeli Settlements under
Article 8(2)(b)(viii) of the Rome Statute   33
   Uzay Yasar Aysev

Whither the Principle of Self-determination in the Post-colonial Era? Building
the Case for a Policy-oriented Approach   84
   Daniele Amoroso

Procedural Haze: The ICC's Jurisdiction over the Situation in Palestine   117
   Yassir Al-Khudayri

Re-centering Justice as the End Goal of Our Struggle   148
   George Bisharat

The Tragic Interplay of International Law and Geopolitics   153
   Richard Falk

Settler-colonial and Anti-colonial Legalities in Palestine   171
   Markus Gunneflo

PART 2
Book Review

Book Review: On Self-Determination, Statehood, and the Law of Negotiation:
The Case of Palestine by Robert P. Barnidge, Jr.   191
   Diana Buttu

PART 3
Materials

SECTION A
United Nations Documents

Falk & Tilley (ECSWA), Israel Practices towards the Palestinian People and the Question of Apartheid   201

Report of the Special Rapporteur on the Situation of Human Rights in the Palestinian Territories Occupied Since 1967 (Oct. 23, 2017)   264

Report of the Special Rapporteur on the Situation of Human Rights in the Palestinian Territories Occupied Since 1967 (Apr. 13, 2017)   294

SECTION B
United Nations Resolutions

Draft United Nations Security Council Resolution S/2017/1060 (Dec. 17, 2017)   325

United Nations General Assembly Resolution A/RES/ES-10/19 (Dec. 21, 2017)   327

United Nations General Assembly Resolution A/RES/72/11 (Dec. 5, 2017)   329

United Nations General Assembly Resolution A/RES/72/12 (Dec. 6, 2017)   331

United Nations General Assembly Resolution A/RES/72/13 (Dec. 6, 2017)   334

United Nations General Assembly Resolution A/RES/72/14 (Dec. 7, 2017)   339

United Nations General Assembly Resolution A/RES/72/15 (Dec. 7, 2017)   352

United Nations General Assembly Resolution A/RES/72/80 (Dec. 14, 2017)   355

United Nations General Assembly Resolution A/RES/72/81
(Dec. 14, 2017)   358

United Nations General Assembly Resolution A/RES/72/82
(Dec. 14, 2017)   360

United Nations General Assembly Resolution A/RES/72/83
(Dec. 14, 2017)   373

United Nations General Assembly Resolution A/RES/72/84
(Dec. 14, 2017)   375

United Nations General Assembly Resolution A/RES/72/85
(Dec. 14, 2017)   381

United Nations General Assembly Resolution A/RES/72/86
(Dec. 14, 2017)   384

United Nations General Assembly Resolution A/RES/72/87
(Dec. 14, 2017)   391

United Nations General Assembly Resolution A/RES/72/134
(Jan. 15, 2018)   401

United Nations General Assembly Resolution A/RES/72/160
(Jan. 23, 2018)   408

United Nations General Assembly Resolution A/RES/72/240
(Jan. 18, 2018)   410

United Nations Human Rights Council Resolution A/HRC/RES/34/28
(Apr. 11, 2017)   416

United Nations Human Rights Council Resolution A/HRC/RES/34/29
(Apr. 12, 2017)   421

United Nations Human Rights Council Resolution A/HRC/RES/34/30
(Apr. 11, 2017)   425

United Nations Human Rights Council Resolution A/HRC/RES/34/31 (Apr. 3, 2017)   437

SECTION C
Cases

Amicus Curaie, Submitted by Susan Akram (Redacted) (Sweden) (Jan. 20, 2017)   451

Council v Hamas, Judgement of the Court (Grand Chamber) (European Union) (July 26, 2017)   489

SECTION D
Legislation

Law for the Regularization of Settlement in Judea and Samaria, 5777–2017 (Israel)   507

SECTION E
Other

Statement Issued by the Central Council of the Palestine Liberation Organization (PLO)   517

Statement by (United States) President Trump on Jerusalem   523

Index   527

PART 1

Articles

∴

Palestinian Refugees in South East Asia: New Frontiers of a 70-year Exile

Francesca Albanese*

Preliminary Findings and Observations from On-going Research[1]

    Overview 4
I   Who are the Palestinian Refugees? 5
    A *Genesis of the Palestinian Refugee Question, at a Glance* 5
    B *Ad hoc Semantic, Legal and Institutional Regimes* 7
    C *Multiple Counts of Displacement* 13
II   Palestinian Refugees in South East Asia: A New Phenomenon 15
    A *Safe Haven Without Legal Protection Framework?* 16
        1   Indonesia 21
        2   Malaysia 23
        3   Thailand 25
III Preliminary Observations on the Inflow of Palestinian Refugees in South East Asia 26
IV Conclusions 31

---

* Francesca Albanese is an international lawyer and the author, with Lex Takkenberg, of *The Status of Palestinian Refugees in International Law: A Tale of Fragmentation and Opportunity* (Oxford University Press, forthcoming). Francesca has worked 15 years in the field of human rights and humanitarian affairs, mostly with the United Nations, including the UN Office of the High Commissioner for Human Rights and the UN Agency for Work and Relief to Palestine Refugees in the Near East. She is an Affiliate Researcher at the Institute for the Study of International Migration, Georgetown University and Visiting Scholar at the Issam Fares Institute, American University of Beirut. She holds an LL.M in Human Rights from the School of Oriental and African Studies, University of London.

1 This study is the revisited version of a paper presented at the Middle East Institute, National University of Singapore in March 2017. It is based on ongoing research for one of the chapters of the forthcoming new edition of: L. Takkenberg, The Status of Palestinian Refugees in International Law (1st ed., 1998) [*hereinafter* Takkenberg]. The chapter, titled "Status and treatment of Palestinian refugees around the world", discusses the legal

Overview

After seventy years, the majority of the refugees from the violence that took place in Palestine around 1948 (around the time when the Israel was created) and their descendants, reside in the Middle East. Over time, a number of them have moved further afield, primarily to Europe and North America, fleeing persecution, discrimination, poverty and further instability in the region. In recent years, and presumably owing to increasingly restrictive asylum policies in Europe and the United States (US), Palestinians (often already refugees) have resolved to seek protection in Asia. Available data shows that between 2011–2013, unprecedented numbers of Palestinians were found in Indonesia, Malaysia and Thailand, with smaller numbers in Korea, Pakistan and Sri Lanka.[2]

Despite the general lack of asylum frameworks in the region, some South East Asian countries have relatively favorable visa policies and/or de-facto allow asylum-seekers to remain in the country temporarily pending durable solutions, which may attract asylum-seekers and refugees to travel there either as temporary or permanent destinations. For example, in Indonesia, refugees are allowed to remain in the country on a temporary basis pending refugee status determination and durable solutions. Geographical proximity to Australia may also be a factor affecting individual decisions to travel to South East Asian countries, which are often treated as transit stops and part of an onward journey.

Overall, the South East Asian region presents both protection opportunities and challenges for Palestinian refugees. Given the scant literature and limited data available on the topic, these remain largely unexplored. This paper attempts to fill this gap by exploring the legal status and general treatment (e.g. enjoyment of basic rights) afforded to Palestinian refugees in South East Asia. It also offers some critical reflections in a field of research which is as new as the routes that Palestinian refugees are currently exploring in search of safe haven after 70 years in exile.

---

status and treatment of Palestinian refugees in various regions, including in the Asia Pacific and South East Asia. The author is grateful to Elisa Mosler, for her help on researching the status and treatment of Palestinian refugees in over 40 countries, to Rania Muhareb, Victor Kattan, Ardi Imseis and Lex Takkenberg for useful comments, and to the UNHCR Headquarters, regional and country offices in South East Asia for their thorough review and inputs. The views expressed in the paper are the author's only.

2   The data for this study was gathered by the author as part of her current research on Palestinian refugees. Primary research took place in the form of questionnaires (referred to in the paper as "SPRIL questionnaire") to gather country-specific information, as well as a review of key secondary sources on Palestinian refugees (UN reports and statistics), and publications and data from domestic sources (immigration agencies, academic research) whenever available.

The paper is divided into four sections. The first offers some background on Palestinian refugees and the extent to which they can be 'differentiated' from other refugee groups. The second discusses the available data on Palestinian refugees in South East Asia, particularly Indonesia, Malaysia and Thailand, where sizable numbers are reported and relatively reliable information exists.[3] The third section discusses some preliminary observations on current protection and legal status needs and priorities for these refugees. Finally, the fourth section offers some conclusions on the situation described in the paper.

I   Who are the Palestinian Refugees?

A   *Genesis of the Palestinian Refugee Question, at a Glance*

The Palestinian refugee question lies at the heart of the Israeli-Palestinian conflict.[4] Palestinian refugees[5] are those who were expelled or fled in connection with the events which culminated with the 1947–1949 war over (British

---

3   *Id.*
4   The Israeli-Palestinian conflict dates back to the late 19th century. At that time, the territory called 'Palestine' was inhabited by a majority of Arabs and a minority of Jews, with the two communities reportedly living in harmony. As consistent waves of Jewish immigrants started to move to Palestine from Europe in the 1880s (first to escape the pogroms in Russia and then, progressively, to settle in Palestine as part of the Zionist project), resentment among the Arab majority started to grow. During the British Mandate over Palestine after World War I, tensions among the Arab and the Jewish communities started simmering. The British took control of Palestine from the Ottoman Empire towards the end of World War I in 1917–1918, with the self-proclaimed task of administratively accompanying the Arab inhabitants toward independence (commitment that was further sanctioned by the Mandate over Palestine that the League of Nations conferred upon Britain in 1920). At the same time, rising anti-Semitism in the West had given impetus to the Zionist cause and had increased the flows of Jewish migration to Palestine. These processes pressured the British to officially commit to establishing a "national home for the Jewish people" in Palestine through the Balfour Declaration (1917), which shaped British policy over Palestine over the following three decades and irreversibly changed the fate of Palestine and its Arab inhabitants. For a more complete overview of the origins of the Israeli-Palestinian conflict and the Palestinian refugee problem, *see*: Ilan Pappé, A History of Modern Palestine, One Land, Two Peoples (2nd ed., 2006); Ilan Pappé, The Making of the Arab-Israeli Conflict (2015); Tom Segev & Arlen Weinstein, 1949: The First Israelis (1998); T. Segev, One Palestine, Complete: Jews and Arabs under the Palestine Mandate (2001); Victor Kattan, From Coexistence to Conquest, International Law and the Origins of the Arab – Israeli Conflict, 1891–1949 (2009), Benny Morris, The Birth of the Palestinian Refugee Problem, 1947–1949 (1987) [*hereinafter* Morris]; Benny Morris, Righteous Victims: A History of the Zionist-Arab Conflict, 1881–1999 (1999); Simha Flapan, The Birth of Israel: Myths and Realities (1987).
5   A clear, encompassing definition of 'Palestinian refugee' does not exist. For a discussion around definitions of Palestinian refugees, *see* below.

Mandate) Palestine and the creation of the State of Israel in 1948.[6] As a consequence of the terror spread by Jewish paramilitary groups operations and the war,[7] roughly 750,000 Arab inhabitants of historic Palestine (hereinafter Palestinians) lost their homes and livelihoods in the country that became Israel.[8] In the aftermath of the war, the Israeli Government enacted legisla-

---

6 In November 1947, the UN General Assembly voted in favor of partitioning Palestine in roughly equal parts between an Arab state that would have accommodated the majority of the 1.3 million Arabs (owners of 46 per cent of the land) and a Jewish state, which would have accommodated almost the entirety of the 650,000 Jews (owners of between 6 and 8 per cent of the land). This was considered by the Arabs as a betrayal of the legal and moral obligation towards their full independence. The Partition Plan accelerated the British withdrawal from Mandatory Palestine, which was completed at the time of the creation of the State of Israel.

7 These groups were the Haganah, Irgun and Lehi. The Haganah, which would become the central block of the Israel military forces in 1948, prepared a number of military plans to take control of the territory of Mandate Palestine at the withdrawal of the British troops. *Plan Dalet* (also known as 'Plan D'), devised in December 1947 and adopted in March 1948, was the fourth and most resolute of these documents. It constituted a set of guidelines to take control of Mandatory Palestine, create a Jewish State and defend its borders and people, including the Jewish population outside of the borders, "before, and in anticipation of" the invasion by regular Arab armies. Plan Dalet acted as the call for the conquest of Arab towns and villages inside and along the borders of the area allocated to the proposed Jewish State by the UN Partition Plan. In case of resistance, the population of conquered villages was to be expelled outside the borders of the Jewish state. In principle, if no resistance was met, the residents could stay put, under military rule. Yet, according to Pappé, confrontations with and resistance by local Palestinian militias provided the perfect context to unleash Plan Dalet; *see* Ilan Pappe, The Ethnic Cleansing of Palestine 43 (2007). The full text of Plan Dalet, is available online at: http://www.mideastweb.org/pland.htm. The equation of Plan Dalet to a "political blueprint" for the expulsion of the Palestine Arabs is found in Walid Khalidi, *Plan Dalet: Master Plan for the Conquest of Palestine*, 18 J. Palestine Stud. 4 (1988).

8 This event is inscribed in Palestinian memory as 'al-Nakba' ('the catastrophe' in Arabic). Prior to the declaration of the State of Israel in May 1948, between 200,000 and 300,000 Arabs had already fled the main cities on the Palestine costal area, as well as fertile rural areas across the country, to safer neighboring Arab states (Syria, Jordan, Egypt, and Lebanon). Military operations further intensified after the creation of the State of Israel and the war that Lebanon, Syria, Egypt, and Jordan declared against the new-born State of Israel in opposition to the UN Partition Plan. The war lasted until March 1949 and was concluded with a truce that allowed Israel to retain control over an area considerably larger than that initially designated through the UN Partition Plan. On the ground, the military operations carried out during the war did not spare any remaining Arab villages inside the State of Israel, and included the use of force against civilian populations. By January 1950, over 400 Arab villages had been depopulated and destroyed. Only 150,000 of the close to one million pre-1948 Arab population remained in what became Israel. Many of these were internally displaced and lived under Israeli military rule until 1966. For an account about the destruction and depopulation of Palestinian inhabited areas and villages in 1948, *see*: All That Remains, The Palestinian Villages occupied and depopulated by Israel in 1948 (Walid Khalidi, ed., 1992)

tion to prevent the return of the displaced Arab population,[9] confiscated their assets and property,[10] and razed the majority of their villages.[11]

Despite the practical difficulties with ascertaining accurate numbers of Palestinian refugees,[12] the majority of them, including 5.3 million 'Palestine refugees' registered with the United Nations (UN) Relief and Work Agency for Palestine Refugees in the Near East (UNRWA)[13] still reside in the territories or countries in which they took refuge in the aftermath of the 1947–1949 events. These include the residual territory of former Mandate Palestine which Israel did not take control of in 1948 – *i.e.* the Gaza Strip (1.3 million) and the West Bank (800,000) – Jordan (2 million), Lebanon (400,000)[14] and Syria (438,000).[15] Finally, small numbers of refugees fled to Egypt, Iraq, Kuwait, Libya, and Saudi Arabia.[16]

B *Ad hoc Semantic, Legal and Institutional Regimes*

There is no one encompassing definition of 'Palestinian refugee'. The most common one is that of 'Palestine refugees' – developed by UNRWA – which

---

[hereinafter Khalidi]; Morris. Khalidi and Morris list between 369 and 418 villages depopulated and destroyed in 1948.

9   After enacting a Law of Return in 1950, which encouraged the immigration of Jews from all over the world to the State of Israel, Israel also approved the Nationality Law in 1952 which barred the Arabs of former Palestine to return to the land.

10 Sabri Jiryis, *The legal structure for the expropriation and absorption of Arab lands in Israel*, 2 J. Palestine Stud. 82 (1973).

11 *See, generally*, Khalidi; Morris.

12 The *Special Statistical Bulletin on the 67th Anniversary of the Palestinian Nakba* of the Palestinian Central Bureau of Statistics (2015) indicates that there are about 12 million Palestinians mostly in the diaspora. Among those, BADIL, the Resource Center for Palestinian Residency & Refugee Rights, estimates that there are: 7.98 million Palestinian refugees at the end of 2014, including over 5 million registered with UNRWA, 1 million non-registered 1948 refugees, one million 1967 refugees (or 1967 displaced persons) and an unknown number of refugees who are neither 1948 nor 1967 refugees – primarily displaced outside of the West Bank, East Jerusalem and the Gaza Strip since 1967. About 7 percent of the displaced Palestinians (approximately 530,000) are internally displaced within Israel and the oPt. See BADIL, *Closing the Protection Gap, Handbook on Protection of Palestinian Refugees in States Signatories to the 1951 Convention*, BADIL (2nd ed., 2015), at 7.

13 This includes 1948 refugees and their descendants; *see* UNRWA, https://www.unrwa.org/where-we-work.

14 In fact, only 250,000 are reported to still reside in the country.

15 UNRWA, *Syria: UNRWA – Palestine Refugees Demographics Verification Exercise 2016* (June 12, 2017), https://www.unrwa.org/resources/reports/syria-unrwa-palestine-refugees-demographics-verification-exercise-2016. The prewar population numbered Palestinian refugees around 540,000.

16 Further discussed below.

refers to "persons whose normal place of residence was Palestine during the period 1 June 1946 to 15 May 1948, and who lost both home and means of livelihood as a result of the 1948 conflict."[17] UNRWA's definition, initially developed to determine eligibility criteria (*i.e.* who among the 1948 displaced persons deserved to receive UN assistance) rather than determining a legal status,[18] has been officially endorsed by the UN General Assembly (UNGA).[19] Nonetheless, this definition cannot be considered inclusive of all Palestinian refugees.[20] The lack of a universal definition of Palestinian refugee does not equate to lack of legal status under international law.[21]

17 This definition is included in the Consolidated Eligibility and Registration Criteria (CERI) adopted by UNRWA (last revision in 2009); available at: http://www.refworld.org/docid/520cc3634.html. The CERI are part of the regulatory framework of UNRWA and are developed as part of its institutional law. The definition is part of the corpus of international law concerning Palestinian refugees. The definition is also incorporated in the UNHCR Revised Note on the Applicability of Article 1D of the 1951 Convention relating to the Status of Refugees to Palestinian Refugees, available at http://www.refworld.org/docid/4add77d42.html. Note the focus on Palestine refugee vs. Palestinian refugee; *see* UNRWA, *Who are Palestinian Refugees?*, https://www.unrwa.org/palestine-refugees.
18 The development of UNRWA definition is developed in detail in: Lex Takkenberg, The Status of Palestinian Refugees in International Law 70–76 (1998).
19 Lance Bartholomeusz, *The Mandate of UNRWA at Sixty*, 28 REFUGEE SURV. Q. 452, 457 (2010). The UN General Assembly has tacitly approved it in the annual reports presented by UNRWA since the 1950s.
20 While the majority of the global Palestinian refugee population (5.3 millions) is registered as 'Palestine refugees' with UNRWA (*see*: https://www.unrwa.org/where-we-work), the rest includes non-registered refugees from 1948 (around 1 million), '1967 displaced', namely those displaced by the 1967 Arab-Israeli conflict (around 1 million) and other refugees displaced as a result of subsequent conflicts. The latter data is in BADIL, *Closing Protection Gaps: Handbook on Protection of Palestinian Refugees* (2nd ed., 2015), at 13–16. The term 'Palestinian refugees' also includes persons of Palestinian origin who were not displaced in 1948 but were subsequently displaced and recognized as refugees under the 1951 Refugee Convention (Article 1A[2] on account of a well-founded fear of persecution for one of the five Convention grounds). They fall under the mandate of the United Nations High Commissioner for Refugee (UNHCR), as do the other (above mentioned) categories when they have fled from and are unable to return to UNRWA's area of operations (Jordan, Lebanon, Syria, the Gaza Strip and West Bank). One significant anomaly of UNRWA definition is that it entitles registration of descendants through patrilineal line, inhibiting children born from refugee mothers to be registered like any other refugees. *See* Christine M. Cervenak, *Promoting inequality: Gender-based discrimination in UNRWA's approach to Palestine refugee status*, 16 Hum. Rts. Q. 300 (1994).
21 Guy Goodwin-Gill and Susan Akram, *Amicus Brief*, XI Palestine Y.B. Int'l L. 190 (1999–2000) [*hereinafter* Goodwin-Gill & Akram]:"Their status and the extent of the protections to which they are afforded are determined by the interrelationship of Article 1D of the 1951 Refugee Convention; Paragraph 7 of the Statute of the United Nations High Commissioner for Refugees (UNHCR Statute); and the refugee definition utilized by

Since 1948, the legal status and treatment afforded to Palestinian refugees has seen significant discrepancies and various changes depending on where they fled to, and, as this section will discuss, the UN agency under whose mandate they fall. In many respects, Palestinian refugees are 'a unique people' under the very international refugee regime established by the 1951 Convention Relating to the Status of Refugees ('1951 Refugee Convention') and the mandate of the Office of the UN High Commissioner for Refugees (UNHCR).[22] In December 1948, in the aftermath of the Palestine refugee crisis (and three years before the adoption of 1951 Convention and its refugee definition as included in Article 1A[2] of the Convention were adopted), the UNGA had already attempted to resolve the Palestine refugee situation by passing UNGA Resolution 194. The resolution stipulated that "the refugees wishing to return to their homes and live at peace with their neighbours should be permitted to do so at the earliest practicable date, and that compensation should be paid for the property of those choosing not to return and for loss of or damage to property [...]".[23] Without defining who is a Palestinian refugee, the resolution also stipulated that a UN Conciliation Commission for Palestine (UNCCP), would inter alia facilitate "the repatriation, resettlement and economic and social rehabilitation of the refugees and the payment of compensation".[24] The UNCCP, however, has not been able to find durable solutions for the Palestinian refugees and from the late 1960s' continues to be nothing more than a symbolic landmark in the Palestinians' quest for justice.[25] Meanwhile, in the countries and territories where they sought refuge in large numbers – namely the Gaza Strip (and later the West Bank), Jordan, Lebanon, and Syria – Palestinian refugees have been provided with varying levels of legal status and solutions

---

      the United Nations Relief and Works Agency for Palestinian Refugees in the Near East (UNRWA Statute)."

22   *Id.*, 185.

23   G.A. Res. 194 [III], *Palestine – Progress Report of the United Nations Mediator*, U.N. Doc. A/RES/194 (III) (Dec. 11), para. 11 [emphasis added].

24   *Id.*

25   After various attempts (and failure) to bring the conflicting parties together and to find a common ground to resolve the conflict, the UNCCP has made no more substantial contributions towards the implementation of paragraph 11 of Resolution 194. The agency has since 1951, issued annual reports to the UNGA expressing its hope that "the situation and related circumstances in the region will improve towards the achievement of a comprehensive, just, and lasting peace in the Middle East, thus enabling it to carry forward its work in accordance with its Mandate as defined by the UNGA in its resolution 194 (III)". *See, e.g.*, G.A. Res. 46/46, U.N. Doc. A/RES/46/46 (Dec. 9, 1991). On the relevance of reconfirmation of resolutions, *see* Samuel A. Bleicher, *The Legal Significance of Re-citation of General Assembly Resolutions*, 63 Am. J. Int'l L. 444 (1969).

depending, *inter alia*, on the respective national institutions and domestic legal framework, and influenced by local political climates. With the exception of Jordan, which granted citizenship to Palestinian refugees, the other countries admitted the refugees only on a temporary basis, pending their return to their homeland.[26] Many Arab countries receiving Palestinian refugees afforded them temporary protection under the League of Arab States' brokered Casablanca Protocol.[27] This was, however, unevenly applied, frequently leaving Palestinian refugees in a legal limbo, exposed to discrimination and lack of legal avenues for redress. One common and unifying factor became the assistance and relief services provided by what was then intended to be a temporary agency, but which still serves Palestinian refugees today – UNRWA. In 1949, UNRWA was created, with an initial mandate of 3 years, to provide immediate assistance and relief to the refugees of Palestine, while a political solution was negotiated under UNCCP's auspices.[28] Due to the lack of a durable solution, UNRWA has continued to serve Palestine refugees on a 3-year-renewable mandate for the past sixty nine years.[29] Because Palestinian refugees in Jordan, Lebanon, Syria, the Gaza Strip and the West Bank come under the mandate of

---

26   Palestinian refugees in Jordan have varying legal statuses, from Jordanian citizens possessing a national number, to stateless ex-Gazans (approximately numbering 75,000). This is mainly due to when the Palestinians arrived in Jordan and from where, as well as the changing political conditions. Jordanian Law No. 6 of 1954 officially ensured that Palestinians with Jordanian citizenship were equal under the law, with full rights. However, the vulnerability of Palestinian Jordanian as citizens has been exposed. *See* Anis *Kassim, The Palestinian: From Hyphenated Citizen to Integrated Citizen*, 3 Y.B. Islamic & Middle Eastern L. 69 (1996), Abbas; Terry Rempel, *Rights in Principle – Rights in Practice: Revisiting the Role of International Law in Crafting Durable Solutions for Palestinian Refugees*, BADIL (Dec. 2009), at 224; Hazem Jamjoum, "Palestinian Refugees in Jordan and the Revocation of Citizenship: An Interview with Anis F. Kassim," Jadaliyya (Jan. 28, 2013), http://www.jadaliyya.com/pages/index/9827/palestinian-refugees-in-jordan-and-the-revocation.

27   From the early 1950s onwards, the Arab League adopted a series of resolutions and (non-binding) regional standards on the status and treatment of Palestinian refugees and Palestinians generally. This included the 1965 Protocol on the Treatment of Palestinian Refugees, known as the Casablanca Protocol, to regularize Palestinian in states where they fled after 1948 and afford them some rights, including the right to work, aiming to give Palestinians residency in neighboring states at the same time maintaining their refugee status. *See* Takkenberg, 141–149.

28   The Agency's mandate entailed providing "direct relief and works programmes" to refugees in order to "prevent conditions of starvation and distress among [the refugees] and to further conditions of peace and stability." *See* G.A. Res. 302 (IV), UN Doc. A/RES/302 (IV) (Dec. 8, 1949).

29   UNRWA, Frequently Asked Questions, http://www.unrwa.org/who-we-are/frequently-asked-questions. UNRWA's mandate was most recently renewed until June 2017 in: G.A. Res. 68/76, *Assistance to Palestine refugees*, A/RES/68/76 (Dec. 16, 2013).

UNRWA, they do not automatically fall under the scope of the 1951 Refugee Convention and the mandate of UNHCR. Palestinian refugees are the only group of refugees to whom a specific and separate analysis applies to determine their status under the 1951 Refugee Convention.[30] Because of this unique situation, among others, it is frequently argued that Palestinian refugees are victims of a 'protection gap', *i.e.* they are to various extents *excluded* from the protection regime available to other refugees.[31] While a comprehensive discussion on the protection gap and Article 1D is beyond the scope of this paper, a few considerations are worth sharing.

Article 1D of the 1951 Refugee Convention[32] specifically excludes persons who are *""receiving" from a UN organ or Agency other than UNHCR "protection and assistance"".*[33] This refers to Palestinian refugees who, at the time the 1951 Refugee Convention was drafted, were already served by two parallel UN agencies: UNCCP and UNRWA. However, it goes on to state that if "such protection or assistance has ceased for any reason, without the position of such persons being definitively settled in accordance with the relevant resolutions adopted by the General Assembly of the United Nations, these persons shall *ipso facto*

---

30 According to Article 1A(2) of the 1951 Refugee Convention, "[a] refugee is a person who, owing to a well-founded fear of being persecuted for reasons of race, religion, nationality, membership of a particular social group or political opinion, is outside the country of his nationality and is unable or, owing to such fear, unwilling to avail himself of the protection of that country".

31 "The collapse of UNCCP protection, limited intervention by UNHCR, non-implementation of recommendations of key UN human rights bodies, and inadequate protection by national authorities has resulted in severe gaps in international protection for Palestinian refugees and displaced persons'. BADIL, *Closing the Protection Gap Handbook* (1st ed., 2009) [*hereinafter* BADIL], http://www.badil.org/phocadownload/Badil_docs/publications/Handbook.pdf.

32 For a debate around the meaning of article 1D, *see* Takkenberg; Goodwin-Gill & Akram; Mutaz Qafisheh and Valentina Azarov, *Article 1 D.*, in The 1951 Convention Relating to the Status of Refugees and its 1967 Protocol: A commentary 537 (Andreas Zimmermann, ed., 2011). *Last but not least, see* BADIL. Most notably, UNHCR has issued notes on the interpretation and applicability of Article 1D in 2002, 2009 and 2013; *see Note on UNHCR's Interpretation of Article 1D of the 1951 Convention relating to the Status of Refugees and Article 12(1)(a) of the EU Qualification Directive in the context of Palestinian refugees seeking international protection* (May 2013), http://www.refworld.org/docid/518cb8c84.html.

33 *Convention Relating to the Status of Refugees* art. 1D (July 28, 1951),189 U.N.T.S. 137 [*hereinafter* 1951 Refugee Convention] [emphasis added]. This first sentence is commonly referred to as an exclusion clause. Similarly, UNHCR Statute, paragraph 7, states that "the competence of the High Commissioner [...] shall not extend to a person: [...] [w]ho continues to receive from other organs or agencies of the United Nations protection or assistance". *See also* G.A. Res. 428(V), *Statute of the Office of the United Nations High Commissioner for Refugees,* U.N. GAOR 5th Sess., U.N. Doc. A/1775 (1950).

be entitled to the benefits of this Convention".³⁴ The 1951 Convention afforded Palestinian refugees a distinctive institutional framework to other refugees; one made of alternative protection schemes, which *exclude* Palestinian refugees from the benefits of the 1951 Convention and UNHCR's scope of work when they fall under UNRWA's mandate and *includes* them when UNRWA's protection or assistance has ceased.³⁵ The exclusion from the general regime was meant to be conditional and temporary – the alternative protection system (*i.e.* UNHCR) would apply when Palestinian refugees were no longer receiving assistance or protection from UNRWA (and the today de facto defunct) UNCCP.³⁶ In line with UNHCR's current interpretation, Article 1D serves a dual purpose of avoiding the duplication of assistance and protection between UNRWA and UNHCR and ensuring "continuity of protection" of Palestinian refugees "whose refugee character has already been established and recognized by various [UNGA] resolutions, in circumstances where that protection or assistance has ceased in accordance with the "inclusion clause" contained in the second paragraph of Article 1D".³⁷

While the applicability of the 1951 Refugee Convention to Palestinian refugees is nowadays confirmed by UNHCR (see above), as well as the jurisprudence of the Court of Justice of the European Union (CJEU),³⁸ some States

---

34   1951 Refugee Convention. This second sentence is commonly referred to as an inclusion clause.
35   The complexity of UNRWA's mandate cessation is beyond the scope of this paper.
36   *Note on UNHCR's Interpretation of Article 1D of the 1951 Convention relating to the Status of Refugees and Article 12(1)(a) of the EU Qualification Directive in the context of Palestinian refugees seeking international protection* (May 2013), http://www.refworld.org/docid/518cb8c84.html [*hereinafter* UNHCR Note (2013)]. UNHCR interprets that the distribution of competence between UNRWA and UNHCR follows the areas of operation: UNRWA is responsible for 'Palestine refugees' insides its areas of operations and UNHCR is responsible for them outside UNRWA areas of operation. On the intended continuity of protection, *see* Goodwin-Gill & Akram, 185: "Taking into account the plain language, drafting history, actual historical context and appropriate canons of treaty construction, the actual intent of the interrelated provisions governing the legal status of Palestinian refugees was to provide them with greater protection than that afforded all other refugees in the world, rather than the least protection which they receive under the current regime".
37   *See* UNHCR Note (2013), section 1. On the intended continuity of protection, *see* Goodwin-Gill & Akram, 185: "Taking into account the plain language, drafting history, actual historical context and appropriate canons of treaty construction, the actual intent of the interrelated provisions governing the legal status of Palestinian refugees was to provide them with greater protection than that afforded all other refugees in the world, rather than the least protection which they receive under the current regime."
38   C-31/09, Bolbol v. Bevándorlási és Állampolgársági Hivatal, 2010 E.C.R. L-2925, http://www.refworld.org/docid/4c1f62d42.html. C-364/11, Mostafa Abed El Karem El Kott

still fail to fully comply with article 1D.[39] Influential scholarship has indicated this as a factor which might hamper the enjoyment of the rights Palestinian refugees are entitled to as internationally recognised refugees.[40] The denial of protection can in itself be seen as a marginalizing factor that can cause further displacement. This point is salient in light of the increasing (often forcible) flight of Palestinian refugees including towards new regions in which UNRWA does not operate.

C Multiple Counts of Displacement

In the absence of a resolution of the Israeli-Palestinian conflict, the Palestinian refugee question has remained unresolved. Accordingly, further rounds of displacement have affected Palestinian refugees over time. Far from being an exceptional state of affairs, displacement has become the natural condition for the majority of Palestinians.[41] Not only are they not allowed to return to their land despite their willingness to do so, but during the 70 years of exile, instability and conflict in regions and countries in which they had settled have caused further onward movement and a general worsening of their situation. For example:

- In 1967, between 200,000 and 350,000 Palestinians – including 175,000 registered refugees who had found refuge in the West Bank – fled the West Bank and Gaza Strip[42] as a consequence of the Six Day War between Israel and

---

and Others v. Bevándorlási és Állampolgársági Hivatal, 2012 E.C.R. I-5539, http://www.refworld.org/docid/50d2d7b42.html.

39   In recent years, BADIL has carried out a monumental research on the State practice application of article 1D; see BADIL.

40   Goodwin-Gill & Akram, 185: "[a]lmost all states and international entities have interpreted the relevant provisions in these instruments as severely restricting the rights of Palestinian refugees *qua* refugees in comparison to the rights guaranteed every other refugee group in the world. As a result, Palestinian refugees have been treated as ineligible for the most basic protection rights guaranteed under international law to refugees in general, further exacerbating the precarious international legal guarantees that international human rights and humanitarian law currently extends to this population".

41   According the UNHCR, in 2016 97,796 Palestinian refugees were registered by UNHCR (the total number of Palestinian persons of concern, including pending asylum cases is 105,979). It is acknowledged that the data is not an accurate reflection of the actual numbers of Palestinian refugees living outside UNRWA areas of operation. It is estimated that the population in those locations might be quite substantial, particularly in the Gulf. See UNHCR, *Global Trends – Forced Displacement in 2016* (2017), at 68, http://www.unhcr.org/5943e8a34.pdf.

42   Total figures amount to 200,000–350,000. UNRWA, *Report of the Commissioner-General for 1966–1967*, General Assembly, Official Records, 22nd Session-Supplement No. 13 (A/6713), at 11; Marie-Louise Weighill, *Palestinians in Exile: Legal, Geographical and*

Arab countries, as a result of which Israel took control of the Gaza Strip and the West Bank including East Jerusalem.
- In 1970, between 18,000 and 20,000[43] Palestinian refugees were exiled from Jordan as part of the expulsion of the Palestine Liberation Organization (PLO) from that country.[44]
- During the 1980s, about 100,000 Palestinians, mostly refugees, fled Lebanon to the Gulf countries and northern Europe[45] as a consequence of the country's civil war, which also engulfed Palestinian refugee camps in Lebanon.[46]
- Between 1990 and 1991, 200,000 Palestinians who had found work and residence in Kuwait were forced to flee after brutal and often lethal violence as a result of the First Gulf War, during which Palestinian leadership had supported Saddam Hussein.[47]
- In 1996, President Muammar Gadhafi of Libya expelled 15,000 of the 30,000 Palestinian residents in Libya in protest against the peace talks between Israel and the PLO, which had culminated in the Oslo process.[48]
- During the sectarian conflict in Iraq between 2005 and 2007, approximately 20,000–25,000 of the 35,000 Palestinian refugees residing there were forced to flee widespread violence and targeted persecution following the First Gulf War, on account of their perceived support for, and their preferential treatment by, former President Saddam Hussein.
- Since the beginning of the ongoing Syrian conflict, approximately 110,000 of the 560,000 refugees registered with UNRWA in Syria in 2011 have fled the country, while 280,000 have been internally displaced.[49]

Statistical Aspects, in *The Palestinian Exodus: 1948–1998* 16 (Ghada Karmi & Eugene Cotran eds., 1999).

43 BADIL, *Survey of Palestinian Refugees and Internally Displaced Persons* (2003), at 23.
44 During the events known as Black September, Jordanian King Hussein quashed the Palestinian resistance to restore his monarchy's rule over the country; *see* Yann Le Troquer & Rozenn Hommery al-Oudat, *From Kuwait to Jordan: The Palestinians' Third Exodus*, 28 J. Palestine Stud. 8 (1999). For more on Black September, *see* Mehmood Hussain, *PLO-Jordan Relations*, 21 Econ. Pol. Wkly. (Sep. 13, 1986); Hassan A. Barari, *Four Decades after Black September: A Jordanian Perspective*, 10 Civ. Wars 231–243 (2008); Clinton Bailey, Jordan's Palestinians Challenge 1948–1983: A Political History 46–62 (1984).
45 Mohamed Kamel Doraï, *Palestinian Emigration from Lebanon to Northern Europe: Refugees, Networks and Transnational Practices*, 21 Refuge 23–31, 24 (2003).
46 Joe Stork, *The War of the Camps, the War of the Hostages*, 133 MERIP Rep. 3–7 (1985).
47 By December 1990, only 120,000 to 150,000 Palestinians remained in Kuwait. Today, Palestinians in Kuwait are estimated between 55,000 and 70,000. Anne M. Lesch, *No Refuge for Refugees: The Insecure Exile of Palestinians*, in Exile and Return: Predicaments of Palestinians and Jews 171 (2005).
48 Bassem Sirhan, *The Palestinians in Libya*, IX Palestine Y.B. Int'l L. 363, 372 (1996–1997).
49 UNRWA, Syria Crisis, https://www.unrwa.org/syria-crisis.

– Between 1967 and 2015, over 800,000 Palestinians have been the victims of various types of conflict-induced forced displacement in the occupied Palestinian territory (oPt), due to a number of measures enacted by Israel, the Occupying Power, such as home demolitions, evictions, deportations, and revocations of residency permits.

This account is conservative and does not consider the discrimination experienced by Palestinian refugees because of their status, mostly in Arab countries, nor the casualties they have suffered in the oPt and other conflict-related situations.[50] Over time, lack of security and instability have pushed Palestinian refugees to be on the move anew in search of protection and better opportunities. Following each of the above shocks, Europe and the Americas have become alternative destinations for Palestinian refugees. In recent years though, the political climate in both Europe and America has deteriorated, with rampant xenophobia toward refugees especially from the Middle East.[51] This has forced Palestinian refugees to go further afield in search for a safe haven.

II Palestinian Refugees in South East Asia: A New Phenomenon

The Asia Pacific region is home to 7.7 million "persons of concern" according to UNHCR.[52] Of these, almost 2.8 million are in South East Asia alone.[53] Palestinian refugees[54] are a relatively new phenomenon in this region, especially in the

---

50 On numerous occasions, Palestinian refugees and Palestinian camps have been the target of military and or retaliatory operations in Israel as well as in Arab countries such as Iraq, Lebanon, and Egypt.

51 Human Rights Watch, *World Report 2017* (2017) [*hereinafter* HRW 2017 Report], Introduction, https://www.hrw.org/world-report/2017/.

52 The Asia and Pacific figures include 3.5 million refugees, 1.9 million IDPs and 1.4 million stateless people. The majority of refugees originate from Afghanistan and Myanmar. *See, further*, UNHCR, Asia and the Pacific, http://www.unhcr.org/asia-and-the-pacific.html.

53 This includes persons of concern to UNHCR in Bangladesh, Brunei Darussalam, Cambodia, Indonesia, Lao PDR, Malaysia, Myanmar, the Philippines, Singapore, Thailand, Timor-Leste and Viet Nam. These figures include 1.4 million stateless and over 500,000 internally displaced (source: UNHCR Regional Office for South East Asia, contacted Feb. 2017). *See, also*, UNHCR, *South East Asia Factsheet* (Sep. 2014), http://reliefweb.int/sites/reliefweb.int/files/resources/UNHCR%20Regional%20Office%20for%20SouthEast%20Asia%20Factsheet%20September%202014.pdf.

54 In the collected data, the count of Palestinian refugees and asylum-seekers includes those with either their country of origin, citizenship/nationality, ethnicity or country of birth noted as Palestine. This is broader than the number of those with country of origin "Palestine" in UNHCR's official/ public statistics. The latter only count the country

forms and numbers of their current flight toward South East Asia. Generally, there are no records of Palestinian refugees arriving to the Asia Pacific region in notable numbers before 2010. Since 2011, however, there have been reports of Palestinian refugees seeking protection in various countries in the region, including Australia,[55] Indonesia, Korea, Malaysia, Pakistan, Sri Lanka, and Thailand. A combination of factors might be the reason for this relatively new phenomenon. The violence and displacement in the Middle East, with its epicentre in Syria, Yemen and Iraq, could alone account for the increased inflow of Palestinian refugees. In addition, the historical places of refuge, such as Jordan, Lebanon, Egypt, and to a significant extent the Gulf countries, have ceased to be welcoming or appealing destinations for Palestinian refugees for a number of reasons. As the next section will examine, there may be further reasons that motivate asylum-seekers, including Palestinian refugees, to travel to South East Asia, despite the limited legal framework that exists there to protect them.

A   Safe Haven without Legal Protection Framework?

Asia is the region with the lowest level of ratification of international instruments[56] even though, second to Africa, it has had the highest number of refugees since the Second World War.[57] Unlike Europe, Africa, and the Americas, the majority of Asian States have not signed onto the major

---

of origin, and there may be Palestinian refugees who were habitual residents of another country other than Palestine (*e.g.* Palestinian refugees who were born and habitually resided in Syria or Iraq) and whose country of origin is recorded as Syria. This broader methodology aims to capture the realistic picture of the persons of concern who are of Palestinian origin, including those with Palestinian ancestry (even if they have never lived in Palestine).

55 There is a modest Palestinian community in Australia, estimated between 20,000 and 30,000. It is hard to differentiate between refugees and diaspora. Arrivals registered under the Australian Programme, being 120 in 2011/12, 198 in 2012/13, 24 in 2013/14 – reflecting the flow of the unrest in the Middle East.

56 Simon Chesterman, *Asia's Ambivalence about International Law and Institutions: Past, Present and Future*, 27 Eur. J. Int'l L. 945–978 (2017).

57 Sara E. Davies, Legitimising Rejection: International Refugee Law in Southeast Asia 1–2 (2007) [*hereinafter* Davies]. Davis writes that immediately after the Second World War, ethnic Chinese from Southeast Asia, who had been forced into China during the war, sought to return to the Southeast Asian countries. Approximately 700 000 fled China after the Communist takeover in 1949, while the partition between India and Pakistan led to an estimated 8–10 million displaced people. In 1954, one million Vietnamese fled from the North of their country in the wake of the first French-Indochina War. Conflict and disputed borders kept on displacing people from Afghanistan, Iran, India, Nepal, Bangladesh, Burma (Myanmar), Pakistan and Tibet. The civil wars in Indochina created massive refugee and asylum-seeker population from the 1960s. It is estimated that during the 1980s and 1980s, 2.5 million fled Indochina alone.

international refugee law instruments to promote and protect refugees, namely the 1951 Convention and its 1967 Protocol.[58]

The 1951 Convention and its 1967 Protocol constitute the "magna carta" of international refugee law,[59] aiming to universalize the notion of who can be defined as a 'refugee', as per Article 1A of the Convention, and promote a standardized, uniform framework for asylum responses provided by the state. In addition to the core principle of *non-refoulement*, which prohibits the expulsion and return of "a refugee in any manner whatsoever to the frontiers of territories where his [or her] life or freedom would be threatened on account of his race, religion, nationality, membership of a particular social group or political opinion",[60] from which there can be no derogation, it also sets out a number of important rights which afford refugees the same treatment due to aliens more generally, and in some cases even nationals of the host country.[61]

---

58 Davies, 3; notes that of twenty-nine states in the region, only ten have signed both the 1951 Convention and its Protocol: Azerbaijan, Cambodia, China, Japan, Kazakhstan, Korea (South), Kyrgyzstan, Philippines, Tajikistan and Turkmenistan. Timor Leste also acceded 1951 Convention and 1967 Protocol in 2003. Only five of these have incorporated the instruments into their domestic law: Japan, Kazakhstan, Korea (South), Kyrgyzstan and Tajikistan. The author observes that this is probably explained as for many former USRR countries ratification of the main human rights instruments was a precondition to recognition by the international community (fn17).

59 Davies, 563.

60 1951 Refugee Convention art. 33. The principle of *non-refoulement* is a cornerstone of refugee law, to which no reservations are permitted under the 1951 Convention and its 1967 Protocol. It is largely considered customary law as such it is binding on all states regardless of whether they have ratified the 1951 Convention or its 1967 Protocol. It "includes non-rejection at the frontier, if rejection would result in an individual being forcibly returned to a country of persecution." See UNHCR, *The Principle of Non-Refoulement as a Norm of Customary International Law, Response to the Questions posed to UNHCR by the Federal Constitutional Court of the Federal Republic of Germany in cases 2 BvR 1938/93, 2 BvR 1953/93, 2 BvR 1954/93* (Jan. 31, 2994), at Conclusions, para. 5. *See, also*, paras. 7–8.

61 Refugees are entitled to have their refugee's personal status recognized and protected, including in connection with their marriage (Article 12). They are entitled to the same rights as nationals when it comes to their freedom of religious belief and practice and their right to choose a religious education for their children (Article 4), artistic and industrial property rights (Article 14), their access to courts (Article 16), their access to rationing (Article 20), elementary education (Article 22(1)), public relief and assistance (Article 23), labour legislation and social security (Article 24) and administrative matters (article 25). In other areas, refugees are granted the same treatment as aliens (Article 7(1)), namely when it comes to property rights (Article 13), the right of association (Article 15), the right to engage in wage-earning employment (Article 17) including the right to engage in agriculture, industry, handicrafts and commerce (Article 18), housing rights (Article 21), secondary education (Article 22(2)), and freedom of movement (Article 26). Refugees are entitled to identity papers (Article 27) and travel documents (Article 28). Assistance

In South East Asia, only Cambodia, Timor Leste and the Philippines have become parties to the 1951 Convention or its Protocol. Both the Philippines and Cambodia have incorporated a national asylum legal framework in government acts.[62] Like the vast majority of Asian States, South East Asian countries have signed onto the Bangkok Principles on the Status and Treatment of Refugees (hereinafter 'Bangkok Principles').[63] Although the Bangkok Principles acknowledge the existence of refugees, the principles of asylum and non-refoulement, the impact of the Bangkok Principles has so far been deemed undiscernible.[64] First, security concerns overshadow the rights enshrined in the Principles. Secondly, given the declaratory, non-binding nature of the Principles, they represent a 'guide' for States in the region who are left free to determine whether and how to assist and protect refugees as they see fit.

The phenomenon that Davis calls the "Asian rejection" of international refugee law, even though explicable in historical terms,[65] has little *raison d'être*

---

to transfer their assets (Article 30) as well as the possibility of assimilation and naturalization (Article 34) are also contemplated. If needed and only on the base of essential national security, states are entitled to undertake provisional measures against a refugee (Article 9), which in no case should expose the refugee to a threat for his/her own life and or physical, moral and psychological safety.

62 *Department Circular No. 058 – Establishing the Refugees and Stateless Status Determination Procedure* [Phil.] (Oct. 18, 2012), http://www.refworld.org/docid/5086932e2.html; *Sub-Decree No. 224 of 2009, on Procedure for Recognition as a Refugee or Providing Asylum Rights to Foreigners in the Kingdom of Cambodia* [Cambodia] (Dec. 17, 2009), http://www.refworld.org/docid/4d81f0172.html.

63 They were adopted by the Asian-African Legal Consultative Organization (AALCO), in 1966 and reaffirmed in 1988 and 2001. The Bangkok Principles enlarge the grounds of persecution of the 1951 Convention to include color, ethnic origin, and gender (Article 1(1)), and recognize the additional man-made causes of refugees flows of the 1969 OAU Convention as applying to anyone fleeing such conditions in their country of origin regardless of individual persecution (Article 1(2)). They further recognize as refugees "lawful dependents of a refugee" (Article 1(4)). Another interesting addition of the Bangkok Principles is the recognition of the right of return in Article 6(1) in addition to the corollary duty of states to receive any refugee wishing to return to their country of origin.

64 Davies, page 3–4.

65 Three arguments are commonly used in the region to justify the limited adhesion to international refugee law instruments. General explanations include "good neighborliness", namely the non-interference in sensitive matters pertaining to the sovereignty of a neighboring state, the "economic costs" imposed by the 1951 Refugee Convention and the "social disruption" in countries with delicate ethnic balances. The author challenges these arguments by explaining how limited Asian involvement in the drafting of the international refugee law instrument is one of the reasons causing Asian states to reject "Eurocentric refugee recognition practices". During the drafting process of the 1951 Convention, despite major refugee crises in Asia (*e.g.* India-Pakistan), European countries insisted to apply the Refugee Convention to European refugees only (hence the geographical limitation,

today. In the 21st century, facing the large numbers of refugees and asylum-seekers[66] that South East Asia continues to experience, the lack of a robust, uniform protection framework is very much resented by the refugees and, ultimately – even if not necessarily understood – by host societies alike. In the absence of formal legal frameworks, state authorities in the majority of countries in South East Asia make no differentiation between refugees, asylum-seekers and other irregular (undocumented) migrants and treat all as 'illegal immigrants'. Refugees and asylum-seekers who have arrived in these countries irregularly or have overstayed their visas are generally subject to the same penalties as undocumented migrants for violating immigration laws.[67] They might be subject to arrest, detention and deportation. Thus, many – probably unaware of UNHCR's assistance – may still refuse to report to UNHCR, so as not to have their presence in the country known to the authorities.[68] Prospects for naturalization are very slim.[69] Refugees and asylum-seekers accordingly end up living difficult lives in limbo, on the margins of society and prone to exploitation and abuse. According to Davis, this has created some impetus for refugees and asylum-seekers in the region to seek protection outside the region, in Europe, the US and Australia.[70] Nonetheless, as the paper argues, the challenging environment has not dissuaded persons of Palestinian origin from seeking protection in this part of the world.

which was only removed by the 1967 Protocol, which truly universalized the notion of refugee). Hence Asian countries rejected the international refugee protection framework altogether.

66   According to Davies, Southeast Asia hosts a large number of potential asylum-seekers, who are forced to live as 'illegal migrants' because these states have no refugee recognition policy and many fear being refused refugee status by the UNHCR. *See* Davies, 4–5.

67   Article 31 of the 1951 Convention states that "States shall not impose penalties, on account of their illegal entry or presence, on refugees who, [...] enter or are present in their territory without authorization [....]. States shall not apply to the movements of such refugees restrictions other than those which are necessary". *See, also*, Guy Goodwin-Gill, *Article 31 of the 1951 Convention Relating to the Status of Refugees: non-penalization, detention, and protection*, paper prepared for an expert roundtable discussion on Art. 31 of the 1951 Convention Relating to the Status of Refugees organized as part of the Global Consultations on International Protection in the context of the fiftieth anniversary of the 1951 Convention, http://www.unhcr.org/publications/legal/419c778d4/refugee-protection-international-law-article-31-1951-convention-relating.html.

68   Michael Alexander, *Refugee Status Determination Conducted by UNHCR*, 11 Int'l J. Refugee L., 251–289 (1999). *Cited in* Davies, 6.

69   SPRIL Questionnaire.

70   Davies, 5.

In the absence of national asylum systems, UNHCR conducts registration and Refugee Status Determination (RSD) under its mandate.[71] To the extent that UNHCR is allowed to operate in a country, it engages in both protection interventions, which may include advocacy for alternatives to detention, assistance to individuals with specific vulnerabilities, protection monitoring, and search for durable solution such as resettlement. A primary concern for UNHCR in the region is establishing accessible and efficient registration and RSD systems so as to ensure that persons in need of international protection are identified and documented at the earliest and can be assisted as required. A large number of persons of concern allegedly remains unregistered,[72] which leaves them hard to monitor, assist, and protect.

In countries in South East Asia where there is no national asylum system, UNHCR conducts registration and RSD under its mandate for asylum-seekers, including those of Palestinian origin. As a first step, Palestinian asylum-seekers go through regular RSD assessments, which trigger an examination of the applicability of Article 1D. Should Article 1D be not applicable, the refugee claim is examined under Article 1A(2). This constitutes a proper interpretation and application of article 1D compared to other regions in the world, as a number of countries continue not to recognize the application of Article 1D to Palestinian refugees,[73] and Palestinian refugees are required to prove their refugee status *again* and to apply as any refugee under article 1A of the Convention. Hence, given the uniqueness of their status (and documentation), Palestinians might

---

71   Even if most South East Asian countries have not ratified the major international human rights instruments, they cooperate with UNHCR by virtue of its legal mandate to directly protect and assist persons of concerns. UNHCR was established as a subsidiary organ of the UNGA through resolution 319 A (IV) of 3 December 1949. Its Statute, adopted through UN General Assembly resolution 428 (V) of 14 December 1950, stipulates that the High Commissioner "acting under the authority of the General Assembly, shall assume the function of providing international protection … and of seeking permanent solutions for the problem of refugees." Paragraph 9 of its Statute provides for the further evolution of UNHCR functions and activities. The UNHCR mandate, other than 1951 Convention, 1967 Protocol and UNGA resolutions, includes surrogate function of diplomatic and consular protection for refugees and stateless persons or international human rights protection. The UNHCR is also legally entitled to and responsible for interceding directly on behalf of refugees and stateless persons who would otherwise not be represented legally on the international plane. The effective exercise of his mandate both presupposes and is underpinned by the commitment from states to cooperate with him and his Office.

72   In Malaysia, approximately 25,000 asylum-seekers are estimated as unregistered. *See* UNHCR, *UNHCR Global Report 2009*, Malaysia, http://www.unhcr.org/4c0902ca9.pdf.

73   This applies, for example, to Canada and the United States, Australia, Switzerland, The Netherlands and Poland. *See* BADIL (2015), 80–309. *See also* Goodwin-Gill & Akram, 253; Takkenberg, 86–129.

face additional burdens – namely complication in obtaining valid travel documents in their country of habitual residence – but also have some opportunities in South East Asia, compared to other refugees. For example, Palestinians holding a Palestinian Authority (PA) passport enjoy a free visa with one month stay in Indonesia and Malaysia, and visa upon arrival in Cambodia, Laos, and Timor Leste.[74] Further, Brunei, Myanmar, the Philippines, Thailand and Vietnam require prior visa often on a six-month-valid PA passport. Singapore also grants visa to PA passport and Middle East refugee travel document holders (online application is required).[75] In examining the specificities faced in the South East Asian states, it is useful to focus on the situation and legal framework of the main refugee-receiving countries, namely Indonesia, Malaysia and Thailand.

1   Indonesia

Over the years, Indonesia has increasingly become a recipient country for refugees and asylum-seekers, albeit with a very small caseload compared to the size of its population.[76] In 2008, less than 1,000 persons of concern were registered with UNHCR and, by the end of 2016, the number had risen to nearly 14,500. Indonesia continues to be perceived to be a convenient transit country for refugees from around the world, largely because of its relaxed visa upon arrival policy for some nationalities as well as its well-established smuggling networks. Until 2014, it was considered by asylum-seekers and refugees relatively easy to use boat links from Indonesia to arrive at Christmas Island (Australia), a path many chose to seek asylum in Australia. This also became a common smugglers' route, and many refugees have died on the journey.[77] However, since a policy change in 2013, Australia no longer accepts migrants and refugees arriving without visas on its shores.[78] Since then, boats carrying migrants and asylum-seekers have been intercepted at sea and directed to off-shore

---

74   'Free visa' means that a person is allowed to enter the country without a visa for a specified period of time. A 'visa-upon-arrival' means that the person needs a visa to enter, but can apply for and receives the visa when s/he requests it.

75   See Singapore Immigration and Checkpoint Authority, https://www.ica.gov.sg/page.aspx?pageid=169&secid=166#Procedure.

76   Increased number of arrivals can be seen at: http://www.unhcr.or.id/en/unhcr-inindonesia. However, the increase has somewhat stabilized, and this is quite small compared with the national population and in the region.

77   See Ali Abunimah, *Palestinian refugees forced out of Iraq feared lost at sea en route to Australia*, Electronic Intifada (Aug. 15, 2012), https://electronicintifada.net/blogs/ali-abunimah/palestinian-refugees-forced-out-iraq-feared-lost-sea-en-route-australia.

78   HRW 2017 Report.

processing centres in Nauru and Manus Islands.[79] It is unclear whether this has decreased transit migration in Indonesia overall, however in the short term this has caused an increase of refugees and asylum-seekers in Indonesia, some of whom may have planned to travel to Australia, but who are no longer able to do so. As of January 2017, the number of refugees and asylum-seekers registered with UNHCR Indonesia totals 14,425 individuals, including 8,039 refugees and 6,386 asylum-seekers.[80] The majority are from Afghanistan, Somalia, Myanmar and Iraq, with a total of 47 nationalities represented in the population. As of December 2016, there were approximately 450 Palestinians (compared to 532 in December 2015) seeking protection with UNHCR. The majority of them come from Iraq on travel documents issued by Iraq.[81]

Because of the lack of proper recognition of refugees and ultimate lack of a national refugee regime, Indonesia generally treats persons seeking international protection as illegal migrants. Indonesian authorities have often detained those whom it intercepted, who only become eligible for release to an International Organization for Migration (IOM)-run community housing if they are recognized as refugees by UNHCR, provided that space is available. The Government of Indonesia respects UNHCR's authority to conduct registration, documentation and refugee status determination. However, refugees in Indonesia do not have any formal legal, social or political rights, and are not permitted legally to work. Generally public services such as health and education are available, however there are a number of barriers preventing refugees from accessing these services.[82] The government authorizes UNHCR to help protect and find solutions for persons seeking international protection.[83] As of December 2016, a presidential regulation ensures that refugees and asylum-seekers can access UNHCR services, and allows them to stay temporarily in the country until their refugee status can be confirmed and appropriate solutions can be found for them.[84] The impact of the regulation is still to be seen.[85]

---

79 *Id.* HRW has condemned the deplorable human rights conditions afforded to refugees, asylum seekers and migrants in these processing centers.
80 SPRIL Questionnaire. A marked increase in the number of registrations by UNHCR occurred in May 2015 following the rescue at sea of nearly 1,000 Rohingyas from Myanmar. Over the course of 2015, some 2,044 RSD interviews were conducted while 2,824 decisions were finalized.
81 SPRIL Questionnaire; UNHCR Interview.
82 UNHCR, Indonesia: Factsheet (Feb. 2016), http://www.unhcr.org/50001bda9.pdf.
83 *Id.*
84 UNHCR, Indonesia: Factsheet (Dec. 2016), http://www.unhcr.org/id/wp-content/uploads/sites/42/2017/05/Indonesia-Fact-Sheet-December-2016.pdf.
85 In an interview with a staff member of an NGO providing relief services to refugees, it was stated that "the main challenge in a country like Indonesia, where no legal framework

Meanwhile, to prevent statelessness, UNHCR has been advocating for the government to improve birth registration procedures generally, and to extend birth registration to the children of refugees and asylum-seekers, so far without tangible results.

Indonesia recognizes PA issued passports and has a one-month free entry policy for those holding such documents. There are no laws or policies in Indonesia relating to Palestinian refugees specifically and their treatment generally does not differ from that of other refugees. The granting of refugee status by UNHCR through its RSD has limited recognition by Indonesian authorities and the refugee's immigration status remains the same. Asylum-seekers may be subjected to arrest, detention, and deportation by Indonesian authorities.[86] In 2015, 95 Palestinians were detained by the authorities in immigration detention facilities. Immigration detention facilities are located across the country, making access for the purpose of monitoring challenging. Preliminary research shows that the Palestinians who are currently in detention facilities have either been arrested or rendered themselves to Indonesian authorities owing to the lack of means to support themselves. UNHCR has been able to facilitate the release of some of these individuals on the basis of specific needs, for example people with disabilities and/or those needing urgent medical treatment. Recognized refugees have also been released to be accommodated in IOM-run facilities. Even in this case, however, assistance is limited and not granted to all. Possibilities of self-reliance for Palestinians, as for other refugees, are limited.[87]

2 Malaysia

Over the years, Malaysia has received an increasing number of asylum-seekers/refugees. There may have been various motivations for asylum-seekers/refugees to travel to Malaysia, including employment in Malaysia, or on their way to Indonesia, often to attempt onwards travel to Australia. In 2015, there were approximately 154,000 refugees and asylum-seekers in Malaysia registered with UNHCR, mostly from Myanmar, Sri Lanka, Somalia, Syria, Iraq, and Afghanistan. Of those, some 800 were of Palestinian origin.[88]

---

exist and the government is not taking full care of refugees, is that even private individuals will most likely refrain from helping refugees, as this could be seen as helping foreigners (normally perceived as a "security threat", at the expenses of nationals".

86 SPRIL Questionnaire.
87 Preliminary research shows that, unlike other groups who could rely on ties with fellow nationals, e.g. the Afghans (like pre-existing diaspora and established communities), Palestinians are very much left on their own.
88 SPRIL Questionnaire.

UNHCR registration records show some Palestinians use travel documents issued by the PA, travel documents for Palestinians issued by Syria, Egypt, Lebanon, and Kuwait, and Jordanian passports.[89] The majority are thought to come directly from the oPt using PA issued documents.[90] Malaysia recognizes such documents as well as travel documents issued by Syria, Lebanon, Egypt "*et al.*"[91] Holders of PA travel documents do not require any visa to enter Malaysia and are issued with a 30 days 'Visit Pass' on arrival. On the other hand, holders of travel documents issued by Syria and other countries need to apply for a visa through Malaysian Embassies abroad (the majority of visas for Palestinians are issued by the Malaysian Embassy in Lebanon).

Interestingly, considering the high numbers of Iraqi Palestinians in Indonesia, UNHCR in Malaysia has generally not recorded Palestinians using travel documents issued by Iraq (except for some old expired passports issued under the former regime).[92] There are, however, some reports of Iraqi Palestinians reaching Malaysia,[93] as well as unconfirmed reports of Palestinian refugees deported from neighbouring countries (including Lao PDR and China) being sent to Malaysia.[94]

In the absence of any formal legislative and administrative framework to address refugee matters,[95] UNHCR in Malaysia conducts all activities related to the reception, registration, documentation, and RSD of asylum-seekers and refugees. The treatment of Palestinian refugees generally does not differ from that of refugees from other countries. Lacking any formal recognition, the hundreds of thousands of refugees and asylum-seekers in Malaysia are treated as illegal migrants. They do not have any formal legal, social, or political rights,

---

89 SPRIL Questionnaire. Among those holding a Jordanian passport there could be West Bank residents whose Jordanian passport (renewable every two years) does not equate to a full national passport, hence the impossibility to reside in Jordan. For greater detail about the status of Palestinians in Jordan *see* Anis Kassim, *The Palestinian: From Hyphenated to Integrated Citizens*, 3 Palestine Y.B. Int'l L. 64–84 (1996).

90 UNHCR Interview.

91 SPRIL Questionnaire; UNHCR Interview.

92 SPRIL Questionnaire. Palestinians from Iraq coming to Malaysia normally have transited through Syria allegedly with fake Iraqi passports. They moved onward to Malaysia with PA issued documents. Some of them still hold expired Palestinian travel documents, as well as ID cards issued during Saddam Hussein's regime.

93 Maryam A. Itani, The Suffering of the Palestinian Refugee Volume 6: Am I not a human? 79 (2010).

94 Action Group for Palestinians of Syria, *China Deports Number of Palestinian Refugees to Malaysia* (Dec. 29, 2014), http://www.actionpal.org.uk/en/post/132/news-and-rpot/hn-eot-ubro-aetna-euest-aasa2.

95 UNHCR, *Malaysia: Fact Sheet* (Aug. 2015), http://www.unhcr.org/protection/operations/56167f6b6/malaysia-fact-sheet.html.

and are generally not legally permitted to work. A welcome exception is represented by the recent admission of Rohingya refugees to work in Malaysia through a scheme with UNHCR (set to start in March 2017). Refugees do not have access to public education. Basic healthcare is available in government hospitals and refugee clinics, although many refugees struggle to pay for the healthcare. There is health insurance that is accessible to refugees.

UNHCR assists the refugee population throughout the country. This includes trying to safeguard the security of refugees, for instance through prevention of deportation, detention interventions and legal representation, and improving their living conditions *inter alia* through advocating for access to legal work.[96]

If an individual is recognised as a refugee by UNHCR, this does not result in any change in their immigration status in Malaysia. If an asylum-seeker has his or her claim rejected by UNHCR, he or she may be subjected to arrest for illegal entry or overstay without valid travel documents, detention and/or deportation by Malaysian authorities.[97] Given their precarious status, detention in immigration detention centers is common occurrence among refugees and asylum-seekers in Malaysia. As of mid-2015, UNHCR had conducted 230 missions to detention facilities, meeting 6,600 detainees. Through visits in detention, court actions, and hotline interventions, 6,031 persons of concern were released.[98]

3   Thailand

As of December 2016, there were under half a million persons of concern in Thailand, around 490 of them Palestinian. Over a half of the Palestinians arriving in Thailand prior to 2015 used Syrian travel documents, and approximately a third used Iraqi travel documents. UNHCR has also registered Palestinians from the oPt, Cyprus, United Arab Emirates, Saudi Arabia, Jordan, Lebanon, Kuwait, and Egypt.[99] The Thai authorities recognize passports issued by the Palestinian Authority, even though it appears that those who hold them need to apply for visas in advance.[100]

In Thailand, the protection regime for refugees and asylum-seekers is precarious. Refugees in Thailand do not have any formal legal, social, or political rights, and are not legally permitted to work. They do not have the same level

---

96   *Id.*
97   SPRIL Questionnaire.
98   UNHCR, Malaysia Fact Sheet, http://www.unhcr.org/56167f6b6.pdf.
99   SPRIL Questionnaire.
100 Royal Thai Embassy, http://www.thaiembassy.ca/en/visiting-thailand/visas/general-visa-info).

of access to public health services as nationals. Refugee children have access to primary education in Thai schools, due to its national "Education for All" policy, and this extends to Palestinian refugee children.

There are no laws or policies in Thailand relating to Palestinian refugees specifically, and their treatment generally does not differ from that of refugees from other countries. Similarly, UNHCR assists the refugee population in the country as a whole, and does not specifically target Palestinian refugees. If an individual is recognized as a refugee by UNHCR, this does not result in any change in their immigration status in Thailand. UNHCR registration documentation is not always accepted and the lack of a visa or proper residency documents can lead to arrest and detention and/or deportation by the Thai authorities.[101]

III   Preliminary Observations on the Inflow of Palestinian Refugees in South East Asia

Over the course of a few years (2011–2013), South East Asian countries have received an increasing number of Palestinian refugees and asylum-seekers. While the numbers of arrivals have stabilized, a few observations can be offered.

> A) Should the regional and international status quo continue, Palestinian flows toward South East Asia are likely to continue and/or to rise.

South East Asian countries may depart from the usual destinations chosen by Palestinian refugees, given the absence of pre-existing ties (*e.g.* established Palestinian communities) as well as the limited prospects of integration, even if for temporary purposes, into the local economy.[102] Nonetheless, the arrivals of Palestinians in South East Asia must be contextualized with the events occurring in the Middle East in 2012 and 2013, and in Europe. For example, many Palestine refugees fleeing Syria to neighboring countries were prevented from entering these as of 2012,[103] and there have been reports of *refoulement*

---

101   SPRIL questionnaire.
102   The research conducted so far does not allow to confirm whether religious affiliation might impact the choice of Palestinian refugees to head to South East Asian countries such as Malaysia and Indonesia.
103   Amnesty International, *Families Ripped Apart as Palestinian Refugees from Syria Denied Entry to Lebanon* (July 1, 2014), http://www.amnesty.org/en/news/families-ripped-apart-palestinian-refugees-syria-denied-entry-lebanon-2014-07-01.

and forcible returns, particularly from Jordan.[104] Of those who were allowed to enter, the vast majority faced a precarious, marginalized existence, unable to regularize their legal status or access civil registration procedures and basic social services.[105] They find themselves dependent on aid for basic subsistence needs, including food and shelter, as well as basic education and healthcare. More than anything else, they and their families are exposed to exploitation, violence and abuse.[106] The escalating military operations in Syria and Iraq have created further displacement and insecurity,[107] especially for those whose status is precarious (such as Palestinian refugees).[108] The tightening of the blockade imposed by Israel (and supported by Egypt) in the Gaza Strip, which is in its tenth year, compounded by three major wars launched by Israel over the enclave, has left many without an alternative other than fleeing. Generally, Palestinian refugees who have the means to travel abroad would travel to Europe or North America, seeking to reunite with existing diasporas. Those who reached South East Asia were most probably left with nowhere to go. Hence, South East Asian countries may have become not "an" alternative but the only practicable option to some vulnerable Palestinian refugees fleeing persecution, conflict and other life-threatening situations. As the situation in the Middle East is not likely to normalize in the near future, and European states – increasingly under right wing Governments – are unlikely to relax their policy towards refugees,[109] the South East Asian option will probably continue

---

104 In Jordan, there have been at least 100 cases of forced deportations since mid-2012. Human Rights Watch, *Jordan: Palestinians Escaping Syria Turned Away* (Aug. 7, 2014), http://www.hrw.org/news/2014/08/07/jordan-palestinians-escaping-syria-turned-away. U.N. Comm. against Torture (CAT), *Concluding Observations on the Third Periodic Report of Jordan*, U.N. Doc. CAT/C/JOR/CO/3 (Jan. 29, 2016), paras. 13–14 (c); UN Comm. Rts. Child (CRC), *Concluding Observations on the Consolidated Fourth and Fifth Periodic Reports of Jordan*, U.N. Doc. CRC/C/JOR/CO/4–5 (June 13, 2014), paras. 55–56.
105 ANERA, *Report: Palestinian Refugees from Syria in* Lebanon (Vol. 4, Apr. 2013), www.anera.org/stories/palestinian-refugees-syria-lebanon/.
106 UNRWA Situation report, Lebanon and Jordan (on file with author).
107 For Syria, *see* UNHCR, *International Protection Considerations with regard to people fleeing the Syrian Arab Republic, Update IV* (Nov. 2015), http://www.refworld.org/docid/5641ef894.html, paras. 21–22. On the situation of Palestinian refugees in Syria, *see* UNRWA, Syria Crisis, https://www.unrwa.org/syria-crisis. On the situation of Palestinian refugees in Iraq, *see* UNHCR Update of UNHCR Aide-Memoire of 20061 Protection Considerations for Palestinian refugees in Iraq, http://www.refworld.org/pdfid/500ebeea2.pdf.
108 For example, Palestinians in Iraq, mostly in Baghdad, also come under frequent suspicion of supporting ISIS and have as such been singled out for arbitrary arrests, torture, abduction and extra-judicial killings. *See* UNHCR, *Relevant COI on the Situation of Palestinian Refugees in Baghdad* (Mar. 30, 2017), http://www.refworld.org/docid/58de48104.html.
109 HRW 2017 Report.

to be a meaningful one for refugees desperately seeking protection. An area which deserves further investigation is whether and to what extent other South East Asian countries might be possible new destinations for Palestinian refugees/asylum-seekers. Much might depend on economic prospects, existing frameworks and or practices to protect refugees, and applicable entry policies for Palestinians.

> B) The presence of Palestinian refugees in South East Asian countries might be underreported. Mechanisms to ensure Palestinian persons of concern are properly recorded is essential to their protection.

On a global level, statistics on Palestinian refugees are inconsistent and/or incomplete, making comprehensive data on Palestinians hard to ascertain. Palestinian nationality is not recognized by many countries, who instead classify Palestinians either as 'stateless', or register them under the citizenship of the country where they last migrated from. Also, Palestinians may conceal their origin out of fear of persecution, retaliation or discrimination. This partly explain why Palestinians are to an extent statistically invisible in many countries. Like other refugees and asylum-seekers in South East Asia, they might not register with UNHCR out of lack of awareness or fear of deportation from national authorities.[110] Lack of precise information about asylum-seekers/refugees in the country, e.g. knowledge of their presence, status and situation, might limit UNHCR's ability to ensure their protection. Concerning Palestinian refugees though, South East Asian countries, where UNHCR conducts RSD, may start to represent an exception given the broad methodological spectrum used.[111]

> C) Given the numbers of refugees in South East Asia, the primary concern is with the legal framework available to refugees and asylum-seekers in the region.

There is no specific protection regime for Palestinians, and the treatment of Palestinian refugees is generally the same as that of refugees of other countries of origin. Nevertheless, in the South East Asia countries in which they have found refuge, Palestinian refugees do not experience the level of politicization

---

110 For example, *see* the case of Malaysia above.
111 In the collected data, the count of Palestinian refugees and asylum-seekers includes those with either their country of origin, citizenship/nationality, ethnicity or country of birth noted as Palestine.

they face in other countries, including the Middle East, Europe, and the Americas.[112]

As most countries in South East Asia are not signatories to the 1951 Refugee Convention and its 1967 Protocol, and have no binding regional framework and few national asylum systems in place, UNHCR remains the principal actor in providing international protection. The lack of ratification of any international instruments to protect refugees and asylum-seekers significantly limits the capacity of UNHCR to deliver (or help state authorities deliver) protection in a systematic manner. Therefore, advocacy for the ratification of international refugee law instruments should continue to be pursued. In parallel, opportunities arising from recent developments in some countries, such as the approval by Thailand's Cabinet to implement a refugee screening mechanism framework[113] and the enactment of a presidential regulation in Indonesia in December 2016, need to be explored further.

Concomitantly, other solutions to ensure respect of the rights of refugees and asylum-seekers need to be considered. First, Indonesia has ratified most of the core international human rights law instruments with the exception of the International Convention for the Protection of all Persons from Enforced Disappearance, which it has nevertheless signed. The same holds true for Thailand with the difference that Thailand is yet to ratify the International Convention on the Protection of the Rights of All Migrant Workers and Members of their Families. However, Malaysia has ratified very few of the core international human rights law instruments and notably is not a party to the International Covenant on Civil and Political Rights (ICCPR), the International Covenant on Economic, Social and Cultural Rights (ICESCR), or the Convention against Torture and Other Cruel, Inhuman or Degrading Treatment or Punishment (CAT). It has only ratified the Convention on the Rights of the Child (CRC) and the Convention on the Rights of Persons with Disabilities (CRPD).[114] These treaties, most particularly CAT and the ICCPR[115] impose on states the obligation of *non-refoulement*, which – as explained

---

112 Interestingly, other groups of asylum-seekers and refugees in the region tend to be singled out for political reasons and may suffer unfavourable treatment – such as the Rohingya, Pakistanis and Sri Lankans – however, Palestinians do not experience this. Ironically, the world's most political refugees are fairly apolitical in Asia.
113 UNHCR, *UNHCR welcomes Thai Cabinet approval of framework for refugee screening mechanism* (Jan. 16, 2017), https://www.unhcr.or.th/en/news/TH_refugee_screening_mechanism.
114 OHCHR, Status of ratification interactive dashboard, http://indicators.ohchr.org/.
115 In the South East Asia region, only Myanmar and Malaysia have not ratified the ICCPR and CAT.

above – imposes an absolute prohibition on the return or expulsion of aliens to places where their lives or freedoms could be at risk. As the principle of *non-refoulement* is generally regarded as being part of customary international law and thus binding even on states not parties to any of the treaties previously mentioned, it should be rigorously upheld with authorities who threaten to deport or expel people whose life would be at risk in the country they flee from. Moreover, since international human rights law generally applies to all persons within a state's jurisdiction regardless of nationality status, that law "supplements the protection regime set out in the 1954 Convention [Relating to the Status of Stateless Persons]" and it helps provide higher standards of protection.[116] Also, even if not binding under international law, the Bangkok Principles should be invoked as a moral obligation of State Parties.

Application of international standards to improve the living conditions and access to basic services for refugees and asylum-seekers should be addressed. People seeking international protection are vulnerable and prone to exploitation, abuse, and violence. Continued neglect of their humanitarian and developmental needs including in countries where they are seeking safe haven will produce further challenges to governance, security, and stability in the latter's societies. Legal instruments for refugees are intended to provide a safety net for the individuals and create a harmonious environment for the host societies (to a large extent, Palestinian refugees and their experience of multiple displacements over 70 years of exile, prove to be an illustrative case in point). Development agendas have goals that are not dissimilar. The UN's Sustainable Development Goals are also applicable to refugees as with all persons in the territory of a country. Unlike the conventional refugee protection framework, they have longer term impact and different enforceability mechanisms. Hence, development agencies should encourage inclusion of refugees and asylum-seekers in their development projects with South East Asian governments, in addition to encouraging national authorities to develop legal frameworks to protect them effectively.[117]

---

116 UNHCR, *Handbook on Protection of Stateless Persons under the 1954 Convention Relating to the Status of Stateless Persons* (2014), para. 141.

117 It is widely recognized that advocacy to promote adherence to international law, especially human rights norms, is an essential part of development, often conflated in the rule of law mission of UN agencies.

IV   Conclusions

Ongoing research suggests that South East Asia has become an increasingly resorted to destination for Palestinian refugees fleeing new waves of displacement in the Middle East (Iraq, oPt, Syria, Yemen). While there is no record of Palestinian refugees seeking protection in South East Asia until 2010, nearly two thousand Palestinians have reportedly done so between 2011 and 2013, heading to Indonesia, Malaysia and Thailand primarily. Indonesia and Malaysia have a relatively favorable visa policy, granting one month free entry to Palestinians holding PA travel documents. While geographical proximity to Australia and possibly, to some extent in the case of Malaysia and Indonesia, common religion might account for the increasing consideration of such destinations among Palestinian refugees, lack of other opportunities remain an important factor. In particular, the increasing closure to refugees in Europe and North America might have pulled more Palestinian refugees, in an unprecedented move, further eastward. This is a new trend in the history of the Palestinian people, whose exile is about to enter its seventieth year.

To a large extent, Palestinian refugees in Indonesia, Malaysia and Thailand experience the same challenges as other refugees and asylum-seekers. The majority of South East Asian countries are not party to the international refugee protection framework, namely the 1951 Refugee Convention and the 1967 Protocol. Moreover, unlike Europe, Africa and the Americas, none of the regions in Asia including South East Asia has developed its own regional system to protect refugees and asylum-seekers. The Bangkok Principles, useful as they might be in providing a reference framework, are not binding and their effectiveness in ensuring international protection to refugees is yet to be determined. The lack of national and regional refugee regimes in the region means that refugees and asylum-seekers are often categorized and treated as irregular migrants. As a result, they have little recourse for legal protection, limited access to public services (such as health, education) and, as they are not offered work permits, they often join the informal economy and are more likely subject to exploitation. Most worrisome is their being at risk of arrest, detention, and deportation. A positive development is the enactment of a presidential decree in Indonesia that since January 2017 allows refugees and asylum seekers to stay in the country until a solution is found.

The lack of an international protection framework and of comprehensive national asylum systems in these countries leave refugees in a legal limbo. In addition, unlike most of the other refugees in the region (*e.g.* from Afghanistan, Myanmar and Sri Lanka), Palestinians cannot rely on pre-existing diasporic ties in South East Asia. As South East Asian governments do not feel legally responsible for refugees, no effort is made to make their life morally and economically sustainable. Hence these individuals tend to live at the margins of host societies, usually relying on international and charitable support. Integration in host societies might be made even more difficult by the suspicion with which domestic constituencies often view the support refugees receive from civil society and charities. In such a context, UNHCR is faced with the monumental task of monitoring and managing flows and living conditions of refugees and asylum-seekers, assessing their claims and acting as a mediator between these persons and the governments. The lack of international standards compliant asylum systems may hamper UNHCR's ability to provide effective protection to persons of concern.

The exile of Palestinian refugees will soon enter its seventieth year. Palestinian refugees have been 'singled out' in the international protection system since its inception. For historical and political reasons, many of them (especially those residing in the Middle East) have experienced limited or no protection, which has compounded their exile and plunged them into further ways of displacement. Should the situation around the world not improve, it is likely that the numbers of Palestinians heading toward South East Asia will grow in the future. While their ultimate protection can be delivered only through a just and durable solution to the Israeli-Palestinian question, effective international protection in countries of destination is necessary to allow them to live their lives in dignity. In the short term, South East Asian governments should be reminded that they are bound by jus cogens provisions, such as the principle of *nonrefoulement*, as well as the obligations to protect, fulfil and respect the rights of any person in the territory despite his or her nationality, as stemming from human rights treaties they have ratified. This is even more compelling towards those who escape intractable protracted refugee situations, like the Palestinians.

South East Asian societies represent natural harbor of social diversity, hence might offer a favorable ground to integration of new comers. The literature presented in this article has made a convincing case that refugees, once regularized, can contribute to growth and stability in the country of destination. It is essential that South East Asian governments acknowledge the situation and consider practical, international law compliant solutions to address refugees' protection needs. Ultimately, the development of a comprehensive refugee protection framework is a necessary building block of more livable and stable societies.

Continuing or Settled? Prosecution of Israeli Settlements under Article 8(2)(b)(viii) of the Rome Statute

*Uzay Yasar Aysev**

    Abstract   34
I   Introduction   34
II   A Definitional Framework for Instantaneous, Continuing, and Continuous Crimes   37
    A   *The Definitional Gap in the International Criminal Jurisprudence*   37
    B   *A Definitional Framework for Instantaneous, Continuing, and Continuous Crimes*   39
        1   Instantaneous Crimes   39
        2   Continuous Crimes   41
        3   Continuing Crimes   46
III   ICC and Instantaneous, Continuous and Continuing Crimes   52
    A   *ICC's Temporal Jurisdictional Framework*   52
    B   *International Jurisprudence on Temporal Jurisdiction and Instantaneous, Continuous, and Continuing Crimes*   54
    C   *The Implications of Continuous and Continuing Crimes in Relation to ICC's Temporal Jurisdiction*   58

---

* Uzay Yasar Aysev is a legal consultant working with Global Rights Compliance L.L.P. He specialises in international humanitarian law, criminal and refugee law. He completed his Bachelor's degree in international relations at the Middle East Technical University, Ankara, and his LLM in public international law with a specialisation in international criminal law from Leiden University, Netherlands. He also holds a Master's degree in European political economy at the London School of Economics, and a graduate diploma in law at the BPP University, London. Uzay worked in a number of international organisations and NGOs including the International Criminal Court, Special Tribunal for Lebanon, UNHCR, Al-Haq and International Bar Association.

IV   Interpretation of Article 8(2)(b)(viii)   62
    A   *Interpretative Approaches at the ICC*   62
    B   *Possible Interpretations of Article 8(2)(b)(viii)*   65
        1   The Narrow Interpretation: Article 8(2)(b)(viii as an Instantaneous or Continuous Crime   66
        2   The Broad Interpretation: Article 8(2)(b)(viii) as a Continuing Crime   71
    C   *Israeli Settlements in the West Bank as a Continuing Crime*   76
V   Conclusion   81

Abstract

This article provides a definitional framework for the concepts of instantaneous, continuous and continuing crimes, drawing from domestic and international legal authorities and applying these definitions to article 8(2)(b)(viii) of the Rome Statute of the International Criminal Court, which criminalizes transfer of population by the Occupying Power into an occupied territory. The article focuses on the interpretation of article 8(2)(b)(viii) as an instantaneous, continuous or continuing crime with reference to the Israeli settlement activities in the West Bank in order to assess whether the transfer of settlers into the West Bank prior to June 2014 – *i.e.* the date that the temporal jurisdiction of the ICC starts in the territory of the State of Palestine, can be investigated and prosecuted.

I   Introduction

On 15 January 2015, the Prosecutor of the International Criminal Court (hereinafter 'ICC' or the 'Court') announced the opening of a preliminary examination into the situation in Palestine.[1] If the Prosecutor is satisfied that the conditions set out in article 53(1) of the Rome Statute (hereinafter "the Statute") are met, a full investigation will be launched to assess whether crimes within the jurisdiction of the Court have been or is being committed in the territory of Palestine. The Israeli settlement activities in the West Bank, including East Jerusalem (hereinafter 'the West Bank') are likely to be a focus of the

---

[1] International Criminal Court (ICC), *Preliminary Examination: Palestine*, https://www.icc-cpi.int/palestine.

Prosecutor's investigation. Indeed, the Prosecutor is already scrutinizing the Israeli settlement activities in the West Bank as a part of her preliminary examinations, presumably under Article 8(2)(b)(viii) of the Statute:[2]

> The Israeli government has allegedly led and directly participated in the planning, construction, development, consolidation and/or encouragement of settlements on the West Bank territory. The settlement activity is allegedly created and maintained through the implementation of a set of policies, laws, and physical measures. Such activities are alleged to include the planning and authorization of settlement expansions or new construction at existing settlements, including ... a scheme of subsidies and incentives to encourage migration to the settlements and to boost their economic development.[3]

The main challenge that the Prosecutor and the Court will face with regards to the investigation and prosecution of the Israeli settlement activities in the West Bank is related to the temporal jurisdiction of the Court. As per the Palestinian declaration of December 2014 made under article 12(3) of the Statute, the Court's jurisdiction on the territory of Palestine is limited to crimes committed after 13 June 2014.[4] Consequently, the incidents of population transfer into the West Bank that can be investigated and prosecuted under article 8(2)(b)(viii) can be divided into two temporal categories, being those that took place: (i) before 13 June 2014 and (ii) after 13 June 2014. The latter category is unlikely to pose any issues in relation to the Court's temporal jurisdiction, as both the physical movement and the settlement of the population into the occupied territory would have taken place within the temporal confines of the Palestinian article 12(3) declaration. Whether the Court can exercise jurisdiction over the former, which comprises the overwhelming majority of the instances of

---

2 Even though no explicit reference is made, the Prosecutor is presumably scrutinizing the Israeli settlements in the West Bank under article 8(2)(b)(viii) of the Statute which criminalizes "[t]he transfer, directly or indirectly, by the Occupying Power of parts of its own civilian population into the territory it occupies ..."; *see* Rome Statute of the International Criminal Court art. 8(2)(b)(viii), July 17, 1998, U.N. Doc. A/CONF.183/9 [*hereinafter* Rome Statute].
3 ICC-OTP, *Report on Preliminary Examination Activities 2016* (Nov. 14, 2016), para. 130, https://www.icc-cpi.int/iccdocs/otp/161114-otp-rep-pe_eng.pdf.
4 *Declaration Accepting the Jurisdiction of the International Criminal Court*, executed for the Government of the State of Palestine by Mahmoud Abbas, President of the State of Palestine (Dec. 31, 2014), https://www.icc-cpi.int/iccdocs/PIDS/press/Palestine_A_12-3.pdf.

population transfer into the West Bank since 1967, on the other hand, is far from unequivocal.

This article will attempt to provide an answer to the conundrum as to whether the Court has the jurisdiction to scrutinize the transfer of Israeli settlers into the West Bank that transpired before June 2014. Essentially, the Court's interpretation and characterization of article 8(2)(b)(viii) will determine the answer to this question.

In providing an answer to this question, the first part of the article will analyze the international criminal jurisprudence on instantaneous, continuous, and continuing crimes. There is a noticeable lacuna in the international criminal jurisprudence regarding the definitions of these terms. In order to remedy this, the remainder of the first part will provide a definitional framework for these terms by drawing from domestic legal sources, rules of state responsibility for internationally wrongful acts and international human rights law. The second part will assess the different implications of instantaneous, continuous, and continuing crimes in relation to the temporal jurisdiction of the Court. Instantaneous crimes, unlike continuing or continuous crimes, can easily be situated within or outside the temporal jurisdiction of the Court as all the elements of the crime in question often occur within a single moment in time. Continuing or continuous crimes, on the other hand, pose serious questions to the Court regarding its temporal jurisdiction as some elements of the crime might have taken place prior to the entry into force of the Statute (hereinafter "the critical date") and continued thereafter. The third and last part will assess the arguments as to how article 8(2)(b)(viii) fits into these categories and the consequences of adopting one characterization over the other in relation to the investigation and prosecution of Israeli settlements in the West Bank, which will have major implications regarding the breadth and scope of the Court's exercise of jurisdiction on the matter.

Which characterization eventually prevails depends in large part on whether the term "transfer of population" within the context of article 8(2)(b)(viii) will be interpreted as a discreet/instantaneous act or an ongoing/continuing act. Due to the rather ambiguous drafting of the elements of article 8(2)(b)(viii) and the relative silence of the *travaux préparatoires* on the matter, there are convincing arguments for both interpretations, which renders article 8(2)(b)(viii) open to characterization as an instantaneous, continuous, or continuing crime. Nevertheless, the present author opines that article 8(2)(b)(viii) would most appropriately be characterized as a continuing crime, as this is the only option that allows for the realization of the fundamental purpose behind the inclusion of this provision into the Statute.

II A Definitional Framework for Instantaneous, Continuing, and Continuous Crimes

A *The Definitional Gap in the International Criminal Jurisprudence*

The international criminal jurisprudence provides very limited guidance on the definitions of instantaneous, continuous and continuing crimes. Instead, continuous and continuing crimes are treated as synonymous concepts and are often used interchangeably without being properly defined.[5] For instance, both the International Criminal Tribunal for Rwanda (hereinafter 'ICTR') and the International Criminal Tribunal for the former Yugoslavia (hereinafter 'ICTY') qualified conspiracy as a continuing crime.[6] The Special Court for Sierra Leone (hereinafter 'SCSL') found the crimes of enslavement, sexual slavery and use of child soldiers to be continuous in nature.[7] The Extraordinary Chambers in the Courts of Cambodia (hereinafter 'ECCC') similarly found the crime of conspiracy, and additionally, joint criminal enterprise (hereinafter 'JCE') to be continuing in nature.[8] However, in making these findings, the judges never clearly defined what exactly is meant by continuous or continuing crimes.

The sole attempt to define the term 'continuing crime' was made by the ICTR Appeals Chamber in the *Nahimana* case. Accordingly, a continuing

---

5 *See* Prosecutor v Lubanga, ICC-01/04-01/06, Decision on the Confirmation of Charges, para. 248 (Jan. 29, 2007) [*hereinafter* Lubanga Confirmation of Charges]; where the Pre-Trial Chamber held that "the crime of enlisting and conscripting is an offence of a continuous nature- referred to by some courts as a "continuous crime" and others as a "permanent crime""]. *See* Situation in Cote d'Ivoire, ICC-02/11, Judge Fernandez de Gurmendi's separate and partially dissenting opinion to the Decision Pursuant to Article 15 of the Rome Statute on the Authorisation of an Investigation into the Situation in the Republic of Côte d'Ivoire, para. 68, n44 (Oct. 3, 2011) [*hereinafter* Gurmendi Dissent]; where Judge de Gurmendi used the terms 'continuing' and 'continuous' crimes interchangeably.

6 Prosecutor v Nahimana et al., ICTR-99-52-T, Judgement and Sentence, paras. 1017, 1044 (Dec. 3, 2003); Prosecutor v Nsengiyumva, ICTR-96-12-I, Decision on the Defence Motions Objecting to the Jurisdiction of the Trial Chamber on the Amended Indictment, paras. 27–28 (Apr. 13, 2000) [*hereinafter* Nsengiyumva Decision]; Prosecutor v. Popovic et al., IT-05-88-T, Judgement: Volume I, 10 June 2010, (10 June 2010), para. 876.

7 Prosecutor v Brima et al., SCSL-04-16-T, Judgement, paras. 39, 1820 (Jun. 20, 2007); Prosecutor v Sesay et al., Case No. SCSL-04-15-T, Judgement, para. 427 (Mar. 2, 2009) [referring to "continuous crimes pleaded in counts 6 to 9" in relation to crimes of sexual slavery, forced marriages, forced labor constituting enslavement (paras 1380–1494), and to forced marriage (para. 1410, n 2621)].

8 Case No. 002/01, Case File N 002/19/09-2007-ECCC/SC, Appeals Judgement, paras. 215–216 (Nov. 23, 2006) [*hereinafter* ECCC 002/01].

crime was defined as "[a] crime that continues after an initial illegal act has been consummated; a crime that involves ongoing elements. [A]n example is illegal U.S. drug importation. The criminal act is completed not when the drugs enter the country, but when the drugs reach their final destination. [A] crime (such as driving a stolen vehicle) that continues over an extended period."[9] Nevertheless, this finding too conflated the concepts of continuing crimes and continuous crimes, as the ICTR Appeals Chamber used the definition of a 'continuous crime' found in the Black's Law Dictionary to define the concept of 'continuing crimes' in its judgement.[10] As a result, this definition also failed to clearly delineate and illustrate the differing parameters of continuing and continuous crimes.

The ICC's core documents provide no guidance on the matter. Neither the Statute nor the Elements of Crimes (hereinafter 'EoC') or the Rules of Procedure and Evidence (hereinafter 'RPE') provide any reference to instantaneous, continuous, or continuing crimes. The recourse to the *travaux préparatoires* is of no avail either. Continuing crimes were debated at the Rome Conference, but the delegations were unable to come to an agreement on the issue and left it for the Court to resolve.[11] The jurisprudence of the ICC is also silent on the matter and, similar to other international tribunals, conflates continuous and continuing crimes.[12] To date, the Court identified only one crime under the Statute as being continuing or continuous. Both the Pre-Trial Chamber and the Trial Chamber in the *Lubanga* case found the crime of conscription and enlistment of children under the age of 15 to be continuing in nature.[13] Additionally, Judge de Gurmendi, in a dissenting opinion, qualified the crimes of enforced disappearance of persons, enslavement, imprisonment, or other severe deprivation of physical liberty, sexual slavery, enforced prostitution, persecution, and apartheid as continuing crimes.[14] In none of these instances did the judges clearly delineate what constitutes a continuous or continuing crime.

---

9   Prosecutor v Nahimana et al., ICTR-99-52-A, Judgement, para. 721, (Nov. 28, 2007) [*hereinafter* Nahimana Judgement].
10 See Black's Law Dictionary 365 (Bryan A. Garner ed., 9th ed., 2009) [*hereinafter* Black's Law].
11 Carsten Stahn et al., *The International Criminal Court's Ad Hoc Jurisdiction Revisited*, 99 Am. J. Int'l L. 421, 429 (2005) [*hereinafter* Stahn (2005)]; Per Saland, *International Criminal Law Principles*, in *The International Criminal Court: The Making of the Rome Statute: Issues, Negotiations and Results* 189, 196–197 (Roy S.K. Lee ed., 1999).
12 *See* Lubanga Confirmation of Charges, para. 248.
13 *Id.*; Prosecutor v Lubanga, ICC-01/04-01/06, Judgment pursuant to Article 74 of the Statute, para. 618 (Mar. 14, 2012) [*hereinafter* Lubanga Article 74 Judgement].
14 Gurmendi Dissent, para. 44.

The foregoing points to a lacuna in the international criminal jurisprudence regarding what exactly is a continuing or continuous crime and what elements are needed to be satisfied to qualify a particular crime as one or the other. In order to remedy this, the next section will attempt to provide a definitional framework for these concepts, drawing from domestic sources and guidance provided by other international judicial bodies as well as academic literature, especially on state responsibility for internationally wrongful acts and international human rights law.

B   *A Definitional Framework for Instantaneous, Continuing, and Continuous Crimes*

The International Law Commission's (hereinafter 'ILC') Draft Articles on State Responsibility for Internationally Wrongful Acts (hereinafter 'ARSIWA') provides good insights in relation to instantaneous, continuous, and continuing crimes. Accordingly, a breach of an international obligation by a State can either be: (i) instantaneous, meaning resolved immediately; (ii) composite, meaning composed of multiple acts which are considered unlawful by reason of their systematic relation to each other; or (iii) continuing, meaning resulting in a continuing illegal situation.[15] As will be illustrated below, in the context of individual criminal responsibility these categories correspond to instantaneous, continuous or continuing crimes respectively.

1   Instantaneous Crimes

An analogy can be drawn between instantaneous breaches of international obligations committed by States and instantaneous crimes committed by individuals. An instantaneous breach is caused by an instantaneous act which can essentially be narrowed down to a single date or a moment in time.[16] The instantaneous act which constitutes the basis of a particular instantaneous breach ceases to exist at the expiration of the brief time period that is necessary for its completion.[17] Anything that continues thereon is considered to be the effects of the act, rather than its continuation.[18] For instance, shooting

---

15   James Crawford, State Responsibility: The General Part 240 (2013) [*hereinafter* Crawford]; *See* I.L.C., Commentary on the Draft Articles on Responsibility of States for Internationally Wrongful Acts, Nov. 2001, arts. 14(1–3), & 15, 53 U.N. GAOR Supp. (No. 10) at 43, U.N. Doc. A/56/83 (2001) [*hereinafter* ARSIWA Commentary].
16   Crawford, 255.
17   Jean Salmon, *Part III: The Sources of International Responsibility, Ch. 27: Duration of a Breach*, in The Law of International Responsibility 383–384 (James Crawford et al. eds., 2010) [*hereinafter* Salmon].
18   Crawford, 255.

and harming a person is an instantaneous act, even though the harm suffered (physical suffering) may have a continuing character.[19] Similarly, breaches such as shooting down an aircraft lawfully flying over a State's airspace, or torpedoing a neutral ship on the high seas, or killing or wounding the representative of a State are instantaneous in character, and the underlying acts that constitute such breaches are instantaneous, i.e. they cease once they are committed.[20]

Similar to instantaneous breaches, instantaneous crimes are completed by a single or a discreet act that transpires in a single, immediate period of time (such as arson or murder), rather than series of acts.[21] An instantaneous crime may take time to prepare and have lasting effects, but it can only take an instant to commit and its physical elements do not persist in time.[22] The process of commission, *i.e.* the completion of all the defining components or elements of the crime, is finalized in that single defined moment.[23] The harm that the discreet act causes occurs at that moment and does not continue beyond it, even if its effects persist in time.[24] For instance, murder would be an appropriate example of an instantaneous crime, as all the elements that constitute the crime are fulfilled and the crime is completed once the victim is killed by the perpetrator with the requisite *mens rea*.[25]

Even though the definition of instantaneous crimes is relatively straightforward, delineating an act as instantaneous or continuing in nature is not an uncontroversial process. Judges, across different international tribunals working on various subject-matters, often disagree on the temporal nature of a particular act or violation. For instance in the *Phosphates in Morocco* case before the Permanent Court of International Justice (hereinafter 'PCIJ'), two judges of the five-judge bench dissented on the characterization of the formation of

---

19   Salmon, 389.
20   I.L.C., Y.B. Int'l L. Comm., Vol. II(1), 32, at 41, para. 26 (1978).
21   Jeffrey R. Boles, *Easing the Tension Between Statutes of Limitations and the Continuing Offense Doctrine*, 7 Nw. J. L. & Soc. Pol'y 219, 227–228 (2012) [*hereinafter* Boles]. *See also* Black's Law, 428.
22   Alan Nissel, Continuing Crimes in the Rome Statute, 25 Mich. J. Int'l L. 653, 661 (2004) [*hereinafter* Nissel].
23   Case of Miguel Angel Sandoval (Juan Miguel Contreras Sepulveda, et al.) – Rol no 517–04, Corte Suprema, Sala Penal, (Nov. 17, 2004) [Chile] [*hereinafter* Sandoval]; *See* Due Process Law Foundation, *Digest of Latin American Jurisprudence on International Crimes* (2010), at 46 [*hereinafter* Latin American Digest].
24   Boles, 227–228.
25   Elements of Crimes art. 7(1)(a), ICC-ASP/1/3 at 108, U.N. Doc. PCNICC/2000/1/Add, 2 (2000) [*hereinafter* Elements of Crimes].

a monopoly through legislation as an instantaneous act with lasting effects.[26] A similar disagreement took place among the ICTR Appeals Chamber judges in the *Nahimana* case, where Judge Shahabuddeen disagreed with the majority in their qualification of incitement to commit genocide as an instantaneous crime that is completed once the discourse in question is uttered or published.[27] Lastly, in *Loizidou v Turkey*, the European Court of Human Rights (hereinafter 'ECtHR') found Turkey's expropriation of the applicant's property and the subsequent refusal to grant her access to the property to constitute a continuing violation, a finding which prompting six dissenting opinions.[28] These examples are useful to illustrate the fact that it is often not a straightforward exercise to exactly pinpoint the temporal nature of an act and as a consequence, differing interpretations emerge.

2 Continuous Crimes

Regardless of the conflation of continuous and continuing crimes in the international criminal jurisprudence, a number of jurisdictions treat these concepts as distinct from one another.[29] The jurisprudence of the ECtHR is

---

26 Phosphates in Morocco Case (It. v Fr.), P.C.I.J. Ser. A/B No. 74, para. 38 (1938) [*hereinafter* PCIJ Phosphates]; Crawford, 256. Judges van Eysinga & Cheng Tien-Hsi dissented on this conclusion, the latter finding that "[t]he monopoly, although instituted by the legislation of 1920, is still existing today. If it is wrongful, it is wrongful not merely in its creation but in its continuance … This prejudice does not merely continue from an old existence but assumed a new existence every day, so long as the legislation that first created it remains in force".

27 Nahimana Judgement, para. 723. Judge Shahabuddeen disagreed with the assessment of the majority and characterized the crime of incitement to commit genocide as a continuing crime. *See* Prosecutor v Nahimana et al., ICTR-99-52-A, Partly Dissenting Opinion of Judge Shahabuddeen, para. 21 (Nov. 28, 2007) [*hereinafter* Nahimana Shahabuddeen Dissent].

28 In *Loizidou*, the European Court of Human Rights had to decide whether Turkey's expropriation of the applicant's property after the 1974 invasion of Northern Cyprus and the subsequent refusal to grant her access to her property constituted a continuing violation of Protocol 1, Article 1 of the European Human Rights Convention, which came into force for Turkey in 1990. *See* Loizidou v Turk. (Preliminary Objections), Eur. Ct. H.R., App. No. 15318/89, Judgement, paras. 99–100 (1995) [*hereinafter* Lozidou]. The decision came out with eleven judges in favor of making a finding of a continuing violation and six dissenting on this point and regarding the violation as being of instantaneous character. For those who regarded the violation as instantaneous, *see* dissenting opinions of Judge Bernhardt (joined by Judge Lopez Rocha), Judge Baka, Judge Jambrek, Judge Pettiti, and Judge Golcuklu.

29 Other commentators have also treated continuous and continuing crimes as separate concepts. *See* Michael G. Kearney, *On the Situation in Palestine and the War Crime of Transfer of Civilians into Occupied Territory*, 28 Crim. L.F. 1 (2017) [*hereinafter* Kearney].

informative in this regard. Through a comprehensive review of the legal systems of the member states of the European Council,[30] the ECtHR found a continuing crime to be "an act (or omission) which has to last over a certain period time – such as the act of assisting and giving shelter to members of an illegal organization".[31] A continuous criminal offence, on the other hand, was defined as "an offence consisting of several acts all of which contain the elements of the same (or similar) offence committed over a certain period of time, such as the intentional, continuous and large-scale concealment of taxable amounts ...".[32] Following from this distinction, the ECtHR outlined the following elements to identify continuous crimes:

1. The perpetrator commits a number of identical, similar or different criminal acts against the same legally protected interest; in addition, it is often required that the identity of the perpetrator and of the victim be the same on each occasion;
2. There is at least a similarity in the manner of execution of the individual acts (modus operandi), or there are other material circumstances connecting them which constitute a whole (actus reus);
3. There is a temporal connection between the different individual acts, which is to be assessed in the particular circumstances of each case;
4. There is the same, repeated criminal intent or purpose (mens rea) for all the individual acts, although they do not all have the planned *ab initio*;
5. The individual acts comprise, either explicitly or implicitly, the constituent elements of the criminal offence(s).[33]

The distinction between continuing and continuous crimes[34] is recognized in the Latin American criminal doctrine as well.[35] Accordingly, a continuous

---

Continuous crimes were referred to as "composite crimes" by another commentator. *See* Nissel, 653. On analyzing the U.S. doctrine of continuing offences, Graham identified two types of continuing offences for statutes of limitations purposes: pure continuing violations and modified continuing violations. *See* Kyle Graham, The Continuing Violations Doctrine, 43 Gonz. L. Rev. 271, 279–283 (2007–2008) [*hereinafter* Graham].

30 Rohlena v Czech, Eur. Ct. H.R., App. No. 59552/08, Judgement, paras. 30–32 (2015).
31 *Id.*, para. 28.
32 *Id.*
33 *Id.*, para. 33.
34 Note that in the Latin American jurisprudence, the notion of 'continuous crimes' as defined by the ECtHR is referred to as "continuing crimes" (crimen continuado) and conversely the notion of 'continuing crimes' is referred to as "continuous or permanent crimes" (*delito continuo o permanente*). For the sake of consistency, the author adopted the ECtHR's terminology. *See* Latin American Digest, at 47 n40.
35 *See* Review motion (Case Marco Antonio Monasterios Perez) (Masimiro Jose Yanez) (- Sentencia 1474, Expediente 06-1656, MP. Carmen Zuleta de Merchan, Tribunal Supremo de Justicia, para IV.1 (Aug, 10, 2007) [Venez.] [*hereinafter* Perez]; Appeal motion (recurso de apelacion extraordinaria) (Case Jesus Piedra Ibarra)(Luis de la Barreda Moreno,

crime is described as being "constituted by individual conducts or single acts that are understood as a single legal entity since all of them are perpetrated with the same single purpose and violate the same right."[36] In other words, they occur when a perpetrator with a single purpose commits different criminal acts at separate times, each of which represents only the partial perpetration of a single crime.[37] An example would be fraud committed by a person against several people on different occasions, but by means of a single underlying *"modus operandi".*[38]

An analogy can be established between composite acts found in the State responsibility literature and continuous crimes. A composite act "although not consisting of a single conduct, continues in time: it is constituted of a series of individual acts of the State which follow each other, and which all contribute to realization of the global act in question."[39] ECtHR defined a composite act as "an accumulation of identical or analogous breaches which are sufficiently numerous and interconnected to amount not merely to isolated incidents or exceptions but to a pattern or system."[40] In this sense, a composite act is not merely a series of repeated actions, but a "legal entity the whole of which represents more than the sum of its parts ... [which may] be made up of a series of individually unlawful acts."[41] Composite acts translate into continuous crimes in the context of individual criminal responsibility.[42] In this sense, similar to composite acts, for a crime to be qualified as continuous, it has to be continuous in essence and not simply constitute repetition of similar conduct.

In light of the foregoing, a continuous crime can be defined as the amalgamation of a plurality of crimes of a similar nature.[43] Such crimes are treated as

et al.) – Recurso de apelacion extraordinaria 1/2003, MO. Juventino V. Castro y Castro, Suprema Courta de Justicia de la Nacion, (Nov. 5, 2003) [Mex.] [*hereinafter* Ibarra]. Constitutional Court (Consejo Supremo de Justicia Militar), Case no. 494-V-94, Re Barrios Altos, (Jun. 4, 2001) [Peru]; Sandoval]. Even though this distinction is not clearly reflected in the English versions of some international instruments, including the Declaration on the Protection of All Persons from Enforced Disappearance, it is crucial for Latin American criminal law, as the application of many rules, including statutes of limitation, will depend on how the crime is categorized. *See* Latin American Digest, at 47, n40. R.A Kok, Statute Limitations in International Criminal Law 102 (2007) [*hereinafter* Kok].

36 *See* Latin American Digest, at 47 n40.
37 Perez; Latin American Digest, at 47.
38 *Id.*
39 Salmon, 383, 391.
40 Ir. v U.K., Eur. Ct. H.R., App. No. 5310/71, Judgment, para. 159 (1978). *See also* Crawford, 266.
41 Crawford, 266. *See also* ARSIWA Commentary, art. 15, para. 9.
42 *See* Nissel, 653; who terms such crimes as "composite crimes".
43 Héctor Olásolo, The Criminal Responsibility of Senior Political and Military Leaders as Principals to International Crimes 276 (2009) [*hereinafter* Olásolo].

a single crime as they are "only intelligible if all the components are considered together."[44] However, unlike continuing crimes, continuous crimes are not committed through, strictly speaking, a single act the commission of which lasts for a prolonged duration of time. Instead a continuous crime is constituted by a series of discreet acts that are internally and externally connected to one another and fulfil the elements of a single criminalization.[45] This connection is often based on factors such as the repetition of the same kind of criminal acts, the uniformity of the perpetrator's intent, the proximity in time between the acts, the location, the victim or the class of victims, or the object or purpose of the criminal conduct which join such acts together.[46] The ending point of a continuous crime is when the perpetrator ceases the proscribed conduct. For instance, The ECCC Supreme Chamber demonstrated through its analysis on JCE held that:

> The temporal extent of [the JCE] starts with the initial contribution to the common purpose as an expression of the shared criminal intent and ends with either the cessation of any further criminal activity by the enterprise or, as far as individuals contributing to the implementation are concerned, withdrawal from the enterprise, the latter requiring cessation of any further contribution as well as abandonment of the shared criminal intent.[47]

Genocide by killing is an appropriate example for both composite acts and continuous crimes. For a series of State conduct to constitute genocide, killings need to be multiple and accompanied by the specific intent to destroy a national, ethnic, racial or religious group.[48] Similarly, for the type of conduct

---

44 ECCC 002/01, para. 215.
45 Gurmendi Dissent, para. 68 n44. *See also* Prosecutor v Semanza, ICTR-97-20-T, Separate and Dissenting Opinion of Judge Pavel Dolenc, para. 32 (May 15, 2003) [*hereinafter* Semanza Dolenc Dissent].
46 Semanza Dolenc Dissent, para. 32. *See also* Prosecutor v Nahimana et al., ICTR-99-52-A, Partly Dissenting Opinion of Judge Fausto Pocar, para. 2 (Nov. 28, 2007).
47 ECCC 002/01, para. 215.
48 Convention on the Prevention and Punishment of the Crime of Genocide art. 2, Jan. 12, 1951, 78 U.N.T.S. 277; Crawford, 267. Judge Lauterpacht found that "a claim of genocide involves the establishment of a pattern or accumulation of individual claims." *See* Case Concerning Application of the Convention on the Prevention and Punishment of the Crime of Genocide (Bosn. & Herz. v Yugoslavia), Counter-Claims Order, Separate Opinion of Judge Lauterpacht, 1997 I.C.J. Rep. 243, para. 13 (Dec. 17). *See also* William A. Schabas, The International Criminal Court: A Commentary on the Rome Statute 134 (2016) [*hereinafter*

enumerated under article 6 of the Statute to constitute genocide, the perpetrator must intend to "destroy, in whole or in part, [a] national, ethnical, racial or religious group as such" and the conduct must take place "in the context of manifest pattern of similar conduct directed against that group or was conduct that could itself effect such destruction."[49] Therefore, whereas killings perpetrated by an individual may constitute multiple murders, if accompanied by the requisite *mens rea* and the contextual element found in the EoC,[50] they could be amalgamated to constitute a single continuous crime of genocide by killing under article 6(a) of the Statute.

Another example of a continuous crime under the Statute is the crime of using children under the age of fifteen to participate actively in hostilities.[51] This crime was characterized as such by in the *Lubanga* case:

> [E]ach individual instance of enlistment into the FPLC, conscription into the FPLC or use to participate actively in hostilities of children under the age of fifteen gives rise to a crime within the jurisdiction of the Court. However, the Chamber considers that it is advisable to treat (1) all instances of enlistment into the FPLC as a continuous war crime of enlistment of children under the age of fifteen into the FPLC; (2) all instances of conscription into the FPLC as a continuous war crime of conscription of children under the age of fifteen into the FPLC; and (3) all instances of use to participate actively in hostilities of children under the age of fifteen by members of the UPC/FPLC as a continuous war

---

Schabas]; Application of the Convention on the Prevention and Punishment of the Crime of Genocide (Croat. v Serb.), Judgment, 2015 I.C.J. Rep. 3, paras. 137–139 (Feb. 3).

49 Elements of Crimes, art. 6(a)–(e).

50 The majority of the Pre-Trial Chamber (Judge Usacka dissenting) interpreted this element to mean that the conduct "must have taken place in the context of a manifest pattern of similar conduct directed against the targeted group or must have had such a nature so as to itself effect, the total or partial destruction of the targeted group". The majority found that "according to this contextual element, the crime of genocide is only completed when the relevant conduct presents a concrete threat to the existence of the targeted group, or a part thereof. In other words, the protection offered by the penal norm defining the crime of genocide – as an *ultima ratio* mechanism to preserve the highest values of the international community – is only triggered when the threat against the existence of the targeted group, or part thereof, becomes concrete and real, as opposed to just being latent or hypothetical". *See* Prosecutor v Al-Bashir, ICC-02/05-01/09, Decision on the Prosecution's Application for a Warrant of Arrest against Omar Hasan Ahmad Al Bashir, paras. 123–124 (Mar. 4, 2009) [*hereinafter* Bashir Decision]. Note that this finding represents a departure from the case law of ad-hoc tribunals; *see* Schabas 130–131.

51 Rome Statute arts. 8(2)(b)(xxvi) & 8(2)(e)(vii).

crime of use to participate actively in hostilities of children under the age of fifteen.[52]

The underlying conduct that constitutes this crime is telling as to why this is the case. The crime of using children to participate actively in hostilities is constituted by "both direct participation in combat and also active participation in military activities linked to combat such as scouting, spying, sabotage and the use of children as decoys, couriers or at military checkpoints."[53] Accordingly, even though every time a child under the age of 15 is used by the perpetrator to fulfil one of these roles a war crime is completed, all of these individual instances of use can be amalgamated into and treated as a single continuous crime.[54] This example is also useful to illustrate the difference between continuing and continuous crimes. As described above, continuous crimes are made up of discreet acts that are completed and are linked to each other based on their contextual similarities. On the other hand, continuing crimes, as will be described below, encompass situations where an unlawful state of affairs is established and then maintained by the perpetrator. The crime of using child soldiers, in this sense, can be seen as an amalgamation of discreet acts that are completed every time a child under the age of 15 performs a particular task that qualifies as active participation. Enlistment and conscription, in contrast, are continuing crimes as they entail the establishment of an unlawful state of affairs, *i.e.* the membership of the child in the armed group, which continues as long as the child remains within the armed group.

3   Continuing Crimes

Similar to instantaneous and continuous crimes, the State responsibility literature is helpful in understanding continuing crimes. In the State responsibility literature, a continuing wrongful act "denotes a single act, constituting a wrongful act, which is prolonged in time …"[55] For an act to be considered as

---

52   Prosecutor v Lubanga, ICC-01/04-01/06, Decision concerning Pre-Trial Chamber I's Decision of February 2006 and the Incorporation of Documents into the Record of the Case against Mr. Thomas Lubanga Dyilo, para. 91 (Feb. 24, 2006). It should be noted that the Pre-Trial Chamber later on qualified enlistment and conscription as a continuing crime and not a continuous crime. See Lubanga Confirmation of Charges, para. 248 n321.
53   Prosecutor v Lubanga, ICC-01/04-01/06 A 5, Judgment, paras. 334–335 (Dec. 1, 2014) [*hereinafter* Lubanga Appeal Judgment].
54   Olásolo, 276 n321.
55   Salmon, 386.

such, it must be continuing in essence and not merely in terms of its effects.[56] Continuing acts involve the perpetuation of an illegal situation, such as: the maintenance in force of a legislation that constitutes a continuing interference with the right of an individual to respect for his private life;[57] illegal detention of a foreign official;[58] illegitimate occupation of part of the territory of another State; the maintenance of armed contingents on the territory of another State without its consent; and the maintenance of colonial domination by force or the illegal blockade of foreign coasts and ports.[59]

An example from the ILC commentary on ARSIWA lends further support to this contention. Accordingly, the act of wrongful taking of property is a completed act, and not a continuing one, if "the expropriation is carried out by legal process, with the consequence that title to the property concerned is transferred ..."[60] Conversely, in case of a de facto, creeping or disguised expropriation resulting in a denial of status, ownership or possession where no such legal process is undertaken, the expropriation would constitute a continuing wrongful act.[61] This example seems to indicate that the crucial element regarding the continuity of a violation is the persistence of the unlawful state of affairs that is a direct result of the initial wrongful conduct. As long as the legal title has not passed and the denial of status, ownership or possession persists, the act of expropriation is a continuing wrongful act whereas once the legal title has passed, the wrongful act is completed, even if the economic consequences extend over time.[62]

Accordingly, for a continuing wrongful act to be completed, the illegal state of affairs has to come to an end as, for instance, upon the return of the body of a disappeared person to the next of kin, in the case of the crime of enforced disappearance.[63] Similarly, once the hostages are released, or the forces that are unlawfully present in an occupied territory are withdrawn, these acts are considered as no longer having a continuing character, even though their

---

56 Andreas Zimmermann, *Palestine and the International Criminal Court Quo Vadis? Reach and Limits of Declarations under Article 12(3)*, 11 J. Int'l Crim. Jus. 303, 323 (2013) [hereinafter Zimmermann].
57 Dudgeon v U.K., Eur. Ct. H.R., App. No 7525/76, para. 41 (1981).
58 United States Diplomatic and Consular Staff in Tehran (U.S. v Iran), Judgment, 1980 I.C.J. Rep 1980, para. 76–78, (24 May).
59 Salmon 383, 386.
60 ARSIWA Commentary art. 14, 60, para. 4.
61 *Id.*, art. 14, 60, para. 4.
62 *Id.*, art. 14, 60, para. 6.
63 *Id.*, art. 14, 60, para. 5.

effects may persist.[64] One useful practice in distinguishing continuing breaches from instantaneous breaches is, in this sense, is to see whether the remedy of cessation is still available to the perpetrator, or only restitution in kind or compensation suffices to provide reparation for the totality of the conduct.[65] If the former is the case, a continuing violation can be established.[66]

A similar approach in relation to continuing violations is employed in the international human rights jurisprudence. In the aforementioned *Loizidou* case before the ECtHR, Turkey argued that under article 159 of the Constitution of the Turkish Republic of Northern Cyprus of 1985, the property in question had been expropriated, and this had occurred prior to Turkey's acceptance of the Court's jurisdiction in 1990.[67] The ECtHR found the 1985 Constitution to be in contravention of international law as well as the relevant Security Council resolutions, and therefore could not be attributed legal effect, meaning that the expropriation of Ms. Loizidou's property was not legally completed at that time and the property continued to belong to her.[68] Consequently, the ECtHR found the ongoing refusal of Turkey to grant Ms. Loizidou access to her property after 1990 to constitute a continuing violation of its treaty obligations, even though the initial act of confiscation of property took place before the critical date.[69] In contrast, in *X v United Kingdom*, the European Commission of Human Rights (hereinafter 'the Commission') refused to find a continuing situation where the applicant was deprived of his property due to an Act of Parliament abolishing the rights of landowners whose property adjoined that of British Railways.[70] Instead, the Commission characterized the expropriation as an instantaneous act with enduring effects.[71] The distinguishing factor between these two cases, similar to the approach of the ILC, is that in the

---

64   *Id.*
65   Joost Pauwelyn, *The Concept of a 'Continuing Violation' of an International Obligation: Selected Problems*, 66 Brit. Y.B. Int'l L. 415, 420 (1996) [*hereinafter* Pauwelyn]; Nissel, 667.
66   Pauwelyn, 420.
67   Loizidou, para. 99.
68   Loizidou v Turkey, Eur. Ct. H.R, App. No. 15318/89, Judgment, paras. 60–64 (1996) [*hereinafter* Loizidou Judgement].
69   Yearbook of the International Law Commission, Vol. II(2), 32, page 61, para. 10 (2001); Judgment, paras. 60–64. This approach finds support in U.S. domestic case law as well. *See* Bodner v Banque Paribas, 114 F. Supp. 2d 117, page 134–135 (E.D.N.Y. 2000); where, in relation to plaintiffs who sought the reinstitution of their confiscated assets by the Nazis during the World War II, the U.S. courts found that "continued denial of [the plaintiffs'] assets, as well as facts and information relating thereto, if proven, constitutes a continuing violation of international law …". *See also* Graham, 272.
70   X v U.K., European Comm. Hum. Rts., Decisions and Reports, vol. 8, 211, page 212; Pauwelyn, 423.
71   *Id.*

former case the expropriation was *de facto* in nature whereas in the latter it was *de jure*.[72] Accordingly, *de facto* expropriation was treated as a continuing violation due to the perpetuation of an unlawful state of affairs whereas *de jure* expropriation, even if it is a violation, was regarded as a completed act.

Similar to continuing wrongful acts, continuing crimes involve "an ongoing course of conduct that causes a harm that lasts as long as that course of conduct persists"[73] which is "by its nature or by its terms ... a single, ongoing crime."[74] In this sense, a continuing offense is distinguishable from "an offense that continues in a factual sense, as [is the case] where a defendant engages in a course of conduct comprised of repeated criminal violations, such as recurring sales of narcotics or a string of separate robberies."[75] The focus is not on the continuing effect of a ceased instantaneous cause, such as a continuing ailment caused by a serious assault.[76] Instead the focus is on the continuing operation of the cause or, in other words, the influence exerted by the initial conduct itself.[77] This continuing cause or influence entails the creation of an unlawful state of affairs[78] which is then maintained by the subsequent conduct of the perpetrator.[79] The *actus reus* of the crime continues to take place as long as this unlawful state of affairs persists.[80]

In the course of a continuing crime, the legal interest that the prohibition in question aims to protect continues to be infringed and the harm that it was designed to prevent continues to be inflicted.[81] Therefore, for a crime to be

---

72 Pauwelyn, 424.
73 Based on Judge O'Scannlain's definition of a continuing offence in: U.S. v Morales, 11 F 3d at 921, (9th Cir. 1993) (O'Scannlain, J., dissenting); Boles, 228.
74 U.S. v Castellano, 610 F. Supp. 1359, 1408 (S.D.N.Y. 1985); *found in* Boles, 228.
75 U.S. v Rivlin, No. 07-Cr-524, 2007 U.S. Dist. LEXIS 89323, at *6–7 (S.D.N.Y. Dec. 5, 2007); U.S. v Yashar, 166 F.3d 873, page 875 (7th Cir. 1999) [*hereinafter* U.S. v Yashar]; U.S. v Reitmeyer, 356 F.3d 1313, 1321 (10th Cir. 2004), *found in* Boles, 228.
76 Nahimana Shahabuddeen Dissent, para. 26. *See also* Del. State Coll. v Ricks, 449 U.S. 250, 258 (1980) [*hereinafter* Del. State Coll. v. Ricks]; Elad Peled, *Rethinking the Continuing Violation Doctrine: The Application of Statutes of Limitations to Continuing Tort Claims*, 41 Ohio N. Univ. L. Rev., 343, 348–349 (2004–2005) [*hereinafter* Peled]. *See also* PCIJ Phosphates, at 26.
77 ICTR Nahimana Shahabuddeen Dissent, para 26. *See also* Del. State Coll. v Ricks; Peled, 366; PCIJ Phosphates, at 26.
78 Astolfo Di Amato, Criminal Law in Italy 78 (2011); Nissel, 654 (2004). Referred to as an "antijuridicial situation" in the Venezuelan jurisprudence; *see* Perez; Latin American Digest, page 47 (2010).
79 Perez; Ibarra; Latin American Digest, page 47–48.
80 *See* Schabas, 557.
81 U.S. v Yashar, page 875; Toussie v United States, No. 441, United States Supreme Court, page 122; Boles, 229 (2012); Sandoval; Latin American Digest, 46.

continuing in nature, the legal interest which is protected from the crime must be susceptible to harm over a prolonged period,[82] and the harm caused to the victim(s) must accumulate over the consummation period.[83] For instance, in crimes such as kidnapping, abduction and forced disappearance the consummation period begins at "the moment a physical impediment is imposed on the victim's freedom of movement and he is detained or confined in a certain location, and it continues throughout the period of deprivation of freedom."[84] The legally protected interest in these cases can be seen as freedom, which by its very nature continues to exist and be impaired, although not destroyed, throughout the prolonged consummation period of these crimes.[85] In this sense, continuing crimes only come to an end once the perpetrator ceases the proscribed course of act or omission[86] and as a consequence desists from the unlawful state of affairs.[87] For the crime to be considered complete, therefore, the perpetrator must cease acts that cause the maintenance or exacerbation of the unlawful state of affairs, and take affirmative steps to improve the situation of his/her own making, such as by releasing a falsely imprisoned victim.[88] This is the only way the continually reiterated intention of the perpetrator to confirm or perpetuate the wrongful act or situation, an intrinsic feature of continuing violations,[89] would come to an end.

In light of the foregoing, the following five elements can be identified to constitute a continuing crime:

1. A precipitating act of the perpetrator(s) creates an unlawful state of affairs that is prolonged through the consummation period;
2. The actus reus of the crime continues to take place as long as the unlawful state of affairs is maintained by the subsequent conduct of the perpetrator(s);
3. The continuation of the unlawful state of affairs and the consequent harm is contingent upon the will of the perpetrator(s);

---

82   Sandoval; Latin American Digest, 46.
83   Kuhnle Bros., Inc v County of Geauga, 103 F.3d 516, 522 (6th Cir. 1997) [*hereinafter* Kuhnle Bros., Inc v County of Geauga]; Graham, 286; Ibarra; Latin American Digest, 48. *See also* Peled, 348–349.
84   Ibarra; Perez; Latin American Digest, 47–48.
85   Ibarra; Latin American Digest, 49.
86   U.S. v Motz, 652 F. Supp. 2d 284, 293 (E.D.N.Y. 2009); U.S. v McGoff, 831 F.3d 1071, 1079 (D.C. Cir. 1987); Boles, 228; *See* Kok, 30; referring to the decisions of the Netherlands Supreme Court (Hoge Raad).
87   Perez; Latin American Digest, 47.
88   Graham, 285.
89   Pauwelyn, 420; Ibarra; Latin American Digest, 48.

4. The legally protected interest of the victims continues to be infringed over the consummation period;
5. The harm caused to the victim(s) accumulates over time.[90]

This approach towards continuing crimes was implicitly affirmed by the Court in the *Lubanga* case, where for the first time a crime under the Statute was construed as being of a continuing nature. Accordingly, "the crime of enlisting and conscripting [children under the age of fifteen] is an offence of a continuing nature ... [which] continues to be committed as long as the children remain in the armed groups or forces and consequently ceases to be committed when these children leave the groups or reach age fifteen."[91] This finding points to the fact that "although the initial act of recruitment will constitute a discrete event, arguably essence of the [prohibition] is not merely the original moment of conscription or enlistment, but rather the child's continuing membership in the armed group or force ..."[92] This is because the legally protected interest under these provisions, i.e. the protection of vulnerable children from the concomitant risks to their lives and well-being created by the enlistment, conscription or use to participate actively in the hostilities,[93] continues to be infringed and the associated harm continues to be caused as long as the child remains in the armed force. From this point of view, conscription or enlistment is not only a discreet event but also an ongoing process that reoccurs each day that the child remains within the armed group.[94] Accordingly, any active role played by the perpetrator in the continued engagement of the victim in the armed forces or a failure to use his/her capacity to bring an end to the child's participation would incur liability under these provisions.[95] In other words, articles 8(2)(e)(vii) and 8(2)(b)(xxvi) do not only prohibit the discreet act of initial conscription or enlistment, but also includes an implicit prohibition on any conduct that maintains or perpetuates the membership of the child in the armed forces. Any conduct that facilitates the continued membership of

---

90   *See* Kuhnle Bros., Inc v County of Geauga; Graham, 286. *See* Ibarra; Latin American Digest, 48. *See also* Peled, 348–349.
91   Lubanga Confirmation of Charges, para. 248. Pre-Trial Chamber's interpretation was confirmed verbatim by the Trial Chamber in the trial judgment. *See* Lubanga Article 74 Judgement, para. 618.
92   Rod Rastan, *Jurisdiction*, in The Law and Practice of the International Criminal Court 141, 173 (Carsten Stahn ed., 2015) [*hereinafter* Rastan].
93   Lubanga Article 74 Judgement, para. 617; Lubanga Judgment, paras. 324.
94   Rod Rastan and Mohamed Elewa Badar, *Article 11: Jurisdiction Ratione Temporis*, in The Rome Statute of the International Criminal Court: A Commentary 657, 668 (Otto Triffterer and Kai Ambos, 2016) [*hereinafter* Rastan and Badar].
95   Schabas, 557.

the child in the armed forces would, therefore, satisfy the material elements of articles 8(2)(e)(vii) and 8(2)(b)(xxvi).

III ICC and Instantaneous, Continuous and Continuing Crimes

As indicated above, instantaneous crimes generally occur over a very short period of time. Therefore, pinpointing whether they have taken place within or outside the temporal jurisdiction of the Court is relatively straightforward. This is not the case for a continuing or a continuous crime where the crime may have started before the critical date and may unfold over days, months or even years. To date, this has never been the case before the ICC. Thus, the approach that the Court will take towards continuing and continuous crimes that have their origins outside its temporal jurisdiction is still unknown. It is very likely that the Israeli settlements and the prosecution of conduct linked to their establishment is going to be the first situation where the Court will have to decide on what course it will take in this regard. Accordingly, this part of the article will attempt to shed light on how the Court may approach crimes of continuing nature that have their origins outside its temporal jurisdiction without offending the confines of the jurisdictional framework set out in the Statute.

A *ICC's Temporal Jurisdictional Framework*

Pursuant to article 11(1) of the Statute, only crimes committed after the entry into force of the Statute are amenable to the jurisdiction of the Court.[96] The baseline of the temporal jurisdiction of the Court was set as 1 July 2002 with the entry into force of the Statute after achieving 60 ratifications. Hence the Court cannot under any circumstances exercise jurisdiction over crimes committed prior to this date.[97] For individual State Parties, the Court's temporal jurisdiction runs from the date that the Statute entered into force for that State pursuant to article 11(2), unless "that State has made a declaration under [article 12(3)]."[98] This means that a State on becoming a Party to the Statute or anytime thereafter can lodge an article 12(3) declaration to provide the Court with retroactive temporal jurisdiction.[99] In this sense, article 11(2) provides

---

[96] G.M. Pikis, The Rome Statute for the International Criminal Court: Analysis of the Statute, the Rules of Procedure and Evidence, the Regulations of the Court and Supplementary Instruments 51 (2010).

[97] R. Cryer et al, An Introduction to International Criminal Law and Procedure, 169 (2010).

[98] Rome Statute art. 11(2).

[99] Rastan and Badar, 671.

both the States Parties and the non-member States the option to accept the Court's jurisdiction retroactively through an article 12(3) declaration, the absolute limit being July 2002.[100]

Principles of *nullum crimen sine lege* and non-retroactivity ratione personae enshrined in articles 22 and 24 of the Statute respectively supplement this jurisdictional framework. Article 22(1)[101] requires the conduct of the perpetrator to constitute a crime within the jurisdiction of the Court at the time that it takes place.[102] The word jurisdiction in article 22(1) "is to be understood in its full sense as encompassing all articles that the Court would consider in making a jurisdictional ruling under article 19…"[103] Thus, the constituent elements of a crime under the Statute can only be satisfied in relation to a perpetrator if the his/her conduct and the crime have taken place within the temporal jurisdiction of the Court. Accordingly, any conduct (including both actions and omissions)[104] occurring outside the temporal jurisdiction of the Court would not constitute a crime within the jurisdiction of the Court.[105] Article 24(1),[106] similarly, provides that no criminal responsibility can be incurred by an individual for his/her conduct violating the provisions of the Statute prior to the entry into force of the Statute.[107] These safeguards stem from the principle that offences and the relevant penalties in relation to a conduct be clearly defined

---

100 Iain Cameron, *Jurisdiction and Admissibility Issues under the ICC Statute*, in The Permanent International Criminal Court: Legal and Policy Issues 65, 70 (Dominic McGoldrick et al. eds., 2004). *See also* the following decisions where the Court allowed the utilization of article 12(3) declarations in the Gbagbo case to provide the Court with retroactive jurisdiction: Prosecutor v Laurent Gbagbo, Decision on the "Corrigendum of the Challenge to the Jurisdiction of the International Criminal Court on the basis of articles 12(3), 19(2), 21(3), 55 and 59 of the Rome Statute filed by he Defence for President Gbagbo, ICC-02/11/-01/11, paras. 60–65 (Aug. 15, 2012); Prosecutor v Gbagbo, Judgment on the Appeal of Mr. Laurent Koudou Gbagbo against the decision of Pre-Trial Chamber I on jurisdiction and stay of proceedings, ICC-02/11-01/11 OA 2, paras. 82–83 (Dec. 12, 2012).

101 Rome Statute art. 22(1); reads "[a] person shall not be criminally responsible under this Statute unless the conduct in question constitutes, at the time it takes place, a crime within the jurisdiction of the Court."

102 *Id.*

103 Bruce Broomhall, *Article 22: Nullum Crimen Sine Lege*, in The Rome Statute of the International Criminal Court: A Commentary 949, 959 (Otto Triffterer and Kai Ambos, 2016) [*hereinafter* Broomhall].

104 Raul C. Pangalangan, *Article 24: Non-retroactivity ratione personae*, in The Rome Statute of the International Criminal Court: A Commentary 971, 975 (Otto Triffterer and Kai Ambos, 2016).

105 Broomhall, 949, 963.

106 Rome Statute art. 24(1); reads "[n]o person shall be criminally responsible under this Statute for conduct prior to the entry into force of the Statute."

107 *Id.*

so that the individual can know exactly what acts and omissions will make him/her criminally liable, in order to prevent arbitrary prosecutions, convictions and punishments.[108]

B   *International Jurisprudence on Temporal Jurisdiction and Instantaneous, Continuous, and Continuing Crimes*

The approach adopted by the ICTR in relation to continuing or continuous crimes that have their origins outside the temporal jurisdiction of the Tribunal provides helpful guidance in understanding the jurisdictional framework set up by articles 11, 22 and 24 of the Statute. The ICTR Appeals Chamber outlined three conditions to be fulfilled with regards to the temporal jurisdiction of the Tribunal for the imposition of criminal liability on an individual: (i) the crime which the accused is charged with was committed in 1994 [*i.e.* within the temporal jurisdiction of the ICTR]; (ii) the acts or omissions of the accused establishing his responsibility under any of the modes of responsibility occurred in 1994; and (iii) the accused had the requisite *mens rea* in order to be convicted.[109] Accordingly, even for the commission of a continuing or a continuous crime, an accused can only be convicted for his/her conduct that occurred within the temporal jurisdiction of the Tribunal.[110] Any conduct that took place outside its temporal jurisdiction cannot be a basis for conviction before the ICTR.[111]

That being said, the ICTY jurisprudence allows for the examination of acts and admission of evidence related to incidents that took place outside its temporal jurisdiction if they: (i) provide relevant historical background information, (ii) a basis for understanding and establishing the perpetrator's conduct (in particular his/her criminal intent) related to the crimes that occurred within the Tribunal's temporal jurisdiction, or (iii) demonstrate a deliberate pattern of conduct on the part of the perpetrator(s).[112] The Trial Chamber

---

108   S.W. v U.K., Eur. Ct. H.R., App. No. 20166/92, Judgement, para. 34 (1995) [*hereinafter* S.W. v U.K.]; Kafkaris v Cyprus, Eur. Ct. H.R., App. No. 21906/04, Judgment, para. 137 (2008); Cantoni v France, Eur. Ct. H.R., App. No. 17862/91, Judgment, para. 29 (1996).

109   Nahimana Judgement, para. 313.

110   *Id.*, para. 724.

111   Prosecutor v Nzege, Case No. ICTR 96-11-AR72, Decision on the Interlocutory Appeals, at 6 (Sep. 5, 2000) [*hereinafter* Nzege Interocutory Appeals]; Nahimana Judgement, para. 317.

112   Stahn (2005), 430; William A. Schabas, The UN International Criminal Tribunals: The Former Yugoslavia, Rwanda and Sierra Leone 136 (2006). *See* Nsengiyumva Decision, paras. 27–28; Prosecutor v Kabiligi, Case No. ICTR-96-34-1, Decision on the defence motions objecting to a lack of jurisdiction and seeking to declare the indictment void ab initio, paras. 33, 38–39 (Apr. 13, 2000); Nahimana v Prosecutor, Case No. ICTR 96-11-AR72, Decision on the Interlocutory Appeals, at 6 (Sept. 5, 2000) [*hereinafter* Nahimana Interlocutory Appeals]; Prosecutor v Ngeze, Case No. ICTR 97-27-I, Decision on the

in *Nsengiyumva* provided a good summary of the Tribunal's position in this regard:

> The Trial Chamber accepts the Prosecutor's submission that the allegations dating before 1994 do not constitute independent crimes. These allegations merely represent what the Prosecutor intends to offer as relevant and admissible evidence of crimes occurring in 1994, or relate to the continuation of events, clarify, and are supplementary to the substantive charges ... Conspiracy is a "continuing crime." Because [it] is a continuing crime, then events that took place outside the period of the Statute can be taken into account if it can be shown that the conspiracy continued into the relevant period of the Statute. Evidence before 1994 may show when the conspiracy actually commenced. All activities prior to 1 January 1994, so far as they are related to the conspiracy, may be relevant.[113]

This effectively means that any allegation of criminal conduct that falls outside the temporal jurisdiction of the ICTR can only be used in "proving the ingredients of the offences which were allegedly committed within the temporal jurisdiction of the Tribunal ... [as] these allegations may be subsidiary or interrelated allegations to the principal allegation in issue and thus may have probative and evidentiary value."[114] Such evidence, however, cannot be used as the sole basis to prove a count in the indictment.[115]

The practice of international human rights bodies in relation to their temporal jurisdiction is similar to the ICTR's approach. Accordingly, in application of international human rights treaties, only the part of a continuing situation which takes place after the date that treaty in question entered into force can be considered a violation.[116] In this sense, the ECtHR has already "endorsed the notion of a continuing violation of the Convention and its effects as to temporal limitations of the competence of Convention organs."[117] In the seminal *De Becker* case, the Commission had to decide whether the fact that the starting

---

Prosecutor's Request for Leave to Amend the Indictment, para. 3 (Nov. 5, 1999); Nahimana Judgement, para. 315.
113   Nsengiyumva, paras. 27–28. *See also* Nahimana Interlocutory Appeals, at 6.
114   Prosecutor v Nahimana et al., Case No. ICTR-96-11-T, Decision on the Prosecutor's Request for Leave to File an Amended Indictment, paras. 27–28 (Nov. 5 1999). Stahn (2005), 430.
115   Nzege Interlocutory Appeals, at 6.
116   Antoine Buyse, *A Lifeline in Time – Non-retroactivity and Continuing Violations under the ECHR*, 75 Nor. J. Int. L. 63, 75 (2006) [*hereinafter* Buyse].
117   Veeber v Est. (No. 1), Eur. Ct. H.R., App. No. 37571/97, Judgment, para. 54 (2003) [*hereinafter* Veeber v Est.].

point of the denial of right to freedom of expression of the applicant lay before the entry into force of the Convention for Belgium rendered his case inadmissible. The Commission found that "the Applicant had found himself placed in a continuing situation which had no doubt originated before the entry into force of the Convention in respect of [the Respondent] Belgium (14th June 1955), but which had continued after that date, since the forfeitures in question had been imposed for life".[118] Ultimately, the Commission declared admissible only the part of the application in relation to the period subsequent to the date Belgium ratified the Convention.[119] It follows from this finding that an act that has its origins prior to the entry into force of the Convention may constitute a continuing violation extending after that date, allowing the ECtHR to exercise jurisdiction.[120] Nevertheless, similar to the ICTR, where an unlawful continuing act has occurred partly before and party after the critical date, the ECtHR can only exercise temporal jurisdiction in relation to the latter part.[121] Any act, fact or situation prior to the critical date can be taken into account solely for the determination of a violation that took place within the jurisdiction of the ECtHR.[122]

This approach to continuing violations resonates in the jurisprudence of other international human rights bodies as well. The Inter-American Court of Human Rights (IACtHR) held that it had "competence to examine human rights violations that are continuing or permanent even though the initial act violating them took place before the date on which the Court's contentious jurisdiction was accepted, if the said violations persist after the date of acceptance, because they continue to be committed; thus, the principle of non-retroactivity is not violated."[123] The Human Rights Committee also followed

---

118 De Becker v Belgium, Eur. Ct. H.R., App. No 214/5, Judgment, para. 8 (1962).
119 *Id.*
120 Salmon, 387–388. Such situations are referred to as "a continuing situation, which still obtains at the present time" by the Commission, *see* Papamichalopoulos and Others v Greece, ECHR, App. No 14556/89, Judgment, para. 40 (1993); Agrotexim and others v Greece, ECHR, App. No 14807/89, Judgement, paras. 57–58 (1995).
121 Salmon, 383, 387. *See* Courcy v U.K., Decision on admissibility, Dec. 16, 1966 (1967), Y.B Eur. Comm. Hum. Rts., 383; E Com HR, Roy and Alice Fletcher v U.K., App. No. 3034/67, Decision on Admissibility (Dec. 19, 1967).
122 Buyse, 63, 75. *See* Broniowski v Poland, Eur. Ct. H.R., App. No. 31443/96, Decision as to the Admissibility, para. 74 (Dec. 19, 2002); Yağci and Sargin v. Turkey, Eur. Ct. H.R., 6/1994/453/533–534, Judgment (Merits and Just Satisfaction), para. 40 (Jun. 8, 1995); Almeida Garrett, Mascarenhas Falcão and Others v. Portugal, Eur. Ct. H.R., App. No. 29813/96, Judgment, para. 43 (Jan. 11, 2000).
123 Rastan and Badar, 665; Rio Negro Massacres v. Guatemala, Inter-Am. Ct. H.R., Judgment of 4 September 2012, para. 37.

suit in finding that it could consider a violation that has taken place prior to the entry into force of the International Covenant on Civil and Political Rights (ICCPR) "unless it is a violation that continues after that date or has effects which themselves constitute a violation of the [ICCPR] after that date."[124]

The Supreme Court Chamber of ECCC ("the SCC" hereinafter) adopted a different approach in relation to crimes of ongoing nature. Accordingly, for the ECCC to exercise jurisdiction in relation to a JCE:

> The actus rei of the crimes that form the subject of the charges must fall within the [temporal jurisdiction of ECCC], while the conduct giving rise to individual criminal liability based on participation in a joint criminal enterprise may have occurred before, provided it formed part of extended contributions to the implementation of a common purpose which continued after 16 April 1975 ... [G]iven that the contributions of the Accused occurred before 17 April 1975 were part of a cluster of transactions of a joint criminal enterprise that continued over a period of time and brought to fruition the relevant actus rei committed within the jurisdictional period of the ECCC, the crime in question was committed within the temporal jurisdiction of the ECCC, as required by Article 2 new of the ECCC Law.[125]

Accordingly, the ECCC could convict an accused based on his/her contributions to a JCE to the critical date, in case the JCE continued into the temporal jurisdiction of the Chambers and the accused did not distance him or herself from the common criminal purpose or continued to contribute to it.[126] The ECCC, in this sense, distinguishes between the crimes committed by the principal perpetrators and the conduct of an accused who did not personally commit the crimes, but contributed to their commission through, for instance, contributing to a JCE.[127] Consequently, departing from the practice of the ICTR, the SCC allowed the Trial Chamber to rely on the conduct of the

---

124   Rastan and Badar, 665; Hum. Rts. Comm., Ibrahima Gueye et al. v. France, Com No. 196/1986, para 5.3 (Apr. 6, 1989), para 5.3. *See also* Hum. Rts. Comm., Miguel A. Millan Sequeira v. Uruguay, Com. No. R.1/6, U.N. Doc. Supp. No. 40 (A/35/49) (Feb. 6, 1977), at para. 16 (1980); Sandra Lovelace v. Canada, Com. No. 24/1977, U.N. Doc. CCPR/C/13/D/24/1977, (1977), para 7.3; Hum. Rts. Comm., Eugeniusz Kurowski v. Poland, Hum Rts. Comm., No. 872/1999, U.N. Doc. CCPR/C/77/D/872/1999 (2003), at para. 6.4.
125   Case No 002/01, Case File N 002/19/09-2007-ECCC/SC, Appeals Judgement, paras 217, 221 (Nov. 23, 2006).
126   *Id.*, para. 221.
127   *Id.*

accused that took place before the critical date to enter a conviction in relation to crimes that were committed within the temporal jurisdiction of the ECCC.[128]

Arguably, the ICTR's approach in relation to conduct pre-dating the critical date is more in line with the explicit provisions of the temporal framework set up by articles 11, 22(1) and 24(1) of the Statute compared to that of the ECCC. Similar to the ICTR, the Statute does not provide the Court with any scope for considering acts which pre-date the entry into force of the Statute or outside its temporal jurisdiction.[129] Instead "[t]he possibility of relying on events prior to the [temporal jurisdiction of the Court] would remain confined to acts of a continuing nature and to evidentiary matters such as establishing the contextual elements of crimes or the existence of a common criminal plan."[130] Indeed in the *Lubanga* case, the Trial Chamber found evidence relating to the period before the temporal jurisdiction of the Court relevant and admissible as they would "assist in establishing the background and context of the events that fall within the timeframe of the charges."[131]

C   *The Implications of Continuous and Continuing Crimes in Relation to ICC's Temporal Jurisdiction*

An assessment on the nature of the crime of enforced disappearance of persons under Article 7(1)(i) is demonstrative of the implications of continuous and continuing crimes in relation to ICC's temporal jurisdiction. The crime of enforced disappearance consists of two steps: (i) abduction, arrest or detention of one or more individuals and (ii) refusal to acknowledge that deprivation of freedom or to give information on the fate or whereabouts of such persons.[132] Normally, the crime of enforced disappearance begins at the time of the abduction of the victim and extends for the whole period of time that the crime is not complete, that is to say until the State acknowledges the detention or releases information pertaining to the fate or whereabouts if the individual.[133] However, pursuant to the footnote 24 of the EoC, all the material elements of the crime of enforced disappearance under article 7(1)(j) need to take place after the entry into force of the Statute for the Court to exercise jurisdiction.[134]

---

128   *Id.*
129   Rastan, 141, 172.
130   Stahn, (2005) 431.
131   Prosecutor v. Lubanga, ICC-01/04-01/06, Judgement (TC), paras. 1022–1027 (Mar. 14, 2002).
132   Elements of Crimes art. 7(1)(I).
133   U.N. H.R.C., *Report of the Working Group on Enforced or Involuntary Disappearances*, U.N. Doc. A/HRC/16/48, (Jan. 26, 2011), at 11, para. 39. *See also* Case of Blake v Guatemala, Inter-Am. Ct. H.R., Judgment (Preliminary Objections), para 39 (Jul. 2, 1996).
134   Elements of Crimes, art. 7(1)(i), n24.

This can be taken as an indication that the drafters of the Statute did not intend for bifurcated continuing crimes where a part of the *actus reus* was completed before the entry into force of the Statute to fall within the temporal jurisdiction of the Court.[135] For instance, the crime of sexual slavery under article 7(1)(g)(2) of the Statute requires the perpetrator to enslave the victim by creating an unlawful situation of dependence that deprives the victim of all autonomy[136] and cause him/her to engage in one or more acts of a sexual nature.[137] In a situation where the prohibited sexual conduct occurred before the entry into force of the Statute, whereas the state of enslavement persisted thereafter, the Court may be precluded from entering a conviction under article 7(1)(g)(2), as one of the constitutive elements of the crime, the sexual element, would have been taken place and completed outside the temporal jurisdiction of the Court.

Nevertheless, any inference that is made through footnote 24 in relation to the jurisdiction of the Court and continuing/continuous crimes must take into account footnote 25 which provides that for the purposes of the first limb of the crime of enforced disappearance the word "detained" includes a perpetrator who maintained an existing detention.[138] This means that:

> [A] case of enforced disappearance may fall within the temporal jurisdiction of the Court without impacting on article 11 or footnote 24, where a perpetrator detains a person prior to July 2002, continues to hold that person in detention after that date, and thereafter refuses to give information on the fate or whereabouts of the person (i.e. disappearance in custody) – since in this scenario all of the material elements of the crime (i.e. both stages of the crime of enforced disappearance) would occur after the entry into force of the Statute. These same considerations would hold for any other crimes all of whose material parameters continue to occur after the temporal threshold of the Court jurisdiction, even if they formed part of a course of conduct that commenced at an earlier date, without offending articles 11, 22 and 24 of the Statute.[139]

---

135 Rastan and Badar, 668; C.f. Mohammed Zeidy, *The Ugandan Government Triggers the First Test if the Complementarity Principle: An Assessment of the First State's Party Referral to the ICC*, 5 Int'l Crim. L. Rev. 83, 96 (2005); where Zeidy argues that footnote 24 can also be seen as highly specific to the crime of enforced disappearance as any similar indication is lacking in relation to other crimes of the same continuing nature.
136 Prosecutor v Katanga, ICC-01/04-01/07, Judgment, para. 965 (Mar. 7, 2014) [*hereinafter* Katanga Judgement].
137 Elements of Crimes art. 7(1)(g)(2).
138 Elements of Crimes art. 7(1)(i), n25.
139 Rastan and Badar, 668–669.

Accordingly, if a person is arrested or abducted and subsequently murdered by the perpetrator at some point in time before the entry into force of the Statute, even if the refusal to provide information continues thereafter, the Court would not have jurisdiction over the crime as a part of the *actus reus* would have been completed outside the temporal jurisdiction of the Court. This is a peculiar to the ICC due to the addition of footnote 25 in the EoC. For instance in the Blake case, the IACtHR found that it lacked jurisdiction in relation to the abduction, deprivation of liberty and the eventual murder of the victim as they were completed outside the temporal jurisdiction of the court.[140] Nevertheless, the IACtHR found itself to be competent to rule on the question of enforced disappearance, as the crime continued into its temporal jurisdiction due to the fact that the government authorities committed subsequent acts which concealed the victim's arrest and murder from his relatives despite their efforts to discover his whereabouts.[141] This would not have been the case before the ICC due to footnote 24 as a part of the *actus reus*, i.e. the abduction and detention, would have been completed outside its temporal jurisdiction once the victim died. Conversely, if the individual was detained before the critical date but his detention continued thereafter, then both the stages of *actus reus*, i.e. the maintenance of the detention and refusal to acknowledge, would have been taken place within the temporal jurisdiction of the Court, bringing the case within the Court's jurisdiction.

So what does all this mean for continuous or continuing crimes? Within this framework, among the individual and separate acts that constitute a continuous crime, the Court could base a conviction only on those that occurred after the entry into force of the Statute. For instance, the Court would not be able to rely on the killings that constituted the crime of genocide under article 6(a) for convicting an accused in a particular case, if they occurred outside the temporal jurisdiction of the Court. Moreover, the accused would not be criminally responsible for any of his/her conduct which occurred before the entry of the force of the Statute pursuant to article 24(1). Indeed, ICC's jurisdictional framework requires all of the elements of the crime, i.e. the *actus reus* and *mens rea*, as well as the conduct of the accused, to occur within the temporal jurisdiction of the Court to enable the judges to enter a conviction.[142] Any prior fact or conduct could only be relied on as evidence in order to prove the contextual

---

140 Case of Blake v Guatemala, Inter-Am. Ct. H.R., Judgment (Preliminary Objections), para. 33 (Jul. 2, 1996).
141 *Id.*, para 34.
142 Leena Grover, Interpreting Crimes in the Rome Statute of the International Criminal Court 192 (2014) [*hereinafter* Grover].

elements of a crime that took place within the Court's temporal jurisdiction, and cannot form a basis of a conviction per se. Instead, such evidence can only be used to prove the contextual elements and the necessary *mens rea* for a conviction on genocide under article 6 of the Statute.

The same principle applies to continuing crimes. Only those crimes all of whose contextual parameters continue to occur after the temporal threshold of the Court's jurisdiction to may be investigated and prosecuted without offending Article 11 and 22 of the Statute or footnote 24 of the EoC.[143] Even if the precipitating act that created the unlawful state of affairs took place outside its temporal jurisdiction, the Court would still be able to scrutinize any conduct which continued after the critical date if such conduct perpetuated or maintained the unlawful state of affairs. In other words, the perpetrator must have participated in the commission of the crime by contributing or exercising control over the perpetuation or maintenance of the unlawful state of affairs after the critical date. This means that, for instance, an individual who enlisted or recruited a child prior to the critical date could not be convicted of the offence if he/she neither played an active role in maintaining the continued membership of the child past that date, nor had the capacity to terminate it.[144] Although the perpetrator might have been responsible for the initial enlistment or recruitment of a child under the age of 15, he/she may not have contributed to or exercised any control over the child's continuing membership, effectively terminating his contribution to the continuing crime before the critical date. In such a case, the Court would not be able to convict the accused as his/her conduct in relation to the crime would have taken place prior to the critical date, even if the unlawful state of affairs continued thereafter.

Now that a definitional framework for instantaneous, continuing and continuous crimes is set and their implications in relation to the temporal jurisdiction of the Court are illustrated, the next part will assess which category Article 8(2)(b)(viii) belongs to. Due to the rather ambiguous nature of the term "transfer of population" and the lack of clear guidance in the EoC or the *travaux preparatoire* of the Statute, Article 8(2)(b)(viii) can arguably fit in any one of these categories. Which interpretation will eventually prevail depends squarely on the interpretative tendencies of the judges that will be dealing with the question. The Judges of the ICC have so far been open to adopting both narrow/literal and broad/purposive approaches when interpreting the provisions of the Statute. Nevertheless, for the reasons that will be elaborated

---

143   Rastan, 173.
144   Schabas, 557.

below, this author opines that Article 8(2)(b)(viii) would most appropriately be characterized as a continuing crime.

IV   Interpretation of Article 8(2)(b)(viii)

A   *Interpretative Approaches at the ICC*

The judges of the ICC have shown diverse interpretative tendencies in applying the provisions of the Statute. This is mostly due to the tension among different interpretative methods and principles that are available to them, which enables them to pick and choose which approach to use based on their differing legal predispositions. A clear example of this is the rules of interpretation found in the Vienna Convention on the Law of Treaties (hereinafter "VCLT"),[145] which were found to be applicable in interpreting the Statute by the Appeals Chamber of the Court:[146]

> [T]he rule governing the interpretation of a section of the law is its wording read in context and in light of its object and purpose ... Its objects may be gathered from the chapter of the law in which the particular section is included and its purposes from the wider aims of the law as may be gathered from its preamble and general tenor of the treaty.[147]

VCLT does not provide a hierarchy between the text and the purpose of a treaty for the interpretation of its provisions.[148] This being so, the judges are required to give equal consideration to both the purpose and the ordinary meaning

---

[145]   Article 31(1) of the Vienna Convention on Law of Treaties provides that "[a] treaty shall be interpreted in good faith in accordance with the ordinary meaning to be given to the terms of the treat in their context in the light of its object and purpose." Article 32 on the other hand indicates that the preparatory work of the treaty may be taken into account to supplement interpretation under article 31; Vienna Convention on the Law of Treaties, 23 May 1969, 1155 U.N.T.S. 331.

[146]   Situation in Democratic Republic of Congo, ICC-01/04, Judgment on the Prosecutor's Application for Extraordinary Review of Pre-Trial Chamber I's 31 March 2006 Decision Denying Leave to Appeal, para. 33 (Jul. 13, 2006) [*hereinafter* DRC Judgement]; Prosecutor v Katanga, ICC-01/04/01/07, Judgment on the Appeal of Mr. Germain Katanga against the decision of Pre-Trial Chamber I entitled "Decision on the Defence Request Concerning Languages", paras 38–39 (May 27, 2008).

[147]   DRC Judgement, para. 33.

[148]   Joost Pauwelyn and Manfred Elsig, *The Politics of Treaty Interpretation: Variations and Explanations across International Tribunals*, *in* Interdisciplinary Perspectives on International Law and International Relations: The State of the Art 445, 448, (Jeffrey L. Dunoff ed., 2013) [*hereinafter* Pauwelynand Elsig]. *See also* Georges Abi Saab, *The Appellate*

of the text, which provides them with room to exercise judicial discretion in interpreting the provisions of the Statute.[149]

The self-proclaimed purpose of the Statute is to end impunity for the perpetrators of international crimes and thus to contribute to the prevention of such crimes[150] by making them punishable in accordance with the principles and procedure specified within the Statute.[151] Employing the purposive approach aimed at the realization of this objective allows the judges to interpret the provisions of the Statute broadly. There are, however, certain principles in the Statute that operate in the opposite direction, especially in relation to the interpretation of the crimes within the jurisdiction of the Court. The principle of legality or *nullum crimen sine lege* enshrined in Article 22 of the Statute is the main principle in this regard.[152] Article 22(2) requires strict construction of the definitions of crimes under the Statute, and in cases of ambiguity, the adoption of the interpretation which is in favor of the accused,[153] essentially limiting the judicial discretion of the judges to interpret the crimes under the Statute expansively and purposively.[154] In addition, Article 21(3) requires the interpretation and application of the Statute as well as exercise of jurisdiction by the Court to be in accordance with internationally recognized human rights norms.[155] As per the international human rights jurisprudence on the

---

Body and Treaty Interpretation, in Treaty Interpretation and the Vienna Convention on the Law of Treaties: 30 Years (Malgosia Fitzmaurice et al. eds., 2010).

149   Pauwelyn and Elsig, 448.
150   Rome Statute *preamble*.
151   *Id*; Situation in Democratic Republic of Congo, ICC-01/04, Judgment on the Prosecutor's Application for Extraordinary Review of Pre-Trial Chamber I's 31 March 2006 Decision Denying Leave to Appeal, para. 37 (Jul. 13, 2006); Prosecutor v Bemba, ICC-01/05-01/08, Decision Pursuant to Art 61(7)(a) and (b) of the Rome Statute on the Charges of the Prosecutor against Jean-Pierre Bemba Gombo, para. 369 (Jun. 15, 2009) [*hereinafter* Gombo Decision].
152   Grover, 134.
153   Rome Statute art. 22(2); "The definition of a crime shall be strictly construed and shall not be extended by analogy [and] [i]n case of ambiguity, the definition shall be interpreted in favor of the person being investigated, prosecuted or convicted."
154   Alexander Grabert, Dynamic Interpretation in International Criminal Law: Striking a Balance between Stability and Change 106 (2015); Joseph Powderly, *The Rome Statute and the Attempted Corseting of the Interpretative Judicial Function*, in The Law and Practice of the International Criminal Court 444, 447, (Carsten Stahn ed., 2015) [*hereinafter* Powderly].
155   Prosecutor v Gombo, ICC-01/05-01/08, Judgment pursuant to Article 74 of the Statute, para. 82 (Mar. 21, 2016); Prosecutor v Gombo, ICC-01/05-01/08 OA, Judgment on the appeal of Mr. Jean-Pierre Bemba Gombo against the decision of the Pre-Trial Chamber III entitled "Decision on application for interim release, para. 28 (Dec. 16, 2008); Prosecutor v Lubanga, ICC-01/04-01/06 OA 12, Judgment on the appeal of the Prosecutor against the

principle of legality, criminal law must not be extensively construed to an accused's detriment.[156] The tension between these opposing principles requires the judges of the Court to strike a balance between "the ideal of ending impunity with the legalistic protection of the accused from arbitrary application of law",[157] which in some instances leads to the adoption of diverging interpretations on the provisions of the Statute.

The jurisprudence of the Court is replete with examples of due regard being given by the judges of the Court to article 22(2) in interpreting the crimes under the Statute.[158] Nevertheless, there are also numerous instances where the purposive approach was employed leading to a wider interpretation of the statutory provisions,[159] including when interpreting the crimes under

---

decision of Trial Chamber I entitled "Decision on the release of Thomas Lubanga Dyilo", Dissenting Opinion of Judge Georghios M. Pikis, para. 12 (Oct. 21, 2008); Gombo Decision, para. 39.

156   Veeber v Est., para. 31; S.W. v U.K., para. 35 (1995); Kokkinakis v. Greece, Eur. Ct. H.R., App. No. 3/1992/348/421, Judgment, para. 52 (1993). *See also* International Covenant on Civil and Political Rights art. 15(1), Dec. 16, 1966, 999 U.N.T.S. 171; H.R. Comm., David Michael Nicholas v Australia, Communication No. 10/80/2002, paras. 7.4–7.5 (Mar. 19, 2004); American Convention on Human Rights art. 9, Nov. 22, 1969, O.A.S.T.S. No. 36, 1144 U.N.T.S. 123; Case of Lori Berenson-Mejia v Peru, Inter-Am. Ct. H.R., Judgment (Merits, Reparations and Costs), para. 125 (Nov, 25, 2004).

157   Nissel, 657.

158   *See* Bashir Decision, paras. 131–133; Lubanga Article 74 Judgement, para. 620; Prosecutor v Chui, ICC-01/04-02/12, Judgment pursuant to Art 74 of the Statute: Concurring Opinion of Judge Christine Van den Wyngaert, paras. 6–7 (Dec. 18, 2012); Gombo Decision, paras. 369, 423 (Jun. 15, 2009); Prosecutor v Gombo, ICC-01/05-01/08, Judgment pursuant to Article 74 of the Statute, para. 82–84 (Mar. 21, 2016).

159   Michail Vagias, The Territorial Jurisdiction of the International Criminal Court, 63 n9 (2014); Powderly, 467. *See also* Leena Grover, A Call to Arms: Fundamental Dilemmas Confronting the Interpretation of Crimes in the Rome Statute of the International Criminal Court, 21 Eur. J. Int'l L. 543 (2010); Carsten Stahn, *Justice Delivered or Justice Denied? The Legacy of the Katanga Judgment*, 12 J. Int'l Crim. Just 809, 815 (2014) [hereinafter Stahn (2014)]; Lubanga, ICC-01/04-01/06, Judgment pursuant to Article 74 of the Statute: Separate and Dissenting Opinion of Judge Odio Benito, paras. 6–8 (Mar. 14, 2012). *See* Lubanga Confirmation of Charges, paras. 278, 281, 284–285; Prosecutor v. Gombo, ICC-01/05-01/08, Decision Adjourning the Hearing pursuant to Article 61(7)(c)(ii) of the Rome Statute, paras. 34–37 (Mar. 3, 2009); Prosecutor v. Lubanga, ICC-01/04-01/06 OA 9 OA 10, Judgment on the Appeals of the Prosecutor and the Defence against Trial Chamber I's Decision on Victim's Participation of 18 January 2008, para. 97 (Jul, 11, 2008); Prosecution v Katanga, Judgment on the Appeal of Mr. Germain Katanga against the Oral Decision of Trial Chamber II of 12 June 2009 on the Admissibility of the Case, paras. 77–79 (Sep. 25, 2009).

the Statute.¹⁶⁰ The judges have even made explicit reference to article 22(2) and then proceeded to engage in an expansive/purposive interpretation of crimes under the Statute in some instances. One striking example of this is the *Katanga* judgment where the majority of the trial judges recognized the potential conflict between purposive and literal interpretative methods and firmly held that the purposive method cannot be used to create new law that would be incompatible with the text of the Statute.¹⁶¹ Nevertheless, the Chamber then developed significant new elements of the control theory based on scholarly doctrine rather than the ordinary meaning of the text, and adopted far-reaching interpretations of crimes against humanity and modes of liability.¹⁶² This points to the fact that the judges of the Court are willing and able to reconcile the restrictions of article 22(2) with the purposive interpretation of the crimes under the Statute, allowing for the possibility broad interpretation of the crimes under the Statute. Such is the case for article 8(2)(b)(viii), as will be illustrated in the next section.

B   *Possible Interpretations of Article 8(2)(b)(viii)*

Article 8(2)(b)(viii) prohibits "[t]he transfer, directly or indirectly, by the Occupying Power of parts of its own civilian population into the territory it occupies..,"¹⁶³ The EoC indicates that the perpetrator must have "[t]

---

160   *See* Alexander Grabert, Dynamic Interpretation in International Criminal Law: Striking a Balance between Stability and Change 106–110, 118 (2015). The term "the national armed forces" under article 8(2)(b)(xxvi) was interpreted to include non-governmental armed forces operating inside the country, distinct from the armed forces of the state. This was arguably against the clear meaning of the word and the intention of the drafters, *See* Lubanga Confirmation of Charges, para 285; Prosecutor v Katanga & Chui, ICC-01/04-01/07, Decision on the Confirmation of Charges, para. 249 (Sep. 30, 2008). This led the author to conclude that "[overall], the meaning of article 8(2(b)(xxvi) was extensively construed on the basis of a purposive approach [and] in order to do so, the Chamber has ignored all other means of interpretation. *See also* Situation in the Republic of Kenya, ICC-01/09, Decision on the Authorization of an Investigation, paras. 83–93 (Mar. 31, 2010); where the majority of the Pre-Trial Chamber (Judge Hans-Peter Kaul dissenting) adopted a broad interpretation of the notion of 'organizational policy' in relation to the contextual elements of crimes against humanity to include non-state like groups or entities.
161   Katanga Judgement, para. 54 (Mar. 7, 2014); Stahn (2014), 816.
162   Stahn (2014), 816–817. The majority of the Katanga Trial Chamber adopted a broad interpretation of the 'organizational policy' requirement in relation to the contextual elements of crimes against humanity under article 7; *see* Katanga Judgement, para. 1119–1120, (Mar. 7, 2014). The majority also further extended scope of article 25(3) of the Statute, arguably in contravention to the ordinary meaning of the text; *see* Stahn (2014), 823–825; Katanga Judgement, paras. 1410–1412.
163   Article 8(2)(b)(viii). *See also* Elements of Crimes art. 8(2)(b)(viii).

ransferred directly or indirectly, parts of its own population into the territory it occupies ... [footnote omitted]."[164] The operative word of the *actus reus* of Article 8(2)(b)(viii) is "transfer" or "transferred". Therefore, the interpretation of this term in relation to article 8(2)(b)(viii) will dictate whether this provision will be construed as an instantaneous, continuous or continuing crime.

The *travaux preparatoires* of the Statute suggest that the Preparatory Commission for the ICC consciously left the interpretation of the term "transfer" in the context of article 8(2)(b)(viii) to the judges of the Court.[165] The EoC provides ambiguous guidance in this respect. Footnote 44 of the EoC indicates that the word transfer must be "interpreted in accordance with the relevant provisions of international humanitarian law" (IHL hereinafter).[166] No indication is provided as to which provisions among the numerous IHL rules are to be taken into consideration. Arguably, this allows several interpretations to emerge and enable parties to argue their case as to which provisions of IHL are applicable in interpreting his term.[167] This is crucial, as the scope of the IHL provisions applicable to the interpretation of the term "transfer" will have a major impact on the scope of Article 8(2)(b)(viii). If a limited number of IHL provisions are taken into regard, then the term "transfer" would be construed narrowly as a discreet act which is completed once the transferred population settles into the occupied territory, leading to the characterization of Article 8(2)(b)(viii) as an instantaneous or a continuous crime. If, on the other hand, a broader interpretation which takes into account a number of other interrelated IHL provisions is adopted, then the term "transfer" would be construed as an ongoing process, rather than a discreet act, which continues to cause harm as long as the transferred population remains within the occupied territory, *i.e.* a continuing crime. Arguably, the latter approach is the appropriate one, as it better corresponds to the legally protected interest under Article 8(2)(b)(viii) and the harm that the prohibition aims to prevent.

1   The Narrow Interpretation: Article 8(2)(b)(viii as an Instantaneous or Continuous Crime

The conventional view on footnote 44 of the EoC is that it refers to Article 49(6) of the Fourth Geneva Convention (hereinafter 'GCIV') and Article 85(4)(a)

---

164   Elements of Crimes art. 8(2)(b)(viii), element 1(a).
165   Knut Dörmann, Elements of War Crimes under the Rome Statute of the International Criminal Court: Sources and Commentary 209 (2003) [*hereinafter* Dörmann].
166   Elements of Crimes art. 8(2)(viii).
167   Herman von Hebel, *Elements of the Specific Forms of War Crimes: Article 8(2)(b)(viii)*, in The International Criminal Court: Elements of Crimes and Rules of Procedure and Evidence 158, 161 (Roy S. Lee ed., 2001) [*hereinafter* von Hebel].

of the Additional Protocol I to the Geneva Conventions (hereinafter 'API').[168] This is understandable as the wording and formulation of these provisions is almost verbatim to that of Article 8(2)(b)(viii). This inevitably creates a link between the interpretation of these three provisions.

Article 49(6) provides that "[t]he Occupying Power shall not deport or transfer parts of its own civilian population into the territory it occupies."[169] The official ICRC commentary on GCIV does not provide clear guidance on Article 49(6) regarding the scope of the term "transfer". Recourse to *travaux preparatoires* of GC IV is similarly of no avail, as there was virtually no discussion over Article 49(6) during the 1949 Geneva Conference.[170] API, on the other hand, upgraded "the transfer by the Occupying Power of parts of its own civilian population into the territory it occupies ... in violation of the Conventions or the Protocol", which was previously a breach, to a grave breach. The language used in the provision is merely a repetition of Article 49(6), indicating that it continues to apply unchanged.[171] Similarly, there is no guidance in relation to the interpretation of the term transfer in the ICRC commentary on the provision.[172]

Based on its ordinary meaning, the term "transfer" within the context of article 8(2)(b)(viii) can be interpreted as "the movement of persons into an occupied territory with a view to settling there."[173] There is some support for this interpretation in the official commentary on article 49(6) of the GCIV. Accordingly "the meaning of the words "transfer" and "deport" are deemed to be different from that in which they are used in other paragraphs of article 49, since they do not refer to *the movement* of protected persons but to *that* of nationals of the occupying Power [emphasis added]."[174] The focus, therefore, seems to be on the movement of population, rather than their subsequent

---

168 von Hebel, 162.
169 Geneva Convention (IV) Relative to the Protection of Civilian Persons in Time of War, art. 49(6), (Aug. 12, 1949).
170 Christian Tomuschat, *Chapter 73: Prohibition of Settlements*, in The 1949 Geneva Conventions: A Commentary 1551, 1559 (Andrew Clapham et al. eds., 2015) [*hereinafter* Tomuschat].
171 Yves Sandoz et al., Commentary on the Additional Protocols of 8 June 1977 to the Geneva Conventions of 12 August 1949, 1000 (1987) [*hereinafter* Sandoz].
172 *Id.*
173 Yoram Dinstein, The International Law of Belligerent Occupation 240 (2009) [*hereinafter* Dinstein].
174 Jean S. Pictet, Commentary on the IV Geneva Convention Relative to the Protection of Civilian Persons in Time of War Article 49(6), 283 (1958) [*hereinafter* Pictet].

presence.¹⁷⁵ Under this interpretation, transfer is regarded as a discrete event in time that transpires once the movement and settlement of the population into the occupied territory is completed. The language and elements of article 8(2)(viii) lends some support to this view as it only criminalizes "transfer" of population and not the inducement of the continuing presence of those who were already transferred.¹⁷⁶

This interpretation also finds some support in the *travaux preparatoire* of the Statute. Ultimately, the discussions on article 8(2)(b)(viii) boiled down to four options in the 'Zutphen Draft' Statute:

> Option 1: The transfer by the Occupying Power of parts of its own civilian population into the territory it occupies,
> Option 2: The transfer by the Occupying Power of parts of its own civilian population into the territory it occupies, or the deportation or transfer of all or parts of the population of the occupied territory within or outside this territory
> Option 3:
>   i. The establishment of settlers in an occupied territory and changes to the demographic composition of an occupied territory and changes to the demographic composition of an occupied territory;
>   ii. The transfer by the Occupying Power of parts of its own civilian population into the territory it occupies, or the deportation or transfer of all or parts of the population of the occupied territory within or outside this territory.
> Option 4: Exclusion of the provision¹⁷⁷

Arguably, the ultimate rejection of option 3(i) is an indication that the drafters of the Statute intended article 8(2)(b)(viii) to be an instantaneous crime.¹⁷⁸ Accordingly, the use of the term "establishment of settlers" in a separate subparagraph in addition to "transfer" which hints at an ongoing and continuing situation was not preferred by the negotiators.¹⁷⁹ The phrase "changes to the demographic composition of an occupied territory" in option 3(ii) which similarly points towards an ongoing state of affairs which continues as long as the

---

175 Eugene Kontorovich, *When Gravity Fails: Israeli Settlements and Admissibility at the ICC*, 47 Isr. L. Rev. 379, 384 (2014) [*hereinafter* Kontorovich].
176 Zimmermann, 324; Kontorovich, 384.
177 Zutphen Draft, A/AC.249/1988/L.13 (Feb. 4, 1998), at 23–24. *See* Kearney, 15–16.
178 Zimmermann, 324.
179 *Id.*

established population remains in the occupied territory, was also rejected. Instead with the addition of the words "directly or indirectly", option 2 was preferred. This can, arguably, be taken as an indication of the intention of the drafters to solely to criminalize the discreet act of transfer of population, and not necessarily any conduct related to the perpetuation of the situation on the ground that consequently emerges once the transfer is completed.[180]

This narrow interpretation of the term "transfer" also opens up the possibility of characterizing Article 8(2)(b)(viii) as a continuous crime. The formulation of Article 8(2)(b)(viii) lends some support to this view. Accordingly, the transfer of population must be carried out by "the Occupying Power", which implies the necessity of a certain degree of planning and implementation at the State level.[181] This means that isolated instances of population movements into an occupied territory without any direct or indirect involvement of the State authorities would fall outside the scope of Article 8(2)(b)(viii).[182] Such involvement may be based on financial subsidies, planning, public information, military action, recruitment of settlers, legislation other judicial action, and even the administration of justice.[183] The role of the State in facilitating the transfer of population in a systematic, coercive and deliberate manner[184] establishes the contextual link among what would otherwise be regarded isolated and separate instances of population movement. The contextual link among these individual population movements can be demonstrated with reference to the aforementioned ECtHR jurisprudence on continuous crimes:

1. The separate instances of transfer of individuals are identical criminal acts committed by the same perpetrator, i.e. the Occupying Power, against the same class of victims and the legally protected interest, *i.e.* the property and land rights to the natives of the occupied territory, as well as the territorial integrity of the victim State.

---

180   Kontorovich, 384.
181   Michel Cottier and Elisabeth Baumgartner, *Paragraph 2(b)(viii): Prohibited deportations and transfers in occupied territories*, in The Rome Statute of the International Criminal Court: A Commentary 404, 410 (Otto Triffterer and Kai Ambos, 2016) [*hereinafter* Cottier and Baumgartner].
182   *Id.* The same argument was made by Yoram Dinstein in relation to Article 49(6) of the GC IV; *see* Dinstein, 241.
183   U.N. ECOSOC, *The Realization of Economic, Social and Cultural Rights: The human rights dimensions of population transfer including the implantation of settlers*, U.N. Doc. E/CN.4/Sub.2/1993/17 (1993), at para. 15 [*hereinafter* UN Population Transfer Report].
184   *Id.*

2. The similarities in the manner of execution of the individual transfers, *i.e.* the implementation of a set of policies, laws, and physical measures by the Occupying Power,
3. The temporal connection between the individual instances of transfer that make up the overall population transfer project,
4. The repeated criminal intent of the perpetrator(s) to ensure the continuation of the transfer, evidenced by the continuing implementation of measures aimed at facilitating further transfers; and
5. The individual transfers and the conduct of the perpetrator(s) that directly or indirectly facilitate them comprise the constituent elements of article 8(2)(b)(viii).

In this sense, just as genocide by killing is an amalgamation of numerous individual instances of killings committed within certain contextual parameters, transfer of population into an occupied territory can be regarded as an amalgamation of all the individual population movements that are contextually linked to one another.

Adopting the narrow approach would be in line with the requirement under Article 22(2) to construe the definition of Statute crimes strictly and in favor of the person being investigated, prosecuted or convicted. That being said, there are two fundamentally problematic aspects associated with doing so. First and foremost, limiting the meaning of the term 'transfer' solely to initial movement and settlement of the nationals of the Occupying Power completely ignores the fundamental purpose of Article 8(2)(b)(viii), as well as the Statute. The legal interest that is protected and the harm that is envisaged to be offset by this provision are not sufficiently covered by the prohibition solely of the initial movement and settlement of the population into the occupied territory. If the narrow interpretation is adopted, an accountability gap would emerge in relation to the unlawful state of affairs caused by the presence of settlers who moved into an occupied territory before the temporal jurisdiction of the Court, but remained thereafter. Secondly, there is no apparent reason why footnote 44, as the main interpretative guidance for Article 8(2)(b)(viii), should be construed narrowly as to only refer to Article 49(6) GCIV and Article 85(4)(a) API. There is a wealth of IHL provisions that may be deemed as relevant to the interpretation of the term 'transfer' in the context of Article 8(2)(b)(viii). Such an approach would expand the meaning of the term 'transfer' beyond the mere movement and settlement of the nationals of the occupying power into the occupied territory. Arguably, this would be more in line with the fundamental purpose of Article 8(2)(b)(viii) and the Statute. The next section will expound on these arguments and the reason why the interpretation of Article 8(2)(b)(viii) as a continuing crime is the legally sound approach.

2   The Broad Interpretation: Article 8(2)(b)(viii) as a Continuing Crime

Interpretation of Article 8(2)(b)(viii) as a continuing crime necessitates the adoption of a purposive interpretation of the term 'transfer' to include not only the initial movement and settlement of the nationals of the occupying power, but also their continued presence on the occupied territory. This would criminalize not only the conduct that lead to the direct or indirect placement of the settlers into the occupied territory, but also the maintenance of their continued presence thereafter.[185] From this perspective, the term 'transfer of population' can be described as the "implantation of settlers and settlements"[186] with the ultimate "effect or purpose of altering the demographic composition of a territory ... [and] the acquisition or control of territory, military conquest or exploitation of an indigenous population or its resources."[187] This is in line with the ILC's definition of this term as "the establishment of settlers in an occupied territory which involves changing the demographic composition of an occupied territory and the disguised intent of annexation."[188] As succinctly put by a commentator, transfer of population into an occupied territory is often the result of:

> [A] deliberate policy, with the direct or indirect involvement of the government to move people – currently under its jurisdiction- into or away from a certain area, having the purpose or effect of compelling people to leave their territory or accept the implantation of (alien) settlers into that territory, aimed at transforming the demographic composition or political status of the territory concerned ... [which] may be carried out precisely with the aim of altering existing borders through consolidating claims to disputing territories.[189]

These descriptions are also supported by the official commentary on Article 49(6) of the GCIV. Accordingly, the principle intention behind the

---

185   Kearney, 31; C.f. Schabas, 342.
186   U.N. Sub-Commission on Prevention of Discrimination and Protection of Minorities, Report of the Sub-Commission on Prevention of Discrimination and Protections of Minorities on its 45th Session, U.N. Doc. E/CN.4/Sub.2/1993/45 (1993), at para. 7.
187   UN Population Transfer Report, para. 17.
188   Report of the International Law Commission on the work of its forty-third session, Official Records of the General Assembly, Forty-sixth session, Supplement No 10, A/46/10 Article 22(b), at 105, para. 7 (1991).
189   Christa Meindersma, *Legal Issues Surrounding Population Transfers in Conflict Situations*, 41 Neth. Int'l L. Rev. 31, 33 (1994) [*hereinafter* Meindersma].

adoption of this provision was "to prevent a practice adopted during the Second World War by certain Powers, which transferred portions of their own population to occupied territory for political and racial reasons or in order, as they claimed, to colonize those territories."[190] This means that, Article 49(6) was included in GCIV to ensure that an occupying power does not gradually annex the occupied territory by alter by changing the demographic structure of the occupied territory through transferring its own population, which would go against the fundamental principle of the temporary nature of an occupation.[191] The same can be said for Article 8(2)(b)(viii). Similarly, the fundamental purpose behind the inclusion of Article 8(2)(b)(viii) to the Statute was to prevent the annexation of land and demographic change of the occupied territory by the Occupying Power through the transfer of its own population.[192] As one commentator put it, "opposition to colonialism and the prerogative that occupation be temporary ... lie[s] behind the criminalization of transfer [under article 8(2)(b)(viii)]."[193]

The inclusion of previously mentioned footnote 44 also provides support to this contention. One commentator has argued that the inclusion of footnote 44 is redundant, as Article 21 of the Statute already incorporates "the established principles of the international law of armed conflict"[194] to the applicable law of the Court.[195] This argument, however, fails to explain why Article 8(2)(b)(viii) is the only crime where such a clarification regarding the interpretation of the term "transfer" is made by the drafters of the EoC. None of the other crimes

---

190 Pictet, art. 49(6), 283 (1958). In the Nuremberg indictment the accused were charged with "Germanization of Occupied Territories" which was described as "[i]n certain occupied territories purportedly annexed to Germany the defendants methodically and pursuant to plan endeavoured to assimilate these territories politically, socially and economically into the German Reich. They endeavoured to obliterate the former national character of these territories. In pursuance of these plans and endeavours, the defendants forcibly deported inhabitants who were predominantly non-German and introduced thousands of German colonists. This plan included economic domination, physical conquest, installation of puppet governments, purported de jure annexation and enforced conscription into the German Armed Forces." *See* International Military Tribunal, Trial of the Major War Criminals, Volume I: Official Documents, at 63,(1947). *See also* Alfred de Zayas, *The Illegality of Population Transfers and the Application of Emerging International Norms in the Palestinian Context*, 6 Palestine Y. B. Int'l L. 17, 25 (1990/91) [*hereinafter* Zayas].
191 Tomuschat, 1559.
192 Schabas, 275.
193 Kearney, 31.
194 The Appeals Chamber of the ICC has confirmed that the interpretation of war crimes under article 8 of the Statute must be consistent with international law, and international humanitarian law in particular. *See* Lubanga Judgement, paras. 322.
195 C.f. Kearney, 20.

that contain the word "transfer" have the same clarification within their elements of crimes.[196] Addition of explicit guidance to interpret the term "transfer" in line with the unspecified relevant provisions of IHL can, thus, be seen as an indication that the drafters of the EoC regarded this crime as being more than mere movement and settlement of population. As outlined above, such transfers are often part of a larger colonial project aimed at the annexation of the occupied territory through demographic change. This inevitably leads to the violation of numerous IHL norms such as the prohibition on destruction and confiscation of private and public property and natural resources,[197] the inadmissibility of the acquisition of territory by force through creeping annexation contrary to the temporary nature of occupation,[198] the obligation to respect the laws in force in the occupied country,[199] and the prohibition on individual or mass forcible transfers of protected persons from occupied territory.[200] Such transfers often worsen the economic situation of the native population and endanger their separate existence as a race.[201] Indeed, the upgrade of the prohibition on transferring population into an occupied territory

---

196   See Elements of Crimes art. 7(1)(d): Crime against humanity of deportation or forcible transfer of population; art. 6(e), Genocide by forcibly transferring children; and art. 8(2)(a)(vii)-1, War crime of unlawful deportation and transfer.

197   See Hague Convention IV – Laws and Customs of War on Land arts. 46, 47, 52–56, Oct. 18, 1907, 36 Stat. 2277, 1 Bevans 631, 205 Consol T.S. 277, 3 Martens Nouveau Recueil (ser. 3) 461 [*hereinafter* Hague Regulations]; Geneva Convention Relative to the Protection of Civilian Persons in Time of War arts. 33, 46, 53, 147 para 6, Aug. 12, 1949, 75 U.N.T.S 287 [*hereinafter* Fourth Geneva Convention]. *See also* U.N. H.R.C. Res. 34/39, *Israeli Settlements in the Occupied Palestinian Territory, including East Jerusalem and the Occupied Syrian Golan*, U.N. Doc. A/HRC/34/38 (Apr. 13, 2017).

198   U.N. Charter art 2(4); Legal Consequences of the Construction of a Wall in the Occupied Palestinian Territory, Advisory Opinion, 2004 I.C.J. 136 (July 9), para. 87 [*hereinafter* Wall Advisory Opinion]. *See also* Jordan J. Paust, *Ten Types of Israeli and Palestinian Violations of the Laws of War and the ICC*, 31 Conn. J. Intl' L. 27, 43 (2015–2016); on the customary nature of prohibition of annexation of any portion of occupied territory. Ardi Imseis, *On the Fourth Geneva Convention and the Occupied Palestinian Territory*, 44 Harv. Int'l L.J. 65, 67 (2003); Dinstein, 49.

199   Hague Regulations art. 43 (Oct. 18, 1907).

200   Fourth Geneva Convention art. 49.

201   Pictet, art. 49(6), page 283. In the Nuremberg indictment the accused were charged with "Germanization of Occupied Territories" which was described as "[i]n certain occupied territories purportedly annexed to Germany the defendants methodically and pursuant to plan endeavoured to assimilate these territories politically, socially and economically into the German Reich. They endeavoured to obliterate the former national character of these territories. In pursuance of these plans and endeavours, the defendants forcibly deported inhabitants who were predominantly non-German and introduced thousands of German colonists. This plan included economic domination, physical conquest, installation of puppet governments, purported de jure annexation and enforced conscription

to a grave breach under API was a recognition of these dire consequences for the population of the occupied territory concerned from a humanitarian point of view.[202]

In light of the foregoing, the legal interest protected under Article 8(2)(b)(viii) can be identified as the land and property rights of the natives of the occupied land as well as the territorial integrity of the occupied State. The harm that Article 8(2)(b)(viii) was designed to prevent, on the other hand, can be depicted as the economic destitution and physical and mental harm inflicted upon the victims, i.e. the native population, through the confiscation of property, land and their consequent forcible transfer. The violation of these rights and the consequent harm is not inflicted only through the initial placement of the nationals of the Occupying Power into the occupied territory; the rights of the native population continue to be infringed and the harm they suffer continue to be inflicted as long as the settler population remains therein. Accordingly, the protection of these rights and the prevention of the depicted harm cannot be achieved by the criminalization of solely the conduct linked to the initial movement and settlement of population into the occupied territory. Any conduct that facilitates their continuing presence, or in other words their maintenance, in the occupied territory must also be criminalized for the realization of the fundamental purpose of Article 8(2)(b)(viii), i.e. the criminalization and prevention of demographic change and creeping annexation of territory by an Occupying Power.

This may be seen a stretching of the meaning of the term 'transfer' contrary to the interpretative guidance provided by Article 22(2) of the Statute. Nevertheless, this critique can be dispelled by drawing a parallel between the approach adopted by the Court in relation to the crime of enlistment or conscription of children under the age of 15 pursuant to Article (8)(2)(e)(vii) and the interpretation of Article 8(2)(b)(viii). In relation to the former, the EoC requires that the perpetrator "conscripted or enlisted" persons under the age of 15 years into an armed force or group.[203] In defining the term "enlistment" and "conscription" the judges of the Court relied on the Oxford Dictionary definitions of these terms. Accordingly, the term "enlisting" was defined as "to enroll on the list of a military body" and conscripting as "to enlist compulsorily."[204] Based on their ordinary meanings, conscription and enlistment can, therefore,

---

        into the German Armed Forces." *See* International Military Tribunal, Trial of the Major War Criminals, Volume I: Official Documents, 63 (1947). *See also* Zayas, 25.
202   Sandoz, 1000.
203   Elements of Crimes, art. 8(2)(e)(vii).
204   Prosecutor v Lubanga Article 74 Judgement, para. 608 n1777, 1778 (Mar. 14, 2012). *See also* Oxford Dictionary (2002, 5th ed.), 491, 831; Dörmann, 377; Commentary on the Rome

be construed as discreet acts that are completed once the child's is incorporated into the armed forces. Instead, the judges found the initial moment of recruitment of the child under the age of 15 not to be the decisive factor[205] and construed these terms in a wider manner to also cover the continuing membership already recruited children.[206] This is so because the legal interest that is protected and the harm that is sought to be prevented through this provision is not only related to the consequences of the initial act of enlistment or conscription. The continued membership of the child to the armed forces perpetuate this harm and continue to infringe the associated legal interest until he/she leaves the armed forces or reaches 15 years of age. This approach adopted by the judges can be regarded as a purposive interpretation of Article 8(2)(e)(vii), aimed at addressing the potential accountability gap that may arise in situations where a child under the age of 15 is incorporated into the armed group before the entry into force of the Statute, but remained thereafter as a result of the perpetrator's conduct that maintained the child's membership to the armed forces.

The same reasoning applies to Article 8(2)(b)(viii). Just as the crime of conscription and enlistment commences at the moment that a child is enlisted in the armed forces and continues to be committed as long as he/she remains therein or is no longer under 15 years of age, *i.e.* the termination of the unlawful state of affairs, the transfer commences at the moment parts of the civilian population is transferred into the occupied territory and perpetuated until such time as the civilians leave the occupied territory.[207] Accordingly, the transfer of population is not merely a discreet event, but an ongoing process of incorporation of the occupied territory into the land of the Occupying Power. In other words "the transfer of civilians in particular, is most accurately understood not as an event, but as a structural pursuit of a specific end point, namely the erasure of the distinction between the colony (occupied territory) and metropole"[208] which can occur gradually and insidiously over an extended period of time, as in the case of prolonged occupations.[209] The term "transfer" can then be interpreted as a singular ongoing process, rather than a discreet

---

      Statute of the International Criminal Court: Observer's Notes 472 marginal n231 (Otto Triffterer ed., 2008); Julie McBride, The War Crime of Child Soldier Recruitment 57 (2014).
205 Rastan and Badar, 668.
206 Lubanga Confirmation of Charges, para. 248; Prosecutor v Lubanga Article 74 Judgement, para. 618.
207 Kearney, 31.
208 Kearney, 32.
209 Meindersma, 34.

act or an amalgamation of discreet acts, constituting as a single continuing crime.

Under this interpretation, Article 8(2)(b)(viii) would criminalize two categories of conduct: (i) the inducement of the movement and settlement of the population into the occupied territory; or (ii) the maintenance of the settlers already present in the occupied territory. The first limb occurs each time a perpetrator's conduct leads to the movement and settlement of its own nationals into the occupied territory. The second limb, on the other hand, reoccurs each day that the perpetrator's conduct induces such persons to remain in the occupied territory, regardless of the initial date of their settlement. As noted by an observer, such conduct "may range from subtle encouragement to more active inducement of people to settle in a particular territory."[210] This may include "any measures taken by the occupying power in order to organize or encourage transfers of parts of its own population into the occupied territory."[211] Such measures may involve provision of government settlement plans, the construction of housing by the State or any policies and measures (such as economic and financial incentives, subsidies and tax exonerations) to induce and facilitate migration into[212] or to maintain the existing settler population in the occupied territory. Any action that involves conducting, ordering, soliciting or inducing a transfer, as well as aiding, abetting or assisting in the commission of such acts may incur criminal liability under Article 8(2)(b)(viii).[213] It is noteworthy to add that the term directly or indirectly may cover "not only active policies of an occupying State, but also any omissions or failures to take effective steps to prevent the movement of population into occupied territory."[214] Indeed an omission can equally be characterized as a continuing act, as long as the omission remains in contravention with the relevant obligation.[215]

C Israeli Settlements in the West Bank as a Continuing Crime

An assessment of the Israeli settlement project in the West Bank illustrates the appropriateness of characterizing Article 8(2)(b)(viii) as a continuing crime and the pitfalls associated with characterizing it as an instantaneous or continuous crime.

The starting point of the Israeli settlement policy in the West Bank was the establishment of the first Israeli settlement, Kfar Etzion, only a few months

---

210 *Id.*, 5.
211 Wall Advisory Opinion, para. 120.
212 Cottier and Baumgartner, 411.
213 Cottier and Baumgartner, 411.
214 von Hebel, 160.
215 *See* Questions Relating to the Obligation to Prosecute or Extradite, 2012 I.C.J. Rep. 422 (July 20), at paras. 71–117.

after the occupation of the West Bank by Israel following the Six-Day War of 1967.[216] Since then, Israel established over 130 settlements and 100 outposts in the West Bank, leading to the growth of the settler population in West Bank to almost 600,000.[217] This was achieved through the consistent policies of the successive governments of Israel for decades. As reported by an international fact-finding mission:

> Since 1967, the Governments of Israel have openly led and directly participated in the planning, construction, development, consolidation and/or encouragement of settlements by including explicit provisions in the fundamental policy instrument (basic policy guidelines), establishing governmental structures and implementing specific measures. These specific measures include (a) building infrastructure, (b) encouraging Jewish migrants to Israel to move to settlements; (c) sponsoring economic activities; (d) supporting settlements through public services delivery and development projects; and (e) seizing Palestinian land, some privately owned, requisitioning land for military needs, declaring or registering land as State land and expropriating land for public needs.[218]

The design and implementation of these measures constitute the underlying conduct committed by the perpetrators of transfer of population into the West Bank, satisfying the *actus reus* of Article 8(2)(b)(viii).

Under the narrow interpretation, only those measures that had a direct or indirect impact on the building, population and enlargement of Israeli settlements after June 2014 would fall within the jurisdiction of the Court.[219] Considering that the vast majority of the Jewish settlement into the West Bank transpired between 1967 and June 2014, the Court would only be able to adjudicate on the transfer of a relatively small percentage of the hundreds of thousands of Israeli settlers currently living in the West Bank.[220] The smaller

---

216   Diakonia, History of Israeli Settlement Policy (Nov. 13, 2013), https://www.diakonia.se/en/IHL/where-we-work/Occupied-Palestinian-Territory/Administration-of-Occupation/Israeli-Settlements-policy/History/.
217   Bt'Selem, Statistics on Settlements and Settler Population, https://www.btselem.org/settlements/statistics; U.N. Doc. A/HRC/34/39, para. 11.
218   *Report of the independent international fact-finding mission to investigate the implications of the Israeli settlements on civil, political, economic, social and cultural rights of the Palestinian people throughout the Occupied Palestinian Territory, including East Jerusalem,* U.N. Doc. A/RHC/22/63 (Feb 7, 2013).
219   Zimmerman, 324. *See also* Kontorovich, 383.
220   There are conflicting statistics regarding the number of settlers in the West Bank as of June 2014. UN reports on the issue consistently indicate that 500,000 to 650,000 settlers are believed to be already present in the West Bank by 2014; *see* U.N. H.R.C. Res. 25/38,

size of the transferred population under scrutiny would, in turn, significantly reduce the scope of the conduct that the Court can adjudicate in relation to the Israeli settlement activities in the West Bank, and have a negative bearing on the gravity considerations under Article 17 for admissibility of potential cases[221] as well as the sentencing of prospective convicts.[222] This would inevitably create an accountability gap in relation to an unlawful state of affairs that has been maintained by the acts and omissions of the Israeli authorities and has been repeatedly identified as being contrary to international law in the West Bank, *i.e.* the continuing presence and maintenance of the settlers in an occupied territory.[223] As a consequence, the realization of the ultimate

---

Israeli Settlements in the Occupied Palestinian Territory, including East Jerusalem and the Occupied Syrian Golan, U.N. Doc. A/HRC/25/38 (Feb. 12, 2014), at para. 8; U.N. H.R.C., *Israeli Settlements in the Occupied Palestinian Territory, including East Jerusalem and the Occupied Syrian Golan*, U.N. Doc. A/HRC/28/44 (Feb. 12, 2014), para. 13; A more recent UN report found the settler population in the West Bank to be over 594,000 by the end of 2015 based on the data of the Israeli Central Bureau of Statistics; *see* U.N. Doc. A/HRC/34/39, para. 11. The Israeli media, on the other hand, reported that as of 30 June 2014, the settler population in the West Bank stood at 382,031; *see* Josef Federman, *West Bank settler group boasts rapid growth*, Times of Israel (Sep, 16, 2014), https://www.timesofisrael.com/west-bank-settler-group-boasts-rapid-growth/. According to the Israeli media, there are currently 421,000 settlers living in the West Bank; *see Number of Israeli settlers living in West Bank tops 421,000: NGO*, I24 News (Sep. 2, 2017), https://www.i24news.tv/en/news/israel/137225-170209-number-of-israeli-settlers-living-in-west-bank-top-421-000-ngo.

221 Kontorovich, 383.
222 *See* ICTY, Prosecutor v Kunarac, IT-96-23/1-A, Judgement, para. 356, (Jun. 12, 2002); where the Appeals Chamber considered the length of enslavement, which is a continuing crime, to be an aggravating factor and found that "[t]he longer the period of enslavement, the more serious the offence." *See also* Prosecutor v Sesay et al., Case No. SCSL-04–15-T, Sentencing Judgement, para. 167 (Apr. 8, 2009); where the Trial Chamber considered the continual, large scale and for prolonged nature of instances of enslavement as an aggravating factor.
223 The ICJ, for instance, found that "since 1977, Israel has conducted a policy and developed practices involving the establishment of Settlements in the Occupied Palestinian Territory, contrary to the terms of Article 49, paragraph 6 [of the 4th Geneva Convention]"; *see* Wall Advisory Opinion, para. 120. Numerous successive UN reports found the Israeli settlements in the West Bank to be contrary to international law and detailed the illegal Israeli practices that are linked to transfer of population into the West Bank; *see* U.N. Doc. A/HRC/34/39. *See also Israeli settlements in the Occupied Palestinian Territory including East Jerusalem, and the occupied Syrian Golan*, U.N. Doc. A/71/355 (Aug. 24, 2016); U.N. H.R.C. *Israeli Settlements in the Occupied Palestinian Territory Including East Jerusalem and the Occupied Syrian Golan*, U.N. Doc. A/HRC/28/44 (Mar. 9, 2015); *Report of the Special Rapporteur on the situation of Human Rights in the Palestinian Territories Occupied since 1967*, U.N. Doc. A/HRC/25/67 (2014); U.N. Doc. A/HRC/22/63 (2013); *Report of the Special Rapporteur on the Situation of Human Rights in the Palestinian Territories Occupied since 1967*, A/HRC/25/67 (Jan. 13, 2014); *Report of the Special Rapporteur on the situation*

objective of Article 8(2)(b)(viii) as well as the Statute in Palestine would be frustrated.

If, on the other hand, the broad interpretation is favored, a wider scope of conduct related to the settler population in the West Bank would be open to the scrutiny of the Court. In addition to conduct leading to further movement of settlers, any conduct that has a causal link with the continuing presence of the totality of the settler population in the West Bank would fall within the jurisdiction of the Court, regardless of the time of their initial movement and settlement. This is due to the fact that, through such conduct, the Israeli authorities maintain the unlawful state of affairs in the West Bank which was precipitated by the establishment of Kfar Etzion settlement in 1967, rendering the continuation of this unlawful state of affairs contingent upon their will. Furthermore, the legally protected interests of the native population in the West Bank under Article 8(2)(b)(viii), as described above, continues to be infringed and the resulting dispossession and economic destitution they suffer[224] accumulates over time as long as settlers are transferred into the occupied territory and remain therein.

What would be the practical implications of adopting the broad interpretation over the narrow interpretation in relation to the situation in the West Bank then? An assessment of the Israeli policy of provision of subsidies and incentives to the Jewish settlements in West Bank is illustrative in this regard. Through the implementation of a governmental scheme of financial incentives in industrial zones that are designated as National Priority Areas, the Israeli authorities continuously and actively encourage commercial development of Israeli and international businesses in and around the settlements in the West Bank.[225] These incentives include benefits such as tax breaks for individuals and business enterprises[226] and direct incentives to the industrial, agricultural and tourism sectors.[227] In addition to such incentives, Israeli authorities offer construction, housing and education subsidies and benefits to the settlers in the West Bank which are not afforded to Israeli citizens living in Israeli

---

of human rights in the Palestinian territories occupied since 1967, U.N. Doc. A/HRC/4/17 (Jan. 29, 2007). Similarly, a recent decision the UN Security Council reaffirmed "that the establishment by Israel of settlements in the Palestinian territory occupied since 1967, including East Jerusalem, has no legal validity and constitutes a flagrant violation under international law ..."; S.C Resolution 2334, U.N. Doc. S/RES/2334 (Dec. 23, 2016).

224 *Report of the Special Rapporteur on the situation of human rights in the Palestinian territories occupied since 1967*, U.N. Doc. A/67/379 (Sep. 19, 2012), para. 9.
225 U.N. Doc. A/HRC/34/39, para. 24.
226 *Id.*
227 U.N. Doc. A/HRC/22/63, para. 22.

territory.[228] As a consequence of implementation of such policies, the Israeli settler population in the West Bank have seen a steady growth over the years.[229] Reportedly, these privileges have turned many settlements in the West Bank into affluent enclaves for Israeli citizens within an area where Palestinians live under military rule and in conditions of widespread poverty.[230]

The continuing provision of such incentives, benefits and subsidies can be said to have both led to the migration of new settlers into the West Bank since June 2014, while at the same time maintaining or perpetuating the presence of the settler population that was established in the West Bank before that date. Under the narrow interpretation, the provision of these privileges would only fall within the scope of Article 8(2)(b)(viii) if it can be demonstrated that they facilitated the arrival of new settlers into the West Bank after June 2014. Under the broad interpretation, on the other hand, in addition to the facilitation of new arrivals, the provision of such privileges to the totality of the settler population present in the West Bank, regardless of their date of arrival, would also qualify criminal conduct due to the fact that it maintains their continuing presence in an occupied territory. Additionally, and perhaps even more importantly, the Israeli authorities may also incur liability under Article 8(2)(b)(viii) due to their omission regarding the revocation of this governmental incentive scheme. That being said, in line with the jurisdiction framework of the Court discussed above, the conduct of a particular accused must have taken place after June 2014 for the Court to be able to scrutinize it. For instance, if an individual played an active role in the preparation and implementation of a plan to provide subsidies and incentives for Israeli settlements in the West Bank, but his/her active participation or omission in relation to the crime has ceased prior to June 2014, the Court would not be able to scrutinize his/her conduct. The fact that the effects of an initial conduct extended into the period where the Court has temporal jurisdiction is not sufficient for an individual to be culpable for a continuing crime. Adopting this approach would allow the Court to realize the true nature and purpose of Article 8(2)(b)(viii) while remaining within the jurisdictional parameters of the Statute.

Conduct related to the physical expansion of the Israeli settlements in the West Bank, on the other hand, poses a more serious challenge to the Court. Needless to say, any measures taken by the Israeli authorities regarding the physical expansion of the settlements, such as plans for construction

---

228 *Id.*; *Report of the Special Rapporteur on the situation of human rights in the Palestinian territories occupied since 1967*, U.N. Doc. A/67/379 (Sep. 19, 2012), paras. 9–10.
229 U.N. Doc. A/HRC/34/39, para. 24.
230 U.N. Doc. A/67/379, para. 9.

of housing units, that are devised or implemented after June 2014 would fall within the jurisdiction of the Court. For instance, the issuance by Israeli authorities of a tender for 438 housing units in the settlement of Ramat Shlomo, or the advancement of 560 settlement units in Maale Adumim and 240 in East Jerusalem, as well as the issuance of tenders for additional 323 units in those settlements in 2015 and 2016[231] would clearly fall within the jurisdiction of the Court under both interpretations, provided that their connection to the movement and settlement of Jewish settlers into the West Bank can be demonstrated. The same can also be said the efforts of the Israeli authorities to retroactively legalize the settlement outposts erected by the Israeli settlers in the West Bank.[232] Whether the omission of the Israeli authorities to dismantle already existing settlement units and evacuate the settler population living in the West Bank, as was done in the Gaza Strip during the disengagement of 2005, would also fall within the scope of Article 8(2)(b)(viii) under the broad interpretation, on the other hand, is a far more difficult question to answer. Arguably, the inaction of the Israeli authorities to remove the physical infrastructure of the settlements translates into the continuing presence of the settlers in the West Bank. That being said, the Court might be reluctant in interpreting Article 8(2)(b)(viii) as providing the authorities of the Occupying Power with a duty to evacuate the already existing settler population out of the occupied territory due to potential human rights implications of such an undertaking. In the West Bank, this would entail the evacuation of almost 600,000 Israeli settlers, possibly through forcible means similar to those that were employed during the evacuation of the Israeli settlements in the Gaza Strip.[233] How the Court will balance the legally protected interests of and the harm caused to the Palestinian victims, and the potential harm that may be inflicted upon the Israeli settlers will be seen in due course.

V Conclusion

This article attempted to provide a definitional framework to instantaneous, continuing, and continuous crimes and apply these definitions to

---

231 U.N. Doc. A/HRC/34/39, paras. 26–27.
232 *Id.*, paras. 32–33.
233 *See* Steven Erlanger, *Tearfully but Forcefully, Israel Removes Gaza Settlers*, N.Y. Times (Aug. 18, 2005), http://www.nytimes.com/2005/08/18/world/middleeast/tearfully-but-forcefully-israel-removes-gaza-settlers.html; *Israel Begins Forced Removal of Jewish Settlers From Gaza as Deadline Expires*, Democracy Now (Aug. 17, 2005), https://www.democracynow.org/2005/8/17/israel_begins_forced_removal_of_jewish.

article 8(2)(b)(viii) of the Statute and the situation in the West Bank. Essentially the discussion boils down to how the term 'transfer' will be interpreted by the Court. A narrow/literal approach leads to the interpretation of the term 'transfer' as an instantaneous or discreet act completed once the movement and settlement of the population into the occupied territory has transpired. A broad/purposive reading of the term, on the other hand, leads to its characterization as a continuing act that continues to be committed as long as the settled population remains within the occupied territory. If the former interpretation is favored, Article 8(2)(b)(viii) would be construed as an instantaneous crime or a continuous crime. This would significantly reduce the type of conduct that the Court can adjudicate on in connection to this provision. In relation to the situation in Palestine, this would limit the Court's jurisdiction solely to conduct that led to the movement and settlement of individuals that occurred after June 2014. This would go against the fundamental purpose behind the incorporation of Article 8(2)(b)(viii) into the Statute and create an accountability gap in relation to conduct that perpetuates and maintains an ongoing unlawful state of affairs in the West Bank, *i.e.* the presence of settlers in an occupied territory. If, however, the latter option is preferred, then Article 8(2)(b)(viii) would be construed as a continuing crime significantly expanding the scope of the types of conduct that may be amenable to the Court's jurisdiction. Under this interpretation, any conduct that facilitates the maintenance of the Israeli population settled in the West Bank may incur liability under article 8(2)(b)(viii), regardless of the date of settlement. The present author opines that this interpretation is the most appropriate one for the realization of the purpose of Article 8(2)(b)(viii) and consequently of the Statute.

The challenging questions in relation to the investigation and prosecution of Israeli settlement activity in the West Bank are not limited to the temporal jurisdiction of the Court. There are a number of remaining issues related to the nature of Article 8(2)(b)(viii) that the Court will ultimately need to find answers to. For instance, can the part of the settlement population that was born in the occupied territory considered to be transferred? Can Jewish settlers from third countries be considered as Israel's 'own population'? What is the required degree of participation for an individual to be responsible for direct or indirect transfer of population into the territory? Can, for instance, would every member of the Knesset voting for a legislation with the effect of inducing population transfer into the occupied territory be considered as perpetrators of a war crime under Article 8(2)(b)(viii)? Due to the virtual absence of any jurisprudence on the matter, the judges of the Court will have to come to their own conclusions in relation to these questions and ultimately determine the parameters of liability under Article 8(2)(b)(viii). Their determination will not only have an impact over to the Israeli conduct in the West Bank, but will reverberate through other situations of population transfer into occupied territory that may eventually come within the jurisdiction of the Court.[234]

---

234 *See* ICC, *Report on Preliminary Examination Activities* (2017), para. 101; on the alleged transfer of population by Russia into Crimea, Ukraine. *See also* the Article 15 Communication to the Prosecutor of the International Criminal Court regarding the situation in Occupied Cyprus dated 14 July 2014, lodged by Member of the European Parliament Costas Mavrides. Eugene Kontorovich, *International Criminal Court action filed vs. settlements*, Wash. Post (Aug. 7, 2014), https://www.washingtonpost.com/news/volokh-conspiracy/wp/2014/08/07/international-criminal-court-action-filed-vs-settlements/?utm_term=.3d2fcf29bd3d.

Whither the Principle of Self-determination in the Post-colonial Era? Building the Case for a Policy-oriented Approach

*Daniele Amoroso**

	Abstract 84	
I	Introductory Remarks 85	
II	*Hic Sunt Leones*: the Principle of Self-determination and the Cognitive Boundaries of the Traditional Approaches 87	
III	The Policy-oriented Approach of the New Haven School of International Law (and its Detractors) 93	
	A	*International Law as a Policy-oriented Process* 94
	B	*The NHS Analytical Model* 97
IV	Applying the NHS Model to the Law of Self-determination: Delimitation of the Problem and Clarification of the Goals 100	
	A	*Identifying the Participants and Their Perspectives. In Particular: the 'People'* 101
	B	*The Role of the Various Participants in the Decision-making Process* 106
	C	*Past Trends in Decision and Conditioning Factors, in Particular the International Response to Irredentist Claims* 108
	D	*Projection of Future Trends* 111
	E	*The Elaboration of Policy Recommendations* 113
V	Conclusions 115	

Abstract

It is no secret that, since the end of decolonization, the principle of self-determination of peoples has been going through a veritable identity crisis. On the one hand,

---

* Associate Professor of International Law, University of Cagliari (da.amoroso@gmail.com). The author wishes to thank the Editor-in-Chief, Ardi Imseis, for his very helpful comments and suggestions. This paper is current as of Aug. 21, 2017.

inconsistencies and double-standards are so commonplace in international practice as to justify the doubt that the law of self-determination is, in fact, power politics in disguise. On the other hand, a significant portion of the international community maintains that the principle has exhausted its historical function and applies only to a very limited number of cases (*e.g.* Palestine and Western Sahara). Yet self-determination of peoples is still well entrenched in international legal life.

Against this background, international lawyers have been called upon to clarify how the customary principle on self-determination has changed in order to meet the challenges posed by the new global order. So far, however, the various attempts to overcome the colonial paradigm have not led to satisfactory results, being doomed to capitulate in the face of the fact that international practice in this field is either too sparse or is inconsistent.

The main reason for this difficulty lies in the tendency to conceive of the law of self-determination in a traditional, 'static' fashion, as a set of clear-cut rules whose content has to be distilled, ultimately, in the light of accumulated past decisions. I will argue, by contrast, that the principle should be looked at in its 'dynamic' aspect, *viz.* as a ceaseless process through which the international community provides an authoritative response to demands for self-determination. My working hypothesis, specifically, is that a valuable contribution to such an investigation may be offered by the policy-oriented jurisprudence developed by the so-called 'New Haven School' of international law (NHS).

I   Introductory Remarks

Writing in 1952, Sir Hersch Lauterpacht famously said that "if international law is, in some ways, at the vanishing point of law, the law of war is, perhaps even more conspicuously, at the vanishing point of international law".[1] Had the distinguished author witnessed the status of the principle of self-determination in the post-colonial era, he would have probably passed a similar (if not harsher) judgment. Inconsistencies and double-standards are so commonplace in international practice as to have recently induced one author to assume the existence of a (pseudo-) rule whereby self-determination claims, in order to be legally validated, must necessarily gain "the support of the most powerful states on our planet".[2]

---

1   Sir Hersch Lauterpacht, *The problem of the revision of the law of war*, 29 Brit. Y.B. Int'l L. 360, 382 (1952).
2   Milena Sterio, The Right to Self-determination Under International Law: 'Selfistans', Secession, and the Rule of the Great Powers 57 (2012).

The latter contention – which, admittedly, comes across more as an intellectual surrender than as a theoretical construction – is emblematic of the difficulties encountered by international scholarship in dealing with self-determination issues in non-colonial contexts. As aptly noted in a report by the United States Institute of Peace, nowadays, the principle of self-determination of peoples has come "to denote different things to different peoples and governments at different times".[3]

At the same time, however, it is undeniable that this principle still plays a role in international legal life. In the last few years, indeed, self-determination of peoples and its jargon have popped up in different domains of international practice. Just consider, in this respect, extensive references to the principle contained in the 2007 *Declaration on the Rights of Indigenous Peoples*, its recurring invocation by secessionist/irredentist movements (*e.g.* in Kosovo, Catalonia or Crimea), or the widespread recognition of Libyan and Syrian rebels as "the only legitimate representative of their people".[4]

Against this background, international lawyers are called upon to clarify how the principle of self-determination has been changing in order to meet the challenges posed by contemporary international society. So far, however, the various attempts to overcome the colonial paradigm have not led to satisfactory results. These doctrinal endeavors, which include the authoritative advocacy of a right to "remedial secession" or to "democratic governance", have in fact proved insufficient in the face of the paucity and inconsistency of international practice in this field.

In my opinion, the main reason for this difficulty lies in the fact that these authors, despite their valuable effort to 'rethink' the law of self-determination,[5] have continued to conceive of it in a traditional, 'static' fashion, as a set of clear-cut, manageable rules whose content has to be distilled, ultimately, in the light of accumulated past decisions. I will argue, by contrast, that the principle of self-determination should be looked at in its 'dynamic' aspect, *viz.* as

---

3   U.S. Institute for Peace, *U.S. Responses to Self-determination Movements: Strategies for Nonviolent Outcomes and Alternatives to Secession*, (1997), at 1. *See also* Rosalyn Higgins, Problems & Process: International Law and How We Use It 128 (1995) [*hereinafter* Higgins] (speaking of the danger that self-determination ends up with "being all things to all men").

4   Regardless of whether it was appropriate in the circumstances of the case, in fact, the use of this defining formula signals the intention by the recognizing state (or international organization) to qualify an (armed) opposition group as a national liberation movement for the purposes of the application of the self-determination regime. For an analysis of past practice, which includes the recognition of the Palestinian Liberation Organization as the "sole and legitimate representative of the Palestinian people", *see* Brad R. Roth, Governmental Illegitimacy in International Law 227–234 (2000).

5   *See, e.g.*, Hurst Hannum, *Rethinking Self-determination*, 34 Va. J. Int'l L. 1, 3 (1993).

the ceaseless process through which the international community provides an authoritative response to demands for self-determination. My working hypothesis, specifically, is that a valuable contribution to such an investigation may be offered by the policy-oriented jurisprudence developed by Harold D. Lasswell and Myres S. McDougal, commonly known as the New Haven School of international law (NHS) which stands out, in the landscape of international legal theory, precisely for having conceptualized international law as "a process by which members of the world community attempt to clarify and secure their common interests through authoritative decisions and controlling practices".[6]

The present paper aims to discuss the provisional results of an ongoing research project I am carrying out on the basis of the foregoing assumption and will proceed as follows. First, I will try to explain the reason for adopting, in the study of the principle of self-determination, a process-oriented, rather than a rule-oriented, approach (part 2). Then, the main tenets of the NHS model will be spelt out (part 3) and applied to self-determination processes (part 4). Part 5 concludes.

II *Hic Sunt Leones*: the Principle of Self-determination and the Cognitive Boundaries of the Traditional Approaches

A glance at the relevant international texts would leave the cursory reader with the impression that the international community has long agreed upon a workable definition of the principle of self-determination. From the 1960 *Declaration on the Granting of Independence to Colonial Countries and Peoples* to the 2007 *Declaration on the Rights of Indigenous Peoples*, the principle of self-determination is commonly described as endowing "all peoples" with the right to "freely determine their political status and freely pursue their economic, social and cultural development".[7] On closer inspection, however, it appears that there is little in this formula which is amenable to a univocal legal definition.[8]

---

6 Lung-Chu Chen, An Introduction to Contemporary International Law: A Policy-Oriented Perspective xvii (3rd ed., 2015) [emphasis in original] [*hereinafter* Chen].

7 Common Article 1(1) to the International Covenant on Civil and Political Rights and the International Covenant on Economic, Social and Cultural Rights, which provides, at para. 2, that: "All peoples may, for their own ends, freely dispose of their natural wealth and resources without prejudice to any obligations arising out of international economic co-operation, based upon the principle of mutual benefit, and international law. In no case may a people be deprived of its own means of subsistence".

8 *See, e.g.*, James Crawford, *The Right of Self-Determination in International Law: Its Development and Future*, in Peoples' Rights 7, 10 (Philip Alston ed., 2001) [speaking of "*lex lata, lex obscura*"].

In particular, two fundamental (and intertwined) issues are left open, namely: a) what constitutes a "people" under the principle of self-determination;[9] and b) what constitutes a legitimate object of self-determination claims (secession, autonomy within the state, democracy, and so on).

In fact, the construction of this principle has always been the site of an ideological confrontation between three visions of self-determination. The first is the (once dominant) *"lecture anti-coloniale quasi-exclusive"*, fostered by socialist and third-world states since the mid-1950s (and still well entrenched among members of the Non-Alignment Movement), whereby the scope of the principle of self-determination would be confined to colonial domination or analogous situations (such as the apartheid regimes in Rhodesia and South-Africa, Morocco's presence in Western Sahara, or the Israeli military occupation and, according to some authorities,[10] apartheid-like system of government in the Palestinian territories).[11] The second vision, which has emerged in the post-Cold War era, is the one propounded (mainly) by Western states, which construes the principle of self-determination through the lens of liberal-democratic institutions and values, such as the holding of free and fair multi-party elections, the protection of minority rights, and the recognition of wide forms of autonomy and self-government to territorially-based minorities and indigenous peoples.[12] Finally, we have the (far more controversial) ethno-nationalist conception, rooted in Wilson's Fourteen Points and recently championed – not without severe inconsistencies[13] – by the Russian Federation,[14] which in its purest form advocates the redrawing of national boundaries with a view

---

9   This uncertainty famously led Sir Ivor Jennings to label the principle at issue as "ridiculous ... because the people cannot decide until somebody decides who are the people"; *see* Ivor Jennings, The Approach to Self-Government 56 (1956).

10 *See, also* for further references, John Dugard & John Reynolds, *Apartheid, International Law, and the Occupied Palestinian Territory*, 24 Eur. J. Int'l L. 867–913 (2013).

11 Alain Pellet, *Quel avénir droit des peuples à disposer d'eux-mêmes?*, in Liber Amicorum Jimenez de Arechaga 255, 265 (1994).

12 *See, e.g.*, Thomas Franck, *The Emerging Right to Democratic Governance*, 86 Am. J. Int'l L. 46, 91 (1992).

13 It suffices to consider, in this regard, the diametrically opposite attitudes held by Russia in relation to Kosovar and Crimean self-determination claims. *See*, for instance, Marko Milanovic, *Crimea, Kosovo, Hobgoblins and Hypocrisy*, EJIL: Talk! (Mar. 20, 2014), https://www.ejiltalk.org/crimea-kosovo-hobgoblins-and-hypocrisy/.

14 Arguably, Zionist conception of self-determination also falls under this category. *See, for instance*, Ruth Gavison, *Israel as a Jewish and Democratic State: Tensions and Possibilities* 26 (1999) – [in Hebrew, translated in Chaim Gains, *Jewish/Palestinian Self-Determination and Citizenship in Israel/Palestine*, EUI Working Paper RSCAS 2014/35, 2) [*hereinafter* Gains].

to matching the ethnic composition of the population in a given territory;[15] and, according to a less radical reading, envisages such a redrawing as a last resort solution, available to peoples only in the case of widespread and serious human rights violations (so-called 'remedial secession').[16]

As a matter of fact, only the first approach has managed to gather the *diuturnitas* and *opinio iuris* required to give birth to a customary international rule with a clearly discernible scope and prescriptive content, namely the prohibition of colonial, alien or racist domination.[17] On the one hand, indeed, the emergence of a right of the peoples to a (liberal-)democratic governance is fatally hindered by the fact that almost half of the international community is constituted by states governed by non-liberal-democratic regimes.[18] On the other hand, the practice supporting an ethno-nationalist reading of self-determination (also in its milder form of a right to 'remedial secession' for oppressed minorities) is scant and anything but univocal.[19] In a word, the existence of customary 'rules' on post-colonial self-determination may be affirmed solely on the basis of a teleologically-oriented selection of the relevant international materials, which over-stretches the legal significance of some manifestation of practice and plays down the importance of others. This explains why, in

---

15 This view was labelled by Koskenniemi as the "rousseauesque approach" to self-determination; see Martti Koskenniemi, *National Self-Determination Today: Problems of Legal Theory and Practice*, 43 Int'l & Comp. L. Q. 241, 250 (1994).
16 *See, e.g.*, Allen Buchanan, Justice, Legitimacy, and Self-Determination: Moral Foundations for International Law 335 (2004).
17 Antonio Cassese, Self-determination of Peoples. A Legal Reappraisal 129–131 (1995) [*hereinafter* Cassese].
18 According to a recent report by Freedom House, of 195 states reviewed, only 89 were considered "free" (under liberal-democratic standards, of course), while 55 were labelled as "Partly Free" and 51 as "Not Free"; see Freedom House, *Discarding Democracy: Return to the Iron Fist. Freedom in the World 2015* (2015), https://freedomhouse.org/sites/default/files/01152015_FIW_2015_final.pdf. Another element which casts more than a doubt on the existence of a legal entitlement to democratic governance is represented by the ambiguous reactions of the international community to unconstitutional changes of democratically elected governments; see Erika De Wet, *From Free Town to Cairo via Kiev: The Unpredictable Road of Democratic Legitimacy in Governmental Recognition*, AJIL Unbound (Jan. 16, 2015) [*hereinafter* De Wet], https://www.asil.org/blogs/free-town-cairo-kiev-unpredictable-road-democratic-legitimacy-governmental-recognition.
19 Katherine Del Mar, *The Myth of Remedial Secession*, in Statehood and Self-determination: Reconciling Tradition and Modernity in International Law 79 (Duncan French ed., 2013); Jure Vidmar, *Remedial Secession in International Law: Theory and (Lack of) Practice*, 6 St. Antony's Int'l Rev. 37–56 (2010).

legal scholarship, these customary rules are often (if not always) described as 'emerging' or *in statu nascendi*.[20]

The point is that the stabilization of a customary rule through a "general practice accepted as law" by the various members of the international community, while difficult per se, is nearly impossible in the area of self-determination, where the most fundamental, and most jealously protected attributes of state sovereignty (national boundaries, form of state, form of government) are potentially at stake. Indeed, the crystallization of the aforementioned norms on colonial, alien or racist domination was made possible by the unique political conditions which led to the demise of colonial empires – a situation which is unlikely to recur, at least in comparable terms, in the near future.

In the light of the foregoing, it would seem that self-determination, as a legal principle, has somehow exhausted its historical function, its relevance being confined to a handful of well identified situations rooted in classical and neo-colonial struggles (*e.g.* Palestine and Western Sahara); or, alternatively, that it is stuck in an impasse, being unable to overcome its glorious (but now fundamentally outdated) anti-colonialist past because of the persistent lack of coherence in international practice.

This would, however, be a hasty conclusion. In approaching the law of self-determination, indeed, one should take care not to confuse the general 'principle' with the individual 'rules' originating therefrom – a distinction masterfully drawn by Antonio Cassese in his celebrated monograph on self-determination.[21] In his view, the existence of general principles, such as that of self-determination, is "a typical expression of the present world community", which is often too divided to agree upon specific rules but nonetheless needs "some sort of basic guidelines for [its] conduct", a lowest common denominator of "the conflicting views of States on matters of crucial importance".[22]

In relation to self-determination, Cassese identified this lowest common denominator in the "quintessence of self-determination", namely the "need to pay regard to the freely expressed will of the peoples"[23] whenever foundational political decisions are at stake. This is a very loose, open-textured standard, as the author pointed out, since "it does not define either the units of self-determination or areas or matters to which it applies, or the means or methods of its implementation ... nor does it point to the objective of self-determination",

---

20   See, *e.g.*, Daniel Thürer & Thomas Burri, *Self-Determination*, in Max Planck Encyc. Pub. Int'l L. 39 (Rüdiger Wolfrum ed., 2013).
21   Cassese, 126–133.
22   *Id.*, 128.
23   Western Sahara, Advisory Opinion, 1975 I.C.J. Rep 12, 58 (Oct. 16).

but limits itself to indicating "the course of action to be taken when one is confronted with problems concerning the destiny of a people".[24]

What does all this mean in practice? The functions assigned by Cassese to the principle of self-determination thus conceived appear to be two. On the one hand, the principle should operate as a standard of interpretation: when a customary or treaty norm is unclear, it should be construed so as to take into account the freely expressed will of the people. On the other hand, it should be possible to infer from the principle some specific rules of international law,[25] for example the prohibition on territorial cessions carried out contrary to the will of the population concerned, or the ban on military coups overthrowing democratically elected governments. Both functions, however, were rarely resorted to in international practice.[26] This has perhaps been the case because the contribution of international and domestic courts in the field of self-determination has been less significant than in other areas of international law, partly because states have shown a reluctance to refer self-determination matters to third-party adjudicators and partly because the very same adjudicators have preferred to carve out for themselves a secondary role to that of political, state-driven organs.[27] Indeed, Cassese concedes that, because of its "general,

---

[24] Cassese, 128 [emphasis in original].
[25] *Id.*, 132–3.
[26] *But see* ACHPR/Res.10(XVI)94, *Resolution on the Military* (1994); Dawda Jawara v. The Gambia, Comm. Nos. 147/95 and 149/96, African Commission on Human and Peoples' Rights [Afr. Comm'n H.P.R.], 72–73 (2000) [*hereinafter* Jawara v. Gambia] (construing the right to self-determination under Art. 20 of the African Charter of Human and Peoples' Rights as forbidding military coups). Still, it should be noted that such a prohibition is anything but established in state practice (*see* De Wet).
[27] This is particularly true with regard to the ICJ, whose pronouncements on the issue – although not "merely adjectival" – are basically aimed at supporting the activities of UN political organ; *see* James Crawford, *The General Assembly, the International Court and Self-determination*, in Fifty Years of the International Court of Justice: Essays in Honour of Sir Robert Jennings 585, 592–4 (Vaughan Lowe and Malgosia Fitzmaurice eds., 1996). *See also* Legal Consequences of the Construction of a Wall in the Occupied Palestinian Territory, Advisory Opinion, 2004 I.C.J. Rep. 136 (July 9). In this respect, it is worthy of note that, when the ICJ has been called upon to settle a self-determination controversy in the absence of a previous determination by the UN General Assembly or the Security Council, it has shown an overly cautious attitude (*see* Accordance with international law of the unilateral declaration of independence in respect of Kosovo, Advisory Opinion, 2010 I.C.J. Rep. 403 (July 22). Of course, there are some notable exceptions, such as the Supreme Court of Canada, whose advisory opinion on *Reference re Secession of Quebec* ([1998] 2 S.C.R. 217) represents an unavoidable point of reference in approaching self-determination issues, or the African Commission on Human and Peoples' Rights, which has found itself competent to adjudicate individual and collective complaints concerning the violation of the right to self-determination; *see* Katangese Peoples' Congress v. Zaire,

loose and multifaceted" character, the principle of self-determination lends itself to "various and even contradictory applications", because of its attitude "to being manipulated and used for conflicting purposes".[28]

It is at this point that the rule-based approach meets its cognitive boundaries. Faced with the normative ambiguity of the principle and the lack of consistency in past applicative trends, it is difficult to ascertain whether a given course of action actually pursues the principle of self-determination, or is just an expression of power politics. Here we arrive at the crux of the working hypothesis explored in this article. As Rosalyn Higgins put it, where legal standards are uncertain, a "policy-directed choice can be properly made".[29] A more comprehensive understanding of the law of self-determination, therefore, should also include an analysis of the *process* which leads to the adoption of such policy-directed choices. This is why I contend that the traditional analysis of the principle of self-determination needs to be *complemented* through a theoretical model that takes into account its dynamic dimension and the embeddedness of policy factors in the actual making of law.[30]

In this respect, the reference to the NHS is all too obvious. Indeed, while normative ambiguity torments the traditional positivist lawyer, it represents the very point of departure of the process-based, policy-oriented jurisprudence.[31] In the following part, the main tenets of this theory will be briefly presented.

Comm. No. 75/92, African Commission on Human and Peoples' Rights [Afr. Comm'n H.P.R.], (1995); Jawara v. Gambia; Kevin Mgwanga Gunme et al v. Cameroon, Comm. No. 266/03, African Commission on Human and Peoples' Rights [Afr. Comm'n H.P.R.], 203 (2009) [*hereinafter* Gunme et al v. Cameroon]. It should not be overlooked, however, that both the Supreme Court of Canada and the African Commission proved fully aware of the prominent role played, in this context, by policy considerations (*see* Reference re Secession of Quebec, [1998] 2 S.C.R. 217, 100–101; Gunme et al v. Cameroon, 203).

28 Cassese, 128–9. *See also* Enrico Milano, Formazione dello Stato e processi di State-building nel diritto internazionale. Kosovo 1999–2013 63–66 (2013) [*hereinafter* Milano].

29 Higgins, 7.

30 On the viability of such an integrated approach, *see* Tai-Heng Cheng, *Making International Law Without Agreeing What It Is*, 10 Wash. U. Glob. Stud. L. Rev. 1, 25 (2011) [*hereinafter* Tai-Heng Cheng]. In a similar vein, although not fully embracing a policy-oriented perspective, *see also* Milano, 45–76.

31 In fact, NHS scholars usually remind the reader that "inherited general prescriptions commonly travel in pairs of complementary opposites"; *see* Harold D. Lasswell and Myres S. McDougal, Jurisprudence for a Free Society: Studies in Law, Science and Policy 213 (1992) [*hereinafter* Lasswell & McDougal].

III The Policy-oriented Approach of the New Haven School of International Law (and its Detractors)

Nowadays, the NHS cannot be said to be popular among international lawyers, particularly in continental Europe.[32] There are at least three reasons for this idiosyncrasy. First, NHS writings are often couched in an esoteric language, which is perhaps easily understandable by the initiated, but it is sometimes nearly unintelligible for the non-NHS reader.[33] While this is certainly (and regrettably) true, it is quite obvious that it cannot be the sole reason to reject a theoretical model outright.

Second, the NHS has been accused of conceiving international law as the "handmaiden of the national interest of the United States",[34] as it would end up with tailoring the notion of lawfulness around United States (US) foreign policy.[35] This point, too, cannot be denied in its entirety. Admittedly, some NHS scholars seem to be geared towards justifying, at any cost, US action in the international arena. But this should be seen as an expression of a personal, patriotic inclination (a phenomenon which is not limited to NHS, by the way)[36] rather than the natural consequence of a process-based jurisprudence.[37] In fact, other authors belonging to the same school did not refrain from criticizing US choices in relation to specific events.[38]

Third, and crucially, many see NHS jurisprudence as 'anathema' to the international legal discipline because it unacceptably conflates law, politics and

---

32 Ghunter Auth, *Book Review: Die Schule von New Haven*, 12 Eur. J. Int'l L. 1027, 1030 (2001).
33 For a devastating critique on this point, *see* Gerald Fitzmaurice, *Vae Victis or Woe to the Negotiators! Your Treaty or Our 'Interpretation' of It?* 65 Am. J. Int'l L. 360, 367 (1971).
34 Stanley Anderson, *A Critique of Professor Myres S. McDougal's Doctrine of Interpretation by Major Purposes*, 57 Am. J. Int'l L. 378, 382 (1963).
35 Richard Falk, *Casting the Spell: The New Haven School of International Law*, 104 Yale L. J. 1991, 1997 (1995).
36 Curiously enough, NHS scholars have always shown a peculiar attention to minimize subjective biases. Precisely to this end, indeed, they recommend the observer to clarify his/her personal standpoint before proceeding in the analysis. *See* Myres S. McDougal, Harold D. Lasswell & W. Michael Reisman, *Theories About International Law: Prologue to a Configurative Jurisprudence*, 8 Va. J. Int'l L. 188, 199–200 (1968).
37 Tai-Heng Cheng, 19; Denise Wallace, Human Rights and Business: A Policy-Oriented Perspective 21 (Brill, 2014) [*hereinafter* Wallace].
38 *See, e.g.*, Eisuke Suzuki, *Self-Determination and World Public Order: Community Response to Territorial Separation*, 16 Va. J. Int'l L. 779, 855 (1976) (criticizing US choice to side with Pakistan during the Bangladesh Liberation War); W. Michael Reisman, *Why Regime Change Is (Almost Always) A Bad Idea*, 98 Am. J. Int'l L. 504, 516 (2004) (criticizing US military intervention in Iraq).

power.³⁹ This criticism is too sweeping. While it is true that one of the salient features of the NHS approach lies in the recognition of "the essential relationship between law and policy",⁴⁰ it is unfair to argue that they do not distinguish 'law' from other social processes (including power processes).⁴¹ This will become apparent if we have a closer look at the main features of this theory.

A   *International Law as a Policy-oriented Process*

NHS scholars locate international law within the wider 'world social process', to be understood as the totality of interactions among human beings or groups thereof ('participants') through which they pursue their desires or wants ('values'),⁴² by employing a set of strategies ('practices') on the basis of resources available to them ('base values'). Among these interactions, a prominent role is played by the 'world power process', namely the process which determines the actual 'outcomes' of the participants' struggle for the desired values. This process consists of the decisions by which some participants coercively shape ('control') the behavior of the other participants, by effecting specific 'outcomes' (in the sense of 'who gets what'). World power process should not be confused with international law (or, in NHS parlance, the 'world legal process'), which is only a part of it. International law, indeed, is described as the continuing process of *authoritative* and *controlling* decisions. Under this model, therefore, law is made of decisions possessing two elements: 'authority' and 'control'.⁴³ While the second is common to all power processes, 'authority' is typical of the law-making process and indicates the conformity of a given decision to the world community's expectations 'about who is competent to make what decisions, in what structures, by what procedures, and in

---

39   Bruno Simma & Andreas Paulus, *The Responsibility of Individuals for Human Rights Abuses in Internal Conflicts: a Positivist View*, 93 Am. J. Int'l L. 302, 305 (1999).
40   Higgins, 5.
41   Tai-Heng Cheng, 12–20.
42   As is known, Lasswell and McDougal proposed an eight-fold taxonomy of 'values', which includes, in sum: (1) Power: the giving and receiving of support in government, politics, and law; (2) Wealth: the production and distribution of goods and services, and consumption; (3) Enlightenment: the gathering, processing, and dissemination of information; (4) Skill: opportunity to acquire and exercise capability in vocation, professions, and other social activities; (5) Well-being: safety, health, and comfort; (6) Affection: intimacy, friendship, and loyalty; (7) Respect: recognition, whether personal or ascriptive; (8) Rectitude: participation in forming and applying norms of responsible conduct. *See* Lasswell & McDougal, 335. McDougal recognized, however, that "any other categorization which offers operational indices in terms of the concrete demands of individual human beings will serve equally well"; *see* Myres S. MacDougal, *Law as a Process of Decision: A Policy-Oriented Approach to Legal Study*, 1 Nat. L. F. 53, 56 (1956).
43   Anthony C. Arend, Legal Rules and International Society 76 (1999) [*hereinafter* Arend].

accordance with what goals and criteria.'⁴⁴ The notion of 'authority', therefore, is crucial in discerning law from decision-making processes resulting in the exercise of 'naked power'.⁴⁵ Contrary to what its critics seem to imply, therefore, NHS jurisprudence does not equate law with power, although it realistically acknowledges that the latter is a constitutive element of the former (because authority without control is not law, but mere 'pretense').⁴⁶

Two aspects, however, need to be clarified, namely *i*) what is the 'community' whose expectations create a base of authority for controlling decisions; and *ii*) what is the precise content of these expectations. With regard to the former, it is worth underlining how, under the NHS model, the relevant community extends beyond the decision-making elites of states and international organizations so as to include also 'politically relevant groups', such as NGOs, political movements, transnational corporations, and so on.⁴⁷ Sure, the weight accorded to the latter's expectations is less than that accorded to states and international organizations; and will vary considerably depending on several factors, such as the subject matter or the group's actual interest and influence. The fact remains, however, that such expectations are not ignored under the NHS model – which explains why the latter is described as "especially empowering" for non-state actors.⁴⁸

In relation to the *content* of such expectations, as seen above, they concern both the procedure ('who is competent', 'in what structures', 'by what procedure') and the substance ('in accordance with what goals and criteria') of the decision-making process. While the former does not raise particular problems, the substantial aspect needs further elaboration. When NHS scholars refer to the 'goals and criteria' by which the decision-making process should be carried out, they have in mind two different, but intermingled problems. In the first

---

44   Chen, 17; Harold D. Lasswell, Myres S. MacDougal & W. Michael Reisman, *The World Constitutive Process of Authoritative Decision*, 19 J. Legal Educ. 253, 256 (1967) [hereinafter Lasswell, MacDougal & Reisman] (speaking in this regard of "expectations of appropriateness").
45   Lasswell, MacDougal & Reisman, 257.
46   *See* Higgins, 4 ("Law ... is the interlocking of authority with power").
47   W. Michael Reisman, *International Lawmaking: A Process of Communication*, 75 Am. Soc'y Int'l L. Proceedings 101, 107 (1981).
48   Eisuke Suzuki, *The New Haven School of Jurisprudence and Non-State Actors in International Law in Policy Perspective*, 42 J. Pol'y Stud. 41 (2012); [hereinafter Suzuki (2012)]; Math Noortmann, *Understanding Non-state Actors in the Contemporary World Society: Transcending the International, Mainstreaming the Transnational, or Bringing the Participants back in?*, in Non-State Actor Dynamics in International Law: From Law-Takers to Law-Makers 153 (Math Noortmann, August Reinisch & Cedric Ryngaert, eds., 2010).

place, the conformity of a given course of action to 'trends in past decisions' is taken into account. Reliance on past trends introduces into the analysis a significant element of stability, which is crucial in any legal theory;[49] it also brings the NHS and the rule-based approach closer, to the extent that the notion of 'past trends' includes a series of legal materials which positivist scholars are well acquainted with (*e.g.* treaties, state practice, international resolutions, international case law, and so on).[50]

Past trends, however, are not the only relevant factor. When a decision based on past trends would not allow the pursuance of a preferred objective; or when past trends are sufficiently ambiguous to enable a policy-directed choice, the 'authority' of decision-making will alternatively ensue from congruence with the basic policy goals of the international community, namely: a) the minimization of the use of unauthorized coercion and violence ('minimum public order'); and b) the full realization of human dignity, *i.e.* 'the greatest production and the widest possible distribution of all human values' ('optimum public order').[51] In practice, this means that the failure to meet the expectations of the world community as to the fostering of these policy goals may deprive a decision of its basis of 'authority', despite compliance with past trends.[52] Conversely, an unprecedented decision, which is contrary to established patterns of behavior, may nevertheless be deemed as lawful because of its attitude to secure both minimum and optimum public order.[53]

Understandably enough, the latter contention has appalled positivist international lawyers who are somehow 'shocked' by a theory enabling policy to trump established rules. This point, however, is less destabilizing than it might at first appear. On the one hand, positivist scholars are ready to acknowledge that, when the law is uncertain, the decision-maker will inevitably be driven

---

49   Chen, 101 ("In the most comprehensive sense, the function of law in any community is to maintain uniformity in decision in clarifying and securing common interests").
50   Higgins, 6.
51   For an excellent analysis of these two goals and their relationship, *see* Steven R. Ratner, *Between Minimum and Optimum Public Order: An Ethical Path for the Future*, in Looking to the Future: Essays on International Law in Honor of W. Michael Reisman 195 (Mahnoush H. Arsanjani *et al.*, eds., 2011).
52   This was the fate, for instance, of the position of equidistance taken by UN organs during the Bangladesh Liberation War, which was somehow 'overruled' by the "smooth flow of decisions in favor of recognition of Bangladesh"; *see* Suzuki (2012), 811.
53   In this respect, a (relatively unproblematic) example is offered by the non-consensual airstrikes carried out by the US (and other Western powers) against the Islamic State of Iraq and the Levant on Syrian territory. While certainly deviant from the traditional norms on the use of force, they have been met with little opposition within the world community at large.

by other than purely legal factors.[54] On the other hand, it is generally accepted that a breach of existing law may constitute the first act of a process eventually leading to the formation of a new customary norm, provided that the law-breaker is convinced of the 'social necessity' (*opinio necessitatis*) of such a breach.[55] What the NHS approach tries to do, accordingly, is only to provide an analytical model through which it is possible to examine and assess "systematically and openly"[56] such a process, making "candid"[57] the policy factors which underlie it. It is worth adding that the time-honored notion of *opinio necessitatis* is far more elusive than the basic policy goals identified by NHS scholars. After all, the pursuance of a peaceful world order where human dignity is fully realized was not just a personal hope of MacDougal and his acolytes, but represents the fundamental goal of the world community since the very adoption of the United Nations (UN) Charter.[58]

B   *The NHS Analytical Model*

The process of authoritative and controlling decision-making described above is studied and evaluated under the NHS model through an analytical grid, made up of two elements: a) which factors should be taken into account ('principles of substance'); and b) how they should be treated ('principles of procedures').

As to the first element, NHS scholars suggest focusing on the following structure. From the outset the *participants* in the decision-making process should be identified. By 'participants', NHS scholars mean any individual or entity "which has at least minimum access to the process of authority in the sense that it can make claims or be subjected to claims".[59] Therefore, this category is not limited to states and international organizations but will also include other relevant stakeholders. This is because, according to the NHS approach, the decision-making process – and, as a consequence, the participation therein – does not reflect the tripartite distinction between legislative, executive and judicial power; but is dissected into seven functions, namely: the gathering and dissemination of information relevant to the decision-making

---

54   *See* Tai-Heng Cheng (discussing 'soft positivism').
55   Benedetto Conforti & Angelo Labella, An Introduction to International Law 35 (2011). Similar observations could be made with regard to 'creative' interpretation of treaty clauses or the superseding of treaty obligations by subsequent customary rules.
56   Higgins, 5.
57   Iain Scobbie, *A View of Delft: some Thoughts about Thinking about International Law*, in International Law 53, 76 (Malcolm Evans, ed., 4th ed., 2014) [*hereinafter* Scobbie].
58   Lasswell & McDougal, 34–35; Chen, 101–103.
59   Lasswell, McDougal & Reisman, 262.

process (intelligence); the advocacy of alternatives to the *status quo* (promotion); the creation of binding norms (prescription); the invocation of an authoritative response in reaction to a breach of prescriptions (invocation); the concrete application of prescriptions, if the case by imposing sanctions (application); the repeal of existing prescriptions that no longer reflect public order goals (termination); the assessment of the performance of the decision-making process with respect to the achievement of the basic policy goals of the international community (appraisal).[60]

It is evident that while states and international organizations may potentially perform any of the aforementioned functions, the role of other participants is more limited. NGOs, for instance, may be crucial in carrying out intelligence, promotion, invocation, and appraisal activities, but are normally ruled out of prescription, application and termination tasks.[61] Individuals, on the other hand, are certainly entitled to 'invoke' an authoritative response in the case of deviation from prescriptions (*e.g.* to complain of a human rights violation before the European Court of Human Rights), whereas their participation in the other functions is generally excluded (or of little relevance).

Having identified the participants in a given decision-making process, the NHS model requires that their 'perspectives', 'bases of power' and 'strategies' be analyzed. Focusing on these factors allows the observer to grasp the viewpoint of those who actually *make* the decisions.[62] The 'perspectives' of the participants, in particular, describe the way they situate themselves in relation to the other participants, their expectations, and the concrete outcome they pursue by participating in the process.[63] The 'bases of power', on the other hand, represent the resources which each participant may rely on in order to influence or determine the outcome of the process. In this respect, one should take into account both the extent to which the participant has access to the decision-making functions detailed above (namely, its 'basis of authority') and its ability to affect their performance *from outside* by leveraging on political, economic, military, religious or cultural pressure.[64] Finally, by 'strategies', NHS scholars indicate the precise course of action taken by each participant to reach its objectives,[65] which may range from pure persuasion (*e.g.* the 'naming

---

60   Lasswell & MacDougal, 205.
61   Suzuki (2012), 56.
62   Wallace, 200.
63   Siegfried Wiessner & Andrew R. Willard, *Policy-oriented jurisprudence and human rights abuses in internal conflict: toward a world public order of human dignity*, 93 Am. J. Int'l L. 316, 323 [*hereinafter* Wiessner & Willard].
64   *Id.*, 324.
65   *Id.*

and shaming' procedures by UN organs and NGOs) to pure coercion (*e.g.* humanitarian intervention), passing through a wide variety of intermediate practices (such as resort to third-party dispute settlements, adoption of non-forcible countermeasures, and so on).

Along with assessing 'participants' by investigating who they are, what they want, what resources they hold and how they act, the NHS model also considers the 'situations' (or 'arenas') in which these processes take place and the 'effects' of their specific 'outcomes' upon the world community at large. On the one hand, each process is examined in its "spatial, temporal, institutional and crisis dimensions".[66] On the other hand, the scope of the analysis should be enlarged so as to gauge what effects would (potentially or actually) ensue, in the long run, from the concretization of the outcomes pursued by the participants.[67]

To recapitulate, any analysis under the NHS model should investigate who are the relevant actors in the case under analysis (*participants*), how they perceive themselves and what they seek for (*perspectives*), in what context they are interacting (*situation*), what (political, economic, military or legal) resources they can count on in order to pursue their objectives (*bases of power*), how these resources are concretely used (*strategies*), and with what short-term (*outcomes*) and long-term consequences (*effects*).[68]

The foregoing, however, tells us little as to how to piece together all the parts of this complex puzzle. This brings us to the second element of the NHS analytical grid, namely the 'principles of procedures', which connotes what NHS scholars have identified as the set of intellectual tasks which the academic observer (as well as the responsible decision-maker) should carry out.[69]

This element is predicated on the performance of five activities. First, the observer (or the decision-maker) should delineate the contours of the problem to be addressed. Generally speaking, a problem arises when there is a "discrepancy between predicted and desired future decisions" regarding a given conflict of claims.[70] Accordingly, at this stage of the analysis, an explanation will be required as to why a certain outcome is deemed desirable, in the light of the basic policy goals of minimization of unauthorized violence and full realization of human dignity. Second, the relevant participants, their conflicting perspectives and their roles will be identified. Third, relevant past decisions

---

66 *Id.*, 323.
67 Lasswell & McDougal, 447.
68 Suzuki (2012), 47.
69 Wiessner & Willard, 325.
70 Wallace, 47; Chen, 16 (describing problems "in terms of disparity between demanded values and their achievement in community processes").

will be reviewed, paying particular attention to the contextual factors which influenced their adoption. Fourth, the observer will strive to predict what outcomes and effects are likely to be reached in the future, having regard both to past trends and conditioning factors. Fifth and finally, past trends will be critically assessed, and new alternatives in rules and institutions will be recommended with a view to advancing the basic policy goals of the community.[71]

These are, in brief, the main features of the NHS model. It is now time to see how this model might work in relation to the law of self-determination. Admittedly, the performance of the high-demanding intellectual tasks set out above and, relatedly, the huge amount of data which should be collected and processed, would require a monograph-size study and (ideally, at least) a team working with non-legal specialists. The rest of our analysis, therefore, will be necessarily tentative and will not go beyond an outline as to how a study on the principle of self-determination could be carried out under a policy-oriented approach.

IV Applying the NHS Model to the Law of Self-determination: Delimitation of the Problem and Clarification of the Goals

International law, as defined by NHS scholars, is the continuous process of authoritative and controlling responses by competent decision-makers to claims lodged by participants in the world legal process. In this sense, the law of self-determination may be described as the overall decision-making process through which the world community upholds, reshapes or rejects the peoples' demands to change the *status quo* by freely determining their political status.[72]

In analyzing this process, the scholar who adopts a policy-oriented approach should, in the first place, delimit the problem he/she wants to investigate, by clarifying what policy goals are to be pursued. In this respect, it is submitted that the basic policy goals of minimization of unauthorized violence and full realization of human dignity acquire a specific meaning when

---

71   Wiessner & Willard, 325 ff.
72   Eisuke Suzuki, *Self-Determination and World Public Order: Community Response to Territorial Separation*, 16 Va. J. Int'l L. 779, 782 (1976) [*hereinafter* Suzuki (1976)]. A non-NHS author has evocatively described this process as the '"clash" between the existential political will of the group exercising the *pouvoir constituant* and the negative or positive response of the various actors of the international community'; *see* Achilles Skordas, *Self-Determination of Peoples and Transnational Regimes: a Foundational Principle of Global Governance*, in Transnational Constitutionalism: International and European Models 207, 209 (Nicholas Tsagourias ed., 2007).

self-determination claims are at stake. Notably, the former translates into a policy promoting stability, embodied in the well-established principles of territorial integrity and non-intervention;[73] the latter, into a policy promoting change when the maintenance of the *status quo* ends up hindering the genuine aspirations of the peoples concerned and, thus, the realization of a world order based on human dignity.[74] Contrary to what may appear, these two policies do not necessarily work in opposition: coercive denial of self-determination claims may be problematic in both respects, as such denial may not only lead to human rights deprivations but it may also boost civil unrest.[75]

The inability of the contemporary law of self-determination to foster these policies in a satisfactory manner does not need to be demonstrated in particular detail. It suffices to consider, on the one hand, that the principle of self-determination has been routinely invoked to justify bloody conflict and territorial annexation; and, on the other hand, that the international community has all too often preferred to turn a deaf ear to popular demands for political change, waiting for an escalation of violence before intervening. This discrepancy between current trends and desired policies, therefore, constitutes the 'problem' which policy-oriented research on self-determination should strive to resolve.

A Identifying the Participants and Their Perspectives. In Particular: the 'People'

Having delimited the object of the analysis, it is necessary to describe the participants in self-determination processes, with specific reference to their perspectives, as well as to their degree of access to the decision-making function. Given the non-statist character of the NHS model, the number of potential participants is much greater within it, which makes the task challenging.

At this stage of the analysis, focus must be placed upon the entity whose demand for self-determination is at stake: the group claiming to be a 'people'. Yet, since peoples do not normally formulate their claims in a direct manner, but through the medium of political elites (political parties, insurrectional groups, local government bodies), the focus should be on the latter. At the same time, however, it is necessary to ascertain the degree of identification between these

---

73 Suzuki (1976), 792–793.
74 *Id.*
75 Susanna Mancini, *Secession and Self-determination*, in The Oxford Handbook of Comparative Constitutional Law 481, 482 (Michael Rosenfeld & András Sajó, eds., 2005) ("[t]here are doubtless cases in which *existing state borders* are the actual source of instability", emphasis in original). *See also* Chen, 102 & 116–118 as well as, with specific regard to self-determination, 158).

elites and the groups they purport to represent,[76] as it is evident that demands for self-determination coming from unrepresentative claimants should not be considered by the world community.[77]

The *perspectives* of these participants should then be investigated, having particular regard to their claims, their patterns of identification, and their expectations. This inquiry provides an analytical account of self-determination claims, which may help, at a later stage, the observer or the decision-maker assess whether and to what extent a specific demand for change deserves to be upheld because it actually advances the common interest of the world community,[78] as well as to determine the way(s) to prevent and/or to resolve self-determination crises.

Generally speaking, self-determination claims may be of two kinds, which are commonly (although not always consistently) labeled as claims for external or internal self-determination.[79] On the one hand, claims for external self-determination involve the (re-)acquisition of statehood or the redrawing of national boundaries. They include secessionist and irredentist claims, as well as the demands for liberation from alien/colonial domination, as in the case of Palestine. On the other hand, claims for internal self-determination aim at a domestic redistribution of power, ranging from the removal of barriers to political participation and the recognition of special autonomy within the state to more radical demands, such as 'regime change'.

This classical distinction, however, needs to be complemented by further analysis. To say that a given group pursues a secessionist claim tells us little as to what its demands in terms of human values are. In this respect, secessionist groups may greatly differ among each other. Compare, for instance, the Kosovar Albanian demand for independence with the secessionist claim (intermittently) made by the 'Lega Nord' party in Italy or the Catalans in Spain. Furthermore, it is certainly possible that different political outcomes (*e.g.* secession and regime change) pursue the same values. Similar to many secessionist

---

76   This problem arises with particular force in relation to insurgent groups, given the impossibility to rely on electoral indexes. States and international organizations proved sensitive to this concern, as evidenced by the practice of the Liberation Committee of the Organization of African Unity to make the recognition of insurgent groups as national liberation movements conditional on the ascertainment, among other things, of their effective popular support – an approach which has been recently resumed in relation to the recognition of Libyan and Syrian rebels. See Stefan Talmon, *Recognition of Opposition Groups as the Legitimate Representative of a People*, 12 Chinese J. Int'l L. 219 (2013).
77   Suzuki (1976), 794.
78   Chen, 38.
79   On this distinction *see*, among others, Stefan Oeter, *Self-Determination*, in The Charter of the United Nations: A Commentary Vol I, 327 (Bruno Simma et al., eds., 3rd ed., 2012).

movements, for instance, the Libyan Transitional National Council and the Syrian Opposition conceive(d) their revolutionary claims as a 'remedy' against the severe deprivation of human rights experienced under the Ghaddafi and Assad regimes, respectively.

A policy-oriented analysis, therefore, requires discerning the various claims which lie behind the request for reallocation of political power common to all demands for self-determination. As we have just seen, self-determination is sometimes perceived by the claimant group as the only way to ensure its own survival in the face of brutal repression by the ruling class.[80] At others, self-determination aims at the reallocation of power by the claimant group because of a perceived mismatch between its expectations and those of the dominant group.[81]

In the generality of cases, such a mismatch will concern wealth redistribution and/or ethnic/cultural/religious identification.[82] Groups advocating autonomy or secession are often driven by the concern that their wealth and resources are "drained away for the service and enrichment of others".[83] Likewise, revolutionary movements do not limit themselves to questioning the ruling elite or the form of government, but contest the way wealth is allotted among classes and social groups. Within claims for wealth, a further distinction should be drawn between the hypotheses where claims for redistribution come from rich, economically superordinate groups (*e.g.* Catalonia in Spain) and the hypotheses where such claims originate from subordinate, disadvantaged groups (*e.g.* the Bougainville people in Papua New Guinea). In this way, it is possible to differentiate between the redistributive effects sought by each claimant.

As is well known, autonomist, secessionist, and irredentist claims are often aimed at reasserting the group's sense of self-identification in reaction to assimilationist or otherwise centripetal policies of the dominant group (imposition

---

80   Suzuki (1976), 798.
81   *Id.*, 812.
82   Of course, economic and ethno-cultural issues may well be (and often are) intertwined. The Crimean crisis is a good example. While the hasty approval of a bill making Ukrainian the sole state language was undoubtedly a precipitating factor, the deep cause of the crisis is to be found in the Crimean Russians' unwillingness to follow the Ukrainian majority along the path towards accession to the European Union and, mostly, to adopt the EU economic and social model. Remarkably, similar feelings have been expressed in a referendum held around the same period in the Moldovan region of Gagauzia (*see Gagauzia Voters Reject Closer EU Ties For Moldova*, Radio Free Europe / Radio Liberty's Moldovan Service (Feb. 2, 2014), http://www.rferl.org/content/moldova-gagauz-referendum-counting/25251251.html.
83   Suzuki (1976), 820.

of one official language, curtailment of religious freedom, administrative centralization and so on). Therefore, the intensity of the disidentification with the dominant group plays an important role and needs to be explored in detail. In this analysis, while historic, geographic, ethnic, cultural and religious factors need to be taken into account, the most crucial task must be to ascertain the subjective perception of the 'self' by the community concerned.[84] Various indexes may be employed to this end. One interesting yet under-researched method consists in investigating the patterns of political participation followed within the group. The party system of a given territorial community may be particularly telling, especially as to whether that community identifies itself with the larger state or federal community. A system dominated by non-statewide parties covering the whole political spectrum (as in Catalonia) is a meaningful indicator of disidentification. In contrast, participation in coalitions at the state or federal level normally denotes an overall sense of identification with the national community. This was the case of the Italian 'Lega Nord' party, which routinely entered electoral alliances with statewide center-right parties – a circumstance leading its top members to frequently hold key ministerial offices in the national government.[85]

From a different angle, the sense of identification of the claimant group should be evaluated in the light of its inclinations toward inclusiveness or exclusiveness. First, it should be verified whether and to what extent the 'we-they' dichotomy which is somehow inherent in claims for territorial separation turns into forms of racism or intolerance towards so-called 'trapped minorities', namely people belonging to the dominant (or other) group who happen to live on the territory whose control is demanded by the claimant group (such as, for instance, the Serbs in Kosovo or the Ukrainians and Tatars in Crimea).[86]

---

[84] Final Report and Recommendations of the Meeting of Experts on extending of the debate on the concept of 'peoples' rights' held in Paris, France, from 27 to 30 November 1989 (SHS-89/CONF.602/COL.1) [22]; Gunme et al v. Cameroon, [170]–[171]. This approach provides a possible response to Jennings's criticism, referred above, as to the lack of an established definition of 'people'. It is the people, in the first place, who "should decide who the people should be"; *see* Amandine Catala, *Secession and Annexation: The Case of Crimea*, 16 German L. J. 581, 603 (2015).

[85] Gennaro Ferraiuolo, *Due referendum non comparabili*, 34 Quaderni costituzionali 706, 707 (2014). Significantly enough, since 2017, the 'Lega Nord' renamed itself as just 'Lega' precisely to reach out the electorate of Southern Italy.

[86] Suzuki (1976), 794–795. If discrimination occurs, this would give rise, in turn, to secessionist/irredentist claims on the part of the trapped minority; *see* Aleksander Pavković, *Recursive Secession of Trapped Minorities: A Comparative Study of the Serb Krajina and Abkhazia*, 17 Nationalism & Ethnic Pol. 297 (2011).

Second, the projected identity of the claimant group and its demands should be gauged in the light of the 'range and degree of identification with regional and global communities, and the degree of conformity to regional and global public policies.'[87] Some claimant groups, show an inclination towards exclusiveness, as evidenced by the attitude to maximize their own enjoyment of all values and resources to the detriment of others.[88] Other claimant groups, instead, foster an inclusive identity, which is compatible both with the shared expectations within the region concerned, as well as with those of the world community at large.[89] As an example of a self-determination claim compatible with regional public policies, one may mention the Catalan secessionist movement, whose projected identity fully adheres to European values.[90]

A process-based approach should also consider that the perspectives of a group may change over time. While it is impossible to enunciate here all the possible factors which may come into play, a concrete example should make this point clearer. Let us again consider the Catalan case. The partial annulment by the Spanish Constitutional Court of the 2006 Statute of Autonomy of Catalonia, which had been approved by the population concerned with a large majority, made the Catalan people pessimistic as to how central authorities would treat their autonomist claims in the future, causing a radicalization of their demand for self-determination, which rapidly turned into a claim for full independence.[91] In other words, the group's perspectives (its identification, expectations, claims) are affected by the actual availability of institutional arrangements through which the group may shape and achieve its own demands.[92] The less these arrangements are available to the group, the more their expectations and patterns of identification will be misaligned with

---

87   Chen, 38.
88   In this respect, the Zionist proprietary attitude towards the Land of Israel is a good example in point. *See* Gains, 1.
89   The analysis is further complicated by the coexistence and competition of "diverse systems of public order" (*see* Myres S. McDougal & Harold D. Lasswell, *The Identification and Appraisal of Diverse Systems of Public Order*, 53 Am. J. Int'l L. 1 (1959). *See also* Chen, 104–116); hence, by the possibility that the projected identity of the claimant group is compatible with one of them but not with the other. Just consider the Crimean claim for self-determination, which adheres to the Russian system of public policy in opposition to the European one.
90   *See, e.g.*, 'Declaració de sobirania i del dret a decidir del poble de Catalunya', adopted by the Catalan Parliament on 23 January 2013 (in particular its Sixth Point).
91   *See, also*, for further developments, Ridao Martìn, *The Right to Secession in the Framework of Liberal Democracies and the Legitimacy of a Unilateral Declaration. The Case of Catalonia*, 4 Age Hum. Rts. J. 117, 120 (2015).
92   Suzuki (1976), 39.

those of the dominant group, and the more radical will become their claims for self-determination.[93]

B   *The Role of the Various Participants in the Decision-making Process*

As seen above, NHS scholars dissect the decision-making process into seven functions, namely intelligence, promotion, prescription, invocation, application, termination, and appraisal. This distinction applies also to the process through which the world community authoritatively reviews self-determination claims. Accordingly, the role performed by each participant in self-determination processes with regard to the enumerated functions should be analyzed.

The claimant group is undoubtedly the spark that ignites the overall decision-making engine. Without its claim, the whole self-determination machinery would not be triggered. Its role is not limited to invocation, however, but also extends to the gathering, processing, and disseminating of relevant information and the active advocacy of policy alternatives, either individually (*see, e.g.*, the activities of the Public Diplomacy Council of Catalonia) or in concert with other groups sharing similar aspirations (consider, for instance, the European Free Alliance, or the Unrepresented Nations and Peoples Organization).

Yet, the claimant group cannot determine by itself its political status: to be effective its demand for change has to be authoritatively upheld by the world community. For this reason, the common attitude which conceives of self-determination as an entitlement is misleading. In fact, it is in the discretion of the world community, acting through the competent decision-makers, to establish whether a given self-determination claim should be upheld, rejected, or reshaped in line with its basic policy goals.[94] The problem thus arises as to which participants, according to the expectations of the world community, are competent to perform such a review function.

Among the participants in self-determination processes, one should look at first to the main addressee of the self-determination claim: the target government. Indeed, the latter's decision to uphold the claimant group's demand (by voluntarily resigning from power, strengthening the autonomy of local institutions, organizing a referendum on independence and so on) basically puts an

---

93   Events in Ukraine offer another useful example. Indeed, the circumstance that, in a very short span of time, President Yanukovich – who enjoyed wide popular support in the South and South-East – was ousted, and that the Ukrainian Parliament put on the agenda the repeal the 2012 Law "on the principles of the state language policy" – which safeguard national minority languages (including Russian) – was critical in deteriorating the sense of identification of the Russian-speaking population with the Ukrainian dominant group.

94   Suzuki (1976), 790.

end to the process. In contrast, its refusal to accede to a request for self-determination is not necessarily viewed as final, but could trigger a wider process involving international organizations, third states, and influential stakeholders.[95] Here lies, in effect, the core meaning of the general principle of self-determination: claims for political change coming from peoples no longer fall within the domestic jurisdiction of the states, but are matters of "international concern", on which the world community may (and should) have a say.[96]

The typical authoritative response of the world community to self-determination claims is crafted in terms of recognition/non-recognition. The practice of states gave rise to various forms of recognition which are located along "a continuum in the degree [they realize] group demands for self-determination".[97] Accordingly, a new entity may be recognized only for limited purposes (*de facto* recognition) or as a fully-fledged state (*de jure* recognition), while an insurrectional group may be recognized as 'a political interlocutor', 'the (sole) legitimate representative of its people', 'the *de facto* government', or 'the legitimate government'. Given the decentralized character of the international community, the decision to recognize (or not to recognize) may in principle be taken unilaterally by individual states.[98] I say 'in principle' because, as a matter of fact, self-determination issues are normally dealt with in a concerted manner, in the institutional context of international organizations (either universal or regional) or in less formal, *ad hoc* international fora (*e.g.* Contact Groups, Meeting of Friends, and so on),[99] often with a view to negotiating an agreed solution which is acceptable to all the parties concerned.[100]

---

95   This point was hinted at by the Supreme Court of Canada in *Reference re Secession of Quebec*, where it was maintained, on the one hand, that the Canadian government "cannot remain indifferent to the clear expression of a clear majority of Quebecers that they no longer wish to remain in Canada", as it has the constitutional duty to negotiate an agreed solution ([92]) and, on the other hand, that the breach of such duty "undermines the legitimacy of a party's actions", with "important ramifications at the international level", having particular regard to the issue of recognition ([103]).

96   On the issue of 'international concern' in a NHS perspective, *see* the seminal work by Myres S. McDougal and W. Michael Reisman, *Rhodesia and the United Nations: The Lawfulness of International Concern*, 62 Am. J. Int'l L. 1 (1968). *See also* Chen, 270–5.

97   Suzuki (1976), 817.

98   Chen, 37.

99   Admittedly, however, this aspect is sometimes neglected by NHS authors who tend to overemphasize the decentralized character of the international community; *see* Sean D. Murphy, Humanitarian Intervention: The United Nations in an Evolving World Order 25 (1996).

100 For a detailed analysis of the recent (and less recent) international attempts to solve self-determination conflicts, *see* Marc Weller, *Settling Self-determination Conflicts: Recent Developments*, 20 Eur. J. Int'l L. 111 (2009).

The need for concerted action is all the more pressing when we move on to consider other, more intrusive responses in support of self-determination claims, namely assistance to insurgent groups, direct military intervention, or – as the most recent practice shows – international state-building. In these cases, the shared expectation within the world community is that states should not act unilaterally. A decision which does not meet such an expectation, therefore, may be controlling, but not authoritative, with the consequence that it should not be regarded as 'law' but as an exercise of 'naked power'. While there are clear-cut cases where this expectation will be breached (*e.g.* Russia's behavior in Crimea or Israel's in Palestine), in most cases such an assessment is definitely less straightforward. Reference is made, in particular, to the cases where the decision to coercively uphold a given self-determination claim is jointly (but far from unanimously) taken by large sections of the international community (see, for instance, the Kosovo state-building process, or the international support for Libyan and Syrian rebels). In these uncertain cases, the 'authority' of the international response (and, thus, its lawful character) lies in a 'grey area' and will be appreciated on a normative level, namely in the light of its attitude to foster the basic polices of the world community of minimization of unauthorized violence and full realization of human dignity.[101] In this respect, a policy-oriented study on self-determination should analyze the role played by the influential NGOs composing the so-called 'global civil society': their mark of approval or disapproval may make a difference in the shaping of the expectations which, as seen above, ultimately render a controlling decision authoritative.

C   *Past Trends in Decision and Conditioning Factors, in Particular the International Response to Irredentist Claims*

The third intellectual task predicated by the NHS is represented by the description of past trends in decisions related to a certain issue, coupled with the analysis of the factors conditioning them. This task is largely familiar to the traditionally trained scholar, whose investigation is usually based on past legal materials. Unlike the latter, however, the NHS does not look at the past in order to establish, with reasonable degree of finality, the existence of a general practice accepted as law (or a settled interpretation of a given treaty provision). Rather, the aim is to assess "how the international system performed" in approaching a situation and, mostly, "why it succeeded or failed"[102] in the fulfillment of the basic policy goals of minimum and optimum public order.

---

101   Arend, 82–3.
102   Wiessner & Willard, 327.

It is certainly neither feasible nor advisable to engage here in a detailed examination of the vast international practice concerning self-determination. What I will try do to, instead, is to offer a glimpse as to how this task might be carried out, by focusing on a specific problem, namely the way the international community has reacted to demands for territorial separation aimed at reunification with an existing state, based on ethno-national affinity ('irredentist claims').

In this connection, it should be highlighted that, since the end of World War II, irredentist claims – including when couched in self-determination terms – have always been viewed with suspicion by the international community.[103] This is true also with regard to decolonization processes, notwithstanding the fact that 'integration with an independent state' represented one of three options open to Non-Self-Governing Territories. Indeed, the international validation of the will of a colonial people to integrate with an independent state was subject to stricter conditions than the other options[104] and was seldom granted.[105] The case of Cyprus is a good example in point. The Greek Cypriots' demand for *enosis* (union) with Greece was never upheld by the international community, which instead proved more favorable to the concession of independence to the island of Cyprus. Indeed, the Greek government's choice to shift its goals was met with approval within the UN General Assembly and led to the conclusion of the 1959 London and Zurich Agreements and the proclamation of independence by Cyprus in 1960.[106]

The same trend may be observed beyond the context of decolonization. Let us consider the case of Kosovo. Despite widespread popular support for unification with Albania,[107] the Contact Group on Kosovo made it clear from the outset that "union [...] with any country or part of any country" was not among

---

103 Francesco Palermo, *Irredentism*, in Max Planck Encyc. Pub. Int'l L. 9 (Rüdiger Wolfrum, ed., 2010). Needless to say, things radically change if the state of origin does not oppose territorial transfer as an outcome of the self-determination process (*see, e.g.*, the provisions on self-determination contained in the 1998 Good Friday Agreement).

104 Under the terms of G.A. Res 1541 (XV), on the one hand, integration should have taken place "on the basis of complete equality between the peoples [concerned]" (Principle VIII); on the other hand, "the integrated territory should have attained an advanced stage of self-government with free political institutions, so that its people would have the capacity to make a responsible choice through informed and democratic processes" (Principle IX).

105 Thomas D. Musgrave, Self-determination and National Minorities 73 (2000).

106 Stephen G. Xydis, *The UN General Assembly as an instrument of Greek policy: Cyprus, 1954–58*, 12 J. Conflict Resol. 141 (1968) [*hereinafter* Xydis].

107 Alexandra Channer, *Albanians Divided by Borders: Loyal to State or Nations?*, in Divided Nations and European Integration 182, 183 (Tristan James Mabry et al eds., 2013).

the options on the table.¹⁰⁸ Nor has the progressive consolidation of Kosovo's statehood affected the expectations of the world community in this respect. A 2015 statement by the Albanian Prime Minister describing unification with Kosovo as "unavoidable and unquestionable" was met with strong criticism by EU institutions.¹⁰⁹

Two major factors conditioned this trend. First, irredentist claims are perceived by the states of origin as a more intense threat to their territorial integrity, as they fear (and with good reason) that demands for self-determination conceal the intention, by the receiving states, to annex part of their territories.¹¹⁰ A related – and, again, largely justified – worry is that irredentist claims and struggles are not genuine, being instead propelled and steered (openly or covertly) by the prospective receiving-state(s).¹¹¹ Second, unification with a larger, more or less ethnically homogenous entity may prove particularly disempowering for the trapped minorities, whose numeric consistence (and hence political leverage) is bound to be 'diluted' in a wider community; by contrast, in the case of independence, their demographic and political weight will be comparatively greater. In the case of Cyprus, for instance, *enosis* was opposed not only by the United Kingdom, but also by Turkey because of the severe risk of marginalization faced by the Turkish Cypriot minority.

Does this trend actually foster the basic policies of the world community? A dramatic answer to this question is provided by the subsequent developments of the Cyprus issue. As is sadly known, the delicate (and largely imperfect) bicommunal balance enshrined in the 1960 Constitution was put under severe pressure in the following years and was swept away in 1974, after a Greece-backed military coup brought the pro-*enosis* nationalist Nikos Sampson to power. This triggered the military reaction by Turkey which invaded the northern part of the island. Notwithstanding the fact the nationalist junta rapidly collapsed and democratic institutions in Cyprus solemnly renounced any intent of unification with Greece, Turkey's occupation persisted and in 1983 Turkish Cypriots unilaterally declared independence, giving birth to the (unrecognized) Turkish Republic of Northern Cyprus. After some forty years of peace talks conducted under the auspices of the United Nations, the contending parties have recently come close to an agreement. On 11 February 2014, the leaders of the Greek and

---

108   Guiding principles of the Contact Group for a settlement of the status of Kosovo, Oct. 7, 2005, Principle 6.
109   Andrew Rettman and Ekrem Krasniqi, *EU says Albania comment on Kosovo unification 'not acceptable'*, EU Observer, Apr. 9, 2015, https://euobserver.com/foreign/128273.
110   Xydis, 157.
111   Donald L. Horowitz, *Self-determination: Politics, Philosophy, and Law*, in National Self-Determination and Secession 181, 183 (Margaret Moore ed., 1998).

Turkish Cypriot communities released a Joint Declaration characterizing the *status quo* as "unacceptable" and expressing their determination to resume negotiation in order "to reach a settlement ... based on a bi-communal, bi-zonal federation with political equality".[112] The bi-communal philosophy underlying the 1960 Constitution, therefore, was basically reaffirmed as the best way to guarantee a durable solution to the Cyprus conflict.

In light of the foregoing, the trend in decisions disfavoring irredentist outcomes and supporting alternatives to it (including independence) appears to be apt to further the basic policy goals of minimizing unauthorized coercion and promoting human dignity. As we have seen, the short-lived attempt by irredentist elites to put into question the settlement reached at the end of the 1950s (coupled, of course, with Turkey's policy of aggression) generated a series of chain reactions which ended up splitting the island of Cyprus, thus provoking both military tension and serious human rights deprivations.

D *Projection of Future Trends*

As a fourth task, the observer is required to predict future trends in decision-making, on the basis of the assessment of past trends and conditioning factors. This is instrumental to testing whether the current manner of coping with a given problem is able to advance the basic policies of the world community. Of course, these projections cannot be made in a mechanical way, in terms of 'inevitability': many variables may influence the world process in ways that are impossible to foresee with absolute certainty.[113] Aware of this, NHS scholars have worked out an intellectual tool, which they call "developmental constructs", consisting in the projection of a spectrum of possibilities from the most optimistic/utopian to the most pessimistic/dystopian ones.[114]

Before applying this tool to self-determination processes, two caveats need to be entered. First, at the present stage of my research, it is not possible to embark on a detailed analysis of the full range of possible scenarios. Therefore, I will limit myself to sketching only the two basic constructs, which lie at opposite extremes of the spectrum. Second, a comprehensive performance of this task would require a much wider assessment of past trends than the one undertaken in the preceding paragraph. Nevertheless, it would be possible to formulate credible predictions by adopting, as alternative starting points, the

---

112 Joint Declaration, respectively at Points 1, 2, and 3. For the text of the Joint Declaration and updates on the peace process, *see* http://www.uncyprustalks.org/nqcontent.cfm?a_id=6753.

113 Chen, 545.

114 Heinz Eulau, *H. D. Lasswell's Developmental Analysis*, 11 Western Pol. Q. 229 (1958).

three competing 'visions' of self-determination outlined above (anti-colonial, liberal-democratic, ethno-nationalist).

a. Anti-colonialist vision. Legitimate self-determination claims are only those aimed at overthrowing (neo-)colonial, alien or racist domination. Any other international interference in domestic political processes is barred by the principles of territorial integrity and non-intervention.

Optimistic construct. The number of states stabilizes, after residual hypotheses of colonial and/or alien domination (*e.g.* Palestine) have been put to an end. Domestic patterns of political participation, notwithstanding their variety, conform to the preferences of the peoples concerned.

Pessimistic construct. Claims for external self-determination outside the anti-colonialist paradigm are systematically rejected, igniting bloody secessionist conflicts throughout the world. The international community intervenes only upon request and in support of the incumbent governments. Authoritarian regimes stay in power, while popular demands for greater participation in the political process are forcibly denied amid general indifference of the international community.

b. Liberal-democratic vision. The principle of self-determination is to be implemented in the light of liberal-democratic institutions and values, such as the holding of free and fair multi-party elections, the protection of minority rights, and the recognition of wide forms of autonomy and self-government for territorially based minorities and indigenous peoples. The international community may intervene in the domestic political processes (if need be, coercively) with a view to assuring compliance with these values. Except for residual cases of alien or colonial domination, external self-determination is generally ruled out.

Optimistic construct. The world community manages to channel secessionist claims into demands for enhanced autonomy. Authoritarian regimes progressively disappear under the supervision of international institutions or following coercive intervention.

Pessimistic construct. Secessionist conflicts are not settled, due to the *a priori* exclusion of independence from the options on the table. In many cases, the conflict remains 'frozen', since the international community proves unable to modify the *de facto* situation and limits itself to denying recognition to it. As a consequence of this state of affairs, the concerned people are somehow insulated from the rest of the world, and are prevented from fully pursuing their needs, desires, and aspirations. On the other hand, pro-democratic interventions are carried out in a selective and biased way, being ultimately aimed at overthrowing leaders who, for their policies, are inimical to the interests of the great powers.

c. Ethno-nationalist vision. In the light of the principle of self-determination, claims for territorial separation based on ethnic, cultural or religious grounds should be validated at the international level.

Optimistic construct. The creation of nationally homogeneous states contributes to the end to interethnic conflict. Within each state, political institutions are tailored on national historical and cultural traditions.

Pessimistic construct. Secessionist conflicts proliferate, causing deep international tensions and human rights violations. Great powers exploit these conflicts to expand their zone of influence. National unity is routinely invoked to legitimize the ruthless crackdown of any political dissent. Trapped minorities experience serious human rights violations.

E *The Elaboration of Policy Recommendations*

The fifth and last operation – in the words of NHS scholars, the "culminating task in the procedure for solving problems"[115] – consists in the invention, evaluation and selection of alternatives, which should be built upon the results reached during the preceding stages of the analysis.

From the above, a general recommendation logically ensues: in reviewing self-determination claims, the competent decision-maker should not content itself with ascertaining, in line with consolidated past trends in decision, whether the claimant group is subject to colonial, racist or alien domination; but should establish whether its decision may move the situation closer to the basic policies of minimizing unauthorized violence and promoting human dignity, having regard to both the claimant group and the larger communities affected.[116]

More specific recommendations will be drawn from this general policy as a culmination of the accurate performance of the other intellectual tasks. Still, even on the basis of the limited analysis conducted so far, it is possible to develop some tentative suggestions. First, the basic policies of promoting human dignity and minimizing unauthorized coercion dictate that the international community should support the demands for self-determination coming from groups suffering immense deprivation of human rights (even if precedents do not consistently converge in this direction). Conversely, as shown by past trends in decision, irredentist claims should be rejected, unless territorial separation occurs with the consent of the state of origin.

Secondly, when self-determination claims aim at reallocating wealth and resources, it will be necessary to ascertain in which direction such redistribution

---

115 Wiessner & Willard, 333.
116 Chen, 35–8; Lee C. Buchheit, Secession: The Legitimacy of Self-Determination 238 (1978).

would go. Claims for wealth coming from economically superordinate classes or territorial communities should be discouraged, as a matter of principle, because they carry the risk of further impoverishment of subordinate groups (so hindering the policy goal of 'the widest possible distribution of all human values'). In contrast, and for the very opposite reason, demands for self-determination seeking a fairer distribution of resources within the community and/or the removal of forms of economic domination should be looked on with favor.[117]

Thirdly, self-determination claims based on disidentification with the dominant group should be reviewed in the light of the following criteria. On the one hand, it should be established whether the group's disidentification is 'real'.[118] In this analysis, while objective factors such as geographical, cultural, ethnic, religious ties inevitably play a role, the subjective perception of the 'self' by the claimant group, as evidenced – among other things – by its patterns of political participation, should be paramount.[119] On the other hand, the degree of inclusiveness of the identity projected by the claimant group should be assessed, having regard both to the community they aspire to govern and the wider regional and world communities. Accordingly, support should be denied to claimant groups when a) their disidentification with the dominant group is not genuine; b) their patterns of self-identification are conducive to discriminatory policies against non-members; c) their claims are incompatible with basic regional and world policies.

Support for self-determination claims, however, does not automatically mean that the community response should perfectly conform to them (*e.g.* by promoting secession or regime change).[120] The basic policy fostering stability requires consideration of whether less radical alternatives are available which equally (or, at least, comparably) fulfil the desires of the claimant group (*e.g.* autonomy/federalism, participation in the national government, enhanced protection of minority rights, wealth redistribution). The same basic policy, moreover, requires paying due attention to the potential upheaval that may result in the concerned region and recommends the adoption of community responses able to minimize the spread of violence and/or unwanted 'domino effects'.

As I have anticipated, these are only a limited number of tentative guidelines. More in-depth analysis would allow expanding the number of

---

117   Suzuki (1976), 825–6.
118   *Id.*, 784.
119   Chen, 38 (speaking of 'intensity' of the claim).
120   Suzuki (1976), 790.

recommendations and addressing issues which have been omitted here (for instance, the evaluation of demands for self-determination coming from small territorial communities). Similarly, case-specific studies would lead to the elaboration of contextual, case-sensitive solutions which have not been possible to discuss in this paper.

V Conclusions

The foregoing discussion does not purport to advocate the adoption of a policy-oriented approach *en bloc*, as a comprehensive theory of international law. As Iain Scobbie seems to suggest, since "[t]he application of most international law is not problematic",[121] reliance on the complex analytical apparatus worked out by NHS scholars would often entail a pointless intellectual effort. Furthermore, the NHS model is more appropriate to explain (and, in some cases, influence) the behavior of political actors than that of judicial bodies.[122] Nevertheless, as I have tried to demonstrate, in the case of self-determination – where rules are not clear and judicial organs carry out a secondary role – a process-based, policy-oriented analysis may prove beneficial in many respects.

First, it shines light on the role played by non-state entities which, while not enjoying the formal status of international subjects, have some say in self-determination processes. I refer, in particular, to political parties, insurrectional groups, and local government bodies whose patterns of self-identification represent an inescapable point of reference in defining the 'self' in self-determination claims.

Second, the dissection of the decision-making functions carried out by the NHS model provides a workable cognitive grid which may help in clarifying the allocation of competences among the various participants in self-determination processes (claimant group, international organizations, target government, third states, influential NGOs, and so on).

---

121 Scobbie, 76.
122 Of course, this is not to rule out that international judges could endorse such an approach. Just consider, in this respect, the scholarly writings by Judge Rosalyn Higgins (former President of the International Court of Justice) and Florentino P. Feliciano (former Chairman of the Appellate Body of the World Trade Organization). However, as it has been convincingly pointed out, '[w]hen the policy-oriented jurist serves as a judge, arbitrator, or counsel, in the normal case, his references to policy in identifying and applying the applicable laws go only as far as permitted by the same secondary legal rules that positivists apply, except in situations where the putative laws would lead to repugnant outcomes' (*see* Cheng, 10).

Third, by questioning the 'sanctity' of past trends, the NHS approach frees the principle of self-determination from the 'chains' of its glorious (but largely outdated) anti-colonialist past and paves the way for an overall rethinking of what constitutes, at present, a legitimate self-determination claim.

Fourth and finally, being committed to normative values (which may be summed up with the binomial 'peace and human dignity'), NHS jurisprudence – contrary to what is commonly believed – does not equate international law with naked power or self-serving political interests, but provides a critical theoretical framework through which to discuss and scrutinize the international behavior of all participants in the decision-making process.

Procedural Haze: The ICC's Jurisdiction over the Situation in Palestine

*Yassir Al-Khudayri**

    Abstract 118
I   Introduction 118
II   Background: Contextualizing Palestine and the ICC 119
    A   *Premises to the Situation in Palestine* 119
    B.   *Palestine's Engagement with the ICC* 123
    C.   *Preliminary Examination into the Situation in Palestine* 125
III   Jurisdiction of the ICC 127
    A   *Territorial Jurisdiction* 128
        1   Obstacles from Oslo – Jurisdiction over Israeli Nationals 128
            i   *Opposing the Ability to Prescribe and Enforce Jurisdiction* 128
            ii   *Safeguards from the Fourth Geneva Convention* 131
        2   Territorial Uncertainty – ICC and the Palestinian Territory 133
        3   Determining Palestinian Territory – Jurisdiction over what? 135
        4   The Palestinian Authority and Hamas Quarrel – Division among Palestinian Factions 139
    B   *Temporal Jurisdiction* 142
IV   Looking to the Future and Conclusion 146

---

*   The author is deeply appreciative to Julianne Romy, Francesca Albanese, Ken Roberts, Victor Kattan, Sara Erjavec, Chitrrangada Singh and James Douglas for their helpful comments and suggestions. This article was last updated in May 2018.

Abstract

Palestine's ratification of the Rome Statute, and limited retroactive acceptance of the jurisdiction of the International Criminal Court (ICC, or the Court), constitutes one of the major legal developments of the Israeli-Palestinian conflict in the past decade. But such a milestone does not come without contentious legal and political challenges. Several procedural obstacles are likely to arise, especially relating to jurisdiction and admissibility, which will determine whether the ICC even gets to substantive questions of accountability. No matter which cases might ultimately be prosecuted, any ICC investigation – and perhaps even the preliminary examination – is thus likely to confront the antagonisms surrounding Palestinian statehood, bilateral agreements between Israel and the Palestinians, border disputes, and domestic criminal proceedings.

I   Introduction

This paper seeks to address the various procedural obstacles that are likely to arise within the ICC situation in Palestine for crimes allegedly committed in the occupied Palestinian territory (oPt).[1] Specifically, the article examines whether the legal framework of the Rome Statute allows the Court to exercise jurisdiction in Palestine, not only following Palestine's ratification of the Statute in 2015,[2] but also in the preceding months, for which respect Palestine delegated retroactive acceptance.[3]

The most contentious legal issues in addressing the Situation in Palestine are likely to concern jurisdiction. It may also be anticipated that these procedural obstacles will arise in the context of addressing crimes allegedly perpetrated by Israeli nationals. Whereas Palestine has ratified the Rome Statute,

---

1   The oPt includes the territories that were occupied by Israel in 1967 (excluding the Egyptian Sinai and the Syrian Golan Heights).
2   ICC, *The State of Palestine accedes to the Rome Statute*, ICC-ASP-20150107-PR1082 (Jan. 7, 2015), https://www.icc-cpi.int/Pages/item.aspx?name=pr1082_2; ICC-OTP, *The Prosecutor of the International Criminal Court, Fatou Bensouda, opens a preliminary examination of the situation in Palestine*, ICC-OTP-20150116-PR1083 (Jan. 16, 2015), https://www.icc-cpi.int/Pages/item.aspx?name=pr1083.
3   *Declaration Accepting the Jurisdiction of the International Criminal Court*, executed for the Government of the State of Palestine by Mahmoud Abbas, President of the State of Palestine (Dec. 31, 2014) [*hereinafter* 2014 Declaration], https://www.icc-cpi.int/iccdocs/PIDS/press/Palestine_A_12-3.pdf; ICC, *Palestine declares acceptance of ICC jurisdiction since 13 June 2014*, ICC-CPI-20150105-PR1080 (Jan. 5, 2015), https://www.icc-cpi.int/Pages/item.aspx?name=pr1080.

and thus in principle accepted the Court's jurisdiction,[4] Israel has not done so, and is not a State Party to the ICC. For this reason, this paper focuses on these anticipated obstacles, as opposed to those arising from crimes allegedly perpetrated by Palestinians. This does not suggest that individuals of any nationality warrant greater or lesser attention in investigating and prosecuting possible international crimes.

Possible jurisdictional concerns include the territorial scope of the Court's mandate. In particular, bilateral agreements potentially affecting delegation of jurisdiction and border feuds between the conflicting parties may be said to exclude the ICC's exercise of jurisdiction. Relatedly, due consideration must be given to whether the ICC may address these issues in the first place. Matters may also be complicated by the political and territorial divide between Palestinian ruling factions. The temporal dimension of the commission of certain alleged crimes should equally be considered, such as the construction of Israeli settlements in the West Bank, many of which began and were completed prior to the Court's temporal jurisdiction.

Finally, although all these legal issues are likely to require resolution by the Court (and are the focus of this discussion), the political dimension of Palestine's accession should not be underestimated. Political decisions – particularly by the United Nations (UN) Security Council (UNSC), Israel, and Palestine itself – may have important consequences on the development of the ICC's ability to act in the Palestine situation. In particular, the UNSC has the power, temporarily, to defer prosecutions or investigations by the ICC Office of the Prosecutor (OTP).[5] Furthermore, the Court may also encounter political challenges in conducting any potential investigation or enforcing possible arrest warrants, since it depends heavily on state cooperation. The unique context of Palestine, where even access to its territory is largely conditioned on the consent of another state, may raise particular complications in this area.

II   Background: Contextualizing Palestine and the ICC

A   *Premises to the Situation in Palestine*

The oPt includes the Gaza Strip and the West Bank (including East Jerusalem) – territories that have been occupied by Israel since the Six Day War of 1967.[6]

---

[4] *See, e.g.*, Rome Statute of the International Criminal Court art. 12(1), July 17, 1998, U.N. Doc. A/CONF.183/9 [*hereinafter* Rome Statute].
[5] Rome Statute art. 16.
[6] Prior to 1967 and following 1948, the West Bank and Gaza had been administered by Jordan and Egypt, respectively.

Since the genesis of the occupation, Israel has built Israeli-populated settlements in the occupied territory. In 1994, the Palestinian Authority (PA) – the Palestinian People's interim self-governing authority with executive, judicial and legislative powers – was created by the Agreement on the Gaza Strip and the Jericho Area between the Israeli government and the Palestine Liberation Organization (PLO).[7] In 1995, the Oslo II Accords divided the West Bank's territory into Areas A, B, and C,[8] with varying degrees of control exercised by the PA. Over 594,000 Israeli settlers currently reside in West Bank settlements.[9] The vast majority of settlements in the West Bank are located in Area C – comprising approximately 61% of the West Bank – where Israel retains full control over administrative and security-related matters.[10]

Israeli settlement areas in the West Bank are mostly declared closed military zones and are generally off limits to Palestinians. They emerge via the transfer of Israeli civilians into urban areas constructed within the oPt, often following dispossession and displacement of Palestinian population. Settlements may arguably be part of an Israeli policy establishing long-term physical presence

---

7   Agreement on the Gaza Strip and the Jericho Area art. III, signed by the Government of the State of Israel and the Palestine Liberation Organization, May 4, 1994 (Cairo, Egypt), available at: http://www.unsco.org/Documents/Key/AGREEMENT%20ON%20THE%20GAZA%20STRIP%20AND%20THE%20JERICHO%20AREA.pdf; Israeli-Palestinian Interim Agreement on the West Bank and the Gaza Strip ch. 3, arts. XVII (1.a),(2.c),(3) and (4), signed by the Government of the State of Israel and the Palestine Liberation Organization, Sept. 28, 1995 (Washington, D.C., USA) [*hereainfter* Oslo II].

8   Oslo II arts. I(2), XI and XIII; ICC-OTP, *Report on Preliminary Examination Activities (2017)* (Dec. 4, 2017), [hereinafter, ICC-OTP PE Report], para. 55, https://www.icc-cpi.int/itemsDocuments/2017-PE-rep/2017-otp-rep-PE_ENG.pdf; UN OCHA (oPt), *Restricting Space: The Planning Regime Applied by Israel in Area C of the West Bank* (Dec. 2009), at 3, https://www.ochaopt.org/documents/special_focus_area_c_demolitions_december_2009.pdf.

9   UN HRC, Israeli settlements in the Occupied Palestinian Territory, including East Jerusalem, and the occupied Syrian Golan: Annual Report of the United Nations High Commissioner for Human Rights and reports of the Office of the High Commissioner and the Secretary-General, U.N. Doc. A/HRC/34/39 (Mar. 16, 2017), para. 11; B'Tselem, Land Expropriation and Settlements (Jan. 1, 2011, last updated Nov. 23, 2015) [*hereinafter* B'Tselem Settlements], http://www.btselem.org/settlements; Human Rights Watch, *Occupation, Inc.: How Settlement Businesses Contribute to Israel's Violations of Palestinian Rights* (Jan. 19, 2016) [*hereinafter* HRW Occupation Inc.], https://www.hrw.org/news/2016/01/19/occupation-inc-how-settlement-businesses-contribute-israels-violations-palestinian; Israeli Central Bureau of Statistics (Sep. 10, 2015) [*hereinafter* Israeli CBS], http://www.cbs.gov.il/shnaton66/st02_16x.pdf.

10 Oslo II art. XI (3) (c) and annexed map no. 1; World Bank, *West Bank and Gaza: Area C and the Future of the Palestinian Economy* (Oct. 2, 2013), at 3, https://openknowledge.worldbank.org/bitstream/handle/10986/16686/AUS29220REPLAC0EVISION0January02014.pdf.

and control over extensive amounts of land in strategic locations of the West Bank.[11] In the context of the West Bank, such policy has been widely described as illegal under international law, notably by the International Court of Justice (ICJ)[12] and the UN.[13] At the ICC, the Chief Prosecutor confirmed that the OTP would be considering Israeli settlements in its preliminary examination of the situation in Palestine.[14]

In 2005, Israel formally disengaged from, and dismantled its settlements in, the Gaza Strip. Nevertheless, Israel still maintains control over the Gaza Strip, namely its air and maritime spaces, as well as six of Gaza's seven land crossings.[15] Gaza is also strictly dependent on Israel for water, electricity, telecommunications and food imports, as well as for its population registry and tax system. The Gaza Strip is currently governed by the group and political party Hamas, since its election in 2006.[16] Since 2007, the Gaza Strip has been under siege by the Israel Defense Forces (IDF) and has suffered immense human and infrastructural loss as a result of the blockade and of Israel's military incursions in 2008–2009, 2012 and 2014 (known as Operations Cast Lead, Pillar of Defense, and Protective Edge, respectively). Hamas and other Palestinian armed groups are alleged to have fired around 4,881 rockets into Israel, including civilian

---

11   *See, generally,* B'Tselem Settlements; HRW Occupation, Inc.; Israeli CBS.
12   Legal Consequences of the Construction of a Wall in the Occupied Palestinian Territory, Advisory Opinion, 2004 I.C.J. Rep. 136 (July 9), paras. 52–54, 79, 120 [*hereinafter* ICJ Wall].
13   S.C. Res. 446, *Territories occupied by Israel*, U.N. Doc. S/RES/446 (Mar. 22, 1979), para. 1; S.C. Res. 242, *Middle East*, U.N Doc S/RES/242 (Nov. 22, 1967); S.C. Res 478, *Territories occupied by Israel*, U.N. Doc. S/RES/478 (Aug. 20, 1980); UN HRC, *Human rights situation in Palestine and other occupied Arab territories: Report of the Independent International Fact-finding Mission to Investigate the Implications of the Israeli Settlements on the Civil, Political, Economic, Social and Cultural Rights of the Palestinian People Throughout the OPt, including East Jerusalem*, U.N. Doc. A/HRC/22/63.7 (Feb. 7, 2013); UN HRC, *Report of the United Nations Fact-Finding Mission on the Gaza Conflict*, U.N. Doc. A/HRC/12/48 (Sep. 25, 2009).
14   P. Beaumont, *ICC Urges Israel to Cooperate in Inquiry into Possible Breaches in Palestine*, The Guardian (May 13, 2015), http://www.theguardian.com/law/2015/may/13/icc-urges-israel-to-cooperate-in-inquiry-into-possible-breaches-in-palestine.
15   UN HRC, Report of the independent commission of inquiry established pursuant to Human Rights Council resolution S21/1, U.N. Doc. A/HRC/29/52 (June 25, 2015), para. 15 [*hereinafter* CoI Report].
16   B'Tselem, Background on the Gaza Strip (Jan. 1, 2011, last updated July 14, 2014), http://www.btselem.org/gaza_strip; *Hamas Sweeps to Election Victory*, BBC News (Jan. 26, 2006), http://news.bbc.co.uk/2/hi/middle_east/4650788.stm; Gisha, *Scale of Control: Israel's Continued Responsibility in the Gaza Strip* (Nov. 2011), http://www.gisha.org/UserFiles/File/scaleofcontrol/scaleofcontrol_en.pdf.

populated areas in Israel, particularly in the country's south.[17] Such attacks have struck residential and commercial centers, and have resulted in six civilian deaths, including children, during the 2014 hostilities.[18] Palestinian armed groups are also alleged to have used protected persons and property such as civilians, hospitals and schools as shields from attacks in order to protect their personnel and assets from attacks.[19]

The destruction carried out during the 51-day Operation Protective Edge of 2014 was unprecedented in Gaza. According to the UN Human Rights Council-mandated Independent Commission of Inquiry (the Commission of Inquiry) appointed in the aftermath of Operation Protective Edge, about 2,251 Palestinians, including 551 children, were killed in the conflict and a further 11,231 Palestinians, including 3,436 children, were injured as a result of 6,000 airstrikes and extensive use of explosive devices in Gaza's densely-populated areas during the ground assault.[20] Added to this was the loss of civilian infrastructure. UN-based sources state that about 18,000 houses were destroyed along with water and sanitation infrastructure, as well as schools and other essential services.[21] The UN Commission of Inquiry, as well as leading civil society groups, found that acts committed during Operation Protective Edge are susceptible of constituting violations of international humanitarian law and international crimes.[22] As per its Report on Preliminary Examinations, the OTP has received information on and/or is examining actions in Gaza related to attacks against residential buildings and civilians; attacks against medical facilities and personnel; attacks against UN schools; and attacks against other civilian objects and infrastructures.[23]

---

17 CoI Report, paras. 27–31; ICC OTP, *Report on Preliminary Examination Activities (2017)* (Dec. 4, 2017), [*hereinafter* ICC OTP PE Report 2017], para. 66, https://www.icc-cpi.int/itemsDocuments/2017-PE-rep/2017-otp-rep-PE_ENG.pdf.

18 CoI Report, para. 21; ICC OTP, Report on Preliminary Examination Activities (*2016*) (Nov. 14, 2016), paras. 120, 123, https://www.icc-cpi.int/iccdocs/otp/161114-otp-rep-PE_ENG.pdf; ICC OTP, Report on Preliminary Examination Activities (*2015*) (Nov. 12, 2015), para. 64, https://www.icc-cpi.int/iccdocs/otp/OTP-PE-rep-2015-Eng.pdf.

19 ICC OTP PE Report 2017, para. 66.

20 CoI Report, paras. 20, 38, 48.

21 UN OCHA (oPt), *Gaza Initial Rapid Assessment* (Aug. 27, 2014), at 4, https://www.ochaopt.org/documents/Gaza_MIRA_report_9September.pdf.

22 CoI report, paras. 44, 50, 52; FIDH, *Trapped and Punished: The Gaza Civilian Population under Operation Protective Edge* (Oct. 2014), at 14, 30, 45, 47 [*hereinafter* FIDH Report], https://www.fidh.org/IMG/pdf/report_gaza_fidh_march_2015.pdf.

23 ICC OTP PE Report 2017, paras. 57–66. Such action may arguably fall within the subject-matter jurisdiction of the ICC, *see*: Rome Statute article 7(1) (as a crime against humanity, part of a widespread and systematic attack against a civilian population); Rome Statute article 8(2)(b)(i), (ii), (iv) (as war crimes, part of direct attacks against civilian

B.   *Palestine's Engagement with the ICC*

Palestine's engagement with the ICC began almost a decade ago. On 22 January 2009, following Operation Cast Lead, the PA lodged a declaration under Article 12(3) of the Rome Statute accepting the ICC's jurisdiction for "acts committed on the territory of Palestine since 1 July 2002",[24] even though it was not a State Party to the Statute.[25] After some three years, then-ICC Prosecutor Luis Moreno Ocampo stated the OTP's view was that such a declaration could only be lodged by a *state*, and that the OTP was not competent to determine whether Palestine constituted a state. He thus referred the question to the UN Secretary General (UNSG) and the UN General Assembly (UNGA), with the proviso that, should the issue of Palestinian statehood be resolved by

---

objects or civilians and breach of the principle of proportionality). For more information on alleged activities by Israelis and Palestinians potentially amounting to international crimes in the West Bank and Gaza, *see*, *e.g.*: CoI Report; Israel Ministry of Foreign Affairs, *The 2014 Gaza Conflict: Factual and Legal Aspects* (May 2015), at 218–242, http://mfa.gov.il/ProtectiveEdge/Documents/2014GazaConflictFullReport.pdf; H.R.C. Res. S-21/1, *Ensuring respect for international law in the Occupied Palestinian Territory, including East Jerusalem* (July 23, 2014), U.N. Doc. A/HRC/S-21/1; Human Rights Watch, Palestine/Israel Indiscriminate *Palestinian* Rocket Attacks, News Release (July 9, 2014), https://www.hrw.org/news/2014/07/09/palestine/israel-indiscriminate-palestinian-rocket-attacks; UN OCHA (oPt), *Gaza Initial Rapid Assessment* (Aug. 27, 2014), at 4; WHO, Gaza Strip: *Joint Health Sector Assessment Report* (Sep. 2014), http://reliefweb.int/sites/reliefweb.int/files/resources/Joint_Health_Sector_Assessment_Report_Gaza_Sept_2014.pdf; FIDH Report; UN OCHA, *Protecting civilians from the use of explosive weapons in populated areas* (Aug. 11, 2016), https://docs.unocha.org/sites/dms/Documents/EWIPA%20fact%20sheet%20final.pdf; Human Rights Watch, *Israel: In-Depth Look at Gaza School Attacks*, News Release (Sep. 11, 2014), https://www.hrw.org/news/2014/09/11/israel-depth-look-gaza-school-attacks; Human Rights Watch, *Separate and Unequal – Israel's Discriminatory Treatment of Palestinians in the Occupied Palestinian Territories* (Dec. 2010), https://www.hrw.org/sites/default/files/reports/iopt1210webwcover_0.pdf; UN OCHA (oPt), *Direct Israeli-Palestinian conflict related casualties*, Annex: Monthly Indicator Tables (Jan. 2016), https://www.ochaopt.org/documents/ocha_opt_the_humanitarian_monitor_tables_january_2016_english.pdf; UN OCHA (oPt), *Record number of demolitions in 2016; casualty toll declines*, Annex: Monthly Indicator Tables (Dec. 29, 2016), http://www.ochaopt.org/content/record-number-demolitions-2016-casualty-toll-declines; Israeli CBS; B'Tselem Settlements; HRW Occupation Inc.

24   2014 Declaration.

25   ICC, *Ukraine accepts ICC jurisdiction over alleged crimes committed between 21 November 2013 and 22 February 2014*, ICC Press Release ICC-CPI-20140417-PR997 (Apr. 17, 2014), https://www.icc-cpi.int/Pages/item.aspx?name=pr997&ln=en. Ukraine is not a state party to the Rome Statute. Nevertheless, the OTP opened a preliminary examination as a result of the declaration lodged by the government of Ukraine pursuant to Article 12(3) of the Rome Statute. *See also* ICC (Registrar), *Acknowledgment of receipt of Côte d'Ivoire Declaration under Article 12(3)*, ICC Registry/0640 (Oct. 31, 2003), https://www.icc-cpi.int/NR/rdonlyres/74EEE201-0FED-4481-95D4-C8071087102C/279845/IC_NVENG.pdf.

the "competent organs of the United Nations", the OTP would consider future allegations of crimes committed in Palestine.[26] Towards the end of 2012, the UNGA granted observer state status to the State of Palestine – altering the observer status held by the PLO.[27] Importantly, this resolution indicated to the UNSG, as the depository for many multilateral treaties, that Palestine has full capacity to accede to international treaties – including the Rome Statute. Accordingly, the current Chief Prosecutor of the ICC, Fatou Bensouda, declared that the OTP "examined the legal implications of this development and concluded that while this change did not retroactively validate the previously invalid 2009 declaration, Palestine could now join the Rome [S]tatute".[28]

Palestine promptly did just that,[29] becoming the 123rd State Party of the ICC on 1 April 2015.[30] This brought the provisions of the Statute into force for Palestine *prospectively*. But in addition, before its accession, Palestine also made a second Article 12(3) declaration, accepting the ICC's jurisdiction *retrospectively* with respect to alleged crimes committed "in the occupied Palestinian territory, including East Jerusalem, since June 13, 2014".[31] By this means, Palestine presumably elected to give the ICC additional jurisdiction over the events of Operation Protective Edge.

---

26 ICC OTP, *Updated Situation in Palestine* (3 April 2012), paras. 5–8, https://www.icc-cpi.int/NR/rdonlyres/C6162BBF-FEB9-4FAF-AFA9-836106D2694A/284387/SituationinPalestine030412ENG.pdf.

27 G.A. Res 67/19, *Status of Palestine in the United Nations*, U.N. Doc. A/RES/67/19 (Dec. 4, 2012), http://www.un.org/en/ga/search/view_doc.asp?symbol=A/RES/67/19. *See also* U.N. Interoffice Memorandum entitled 'Issues Related to General Assembly Resolution 67/19 on the Status of Palestine in the United Nations' (Dec. 2012), at 3–4, paras. 13–16, http://palestineun.org/wp-content/uploads/2013/08/012-UN-Memo-regarding-67-19.pdf.

28 F. Bensouda, *Fatou Bensouda: The Truth about the ICC and Gaza*, The Guardian (Aug. 29, 2014), https://www.theguardian.com/commentisfree/2014/aug/29/icc-gaza-hague-court-investigate-war-crimes-palestine.

29 The UNSG Depositary notification of Accession to the Rome Statute by the State of Palestine is available at: https://treaties.un.org/doc/Publication/CN/2015/CN.13.2015-Eng.pdf.

30 ICC, *ICC welcomes Palestine as new State Party*, ICC Press Release ICC-CPI-20150401-PR1103 (Apr. 1, 2015), https://www.icc-cpi.int/Pages/item.aspx?name=pr1103.

31 2014 Declaration; ICC, *Palestine declares acceptance of ICC jurisdiction since 13 June 2014*, ICC Press Release ICC-CPI-20150105-PR1080 (Jan. 5, 2015), https://www.icc-cpi.int/Pages/item.aspx?name=pr1080. ICC, *The State of Palestine accedes to the Rome Statute* (ICC Press Release ICC-ASP-20150107-PR1082 (Jan. 7, 2015), https://www.icc-cpi.int/Pages/item.aspx?name=pr1082_2.

C. Preliminary Examination into the Situation in Palestine

Acting *proprio motu*, ICC Prosecutor Fatou Bensouda immediately opened a preliminary examination into the Situation in Palestine on 16 January 2015, considering events since 13 June 2014.[32] This does not necessarily imply that an investigation will be opened. Rather, it is the OTP's initial consideration of the available information to determine whether the minimum conditions for an investigation – prescribed by Article 53 of the Statute – are met.[33] There is no prescribed timeline for the OTP to complete this analysis, which may entail the OTP monitoring the progress of any relevant domestic judicial proceedings.[34] Indeed, several of these examinations have been lasting for years, such as the examples of Afghanistan, Columbia, Georgia, and Guinea.[35] The preliminary examination in Palestine may therefore well linger for the foreseeable future.[36]

Palestine had not initially referred the situation to the ICC under article 14(1).[37] However, on 15 May 2018, the State of Palestine referred the situation to the ICC. This implies that the Prosecutor no longer requires

---

32 ICC OTP, The Prosecutor of the International Criminal Court, Fatou Bensouda, opens a preliminary examination of the situation in Palestine, ICC Press Release ICC-OTP-20150116-PR1083 (Jan. 16, 2015), https://www.icc-cpi.int/Pages/item.aspx?name=pr1083.

33 *Id.* Article 53(1) requires the Prosecutor to be satisfied there is a reasonable basis to believe that crimes within the jurisdiction of the Court were committed, that at least one potential case would be admissible, and that opening an investigation would not be contrary to the interests of justice. Presently, in this preliminary examination, the OTP appears to be considering jurisdictional matters: ICC OTP PE Report 2017, paras. 51–78. *See further* ICC OTP, *Policy Paper on Preliminary Examinations* (Nov. 2013) [*hereinafter* OTP PE Policy Paper], para. 5, https://www.icc-cpi.int/iccdocs/otp/OTP-Policy_Paper_Preliminary_Examinations_2013-ENG.pdf; ICC OTP, *Policy Paper on the Interests of Justice* (Sept. 2007), at 2, https://www.icc-cpi.int/NR/rdonlyres/772C95C9-F54D-4321-BF09-73422BB23528/143640/ICCOTPInterestsOfJustice.pdf.

34 OTP PE Policy Paper, para. 5, section III, para. 14. *See also* David Bosco, *Palestine in the Hague: Justice, Geopolitics, and the International Criminal Court*, 22 Global Governance 155, 166 (2016).

35 ICC OTP, *Report on Preliminary Examination Activities 2014* (Dec. 2, 2014), https://www.icc-cpi.int/iccdocs/otp/OTP-Pre-Exam-2014.pdf. See the ICC's preliminary examinations in Afghanistan, Columbia, Georgia and Guinea.

36 Yonah Jeremy Bob, *JPost speaks to ICC Prosecutor Bensouda about Israel's fate on war crimes*, Jerusalem Post (Feb. 23, 2016), http://www.jpost.com/Israel-News/Politics-And-Diplomacy/Exclusive-JPost-speaks-to-ICC-Prosecutor-Bensouda-about-Israels-fate-on-war-crimes-445806. When approached on this issue, the Chief Prosecutor of the ICC stated that she "cannot ... say that it will take seven years, or it will take ten years or it will take any number of years ... all of this depends on the facts and the circumstances. The preliminary examination cannot be given a timeline".

37 2014 Declaration.

authorization of the ICC Pre-Trial Chamber to open a formal investigation once the legal requirements are met.[38] Should it choose to do so, Israel would also be entitled to make observations in this process.[39]

Should the OTP find that the jurisdictional requirements of the Court have been met, the preliminary examination may move onto the next phase, which deals with issues of admissibility. In this regard, the OTP may also find obstacles when assessing matters of complementarity and gravity of alleged crimes.[40] When looking into complementarity, it will likely be found that the Palestinian government is unable to prosecute alleged Israeli perpetrators, namely since it lacks the legal, financial and infrastructural means to do so. Israel, on the other hand, has a sophisticated judicial system which has recently adopted the recommendations of the Turkel Commission in view of solidifying the independence and impartiality of military investigations into war crimes.[41] Accordingly, the OTP would have to demonstrate that the Israeli judiciary is 'unwilling' to carry out investigations or prosecutions into potential crimes under the ICC's jurisdiction, as per the requirements of Article 17(2) of the Rome Statute.[42] In this respect, it is notable that the Commission of Inquiry pointed out flaws in Israel's ability or willingness to "investigate, prosecute and hold perpetrators accountable for violations of international humanitarian law and international human rights law" in the context of its activities during Operation Protective Edge in the Gaza Strip.[43] As for West Bank settlements, the Israeli policy surrounding the construction of settlements in the oPt has not undergone any kind of judicial review, while the legislative and administrative scheme supporting these settlements derives from actions

---

38   Rome Statute Art. 15(3). *See also*: State of Palestine, Referral of the State of Palestine Pursuant to Articles 13(a) and 14 of the Rome Statute (May 15, 2014).
39   *See also* Rome Statute arts. 18, 19.
40   *Id.*, art. 17(1).
41   Turkel Commission, Israel's Mechanisms for Examining and Investigating Complaints and Claims of Violations of the Laws of Armed Conflict According to International Law (Summary of second report) (Feb. 2013), http://www.turkel-committee.gov.il/files/newDoc3/Summary.pdf. The Turkel Commission was appointed by the Israeli Government to examine "whether the mechanism for examining and investigating complaints and claims raised in relation to violations of the laws of armed conflict ... conforms with the obligations of the State of Israel under the rules of international law" (*see* para 1).
42   For more on the principle of complementarity, International Centre for Transitional Justice, *What is Complementarity? National Courts, the ICC, and the Struggle against Impunity*, https://www.ictj.org/sites/default/files/subsites/complementarity-icc/.
43   CoI report, para. 72.

stemming from the highest ranks of the Israeli government.[44] These factors are likely to come into play should the OTP's preliminary examination ever reach the point of dealing with matters of complementarity. As for the gravity requirement, such an analysis would likely have to consider "quantitative and qualitative"[45] aspects of the "scale, nature, manner of commission and impact of the crimes",[46] namely the number of child victims and the long-term impact of the destruction of housing units, hospitals, schools and clean water and electricity supplies.[47] Similarly, the overall impact of activities on the territorial integrity of the State of Palestine – as the self-determination unit within which the Palestinian people are entitled to exercise self-determination – will likely be considered.

III   Jurisdiction of the ICC

The ICC has jurisdiction over acts committed by Palestinians, as well as acts committed by individuals of any nationality on Palestinian territory.[48] Jurisdiction over nationals of non-member states (or of states that have not accepted the Court's jurisdiction) is potentially one of the most controversial aspects of the ICC's mission. So far, the only other actions in which a preliminary examination was opened concerning nationals of a non-State Party were in the *Situation on Registered Vessels of the Union of the Comoros, the Hellenic Republic and the Kingdom of Cambodia*, also known as the Gaza Flotilla raid of 2010, and

---

44   *Netanyahu affirms support for 'courageous' West Bank settlers*, Middle East Eye (Jan. 24, 2016), http://www.middleeasteye.net/news/netanyahu-supports-settlements-west-bank-1963021862; *Netanyahu says Israeli government 'supports settlement at any time' after Hebron incident*, ABC (Jan. 24, 2016), http://www.abc.net.au/news/2016-01-25/netanyahu-says-supports-settlement-at-any-time/7110874; Barak Ravid, *Netanyahu: We are Considering Unilateral Moves in West Bank*, Ha'aretz (May 23, 2014), http://www.haaretz.com/israel-news/.premium-1.592382; Judi Rudoren & Jeremy Ashkenas, *Netanyahu and the Settlements*, N.Y. Times (Mar. 18, 2015), http://www.nytimes.com/interactive/2015/03/12/world/middleeast/netanyahu-west-bank-settlements-israel-election.html?_r=1; Isabel Kershner, *Israel Approves Additional Funding for Settlements in West Bank*, N.Y. Times (June 19, 2016), http://www.nytimes.com/2016/06/20/world/middleeast/israel-west-bank-settlements-palestinians.html.
45   ICC OTP, Report on Preliminary Examination Activities 2014 (Dec. 2, 2014), para 61.
46   ICC OTP, Regulations of the Office of the Prosecutor Regulation 29(2), ICC-BD/05-01-09 (Apr. 23, 2009), https://www.icc-cpi.int/nr/rdonlyres/fff97111-ecd6-40b5-9cda-792bcbe1e695/280253/iccbd050109eng.pdf.
47   OTP PE Policy Paper, para. 5.
48   Rome Statute art. 12(2)(a).

Situation in the Republic of Korea. The latter situation did not pass the preliminary examination phase, whilst the former is currently under reconsideration.[49]

A   *Territorial Jurisdiction*
1   Obstacles from Oslo – Jurisdiction over Israeli Nationals

One of the procedural obstacles that the ICC may face in exercising jurisdiction in the Situation in Palestine arises from the Oslo Accords. The Oslo Accords grant Israel a wide array of prerogatives in the oPt, namely exclusive exercise of criminal jurisdiction over acts committed by Israelis in Areas A, B, and C of the West Bank.[50] In practice, the Oslo Accords would effectively prevent Palestine from delegating powers of personal criminal jurisdiction over Israelis to the ICC, since it itself is unable to exercise such jurisdiction.

i   *Opposing the Ability to Prescribe and Enforce Jurisdiction*

This is what Eugene Kontorovich and Michael Newton, in particular, have argued. The authors consider that the principle of delegated jurisdiction and treaty law render the Palestinian government unable to delegate personal criminal jurisdiction over Israelis to the ICC.[51] They insist on the need for symmetry between the domestic jurisdiction and the ICC's jurisdiction, since the powers of the latter strictly derives from sovereign national jurisdictions.[52] Following on from their interpretation, this would mean that Israeli civil and military leadership (and over 500,000 Israeli settlers in the West Bank, including East Jerusalem) are out of Palestinian jurisdictional reach. Indeed, by adhering to the idea that the ICC operates on the basis of delegated jurisdiction, questions arise as to whether the Palestinian government can delegate to the Court powers that it itself could not exercise in the first place – namely that of criminal jurisdiction over Israeli nationals.[53]

---

49 The Pre-Trial Chamber requested the OTP to reconsider its determination not to open a preliminary examination in the *Situation on Registered Vessels of the Union of the Comoros, the Hellenic Republic and the Kingdom of Cambodia*.

50 Oslo II, Chapter 3, Article XVII (1.a),(2.c),(3) and (4) and Annex IC, Article 1(2)(b). *See also* Human Sciences Research Council, Occupation, Colonialism, Apartheid? A re-assessment of Israel's practice in the Occupied Palestinian Territories under international law (May 2009), at 71–81.

51 Eugene Kontorovich, *Israel/Palestine – The ICC's Uncharted "Territory"*, 11 J. Int'l Crim. Just. 979, 989–992 (2013) [*hereinafter* Kontorovich]; Michael A. Newton, *How the International Criminal Court Threatens Treaty Norms*, 49 Vand. J. Transnat'l L. 371, 373, 404, 429–430 (2016) [*hereinafter* Newton].

52 Newton, 398.

53 Dapo Akande, The Jurisdiction of the International Criminal Court over Nationals of Non-Parties: Legal Basis and Limits, 1 J. Int'l Crim. Just. 618, 621–634 (2003).

Carsten Stahn rejects these requirements of symmetry, arguing that the main purpose of international criminal justice is to complement domestic jurisdictional gaps.[54] Stahn notes that "the very rationale of accession to the Rome Statute may lie in the prospect that it offers greater options of prescription and enforcement jurisdiction".[55] Similarly, Rod Radstan rejects the imperative of matching legislation for the exercise of the ICC's jurisdiction.[56] Indeed, if the understanding that strict symmetry of jurisdiction were to be sustained, the purpose of complementarity under the Rome Statute would be void. Complementarity, as per Article 17 of the Rome Statute, covers the very situation in which a state is unable to prosecute a core-crime.[57] Stahn convincingly goes on to argue that the ICC's jurisdictional powers are "grounded in the competence of the state to adhere to treaties, rather than delegation of equivalent jurisdictional titles by the state".[58] Here, it is argued that the ICC operates under the idea of "automatic jurisdiction",[59] meaning that the ICC's ability to exercise jurisdiction is obtained once a state becomes party to the Rome Statute and that "no additional consent or parallelism of jurisdictional titles is necessary".[60]

The issue may also be approached by opposing the concepts of prescriptive jurisdiction and enforcement jurisdiction,[61] and arguing that bilateral jurisdictional agreements can only limit the latter.[62] The term "prescriptive jurisdiction" refers to a state's capacity to "make its law applicable to the activities, relations,

---

54 Carsten Stahn, *Response: The ICC, Pre-Existing Jurisdictional Treaty Regimes, and the Limits of the Nemo Dat Quod Non Habet Doctrine – A Reply to Michael Newton*, 49 Vand. J. Transnat'l L. 443, 448 (2016) [hereinafter Stahn].
55 Id., 449.
56 Rod Rastan, *The Jurisdictional Scope of Situations Before the International Criminal Court*, 23 Crim. L. F. 1, 20 (2012).
57 For a more detailed explanation, *see* Stahn, 449.
58 *Id.*, 449.
59 William Schabas, Article 12: Preconditions to the Exercise of Jurisdiction, in *The International Criminal Court: A Commentary on the Rome Statute* 280–282 (1st ed., 2010).
60 For a more detailed explanation, *see* Stahn, 449.
61 *See* Roger O'Keefe, *Universal Jurisdiction: Clarifying the Basic Concept*, 2 J. Int'l Crim. Just. 735, 736–737 (2004). The expression "enforcement jurisdiction" is interchangeable with term "exercise of jurisdiction:, *see* Roger O'Keefe, *Response: "Quid," Not "Quantum": A Comment on "How the International Criminal Court Threatens Treaty Norms"*, 49 Vand. J. Transnat'l L. 493 (2016) [hereinafter O'Keefe].
62 Kai Ambos, *Palestine, UN Non-Member Observer Status and ICC Jurisdiction*, EJIL: Talk! (May 6, 2014) [hereinafter Ambos], http://www.ejiltalk.org/palestine-un-non-member-observer-status-and-icc-jurisdiction/.

or status of persons, or the interests of persons in things".[63] "Enforcement jurisdiction", on the other hand, concerns the ability "to enforce or compel compliance or to punish noncompliance with its laws or regulations".[64] Indeed, bilateral jurisdictional agreements such as Oslo could arguably only affect a state's enforcement jurisdiction.[65] It is submitted that the ability to delegate jurisdiction does not derive from the ability to exercise jurisdiction, but an internationally recognized legal authority over a territory or individuals within that territory.[66] Any other understanding would open way for notable accountability gaps by implying that a state that is unable to exercise jurisdiction over certain parts of its territory would no longer be able to investigate or prosecute perpetrators, or reach out to international jurisdiction. Similarly, this would also render the Rome Statute's provision on complementarity void.[67]

In this respect, Oslo II does not seem to have stripped Palestinians of their inherent jurisdiction over the oPt, but simply of the exercise of that jurisdiction by means of a bilateral agreement delegating powers to Israel. Indeed, if Israel legally acquired exclusive enforcement jurisdiction, it is because those powers rested in the hands of the Palestinians in the first place, and were then delegated. Such previous delegation of jurisdictional powers to Israel should not eliminate Palestine's ability to do so in favor of another institution.[68] By maintaining its prescriptive jurisdiction over its territory, the State of Palestine could very well delegate that same jurisdiction to the ICC, thus granting the ICC at least those same prescriptive powers. Whether or not the ICC would be able to act on the basis of that jurisdiction becomes then a matter of exercise of jurisdiction – *i.e.* admissibility under the Rome Statute. Given that the Court is not party to the Oslo Accords, the exercise of its jurisdiction would have to be resolved by the law governing the ICC – through an assessment of complementarity and cooperation: in particular, whether Israel is effectively investigating and prosecuting alleged perpetrators of core-crimes under the Rome

---

63 Restatement (Third) of the Foreign Relations Law of the United States (1987), Am. Law. Inst., § 401(a).
64 *Id.*, § 401(a), (c).
65 Ambos; Stahn, 451; O'Keefe, 437–439.
66 Yuval Shany, *In Defence of Functional Interpretation of Article 12(3) of the Rome Statute*, 8 J. Int'l Crim. Just. 329, 339 (2010). This perspective seems to have been equally endorsed by the Pre-Trial Chamber in the *Situation in Georgia* when Georgia could not exercise jurisdiction over parts of its territory due to Russian military presence, *see* ICC, Situation in Georgia, *ICC-01/15-12*, Pre-Trial Chamber, Decision on the Prosecutor's request for authorization of an investigation (Jan. 27, 2016), paras. 54–62.
67 Stahn, 449.
68 *Id.*, 451.

Statute in Palestinian territory. As far as jurisdiction goes, the Oslo Accords should therefore not limit delegation to the ICC.

ii   *Safeguards from the Fourth Geneva Convention*

In any event, the same conclusion can also be reached based on the Palestinian government's ability to exercise jurisdiction by reference to the Fourth Geneva Convention's regime on grave breaches and belligerent occupation, which is part of customary international law.[69]

As a signatory to the Geneva Conventions, Palestine is bound to its entire body of law. In this respect, Article 146(2) of the Fourth Geneva Convention requires states to search for and try or extradite persons suspected of committing grave breaches, regardless of their nationality:

> Each High Contracting Party shall be under the obligation to search for persons alleged to have committed, or to have ordered to be committed, such grave breaches, and shall bring such persons, regardless of their nationality, before its own courts. It may also, if it prefers, and in accordance with the provisions of its own legislation, hand such persons over for trial to another High Contracting Party concerned, provided such High Contracting Party has made out a 'prima facie' case.

Jean-Marie Henckaerts argues that the principle of *aut dedere aut iudicare* (to either extradite or prosecute) creates an obligation that is "fundamental for the protection of the human person and, as such, has become part of customary international law through extensive and virtually uniform practice, including ratification of the Geneva Conventions".[70]

As such, although the Fourth Geneva Convention does not create enforceable individual rights to Palestinians, it does limit the legal effect of the Oslo Accords insofar as they strip Palestinians of their guarantees. Accordingly, Palestinian judicial authorities would legally maintain full jurisdiction over grave breaches of the Geneva Conventions committed within their sphere of territorial jurisdiction.[71]

In addition, according to Articles 8 and 47 of the Fourth Geneva Convention, belligerents cannot conclude agreements which denigrate or deprive protected

---

69 ICJ Wall, para. 79.
70 Jean-Marie Henckaerts, *The grave breaches regime as customary international law*, 7 J. Int'l Crim. Just. 683, 697 (2009).
71 Any non-legal or practical limitation to the exercise of this jurisdiction (*e.g.* economic, logistical) is beyond the scope of this study and should not affect its relation to the ICC.

persons of the benefits of the Convention. No legal effect can arise from the renunciation of such rights. Article 8 of the Fourth Geneva Convention provides:

> Protected persons may in no circumstances renounce in part or in entirety the rights secured to them by the present Convention and by the special agreements referred to in the foregoing Article.

Article 47 of the Fourth Geneva Convention provides:

> Protected persons who are in occupied territory shall not be deprived, in any case or in any manner whatsoever, of the benefits of the present Convention by any change introduced, as the result of the occupation of a territory, into the institutions or government of the said territory, nor by any agreement concluded between the authorities of the occupied territories and the Occupying Power, nor by any annexation by the latter of the whole or part of the occupied territory.

Protected persons are those "who at any given moment and in any manner whatsoever, find themselves, in cases of a conflict or occupation in the hands of a Party to the conflict or Occupying Power of which they are not nationals".[72] The drafters of the Fourth Geneva Convention, recognizing that protected persons could come under pressure to relinquish certain protections afforded by the Geneva Conventions, included these aforementioned provisions.[73] Indeed, drafters purposely emphasized the non-derogative nature of these protections in order to avoid states taking "refuge behind the will of the protected persons" when justifying their violations of the Conventions.[74] As the representative body of the Palestinian people, it could be understood that the State of Palestine is prevented from depriving those under its governance from the benefits of the Fourth Geneva Convention. Indeed, if the Palestinian people – as protected persons – cannot waive such rights, then, *a forteriori*, neither should the State of Palestine.

---

72   ICRC Commentary to the Geneva Convention relative to the Protection of Civilian Persons in Time of War, art. 4, https://www.icrc.org/ihl.nsf/7c4d08d9b287a42141256739003e636b/6756482d86146898c125641e004aa3c5?OpenDocument; Jean S. Pictet, Commentary to the Geneva Convention relative to the Protection of Civilian Persons in Time of War 46 (1958) [*hereinafter* Pictet].
73   *Id.*; Pictet 69–70; Yoram Dinstein, The International Law of Belligerent Occupation 57 (2009).
74   Pictet, 75.

Accordingly, the Oslo process and its subsequent practice should not deprive Palestinians from the protections of the Geneva Conventions,[75] namely that of bringing persons alleged to have committed grave breaches before their own courts.[76] The provisions of the Fourth Geneva Convention appear to prevent Palestinians from denouncing their jurisdiction over grave breaches. It is unlikely that the practice arising from the Oslo process will change the status of these rights under the Fourth Geneva Convention.[77] This being said, the law should not condone the idea that the Oslo Accords deprive the Palestinian government from exercising jurisdiction over international crimes in the oPt against anyone, including Israelis. The Oslo Accords would therefore be interpreted as *also* – not *exclusively* – conferring jurisdiction to Israel. It could therefore be argued that the provisions contained in the Fourth Geneva Convention guarantee the Palestinian government's inherent jurisdiction over these matters in the oPt, and consequently the validity of its delegation of powers to the ICC.

2 Territorial Uncertainty – ICC and the Palestinian Territory

A great part of the Israeli/Palestinian conflict is based on land disputes.[78] A major issue that may arise when assessing territorial jurisdiction is the concept of *Palestinian territory* for the purposes of the Court's territorial jurisdiction.

The oPt typically refers to the lands occupied by Israel since the 1967 six-day war,[79] which follows the Armistice Declaration of 1949 (also known as the *Green Line*). It is however said that its borders are not permanent and that a definitive peaceful solution to the conflict will entail land swaps "on the basis of the pre-1967 borders", presumably in order to accommodate settlements into Israeli territory. Indeed, the UN General Assembly resolution recognizing

---

75 Geneva Convention Relative to the Protection of Civilian Persons in Time of War arts. 8, 47, Aug. 12, 1949, 75 U.N.T.S 287 [*hereinafter* Fourth Geneva Convention].

76 Id., art. 146(2).

77 Adam Roberts, *What is Military Occupation?*, 55 Brit. Y.B. Int'l L. 249, 288; Yutaka Arai-Takahashi, The Law of Occupation: Continuity and Change of International Humanitarian Law, and its Interaction with International Human Rights Law 274 (2009).

78 The first large-scale armed conflict broke out following the UN Partition Plan of 1947, which resulted in an Arab/Israeli war. This war ended in 1948, with the State of Israel conquering the majority of the land within the former-British Mandate of Palestine and the consequent displacement of about 700,000 Palestinians. In 1967, the Six Day War took place, thus displacing hundreds of thousands of other Palestinians. Much of the conflict and violence that followed is said to have found its genesis in these two major events; and the right of return of Palestinian refugees, in addition to Israel's control over the West Bank and Gaza are regarded as two of the main issues within the conflict.

79 S.C. Res. 242 (1967), *Middle East*, U.N. Doc. S/RES/242 (Nov. 22, 1967).

the State of Palestine does not expressly define the territorial boundaries of Palestine. For the ICC, this could cause ambiguity as to whether crimes have been committed within Palestinian territory – and consequently whether the Court has jurisdiction over the matter. The Rome Statute does not provide a clear formula to solve this issue.

It has been argued that the ICC is not a border-determination body, and that, should it engage in this matter, the Court would be exceeding its purpose as originally envisioned by the drafters of the Rome Statute.[80] Such arguments against the ICC's ability to make findings on Palestinian territory should be questioned. Indeed, there is no global border determination body – perhaps the closest to such an institution is the ICJ, with limited jurisdiction itself. However, making a legal determination on Palestine's territory, as a necessary exercise for its jurisdiction, could arguably fall within the ICC's mandate. In this regard, the Kampala amendments enshrine the Court's ability to determine the existence of the act of aggression for the prosecution of the crime of aggression. There seems to be no legal prohibition on the ICC's ability to determine whether a certain act was committed within the territory of a given state. In fact, this power is already entrusted to the Court in the context of its ability to determine the existence of the elements of the crime of aggression – namely the violation of a state's territorial integrity.

The Kampala amendments require the ICC to determine the existence of an act of aggression when looking into the respective crime. The Rome Statute establishes that the Court may make its own findings in determining an act of aggression, regardless of any such exercises by organs outside the Court.[81] The Special Working Group in the Kampala revision purposely removed the provisions establishing the binding nature of external bodies' decisions in the ICC's assessment of the existence of the elements of the act of aggression.[82] Although the UNSC would arguably have *primary* responsibility in these matters, the final word seems to lay in the hands of the Court. Any other understanding would strip the ICC from deciding itself on the elements of the crime,

---

80   William Schabas, An Introduction to the International Criminal Court 82 (4th ed., 2011); Iain Scobbie, Alon Margalit and Sarah Hibbin, *Recognizing Palestinian Statehood*, Yale. J. Int'l Aff. (online post) (Aug. 25, 2011); Kontorovich, 984.

81   Rome Statute art. 16 *bis* (9).

82   U.N. Doc. PCNICC/2002/2/Add.2, discussed in: Roger S. Clark, *Rethinking Aggression as Crime and Formulating its Elements: The Final Work-Product of the Preparatory Commission for the International Criminal Court*, 15 Leiden L. J. 859–890 (2002); Roger S. Clark, *Amendments to the Rome Statute of the International Criminal Court Considered at the first Review Conference on the Court, Kampala, 31 May-11 June 2010*, 2 Goettingen J. Int'l L., 689, 700 (2010) [hereinafter Clark].

and consequently of its effective judicial function. This is particularly the case when external determinations are assessed in light of political considerations, as is often the case with the UNSC.[83]

The Rome Statute establishes the violation of territorial integrity as an element of the act of aggression.[84] It stands to reason that, in order to determine the existence of that element, the Court must assess the territorial nature of the location in which an act occurred (*locus delicti*) – i.e. whether an act was committed within the territory of one state or the other. It is an essential preliminary exercise intrinsic to the Court's ability to determine the existence of the elements of the act of aggression. Accordingly, it could be argued that the ICC is indeed able to make certain territorial findings when such assessments are necessary for the exercise of its judicial functions. The contrary would run counter the purpose of the Rome Statute and would render the Court's judicial exercise over the crime of aggression useless.

In the context of the situation in Palestine, such powers should not necessarily extend to the entirety of the Palestinian territory, nor should it be used to resolve border disputes between the parties – this indeed would transcend the scope of the Court's powers. This capacity must be solely limited to determining whether an alleged core-crime under the Rome Statute was committed within the ICC's sphere of territorial jurisdiction, which in this case would be Palestinian territory. To a less complex extent, in the *Situation in Georgia*, the Pre-Trial Chamber made a finding that South Ossetia was part of Georgian territory for the purposes of establishing jurisdiction over a *locus delicti*, regardless of claims to the contrary and belligerent occupation by the Russian Federation.[85] It could therefore be argued that, in the context of Palestine, the ICC would not be exceeding its mandate when making limited territorial findings necessary to the exercise of its jurisdiction.

3   Determining Palestinian Territory – Jurisdiction over what?

Having established that the ICC could potentially make findings concerning Palestine's territory in the exercise of its judicial function, difficulties remain in determining what the relevant Palestinian territory consists of.

---

83   Clark, 700.
84   Rome Statute art. 8 *bis* (2).
85   To a less complex extent, in the *Situation in Georgia*, the Pre-Trial Chamber made a finding that South Ossetia was part of Georgian territory, regardless of claims to the contrary. *See*: International Criminal Court, Situation in Georgia, *ICC-01/15-12*, Pre-Trial Chamber, Decision on the Prosecutor's request for authorization of an investigation, 27 January 2016, para. 6.

To exercise its judicial function, the Court need not define the entire Palestinian territory, but only those parts relevant to the alleged crimes of concern. Several recent inter-party agreements and UN resolutions on the conflict have been thought out with future land swaps in mind, purposely avoiding defining permanent borders. However, this should not preclude the ICC from identifying the oPt – or at least certain relevant parts of it – as Palestinian territory for the exercise of its judicial mandate (namely that of determining the liability of individuals). It would be difficult to support the understanding that there is no Palestinian territory. This would not only suggest that the General Assembly simply ignored the Montevideo criteria for statehood,[86] but would possibly ignore the reality on the ground – especially in Area A of the West Bank and in Gaza, which are under Palestinian administration on both civil and security-related issues. International law does not require that a state's territory be fully defined. The ICJ established that "there is (…) no rule that the land frontiers of a state must be fully delimited and defined, and often in various places and for long periods they are not".[87] It is unnecessary and excessive to permanently determine the entire Palestinian territory – to do so would lay outside the scope of the Court. What should be required is the recognition that the relevant crimes have been committed within Palestinian territory.[88]

The disputed nature of the territory may come into play when assessing land ownership. The Permanent Court of International Justice established that a territory need not be undisputed in order for it to be attributed to a state.[89] As stated by James Crawford, this would grant states veto power over other states' territorial boundaries or existence by unilaterally asserting territorial rights.[90] The ICC would have to assess certain criteria in order to determine whether an alleged crime was committed on Palestinian territory. A state's right over its territory can be determined either by effective control or by international recognition of its legal entitlement to a territory. In the case of Palestine, both of these criteria can be noted in relation to the oPt. Indeed, the status of Area

---

86   Montevideo Convention on the Rights and Duties of States, Dec. 26, 1934, 165 L.N.T.S. 19.
87   International Court of Justice, North Sea Continental Shelf Cases, Judgement, 1969 I.C.J. Rep. 3 (Feb. 20), at 3, 32.
88   Rome Statute art. 12(2)(a).
89   Permanent Court of International Justice, Delimitation of the Polish-Czechoslovakian Frontier (Question of Jaworzina), Advisory Opinion, 1923 P.C.I.J. Series B No. 8 (Dec. 6); James. Crawford, The Creation of States in International Law 48 n48 (2nd ed., 2006) [hereinafter Crawford]: The point was assumed by the Permanent Court in two cases:" Monastery at St Naoum (Albanian Frontier) and Polish-Czechoslovakian Frontier (Question of Jaworzina).
90   Crawford, 48–50; Yael Ronen, *Israel, Palestine and the ICC – Territory Uncharted but not Unknown*, 12 J. Int'l Crim. J. 7, 11 (2014) [hereinafter Ronen].

A of the West Bank and the Gaza Strip reflects a reality distinct from that of the remainder of the West Bank (Areas B and C). Palestine's entitlement to its territory arguably stems from its *effective control* over Area A of the West Bank and the Gaza Strip (although not directly by the PA), as well as its legal entitlement to statehood over *at least* certain parts of the West Bank and Gaza, based on the Palestinian people's right to self-determination. Thus, the Palestinian case could present a combination of both factual factors (effective control) and legal factors (right to self-determination) granting a state's entitlement to a territory. It is reiterated that the exercise of assessing whether a certain area is Palestinian territory should be limited to the specific territory in which a crime was allegedly committed, thus enabling the exercise of the Court's jurisdiction.[91]

As stated, Palestine's entitlement over the West Bank and the Gaza Strip may stem from its effective control within these territories. A state's territory finds its core in areas where it exercises effective control.[92] However, mere effective control could be insufficient to assert sovereignty over an entire territory. This is reflected, for instance, by the prohibition of acquiring sovereignty by force or occupation. The prolonged military occupation of the oPt should not legally grant Israel sovereignty, nor should it withdraw the Palestinian people's legal entitlement to it. Nevertheless – as demonstrated in the case of Croatia – sovereignty can extend beyond that core territory in which the state exercises effective control.[93]

Palestine's sovereignty may extend beyond the territory under its effective control due to the Palestinian people's right to self-determination. The ICC would not itself have to make its own findings on the Palestinian people's right to self-determination over certain parts of the West Bank where alleged crimes have been committed, as it is widely acknowledged in international law, notably by the ICJ. In its Advisory Opinion, the ICJ criticized the construction of the Israeli wall in the oPt, stating that it contributed to the departure of Palestinians between the Green Line and the separation barrier, thus easing the absorption of those areas into Israel and "severely imped[ing] the exercise

---

91 Ronen, 7, 11 (2014).
92 Crawford, 48.
93 *Id.*, 50. Here, Crawford states that "the borders of the new State in 1991 were sufficiently certain ... but effective control fluctuated with military conflict between the new State and Serbian forces, local and federal. The rule applied ... when Croatia was recognized notwithstanding the occupation of Eastern Slavonia by the Yugoslav National Army and operations by Serbian irregulars elsewhere". Crawford goes on to give further examples such as the territorial uncertainty of the Polish republics between the World Wars.

by the Palestinian people of its right to self-determination".[94] This arguably implies that at least those parts of the territory between the separation wall and the Green Line – which are mostly border areas – fall within the legal entitlement of the Palestinians by virtue of their right to self-determination. Moreover, several resolutions and declarations by the UNGA, UNSC and Secretary General have urged Israel to withdraw from territories occupied since 1967, reiterating the Palestinians' right to self-determination.[95] Israel itself has recognized this right.[96] As mentioned by Yael Ronen, the UNGA resolution 67/19 recognizing Palestinian statehood in 2012 "did not define Palestine, it merely transformed it from a prospective state to an existing one".[97] The depth and extent of a state's sovereignty greatly depends on internationally recognized legal entitlement. Palestine's sovereignty over its territory could then stem from its effective control over a core territory *and* from its internationally recognized legal entitlement to at least certain or particular parts – if not all – of the oPt based on the right to self-determination.

As for the specific case of the territory on which Israeli settlements are located, its status is the same as that of the rest of the West Bank and should not require a different assessment criteria. The Israeli government has claimed that the territory is not occupied but *disputed*, and that "Israel's claim to this disputed territory is no less valid than that of the Palestinians".[98] This argument's legal standing may be put into question. As mentioned by Yael Ronen, *disputed* is merely a factual description of a political situation and not a legal category.[99] Israel's aspirations to these lands, should they occur, are likely political and there should be no competing legal claims of sovereignty nor a legal dispute over the current status of the settlements. The illegal presence, as defined by the ICJ and UN resolutions, of Israeli settlers in West Bank settlements would

---

94   ICJ Wall, paras. 121–122.
95   S.C. Res. 242 (1967), *Middle East* (22 November 1967) UN Doc S/RES/242; UNSC & UNGA, *Report of the Secretary-General on Peaceful Settlement of the Question of Palestine*, U.N. Doc. A/68/363-S/2013/524 (Sep. 4, 2013), para. 21; G.A. Res. 32/20, *The situation in the Middle East*, U.N. Doc. A/RES/32/20 (Nov. 25, 1977); G.A. Res. 33/29, *The situation in the Middle East*, U.N. Doc. A/RES/33/29 (Dec. 7, 1978); G.A. Res. 34/70, *The situation in the Middle East*, UN Doc A/RES/34/70 (Dec. 6, 1979); ICJ Wall, para. 159.
96   Declaration of Principles on Interim Self-Government Arrangements, signed by the Government of the State of Israel and the Palestine Liberation Organization (Washington, D.C., USA), Sep. 13, 1993) [*hereinafter* Oslo I].
97   Ronen, 13.
98   Israel Ministry of Foreign Affairs, *Israel, the Conflict and Peace: Answers to frequently asked questions* (Nov. 2007), http://mfa.gov.il/MFA/MFA-Archive/2003/Pages/Israel-%20the%20Conflict%20and%20Peace-%20Answers%20to%20Frequen.aspx#how.
99   Ronen, 16.

not grant a legal claim upon which Israeli entitlement to that territory can be founded. In fact, the ICJ has expressly noted that situations resulting from the construction of the wall, of which Israeli settlements are an intrinsic part of, are not to be recognized by the international community.[100]

In short, it is defensible that Israel's disagreement over the lands constituting Palestinian territory does not affect Palestine's legal entitlement over the relevant portions of the oPt. The territory in which Israeli settlements are located could potentially be legally considered part of the State of Palestine for the purposes of territorial criminal jurisdiction to be delegated to the ICC. In other words, the existence of settlements in the oPt should not, under international law, subject settlement territories to different standards than those of the rest of the oPt when assessing Palestinian territory.[101] It could therefore be reasonable for the ICC to exercise territorial jurisdiction over these territories without engaging in border determination and exceeding its mandate. Indeed, at least for the purposes of the ICC's exercise of jurisdiction, it seems legally sound to qualify Palestinian territory as the territory over which *only* Palestine claims sovereignty and holds international recognition of legal entitlement – which may or may not include the entirety of the West Bank. This does not appear to preclude future land swaps and peace agreements.

4   The Palestinian Authority and Hamas Quarrel – Division among Palestinian factions

The political discord between leading Palestinian factions may raise issues concerning the extent of the State of Palestine's jurisdiction over the entire Palestinian territory. As mentioned above, the PA administers the West Bank and Hamas controls the Gaza Strip. At the time of writing, reconciliation

---

100   The illegality of Israeli settlements has been reiterated above. Also, in ICJ Wall, para. 159, the Court stated that "the Court is of the view that all States are under an obligation not to recognize the illegal situation resulting from the construction of the wall in the Occupied Palestinian Territory, including in and around East Jerusalem. They are also under an obligation not to render aid or assistance in maintaining the situation created by such construction. It is also for all States, while respecting the United Nations Charter and international law, to see to it that any impediment, resulting from the construction of the wall, to the exercise by the Palestinian people of its right to self-determination is brought to an end." For the ICJ finding that the construction of Israeli settlements forms a part of the wall-related policy of the Israeli government, see ICJ Wall, para. 122.

101   Indeed, under international law, legal rights cannot derive from an illegal act (*ex injuria jus non oritur*). See Martin Dawidowicz, *The obligation of non-recognition of an unlawful situation*, in The Law of International Responsibility 677, n1 (J. Crawford, A. Pellet, S. Olleson eds., 2010).

efforts between the two have been underway.[102] Whether such efforts will have any bearing on the matter at hand will highly depend on the success, as well as on the terms of the reconciliation. Based on the *status quo* of early 2018, it could be argued that the PA's lack of full direct control over the Gaza Strip could negatively condition the ICC's jurisdiction over this territory by virtue of the requirements of delegated jurisdiction. Indeed, questions arise as to how the PA is able to delegate jurisdiction over territory that it itself does not control – in this case the Gaza Strip.

These questions can arguably be answered by looking into the instrument of ratification of the Rome Statute and into the unique aspects of the structure of Palestinian governance. In particular, it was not the PA but the State of Palestine that ratified the Rome Statute.[103] Also, it may be found that the State of Palestine *absorbed* the roles of the PA as the domestic administration of the oPt, and of the PLO in its role to represent all Palestinians in international fora, particularly through its capacity to enter international agreements in representation of the entire oPt.[104] According to this, by ratifying the Rome Statute, the State of Palestine would have validly delegated territorial jurisdiction to the ICC through the capacity that it has acquired via the PLO within the international community.

In this respect, an important distinction to be made is that between the external and internal governance of the State of Palestine. As we know it today, the Palestinians' internal governance – *i.e.* their administration over the territory they claim as their own – was born out of the Oslo Peace Process between the PLO and Israel, with the creation of the PA.[105] As an essentially domestic entity, the PA's exercise of practical governance is limited to internal matters within the parts of the oPt it administers. However, as far as foreign relations are concerned, it is the PLO that is recognized as the legitimate representative of the Palestinian people with the capacity to enter international relations, and not the PA or Hamas.[106] Within the UN system, it is the PLO

---

102 Nidal Mughrabi, *Palestinians see Gaza peace dividend pass them by*, Reuters (Jan. 16, 2018) https://www.reuters.com/article/us-israel-palestinians-gaza/palestinians-see-gaza-peace-dividend-pass-them-by-idUSKBN1F51DO.

103 ICC, *The State of Palestine accedes to the Rome Statute*, ICC-ASP-20150107-PR1082 (Jan. 7, 2015), https://www.icc-cpi.int/Pages/item.aspx?name=pr1082_2.

104 The PLO was founded during the first Palestinian National Council on 28, May 1964, in Jerusalem to address the Palestinian national cause; *see* Rashid Hamid, *What is the PLO?* (1975), 4 J. Palestine Stud. 90–109 (1975).

105 Agreement on the Gaza Strip and the Jericho Area, signed by the Government of the State of Israel and the Palestine Liberation Organization (Cairo, Egypt), May 4, 1994, Article III.

106 The Palestinian people have been represented in the UNGA by the PLO since 1974, *see*: G.A. Res. 3210 (XXIX), *Invitation to the Palestine Liberation Organization*, U.N. Doc. A/RES/3210 (Oct. 14, 1974).

that is entrusted with the powers and responsibilities of the State of Palestine, and the State of Palestine acts on the basis of the PLO.[107] Indeed, the PLO has represented the Palestinian people in the UN since 1974, and has also done so in several other international bodies such as the Movement of Non-Aligned Countries, the Organization of the Islamic Conference and the Arab League.[108] More recently, Palestine – through the powers conferred to the PLO – became a member of UNESCO.[109]

The extent of the PLO's representative mandate includes those residing in the Gaza Strip, the West Bank (including East Jerusalem) and those who make up the Palestinian diaspora.[110] Thus, it is the PLO, as the entity from which the Government of Palestine draws its international capacity – not the PA or Hamas – that represents the full array of Palestinians residing in and out of the oPt. Internal political struggles should not interfere with the PLO's capacity to represent the Palestinian people in international fora or to accede to international treaties, as it has done since times pre-dating both the PA and Hamas.[111]

In sum, *at least* since 2012, with UN General Assembly Resolution 67/19, the PLO's role in international affairs has been engaged in under the veil of the Government of the State of Palestine. It was not the PA, but the State of Palestine, acting through the PLO, that ratified the Rome Statute. The PLO's status and function within the international community, as representatives of the Palestinian people, was succeeded by the State of Palestine. Accordingly, regardless of effective internal control of either domestic faction, the Government of the State of Palestine – as an entity operating through the PLO – has validly ratified the Rome Statute and delegated jurisdiction to the ICC,

---

107   In 1988, the designation of the observer-entity PLO was succeeded by observer-entity *Palestine* in the UNGA, without prejudice to the PLO's status and function within the UN system; *see* G.A. Res. 43/177, *The Question of Palestine*, U.N. Doc. A/RES/43/177 (Dec. 15, 1988). In 2012, the observer-state *State of Palestine* succeeded the observer-entity *Palestine* in the UNGA, both represented by the PLO, *see* G.A. Res. 67/19, *Status of Palestine in the United Nations* (Dec. 4, 2012), U.N. Doc. A/RES/67/19; Letter dated 9 December 1988 from the Permanent Observer of the Palestine Liberation Organization to the United Nations addressed to the Secretary-General, U.N. Doc. A/43/928 (9 December 1988), para. 15.
108   The Palestinian people have been represented in the UN General Assembly by the PLO since 1974, *see*: G.A. Res. 3210 (XXIX), *Invitation to the Palestine Liberation Organization*, U.N. Doc. A/RES/3210 (Oct. 14, 1974); G.A. Res. 3237 (XXIX), *Observer Status for the Palestine Liberation Organisation*, UN Doc A/RES/3237 (Nov. 22, 1974); G.A. Res. 67/19, *Status of Palestine in the United Nations*, U.N. Doc. A/RES/67/19 (Dec. 4, 2012), para. 22.
109   UNESCO General Conference, 36th Session (2011), *Admission of Palestine as a Member of UNESCO* (Oct. 25–Nov. 12, 2011), 36 C/Resolution, para. 76.
110   G.A. Res. 3210 (XXIX) invited the PLO to participate in the UNGA as "the representative of the Palestinian people".
111   The PA was created during the Oslo Peace Process in 1994; Hamas was formally established in 1987, *see* Paola Caridi, Hamas: From Resistance to Government 48 (2010).

representing Palestinians in the territory of Palestine and across the domestic political spectrum.

This status enjoyed by the PLO is arguably reinforced by the fact that both factions support the PLO as an institution whose representative powers lengthens throughout the oPt. This support was reiterated by Palestinian President Mahmoud Abbas with Hamas's backing in August 2014.[112] Indeed, Hamas's support for a Palestinian bid to the ICC has been widely reported and, regardless of the issues over which these factions disagree, there is a unified Palestinian stance regarding the Court's role in the oPt by means of the PLO's representation of the State of Palestine.[113] Even during the more recent disagreements between the PA and Hamas, neither party has withdrawn its support for Palestine's bid to the ICC. Consequently, internal domestic differences – subject to ongoing negotiations – are unlikely to constitute an obstacle to the PLO's ability to represent Palestine across the West Bank and Gaza for the purpose of delegation of jurisdiction to the ICC. Domestic discord should therefore not affect the ICC's jurisdiction over the oPt.

B   *Temporal Jurisdiction*

The ICC may exercise its jurisdiction over crimes committed after the entry into force of the Rome Statute for a state, "unless that State has made a declaration under article 12, paragraph 3".[114] The Rome Statute entered into force for Palestine on 1 April 2015, following the Palestinian government's accession

---

112 Avaneesh Pandey, *Hamas Pledges Support for International Criminal Court Bid as Abbas Urges Resumption of Talks*, I.B. Times (Aug. 23, 2014), http://www.ibtimes.com/hamas-pledges-support-international-criminal-court-bid-abbas-urges-resumption-talks-1667212; *Hamas Backs Palestinian Bid to Join International Criminal Court*, N.Y. Post (Aug. 23, 2014), http://nypost.com/2014/08/23/hamas-backs-palestinian-bid-to-join-international-criminal-court/.

113 Nidal Al-Mughrabi, *Hamas backs Palestinian push for ICC Gaza war crimes probe*, Reuters (Aug. 23, 2014), http://www.reuters.com/article/us-mideast-gaza-icc-idUSKBN0GN09320140823; Nidal Al-Mughbrabi and Ari Rabinovitch, *Hamas welcomes ICC inquiry into Israeli-Palestinian conflict*, Reuters (Jan. 17, 2015), http://www.reuters.com/article/us-israel-palestinians-icc-idUSKBN0KQ0KG20150117; *Hamas Welcomes ICC Probe Into Possible War Crimes in Palestinian Territories*, Ha'aretz (Jan. 17, 2015), http://www.haaretz.com/israel-news/1.637615; *Hamas declares support for Palestinian bid to join international criminal court*, The Guardian (Aug. 23, 2014), https://www.theguardian.com/world/2014/aug/23/hamas-back-palestinian-bid-international-criminal-court; Yasser Okbi and Maariv Hashavua, *Hamas says willing to cooperate with ICC to advance Palestinian cause*, Jerusalem Post (Apr. 10, 2015) http://www.jpost.com/Arab-Israeli-Conflict/Hamas-says-willing-to-cooperate-with-ICC-to-uphold-Palestinian-rights-396707.

114 Rome Statute art. 11(2).

to the Rome Statute on 2 January 2015.[115] Along with the accession to the ICC, the State of Palestine lodged an Article 12(3) declaration accepting the Court's jurisdiction for acts committed on its territory since 13 June 2014.[116] The Declaration likely sought to give the ICC jurisdiction over Israel's most recent military incursion in the Gaza Strip, Operation Protective Edge.

As a result of Palestine's most recent Article 12(3) declaration, the Court should not encounter any major obstacles in asserting its temporal jurisdiction over acts committed during and after Operation Protective Edge in the summer of 2014. However, questions may arise regarding the construction of settlements in the West Bank – namely the transfer of population and destruction of property that occurred before 13 June 2014. Indeed, hundreds of thousands of Israeli settlers have been transferred into the oPt and a similar number of Palestinians were displaced before the time-frame in which the ICC can legally exercise its jurisdiction. The crime of transfer and displacement of population can arguably be identified as a continuing crime, at least until the return of displaced civilians and the withdrawal of settlers from the occupied territory. To consider this scenario in light of continuing crimes, certain acts in support of the construction or maintenance of settlements should have been committed within the time-frame of the ICC's temporal jurisdiction – in this case, since 13 June 2014. Such acts may include the construction of settlements, the non-withdrawal of settlers or any of the supporting acts by the Israeli authorities.

The Rome Statute does not provide clear solutions on how to approach continuing crimes. However, the ICC's Elements of Crimes does contain a footnote suggesting that continuing crimes do not fall within the jurisdiction of the Court in the context of enforced disappearances.[117] Whether or not the Court will extend this principle to other potential continuing crimes remains to be seen, as the Elements of Crimes contain no such express limitation in regard to any other core-crime.

Should the Court find that continuing crimes may apply to other core-crimes, relevant jurisprudence may be drawn from similar judiciaries. The

---

115   Rome Statute art. 126(1); the UNSG Depositary notification of Accession to the Rome Statute by the State of Palestine is available at: https://treaties.un.org/doc/Publication/CN/2015/CN.13.2015-Eng.pdf.

116   2014 Declaration; ICC, *Palestine declares acceptance of ICC jurisdiction since 13 June 2014*, ICC-CPI-20150105-PR1080 (Jan. 5, 2015), https://www.icc-cpi.int/Pages/item.aspx?name=pr1080.

117   International Criminal Court, Elements of Crimes n 24, Official Records of the Assembly of States Parties to the Rome Statute of the International Criminal Court, First session (New York), Sep. 3–10, 2002; Official Records of the Review Conference of the Rome Statute of the International Criminal Court, Kampala, 31 May -11 June 2010 (ICC, RC/11).

Appeals Chamber and Trial Chamber of the International Criminal Tribunal for Rwanda (ICTR) in *Nahimana* have identified continuous crimes as those that "[continue] in time until the completion of the acts contemplated".[118] Black's Law Dictionary, which was also relied on by the Appeals Chamber of the ICTR, defines a continuing crime as "a crime that continues after an initial illegal act is consummated; a crime that involves ongoing elements (...) A crime (...) that continues over an extended period of time",[119] and that implies an ongoing criminal responsibility.[120] In the aforementioned case, the Trial Chamber of the ICTR had considered an accused culpable of a continuing crime for re-circulating (during the time within the Tribunal's temporal jurisdiction) material that incited genocide which had been originally published before its temporal jurisdiction (pre-1994). The Appeals Chamber later rejected the argument that these acts constituted continuing crimes, but on the basis that speeches, emissions and articles were discrete actions which ended once they were dispersed.[121] Conversely, in the Situation in Palestine, it could be argued that the construction and maintenance of settlements in the West Bank are no such "discrete actions", namely due to its supporting political apparatus.

Acts supporting Israeli settlements in the oPt constructed prior to 13 June 2014 do not end with the construction of the last housing unit. A plurality of government-led acts follows in continuation of the policy, namely in granting financial benefits to families who choose to move to West Bank settlements, the highly complex security apparatus set-up by the IDF surrounding Israeli-only residential areas, the ongoing expulsion of Palestinians who attempt to return to their previous homes or farm lands, and even the maintenance of settler roads and physical infrastructure. There are various instrumental acts that are actively put into effect in order to maintain these settlements.[122] Israel's

---

118   *The Prosecutor v. Nahimana*, Case No. ICTR 99-52-T, Trial Chamber I, Judgment and Sentence (International Criminal Tribunal for Rwanda, May 12, 2003), para. 1017.
119   *Nahimana v. The Prosecutor*, Case No. ICTR-99-52-A, (ICTR-99-52-A), Appeals Chamber, Appeals Judgment (International Criminal Tribunal for Rwanda, 28 November 2007), para. 721 [*hereinafter* Nahimana Appeal]; H.C. Black, Black's Law Dictionary (8th ed., 2004).
120   *Id.*, para. 721.
121   *Id.*, paras. 691–716.
122   *See* Preliminary report prepared by Mr. A.S. Al-Khasawneh and Mr. R. Hatano on the Human Rights Dimensions of Population Transfer, including the implantation of settlers and settlements, U.N. Doc. E/CN.4/Sub.2/1993/17 (July 6, 1993), paras. 14–15; *Netanyahu affirms support for 'courageous' West Bank settlers*, Middle East Eye (Jan. 24, 2016), http://www.middleeasteye.net/news/netanyahu-supports-settlements-west-bank-1963021862; *Netanyahu says Israeli government 'supports settlement at any time' after Hebron incident*, ABC (Jan. 24, 2016), http://www.abc.net.au/news/2016-01-25/

settlement policy is not made of singular discrete actions which suddenly dissipate once an odd deed is carried out. It is based on a complex system of continuous actions that are planned and/or endorsed by the highest levels of government which last for as long as the settlements themselves.

Moreover, acts committed in the time preceding the Court's temporal jurisdiction may also be relevant to the extent that they could serve as evidence to support or clarify a particular context on conducts occurring within its jurisdiction.[123] This may contribute to evidence of a policy of population transfer that continues into the time-frame of the ICC's temporal jurisdiction. It therefore seems highly plausible that alleged crimes of transfer and displacement of population beginning before 13 June 2014 may be relevant, at least as evidence of past conduct and policy.

In any event – even if one is to set aside the applicability of the doctrine of continuing crimes under the Rome Statute – there is arguably tenable evidence that since 13 June 2014 several housing units have been planned and constructed, hundreds of Israeli settlers have been transferred into the West Bank and numerous Palestinians have had their homes and places of business destroyed or confiscated.[124] These events could very well fall within the ICC's

---

netanyahu-says-supports-settlement-at-any-time/7110874; Barak Ravid, *Netanyahu: We are Considering Unilateral Moves in West Bank*, Ha'aretz (May 23, 2014), http://www.haaretz.com/israel-news/.premium-1.592382; Judi Rudoren & Jeremy Ashkenas, *Netanyahu and the Settlements*, N.Y. Times (Mar. 18, 2015), http://www.nytimes.com/interactive/2015/03/12/world/middleeast/netanyahu-west-bank-settlements-israel-election.html?_r=1; Isabel Kershner, *Israel Approves Additional Funding for Settlements in West Bank*, N.Y. Times (June 19, 2016), http://www.nytimes.com/2016/06/20/world/middleeast/israel-west-bank-settlements-palestinians.html.

123 Nahimana Appeal, para. 315.

124 *Israel approves 454 new settlement homes in East Jerusalem*, Al-Jazeera English (Nov. 17 2015), http://america.aljazeera.com/articles/2015/11/17/israel-approves-454-new-settlement-homes-in-east-jerusalem.html; *Israel re-mapped West Bank land to expand settlement construction – report*, RT (May, 31 2016), https://www.rt.com/news/344926-israel-west-bank-settlements/; Barak David, *Israel Approves Construction of 42 Units in West Bank Settlement Home to Slain 13-year-old*, Ha'aretz (July 2, 2016), http://www.haaretz.com/israel-news/1.728476; *Israel accelerates settlement construction in West Bank: Peace Now*, Press TV (Apr. 13, 2016), http://www.presstv.com/Detail/2016/04/13/460541/Israel-settlement-construction-West-Bank-Peace-Now-Tel-Aviv; Tovah Lazaroff, *State Comptroller: Only 30% of illegal West Bank construction demolished*, Jerusalem Post, 30 March 2016), http://www.jpost.com/Israel-News/State-Comptroller-Only-30-percent-of-illegal-West-Bank-construction-demolished-449665; John Hall, *Israel to resume building controversial settlements in the West Bank after 18-month moratorium*, The Independent (Jan. 25, 2015), http://www.independent.co.uk/news/world/middle-east/israel-to-resume-building-controversial-settlements-in-the-west-bank-after-18-month-moratorium-a6832881.html; Philip Weiss, *Israel announces yet another new*

temporal jurisdiction and it is doubtful that the OTP will have great difficulties in making its case in this regard.

IV   Looking to the Future and Conclusion

Palestine's non-member state status at the UNGA in 2012 appears to have granted the OTP an entirely new legal spectrum compared to that of 2009. With matters of Palestinian statehood arguably laid to rest in respect to ICC membership, the OTP is now undertaking its preliminary examination into the Situation in Palestine. However, such a step remains a long way from opening a formal investigation.

Having identified some of the major procedural obstacles that may arise during the pre-trial phases of the Situation in Palestine, it seems likely that any decision will be far from universally appeasing. The Oslo Accords, territorial uncertainties, and internal conflicts among leading Palestinian factions raise questions about the validity of the ICC's territorial jurisdiction. Also, limits established by the Court's temporal scope could lay tens of thousands of settlement housing units in the West Bank outside the jurisdictional grasp of the ICC. However, as established above, reference to a wide array of sources may very well serve as pillars for overcoming these apparent procedural hurdles.

It has been demonstrated that, by carefully analyzing the nuances of the theory of delegated jurisdiction in treaty law, as well as fundamental bodies of international law – namely the Fourth Geneva Convention – the Oslo Accords may arguably not bar the ICC's jurisdiction over alleged perpetrators in Palestinian territory. Also, the Court should not need to overcome its original mandate by determining the entirety of Palestinian territory. It could be sufficient and within its judicial powers to make limited findings that are necessary to the exercise of its judicial function, by drawing from acknowledged sources. It has also been illustrated that political quarrels between leading Palestinian factions should not affect the Government of the State of Palestine's ability to represent the entire Palestinian territory.

As for the ICC's temporal jurisdiction, it cannot be said with certainty that the Court will include West Bank settlement housing units initiated before

settlement, as U.S. plans to join Europe in fresh criticism, Mondoweiss (May 9, 2016), http://mondoweiss.net/2016/05/announces-settlement-criticism/; Peter Beaumont, *Netanyahu approves more West Bank construction after demolition ruling*, The Guardian (July 29, 2015), https://www.theguardian.com/world/2015/jul/29/netanyahu-approves-west-bank-settlement-construction-demolition.

13 June 2014 by applying the doctrine of continuous crimes. However, there seems to be no major hurdle in recognizing its own jurisdiction over housing units initiated after that date.

Additionally, admissibility under the Rome Statute will require that the conditions set by the principle of complementarity and the gravity requirements undergo a close look by the OTP. Particularly, the existence of prosecutorial or investigative action within the Israeli courts, as well as the very structure of the judicial system, will need to fall under candid scrutiny. Israeli domestic courts have yet to pronounce themselves on the legality of West Bank settlement construction and its consequences.

The involvement of the ICC in this long-lasting conflict is unlikely to have a catalyzing effect in the big picture. Nevertheless, it is inconceivable that ignoring the commission of atrocities – wherever they may occur – is a preferable route to advocating against impunity. Accountability, should it occur in this case, will likely have the limited value it often has: a *post facto* intervention that serves as a comfortable alternative to pre-emptive measures. Whether acknowledgment and accountability for the harm suffered by Palestinian and Israeli civilians will bring moral redress to the victims and their families, as well as prevent future atrocities, is something that remains to be seen. In any case, merited prosecutorial action will necessarily entail impartial assessments into the actions of every party to the conflict, guided and limited by the legal framework in which it operates.

Re-centering Justice as the End Goal of Our Struggle

George Bisharat*

Law always has two faces: the face of justice and the face of power. My message this afternoon is simple: that in envisioning alternative futures in Israel/Palestine, while we cannot afford to neglect law, it is justice that must always remain our guiding light.

This may strike you as a platitude: no one opposes justice. But I would not raise it here if there were not strong evidence that this central pillar of our movement has been obscured.

In particular, the quest for a state that began as a means to realize Palestinian rights has morphed into a quest for a state as an end in itself, virtually without regard to the nature of that state nor its capacity to actually accomplish justice for Palestinians. We have two Palestinian regimes with authoritarian tendencies, that seem more likely to serve as coffins for the burial of Palestinian rights than vessels for their fulfillment.

Re-centering justice at this time is both a moral imperative and a pragmatic political necessity.

But beyond this general call, I also suggest a more multi-faceted conception of justice than we have fielded in the past. So I am not just advocating a return to the sense of justice that animated the movement for Palestinian rights historically. I am also proposing that we expand to a more encompassing one – call it a 21st century justice reboot.

---

* George E. Bisharat is an Emeritus Professor of Law at the University of California Hastings College of the Law, and a former deputy public defender in San Francisco. In addition to his academic publications, he is a frequent commentator on law and politics in the Middle East for both print and broadcast media throughout the globe. This piece is based on a presentation delivered by the author at the conference titled "The State of Israel and International Law: Legitimicacy Exceptionalism and Responsibility", held between the 31st of March and the 2nd of April 2017 at University College Cork, a constituent university of the National University of Ireland.

Here's how I will proceed:

First, a few words about justice in the early days of the Palestinian movement.

Then, I will explain why I claim that justice is both a moral imperative and political necessity.

Following that, I will briefly review seven facets of justice that we might be wise to consider.

I will finish with a few words about the role of international law and question whether its capacity to deliver justice for Palestinians and others would be enhanced by a principle of state illegitimacy.

The Palestinian opposition to Zionist colonization began as a struggle for justice, first and foremost against the forced displacement of Palestinians in favor of Zionist settlers and the denial of our right to return – commemorated in what we call the Nakba. In truth, the Nakba, defined as the forced displacement of Palestinians for Jewish settlement, continues, as several have observed here, albeit in shifting forms.

The struggle for justice, therefore, has been at its core a struggle to halt the Nakba and to reverse its effects to the maximum extent possible. Understandably, it has focused on righting the wrongs committed against the Palestinian people.

But Palestinians have also embraced broader goals. Particularly in the Palestine Liberation Organization's early adoption of its goal of a democratic secular state in Palestine, we upheld a vision of a progressive society in which all peoples could live in peace, security, and prosperity under a regime of equal rights and mutual respect.

That was the vision that, in the early days of our movement, captured the imaginations of millions throughout the world.

Why is re-centering justice as our end goal a prescription for the ills we currently face, especially as we witness the Zionist colonizing juggernaut rolling forward, with nothing on the horizon to even slow its advance? Does it make sense to double down on justice and even expand our ambitions when we have failed to achieve justice in even a minimal form? Is it right to affirm tolerance and inclusion against the headwind of rising right-wing ethnic nationalism, in which Israel is ahead of the global curve by a decade or two?

These are serious questions. My instinct is that part of our current weakness is precisely that we have been too compromising on matters of principle. The result has been the internal division and deflation of our movement, and lesser international solidarity. Our soft power, to recall Richard Falk's phrase, can only be enhanced by adopting a broad vision of justice.

But invoking "justice" in the abstract is not enough. So here are seven facets or dimensions of justice that, to my mind, merit consideration. This list is provisional and not exhaustive.

The first is *original justice* – by this I mean that while a broader conception of justice is called for today than in the past, the original core rights of the Palestinian people remain the bedrock of a just resolution. It is the Palestinians who were the first and remain the primary victims of Zionism, and whose rights remain in most urgent need of restoration. We are building on, not discarding, earlier conceptions of justice.

I underscore here that I mean the entire Palestinian people, including the majority who are refugees living in internal or external exile and those who live as second-class citizens within Israel.

Early on, Palestinians recognized that justice for us could not be injustice for others, but there is a need to more fully elaborate a conception of what might be called *protective justice*. We would benefit by a compassionate declaration along the lines of South Africa's Freedom Charter outlining how our conception of justice also includes Israeli Jews, who will continue to inhabit Israel/Palestine.

Whether the land is shared in one state, two, or two dozen, we need a vision of a future society that respects and strives for justice for all. The more concrete we can be, the better – for example, in addressing the status and rights of secondary occupants (Israeli Jews) who currently inhabit former Palestinian homes, and to outline a process that treats them justly and with respect and dignity.

We also must think beyond the binary of Israeli Jews/Palestinian Arabs, which flattens and masks diversity on both sides. There are many considerations here, but the salient one to me involves Mizrahi Jews, who I would count as Zionism's second major category of victims. From the destabilization of their communities in the Arab world that Zionism caused, to the discrimination and racism those who settled in Israel have faced from Jews of Ashkenazi descent, Mizrahi Jews have suffered largely in obscurity. Mending their wounds will be a complex challenge and, in part, implicates regional considerations, to which I will return shortly.

South Africa provides us a model for thinking about other facets of justice as well. South Africans conducted a partially successful experiment in what is sometimes called *transitional justice.*

While our transition still lies ahead, we can start conceptualizing how we will deal with truth and reconciliation. There is scope for acknowledgments and apologies for suffering inflicted on multiple sides, including by Palestinians.

Post-apartheid South Africa, as you also doubtlessly know, is riven with problems of crime and deep social and economic inequalities. Many critics of the transition from apartheid trace these problems to the failure to consider questions of *social justice* in that transition.

Israel suffers acute income inequality, as became vividly apparent in the 2011 protest movement in Tel Aviv. The neoliberal policies of the Palestinian Authority have also exacerbated deep class divisions in the West Bank. Poverty rates in the Gaza Strip are terrible, due to the ruinous siege now in its tenth year, three major Israeli attacks, and nearly continuous low grade violence. Out of this, how do we not just end the Nakba, but also build a humane society in which any of us would be proud to live?

Gender and sexual preference justice, both Israeli and Palestinian societies, manifest patriarchy and sexual preference oppression in their specific ways. This is not just me importing my San Francisco values to Israel/Palestine. Rather, I take my cue from local feminists and queers. On the Palestinian side, women have long been expected to subordinate gender rights to national struggle, for no good reason. We must stand for gender and sexual preference justice everywhere, and now.

In a place where injustices against humans abound, it is easy to neglect damages to the natural environment. Gaza, as you no doubt have read, may well be unlivable from an environmental perspective as soon as 2020, according to some experts. So we must account at some level for *environmental justice*.

Israel has alternately plundered the occupied Palestinian territories of water or stone, and used them as dumping grounds for pollutants. Neither has the Palestinian Authority proved itself a responsible steward of the environment. Yet justice to the land, if we may call it that, is a matter of urgent concern to all life in the region.

This brings us to the last facet of justice I will address today, namely *regional justice*. Israel has inflicted harm in varying degrees on all of its neighbors at one time or another. Just to start, Israel cast hundreds of thousands of destitute refugees onto neighbors ill-equipped to absorb them. Arab societies were disfigured, robbed of vitality and diversity, by the loss of their Jewish communities following Israel's establishment. And while the circumstances of the departures of Mizrahi Jews from Arab countries varied widely, there is no doubt that some suffered grave injustices that should be acknowledged and rectified.

Is consideration of these multiple facets of justice premature? Possibly. But the more we flesh out the meaning of justice, the more we will ignite support and enthusiasm. We can offer the world the model of another Arab police state, or two, as the case may be; or one of an enlightened and just society, that fosters diversity and sustainability in our relationship to the natural environment. Which do you think is more likely to inspire support, and to mobilize people to action?

Now to the last part of my presentation, about the role of international law as a medium for accomplishing justice and whether it should include a principle of state illegitimacy.

It may surprise you to learn that I, an organizer of this conference, came here agnostic as to that question. Frankly, I doubt that international law currently lacks the tools to encourage justice in Israel/Palestine. Many liberation struggles, including the struggle against apartheid, have succeeded without a principle of state illegitimacy.

Here we have to be careful not to be bewitched by law's promise – not to expect law to outrun politics, and deliver victories that have not been earned on the field of political struggle. I say this because some of us may have high expectations, for example, of the International Criminal Court.

I recently visited the United States National Civil Rights Museum in Memphis, Tennessee, housed in the Lorraine Hotel, where the Reverend Martin Luther King was assassinated in 1968. I was struck in particular by a quote I read there from Bayard Rustin, a prominent strategist of the civil rights movement that said:

Unjust social laws and patterns do not change because supreme courts deliver just decisions ... Social progress comes from struggle: all freedom demands a price.

Rustin reminds us that courts make socially and politically progressive decisions only when forced to do so by a mobilized citizenry. This, I would argue, is just as true of international courts as it is of domestic courts. So we must be guarded in our expectations of what to expect from law.

This is far from saying, however, that international law is inconsequential. No South African official was ever tried under the International Convention on the Suppression and Punishment of the Crime of Apartheid, but its adoption by the United Nations General Assembly in 1973 was surely not an idle act. On the contrary, it dramatically expressed the moral outrage of a segment of the international community that helped to transform public discourse about South African apartheid. The same is true of Richard Falk's and Virginia Tilley's recent report on Israel's treatment of the Palestinian people as constituting the crime of apartheid – which is precisely why it has been officially suppressed.

Law may not deliver us salvation. We who work in the legal field must put our shoulders to the wheel along with others pushing in their own domains. In other words, if we effectively integrate the legal with other forms of struggle, justice will at least come a little closer.

The Tragic Interplay of International Law and Geopolitics

Richard Falk*

I   Palestine/Israel as Anomaly   153
II Against the Rising Tide of Anti-colonialism   159
III Establishing Israel Did Not Complete the Zionist Project   163
IV Some International Law Considerations   166
V   Concluding Comments   168

I   Palestine/Israel as Anomaly

The Israel/Palestine relationship can be partially appreciated – but only partially – as an unresolved remnant of the decolonizing struggles that took place in the period between 1945 and 1975. These struggles brought political independence and self-determination to almost all major colonized peoples throughout the Global South during the latter half of the 20th century, but not to the Palestinian people, regardless of whether their colonized status is associated with the Ottoman Empire, the British Empire, or Israel.[1] This failure is a historical anomaly that needs further exploration. Of course, it is obvious that the connections between Europe, world Jewry, and the Holocaust were a distinctive conjuncture of forces that helps explain why Palestine never achieved

---

*   Albert G. Milbank Professor of International Law Emeritus, Princeton University; author of *Palestine: The Legitimacy of Hope* (2017). Based on keynote address at conference, "International Law & the State of Israel: Legitimacy, Exceptionalism, Responsibility," 31 March–2 April, 2017, University of Cork, Cork, Ireland.

1   There are also a series of captive nations that are controversial byproducts of what might be called incomplete decolonization and failures to implement norms of self-determination. Among the many examples, generally contested, are the struggles of the Kurds, Tamils, Kashmiris, and Tibetans. Palestine stands out as a major country, bisected by the establishment of Israel in 1948, which has been unable to achieve self-determination for its indigenous population for a series of complex reasons.

political independence and why the Palestinian people have been denied the right of self-determination for more than seven decades.

The Israel/Palestine relationship has evolved into a struggle between two unevenly endowed national movements pursuing contradictory claims of sovereign rights and nationalist supremacy in the same territory, with one movement exerting predominant, prolonged, discriminatory, and punitive control over the other. As a result, the struggle needs to be considered as a form of asymmetric conflict. Such a structuring of the conflict has several normative implications that have affected the nature of the Israeli state as it emerged and evolved since its establishment in 1948.

It also is to be noted that Israel arose out of a specific category of colonial projects, as constituted by its character as a 'settler-colonial state'. The settler nature of Israel is at the very core of the Zionist movement since its inception in Europe toward the end of the 19th century. The language and goal of settlement was tied to the promise of a Jewish homeland from its inception, the feasibility of which depended on achieving a certain density of Jewish presence in the territory then known as Palestine that did not exist when the Balfour Declaration was made in 1917.[2]

Unlike other colonial projects, the Zionist movement connected its ideological commitment and claim to the particular land of Palestine on a basis that emphasized the depth of *connection* rather than the length of *presence*. Palestine was affirmed by Zionists as the sacred and necessary resting place, sanctuary, and 'promised land' of the Jewish people.[3] As such, it could not, under any conditions be given an alternate geographic and national destiny. The ethical and political complexity of this Zionist undertaking during its early stages arose due to the overwhelming Arab majority presence in the land.[4] This complicating feature surfaced as soon as the vision of a Jewish Homeland

---

2 It is illuminating that Jewish immigrants to Palestine prior to 1948 were called 'settlers', as are those Israelis who establish unlawful settlements on occupied Palestinian territory since 1967. In some usages, especially in Europe, both categories are referred to as 'colonists' and 'colonies'.

3 In Jewish religious ritual, Israel is 'promised' by God, thus transcending and circumventing any secularly based claim of entitlement, including contrary self-determination rights asserted on behalf of the territorial majority population.

4 Such a complexity was accentuated by the fact that the early Zionist leadership was committed not only to establishing a Jewish state, but a *democratic* Jewish state. As such, Zionism was always faced with the primary challenge of reducing the large Arab majority to a subordinate minority, and the secondary challenge of devising ways to disguise privileging of Jews over non-Jews without seeming to violate notions of equality and the dignity of the individual.

began to gain political momentum a century ago.[5] This awkward reality posed a formidable challenge. In practical terms, it meant that the Arab population would have to be pacified and subjugated, dispossessed and displaced, and/or exterminated, while at the same time the Jewish demographic presence was being increased by all possible means.[6] It is a matter of historical experience that all settler-colonial projects, if enduringly successful, rely on one or more of these instruments of control over the indigenous or native population.[7] Over the course of its existence, Israel has created an elaborate structure of subjugation and dispossession as its main instruments of control, although given a special character by the deliberate fragmentation of the Palestinian population into distinct domains of control.[8]

This unfolding of Palestine's modern history can also be explained by reflecting upon the truly tragic legacy of both world wars so far as the Palestinian people are concerned.[9] World War I gave rise to Britain according its colonial blessings upon an early version of the Zionist Project in the principal form of the Balfour Declaration issued even before it managed to gain control itself over Palestine in the aftermath of the Ottoman collapse. World War II continued and accelerated this dynamic in new forms, severely victimizing the Palestinian people by inflicting mass suffering remembered and observed by Palestinians as the *Nakba* (or 'catastrophe'), centering on a process of violent dispossession and displacement on a scale comparable to what the Jews

---

5 It is convenient to associate the inception of political momentum of the Zionist Project with the issuance of the Balfour Declaration in 1917.
6 A scholarly account of this Zionist push to encourage Jewish settlement in Israel is one of the many achievements of Thomas Suarez, State of Terror: How Terrorism Created Modern Israel (2017) [*hereinafter* Suarez].
7 In rare instances, the settler community is neither expelled nor fully effective in subjugating the indigenous population. South Africa is the most outstanding example of achieving relative stability by way of reconciliation between the native population and the settler community. In effect, political apartheid was dismantled, while the social and economic interests of the white minority was maintained. Whether this kind of accommodation will stand the tests of time remains to be seen, and undoubtedly hinges on whether the material conditions of the African majority can be significantly improved.
8 This fragmentation as an element of control is explored by Richard Falk and Virginia Tilley in their report submitted to the UN Economic and Social Commission for Western Asia (ESCWA), released on March 15, 2017 under the title, "Israeli Practices Towards the Palestinian People and the Question of Apartheid" [*hereinafter* ECSWA Report]. The text of the report was removed from the ESCWA website by order of the UN Secretary-General, but is available via the website of Southern Illinois University Carbondale, Open SIUC.
9 This tragic legacy should also be extended to the Middle East as a whole, and can be traced to Anglo-French colonial diplomacy culminating in the originally secret Sykes-Picot Agreement of 1916.

themselves had experienced in Europe during the Nazi period, although without the accompaniment of German genocide.[10] This dynamic associated with the Nakba as both event and ongoing process has resulted in the continuing collective victimization of the Palestinian people for seventy years with no end in sight.

In the background of this Palestinian ordeal is a haunting question, "Why did this historical anomaly take place?" That is, why did the Palestinians, almost alone among colonized people, not gain their freedom, achieve their basic rights, when all other societies in the Middle East, and elsewhere, for better and worse, became sovereign states admitted to membership in the United Nations (UN) and treated as legitimate independent participants in international society.

And not only was there this Palestinian failure to gain political independence, but there was the related opposite and counter-current phenomenon of Israel being able in the midst of global decolonization to establish and sustain an expanding state that has become over time even able to secure a political enclave of tactical and opportunistic acceptance in the wider Arab World.[11] As Israeli military analysts agree, the only genuine current international threat to Israeli security is posed by some revival of mass resistance by Palestinians living under occupation in conjunction with an enlarged and more militant global solidarity movement.[12] In other words, at least for now, Israel's security is not threatened by armed resistance or hostile military attacks by neighbors as it was in the early period of its existence, roughly 1948–1973.

An obvious, yet instructive, realist explanation for this historical anomaly is that respect for Palestinian rights and wellbeing contradicted the fundamental goals, military capabilities, and diplomatic skills of the emergent Zionist project, and continue to do so more than one hundred years after the issuance of the Balfour Declaration. As long as Palestinians were and are seen as standing

---

10   Although it should be noted that Zionist doctrine and practice neither did not rest explicitly on an overt racist rationale, nor did it ever officially embrace genocidal tactics or advocacy. But *see* Ilan Pappe, Ethnic Cleansing of Palestine (2006); *see also* Edward Said, The Politics of Dispossession: The Struggle for Palestinian Self-Determination, 1969–1994 (1994).

11   *See* Jeff Halper's important partial explanation of this extraordinary Israeli counter-historical success by reference to the Israeli arms industry, augmented by claims of field tested weaponry, and counterinsurgency experience, as providing the basis for a robust arms diplomacy that has created networks of dependency with more than one hundred countries. Jeff Halper, The War Against the People: Israel, the Palestinians and Global Pacification (2015).

12   For assessments of Palestinian prospects, *see* Ali Abunimah, The Battle for Justice in Palestine (2014); and Richard Falk, Palestine the Legitimacy of Hope (2014).

in the way of achieving a Jewish state that extends to the whole of historic or biblically envisioned Palestine, the aspirations of the Palestinian people will be viewed as an obstacle to the completion of the Zionist project in its post-Israeli phase. As such, Palestinian rights must be denied, and trampled upon as a supposedly necessary dimension of continuing Israeli state-building and territorial expansion that will continue as long as the Zionist leadership retains its maximalist commitment.[13] There is confusion about this 'red line' as the Israeli government has on several occasions seemed to accept the United States (US)-led international consensus in support of the two-state solution. Viewed more critically, Israel's public diplomacy on solving the conflict is more accurately viewed as a tactical and public relations international imperative that is offset by taking a variety of steps to ensure that no viable and genuinely sovereign Palestinian state will ever be established on *Eretz Israel*, or historic Palestine.

The weight of scholarly research appears to confirm the still somewhat contested conclusion that the dominant Zionist approach has been to establish a Jewish beachhead state within a part of Palestine as a first step, and then continuously agitate and press to extend ever further the contours of its geographic reality until the dream of Israel as a fully realized and ethnically pure Jewish state is achieved.[14] While doing this, it seems to have been deemed tactically necessary and politically effective to disguise the full extent of this strategic plan to avoid an international pushback, and even to quell a critical backlash from non-Zionist Jews and liberal secular Zionists, especially in the Jewish diaspora. In this fundamental respect, the Palestinian people have been long victimized by what might be identified as their 'negative exceptionalism'. By this, I mean that distinctive religio-historical-political circumstances, location, and geopolitical priorities combined to deprive the Palestinian people of attaining their national goals despite the collapse of European colonialism the world over, including throughout the Middle East.

To bring the understanding into sharper relief, the fact that the Zionist movement decided that the fulfillment of their commitment to create a Jewish homeland could only be satisfied in biblically sanctified Palestine was a crucial contributor to this process.[15] Another contributing factor relates to European

---

13 The assassination of Yitzhak Rabin in 1995 was a warning from within Zionist circles that any move toward establishing a Palestinian state on biblically sacred Jewish land was totally unacceptable.

14 *See* Suarez; and Victor Kattan, From Coexistence to Conquest: International Law and the Origins of the Arab-Israeli Conflict, 1891–1949 (2009) [*hereinafter* Kattan].

15 As is well-known, other possible sites for the Jewish homeland were considered and rejected at the early stages of Zionism in deference to the symbolic and religious association of Jewish tradition with Palestine.

anti-Semitism in the nineteenth and twentieth centuries, climaxing with the Holocaust, generating European and North American sympathy and support for this Zionist project (including ironically among many anti-Semites), as well as lending an urgent impetus to Jewish emigration to Israel. This sympathy and support gained further political traction after 1945 due to the strong feelings of guilt among the liberal democracies of Europe and North America, especially the widespread awareness that these governments had done far too little to oppose the Nazi genocide being carried out against Jews, as well as from Zionist pressures to discourage Jews in Europe from remaining or emigrating to the US. From this vantage point, the least that the victorious allies could do was accept the emergence of a Jewish state in Palestine even if it involved cruelly overriding the legitimate grievances, aspirations, and concerns of the indigenous Palestinian population. In this sense, Western hegemonic thinking after World War II remained tainted by civilizational racism even as European colonialism was proving itself to be a spent force throughout Asia and Africa.[16]

The critical interplay between international law and geopolitics exerted a strong influence on the formation and maintenance of the Israeli state. It is an inevitably complicated and contested narrative, made more so by twists and turns through time. This complexity arises, in large part, from the relevance and plausibility of competing normative logics that have varied in their influence as the narrative has unfolded. What this has meant as a practical matter is that the normative perspectives of international law and international morality have been challenged and disregarded, and generally overwhelmed, by normative logics associated with geopolitics and associated historical and religious claims of right.[17]

Further, confusion has arisen as discussion has become blurred by strong advocacy of diverse ideological positions under contradictory historical circumstances. For instance, the Balfour Declaration at the time of its utterance a hundred years ago did not violate prevailing norms as colonial prerogatives that were in 1917 embedded in international law and state practice. The Declaration was in the spirit of paternalistic international norms that supposedly showcased the moral superiority of Western civilization, and was only controversial to the extent that some in Britain thought that such a maneuver might complicate wider British objectives in the Arab World. This was reinforced by the

---

16   The pertinence of Edward W. Said's *Orientalism* (1978) seems almost too obvious to mention.
17   This question of interacting normative logics deserves wider exploration and discussion in the context of the Palestinian struggle, as well as from the perspective of the Zionist project.

acceptance, without notable friction, of the Balfour pledge by the League of Nations in its establishment of the Palestine Mandate under British administrative authority.

II   Against the Rising Tide of Anti-colonialism

Such an overtly colonialist initiative had become inconceivable after World War II.[18] However, in the aftermath of World War I although the legitimacy of colonialism was facing growing international pressures, its legality and diplomatic impact was not seriously challenged. As a result, the European colonial powers successfully pursued their ambitions in shaping the postwar regional order of the Middle East, but not nearly as much as would have been the case fifty years earlier when the colonialist undertaking was such an established aspect of world order as to be uncontested in dominant diplomatic venues. What then preoccupied world politics were inter-colonial rivalries.

There were three main sources of opposition to the legitimacy of colonialism as emergent after World War I: first, the anti-colonialism arising out of the Russian Revolution, and articulated powerfully by Lenin and Trotsky; secondly, the commitment of American diplomacy under the leadership of Woodrow Wilson to 'self-determination' of those peoples in the Arab world previously subject to Ottoman rule, which encompassed the population of Palestine; thirdly, the growing nationalist consciousness of colonized peoples that was beginning to give rise to significant resistance and anti-colonial movements. Against this background of friction and ambivalence the Mandates System was devised as a hegemonic instrument of international law, masking the persistence of colonialist outcomes while still acknowledging the impact of new social forces relevant to the normative evolution of world order in an anti-colonial direction, but still incapable of successfully challenging the de facto realities of colonial governance.

European colonial maneuvers underlay this special compromise struck between appearance and reality after World War I. Two such initiatives were particularly relevant to the Palestinian narrative as shaped by British colonial interests. Above all, the Sykes-Picot Agreement of 1916 gave Britain a favorable

---

18   Maybe 'inconceivable' is too strong. After all, Teresa May, the current British prime minister, proposes to celebrate the centenary of the Balfour Declaration, an initiative applauded by Netanyahu. This refurbishing of the colonial mentality, along with an accompanying indifference to the suffering imposed on the Palestinian people in the ensuing century, will undoubtedly be disguised by treating the Balfour Declaration as a humanitarian and cultural initiative that resulted in a robust 'democratic' state adhering to Western values.

prospect that its strategic interests in safeguarding the Suez Canal and its overland trade routes to Asia would be recognized by giving the British Crown colonial title in post-Ottoman Palestine. The Balfour Declaration performed a complementary role for Britain. By giving the fledgling Zionist movement a normative and operational leg to stand upon in Palestine, the British could rely on its characteristic divide and rule approach to colonial governance as well as induce critical Jewish support in several key countries engaged on the Allied side in World War I.[19]

In the case of the Middle East, and Palestine in particular, the British had most opportunistically acknowledged and manipulated nationalist aspirations by promising Arab leaders independence and sovereignty in exchange for joining the fight against the Ottoman Empire.[20] Although the promise was being cynically broken behind the scenes, even while the fighting continued, the betrayal of these earlier expectations of Arab independence later served to legitimate Zionist and nationalist movements of resistance to colonial and European political arrangements as well as to underscore the illegitimacy of continued colonial rule in the region. As is widely understood, Sykes-Picot was never implemented as it was originally envisioned, that is, in an overt colonialist format, but was rather reconfigured in a disguised and superficially tutelary form presented to the world as an idealistic project known as the Mandates System. In effect, the persisting realities of colonial rule were hidden beneath the mantle of a weak trusteeship-style arrangement supposedly based on the temporary administering mandatory power accepting a responsibility to the League of Nations to prepare administered peoples supposedly not able to stand on their own feet for eventual independence – an obligation heralded as 'a sacred trust of civilization'.[21]

It was in this context that the Israeli state-building project began to be planned and developed, matured, and adapted. Prior to the establishment of Israel during the early mandate period, the Zionist political community was incubated by British colonial motives. But as time passed, tactics and policy priorities shifted, and the Zionist leadership came to regard the British presence in Palestine as an obstacle standing in the way of establishing a sovereign Jewish state in Palestine. Zionist ingenuity, unscrupulousness, and incredible

---

19 *See* Jonathon Schneer, The Balfour Declaration: The Origins of the Arab-Israeli Conflict (2012) [*hereinafter* Schneer].

20 *See* the Sir Henry McMahon-Ibn Ali Hussein correspondence as discussed in Schneer, 62–74; Kattan.

21 *See* Covenant of the League of Nations, art. 22, which sets forth a paternalist rationale for the imposition of the mandates system upon the former Middle East territories of the Ottoman Empire.

dedication were all evident during the pre-state years, especially in the last decade of the British mandate.[22] Zionist priorities in this pre-state Israel were two-fold: first, a feverish all-out effort to increase the density of the Jewish presence in Palestine so as to mitigate the unfavorable demographic balance; and second, to make the costs of governance for Britain so high in Palestine as to prompt its early withdrawal from the scene, clearing the way for a show of superior force by Zionist militias in relation to the majority Arab population.

During the mandate period, the Palestinian people (or the Arab majority inhabitants) did not enjoy or articulate any international right of self-determination as against the quasi-colonial rule to which they were subjected. The Balfour Declaration contains a forgotten proviso purporting to reassure the Palestinian people by stating "that nothing shall be done which may prejudice the civil and religious rights of existing non-Jewish communities in Palestine". Of course, this hollow promise embedded in the Balfour language was no more than a gesture, which Britain never showed the slightest interest in upholding. Rather, in keeping with its colonial practice, Britain adopted a divide-and-rule approach that initially supported Jewish immigration and Zionist claims so as to create useful leverage against the Arabs. This pattern increasingly worried the indigenous majority population of Palestine, giving rise to early signs of Palestinian opposition to Zionism and to the dilemmas facing British administration. In this regard, self-determination played no direct role in the national movement leading to the emergence of the state of Israel, which rested its initial claims to a Jewish homeland on this colonial initiative backed up by the Zionist sense of religious entitlement to the land. A few years later, these early Zionist aspirations for a Jewish homeland were given the legitimating blessings of the international community through the inclusion of Palestine in the Mandate System and of the Balfour Declaration in the Mandate Agreement between Britain and the League of Nations. Although from the perspective of the present such formal acknowledgements seem to defy the prevailing normative logic of self-determination of a people, as of the 1920s such a step was seen as a 'progressive' move that seemed to envision an end to the colonial era, but without a time horizon.

It should be remembered that several earlier major settler-colonial projects in the United States, Canada, Australia, and New Zealand had broken free from their British colonial origins by varying means to establish their own sovereign states. In each of these instances, the native pre-settler population was displaced, dispossessed, cleansed, subjugated, and even, in some instances, exterminated in the course of the process by which these societies sought their own

---

22   *See* Suarez, for a detailed account of Zionist tactics in this pre-state period.

national independence and exclusive sovereign control over those territories. In this regard, the Zionist revolt against British governance has a trajectory in some ways similar to these earlier examples of settler-colonial nationalism. The Zionist project also unfolded in two stages: first, a preliminary validation of settlement and privilege by adopting the colonialist identity; and, secondly, a revolt against colonial rule so as to achieve independent statehood followed by the expulsion and subjugation of the native pre-colonial population. Of course, in Palestine, the colonial nature of the British presence was somewhat qualified by its mandate trappings.

Despite the record of abusing native communities, each of these settler polities were admitted into international society as fully sovereign and legitimate states with no objections when they claimed and achieved independence. It should also be remembered that the normative context at the time meant that there were no operative international legal or moral constraints prohibiting the abuse of native peoples and disregard of their claimed sovereign rights although, on occasion, hidden behind unenforced treaties with settler representatives and exploitative land purchases and acquisitions. Instead, the normative atmosphere reflected moralizing racist claims to the effect that colonization was a matter of the 'white man's burden,' the civilizing mission of the West, and the manifest destiny of European territorial expansion. In fact, the dispossession, displacement, and erasure of native populations was actually claimed to be an expression of the forward progress of history. The Zionist movement, which in its early phase employed such rationalizations of civilizational superiority, adopted in the post-colonial period more modernizing idioms, publicizing its positive impact on Palestine by claims of 'making the desert bloom'. Such claims were also assertions of an invidious contrast with traditions of Arab land management as backward and passive. Implicitly, this meant that dispossessing and displacing a large proportion of the indigenous inhabitants was part of the progressive march of history as interpreted through a modernist optic.

What is striking about the success of Zionism is that it effectively realized its colonialist ambitions while swimming against a strong tide of history. To be sure, Zionism never validated its undertaking by invoking its colonialist credentials alone, but relied for its primary justification on Jewish religious and ethnic destiny associated with the long suppressed connections of the Jewish people as a people with the 'promised' land of Israel. Yet the early articulation and recognition of these claims depended on British colonial mentality and support for its initial international acceptance, and more generally on European ideas of superiority – ideas that completely disregarded the political will and national rights of the Arab majority population.

III Establishing Israel Did Not Complete the Zionist Project

The distinctive nature of the Zionist claim to statehood is clearly set forth in the 1948 declaration establishing the state of Israel, which provides that:

> *The Land of Israel was the birthplace of the Jewish people. Here their spiritual and political identity was shaped. Here they first attained to statehood, created cultural values of national and universal significance and gave to the world the eternal Book of Books.*
>
> *After being forcibly exiled from their land, the people kept faith with it throughout their Dispersion and never ceased to pray and hope for their return to it and for the restoration in it of their political freedom.*
>
> *Impelled by this historical and traditional attachment, Jews strove in every successive generation to re-establish themselves in their ancient homeland. In recent decades they have returned in their masses.*

Note that in this Declaration there is no reference to international law or the principle of self-determination, or even to an ethical claim of the urgency of creating what might be called a 'Jewish sanctuary state'. The legitimacy of Israel formally premised on religious roots and the singular attachment of Jews to the land of Palestine as evidenced by tradition and a continued Jewish presence however small until the twentieth century. The credibility of the movement for Jewish statehood was further validated by successive waves of Jewish immigration dating back to the 1920s that managed to raise the demographic profile of Jews in Palestine, while still falling far short of achieving a majority.

Another feature of Israeli state formation that is distinctive, although bearing minor resemblances to the emergence of such states as Pakistan and Northern Ireland, involves a decidedly ambivalent attitude toward the colonial power. The Zionist Project during the Mandate period shifted its primary goal from the possibility of a homeland in British controlled Palestine to the necessity of establishing a fully sovereign Jewish state in Palestine. This shift required either the consent of the British or their expulsion. In this pursuit, Zionism indirectly rejected the approach taken in Palestine by its original benefactor, Great Britain, and in the late 1930s began to mount a concerted violent campaign to make Palestine ungovernable by Britain at acceptable costs, and even to threaten public order in Britain itself with terrorist acts so as to make British withdrawal the only sensible course of action. In the face of this coordinated armed and diplomatic resistance to its Mandatory role, Britain itself modified its approach to governance of Palestine, favorably entertaining the idea of partition as it almost always did when British colonial strategy of 'divide and rule' was being superseded by an end game that effectively challenged colonial rule.[23]

As the Zionist opposition to British governance gained momentum, and Britain found itself greatly weakened by World War II, Britain turned to the fledgling UN with a recommendation of partition, which was then fleshed out within the UN, presented to the General Assembly, and adopted in 1947 by a majority vote in the form of UN General Assembly Resolution 181. This proposed territorial partition of Palestine was vigorously opposed by all of the Arab countries represented in the UN as well as by other non-Western states.

It has never been clearly enough argued that this international partition arrangement was incompatible with the prevailing normative idea then embedded in international law. From a legal perspective decolonization implied a sovereign state within the full extent of its colonial borders with whatever distinct ethnicities were present to be incorporated on a formal basis of equality. The British approach adopted by the UN meant that a colony would be divided as a result of international decision-making rather than reflecting either the internal preferences of the majority resident population or the coercive secession of a captive minority as in India.[24]

It is somewhat perverse to condemn the Palestinians due to their rejection of partition, and praise Zionist leadership for its supposedly realistic acceptance of partition. Recent scholarship, most authoritatively in Thomas Suarez's book, *State of Terror: How Terrorism Created Modern Israel*, documents beyond a reasonable doubt that the Zionist acceptance of partition was a cynical and intelligently expedient and tactical move designed to advance a step further toward their eventual and never abandoned goal of Greater Israel.[25] Contrary to public protestations of accepting the UN plan, Zionist leaders never saw their action as anything more than an intermediate and pragmatic stage in an ongoing Zionist quest for a Jewish state that corresponded in size with the imagined, historically highly uncertain boundaries of biblical Palestine or 'the land of Israel'.

The public acceptance of partition was insincere, and could not obscure the Zionist resolve to minimize the Arab presence in the territorial polity under its control so as to advance the plan to become a 'Jewish state' in the whole of the country. This meant that the Zionists ultimately regarded the territorial delimitations of partition as temporary. It has become clear that at all stages

---

23 *See* discussion of partition proposals under British mandate and at the United Nations in: Kattan, 146–168.
24 *See* Radha Kumar, Making Peace with Partition (2005).
25 *See* Suarez.

of the conflict the minimally acceptable 'final' boundaries that would be acceptable to the dominant tendency in the Zionist leadership would encompass all or nearly all of historic Palestine, and by some grandiose Zionist visions extending beyond modern Palestine to include Jordan and parts of Lebanon. Since its inception, Israel has always avoided indicating the boundaries of the state in its official maps. From an international law standpoint, and even an international politics perspective, we can ask why such claims have been effectively pursued over so many decades while colonialism as a whole was in free fall collapse.

The main answer seems to rest in the agency of hard power, reinforced by a very skillful deployment of soft power assets, including geopolitical leverage and the manipulation of international public opinion, thereby shaping the mainstream discourse. Zionist military forces were extremely well trained and equipped in a manner that allowed them to control combat zones during their struggle for statehood, and subsequently when confronting hostile Arab neighbors. This record of militarily achieved political victories was also contrary to the historical tide. Settler colonies that had not completely sidelined indigenous populations, put up a strong fight against nationalist movements as in Indochina and Algeria, but eventually were defeated, not by superior military forces, but by nationalist perseverance, and the settler option to retreat to the metropole. The psycho-politics of Israeli settler colonialism is different from others. For there is no home country that could preserve Jewish national coherence and there persists a belief among Zionists in a sacred Jewish connection with the land of Palestine that both bestows an exclusive right to Jewish statehood and establishes a contradictory hierarchy between the opposing normative logics of Jews and Arabs that can be resolved only on the battlefield; a predicate of national tragedy for the losing side, or for both sides, if the struggle ends in a stalemate.[26] To reinforce this show of Israeli resolve, Zionist militants often refer to a 'Masada Complex' suggesting that Israelis would sooner die than either surrender or quit the land.[27]

As suggested, Israel defied self-determination norms by initially gaining statehood via the instrumentality of partition, which was rejected by the Palestinian Arabs as it had been when proposed by the British Royal

---

26   The Jewish normative logic is based on biblical entitlement as reinforced by moral necessity in the aftermath of the Holocaust, while the Arab normative logic is premised on indigenous presence over many generations.
27   The so-called 'Masada Complex' is an Israeli reference to the historical incident in which an estimated 960 Jews committed suicide rather than surrender to the Roman Empire in approximately 74 AD in a battle fought on the Masada cliffs. The reference is invoked to demonstrate the absolute resolve of Israel to defend its sovereignty.

Commission of Inquiry, also known as the 'Peel Commission', in 1937. In reality, neither the Zionists nor the Palestinians wanted partition, each wanted to establish a state encompassing the entire territory. The Zionists were more sophisticated and calculated in their approach and far better connected with Western elite sources of geopolitical influence, finally agreeing to accept the partition conception embodied in the UN Plan, then taking full and irreversible advantage of the Palestinian rejection, their weak national movement, and much inferior military capabilities even as abetted by the intervening armies of Arab neighbors. The net result was a kind of de facto partition, which was actualized around the armistice borders of 1949, expanding Israeli territorial control from around 56% as conferred by the UN plan to 78% of Palestine. But even this 78% was not accepted by Israel as its final borders, although these borders – the so-called Green Line – have been accepted by the international community in the form of UN Security Council Resolution 242, which was the foundation on which the two-state solution was built. In 1988, the Palestine Liberation Organization (PLO) also formally endorsed this approach.[28]

The PLO dropped its objection to the existence of Israel and proposed normalization and legitimation, provided Israel would withdraw to the Green Line. This general outline of a peaceful solution was also accepted by the Arab League in its 2002 peace initiative, subsequently twice modified in Israel's favor, initially in 2007, and then in 2014, in response to diplomatic pressure exerted by John Kerry acting on behalf of the Obama presidency in response to Israeli demands resting on alleged security requirements.

IV Some International Law Considerations

The Mandate System was internationally legalized and legitimized by being inserted into the Covenant of the League of Nations, and more concretely in a Mandate Agreement for Palestine.[29] At the time, a Palestinian right of self-determination was not even firmly recognized as a moral or political right, much less as a legal right, and was not mentioned in the Covenant. By the time the UN Charter was drafted, the right of self-determination was at least acknowledged as an aspirational political right in the ambiguous and vague language of Article 1(2) devoted to UN Purposes: "[t]o develop friendly

---

28   This dynamic of deliberate fragmentation of the Palestinian people is treated as the main feature of Israeli apartheid as analyzed in the ESCWA study. *See also* Richard Falk, Palestine's Horizon: Toward a Just Peace 44, 139 (2017).

29   *See* League of Nations Covenant, art. 22.

relations among nations based on respect for the principle of equal rights and self-determination of peoples." Such a formulation did not pretend that the right of self-determination had attained the status of law or even that its articulation in this form was incompatible with the continuation of the European colonial system. The legalizing of the right of self-determination was a subsequent development that came gradually, as expressed by way of a series of UN General Assembly resolutions and through the cascade of successful anti-colonial struggles in the 1960s and 70s.[30] It was authoritatively incorporated into international law in the form of UN General Assembly Resolution 2625, entitled Declaration of Principles of International Law Concerning Friendly Relations and Cooperation in Accordance with the Charter of the UN.[31] Self-determination was deemed one of seven principles providing the international law foundation for the conduct of relations among sovereign states in an ideologically polarized world. The substance of self-determination was spelled out in the body of the resolution, being constrained by the proviso that the right of self-determination could not be validly interpreted as "authorizing or encouraging" any action to break up any existing state provided only that existing states were obliged to respect the principle of self-determination – which really meant little more than that colonial claims were no longer legitimate from the perspective of international law.

Self-determination as a legal right is authoritatively set forth in common Article 1(1) of the two human rights covenants adopted for ratification in 1966, which reads as follows: "All peoples have the right of self-determination. By virtue of that right they freely determine their political status and freely pursue their economic, social and cultural development." Not only is the legal status of self-determination confirmed; the right of self-determination has ascended the normative ladder to become the right of rights, the precondition for the exercise of other rights.[32]

The formation of the Israeli state is premised on the initial legitimacy and effectiveness attaching to colonial policies as of the early decades of the 20th

---

30   Give citations of important UN resolutions (in Catalonia Report).
31   See G.A. Res. 2625 (XXV), Declaration of Principles of International Law Concerning Friendly Relations and Co-Operation of States in Accordance with the Charter of the United Nations, U.N. Doc. A/Res/25/2625 (Oct. 24, 1970); incorporating the principle of self-determination as one six guiding principles of international law during the Cold War period. See also Final Act of the Conference on Security and Cooperation in Europe, adopted 1 August 1975.
32   This legal status is also confirmed by the International Court of Justice in its Advisory Opinion in Western Sahara, Advisory Opinion, 1975 I.C.J. Rep. 12 (Oct. 16), on self-determination case; as reaffirmed Legal Consequences of the Construction of a Wall in the Occupied Palestinian Territory, 2004 I.C.J. Rep. 136 (July 9).

century, allowing the Zionist movement to augment Jewish settlement even in the face of Palestinian displacement and the clear intentions of Zionism to settle for nothing less than a state. Here is where competing normative logics complicate the story. Zionists, although tactically willing to moderate the public enunciation of goals at each stage of state formation and development, predominantly relied on biblical and historical arguments for their animating claims and motivating support among diasporic Jews.

The 19th century Zionist project would have long ago vanished from the scene, likely discounted as one more utopian example of 'messianic nationalism' if it had not acquired political traction as a result of a combination of factors: the early encouragement given by the issuance of the Balfour Declaration; Zionist diplomatic maneuvers abetted by violence, a concerted terrorist campaign within Palestine against the British and less so, against the Arabs, and internationally; and most of all, due to various effects during the 1930s of the persecution of Jews in Europe that reached its genocidal climax during the closing years of World War II. These contextual factors were reinforced by European and American support for the establishment and security of Israel.

Later on, Israel's unexpected military prowess – expressed both in conventional forms of combat and via counterterrorist warfare – managed to align its ambitions with its capabilities and allowed it to achieve security.[33] It is this tactical flexibility and ingenuity that has allowed Israel to defy the odds, and produce a series of outcomes that accord with principles of effectiveness, undergirding the realist view of international legality and legitimacy. As such, statehood is a factual condition, essentially outside the domain of law or morality.

V   Concluding Comments

In reviewing this history of the emergence of Israel in Palestine, we take particular note of the tension between competing normative logics, and the degree to which the political outcome reflects, above all, military effectiveness and geopolitical primacy. In other words, adherents of Zionism used diplomatic skill and fashioned a nationalist movement to create the conditions under which they claimed statehood in 1948 and realized Israel's admission to the

---

33   *See* Timothy Snyder, Black Earth: The Holocaust as History and Warning (2015); for valuable insight into the development of Zionist military capabilities in collaboration with an anti-Semitic Polish Government that regarded a Jewish homeland in Palestine as a desirable way to diminish the Jewish presence in Europe.

UN as a legitimate state. As with the British who gave Zionism its initial legitimating claim in the Balfour Declaration, but then gradually became the enemy of Zionist ambition, so with Israel and the UN. Initially, admission to membership in the UN was a major diplomatic victory for Israel. Later when the UN served as a vehicle for demanding implementation of Palestinian rights and censuring Israel for their denial, the UN became a biased organization to be delegitimized to the extent possible. UN-bashing has been an early signature issue of the US Republican congress and the Trump presidency, and yet this is not a departure from the approach adopted by all American presidents over the course of the last half-century. At the same time, in the spirit of double-coding, Israel does its utmost to gain influence and enhance its international stature within the UN and is now even competing for term membership in the UN Security Council.

What do the evolving normative logics in the present historical context tell about the future of Israel/Palestine? If the analysis is correct, then so long as Israel's military matrix of control over the Palestinians is sustained and reinforced by geopolitical support, Israeli dynamics of expansionism will continue until the full extent of the purported biblical entitlement is absorbed by Israel. This dynamic will necessarily be coupled with the denial of Palestinian rights, above all, the right of self-determination and return. Whether a growing global civil society solidarity movement exerting delegitimizing pressures through the 'Boycott, Divestment and Sanctions' campaign is sufficiently persuasive to alter these expectations is highly uncertain at this point. The challenge to those supporting the Palestinian struggle is to change the legitimacy climate sufficiently to induce important countries to support meaningful sanctions against Israel. Only in this way can the geopolitical balance be sufficiently altered to induce Israel to join the quest for a just resolution of Palestinian claims.

We do know that persevering national movements have generally prevailed over militarily superior forces during the latter stages of the struggle against European colonial rule. The question posed is whether Israel is an exception to this trend because of its governmental, military, paramilitary, diplomatic ingenuity, psycho-political mentality of unconditional commitment, and absolute ideological claim of right and of necessity. So far, Israel has successfully defied the decolonizing trend, while being perceived in the West as a normal, legitimate state that is not viewed as part of the unfinished business of the anti-colonial movement. At this point, acknowledging context and evolution, delegitimizing challenges are principally directed at Israel's policies and practices, having moved away from its existence as a state. In this regard, as of the present, both peoples can be seen from the perspective of international law to have mutually valid claims of self-determination. The question confronting all concerned with peace and justice is whether these overlapping claims of self-determination can be sufficiently reconciled to allow the two peoples to live together on the basis of equality.

From an international law perspective, does legality continue to reflect the asymmetric hard power realities of the Israel/Palestine relationship or will it yield to the soft power leverage arising from Palestinian grievances and legitimacy claims. The unraveling of this dynamic in coming years will be initially shaped by political developments internal and external to the disputed territory of Israel/Palestine, and only after the political struggle has been resolved will a legal framework be stabilized. If Israelis prevail, then the present apartheid structures will indefinitely govern the relations of Jews and Palestinians. If Palestinians prevail, then it is likely that modalities of coexistence based on either separation or integration will govern the political future of the two peoples. The peace envisioned here presupposes the *prior* dismantling of Israeli apartheid structures now in place to ensure the stability of Israel as a Jewish state confronted by Palestinian resistance.[34]

---

34 For the full elaboration of argument that Israel should be viewed as an apartheid state from the perspective of international law, *see* Falk & Tilley, ESCWA Report.

Settler-colonial and Anti-colonial Legalities in Palestine

Markus Gunneflo*

I   Introduction   171
II   Positive Law: Disciplining Means and Reifying the Ends of the State   174
III IHL and the 1967 Occupation   176
IV   International Law and the 1948 *Nakba*   181
V   Anti-colonial Legalities: The Prohibition of Apartheid   185
VI   Conclusion   187

I   Introduction

In May 2013, the conference *Law and Politics: Options and Strategies of International Law for the Palestinian People* was held at Birzeit University. The aim was to "examine the currently dominant international law paradigm, its merits, limitations and possible alternatives".[1] The concept note for the conference further stated:

---

*   Markus Gunneflo is a Senior Lecturer of public international law at Lund University, Sweden. His research is in the theory, history and politics of international law. The ideas in this paper have benefited from being presented and discussed at the following conferences: *Walter Benjamin in Palestine: The Place and Non-place of Radical Thought*, Ramallah 2015; *International Law and the State of Israel: Legitimacy, Responsibility and Exceptionalism*, Cork 2017; *International Law in a Dark Time*, Helsinki 2017 and the *Law and Disaster* workshop, Melbourne 2017. I am very grateful to the organizers of these events and would like to especially mention Sami Khatib, George Bisharat, Martti Koskenniemi & Anne Orford and Adil Hasan Khan. The first steps were taken when Vasuki Nesiah, John Reynolds, Nahed Samour and myself decided to put together a panel for the *Benjamin in Palestine* conference and this collective have provided inspiration, encouragement and critical insights throughout the project. Many thanks to Vasuki Nesiah, Sundhya Pahuja, Gregor Noll and Jens Bartelson for close engagement with earlier versions of the paper and to Ardi Imseis for taking interest in it, for very helpful comments and for guiding it to completion. Mistakes and views are mine alone.

1   Birzeit Institute of Law, Civic Coalition for Palestinian Rights in Jerusalem and the Decolonizing Palestine Project, *Law and Politics: Options and Strategies of International Law*

> The Israeli occupation – which operates under the legal premise that it is temporary – has developed into almost half a century of military control and Israeli colonies. Still, Israel's occupation regime *per se* has never been declared illegal by the United Nations [UN]. The assumption of the lawful, temporary character of Israel's occupation is being upheld despite ample evidence of Israeli policies and practices of colonialism and forced population transfer which systematically discriminate and oppress Palestinians ... These Israeli policies and practices have been documented by UN human rights treaty committees, UN Special Rapporteurs and fact-finding missions ... Under the dominant IHL [international humanitarian law] paradigm, however, although occasionally condemned, they are treated as single incidents and exceptional acts of an otherwise lawful occupation regime, justified by Israel on grounds of public order, security or military necessity.[2]

This article is an attempt to think with the organizers and participants of the *Law and Politics* conference about international law's complicity in Israeli settler colonialism and, ultimately, about what is required, in terms of international law, to unsettle this status quo.

The argument is that the disciplining of state *means* – the extensive practices of documentation and condemnation discussed in the concept note – at the same time reifies the settler colonial *ends* of the Israeli state, and that this impasse holds true both in and beyond the occupation. What is needed is a legal framework that breaks with this structure. To that end, this paper is divided into four parts. The first section develops a theoretical framework for understanding international law's complicity in the continuing Palestinian *Nakba*, drawing on the heterodox Marxist Walter Benjamin's critique of positive law in terms of the dialectics of means and ends sketched out in the foregoing. Drawing on this framework, the second section takes on the occupation and the IHL-centrism marked out as the problem to be addressed by the *Law & Politics* conference. The fateful transformation of the "Question of Palestine" in international law into the terms of communication and substantive content of the laws of occupation in and after 1967 is examined through 1967 United Nations (UN) Security Council (UNSC) deliberations around Resolution 242 and by considering Hani Sayed's clear-sighted account of the place of the occupation in the wider Israeli settler-colonial project. The third section considers

---

  for the Palestinian People: Concept Note [on file with author] [*hereinafter* Birzeit Concept Note].
2 *Id.*

if the criticism levelled against international law and international legal institutions for treating Israeli transgressions on the West Bank and Gaza as single incidents and exceptional acts of an otherwise lawful occupation regime, cannot also be applied to the state of Israel itself, in its treatment of the Palestinian population from 1948 up until today. As a starting point, I return here to 1948 deliberations in the UNSC on the status in international law of the newly proclaimed state. This is complemented by an appraisal of Antony Carty's account of the continuing relevance of 1948 for Israel as a subject of international law. The fourth section turns to the significance of the international law of anti-colonialism, in particular the prohibition against apartheid, for breaking with the dialectics of means and ends found to be propping up Israeli settler-colonial structures even in the act of criticizing Israel for violations of international law. The recent UN Economic and Social Commission for Western Asia (ESCWA) report written by Richard Falk and Virginia Tilley – *Israeli Practices Towards the Palestinian People and the Question of Apartheid* – is considered for its uncovering of this problem and, in particular, for marking out not the *means*, but the settler-colonial *ends* of the Israeli state as prohibited by international law.

Based on a particular strand of Marxist legal theorizing, the conclusions from this article do not follow the usual pattern of optimism or cynicism, where international law's indeterminacy is either seen as an opportunity for waging "lawfare" against the occupation or the state of Israel itself[3] or, alternatively, as a reason to abandon international law as a tool for progressive politics in Palestine and beyond.[4] Instead, I describe the legal politics of Palestine today as a contest between settler-colonial and anti-colonial legalities, where international law plays a significant part in both.[5] Thus, the question of the indeterminacy of international law is raised from the level of norms to the level of the international legal order itself.

---

3 This ranges from mainstream to more critical approaches. Richard Falk's most recent book on this topic is a fine example of the latter; *see* Richard Falk, Palestine's Horizon: Toward a Just Peace (2017).
4 China Miéville is perhaps the best example; *see* China Miéville, Between Equal Rights: A Marxist Theory of International Law (2005) [*hereinafter* Miéville]. *See, in particular,* the concluding chapter "Against the Rule of Law".
5 This framing is indebted to John Reynolds; *see* John Reynolds, *Anti-Colonial Legalities: Paradigms, Tactics & Strategy*, 18 Palestine Y.B. Int'l L. 8–52 (2015) [*hereinafter* Reynolds].

II   Positive Law: Disciplining Means and Reifying the Ends of the State

At the outset, I emphasized how the 2013 *Law and Politics* conference highlighted how, in the context of the occupation, more law – more authoritative statements and monitoring of violations of humanitarian law – may entrench the status quo. The key to this reading of the situation is to be found in the concept note when it speaks about an assumption of the lawful, temporary character of Israel's occupation – an assumption upheld despite ample evidence of Israeli policies and practices of colonialism and forced population transfer, systematically discriminating and oppressing Palestinians – and, toward the end, that violations are treated as single incidents and exceptional acts of an otherwise lawful occupation regime.

I will argue that Walter Benjamin in his iconic 1921 essay *Critique of Violence* provides, through a Marxist critique of law, a simple way of understanding why such situations evolve. Indeed, the other projects that Benjamin was working on in the context of writing his *Critique*, shows that he was studying jurisprudential texts but also commodity fetishism in Karl Marx's *Capital*.[6] Benjamin's writings – stretching across, or rather defying, the disciplinary boundaries of literary theory, art criticism, political theory, even fiction – offers a sustained criticism of modern society's idolatrous forms of representation.[7] In *Critique of Violence* Benjamin brings this general concern to bear on the "justice" of positive law.[8] In this context he criticizes positive law for being entirely consumed with disciplining state means and, in the same instance, of fetishizing the state and its "justice".

In Marx's *Capital*, the structural separation between the spheres of production and exchange by means of fetishism is described as the valorizing of something that is a contrivance of market forces; reifying, "thingifying" an object as "valuable" in and of itself, independent of its historical origins and conditions of production. In the capitalist economy, commodities are fetishized

---

6   See Walter Benjamin, *The Right to Use Force & Capitalism as Religion*, in Walter Benjamin: Selected Writings, 1: 1913–1926 (Marcus Bullock, Michael W. Jennings eds., 2004) [fragment written between 1920 and 1921, unpublished in Benjamin's lifetime]. Howard Eiland & Michael W. Jennings, Walter Benjamin: A Critical Life 149 (2016). I will seize on these aspects of the text leaving significant political theological motifs aside that Benjamin develops in conversation with, *inter alia*, Erich Unger, Gorge Sorel and Hermann Cohen.

7   See James Martel, Divine violence: Walter Benjamin and the Eschatology of Sovereignty (2012).

8   Walter Benjamin, *Critique of Violence*, in Reflections, Essays, Aphorisms, Autobiographical Writings 277–300 (Peter Demetz ed., 1986) [originally published in German in 1921] [*hereinafter* Benjamin].

so as to make them something other than social products of concrete labor (*i.e.* the difference between exchange- and use value).[9]

Hedrick argues that just as consumers in a capitalist economy are compelled to fetishize commodities – a process through which they assume "magical", "larger-than-life" properties[10] – legal actors fetishize the objectiveness of legal outcomes, the legal order and ultimately state "justice" itself.[11] Legal actors know, of course, that the materials they work with are indeterminate human creations but are structurally compelled to consider the process as one of discovering fixed and objective meanings. Moreover, insofar as they accept the process of application as *de facto* legitimate, legal subjects habitually accede to the idea of justice in law.[12] On an aggregate level this has effects that Marx himself points to in *Notes for a Critique of Hegel's Philosophy of Right* – "All told, the whole legal order acquires a petrified, think-like visage: 'sovereignty, the essence of the state is here conceived to be an independent being; it is objectified'".[13]

Russian legal theorist Evgeny Pashukanis's commodity-form theory of law has become the foremost reference point in Marxist jurisprudence.[14] I will take a different path here: one that leads to Frankfurt School critical theory. In this tradition, commodity exchange is understood to saturate not just the economy and law but all dimensions of social experience. The commodity structure penetrates society in all its aspects and remolds it in its own image, in the expression of Georg Lukács.[15] I argue that it is possible to conceive of Walter Benjamin's *Critique of Violence* as part of this tradition.

Right at the beginning of the text, Benjamin writes that distinctions in law between legitimate and illegitimate force will be based on the presence or absence of a "general historical acknowledgment" of the ends to which specific uses of force serve as means.[16] Building on the basic distinction between

---

9   Karl Marx, Capital: A Critique of Political Economy (Vol. I, 1990, first published in German in 1867).
10 Alan How, Critical Theory (2003), 65.
11 Todd Hedrick, *Reification in and Through law: Elements of a Theory in Marx, Lukács and Honneth*, 13 Eur. J Pol. Theory 178–198 (2014).
12 Ibid p. 185.
13 *Id.*, 185 (Marx's quote).
14 Evgeny Bronislavovich Pashukanis, The General Theory of Law & Marxism (2003) [originally published in Russian in 1924]. For recent uptakes in international law, *see* Miéville. Robert Knox, *Valuing Race? Stretched Marxism and the Logic of Imperialism*, 4 London Rev. Int'l L. 81–126 (2016); Robert Knox, *Strategy and Tactics*, 21 Finnish Y.B. Int'l L. 193–229 (2010).
15 Georg Lukács, History and Class Consciousness 85 (1971) [originally published 1923]–.
16 Benjamin, 280.

means and ends Benjamin scolds the "justice" of natural law for only being concerned with just ends and therefore of being apologetic about the means that achieve them, and, conversely, the "justice" of positive legal systems for being entirely consumed with disciplining means, and therefore of reifying the historically constituted ends those means serve.

The connection to Palestine and the prefatory observations about occupation law from the *Law & Politics* conference concept note will be immediately clear. Even more so when considering the multiple indications in the text about how law's "justice" covers up historical injustices in this way. Benjamin writes that violence crowned by fate is the origin of law and military violence is a primordial condition, paradigmatic of the violence that makes it.[17] He also writes about how, when the highest form of violence – that which can impact life and death – occurs in the legal system, the origins of law jut manifestly and fearsomely into existence, something "rotten" in law revealed.[18]

III   IHL and the 1967 Occupation

In this section, the use of IHL as the dominant paradigm for Palestine will be scrutinized. The historical dimension is given to us already in the *Law & Politics* conference concept note where the 1967 UNSC Resolution 242[19] is said to have laid the foundations for this significant shift. For reasons I will come back to, I see Resolution 242 less as laying the foundation for this paradigm and more as symptomatic of the structural problem of international law discussed in this article: of disciplining *means* while reifying the *ends* of the state.

On 22 November 1967, the UNSC held its 1382nd meeting. On the agenda, was a UK proposal to deal with the then 5-month-old Israeli occupation of what remained of mandate Palestine after the 1948 war – resulting in the passage of Resolution 242.

From 1948 to 1967, the question of Palestine in international law was understood as encompassing the entire territory and population of the former British Mandate. Resolution 242 established that the West Bank, including East Jerusalem and the Gaza strip were occupied territory and, as such, they could never become Israeli territory absent Palestinian acquiescence and that Israeli withdrawal from them was a requirement for peace.[20] Under the legal

---

17   *Id.*, 283.
18   *Id.*
19   S.C. Res. 242, U.N.Doc. S/RES.242 (Nov. 22, 1967).
20   Birzeit Concept Note.

paradigm that evolved out of Resolution 242, however, "the Palestine question became the question of the future status of the Israeli occupied West Bank and Gaza Strip, rather than the issue of the indigenous Palestinian people and citizens of former British Mandate Palestine with substantial outstanding rights and claims in their homeland".[21] This shift did not go unchallenged.

The United Kingdom (UK) proposal followed the vote on two resolutions in the UN General Assembly (UNGA). One was introduced by a group of Latin American and Caribbean countries, the other by Yugoslavia on behalf of several non-aligned states. Both affirmed the inadmissibility of the acquisition of territory by conquest and a complete Israeli withdrawal,[22] but failed to achieve the two-thirds majority required, according to the Charter, for recommendations with respect to the maintenance of international peace and security. The different draft resolutions that would later be circulated in the UNSC followed the same principle but differed in relation to the use of definite language or indefinite language in the withdrawal provision. Israeli representative Abba Eban insisted on indefinite language – no use of "the" or "all" in relation to the territories from which a demand would be made of Israel to withdraw.[23]

George Tomeh, representative from Syria, (invited to take part in the meeting without vote) would be first to speak in the 22 November 1967 meeting in the UNSC. At the outset, he noted that the session may prove to be a crucial turning point in the tragic history of Palestine and that "whether it may be so depends basically on the safeguarding of Arab rights, so far ignored or disregarded". Tomeh continues:

> But as one looks around this Council table, when the future of a whole area and the destiny of a whole people are being decided on, one is struck by an anomalous fact, namely, that the party directly concerned, the Arab people of Palestine, who should themselves be the first speakers to be heard – since they have never ceded their inalienable rights to anybody nor forfeited them – are totally absent from the picture. No reference is made to them in the draft resolution, except, belatedly, in sub-paragraph (b) of operative paragraph 2, as constituting the refugee problem. Yes, this is the Arab people of Palestine, the uprooted, dispossessed people in

---

21 *Id.*
22 Michael Lynk, *Conceived in Law: The Legal Foundations of Resolution 242*, 73 J. Palestine Stud. 7–23 (2007) [*hereinafter* Lynk].
23 *Id.*, 11.

exile, crying for justice for over twenty years now, without so far finding justice in the councils of the world.[24]

The absence of the Palestinian people at the table of the UNSC and the failure to take the Palestinian perspective into account serves as a reminder of how the international legal regime "reflects and reifies the status, rights, and obligations of states".[25]

Another criticism towards the process was how it opened for the resolution to be instrumentalized to serve the Israeli interest of a prolonged occupation. This could already be gleaned from the Israeli vetting of the issue in preparing the draft resolutions and by statements in the UNSC. Tomeh argues that "it goes without saying" that the withdrawal of Israel from the occupied territories should be a key focus of the attention and efforts of the international community, but that this requirement is "almost nullified" by the absence of both time-limits and that the withdrawal is to be to the pre-June 5 armistice lines"[26] Michael Lynk, current UN special rapporteur on the situation of human rights in the Palestinian territories occupied since 1967, would later opine that "the missing definite terms – 'the', 'all' or '4 June 1967 lines' [constituted] the slender hook that Eban, Israel and its supporters would ... hang their interpretative hats to employ Resolution 242 as a justification for its prolonged occupation and colonization of the 1967 lands".[27]

Tomeh, in the UNSC, gives even more space to *what is not* in the UK draft proposal and, as far as I know, not in the other draft proposals either. First and foremost, there is no mention of a Palestinian right to self-determination as enshrined in the UN Charter and the Universal Declaration of Human Rights. Tomeh also makes reference to the fact that the UNGA, at its very first session held after the expulsion of the majority of the Arab inhabitants of Palestine, had endorsed the recommendation of the assassinated Swedish mediator, Folke Bernadotte: that the refugees wishing to return to their homes and live at peace with their neighbors shall be permitted to do so at the earliest practicable date, and that compensation should be paid for the property of those choosing not to return and for loss of or damage to property.[28] Instead, Resolution 242 speaks in characteristically vague terms of "a just resolution of the refugee problem". Tomeh continues:

24 S.C. Verbatim Record, U.N. Doc. S/PV. 1382 (1967).
25 Roger Normand & Chris Jochnick, *The Legitimation of Violence: A Critical History of the Laws of War*, 35 Harvard Int'l L. J. 49–95 (1994), 58.
26 S.C. Verbatim Record, U.N. Doc. S/PV. 1382 (1967).
27 Lynk, 15.
28 G.A. Res 192, U.N. Doc. A/RES/194 (Dec. 11, 1948).

but what has happened to those rights, affirmed regularly every year since 1948? Why have they been glossed over in the present draft? Why is no reference whatsoever made to those resolutions, as if they did not exist at all? It is in the light of this experience and of Israel's disregard of those resolutions that we consider the present United Kingdom draft resolution ... It is inconceivable to Syria that this draft resolution be accepted because it ignores the roots of the problem, the various resolutions adopted by the United Nations on the Palestine question and the right of the Palestinian people to self-determination, and goes further than that; it crowns all those failures by offering to the aggressors' solid recognition of the illegitimate truths of their wanton aggression when it speaks of "secure and recognized boundaries".[29]

The theoretical framework adopted here suggests that there are structural reasons not just for the absence of Palestinians in the UNSC deliberations but for the change of approach to the question of Palestine in international law announced by Resolution 242. Once effective control over foreign territory is a fact and an occupation regime established, the attention it gets from the patrons of international law is one of disciplining this legal power through the means provided by IHL, at the same time, then, naturalizing the occupation and limiting the ways in which Israeli governance of the West Bank and Gaza can be thought of. In this way, the question of Palestine was transformed into the terms of communication and substantive content of the laws of occupation.[30]

Hani Sayed's *The Fictions of the "Illegal" Occupation in the West Bank and Gaza* is a remarkably clear-sighted analysis of the consequences of this shift. Sayed starts out by noticing how academic and policy discussions around the State of Israel's control of the West Bank and Gaza Strip centers on legality, particularly the laws of occupation.[31] Sayed notices how, in this mainstream approach, the laws of occupation provide a grid of intelligibility for all the concrete practices of Israel as an occupying power and legal analysis becomes a matter of comparing the concrete practices of the occupying power with the abstract norms of the law.

---

29 S.C. Verbatim Record, U.N. Doc. S/PV. 1382 (1967).
30 This is Peter Fitzpatrick's formulation of the work of reification in law; *see* Peter Fitzpatrick, *Law and Societies*, 2 Osgoode Hall L. J. 115–138 (1984), 126.
31 Hani Sayed, *The Fictions of the Illegal Occupation in the West Bank and Gaza*, Oregon Rev. Int'l L. 16, 79–126 (2014) [*hereinafter* Sayed].

Sayed further notes that others have pointed to how a discourse of condemnation vs. justification from within this grid of intelligibility paradoxically has served so as to legitimize the occupation and resulted in a situation where the more the practices of the occupying power are audited for compliance with the laws of occupation, the more the systemic connections between them are made difficult to discern and are immunized from critique.³²

Sayed's suggestion is that in order to get around this, the question of how the West Bank and Gaza is governed will need to be studied outside of the grid of intelligibility provided by occupation law. Deducing the elements of Israeli governance from the legal regime applicable according to the international law of occupation will need to be avoided. In other words, occupation law cannot be seen as a framework for speaking truth to power but as a legal regime which is constitutive of systems of social control.³³ What he finds, when doing so, is conveniently summed up like this:

> The government of Israel maintains a strategic control over the territories and Palestinian populations of the WBGS [West Bank and Gaza Strip] with the ability to project military power at will. In international law such level of control satisfies the legally accepted definition of *effective control*; In the territories under its effective control, the government of Israel has set up a dual governance regime that distinguish between Palestinian-Arab persons and places and Israeli-Jewish persons and places; and the government of Israel has abdicated any responsibility over civilian affairs of the Palestinian Arabs in the WBGS. Jewish residents are Israeli citizens, and Jewish places are effectively integrated in the Israeli legal system, administration, and economy. International donors and humanitarian agencies are by default responsible for the welfare [of] the Palestinians in the WBGS.³⁴

As we can see, Sayed agrees that the level of control exercised by Israel in the West Bank and Gaza fulfil the criterion of effective control. However, in suspending occupation law for the purpose of understanding Israeli governance, a different image of the "occupation" emerges. It becomes possible to see that conceiving of Israeli governance of the West Bank and Gaza as an occupation covers up the links to internal state policies and to an overarching settler

---

32   *Id.*, 81.
33   *Id.*, 110.
34   *Id.*, 110–111.

colonial project that does not accept the 1967 armistice line as a limit.[35] As put by Darryl Li, "occupation law's assumption of otherness, premised on a simple dichotomy between occupied territory and occupying states, are not particularly helpful in grasping a basic fact: since the 1967 war, the territory of the British Mandate has been ruled by a single supreme authority".[36]

The legal order of the occupation is key for understanding how it is possible to maintain this situation, even if the authorities are constantly charged with illegal acts, according to that same legal regime. In fact, the use of occupation law to regulate the occupation, rein in the most egregious policies or actions by the authorities – as important as it is – serves exactly to thingify the occupation; makes it not just regulative but constitutive of a regime for acquisition of land and domination of the Palestinian population.

Sayed is not saying that we therefore should turn our attention to the lawfulness of the occupation per se.[37] He sees a number of problems with simply scaling up the question of the legality and the occupation in this way: it reinforces the assumption that as occupied territories, Gaza and the West Bank are distinct territorial units with a special governance regime, in other words, it suffers from the same problem of concealing systemic links to internal state policies as the mainstream approach. The other, associated, problem is that it leads to a narrowing of the field of vision to an, increasingly untenable, two-state political solution to the conflict.[38]

In the next section I will consider if the criticism of how international lawyers and international legal institutions have dealt with the occupation – treating Israeli transgressions as single incidents and exceptional acts of an otherwise lawful regime – cannot be applied to the state of Israel itself. This brings us back to 1948 and the settler-colonial terms on which the state of Israel was founded; terms – if the argument holds – that are reified when international law is used to discipline the Israeli state.

---

35 On settler-colonialism in Israeli constitutional law, see Mazen Masri, The Dynamics of Exclusionary Constitutionalism (2017).
36 Darryl Li, *Occupation Law and the One-State Reality*, Jadaliyya (Aug. 22, 2011), http://www.jadaliyya.com/pages/index/2295/occupation-law-and-the-one-state-reality.
37 Aeyal Gross has contributed to this discourse in important ways and his recent book provides the most sophisticated account of it, in and beyond the context of Israel/Palestine: Aeyal Gross, The Writing on the Wall: Rethinking the International Law of Occupation (2017).
38 Sayed, 83.

IV   International Law and the 1948 *Nakba*

The 1948 UNSC deliberations on the newly proclaimed Israeli state provide a useful starting point for understanding the terms on which the Israeli state was founded and their relationship to international law.

On the agenda for the 339th meeting on 27 July 1948 was a proposal from Syria that, because the UK had abandoned its mandate without having established any governmental organization to resume power of administration, the International Court of Justice (ICJ) should give an advisory opinion as to the status of Palestine. Israel had declared its independence just two months earlier and the civil war in the former mandate had entered its inter-state phase between the nascent Israeli state and a coalition of Arab neighbors. Israel was in the process of claiming significantly more than was reserved for the Jewish state in UN Resolution 181 (on the partition) and hundreds of thousands (the numbers 750,000 or 800,000 are often used by historians) of Palestinians were in the process of becoming the first of many generations of refugees while others would be subjected to a discriminatory military rule inside the state of Israel itself.

In this context, the Israeli representative Abba Eban, who was invited to take part in the deliberations without vote, was able to exploit the international law of statehood operative at the time to push back against the resolution, and the idea that the UNSC should request an advisory legal opinion. He did this in the following terms:

> All States known to history have become States by their own unilateral assertion, without any injunction or permission from the organized international community ... If legitimate origin were relevant – which it is not – in determining statehood, there would be only one instance in which it could be established, for the General Assembly required and demanded the establishment of the State of Israel ... Israel, in fact, possesses the only international birth certificate in a world of unproven virtue, and by a strange irony, it is precisely in this instance – the only instance in which the international community has pronounced itself – that the legitimacy of statehood is to be submitted to the International Court of Justice for investigation. It is not within the capacity of the International Court of Justice to determine the existence or the non-existence of the State of Israel, which is a question of fact and not of law, based on criteria of effectiveness and not of legitimacy.[39]

---

39   S.C. Verbatim Record, U.N. Doc. S/PV.339 (July 27, 1948).

The question was never referred to the ICJ. The failure of the Syrian resolution to obtain the necessary affirmative votes cannot be taken as proof of the extreme position on the pure fact of statehood in international law taken by Eban but it is a fact that international law authorities understand Israel to have become a subject of international law sometime between 1948 and 1949 on terms that later would be implicitly or explicitly accepted in international fora.[40]

Experts disagree whether international law prohibited the *Nakba*[41] but not over whether Israel became a subject of international law on the terms established through its war of independence.[42] In the UNSC, the representative of Egypt, Mahmoud Bey Fawzi (also invited to take part in the deliberations, without vote) underlined the long-term consequences of those terms, and of the establishment of a Jewish state for the Palestinian population.

> On every occasion when we speak to them of our fairness, of our rights, of our justice; they will say, 'But we have a State.' Even when we point out that there are already immigration laws governing all Palestine, that those laws are not yet repealed, and that neither the Mediator, nor the Security Council, nor the so-called Jewish authorities in Palestine, are in law empowered in the present situation to legislate for Palestine or any part of it, the Zionists, will again say, 'But we have a State.' This is their only retort. They have extorted what they wanted and they are simply sitting tight with, so far, no means of redress for the Arabs.[43]

Anthony Carty has seized on the question of the continuing normative significance of the events of 1948 in the case of Palestine. He points to a debate in the UNSC in 1966 where the Israeli representative stated:

> And whatever we do, whatever our Government decides to do, it is done in order to defend and protect our national independence and our national

---

40 Roger O'Keefe, *Israel/Palestine Sixty Years On*, in Krisenherde im Fokus des Völkerrechts – Trouble Spots in the Focus of International Law 13–55 (Thomas Giegerich, Alexander Proelß & Ursula E. Heinz eds., 2010) [*hereinafter* O'Keefe], 17.
41 *See* the different conclusions drawn by O'Keefe and Victor, Kattan, From Coexistence to Conquest, International Law and the Origins of the Arab-Israeli Conflict, 1891–1949 (2009). *See also* Anthony Carty, *Israel's Legal Right to Exist and the Principle of the Self-Determination of the Palestinian People?*, 76 Modern L. Rev. 158–177 (2013) [*hereinafter* Carty].
42 *See* James Crawford, The Creation of States in International Law (2007), 432–434.
43 S.C. Verbatim Record, U.N. Doc. S/PV.339.

security – on the sole responsibility of our Government and not on behalf of anybody else or on behalf of any other considerations but our own.[44]

Carty also notes how the words from the *Declaration of the Establishment of the State of Israel* – that Israel must be the master of its own fate, how the Jewish state exists to protect the Jewish people and so forth – continues to be commonplace in official political discourse. In this context, Carty refers to a "dynamic or drive underlying state action ... for the state to sustain and preserve itself precisely with the same independent force and energy with which it originally established itself".[45] Carty makes clear the effects of this "meta-legal drive" on the international legal order; when law is completely determined by the factual in this way, he argues, it is more intellectually honest to accept that we find ourselves in the "absence of any international legal order".[46]

Elsewhere I have drawn on Carty, and on the 1948 events in the UNSC just mentioned, to make a similar point.[47] The argument about how international law disciplines means while reifying the ends of the state, is a different one, however; one that can be used to understand the situation in Palestine not as *absence*, but *presence*, of international legal order.

The recent ESCWA report entitled *Israeli Practices Towards the Palestinian People and the Question of Apartheid*, written by Richard Falk and Virginia Tilley helps us understand how.[48] The report argues that Israel has established an apartheid regime that dominates the Palestinian people as a whole and that the core method of doing so is upholding the separation of Palestinians into the categories of refugee, occupied and minority populations. Most importantly, the report charges the international community of having unwittingly collaborated with this regime by distinguishing between Palestinian citizens of Israel and Palestinians in the occupied territories and those outside the country as

---

44   S.C. Verbatim Record, U.N. Doc. S/PV. 1321.
45   Carty, 158.
46   *Id.*
47   Markus Gunneflo, Targeted Killing: A Legal and Political History (2016).
48   Richard Falk & Virginia Tilley, *Israeli Practices towards the Palestinian People and the Question of Apartheid*, UN Economic and Social Commission for Western Asia (2017) [*hereinafter* ESCWA Report], available at: https://electronicintifada.net/sites/default/files/2017-03/un_apartheid_report_15_march_english_final_.pdf. The backlash against the report is discussed in: Richard Falk, *The Inside Story on Our UN Report Calling Israel an Apartheid State*, The Nation (Mar. 22, 2017), https://www.thenation.com/article/the-inside-story-on-our-un-report-calling-israel-an-apartheid-state/; Richard Falk & Virginia Tilley, *Open Letter to UN Ambassador Nikki Haley on Our Report on Apartheid in Israel*, The Nation (Apr. 25, 2017), https://www.thenation.com/article/open-letter-to-un-ambassador-nikki-haley-on-our-report-on-apartheid-in-israel/.

"the refugee problem".[49] International law's focus on discrete illegalities in these different spheres, has obscured the fact that what we are dealing with is one, not many, legal regimes.

V Anti-colonial Legalities: The Prohibition of Apartheid

Mazen Masri notes that in Arabic language literature going as far back as the founding of the Israeli state, distinctions are made between the colonialism that other countries in the region suffered from and Zionist settler-colonialism, which "aims to substitute one homeland for another, and eliminate one group so that another can settle in its place".[50]

In the history of colonialism, Israel is characterized not just by its settler-colonial characteristics but by the fact that this state project was realized at the same time as decolonization took place around it. In an article published in the *Palestine Yearbook of International Law* (Vol. XV), Laura Ribeiro describes Palestine as the "last colonial encounter".[51] After the First World War, Palestine found itself at the center of the project of the transformation of colonial territories into independent states and a key concern of the newly formed international institutions set to achieve it. Eventually the state would receive its international legal "birth certificate" by the UN but equally significant is the fact that the discussions around recognition of Israeli statehood show that states indeed were preoccupied with determining whether the Montevideo Convention criteria were fulfilled or not.[52] These criteria were a product of the

---

49 ESCWA Report, 37.
50 From Constantin Zureiq "the Meaning of the Nakba", translated in: Mazen Masri, The Dynamics of Exclusionary Constitutionalism 16 (2017). The description of Israel as a settler colonial state, pivots on the fact that the founding and preserving of a Jewish state in Palestine implies what Patrick Wolfe has described as a 'logic of elimination': replacing indigenous society with the society of the colonizer. In his theory, this need not involve events of physical violent elimination, although this has certainly been the case in Palestine, but is rather to be understood as a structure to be found in the economy, the political system and the law. Patrick Wolfe, Settler Colonialism and the Transformation of Anthropology: The Politics and Poetics of an Ethnographic Event (1999). On Palestine *see also* chapter 8 of Patrick Wolfe, Traces of History: Elementary Structures of Race Ch. 8 (2016).
51 Ribeiro, Laura, *International Law, Sovereignty and the Last Colonial encounter: Palestine and the New Technologies of Quasi-sovereignty.* Palestine Y.B. Int'l L., 15, 67–93 (2009). The article is influenced by Anghie, Antony. Imperialism, Sovereignty and the Making of International Law (2004).
52 Mikulas Fabry, Recognizing States: International Society and the Establishment of New States since 1776 (2010), 156–157.

efforts of subjugated peoples to achieve the sovereignty they had been denied under the earlier standard of civilization and was used for purposes of liberation elsewhere at this time.[53] According to Ribeiro,

> The case of Palestine marks a duplicitous break in international law. Post-WWII international law became the dominant language and institutional means through which de-colonization was articulated, while in Palestine, it reproduced colonial structures and legitimized a new colonial outpost. Moreover, this contradiction was not dichotomized – international law did not just allow decolonization for some while facilitating colonization for others – it colonized and liberated at the same time, in the same place. In the case of Palestine, international law recognized Israel as both the native and colonizer at the same time. It was a settler-colonial project facilitated and validated through international laws and institutions, while simultaneously being an act of de-colonization ...[54]

The argument in this article about the complicity of international law in Israeli settler-colonialism concerns the failure to understand the Israeli state in terms of this duplicitous break. Even taking the extensive international legal criticism directed towards it into account, this failure consists in the normalization of Israel during a time in which the international legal order became increasingly adversely related to colonialism.

Although this era of anti-colonialism in international law is over, the prohibition of colonialism, population transfer and apartheid is still part of positive international law and for the last few decades has increasingly been brought to bear on Israel.[55] This gives me good reason to offer a few words about the nature and role of that law from the perspective advanced here. I will do so by focusing on the 2017 ECSWA report written by Falk and Tilley.

The key finding of the Falk and Tilley report is that Israel has established an apartheid regime that dominates the Palestinian people as a whole – meaning not just Palestinians ruled by military law in the West Bank and Gaza Strip, but also citizens of Israel, residents of Jerusalem and refugees and exiles living outside historic Palestine.[56] The report finds that, although fragmented through a

---

53   *See* Arnulf Becker-Lorca, Mestizo International Law: A Global Intellectual History (2014).
54   Laura Ribeiro, *International Law, Sovereignty and the Last Colonial Encounter: Palestine and the New Techonologies of Quasi-Sovereignty*, 15 Palestine Y.B. Int'l L. 67–93 (2009), 68.
55   For an excellent overview, *see* Reynolds.
56   ECSWA Report. Previous efforts of applying the international law of apartheid against Israel are usefully surveyed and analyzed in John Dugard & John Reynolds, *Apartheid, International Law, and the Occupied Palestinian Territory*, 24 Eur. J. Int'l L. 867–913 (2013) [*hereinafter* Dugard & Reynolds]. *See also* John Reynolds, *The Spectre of South*

history of wars and expulsions and treated according to different laws in these four spheres, ultimately the four domains make up one comprehensive regime. The core method of controlling the Palestinian population and to preserve Israel as a Jewish state is upholding, as Falk puts it in another context, the "discriminatory separation of Palestinians into such subordinated categories as occupied, refugee, terrorist and minority in a Jewish state."[57] This is also where the report charges the international community for having collaborated with this regime by mimicking this separation in its treatment of the Israeli state. This extends the criticism of Hani Sayed on the reliance of occupation law for understanding the Israeli governance of the West Bank and Gaza, to the conceptualization in international law of the Israeli state's historical treatment of the Palestinian population as a whole. The reasoning applied there also applies here: the more Israeli policies and actions are audited for compliance in these different spheres, the more the systemic connections between them are obscured and the regime itself is immunized from critique.

The significance of the international law prohibition against apartheid is that it allows us to expose and consider this from the point of view of positive international law. Apartheid, according to the report's understanding of the Apartheid Convention[58] and the Rome Statute definition,[59] can be established only if discrete acts are part of an institutionalized regime with the intention or purpose of racial domination and oppression.[60] Ultimately, the prohibition against apartheid deals with apartheid as an *end* of the state, not as a *means*. This can be understood from the Apartheid Convention prohibiting a list of "inhuman acts", "committed *for the purpose*" of racial domination and when a people are *systematically* oppressed. Similarly, the Rome Statute crime of apartheid hinges on an "*institutionalized regime*" of systematic oppression and domination ... committed with the *intention* of maintaining that regime". The application of these norms to Israel is examined in the historical makeup of the geography of Israel-Palestine, state discourse and laws on Israel as a Jewish state, policies for demographic engineering, Jewish-national institutions and the above-mentioned fragmentation of the Palestinian population.[61]

Africa. Jadaliyya (Oct. 29, 2011), http://quickthoughts.jadaliyya.com/pages/index/3006/the-spectre-of-south-africa.

57   Richard Falk, Palestine's Horizon: Toward a Just Peace 79 (2017).
58   International Convention on the Suppression and Punishment of the Crime of Apartheid, July 18, 1976, 1015 U.N.T.S. 243.
59   Rome Statute of the International Criminal Court, July 1, 2002, 2187 U.N.T.S. 90.
60   For the customary law status of the prohibition of Apartheid, *see* Dugard & Reynolds.
61   ECSWA Report.

VI Conclusion

The power of international law simultaneously sustains individual states, the state system and the existing power structures determining that system at any particular point in time.[62] For a very long time, those existing power structures served the ends of imperialism and colonialism. The statehood secured by international law was a proxy for civilization and a license for the violent European civilizing mission. At the time of the founding of the Israeli state, this was changing. Similar to Ribeiro, David Theo Goldberg has described Israel as an anomaly at its founding, "reflecting conflicting logics of world historical events between which its declarative moment was awkwardly wedged". It mimicked rather than properly mirrored the logics of independence that could be seen in decolonizing societies of the day while embodying "*in potential*, by the structural conditions of its very formation, *some* key features of the apartheid state".[63] What I have been trying to show in this short paper is that the complicity of international law in Israeli settler-colonialism, and its derivative apartheid,[64] is premised not just on the establishment of the Israeli state on settler-colonial terms in 1948, but on the way in which international law disciplines means while reifying the settler colonial ends of the state and that this is true both in and beyond the occupation. This is captured in the Falk and Tilley report when they charge the international community for being complicit with this regime in so far as distinguishing between Palestinian citizens of Israel, permanent residents of Jerusalem, Palestinians in the occupied territories and those outside the country as "the refugee problem". The focus on discrete illegalities in each of these spheres has not just obscured what they have in common but normalized the separation of the Palestinian population that is a key feature of Israeli apartheid. This explains the paradox where Israel is so often criticized for violating international law, yet the status quo is maintained. In contrast, the prohibition of apartheid, as part of a legacy of anti-colonial international legal power structures, directly address such ends as prohibited by international law. This is an anti-fetishist international law directly addressing the question of the "presence or absence of a general historical acknowledgment of ends" that Walter Benjamin refers to, and, as such, is calling into question the very basis upon which questions of legality are presently determined in historic Palestine.

---

62 Jennifer Beard, *The International Law in Force: Anachronistic Ethics and Divine Violence*, in Events: The Force of International Law 18–28 (Fleur Johns, Richard Joyce & Sundhya Pahuja eds., 2010), 18.

63 David Goldberg, *Racial Palestinianization*, in Thinking Palestine 25–45 (Ronit Lentin ed., 2008), 26.

64 *See* Reynolds, 10.

PART 2

Book Review

Book Review: On Self-Determination, Statehood, and the Law of Negotiation: The Case of Palestine by Robert P. Barnidge, Jr.

*Diana Buttu**

This year marks the 25th anniversary of the signing of the Declaration of Principles, launching the negotiations process between Israel and the Palestine Liberation Organization (PLO) and culminating in the signing of several interim agreements between Israel and the PLO, collectively dubbed the Oslo Agreements after the name of the capital in which Israeli security officials and PLO members secretly met. The thousands of pages of these agreements[1] signed between 1993 and 2000, had, at their core, a few main principles: (i) Palestinian recognition of Israel; (ii) Israeli redeployment from parts

---

* Diana Buttu is a Palestinian-Canadian lawyer who served as a legal advisor to the Palestinian negotiating team from 2000–2005.
1 These agreements include the following:
    - 1993: Israel-PLO Letters of Recognition. In these letters, the PLO affirms that it: (i) recognizes Israel's right to exist in peace and security; (ii) accepts UN Security Council Resolutions 242 and 338; (iii) agrees to engage in negotiations with Israel; (iv) renounces terrorism and (v) agrees to amend the Palestinian National Covenant. Israel, in exchange, recognizes the PLO and agrees to commence negotiations. *See*: http://unispal.un.org/UNISPAL.NSF/0/36917473237100E285257028006C0BC5.
    - 1993: Declaration of Principles on Interim Self-Government Arrangements ("DOP"). This Agreement outlines the permanent status issues to be negotiated: Jerusalem, borders, settlements, water, security and refugees. The DOP spells out that the "transitional period" is to last no more than 5 years and lead to the implementation of UN Resolutions 242 and 338. The DOP also calls for elections and outlines the first redeployment. *See*: http://avalon.law.yale.edu/20th_century/isrplo.asp.
    - 1994: Gaza-Jericho Agreement. This Agreement outlines the limited powers and responsibilities of the Palestinian Authority and specifies the redeployment of the Israeli army from parts of Gaza and Jericho city. It also launches the start of the five-year transitional period and the transfer of limited power to the Palestinian Authority. Part of this Agreement includes the Paris Protocol on Economic relations which integrates the Palestinian economy into that of Israel. *See*: http://avalon.law.yale.edu/20th_century/transfer_powers.asp.
    - 1995: The Interim Agreement: This agreement was superseded by the Oslo II Accord, except for Article XX (Confidence-Building Measures). Article XX dictated the release or

of the West Bank and Gaza Strip and the concomitant division of the West Bank into Areas A, B and C, (iii) the establishment of the Palestinian Authority to govern Palestinians in those areas, while simultaneously entrenching security collaboration with Israel to ensure that Palestinians would not carry out armed attacks against Israeli civilians, settlers and even soldiers; and (iv) the entrenchment of the "two state" framework, with negotiations as the means of ending Israel's military rule.

In addition to the stated principles of these Agreements, the Oslo Agreements also had side effects – intended by Israel – namely the rapid pace of settlement expansion. Due primarily to massive Israeli government subsidies, the total Jewish settler population nearly doubled from 1993 to 2000, increasing from 210,000 to 380,000 including East Jerusalem and the number of housing units rose by 50 percent (excluding East Jerusalem). During these "peace process" years, settler activity proceeded at a faster pace than under any other period that preceded it. Today, the Israeli Central Bureau of Statistics reports that there are 610,000 settlers in the West Bank including East Jerusalem, nearly tripling the settler population. The starkest rise in settlement growth was in the West Bank, excluding East Jerusalem, which witnessed a rise in the settler population from 52,000 in 1993 to over 399,000 at the end of 2016. Illegal under international law and built on land illegally seized from Palestinians, these settlements now control nearly 60 percent of the land surface of the West Bank, including East Jerusalem.[2]

Alongside the scarring of Palestine's landscape and its political decision-making, the Oslo process ushered in new language – a language that persists today. For example, the word "anti-imperialism" was replaced with "conflict" requiring "logframes"; the word "Palestine" replaced with the oddly-phrased and awkwardly capitalized "occupied Palestinian territory"; and, for the purposes of this book, the words "revolution" and "liberation" were replaced with the term "negotiations."

In addition to changing terminology, "negotiations" for some became a "way of life" (for example as outlined in Saeb Erekat's book *Life is Negotiations*), with Palestinian leaders such as Mahmoud Abbas, Saeb Erekat, Nabil Sha'ath and others viewing negotiations as "sacred." So entrenched have negotiations become in the psyche of the above-mentioned individuals (and others not named) that talk of negotiations by the current Palestinian leadership persists,

---

      turn over of Palestinian detainees and prisoners by Israel. The Paris Protocol was incorporated in Article XXIV of Oslo II.

2 *See* OCHA, *Humanitarian Factsheet on Area C of the West Bank* (July 2011), https://www.ochaopt.org/documents/ocha_opt_area_c_fact_sheet_july_2011.pdf.

even in the face of a Netanyahu government which has both made it clear that it will never end Israel's military occupation[3] or dismantle settlements,[4] and has taken steps to formally annex settlements into Israel.[5] Even the United States government, once a champion of the negotiations process, has spoken of the "deal of the century" has resorted to unilateralism by declaring Jerusalem as Israel's capital and halting aid to a flailing UNRWA in order to do away with Palestinian refugees.

To be clear, while a quarter century has passed since the signing of the Declaration of Principles, the majority of this time has been marked by periods *lacking* any negotiations, in which Israeli and Palestinian negotiators have not even feigned that meaningful negotiations are underway or that progress has been achieved. Yet, despite this lack of progress, Israeli political parties continue to laud the negotiations process and have continued to demand negotiations "without pre-conditions" (*i.e.* a settlement freeze) while demanding conditions of its own (*i.e.* Palestinian recognition of Israel as a "Jewish state"). The reasons for Israel's continued insistence on negotiations are clear. The Oslo Agreements facilitated Israel's settlement expansion, paved the way for international acceptance of Israel,[6] improved Israel's economy and, most importantly, undermined other strategies such as BDS, transforming a situation of settler-colonial apartheid into an issue to be resolved by "both sides" despite the power imbalance and inappropriateness of negotiations to a situation of settler-colonialism.

---

3   Alon Ben Meir, *There Will Be No Palestinian State Under Netanyahu's Watch*, HuffPost (Feb. 15, 2008), https://www.huffingtonpost.com/alon-benmeir/there-will-be-no-palestin_b_14746310.html.
4   Noga Tarnopolsky, *Netanyahu says Israel won't retreat on Jewish settlements: 'We are here to stay forever'*, L.A. Times (Aug. 28, 2017), http://www.latimes.com/world/middleeast/la-fg-israel-netanyahu-settlements-20170828-story.html.
5   Jeffrey Heller, *U.S. pressure delays Israel's 'Greater Jerusalem' bill: legislator*, Reuters (Oct. 29, 2017), https://www.reuters.com/article/us-israel-palestinians-settlement/u-s-pressure-delays-israels-greater-jerusalem-bill-legislator-idUSKBN1CY0CB.
6   The Oslo Agreements paved the way for additional international acceptance of Israel. Between 1992 and 1999, 45 countries established diplomatic ties with Israel, more than in the four preceding decades combined. Moreover, Israel signed a peace treaty with Jordan in 1994, an agreement that likely would not have been signed without the Oslo Agreements. In addition to these diplomatic ties, the Oslo Agreements ushered in new economic prosperity for Israel, which opened trade offices in Morocco, Tunisia, Oman, Qatar, Mauritania – all members of the Arab League. Moreover, US assistance to Israel increased with Israel receiving its largest aid package under the Obama Administration; *see* Peter Baker and Julie Hirschfeld Davis, *U.S. Finalizes Deal to Give Israel $38 Billion in Military Aid*, N.Y. Times (Sept. 13, 2016), https://www.nytimes.com/2016/09/14/world/middleeast/israel-benjamin-netanyahu-military-aid.html.

It is in the context of "both sides" that Barnidge writes this book. Specifically, Barnidge begins by exploring Palestinian self-determination and conveniently dismisses the notion – adding that it serves a "mythic function" – while simultaneously accepting Israel's ethnic cleansing of Palestine as being the "rebirth of the Jewish State"[7] and noting that the UN's embrace of Palestinian self-determination "came at the expense of Jewish self-determination".[8] Barnidge ignores how the expression of "Jewish self-determination", that he is at pains to support, came at the expense of Palestinian rights and, in particular, led to the ethnic cleansing of Palestine, the continued denial of the Palestinian right to return by Israel and an ongoing attempt to rid Palestinians of their homeland.

In his subsequent chapters, Barnidge aims to lay out what he refers to as the "negotiation imperative" in which he argues that Palestinians not only began a process of negotiations dating back to the 1970s but, from this, that Palestinians are legally obliged to continue to negotiate even in the face of continued illegal actions on Israel's behalf.

While laying out this "negotiation imperative," Barnidge is certain to highlight that, while Palestinians are required to negotiate with their oppressor and colonizer, the Palestinian Authority is neither a sovereign entity but "increased forms of internal self-determination to the Palestinians" and "did not create, or somehow deterministically foresee the creation of, a sovereign Palestinian entity". Stated differently, what Barnidge argues is precisely what Israeli officials, and Israel's supporters perpetually seek: a Palestinian body that is neither sovereign (nor capable of being sovereign); the denial of self-determination (and questioning whether Palestinians are even entitled to self-determination); and a demand that Palestinians continue to negotiate even in the face of Israel's repeated violations of international law.

Barnidge's position is best summarized in his chapter titled *Palestinian Applications for Admission to the United Nations* in which he states:

> The Israeli-Palestinian instruments, by contrast, reaffirm negotiation as a means to an end, "peace" the contours of which, both juridically and philosophically, are by no means settled, and that cannot with certainty be predicted *ex ante*. In other words, a final settlement will necessarily reflect the outcome of "horsetrading" between the two sides of their respective rights and obligations.[9]

---

7 Robert P. Barnidge, Self-Determination, Statehood, and the Law of Negotiation: The Case of Palestine 41 & 84 (2016) [*hereinafter* Barnidge].
8 *Id.*, 87.
9 *Id.*, 153.

Stated differently, for Barnidge, international law is irrelevant: it matters little that Israel continues to carry out war crimes by building settlements in the West Bank; it matters little that Israel continues to deny Palestinians their right to return to their homes because they are not Jewish; it matters little that Israel acquired territory by force and that the UN has repeatedly condemned Israel's actions. Rather, for Barnidge, what matters is that Palestinians continue negotiating in the face of these actions.

The latter part of Barnidge's book is an attempt to assess the Palestinian applications for admission to the UN. While this reviewer views these attempts as a futile measure to return to a failed negotiations process rather than as an attempt to hold Israel accountable for its continued violations of international law, Barnidge believes that "it is doubtful that the Palestinian applications can be interpreted as either permissible responses to an Israeli material breach or the PLO's suspension or termination of the bilateral negotiation imperative."[10] He goes on to state that neither party has renounced Oslo, conveniently ignoring Sharon's 2001 statements to that effect[11] and Israel's repeated violations of it. Placing Israel's continued settlement expansion on the same plane as the Palestinian Authority's applications to the UN for full membership, Barnidge concludes that:

> Similarly, the Palestinian applications of autumn 2011 and autumn 2012 no more facilitate a sustainable settlement than Israel's withholding of tax revenue to the Palestinian Authority or the presence of Jews beyond the 1949 armistice lines impedes it.[12]

Barnidge concludes his book by repeating Israel's oft-stated line in which they call for "both sides" to "negotiate with one another without preconditions according to the exacting international law of negotiation".[13] While purporting to focus on international law, Barnidge's book falls strikingly short. He fails to engage in any analysis of Israel's continued colonization of the West Bank, Israel's continued siege over the West Bank and Israel's 50-year military occupation and denial of freedom. Rather, he simultaneously ignores these issues and holds the Palestinian Authority to international legal standards (such as the Vienna Convention on the Law of Treaties) while going to great lengths to deny

---

10 *Id.*, 180.
11 John Podhoretz, *Sharon's landslide – Israel's choice, the soldier's peace*, N.Y. Post (Feb. 7, 2001), https://nypost.com/2001/02/07/sharons-landslide-israels-choice-the-soldiers-peace/.
12 Barnidge, 181.
13 Barnidge, 188.

Palestinian self-determination and highlighting that the Palestinian Authority is not a state. In other words, he demands that Palestinians negotiate – and only negotiate – in the face of Israel's actions and fails to engage in any analysis of the history of negotiations and, particularly, why this process has lingered for 25 years.

Barnidge's conclusion will certainly appeal to some, namely members of the diplomatic community, who seek to do nothing while making mealy-mouthed statements calling for a resumption of negotiations and imploring "both sides" not to take "prejudicial" actions (code for calling on Israel not to continue settlement activity but too afraid to say so directly). It certainly will appeal to Israel who wants nothing more than a continued negotiations process as it allows them to continue to deflect from its ongoing war crimes by stating that it is in engaging in conflict resolution. Sadly, this is where the Palestinian Authority has taken Palestinians: entrenched in a failed process with virtually nowhere to go, and with academics writing about how we must remain bound to this futile process.

PART 3

Materials

SECTION A

United Nations Documents

Falk & Tilley (ESCWA), Israel Practices towards the Palestinian People and the Question of Apartheid

Economic and Social Commission for Western Asia
Israel Practices towards the Palestinian People and the Question of Apartheid[1]
Palestine and the Israeli Occupation, Issue No. 1
E/ESCWA/ECRI/2017/1

© 2017 United Nations

All rights reserved worldwide

Photocopies and reproductions of excerpts are allowed with proper credits.

All queries on rights and licenses, including subsidiary rights, should be addressed to the United Nations Economic and Social Commission for Western Asia (ESCWA), e-mail: publications-escwa@un.org.

The findings, interpretations and conclusions expressed in this publication are those of the authors and do not necessarily reflect the views of the United Nations or its officials or Member States.

The designations employed and the presentation of material in this publication do not imply the expression of any opinion whatsoever on the part of the United Nations concerning the legal status of any country, territory, city or area or of its authorities, or concerning the delimitation of its frontiers or boundaries.

Links contained in this publication are provided for the convenience of the reader and are correct at the time of issue. The United Nations takes no responsibility for the continued accuracy of that information or for the content of any external website.

References have, wherever possible, been verified.

Symbols of United Nations documents are composed of capital letters combined with figures. Mention of such a symbol indicates a reference to a United Nations document.

---

[1] PDF available at: https://electronicintifada.net/sites/default/files/2017-03/un_apartheid_report_15_march_english_final_.pdf.

United Nations publication issued by ESCWA, United Nations House, Riad El Solh Square, P.O. Box: 11–8575, Beirut, Lebanon.

Website: www.unescwa.org.

Acknowledgements

This report was commissioned by the Economic and Social Commission for Western Asia (ESCWA) from authors Mr. Richard Falk and Ms. Virginia Tilley.

Richard Falk (LLB, Yale University; SJD, Harvard University) is currently Research Fellow, Orfalea Center of Global and International Studies, University of California at Santa Barbara, and Albert G. Milbank Professor of International Law and Practice Emeritus at Princeton University. From 2008 through 2014, he served as United Nations Special Rapporteur on the situation of human rights in the Palestinian territories occupied since 1967. He is author or editor of some 60 books and hundreds of articles on international human rights law, Middle East politics, environmental justice, and other fields concerning human rights and international relations.

Virginia Tilley (MA and PhD, University of Wisconsin-Madison, and MA in Contemporary Arab Studies, Georgetown University) is Professor of Political Science at Southern Illinois University. From 2006 to 2011, she served as Chief Research Specialist in the Human Sciences Research Council of South Africa and from 2007 to 2010 led the Council's Middle East Project, which undertook a two-year study of apartheid in the occupied Palestinian territories. In addition to many articles on the politics and ideologies of the conflict in Israel-Palestine, she is author of *The One-State Solution* (University of Michigan Press and Manchester University Press, 2005) and editor of *Beyond Occupation: Apartheid, Colonialism and International Law in the Occupied Palestinian Territories* (Pluto Press, 2012).

This report benefited from the general guidance of Mr. Tarik Alami, Director of the Emerging and Conflict-Related Issues (ECRI) Division at ESCWA. Mr. Rabi' Bashour (ECRI) coordinated the report, contributed to defining its scope and provided editorial comments, planning and data. Ms. Leila Choueiri provided substantive and editorial inputs. Ms. Rita Jarous (ECRI), Mr. Sami Salloum and Mr. Rafat Soboh (ECRI), provided editorial comments and information, as well as technical assistance. Mr. Damien Simonis (ESCWA, Conference Services Section) edited the report.

Appreciation is extended to the blind reviewers for their valuable input.

We also acknowledge the authors of and contributors to Occupation, Colonialism, Apartheid? A Reassessment of Israel's Practices in the Occupied Palestinian Territories under International Law, whose work informed this report (see annex I) and was published in 2012 as Beyond Occupation: Apartheid, Colonialism and International Law in the Occupied Palestinian Territories.

Preface

The authors of this report, examining whether Israel has established an apartheid regime that oppresses and dominates the Palestinian people as a whole, fully appreciate the sensitivity of the question.[2] Even broaching the issue has been denounced by spokespersons of the Israeli Government and many of its supporters as anti-Semitism in a new guise. In 2016, Israel successfully lobbied for the inclusion of criticism of Israel in laws against anti-Semitism in Europe and the United States of America, and background documents to those legal instruments list the apartheid charge as one example of attempts aimed at "destroying Israel's image and isolating it as a pariah State".[3]

The authors reject the accusation of anti-Semitism in the strongest terms. First, the question of whether the State of Israel is constituted as an

---

2   This report was prepared in response to a request made by member States of the United Nations Economic and Social Commission for Western Asia (ESCWA) at the first meeting of its Executive Committee, held in Amman on 8 and 9 June 2015. Preliminary findings of the report were presented to the twenty-ninth session of ESCWA, held in Doha from 13 to 15 December 2016. As a result, member States passed resolution 326 (XXIX) of 15 December 2016, in which they requested that the secretariat "publish widely the results of the study".

3   Coordinating Forum for Countering Antisemitism (CFCA): FAQ: the campaign to defame Israel. Available from http://antisemitism.org.il/eng/FAQ:%20The%20campaign%20to%20defame%20Israel. The CFCA is an Israeli Government "national forum". "The new anti-Semitism" has become the term used to equate criticism of Israeli racial policies with anti- Semitism, especially where such criticism extends to proposing that the ethnic premise of Jewish statehood is illegitimate, because it violates international human rights law. The European Union Parliament Working Group on Antisemitism has accordingly included in its working definition of anti-Semitism the following example: "Denying the Jewish people their right to self-determination, e.g., by claiming that the existence of the State of Israel is a racist endeavour" (see www.antisem.eu/projects/eumc-working-definition-of-antisemitism). In 2016, the United States passed the Anti-Semitism Awareness Act, in which the definition of anti-Semitism is that set forth by the Special Envoy to Monitor and Combat Anti-Semitism of the Department of State in a fact sheet of 8 June 2010. Examples of anti-Semitism listed therein include: "Denying the Jewish people their right to self-determination, and denying Israel the right to exist." (Available from https://2009-2017.state.gov/documents/organization/156684.pdf).

apartheid regime springs from the same body of international human rights law and principles that rejects anti-Semitism: that is, the prohibition of racial discrimination. No State is immune from the norms and rules enshrined in the International Convention on the Elimination of All Forms of Racial Discrimination, which must be applied impartially. The prohibition of apartheid, which, as a crime against humanity, can admit no exceptions, flows from the Convention. Strengthening that body of international law can only benefit all groups that have historically endured discrimination, domination and persecution, including Jews.

Secondly, the situation in Israel-Palestine constitutes an unmet obligation of the organized international community to resolve a conflict partially generated by its own actions. That obligation dates formally to 1922, when the League of Nations established the British Mandate for Palestine as a territory eminently ready for independence as an inclusive secular State, yet incorporated into the Mandate the core pledge of the Balfour Declaration to support the "Jewish people" in their efforts to establish in Palestine a "Jewish national home".[4] Later United Nations Security Council and General Assembly resolutions attempted to resolve the conflict generated by that arrangement, yet could not prevent related proposals, such as partition, from being overtaken by events on the ground. If this attention to the case of Israel by the United Nations appears exceptional, therefore, it is only because no comparable linkage exists between United Nations actions and any other prolonged denial to a people of their right of self-determination.

Thirdly, the policies, practices and measures applied by Israel to enforce a system of racial discrimination threaten regional peace and security. United Nations resolutions have long recognized that danger and called for resolution of the conflict so as to restore and maintain peace and stability in the region.

To assert that the policies and practices of a sovereign State amount to apartheid constitutes a grave charge. A study aimed at making such a determination should be undertaken and submitted for consideration only when supporting evidence clearly exceeds reasonable doubt. The authors of this report believe that evidence for suspecting that a system of apartheid has been imposed on the Palestinian people meets such a demanding criterion. Given the protracted suffering of the Palestinian people, it would be irresponsible not to present the evidence and legal arguments regarding whether Israel has established an apartheid regime that oppresses the Palestinian people as a whole, and not to

---

4 The Council of the League of Nations, League of Nations Mandate for Palestine, December 1922, article 2. Available from www.mandateforpalestine.org/the-mandate.html.

make recommendations for appropriate further action by international and civil society actors.

In sum, this study was motivated by the desire to promote compliance with international human rights law, uphold and strengthen international criminal law, and ensure that the collective responsibilities of the United Nations and its Member States with regard to crimes against humanity are fulfilled. More concretely, it aims to see the core commitments of the international community to upholding international law applied to the case of the Palestinian people, in defence of its rights under international law, including the right of self-determination.

Contents

Acknowledgements   iii
Preface   v
Executive Summary   1
Introduction   9

1   The Legal Context: Short History of the Prohibition of Apartheid   11
    Alternative definitions of apartheid   12

2   Testing for an Apartheid Regime in Israel-Palestine   27
    A   *The Political Geography of Apartheid*   27
    B   *Israel as a Racial State*   30
    C   *Apartheid through Fragmentation*   37
    D   *Counter-arguments*   49

3   Conclusions and Recommendations   52
    A   *Conclusions*   52
    B   *Recommendations*   53

Annexes
I   Findings of the 2009 HSRC Report   58
II   Which Country?   64

[1]

Executive Summary

This report concludes that Israel has established an apartheid regime that dominates the Palestinian people as a whole. Aware of the seriousness of this allegation, the authors of the report conclude that available evidence establishes beyond a reasonable doubt that Israel is guilty of policies and practices that constitute the crime of apartheid as legally defined in instruments of international law.

The analysis in this report rests on the same body of international human rights law and principles that reject anti-Semitism and other racially discriminatory ideologies, including: the Charter of the United Nations (1945), the Universal Declaration of Human Rights (1948), and the International Convention on the Elimination of All Forms of Racial Discrimination (1965). The report relies for its definition of apartheid primarily on article II of the International Convention on the Suppression and Punishment of the Crime of Apartheid (1973, hereinafter the Apartheid Convention):

> The term "the crime of apartheid", which shall include similar policies and practices of racial segregation and discrimination as practiced in southern Africa, shall apply to ... inhuman acts committed for the purpose of establishing and maintaining domination by one racial group of persons over any other racial group of persons and systematically oppressing them.

Although the term "apartheid" was originally associated with the specific instance of South Africa, it now represents a species of crime against humanity under customary international law and the Rome Statute of the International Criminal Court, according to which:

> "The crime of apartheid" means inhumane acts ... committed in the context of an institutionalized regime of systematic oppression and domination by one racial group over any other racial group or groups and committed with the intention of maintaining that regime.

Against that background, this report reflects the expert consensus that the prohibition of apartheid is universally applicable and was not rendered moot by the collapse of apartheid in South Africa and South West Africa (Namibia). [2]

The legal approach to the matter of apartheid adopted by this report should not be confused with usage of the term in popular discourse as an expression of opprobrium. Seeing apartheid as discrete acts and practices (such as the "apartheid wall"), a phenomenon generated by anonymous structural conditions like capitalism ("economic apartheid"), or private social behaviour on the part of certain racial groups towards others (social racism) may have its place in certain contexts. However, this report anchors its definition of apartheid in international law, which carries with it responsibilities for States, as specified in international instruments.

The choice of evidence is guided by the Apartheid Convention, which sets forth that the crime of apartheid consists of discrete inhuman acts, but that such acts acquire the status of crimes against humanity only if they intentionally serve the core purpose of racial domination. The Rome Statute specifies in its definition the presence of an "institutionalized regime" serving the "intention" of racial domination. Since "purpose" and "intention" lie at the core of both definitions, this report examines factors ostensibly separate from the Palestinian dimension – especially, the doctrine of Jewish statehood as expressed in law and the design of Israeli State institutions – to establish beyond doubt the presence of such a core purpose.

That the Israeli regime is designed for this core purpose was found to be evident in the body of laws, only some of which are discussed in the report for reasons of scope. One prominent example is land policy. The Israeli Basic Law (Constitution) mandates that land held by the State of Israel, the Israeli Development Authority or the Jewish National Fund shall not be transferred in any manner, placing its management permanently under their authority. The State Property Law of 1951 provides for the reversion of property (including land) to the State in any area "in which the law of the State of Israel applies". The Israel Lands Authority (ILA) manages State land, which accounts for 93 per cent of the land within the internationally recognized borders of Israel and is by law closed to use, development or ownership by non-Jews. Those laws reflect the concept of "public purpose" as expressed in the Basic Law. Such laws may be changed by Knesset vote, but the Basic Law: Knesset prohibits any political party from challenging that public purpose. Effectively, Israeli law renders opposition to racial domination illegal.

Demographic engineering is another area of policy serving the purpose of maintaining Israel as a Jewish State. Most well known is Israeli law conferring on Jews worldwide the right to enter Israel and obtain Israeli citizenship regardless of their countries of origin and whether or not they can show links to Israel-Palestine, [3] while withholding any comparable right from Palestinians, including those with documented ancestral homes in the country. The World Zionist Organization and Jewish Agency are vested with legal authority as agencies of the State of Israel to facilitate Jewish immigration and preferentially serve the interests of Jewish citizens in matters ranging from land use to public development planning and other matters deemed vital to Jewish statehood. Some laws involving demographic engineering are expressed in coded language, such as those that allow Jewish councils to reject applications for residence from Palestinian citizens. Israeli law normally allows spouses of Israeli citizens to relocate to Israel but uniquely prohibits this option in the case of Palestinians from the occupied territory or beyond. On a far larger scale, it is a matter of Israeli policy to reject the return of any Palestinian refugees and exiles (totalling some six million people) to territory under Israeli control.

Two additional attributes of a systematic regime of racial domination must be present to qualify the regime as an instance of apartheid. The first involves the identification of the oppressed persons as belonging to a specific "racial group". This report accepts the definition of the International Convention on the Elimination of All Forms of Racial Discrimination of "racial discrimination" as "any distinction, exclusion, restriction or preference based on race, colour, descent, or national or ethnic origin which has the purpose or effect of nullifying or impairing the recognition, enjoyment or exercise, on an equal footing, of human rights and fundamental freedoms in the political, economic, social, cultural or any other field of public life". On that basis, this report argues that in the geopolitical context of Palestine, Jews and Palestinians can be considered "racial groups". Furthermore, the International Convention on the Elimination of All Forms of Racial Discrimination is cited expressly in the Apartheid Convention.

The second attribute is the boundary and character of the group or groups involved. The status of the Palestinians as a people entitled to exercise the right of self-determination has been legally settled, most authoritatively by the International Court of Justice (ICJ) in its 2004 advisory opinion on Legal Consequences of the Construction of a Wall in the Occupied Palestinian Territory. On that basis, the report examines the treatment by Israel of the Palestinian people as a whole, considering the distinct circumstances of geographic and juridical fragmentation of the Palestinian people as a condition imposed by Israel. (Annex II addresses the issue of a proper identification of the "country" responsible for the denial of Palestinian rights under international law.)

This report finds that the strategic fragmentation of the Palestinian people is the principal method by which Israel imposes an apartheid regime. It first examines [4] how the history of war, partition, de jure and de facto annexation and prolonged occupation in Palestine has led to the Palestinian people being divided into different geographic regions administered by distinct sets of law. This fragmentation operates to stabilize the Israeli regime of racial domination over the Palestinians and to weaken the will and capacity of the Palestinian people to mount a unified and effective resistance. Different methods are deployed depending on where Palestinians live. This is the core means by which Israel enforces apartheid and at the same time impedes international recognition of how the system works as a complementary whole to comprise an apartheid regime.

Since 1967, Palestinians as a people have lived in what the report refers to as four "domains", in which the fragments of the Palestinian population are ostensibly treated differently but share in common the racial oppression that results from the apartheid regime. Those domains are:

1. Civil law, with special restrictions, governing Palestinians who live as citizens of Israel;
2. Permanent residency law governing Palestinians living in the city of Jerusalem;
3. Military law governing Palestinians, including those in refugee camps, living since 1967 under conditions of belligerent occupation in the West Bank and Gaza Strip;
4. Policy to preclude the return of Palestinians, whether refugees or exiles, living outside territory under Israel's control.

Domain 1 embraces about 1.7 million Palestinians who are citizens of Israel. For the first 20 years of the country's existence, they lived under martial law and to this day are subjected to oppression on the basis of not being Jewish. That policy of domination manifests itself in inferior services, restrictive zoning laws and limited budget allocations made to Palestinian communities; in restrictions on jobs and professional opportunities; and in the mostly segregated landscape in which Jewish and Palestinian citizens of Israel live. Palestinian political parties can campaign for minor reforms and better budgets, but are legally prohibited by the Basic Law from challenging legislation maintaining the racial regime. The policy is reinforced by the implications of the distinction made in Israel between "citizenship" (*ezrahut*) and "nationality" (*le'um*): all Israeli citizens enjoy the former, but only Jews enjoy the latter. "National" rights in Israeli law signify Jewish-national rights. The struggle of Palestinian citizens of Israel for equality and civil reforms under Israeli law is thus isolated by the regime from that of Palestinians elsewhere. [5]

Domain 2 covers the approximately 300,000 Palestinians who live in East Jerusalem, who experience discrimination in access to education, health care, employment, residency and building rights. They also suffer from expulsions and home demolitions, which serve the Israeli policy of "demographic balance" in favour of Jewish residents. East Jerusalem Palestinians are classified as permanent residents, which places them in a separate category designed to prevent their demographic and, importantly, electoral weight being added to that of Palestinians citizens in Israel. As permanent residents, they have no legal standing to challenge Israeli law. Moreover, openly identifying with Palestinians in the occupied Palestinian territory politically carries the risk of expulsion to the West Bank and loss of the right even to visit Jerusalem. Thus, the urban epicentre of Palestinian political life is caught inside a legal bubble that curtails its inhabitants' capacity to oppose the apartheid regime lawfully.

Domain 3 is the system of military law imposed on approximately 4.6 million Palestinians who live in the occupied Palestinian territory, 2.7 million of them in the West Bank and 1.9 million in the Gaza Strip. The territory is administered in a manner that fully meets the definition of apartheid under the Apartheid Convention: except for the provision on genocide, every illustrative "inhuman act" listed in the Convention is routinely and systematically practiced by Israel in the West Bank. Palestinians are governed by military law, while the approximately 350,000 Jewish settlers are governed by Israeli civil law. The racial character of this situation is further confirmed by the fact that all West Bank Jewish settlers enjoy the protections of Israeli civil law on the basis of being Jewish, whether they are Israeli citizens or not. This dual legal system, problematic in itself, is indicative of an apartheid regime when coupled with the racially discriminatory management of land and development administered by Jewish-national institutions, which are charged with administering "State land" in the interest of the Jewish population. In support of the overall findings of this report, annex I sets out in more detail the policies and practices of Israel in the occupied Palestinian territory that constitute violations of article II of the Apartheid Convention.

Domain 4 refers to the millions of Palestinian refugees and involuntary exiles, most of whom live in neighbouring countries. They are prohibited from returning to their homes in Israel and the occupied Palestinian territory. Israel defends its rejection of the Palestinians' return in frankly racist language: it is alleged that Palestinians constitute a "demographic threat" and that their return would alter the demographic character of Israel to the point of eliminating it as a Jewish State. The refusal of the right of return plays an essential role in the apartheid regime by ensuring that the Palestinian population in Mandate Palestine does not grow to a point that would threaten Israeli military control of the territory and/or provide the [6] demographic leverage for Palestinian citizens of Israel to demand (and obtain) full democratic rights, thereby eliminating the Jewish character of the State of Israel. Although domain 4 is confined to policies denying Palestinians their right of repatriation under international law, it is treated in this report as integral to the system of oppression and domination of the Palestinian people as a whole, given its crucial role in demographic terms in maintaining the apartheid regime.

This report finds that, taken together, the four domains constitute one comprehensive regime developed for the purpose of ensuring the enduring domination over non-Jews in all land exclusively under Israeli control in whatever category. To some degree, the differences in treatment accorded to Palestinians have been provisionally treated as valid by the United Nations, in the absence of an assessment of whether they constitute a form of apartheid. In the light of this report's findings, this long-standing fragmented international approach may require review.

In the interests of fairness and completeness, the report examines several counter- arguments advanced by Israel and supporters of its policies denying the applicability of the Apartheid Convention to the case of Israel-Palestine. They include claims that: the determination of Israel to remain a Jewish State is consistent with practices of other States, such as France; Israel does not owe Palestinian non-citizens equal treatment with Jews precisely because they are not citizens; and Israeli treatment of the Palestinians reflects no "purpose" or "intent" to dominate, but rather is a temporary state of affairs imposed on Israel by the realities of ongoing conflict and security requirements. The report shows that none of those arguments stands up to examination. A further claim that Israel cannot be considered culpable for crimes of apartheid because Palestinian citizens of Israel have voting rights rests on two errors of legal interpretation: an overly literal comparison with South African apartheid policy and detachment of the question of voting rights from other laws, especially provisions of the Basic Law that prohibit political parties from challenging the Jewish, and hence racial, character of the State.

The report concludes that the weight of the evidence supports beyond a reasonable doubt the proposition that Israel is guilty of imposing an apartheid regime on the Palestinian people, which amounts to the commission of a crime against humanity, the prohibition of which is considered *jus cogens* in international customary law. The international community, especially the United Nations and its agencies, and Member States, have a legal obligation to act within the limits of their capabilities to prevent and punish instances of apartheid that are responsibly brought to their attention. More specifically, States have a collective [7] duty: (a) not to recognize an apartheid regime as lawful; (b) not to aid or assist a State in maintaining an apartheid regime; and (c) to cooperate with the United Nations and other States in bringing apartheid regimes to an end. Civil society institutions and individuals also have a moral and political duty to use the instruments at their disposal to raise awareness of this ongoing criminal enterprise, and to exert pressure on Israel in order to persuade it to dismantle apartheid structures in compliance with international law. The report ends with general and specific recommendations to the

United Nations, national Governments, and civil society and private actors on actions they should take in view of the finding that Israel maintains a regime of apartheid in its exercise of control over the Palestinian people. [8–9]

Introduction

This report examines the practices and policies of Israel with regard to the Palestinian people in its entirety. This is not an arbitrary choice. The legal existence of the "Palestinian people" and its right, as a whole people, to self-determination were confirmed by the International Court of Justice (ICJ) in its advisory opinion on the separation wall in occupied Palestinian territory:[5]

> As regards the principle of the right of peoples to self-determination, the Court observes that the existence of a "Palestinian people" is no longer in issue. Such existence has moreover been recognized by Israel in the exchange of letters of 9 September 1993 between Mr. Yasser Arafat, President of the Palestine Liberation Organization (PLO) and Mr. Yitzhak Rabin, Israeli Prime Minister. In that correspondence, the President of the PLO recognized "the right of the State of Israel to exist in peace and security" and made various other commitments. In reply, the Israeli Prime Minister informed him that, in the light of those commitments, "the Government of Israel has decided to recognize the PLO as the representative of the Palestinian people". The Israeli-Palestinian Interim Agreement on the West Bank and the Gaza Strip of 28 September 1995 also refers a number of times to the Palestinian people and its "legitimate rights" (preamble, paras. 4, 7, 8; article II, para. 2; article III, paras. 1 and 3; article XXII, para. 2). The Court considers that those rights include the right to self-determination, as the General Assembly has moreover recognized on a number of occasions (see, for example, resolution 58/163 of 22 December 2003).

The status of the Palestinians as a people is therefore legally settled (although Israel contests it), and so the practices and policies of Israel towards the whole Palestinian people, despite the Palestinians being fragmented geographically and politically, should be addressed as a single, unified matter. That view is

---

5   Legal Consequences of the Construction of a Wall in the Occupied Palestinian Territory, Advisory Opinion, I.C.J. Reports 2004, p. 136. Available from www.icj-cij.org/docket/files/131/1671.pdf.

reinforced by the realization that there is no prospect for achieving fundamental Palestinian rights, above all the right of self-determination, through international diplomacy as long as this question remains open.

The authors hope that this report will assist United Nations Member States in making responsible and full use of their national legal systems in the service of the [10] global common good. Civil society organizations are also urged to align their agendas and priorities with the findings of this report. Nonetheless, it is primarily incumbent on Israel to comply with international criminal law. Apartheid as an international crime is now viewed by jurists as a peremptory norm (*jus cogens*) of international customary law, which creates obligations *erga omnes*. In other words, it is an overriding principle, from which no derogation is permitted, and which is therefore binding, regardless of the consent of sovereign States, and cannot be renounced by national Governments or their representatives.[6] In effect, this means that even States that do not accede to the International Convention on the Suppression and Punishment of the Crime of Apartheid (hereinafter the Apartheid Convention) are responsible for adhering to its obligations. Israel is thus bound by its obligations to end a crime of apartheid if authoritative findings determine that its practices and policies constitute such a criminal regime. [11]

1   The Legal Context: Short History of the Prohibition of Apartheid

The prohibition of apartheid in international human rights law draws primarily from two areas: (1) prohibitions of discrimination on the basis of race; and (2) rejection of the racist regime that governed in the Republic of South Africa between 1948 and 1992.[7]

The prohibition of racial discrimination traces to the earliest principles of the United Nations. While a full list would overburden this report, foundational statements include Article 55 of the United Nations Charter and article 2 of

---

6 John Dugard, "Introductory note to the Convention on the Suppression and Punishment of the Crime of Apartheid", United Nations Audiovisual Library of International Law, 2008. Available from http://legal.un.org/avl/ha/cspca/cspca.html.

7 The precise date given for the end of apartheid varies with the benchmark used: decriminalization of the African National Congress (ANC) in 1990; the launching or closure of the CODESA (Convention for a Democratic South Africa) talks in 1991 or 1993 respectively; the assassination of Chris Hani in 1993, which triggered the capitulation of the apartheid regime; the election of Nelson Mandela as President in 1994; or passage of the new Constitution in 1995. Taking the meaningful collapse of apartheid's legitimacy as a rough signpost, the fall of apartheid is here dated to 1992.

the Universal Declaration of Human Rights (1948). Later instruments, particularly the International Convention on the Elimination of All Forms of Racial Discrimination, spelled out the prohibition in greater detail. Thus Member States of the United Nations are obligated to abide by the prohibition of apartheid whether or not they are parties to the Apartheid Convention.

The juridical history of international rejection of apartheid in South Africa dates to the early years of the existence of the United Nations. General Assembly resolution 395(V) of 1950 was the first to make explicit reference to apartheid in southern Africa, which it defined as a form of racial discrimination.[8] Resolution 1761(XVII) of 1962 established what came to be called the Special Committee against Apartheid.8 In the preamble to the 1965 International Convention on the Elimination of All Forms of Racial Discrimination, alarm is expressed about "manifestations of racial discrimination still in evidence in some areas of the world ... such as *policies of apartheid*, segregation or separation" (emphasis added). In article 3, signatories to the Convention "particularly condemn *racial segregation and apartheid* and [12] undertake to prevent, prohibit and eradicate all practices of this nature in territories under their jurisdiction" (emphasis added).

The Apartheid Convention of 1973 classifies apartheid as a crime against humanity (in articles I and II) and provides the most detailed definition of it in international law.[9] It also clarifies international responsibility and obligations with regard to combating the crime of apartheid. In the 1977 Protocol Additional to the Geneva Conventions of 12 August 1949, and Relating to the Protection of Victims of International Armed Conflicts (hereinafter Additional Protocol I to the 1949 Geneva Conventions), apartheid is defined as a war crime. The 1998 Rome Statute of the International Criminal Court (ICC), hereinafter the Rome Statute, lists apartheid as a crime against humanity (article 7 (1) (j)), bringing its investigation and possible prosecution under the jurisdiction of the ICC.

Although only 109 States are parties to the Apartheid Convention, most States (currently 177) are parties to the International Convention on the Elimination of All Forms of Racial Discrimination, under which they commit themselves to "prevent, prohibit and eradicate" apartheid (article 3). As of 31 January 2017, 124 States had ratified the Rome Statute. Hence, most States

---

8 Resolution 395(V) addressed racial discrimination against people of Indian origin in South Africa (A/RES/395(V)). Concern for that population had been expressed earlier, beginning with resolution 44 (I) of 1946 (A/RES/44(I)).
9 When the Convention was drafted, apartheid had already been described as a crime against humanity by the General Assembly, as in resolution 2202 (XXI) of 1966 (A/RES/2202(XXI) A–B).

have a legal responsibility to oppose apartheid and take measures to end it wherever it may arise. That responsibility concerns not only human rights violations resulting from apartheid but the threat it poses to international peace and security. The Apartheid Convention further provides that States parties should act at the national level to suppress and prevent the crime of apartheid, through legislative action and prosecutions and legal proceedings in any competent national court.

This report proceeds on the assumption that apartheid is a crime against humanity and that all Member States of the United Nations are legally responsible for acting to prevent, end and punish its practice.

Alternative Definitions of Apartheid

Arguments about whether a State practices apartheid rest on how apartheid is defined. Several definitions are currently used in polemical debate with regard to Israel, which is frequently labelled an "apartheid State" for its practice of discrete [13] "acts of apartheid", such as the "apartheid wall".[10] Those who insist that Israel cannot be held culpable for apartheid argue that the country's laws are fundamentally different from those of apartheid South Africa: for example, because Palestinian citizens of Israel have the right to vote.[11] These diverse arguments arguably fall outside a study grounded in the tenets of international law as set forth in the pertinent instruments, but a quick overview of them here is warranted. This brevity should not be taken to imply a dismissal of such definitions, which have their place beyond strict considerations of international law. Rather, the overview serves to explain why they are not employed in this report. Neat divisions cannot always be made between these definitions, and some clearly overlap, but they can be identified as types or tendencies.

1. Defining only regimes consistent with the apartheid regime in South Africa as being apartheid, so that, by definition, digressions from South African practices preclude any charge of apartheid.
2. Treating discrete practices considered to have qualities of apartheid, such as the so-called "apartheid wall" ("separation fence" or "separation barrier" in official Israeli discourse), as signifying that a State has established a comprehensive apartheid regime.
3. Defining apartheid as the outcome of anonymous structural global forces, such as global corporate influences or neoliberalism, as enforced by Bretton Woods institutions.

---

10 A literature review of such references exceeds the scope of this report.
11 CERD/C/ISR/14–16.

4. Defining apartheid as the aggregate body of private racist practices by the dominant society as a whole, whereby State involvement is a contingent tool for enforcing a draconian social system based on racial hierarchy, discrimination and segregation.
5. Treating apartheid as pertaining only to Palestinian citizens of Israel, or only to Palestinians in the occupied territory, or excluding Palestinian refugees and involuntary exiles living outside territory under Israeli control.[12]

These types of definition, and the reasons that make them unsuitable for this report, are elaborated upon below. [14]

1   The Comparison with Southern Africa

Arguments about whether Israel has established an apartheid regime often compare the policies and practices of Israel with the system of apartheid in southern Africa (South Africa and Namibia).[13] The very term "apartheid" may suggest that the system of racial discrimination as practised by the South African regime constitutes the model for a finding of apartheid elsewhere.[14] The comparison does sometimes provide illuminating insights: for instance, by clarifying why existing proposals for a two-State solution in Mandate Palestine are most likely to generate a Palestinian Bantustan.[15] Such insights are found by examining the South African distinction between so-called "petty apartheid" (the segregation of facilities, job access and so forth) and "grand apartheid", which proposed solving racial tensions with the partition of South African territory and by establishing black South African "homelands" delineated by the regime. Be that as it may, the South African comparison will be mostly avoided in this report, because (1) such comparison contradicts the universal character of the prohibition of apartheid and (2) because apartheid systems that arise in different countries will necessarily differ in design. Nonetheless, because they tend to have much in common, this approach requires brief elaboration.

---

12   Palestinians expelled from the occupied Palestinian territory by Israel and not allowed to return.
13   The term "southern" Africa reflects the practice of South Africa in extending apartheid to South West Africa (now Namibia), which South Africa had held under a League of Nations mandate and refused to relinquish after the Second World War.
14   Afrikaans is the adapted Dutch of the indigenized Dutch-European "Afrikaner" settler society in southern Africa.
15   For a study of how arrangements for the Palestinian Interim Self-Government Authority replicate the South African "homelands", or Bantustans, see Virginia Tilley, "A Palestinian declaration of independence: implications for peace", Middle East Policy, vol. 17, No. 1 (March 2010). Available from http://mepc.org/journal/middle-east-policy-archives/palestinian-declaration-independence-implications-peace.

(a)   *Reasons for the Error of Comparison*

The first reason people turn to the South African case is that the collective memory of the South African struggle and the term "apartheid" itself encourage this error. On coming to power in 1948, the Afrikaner-dominated Nationalist Party translated its constituency's long-standing beliefs about racial hierarchy into a body of racial laws designed to secure white supremacy and determine the life conditions and chances of everyone in the country on the basis of race. The Nationalists' term for this comprehensive system was apartheid (Afrikaans for "apart-hood" or "separate development").[16] The opposition to apartheid (coordinated by the African National [15] Congress, the Pan-African Congress, the domestic United Democratic Front and other southern African actors, as well as sympathetic international human rights networks) accordingly adopted the term in order to denounce it. The General Assembly did the same, using the term for a series of measures concerning South Africa. For many people, this long history of legal activism naturalized the association between apartheid and South Africa to the point of conflation.

That this conflation is a legal error can be seen in the history of usage through which the term gained universal application:

- 1962 – The General Assembly established the Special Committee on the Policies of Apartheid of the Government of South Africa, later renamed the Special Committee against Apartheid;
- 1965 – Under the International Convention on the Elimination of All Forms of Racial Discrimination, apartheid was classified as a form of racial discrimination (preamble and article 3) with no mention of South Africa;
- 1973 – The Apartheid Convention clarified that "inhuman acts" that constitute the crime of apartheid would "include" acts that are "similar to" those of apartheid South Africa;
- 1976 – The Secretariat of the United Nations set up the Centre against Apartheid;
- 1998 – Apartheid was listed in the Rome Statute as a crime against humanity, with no mention of South Africa.

That the term has come to have universal application is clarified by South African jurist John Dugard (a leading legal scholar of apartheid):

---

16 The National Party was the principal party in South Africa expressing the Afrikaner worldview and white-nationalist political goals. Hold-outs against United Nations denunciations of apartheid in South Africa included Israel, which maintained a close alliance with the regime throughout its duration, and the United States of America, which had close business ties with South Africa.

That the Apartheid Convention is intended to apply to situations other than South Africa is confirmed by its endorsement in a wider context in instruments adopted before and after the fall of apartheid ... It may be concluded that the Apartheid Convention is dead as far as the original cause for its creation – apartheid in South Africa – is concerned, but that **it lives on as a species of the crime against humanity**, under both customary international law and the Rome Statute of the International Criminal Court (emphasis added).[17] [16]

This report assumes that the term "apartheid" has come to have universal application in international law and is accordingly not confined to the South African case.

(b)   *The Paucity of Precedents*
A second reason people turn to the South African comparison is that, because no other State has been accused of the crime of apartheid, South Africa stands as the only case providing a precedent. Given the importance of precedents in the interpretation of law, it is arguably natural for people to look at the "inhuman acts" of apartheid in southern Africa as the models or benchmarks for what apartheid "looks like". For example, some claim that Israel clearly does not practise apartheid because Palestinian citizens of Israel have the right to vote in national elections, while black South Africans did not. That the design of apartheid regimes in other States must necessarily differ – due to the unique history of their societies and the collective experience shaping local racial thought, such as settler colonialism, slavery, ethnic cleansing, war or genocide – is neglected in such a simplified search for models.

Nevertheless, the case of southern Africa does serve to expose some legal arguments as specious. For example, it might be argued that the treatment by Israel of Palestinian populations outside its internationally recognized borders (that is, in the occupied Palestinian territory and abroad) falls beyond the scope of the question, making its policies on Palestinian refugees and Palestinians living under occupation irrelevant to a charge of apartheid. That this argument is unsupportable is confirmed by reference to ICJ advisory opinions regarding the behaviour of South Africa in South West Africa (Namibia).[18] In 1972, the

---

17   John Dugard, "Introductory note to the Convention on the Suppression and Punishment of the Crime of Apartheid". Available from http://legal.un.org/avl/ha/cspca/cspca.html.
18   In the 1960s, South Africa administered South West Africa (Namibia) as a fifth province and applied to it its doctrine of apartheid, complete with Bantustans. The policy attracted repeated criticism from the General Assembly.

ICJ found South African rule over Namibia illegal partly on the grounds that it violated the rights of the Namibian people by imposing South African apartheid laws there.[19] South Africa was thus held to account for apartheid practices outside its own sovereign territory and in respect to non-citizens. [17]

This report assumes that the question of formal sovereignty is not germane to a finding of apartheid.

2   Apartheid as Discrete Practices

Discrete acts by Israel are frequently labelled as examples of "apartheid": for example, as noted earlier, in references to the "apartheid wall". Such references are useful to those wishing to highlight how the forcible segregation of groups strongly suggests apartheid. Yet it would be erroneous to take such isolated practices as indicative that a State is constituted as an apartheid regime.[20] Rather, the Apartheid Convention provides a definition that stresses the combination of acts with their "purpose" or intent:

> For the purpose of the present Convention, the term "the crime of **apartheid**", which shall include similar policies and practices of racial segregation and discrimination as practiced in southern Africa, shall apply to the following inhuman acts **committed for the purpose of** (emphasis added) establishing and maintaining domination by one racial group of persons over any other racial group of persons and systematically oppressing them (article II).

---

19   The ICJ was addressing the legality of South Africa's continued rule of South West Africa in violation of a Security Council resolution calling for its withdrawal. *See* especially the last of four opinions issued between 1950 and 1971: *International Status of South-West Africa, Advisory Opinion, I.C.J. Reports 1950*, p. 128; *Voting Procedure on Questions Relating to Reports and Petitions Concerning the Territory of South West Africa, Advisory Opinion, I.C.J. Reports 1955*, p. 67; *Admissibility of Hearings of Petitioners by the Committee on South-West Africa, Advisory Opinion, I.C.J. Reports 1956*, p. 23; *Legal Consequences for States of the Continued Presence of South Africa in Namibia (South West Africa) Notwithstanding Security Council Resolution 276 (1970), Advisory Opinion, I.C.J. Reports 1971*, p. 16 (especially paras. 131 and 133).

20   Former special rapporteurs John Dugard and Richard Falk highlighted the problem of determining when "features of apartheid" signify that an apartheid regime is operating, which would constitute a matter that might be referred to the ICJ. For both rapporteurs, the question arose with regard to the legality of the Israeli occupation. Mr. Dugard described "road apartheid" in the occupied Palestinian territory and noted that the Israeli occupation has "features" or "elements" of apartheid. However, whether Israel is constituted as an apartheid regime remained for Mr. Dugard a question still to be legally determined (A/62/275). Mr. Falk adopted a similar position (A/HRC/25/67, p. 21).

The Convention then lists six categories of such "inhuman acts". In article 7 (2) (h), the Rome Statute formulates the same concept differently, but again places emphasis on such acts as reflecting an "intention":

> "The crime of apartheid" means inhumane acts of a character similar to those referred to in paragraph 1 [i.e., "when committed as part of a widespread or systematic attack directed against any civilian population, with knowledge of the attack"], committed in the context of an institutionalized regime of systematic oppression and domination by one racial group over any other racial group or groups and committed with the intention of maintaining that regime.

Both instruments thus establish that discrete acts are crimes of apartheid only if they are part of an institutionalized regime and have the "intention" or "purpose" of racial domination and oppression. The same acts, if not observably part of such a regime or lacking such a clear purpose, may be denounced as reprehensible [18] instances of racism but do not meet the definition of a crime of apartheid. For that reason, a check-list method alone – such as looking for the "inhuman acts" mentioned in the Apartheid Convention – would be a misreading of the Convention's intention. In article II, it explicitly establishes that such acts are illustrative, not mandatory, and are crimes of apartheid only if they serve the overarching purpose of racial domination. Hence, such acts can be considered crimes of apartheid only after the existence of an "institutionalized regime of systematic oppression and domination" has been conclusively established.

The very existence of the Apartheid Convention indicates that apartheid is rightly distinguished from other forms of racial discrimination, already prohibited under instruments such as the International Convention on the Elimination of All Forms of Racial Discrimination, by its character as a regime. The Rome Statute expressly refers to apartheid as a regime. In political science, a State regime is the set of institutions through which the State is governed, principally regarding its arrangements for exercising power. In the oft-cited formulation by political scientist Robert Fishman:

> A regime may be thought of as the formal and informal organization of the centre of political power, and of its relations with the broader society. A regime determines who has access to political power, and how those who are in power deal with those who are not ... Regimes are more

permanent forms of political organization than specific governments, but they are typically less permanent than the State.[21]

On the basis of this definition, relevant evidence for an apartheid regime in Israel- Palestine must go beyond identifying discrete acts and determine whether the regime blocks access to "the centre of political power" on the basis of race. Moreover, the Apartheid Convention specifies that "organizations, institutions and individuals" may be culpable for the crime of apartheid (article I, para. 2). This, too, means that the State as a whole may be held accountable for committing that crime.

Finally, identifying apartheid as a regime clarifies one controversy: that ending such a regime would constitute destruction of the State itself. This interpretation is understandable if the State is understood as being the same as its regime. Thus, some suggest that the aim of eliminating apartheid in Israel is tantamount to aiming to "destroy Israel". However, a State does not cease to exist as a result of regime change. The elimination of the apartheid regime in South Africa in no way affected the country's statehood. [19]

To determine whether specific acts constitute evidence of apartheid, this report examines whether they contribute to the overarching purpose of sustaining an institutionalized regime of racial oppression and domination.

3   Apartheid as Generated by Anonymous Structural Conditions

Some writers have begun to define apartheid as the racialized impact of anonymous socioeconomic forces, such as the capitalist mode of production. It may indeed be heuristically useful to use the term "economic apartheid" to describe situations where economic inequality feeds into racial formation and stratification, even in the absence of any deliberate State policy to achieve this result.[22] (Scholars of race relations will identify this as the illimitable race-class debate.) In this model, "apartheid" is used to flag discrimination that emerges spontaneously from a variety of economic conditions and incentives. Some argue that the entire global economy is generating a kind of "global apartheid".[23]

---

[21] Fishman, Robert M., "Rethinking State and regime: Southern Europe's transition to democracy", *World Politics*, vol. 42, No. 3 (April 1990).

[22] For more on this, *see* Cass Sunstein, "Why markets don't stop discrimination", *Social Philosophy and Policy*, vol. 8, issue 2 (April 1991).

[23] Anthony H. Richmond, *Global Apartheid: Refugees, Racism, and the New World Order* (Toronto, Oxford University Press, 1994).

The trouble with this hyper-structural approach is that it renders agency, particularly the role of a given State, unclear or implicitly eliminates it altogether. International law interprets apartheid as a crime for which individuals (or States) can be prosecuted, once their culpability is established by authoritative legal procedures. No such criminal culpability could pertain when treating apartheid as the product of the international structure itself, as this would not signify whether the State regime is configured deliberately for the purpose of racial domination and oppression – the distinguishing quality of apartheid according to the Apartheid Convention and Rome Statute.

This report considers that the question of whether or not an apartheid system is in place should be analysed at the level of the State, and that the crime of apartheid is applicable only to that level.

4   Apartheid as Private Social Behaviour

The term apartheid is also used to describe racial discrimination where the main agent in imposing racial domination is the dominant racial group, whose members [20] collectively generate the rules and norms that define race, enforce racial hierarchy and police racial boundaries. The primary enforcers of such systems are private, such as teachers, employers, real estate agents, loan officers and vigilante groups, but they also rely to varying degrees on administrative organs of the State, such as the police and a court system. It follows that maintaining these organs as compliant with the system becomes a core goal of private actors, because excluding dominated groups from meaningful voting rights that might alter that compliance is essential to maintaining the system.

Social racism doubtless plays a vital role in apartheid regimes, by providing popular support for designing and preserving the system, and by using informal methods (treating people with hostility and suspicion) to intimidate and silence subordinated groups.[24] Social racism is rarely entirely divorced from institutionalized racism. Law and practice are so interdependent that the difference between them may seem irrelevant to those oppressed by the holistic system they create.

Nonetheless, one significant difference distinguishes the two: the role of constitutional law. Where a State's constitutional law provides equal rights to the entire citizenry, it can provide an invaluable resource for people challenging discrimination at all levels of the society. However, if constitutional law

---

24   Surveys of Jewish Israeli attitudes towards "Arabs" and Palestinians are omitted here because they do not pertain to a study of the State's institutionalized regime. This omission in no way intends to suggest that popular views are not key guardians and enforcers of that regime.

defines the State as racial in character – as in Israel (as a Jewish State), and apartheid South Africa (as a white-Afrikaner State) – movements against racial discrimination not only lack this crucial legal resource but find themselves in the far more dangerous position of challenging the regime itself. Such a challenge will naturally be seen by regime authorities as an existential threat and be persecuted accordingly.[25]

In short, it is crucial for a finding of apartheid to establish whether the State's constitutional law (the Basic Law in Israel) renders discrimination illegal or renders resistance to discrimination illegal. The latter case fits the definition of apartheid in the Apartheid Convention, which lists as a crime against humanity "persecution of organizations and persons, by depriving them of fundamental rights and freedoms, because they oppose apartheid" (article II (f)). [21]

5   Apartheid and the Question of Race

The Apartheid Convention defines apartheid as "domination by one racial group of persons over any other racial group of persons...". The Rome Statute uses similar wording: "... systematic oppression and domination by one racial group over any other racial group or groups...". However, neither Jews nor Palestinians are referred to as "races" today. Moreover, Jews are correctly argued to include many "races" in the sense of the old colour categories: black, white, Asian and so forth. Thus, one challenge to any accusation that Israel maintains an apartheid regime is that the Israeli-Palestinian conflict is not racial in nature. Hence, the argument goes, Jews cannot be racist toward Palestinians (or anyone else) because Jews themselves are not a race.

Such arguments reflect a mistaken and obsolete understanding of race. Through the first half of the twentieth century, the idea of race was seen as scientifically established and measurable. Since the Second World War, however, it has come to be recognized as a social construction that varies over time and may be contested within each local context. One illustration of such variability is the North American "one-drop rule", which has long operated to label as "black" anyone with a perceptible element of African phenotypes or known black ancestry. Yet the same "black" person, travelling to Latin America, finds the one-drop rule working in reverse, such that s/he is not considered "black" if

---

25   Although the Constitution of the United States of America states that "We hold these truths to be self-evident, that all men are created equal", race relations always complicated this principle in practice. Constitutional law favouring white supremacy included the key "separate but equal" provisions in *Plessy v. Ferguson*, 163 US 537 (1896). They were overturned only in 1954, in *Brown v. Board of Education of Topeka*, 347 US 483, which was later followed by the Civil Rights Act of 1964 and the Voting Rights Act of 1965.

s/he has any portion of "white" blood, instead being called *mestizo* or *mulatto*. Thus racial identity changes with the setting.

Consequently, there can be no single, authoritative, global definition of any race. The only way to determine how racial identities are perceived and practiced locally is through historical studies of racial thought and by field observations in each local setting. The question is therefore not whether Jewish and Palestinian identities are innately racial in character wherever they occur, but whether those identities function as racial groups in the local environment of Israel-Palestine.

This point raises another question on how race is handled in United Nations instruments.[26] For the purposes of human rights law, a finding of racial discrimination is based less on how groups are labelled than how they are treated. For example, although Jews today are not normally referred to as a "race", anti-[22] Semitism is correctly seen as a form of racism. It would indeed be unethical and politically regressive sophistry to argue that Jews cannot be subject to racial discrimination simply because they are not normally referred to as a "race". The International Convention on the Elimination of All Forms of Racial Discrimination captures that point by defining "racial discrimination" as embracing a range of identities:

In this Convention, the term "racial discrimination" shall mean any distinction, exclusion, restriction or preference based on **race, colour, descent, or national or ethnic origin** which has the purpose or effect of nullifying or impairing the recognition, enjoyment or exercise, on an equal footing, of human rights and fundamental freedoms in the political, economic, social, cultural or any other field of public life (part I, article 1) (emphasis added).

By invoking that Convention in its preamble, the Apartheid Convention suggests that its language regarding "racial group or groups" embraces the same range of identities.

Recognizing this contextual meaning of "race" is not haphazard. Since the mid-twentieth century, scholars of international law have joined social scientists in coming to understand racial identity as fundamentally a matter of perception, rather than objectively measurable qualities. Racial identities are usually signally somatic and so are *seen* as stable and permanent, acquired at birth and thus immutable. That races are actually *social constructions* is evidenced by how such constructions vary from society to society: that is, the significance of specific somatic criteria, such as skin colour or eye shape, to

---

26 The exception that proves the rule regarding definitions of race is the isolated effort by the International Criminal Tribunal for Rwanda: *see Prosecutor v. Jean-Paul Akayesu*, case No. ICTR-96-4-T, Judgement (TC), 2 September 1998, Akayesu Trial Judgment, paras. 511–515.

a racial typology. Where such perceptions of an essential identity persist, the difference disappears between language about groups understood as racial or "ethnic", as descent groups, and that which sees them as sharing a particular national or ethnic origin. What matters in all those cases is that all members of a group – including infants and others who cannot possibly constitute a "racial threat" – are embraced by one policy. A pertinent example of this conflation of terms has been discrimination against Jews, for whom a mix of labels (race, religion and ethnicity) has been used by those pursuing anti-Semitic segregation, persecution or genocide. The question here is, therefore, whether relations between Jews and Palestinians in Mandate Palestine rest on ideas that each group has an immutable character, such that their relations fit the definition of "racial" discrimination.

A comprehensive review of how Jewish and Palestinian identities are understood locally in Israel-Palestine would overburden this report. Fortunately, one factor confirms the racial quality of both identities in this context: both are considered *descent* groups (one of the categories in the International Convention on the [23] Elimination of All Forms of Racial Discrimination). Palestinian identity is explicitly based on origins or ancestral origins in the territory of Mandate Palestine. The 1964 Charter of the Palestinian Liberation Organization (PLO)[27] expresses this principle by affirming that Palestinian identity is passed down through the paternal line and is intergenerational:

> Article 5: The Palestinian personality is a permanent and genuine characteristic that does not disappear. It is transferred from fathers to sons.

Palestinian national identity has always been nested within pan-Arabism, an ethno- national identity formulated first as a modern territorial nationalism by Sherif Hussein of Mecca. "Arab" was certainly the generic term for Arabic-speaking people in Palestine when the Zionist movement began to settle the area. General Assembly resolution 181(II) of 1947,[28] which recommended the partition of Mandate Palestine into an "Arab State" and a "Jewish State", drew from that discourse. Updated and promoted especially by Egyptian President Gamal Abdul Nasser to craft an anticolonial Arab identity bloc across the Middle East and North Africa, Arab identity became a vital identity and political resource for the PLO, as reflected in its Charter:

---

27   *See*   https://web.archive.org/web/20101130144018/http://www.un.int/wcm/content/site/palestine/pid/12363.

28   A/RES/181(II).

Article 1: Palestine is an Arab homeland bound by strong Arab national ties to the rest of the Arab countries and which together form the great Arab homeland.

... Article 3: The Palestinian Arab people has the legitimate right to its homeland and is an inseparable part of the Arab Nation. It shares the sufferings and aspirations of the Arab Nation and its struggle for freedom, sovereignty, progress and unity ...

In this conception, Palestinians are integral members of the Arab "Nation", but it is the "Palestinian people" that holds the right to self-determination in Mandate Palestine, thus conveying the international legal meaning of "nation" to the Palestinian people.

In contrast, Jewish identity combines several contradictory elements.[29] "Jewish" is certainly a religious identity in the sense that Judaism is a religious faith to which [24] anyone may convert if willing and able to follow the required procedures. On that basis, opponents of Israeli policy insist that Jewishness is not a national identity but simply a religious one, and so Jews *qua* Jews are not a "people" in the sense of international law and therefore lack the right to self-determination. Supporters of Israel use the same point to deny that Jewish statehood is racist, on the grounds that Zionism and Israel cannot be racist if Jews are not a race. However, those arguments are flawed, even disingenuous, as religious criteria alone are not adequate for defining what it is to be "Jewish".

Like many other groups that today are now commonly called "ethnic" or "national", until the mid-twentieth century Jews were often referred to as a "race". Jewish-Zionist thinkers adopted the same approach, reflecting contemporary concepts of what races were, how races composed peoples and nations, and how on that basis they had the right to self-determination. For example, Zionist philosopher and strategist Max Nordau commonly used the term "race" for Jews in speaking of Jewish interests in Palestine.[30] For decades, the founder of Revisionist Zionism, Vladimir Jabotinsky, wrote passionately about the Jewish "race" and how the "spiritual mechanism" associated with it granted transcendental value to a Jewish State.[31] Today, this usage persists in

---

29 Internal debates about "who is a Jew" are irrelevant to the State's construction of Jewishness as a single people, and thus not pertinent to this report. On such debates, *see*, for example, Noah Efron, *Real Jews: Secular Versus Ultra-Orthodox: The Struggle For Jewish Identity In Israel* (New York, Basic Books, 2003).

30 *See*, for example, Max Nordau, "Address to the First Zionist Congress", 29 August 1897. Available from www.mideastweb.org/nordau1897.htm.

31 *See* Vladimir Jabotinsky, A lecture on Jewish history (1933), cited in David Goldberg, *To the Promised Land: A History of Zionist Thought* (London, Penguin, 1996), p. 181.

the Memorandum of Association of the Jewish National Fund (JNF), which in article 2 (c) cites one of its objectives as being to "benefit, directly or indirectly, those of Jewish race or descent". In none of those sources is religious faith even mentioned (because it is recognized to vary): the concern is entirely with descent. Halachah (often translated as "Jewish law") and social norms in Jewish communities provide that Jewish identity is conveyed from mother to child, irrespective of the individual's actual religious beliefs or practice. The State of Israel enshrined the central importance of descent in its Law of Return of 1950 (amended in 1970),[32] which states that:

> For the purposes of this Law, "Jew" means a person who was born of a Jewish mother or has become converted to Judaism and who is not a member of another religion.

Descent is crucial to Jewish identity discourse in Israel because direct lineal descent from antiquity is the main reason given by political-Zionist philosophers [25] for why Jews today hold the right to self-determination in the land of Palestine. In this view, all Jews retain a special relationship and rights to the land of Palestine, granted by covenant with God: some schools of Zionism hold that Israel is the successor State to the Jewish kingdoms of Saul, David and Solomon. That claim is expressed, inter alia, in the Declaration of Independence of Israel,[33] which affirms that Jews today trace their ancestry to an earlier national life in the geography of Palestine and therefore have an inalienable right to "return", which is given precedence over positive law:

> The Land of Israel[34] was the birthplace of the Jewish people. Here their spiritual, religious and political identity was shaped. Here they first attained to statehood, created cultural values of national and universal significance and gave to the world the eternal Book of Books.

After being forcibly exiled from their land, the people kept faith with it throughout their Dispersion and never ceased to pray and hope for their return to it and for the restoration in it of their political freedom.

---

32 Passed by the Knesset on 5 July 1950 and amended on 10 March 1970.
33 Provisional Government of Israel, The Declaration of the Establishment of the State of Israel, Official Gazette, No. 1 (Tel Aviv, 14 May 1948). It is also commonly referred to as the Declaration of Independence. Available from https://www.knesset.gov.il/docs/eng/megilat_eng.htm.
34 Eretz-Israel in Hebrew.

Impelled by this historic and traditional attachment, Jews strove in every successive generation to re-establish themselves in their ancient homeland. In recent decades they returned in their masses. [...]

That claim to unbroken lineal descent from antiquity attributes collective rights to the "land of Israel" to an entire group on the basis of its (supposed) bloodlines. The incompatible claim that Jewishness is multiracial, by virtue of its character as a religion to which others have converted, is simply absent from this formula.

The emphasis on descent implicitly portrays all other descent groups – including Palestinians – as lacking any comparable right by virtue of their different descent. Thus the claim to Palestine as the exclusive homeland of the Jewish people rests on an expressly racial conception of both groups. This means that Jews and Palestinians are "racial groups" as defined by the International Convention on the Elimination of All Forms of Racial Discrimination and, accordingly, for the purposes of the Apartheid Convention. [26–27]

2 Testing for an Apartheid Regime in Israel-Palestine

The design of an apartheid regime in any State will necessarily reflect the country's unique history and demography, which shape local perceptions of racial hierarchy and doctrines of racial supremacy. The first task here is, therefore, to consider how local conditions in Israel-Palestine constitute such an environment. The main feature, stemming from the history of wars and expulsions, is the geographic fragmentation of the Palestinian people into discrete populations that are then administered differently by the State regime. Those components include Palestinians living under direct Israeli rule in three categories (as citizens of the State of Israel, residents of occupied East Jerusalem, and under occupation in the West Bank and Gaza) and Palestinians living outside direct Israeli rule: refugees and involuntary exiles expelled from the territory of Mandate Palestine who are prohibited by Israel from returning. The next section clarifies how those four categories have emerged from the territory's history of warfare and incremental annexation.

A *The Political Geography of Apartheid*
The geographic unit of "Mandate Palestine" was established by the League of Nations in 1922 with the stated intention of fostering the future independence of Palestine as a State, as specified in the League of Nations Charter.[35] Famously,

---

35   The borders of Mandate Palestine were derived from the Sykes-Picot agreement, which divided Ottoman imperial territory after the First World War and placed it under British

the Palestine Mandate included contradictory provisions for a Jewish "national home" (not a State) and the special authority of the Jewish Agency in establishing that "home". Later British commissions and white papers specified that "national [28] home" had not been intended to signify a Jewish State, but that position was not accepted by the Zionist leadership. Endemic violence that emerged from this contradictory formula, combined with imperial exhaustion after the Second World War, ultimately led Great Britain to withdraw from its role as Mandatory Power and submit the fate of Palestine to the United Nations. In 1947, the General Assembly passed resolution 181(II) by a modest majority of 36 Member States, recommending the territory's partition into a "Jewish State" and an "Arab State". The same resolution specified conditions and measures deemed essential to make partition viable, including borders that provided for racial majorities in each titular State, constitutional protections for minorities, economic union between the two States and a special international regime for the city of Jerusalem.[36]

In the 1948 war, however, the Zionist movement took over territory far beyond what had been assigned to the Jewish State under resolution 181(II) and, by so doing, rendered moot its labyrinthine provisions, including acquiescence by the internationally recognized representatives of the Palestinian people. In 1948, the Zionist leadership declared the independence of Israel in territory under its military control, although its final borders had yet to be established. In 1949, the General Assembly recommended admission of the State of Israel to membership even though its borders had still not been finalized. Palestinians remaining in Israel, who had not fled or been expelled in the 1948 war, became citizens of Israel, but Israel administered them under emergency laws and denied them civil rights, such as the franchise, until 1966.

From 1948 until 1967, the West Bank (including East Jerusalem) was governed by Jordan, while the Gaza Strip was administered by Egypt. As a result of the 1967 Arab-Israeli war, both territories came under Israeli military

---

or French Mandates. Article 22 of the Covenant of the League of Nations provided for various classes of mandate territory. Palestine was considered one of the most advanced areas, whose "existence as independent nations can be provisionally recognized subject to the rendering of administrative advice and assistance by a Mandatory until such time as they are able to stand alone". In that context, "independent nations" signified independent statehood, thus informing language in the Mandate for Palestine. The early history of Palestine's mandate borders, which combined Transjordan and Palestine, is not considered material to this report, but for that history, *see* especially Victor Kattan, *From Coexistence to Conquest: International Law and the Origins of the Arab-Israeli Conflict, 1891–1949* (London, Pluto Press, 2009).

36 Resolution 181(II) was the result of work by the United Nations Special Committee on Palestine (UNSCOP), with its two subcommittees providing options for a partitioned or unified State.

occupation and rule, yet were not formally annexed.[37] The geographic separation of the West Bank and Gaza Strip has suggested the existence of two discrete territories. However, the United Nations commonly refers to the West Bank and Gaza Strip in the singular as the "occupied Palestinian territory", treating both as geographic fragments of "Palestine" as established under the League of Nations Mandate.[38] Pursuant to [29] article XI of the 1995 Israeli-Palestinian Interim Agreement on the West Bank and the Gaza Strip (also known as the Oslo II Accord or Oslo II), for the purposes of negotiation those areas were considered a "single territorial unit" (article XI). Hence, international jurists and the United Nations consider Palestinians in the West Bank and Gaza Strip to be under one legal category: that is, civilians under belligerent occupation, whose rights and protections are stipulated primarily in the Fourth Geneva Convention Relative to the Protection of Civilian Persons in Times of War (1949).

East Jerusalem (that part of Jerusalem on the east side of the Armistice Line or "green line" of 1949) obtained a special status. Although seamlessly integrated with the West Bank between 1948 and 1967, East Jerusalem retained the aura of the diplomatic character, proposed by resolution 181(II), of a *corpus separatum*, reflecting its vital importance to all three Abrahamic faiths. After the 1967 war, however, Israel passed legislation making East Jerusalem part of the unified city of Jerusalem, radically expanding the city's borders, and extending Israeli civil law throughout. After the second intifada (from September 2000), parts of East Jerusalem were re-segregated from Jewish areas physically by the separation wall and its security gates and Israeli checkpoints. This forced separation has allowed Israel to separate East Jerusalem from the West Bank in juridical terms and so has generated the category of Palestinian "residents"

---

37   Although effectively annexed, the occupied Syrian Golan is excluded from the scope of this report because that territory was not part of the Palestine Mandate and is considered legally to be Syrian territory. However, many of this report's findings could apply to Israeli policy in the Golan and may be consistent with apartheid, as Israel has used Jewish settlement to stake a claim to the land and the population of the four Druze villages there live in conditions of relative deprivation.

38   Steps taken by the General Assembly to recognize a "State of Palestine" have prompted some to suggest that occupied Palestinian territory should now be referred to as "occupied Palestine". However, since recognition of such a State still lacks any final agreement about its borders, the authors here continue to use the term "occupied Palestinian territory" to refer to territory delineated by the 1949 Armistice Agreement and occupied by Israel in the 1967 war.

of East Jerusalem, whose rights stem largely from Israeli law on permanent residency.[39]

The territory's history has further generated the separate case of Palestinian citizens of Israel: people who remained inside the internationally recognized borders of Israel after 1949 and their descendants. Granted Israeli citizenship although not full "national" equality as non-Jews in a Jewish-national State, this Palestinian population now makes up 20 per cent of the country's citizenry.[40] How Israeli law and doctrine has defined this population as citizens but not "nationals" of the State is addressed below. Here it is incumbent only to recognize that Palestinian citizens of Israel comprise a distinct legal category. The situation of refugees and involuntary exiles comprises the final category, distinct from the others in that they are governed by the laws of the other States in which they reside. [30]

By developing discrete bodies of law, termed "domains" in this report, for each territory and their Palestinian populations, Israel has both effected and veiled a comprehensive policy of apartheid directed at the whole Palestinian people.[41] Warfare, partition, de jure and de facto annexation and occupation in Palestine have, over the decades, generated the complex geography in which the Palestinian people have become fragmented into different juridical categories and are administered by different bodies of law. What matters for the purposes of a study of apartheid is how Israel has exploited this fragmentation to secure Jewish-national domination.

B   *Israel as a Racial State*

A test of apartheid cannot be confined, methodologically, to identifying discrete policies and practices, such as those listed under the Apartheid Convention. Such policies and practices must be found to serve the *purpose* or *intention* of imposing racial domination and oppression on a subordinated racial group. In somewhat circular reasoning, international law provides that discrete "inhuman acts" acquire the status of a crime against humanity only

---

39   The Knesset passed Basic Law: Jerusalem, Capital of Israel on 30 July 1980 (published in *Sefer Ha-Chukkim* No. 980 of 5 August 1980, p. 186).

40   Jewish Virtual Library, Vital Statistics: Latest Population Statistics for Israel (January 2017). Available from www.jewishvirtuallibrary.org/latest-population-statistics-for-israel.

41   "Domain" is used in the report in the sense of logic or discourse analysis, in which concepts and actors are understood as part of one "universe" of references. Hence, the domains in Israeli policy consist of definitions of the populations themselves (domestic, foreign, citizens or otherwise, "Palestinians" oriented toward Palestinian self-determination or "Arabs" as an Israeli minority, and so forth), as well as the laws, practices, norms and other measures, formal and informal, by which Israeli definitions of those identities are imposed on Palestinian populations in each domain.

if they intentionally serve that purpose, but establishes that such a purpose requires the identification of related inhuman acts. The solution is to examine the context in which acts and motives are configured: that is, whether the State itself is designed to ensure "the domination of a racial group or groups over any other racial group or groups". (For example, in South Africa, State institutions were designed to ensure incontestable domination by whites and, particularly, Dutch-Afrikaners.)

In this study, it is vital to establish the racial character of the regime that the system of domains is designed to protect. Otherwise, their internal diversity – the laws that comprise them – can convey the incorrect impression of discrete systems.

That Israel is politically constructed as the State of the Jewish people requires no extended explanation here, but will be discussed briefly.[42] Since the turn of the twentieth century, the history of the Zionist movement has been centred on creating and preserving a Jewish State in Palestine. That aim remains the cornerstone of [31] Israeli State discourse. During the Mandate years, the Jewish Agency and Zionist leadership argued that the "Jewish national home" promised under the Mandate was to be a sovereign Jewish State. The Declaration of the Establishment of the State of Israel specifically referred to the new State as a "Jewish State in Eretz- Israel". The Basic Law: Human Dignity and Liberty[43] and Basic Law: Freedom of Occupation[44] specify concerns with "the values of the State of Israel as a Jewish and democratic State".[45] The 1952 World Zionist Organisation – Jewish Agency (Status) Law,[46] which establishes those organizations as "authorized agencies" of the State on a range of responsibilities, including land settlement, specifies that Israel is "the creation of the entire Jewish people, and its gates are open, in accordance with its laws, to every Jew wishing to immigrate to it".

---

42   For a more complete discussion, *see* Tilley (ed.), *Beyond Occupation*, chaps. 3 and 4.
43   Passed by the Knesset on 17 March 1992 (published in *Sefer Ha-Chukkim* No. 1391 of 25 March 1992). Available from https://www.knesset.gov.il/laws/special/eng/basic3_eng.htm.
44   The law amending the original 1992 legislation was passed by the Knesset on 9 March 1994 (published in *Sefer Ha-Chukkim* No. 1454 of 10 March 1994). Available from https://www.knesset.gov.il/laws/special/eng/basic4_eng.htm.
45   A controversial bill to declare this principle as a central tenet had been tabled in the Knesset but not yet passed at the time of writing. *See* Basic Law: Israel as the Nation-State of the Jewish People, Ministry of Justice. Available from http://index.justice.gov.il/StateIdentity/InformationInEnglish/Documents/Basic%20Law%20110911%20(1).pdf. Accessed 5 February 2017.
46   The Status Law was amended in 1975 to restructure this relationship: *see* World Zionist Organisation – Jewish Agency for Israel (Status) (Amendment) Law, 1975.

The mission of preserving Israel as a Jewish State has inspired or even compelled Israel to pursue several general racial policies.

1   Demographic Engineering

The first general policy of Israel has been one of demographic engineering, in order to establish and maintain an overwhelming Jewish majority in Israel. As in any racial democracy, such a majority allows the trappings of democracy – democratic elections, a strong legislature – without threatening any loss of hegemony by the dominant racial group. In Israeli discourse, this mission is expressed in terms of the so-called "demographic threat", an openly racist reference to Palestinian population growth or the return of Palestinian refugees. Related practices have included:

1. A global programme, organized by the World Zionist Organization and Jewish Agency, launched at the end of the nineteenth century and accelerating into the early 1930s, to bring Jewish immigrants to Palestine in numbers large enough to ensure the demographic majority needed for building a Jewish State with democratic characteristics; [32]
2. Ethnic cleansing (forcible displacement) in 1948 of an estimated 800,000 Palestinians from areas that became part of the internationally recognized territory of Israel; 47
3. Subsequent measures undertaken by Israel to maintain an overwhelming Jewish majority within its internationally recognized territory, including by:
    a. Preventing Palestinian refugees from the wars of 1948 and 1967 from returning to homes in Israel or in the occupied Palestinian territory, which they had abandoned due to fighting, dispossession, forced expulsion and terror;[47]
    b. Composing the Law of Return and Citizenship Law (often wrongly translated as Nationality Law) to provide Israeli citizenship to Jews from any part of the world, while denying citizenship even to those Palestinians who have a documented history of residency in the country;
    c. A range of other policies designed to restrict the size of the Palestinian population, including harsh restrictions placed on immigration, the return of refugees, and rules prohibiting Palestinian spouses of Israeli citizens from gaining legal residency rights in Israel.

---

47   Ibid. The right of refugees to return is specified in the International Convention on the Elimination of All Forms of Racial Discrimination (article 5 (d) (ii)).

4. The affirmation in the Basic Law that Israel is a "Jewish and democratic State", thus establishing Jewish-racial domination as a foundational doctrine.

Together, those measures have been highly effective in maintaining an overwhelming Jewish majority in Israel. In 1948, the ratio of Palestinians to Jews in Palestine was approximately 2:1 (some 1.3 million Arabs to 630,000 Jews).[48] Today, Palestinian citizens of Israel constitute only about 20 per cent of the population, rendering them a permanent minority.

2   Bans on Challenges to Racial Domination

Israel reinforces its race-based immigration policy with measures designed to prevent Palestinian citizens of Israel from challenging the doctrine and laws that purport to establish Israel as a Jewish State. Article 7 (a) of the Basic Law: Knesset (1958), for instance, prohibits any political party in Israel from adopting a platform that challenges the State's expressly Jewish character: [33]

> A candidates list shall not participate in elections to the Knesset, and a person shall not be a candidate for election to the Knesset, if the objects or actions of the list or the actions of the person, expressly or by implication, include one of the following:
>
> > (1) Negation of the existence of the State of Israel as a Jewish and democratic State (emphasis added) …[49]

Voting rights lose their significance in terms of equal rights when a racial group is legally banned from challenging laws that perpetuate inequality. An analogy would be a system in which slaves have the right to vote but not against slavery. Such rights might allow slaves to achieve some cosmetic reforms, such as improved living conditions and protection from vigilante violence, but their status and vulnerability as chattels would remain. Israeli law bans organized Palestinian opposition to Jewish domination, rendering it illegal and even seditious.

---

48   Censuses categories under the British Mandate were ordered by "religion" rather than ethnicity. Statistics therefore grouped together Arab and non-Arab Christians. In 1947, Christians and Muslims numbered 143,000 and 1,181,000 respectively.

49   Basic Law: Knesset. Available from https://www.knesset.gov.il/laws/special/eng/basic2_eng.htm.

3 Israeli Jewish-national Institutions

Israel has designed its domestic governance in such a way as to ensure that the State upholds and promotes Jewish nationalism. The term "Jewish people" in political Zionist thought is used to claim the right to self-determination. The quest of an ethnic or racial group for its own State amounts to a national project, and so Israeli institutions designed to preserve Israel as a Jewish State are referred to in this report as "Jewish-national" institutions.

In Israel, an interplay of laws consolidates Jewish-national supremacy. For example, regarding the central question of land use, Basic Law: Israel Lands[50] provides that real property held by the State of Israel, the Development Authority or the Keren Kayemet Le-Israel (JNF-Jewish National Fund) must serve "national" (that is, Jewish-national) interests and cannot be transferred to any other hands. It further establishes the Israeli Lands Authority (ILA) as administrator of such lands. The ILA (as successor of the Israeli Lands Administration) is charged with administering land in accordance with the JNF Covenant, which requires that land held by the JNF be held in perpetuity for the exclusive benefit of the Jewish people. The ILA also operates in accordance with the World Zionist Organization- Jewish Agency Status Law (1952), which sets forth the responsibility of those conjoined organizations for serving Jewish settlement and development. Thus, State land, which accounts for 93 per cent of land within the country's [34] internationally recognized borders, is managed through laws prohibiting its use by non-Jews.[51]

In a legal process that Israeli lawyer Michael Sfard has called "channelling", Israel has extended the application of laws regarding land to the occupied Palestinian territory.[52] Large areas of the West Bank have been declared "State lands", closed to use by Palestinians and administered in accordance with Israeli regime policies that, as described above, by law must serve the Jewish people.[53] In other words, much of the West Bank, including East Jerusalem, is under the authority of an Israeli State institution that is legally bound to administer that land for the exclusive benefit of the Jewish people. The same

---

50   Passed by the Knesset on 19 July 1960 (published in *Sefer Ha-Chukkim* No. 312 of 29 July 1960).

51   ILA website. Available from www.mmi.gov.il/Envelope/indexeng.asp?page=/static/eng/f_general.html.

52   For details on how this is done, *see* Tilley (ed.), *Beyond Occupation*.

53   Provisions of humanitarian law prohibiting the occupant from altering the infrastructure, laws and economic institutions that existed in occupied territory prior to its coming under belligerent occupation include articles 43 and 55 of the 1907 Hague Regulations (Convention (IV) respecting the Laws and Customs of War on Land and its annex: Regulations concerning the Laws and Customs of War on Land) and article 64 of the Fourth Geneva Convention. *See also* Tilley (ed.), *Beyond Occupation*, chap. 2.

arrangement once governed Israeli Jewish settlements in the Gaza Strip, but since the Israeli "disengagement" of 2005 and the withdrawal of Jewish settlements, such laws apply only to small portions of the Strip, such as the unilaterally imposed security zone by the fence.

The Jewish Agency and World Zionist Organisation (hereafter JA-WZO) deserve special attention for their role in establishing the racial character of the Israeli regime. According to Israeli law, they remain the "authorised agencies" of the State regarding Jewish-national affairs in Israel and the occupied Palestinian territory.[54] Their authority is detailed in the Covenant signed on 26 July 1954 between the Government of Israel and the Zionist Executive, representing the JA-WZO.[55] The Covenant provides for a coordinating board, composed half of State officials and half of JA-WZO members, which is granted broad authority to serve the Jewish people, extending to development plans for the entire country. Powers accorded to the JA-WZO by its Covenant are:

> The organising of [Jewish] immigration abroad and the transfer of immigrants and their property to Israel; participation in the absorption of immigrants in Israel; youth immigration; agricultural settlement in Israel; the acquisition and amelioration of land in Israel by the institutions of the Zionist Organisation, the Keren Kayemeth Le-Israel [Jewish National Fund] and the Keren Hayesod [United Jewish Appeal]; participation in the establishment [35] and the expansion of development enterprises in Israel; the encouragement of private capital investments in Israel; assistance to cultural enterprises and institutions of higher learning in Israel; the mobilisation of resources for financing these functions; the coordination of the activities in Israel of Jewish institutions and organisations acting within the sphere of these functions with the aid of public funds.

A principle task of the JA-WZO is to work actively to build and maintain Israel as a Jewish State, particularly through immigration policy:

> ... 5. The mission of gathering in the [Jewish] exiles, which is **the central task of the State of Israel** and the Zionist Movement in our days, requires constant efforts by the Jewish people in the Diaspora; **the State of Israel**, therefore, expects the cooperation of all Jews, as individuals and groups, in building up the State and assisting the immigration to it of the masses

---

54 The World Zionist Organisation – Jewish Agency (Status) Law of 1952 was amended in 1975. Available from https://www.adalah.org/en/law/view/534.

55 *See* www.israellobby.org/ja/12311970_JAFI_Reconstitution.pdf, appendix I.

of the [Jewish] people, and regards the unity of all sections of Jewry as necessary for this purpose (emphasis added).[56]

Such explicit language by the State's authorized agencies conclusively underlines the State's essentially racist character.

The World Zionist Organisation-Jewish Agency (Status) Law is linked to a second body of Israeli law and jurisprudence that distinguishes between citizenship (in Hebrew, *ezrahut*) and nationality (*le'um*). Other States have made this distinction: for example, in the former Soviet Union, Soviet citizens also held distinct "national" identities (Kazakh, Turkmen, Uzbek and so forth), but all nationalities had equal legal standing. In Israel, by contrast, only one nationality, Jewish, has legal standing and only Jewish nationality is associated with the legitimacy and mission of the State. According to the country's Supreme Court, Israel is indeed not the State of the "Israeli nation", which does not legally exist, but of the "Jewish nation".[57] [58] National rights are reserved to Jewish nationality. For instance, the Law of Return serves the "in-gathering" mission cited above by allowing any Jew to immigrate to Israel and, through the Citizenship Law,[58] to gain immediate citizenship. No other group has a remotely comparable right and only Jews enjoy any collective rights under Israeli law. [36]

The operational platform of the JA-WZO, reformulated in 2004 as the Jerusalem Programme, further clarifies how the State of Israel will serve as a "Jewish State". Its language is illuminating, especially in the light of the broad powers held by the JA-WZO, cited above:

> Zionism, the national liberation movement of the Jewish people, brought about the establishment of the State of Israel, and views a **Jewish, Zionist, democratic and secure State of Israel to be the expression of the common responsibility of the Jewish people for its continuity and future**. The foundations of Zionism are:
>
> – The unity of the Jewish people, its bond to its historic homeland Eretz Yisrael, and the centrality of the State of Israel and Jerusalem, its capital, in the life of the nation.

---

56 World Zionist Organisation-Jewish Agency (Status) Law of 1952.
57 *George Rafael Tamarin v. State of Israel* (20 January 1972), Decisions of the Supreme Court of Israel (Jerusalem: Supreme Court, 1972), vol. 25, pt. 1, 197 (in Hebrew). *See also* Roselle Tekiner, "On the inequality of Israeli citizens", *Without Prejudice*, vol. 1, No. 1 (1988), pp. 9–48.
58 Passed by the Knesset on 1 April 1952 and amended in 1958, 1968 and 1971.

- Aliyah to Israel from all countries and the effective integration of all [Jewish] immigrants into Israeli Society.
- Strengthening Israel as a Jewish, Zionist and democratic State and shaping it as an exemplary society with a unique moral and spiritual character, marked by mutual respect for the multi-faceted Jewish people, rooted in the vision of the prophets, striving for peace and contributing to the betterment of the world.
- Ensuring the future and the distinctiveness of the Jewish people by furthering Jewish, Hebrew and Zionist education, fostering spiritual and cultural values and teaching Hebrew as the national language.
- Nurturing mutual Jewish responsibility, defending the rights of Jews as individuals and as a nation, representing the national Zionist interests of the Jewish people, and struggling against all manifestations of anti-Semitism.
- Settling the country as an expression of practical Zionism (emphasis added, bullet points in the original).[59]

This discussion, although incomplete, should suffice to demonstrate that Israel is designed to be a racial regime. To remain a "Jewish State," uncontested Jewish-nationalist domination over the indigenous Palestinian people is essential – an advantage secured in the democracy of Israel by population size – and State laws, national institutions, development practices and security policies all focus on that mission. Different methods are applied to Palestinian populations depending on where they live, requiring variations in their administration. Within Israel that discriminatory feature is exhibited by the deceptive distinction between citizenship laws that treat all Israelis more or less equally, and nationality laws that are blatantly discriminatory in favour of Jews. The distinction allows Israel to continue [37] its insistence on being "a democracy", while discriminating in fundamental ways against its non-Jewish citizens.

Most important here is that Israel uses different methods of administration to control Palestinian populations depending on where they live, generating distinctive conditions. Fragmentation of the Palestinian people is indeed the core method through which Israel enforces apartheid.

C   *Apartheid through Fragmentation*

Different methods of administration are used to control Palestinian populations depending on where they live. The practical onus of that administrative complexity also benefits Israel, as the fragmentation of the Palestinian people is the core method through which Israel enforces apartheid.

---

59   *See* www.wzo.org.il/The-Jerusalem-Program. Accessed 19 February 2017.

It would be an error to assume that, although comprising one regime, apartheid is effected through a single monolithic body of laws, applied everywhere to everyone without variation. The South African case is relevant here: even within the comprehensive body of law that defined life chances for everyone in the country, apartheid included important variations: for instance, different laws for black South Africans living in townships and in the Bantustans and different privileges for Indians and Coloureds. Similarly, the apartheid regime of Israel operates by splintering the Palestinian people geographically and politically into different legal categories.

The international community has unwittingly collaborated with this manoeuvre by drawing a strict distinction between Palestinian citizens of Israel and Palestinians in the occupied Palestinian territory, and treating Palestinians outside the country as "the refugee problem". The Israeli apartheid regime is built on this geographic fragmentation, which has come to be accepted as normative. The method of fragmentation serves also to obscure this regime's very existence. That system, thus, lies at the heart of what is to be addressed in this report.

The four domains

This report finds that Israel maintains an apartheid regime by administering Palestinians under different bodies of law, identified here as constituting four legal domains:
- Domain 1: laws curtailing the capacity of Palestinian citizens of Israel to obtain equal rights within the State's democracy. [38]
- Domain 2: permanent residency laws designed to maintain a highly insecure legal status for Palestinian residents of occupied East Jerusalem.
- Domain 3: military law governing Palestinians in occupied Palestinian territory as a permanently alien population, which rejects any claim they may want to make on Israeli political representation for equal rights and conditions.
- Domain 4: policy preventing Palestinian refugees and involuntary exiles from returning to their homes in Mandate Palestine (all territory under the direct control of Israel).

These domains interplay so as to enfeeble Palestinian resistance to Israeli apartheid oppression in each of them, thereby reinforcing oppression of the Palestinian people as a whole. The following sections describe how the system works.[60] [39]

---

60   Much of the following section represents an edited version of the discussion in Tilley (ed.), *Beyond Occupation*, chap. 4.

Domain 1: Palestinian citizens of Israel

Approximately 1.7 million Palestinians are citizens of Israel and have homes within its internationally recognized borders. They represent those who were not expelled or did not flee in the 1948 or 1967 wars. As citizens, they purportedly enjoy equal rights along with all Israeli citizens. For the first 20 years of the country's existence, however, they were subjected to martial law and they continue to experience domination and oppression solely because they are not Jewish. Empirically, this policy of domination is manifest by the provision of inferior social services, restrictive zoning laws, and limited budget allocations benefitting their communities, in formal and informal restrictions on jobs and professional opportunities, and in the segregated[61] landscapes of their places of residence: Jewish and Palestinian citizens overwhelmingly live separately in their own respective cities and towns (the few mixed areas, as in some neighbourhoods in Haifa, are exceptional).[62]

Those problems are not only the result of discrete policies. The dilemma for Palestinian Muslim, Christian and other non-Jewish citizens is to seek equal rights in a regime that openly privileges Jews. Any actions to weaken or eliminate that regime are considered "national" (that is, Jewish-national) threats. Even constitutional law providing for equal treatment before the law, such as Basic Law: Human Dignity and Liberty and Basic Law: Freedom of Occupation (see above), allows for discrimination on those "national" grounds. Israeli constitutional law therefore, rather than providing tools for combatting oppression, makes resistance to oppression illegal.

The concern of the regime is that Palestinian citizens of Israel could eliminate its discriminatory design if they were able to revise the Basic Law and other key legislation (such as the Law of Return). Such changes require only a simple majority vote in the Knesset. However, as long as Palestinians represent only 20 per cent of the population, they will be unable to win the necessary proportion of Knesset seats. For example, even after forming an unprecedented unity list for elections to the Knesset in 2015, Palestinian parties held only 13 (10.6 per cent) of 120 seats. Because the Basic Law: Knesset disallows political parties from adopting a platform containing any challenge to the identity of

---

61   Druze citizens of Israel have fallen into a different category under Israeli policy. They serve in the military and are accorded rights and treatment superior to those of Palestinian Muslims and Christians.

62   *See* Ian Lustick, Arabs in the Jewish State: Israel's Control of a National Minority (Austin, University of Texas Press, 1980); Nadim Rouhana, Palestinian Citizens in an Ethnic Jewish State: Identities in Conflict (New Haven, Yale University Press, 1997) and Ben White, Palestinians in Israel: Segregation, Discrimination and Democracy (London, Pluto Press, 2011).

Israel as a Jewish State, [40] Palestinian parties can campaign only for minor reforms and better municipal budgets. They are legally prohibited from challenging the racial regime itself. Thus the right to vote is circumscribed by laws regarding party platforms.[63]

Any study of domain 1 will involve interpreting coded language. For example, the Admissions Committee Law of 2011 authorizes the creation of private Jewish councils in small rural Jewish towns to exclude applications for residency on the basis of the applicants' "social suitability". This is a proxy term for Jewish identity and provides a legal mechanism for such communities to reject Palestinian applicants.[64]

Israeli law must be evaluated in its application in order to determine whether a racist agenda lies beneath the apparently neutral legal language. A plethora of Israeli laws reserve public benefits to those who qualify as citizens under the Citizenship Law and the Law of Return – an oblique reference to Jews – thus creating a nested system of covert racism that is invisible to the casual observer.

Effectively interchangeable under international law, the terms "citizenship" (*ezrahut*) as "nationality" (*le'um*) have distinct meanings in Israel, where citizenship rights and national rights are not the same thing. Any citizen enjoys the former, but only Jews enjoy the latter, as only Jewish nationality is recognized under Israeli law. These and other laws comprise a regime of systematic racial discrimination that imposes second-class citizenship on Palestinian citizens of Israel.[65] The broad impact is confirmed even by Israeli data, which detail, for instance, inferior funding for Palestinian schools, businesses, agriculture and health care, as well as limits on access to jobs and freedom of residence.

---

63 The Arab-Israeli party Balad has uniquely adopted an openly anti-Zionist platform and calls for Israel to become a State of all its citizens. The arrests, attacks, investigations and Supreme Court cases involving Balad illustrate the determination of the Israeli authorities not to let this stand spread.

64 Human Rights Watch, "Israel: New Laws Marginalize Palestinian Arab Citizens", 30 March 2011: "The "admissions committee" law requires anyone seeking to move to any community in the Negev and Galilee regions with fewer than 400 families to obtain approval from committees consisting of town residents, a member of the Jewish Agency or World Zionist Organization, and several others. The law empowers these committees to reject candidates who, among other things, "are ill- suited to the community's way of life" or "might harm the community's fabric". Available from https://www.hrw.org/news/2011/03/30/israel-new-laws-marginalize-palestinian-arab-citizens.

65 A particularly valuable source on this discrimination is the database of discriminatory laws maintained by Adalah: Centre for Legal Rights of the Arab Minority in Israel, which in 2016 listed more than 50 discriminatory laws of Israel, and reports on related legal challenges. Available from www.adalah.org/en/law/index.

Thus, domain 1 sustains the myth that one portion of the Palestinian people enjoys the full benefits of democracy, while at the same strengthening the apartheid [41] regime that serves to preserve Israel as a Jewish State. Israel uses the trappings of token universal democracy to lead many observers astray and deflect international opprobrium. The success of this approach depends on limiting Palestinian citizens to a politically ineffectual minority. However, it is impossible to fully appreciate this outcome without examining Israeli policies and practices in the other three domains. Indeed, the success of domain 1 depends on the workings of the other three.

Domain 2: Palestinians in East Jerusalem
Israeli policies towards the some 300,000 Palestinians in East Jerusalem can be addressed more concisely.[66] The discrimination evident in domain 1 is reproduced: Palestinians in East Jerusalem experience discrimination in areas such as education, health care, employment, residency and building rights, experience expulsion from their homes and house demolitions consistent with a project of ethnic engineering of Greater Jerusalem, and suffer harsher treatment at the hands of the security forces.[67]

The central question here, however, is not whether Israel discriminates against Palestinians – amply confirmed by the data – but how the domain for Palestinians in East Jerusalem operates as an integral element of the apartheid regime. In brief, domain 2 situates Jerusalem Palestinians in a separate category designed to prevent them from adding to the demographic, political and electoral weight of Palestinians inside Israel. Specific policies regarding their communities and rights are designed to pressure them to emigrate and to quell, or at least minimize, resistance to that pressure. The "grand apartheid"[68] dimension of this domain can be appreciated by observing how the Israeli Jerusalem municipality has openly pursued a policy of "demographic balance" in East Jerusalem. For instance, the Jerusalem 2000 master plan seeks

---

66   The figure of 300,000 was provided by the Association for Civil Rights in Israel in March 2015.
67   For more details, see A/HRC/31/73; B'Tselem, "Statistics on Palestinians in custody of the Israeli security forces" (January 2017, available from http://www.btselem.org/statistics/detainees_and_prisoners); Office for the Coordination of Humanitarian Affairs (OCHA), *Humanitarian Bulletin* (16 November 2015, available from https://www.ochaopt.org/documents/ocha_opt_the_humanitarian_monitor_2014_12_11_english.pdf); Alternative Information Center (AIC), "OCHA: One in two Palestinians to need humanitarian assistance in 2017" (26 January 2017, available from http://alternativenews.org/index.php/headlines/329-ocha-one-in-two-palestinians-to-need-humanitarian-assistance-in-2017).
68   *See* Tilley, "A Palestinian declaration of independence".

to achieve a 60/40 demographic balance in favour of Jewish residents.[69] As long ago as the 1980s, the municipality had drafted master plans to fragment Palestinian neighbourhoods [42] with intervening Jewish ones, stifling the natural growth of the Palestinian population and pressuring Palestinians to leave.[70] Describing Jewish settlements in East Jerusalem as "neighbourhoods" is part of the wider tactic of disguising violations of international humanitarian law through the use of non-committal language.

Such policies have a significant impact because Jerusalem has such importance for the collective identity of Palestinians as a people. For them, the city is the administrative, cultural, business and political capital of Palestine, home to the Palestinian elite, and site of hallowed places of worship and remembrance. Although many Palestinians in East Jerusalem maintain networks of family and business connections with Palestinian citizens in Israel, the West Bank and (now to a lesser extent) the Gaza Strip, their primary interest is to go about their lives and pursue their interests in the city where they have homes, businesses, a vigorous urban society, strong cultural resonances, and, in some cases, ancestral roots going back millennia.

Israel pursues efforts to weaken the Palestinians politically and contain their demographic weight in several ways. One is to grant Palestinians in East Jerusalem the status of permanent residents: that is, as foreigners for whom residency in the land of their birth is a privilege rather than a right, subject to revocation. That status is then made conditional on what Israeli law terms their "centre of life", evaluated by documented criteria such as home and business ownership, attendance at local schools and involvement in local organizations. If the centre of life of an individual or family appears to have shifted elsewhere, such as across the Green Line, their residency in Jerusalem may be revoked. A Palestinian resident of Jerusalem who has spent time abroad may also find that Israel has revoked his or her residency in Jerusalem.

Proving that Jerusalem is one's "centre of life" is burdensome: it requires submitting numerous documents, "including such items as home ownership papers or a rent contract, various bills (water, electricity, municipal taxes), salary slips, proof of receiving medical care in the city, certification of children's

---

69 A/HRC/22/63, para. 25.
70 For further discussion of the Jerusalem master plans, see Francesco Chiodelli, "The Jerusalem Master Plan: planning into the conflict", *Journal of Palestine Studies*, No. 51 (2012). Available from www.palestine-studies.org/jq/fulltext/78505. For related maps, see Bimkom, *Trapped by Planning: Israeli Policy, Planning and Development in the Palestinian Neighborhoods of East Jerusalem* (Jerusalem, 2014). Available from http://bimkom.org/eng/wp-content/uploads/TrappedbyPlanning.pdf.

school registration".[71] The difficulty in meeting the criteria is suggested [43] by the consequences of failure to do so: between 1996 (a year after the "centre of life" legislation was passed) and 2014, Jerusalem residency was revoked for more than 11,000 Palestinians.[72] To avoid that risk, a growing, albeit relatively low, number of Palestinians are seeking Israeli citizenship. Israel has granted only about half of those requests.[73]

Their fragile status as permanent residents leaves Palestinians in East Jerusalem with no legal standing to contest the laws of the State or to join Palestinian citizens of Israel in any legislative challenge to the discrimination imposed on them. Openly identifying with Palestinians in the occupied Palestinian territory politically carries with it the risk of Israel expelling them, for violating security provisions, to the West Bank and removing their right even to visit Jerusalem. Thus, the urban epicentre of Palestinian nationalism and political life is caught inside a legal bubble that neutralizes Palestinians' capacity to oppose the apartheid regime.[74]

Domain 3: Palestinians in occupied Palestinian territory

The roughly 4.6 million Palestinians who live in the occupied Palestinian territory (2.7 million in the West Bank and 1.9 million in the Gaza Strip) are governed not by Israeli civil law, but by military law, codified as orders issued by the commander of the territories and administered by the Israeli Defence Forces (IDF) and other designated arms of the occupying power.[75] Since the Israeli "disengagement" and withdrawal of settlers in 2005, the Gaza Strip has been internally governed by the Hamas Government (elected in 2006 to head the Palestinian Authority but later deposed). Still, Israeli military law continues to apply for Gaza regarding exclusive Israeli control over Palestinian move-

---

71 B'tselem, "Revocation of residency in East Jerusalem", 18 August 2013. Available from www.btselem.org/jerusalem/revocation_of_residency.
72 Data from B'tselem, Statistics on Revocation of Residency in East Jerusalem. Available from www.btselem.org/jerusalem/revocation_statistics.
73 Maayan Lubell, "Breaking taboo, East Jerusalem Palestinians seek Israeli citizenship in East Jerusalem", *Haaretz*, 5 August 2015. Available from www.haaretz.com/israel-news/1.669643. According to the article, the number of Jerusalem Palestinians applying for Israeli citizenship has grown to between 800 and 1,000 annually, although in 2012 and 2013 only 189 out of 1,434 applications were approved.
74 Nonetheless, Palestinians in Jerusalem have made formidable contributions to critiques of Israeli policies, the more impressive for their having done so under such conditions.
75 Until the Oslo Accords of 1993 and 1995, governance of the occupied Palestinian territory was assigned to a "civil administration" operating within the IDF. In 1994, much of its authority was transferred to the Palestinian Authority (also known as the Palestinian National Authority), an interim self-government body.

ment and trade in and out of the territory, the unilaterally imposed "security zone" along the perimeter fence, and Palestinian [44] access to fishing areas and sea routes. Gaza remains, therefore, under military occupation in the eyes of the United Nations.[76]

In 2009, a comprehensive report by the Human Rights Research Council of South Africa found that Israeli practices in the occupied Palestinian territory were overwhelmingly consistent with apartheid (see annex I). Israel has not accepted those findings, however, on several grounds. Those who claim that Israel does not govern Palestinians in an apartheid regime invariably cite conditions and rights for Palestinians in domain 1 (citizens of Israel). Leaving aside the issue of domain 2, they say that the situation of Palestinians in the occupied territory is irrelevant to the question. That approach can be persuasive at first glance. Palestinians in the occupied Palestinian territory are not citizens of Israel and, under the laws of war (cf. the Fourth Geneva Convention), are not supposed to be. The differential treatment by Israel of citizens and non-citizens in the occupied Palestinian territory could therefore seem admissible or, at least, irrelevant. In this common view, Israel would be practicing apartheid only if it annexed the territory, declared one State in all of Mandate Palestine and, thereafter, continued to deny equal rights to Palestinians. Influential voices such as former Israeli Prime Minister Ehud Olmert, former United States President Jimmy Carter, former United States Secretary of State John Kerry, and a host of Israeli, American and other critics and pundits have warned that Israel should withdraw from the West Bank precisely to avoid that scenario.

However, those warnings rest on flawed assumptions. First, Israel already administers the occupied Palestinian territory in ways consistent with apartheid, given that the territory has not one population but two: (a) Palestinian civilians, governed by military law; and (b) some 350,000 Jewish settlers, governed by Israeli civil law. The racial character of this situation is evidenced by

---

[76] The authors of this report concur with those scholars who have concluded that Gaza remains under military occupation. Although governed entirely by Palestinians, key elements of apartheid as defined by the Apartheid Convention remain. In particular, Israel has exclusive control of the borders of Gaza and, since 2007, has imposed a blockade, which translates into draconian restrictions on Palestinian movement that affect trade, work, education and access to health care (article II (c)), and repression of any resistance to those conditions (article II (f)). The Palestinian Authority has suffered from de facto separation, particularly since the 2006 legislative election victory of Hamas and the clashes that led to its taking effective control over the Gaza Strip in 2007. Between then and 2014, there were two de facto Palestinian Governments, one in Gaza and the other in Ramallah, controlled by Hamas and the Fatah movement respectively. In 2014, they formed a national unity Government, although Hamas retained effective control of the Gaza Strip.

the fact that all West Bank settlers are administered by Israeli civil law on the basis of being Jewish, whether they are Israeli citizens or not.[77] Thus, Israel administers the West Bank [45] through a dual legal system, based on race, which has led to expressions of concern by, among many others, former special rapporteurs Mr. Dugard and Mr. Falk.

Secondly, the character of this dual legal system, problematic in itself, is aggravated by how the State of Israel manages land and development on the basis of race. By denying Palestinians essential zoning, building and business permits, Israeli military rule has crippled the Palestinian economy and society, leaving Palestinian cities and towns (outside the Ramallah enclave) increasingly under- resourced and suffocating their growth and the welfare of their inhabitants. The Israeli blockade of Gaza has resulted in even worse living conditions for the entrapped Palestinian population there.

In contrast, Jewish settlements in the West Bank are flourishing. All State ministries provide support for their planning, funding, building and servicing; some, such as the Ministry of Construction and Housing and the Ministry of Agriculture and Rural Development, have been entirely committed to doing so. They also offer financial incentives for Jews to move to the settlements, including interest-free loans, school grants, special recreational facilities, new office blocks, agricultural subsidies, job training and employment guarantees. State complicity is further demonstrated by measures to integrate the economy, society and politics of Jewish settlements into those of Israel, generating seamless travel and electricity networks, a unified banking and finance system for Jews, Jewish business investment, and, in particular, a customs union.[78]

This vast State involvement belies any claim that the settlements are the work of maverick religious zealots, and challenges the plausibility of claims that Israel will leave the West Bank as soon as a negotiated settlement is achieved.[79] The scale, complexity and cost of the settlement grid, estimated by some researchers at hundreds of billions of United States dollars, further underline the intensity of the Israeli commitment to the settlements. The po-

---

77 Limor Yehuda and others, *One Rule Two Legal Systems: Israel's Regime of Laws in the West Bank* (Association for Civil Rights in Israel (ACRI), October 2014), p. 108. Available from www.acri.org.il/en/wp-content/uploads/2015/02/Two-Systems-of-Law-English-FINAL.pdf.

78 Eyal Benvenisti, *The International Law of Occupation* (Princeton, Princeton University Press, 1993), p. 135.

79 In July 2014, Israeli Prime Minister Benjamin Netanyahu announced: "I think the Israeli people understand now what I always say: that there cannot be a situation, under any agreement, in which we relinquish security control of the territory west of the River Jordan." *See* David Horovitz, "Netanyahu finally speaks his mind", *The Times of Israel*, 13 July 2014.

tential cost of (and political resistance to) withdrawal far exceed the political will or capacity of any Israeli Government.

The dual legal system applied by Israel in the occupied Palestinian territory justifies two brief digressions from the report's method: of eschewing a check-list method (comparing a State's behaviour with the Apartheid Convention's sample [46] "inhuman acts") and avoiding comparisons with southern Africa. A check-list approach helps to clarify how Israel imposes apartheid on one racial group in order to ensure the domination of another. Such an item-by-item comparison of Israeli practices with the "inhuman acts" listed in the Apartheid Convention was undertaken for the Human Sciences Research Council of South Africa (HSRC) report issued in 2009. The findings of that study, summarized in annex I, were conclusive: except for the provision on genocide (which was not practiced in southern Africa either), every "inhuman act" listed in the Apartheid Convention is practiced by Israel in the West Bank.

The architects of South African apartheid adopted a strategy of "grand apartheid" to secure white supremacy in the long term through the country's geographic partition into white areas (most of the country) and disarticulated black areas. That policy inspired the clause in the Apartheid Convention denouncing as a crime the creation of "separate reserves and ghettos for the members of a racial group or groups" (article II (d)). "Bantu" or "black" reserves were controlled by black South Africans appointed as leaders by the State. In the rhetoric of "grand apartheid", those reserves or "homelands" were slated to become independent States that would provide self-determination to black South African peoples (language groups). Black South African governors were authorized (and armed) to suppress resistance by their African inhabitants, many of whom had been forcibly transferred into them, and to govern their territories in ways compatible with white development interests. That model so closely resembles current premises supporting a two-State solution in Palestine that it calls for sober reflection, not least because of the violent and destabilizing effects it had throughout sub-Saharan Africa.

The question arises as to whether Israel has deliberately pursued fragmentation of the West Bank into an archipelago of Palestinian cantons, divided by intervening Jewish-only areas (the Bantustan model). Certainly, this geography will permanently enfeeble any putative Palestinian sovereignty, preserving the prerogative of Israel to administer intervening land for the Jewish people. Oslo II, paradoxically, facilitated this "grand" strategy by establishing borders for the Palestinian autonomy enclaves. The comparison with South Africa helps to clarify an essential observation: with Israeli Jewish-national domination over an area dotted with Palestinian autonomy zones, apartheid is expressed as fully in a partition strategy as it is in a unified State.

In sum, domain 3 has been configured to exclude indefinitely the 4.6 million Palestinians living under Israeli military law from mounting any claim against the State of Israel for rights under Israeli civil law. International law and diplomacy, with its commitment to reject the acquisition of territory by force, has led to the [47] population of the occupied Palestinian territory being projected as a permanently separate and distinct Palestinian-national entity. Well intentioned and based on international law, this approach has had the effect of splitting Palestinians in the occupied territory from the 1.7 million Palestinian citizens of Israel and those in East Jerusalem. In that way, the demographic balance in Israel can be maintained as Jewish and a united Palestinian challenge to its apartheid regime can be avoided.

Domain 4: Palestinian refugees and involuntary exiles

In early 2016, 3,162,602 Palestinians living outside Mandate Palestine were officially registered as refugees by the United Nations Relief and Works Agency for Palestine Refugees in the Near East (UNRWA).[80] Estimates of the entire refugee population, including those not registered with UNRWA and people who left Palestine under other circumstances and are not allowed to return (referred to as "involuntary exiles" in this report), range from six to eight million people. Although an exact count is difficult given the global diaspora of Palestinians now in their fourth and fifth generations, by any responsible estimate more Palestinians live outside Mandate Palestine than in it.[81]

Palestinian refugees are widely distributed. Approximately two million live in the occupied Palestinian territory: 792,000 in camps in the West Bank and 1.3 million in the Gaza Strip. Living under Israeli occupation, these people fall under domain 3, although they benefit from some protections and special services from UNRWA. The rest live mostly in the frontline States of Jordan (around 2.1 million), Lebanon (around 458,000) and the Syrian Arab Republic (around 560,000).[82] Only about 5 per cent live outside the Middle East. Lacking any citizenship, they are subject, without recourse, to the laws of their host State (not always comfortably, as some States – notably Lebanon – impose spe-

---

80   UNRWA lists of total of 5,266,603 refugees, the difference being accounted for by those living in the occupied Palestinian territory. See https://www.unrwa.org/where-we-work. Accessed 8 February 2017.

81   The figure is a middle estimate, as the number of Palestinians who fled in the 1948 war has not been firmly established. Some scholars suggest 700,000 and 750,000 left; the Israelis provide a figure of 520,000; and Palestinian authorities estimate the number at between 900,000 and 1 million.

82   UNRWA, UNRWA in figures as of 1 Jan 2016. Available from https://www.unrwa.org/sites/default/files/content/resources/unrwa_in_figures_2016.pdf.

cial restrictions on Palestinian refugees).[83] Those conditions have contributed to sustaining a strong nationalist nostalgia and sentiment among the great majority of Palestinian refugees regarding their origins [48] in Palestine and a potent sense of enduring injustice resulting from Israeli policies. Their inability to return to their country thus remains a central grievance and a key issue in peace talks. Politically, no Palestinian leadership can acquiesce to a peace agreement that ignores the refugees.

In 1948, General Assembly resolution 194(III) resolved that "the [Palestinian] refugees wishing to return to their homes and live at peace with their neighbours should be permitted to do so" and that compensation should be provided to the rest. Israel has rejected the application of that resolution on security grounds and on the basis of the "demographic threat" of a Palestinian majority: in the unlikely event that the entire Palestinian population of refugees and involuntary exiles returned to Palestine *en masse*, the Palestinian population under Israeli rule would total some 12 million, electorally overwhelming the 6.5 million Jews in Israel. Even if that refugee population returned in numbers sufficient only to generate a Palestinian majority (as is far more likely), Israel would be forced into either adopting an explicitly apartheid policy in order to exclude them, and abandoning democracy altogether, or enfranchising them and abandoning the vision of Israel as a Jewish State. As expressed in an article posted on the Israeli Ministry of Foreign Affairs website:

According to Palestinian sources, there are about 3.5 million Palestinian refugees nowadays registered with UNRWA. If Israel were to allow all of them to return to her territory, **this would be an act of suicide on her part, and no State can be expected to destroy itself** (emphasis added).[84]

Thus, domain 4 plays an essential role in the apartheid regime of Israel. Its refusal to allow refugees and involuntary exiles to return ensures that the Palestinian population never gains the demographic weight that would either threaten Israeli military control of the occupied Palestinian territory, or provide the demographic leverage within Israel to allow them to insist on full democratic rights, which would supersede the Jewish character of the State of Israel. In short, domain 4 ensures that Palestinians will never be able to

---

83 For a short summary of the conditions in which Palestinian refugees live in Lebanon, see Meghan Monahan, Treatment of Palestinian refugees in Lebanon, Human Rights Brief (2 February 2015). Available from http://hrbrief.org/2015/02/treatment-of-palestinian-refugees-in-lebanon.

84 Ruth Lapidoth, "Do Palestinian refugees have a right to return to Israel?", posted on Israeli Ministry of Foreign Affairs, 15 January 2001. Available from www.mfa.gov.il/mfa/foreignpolicy/peace/guide/pages/do%20palestinian%20refugees%20have%20a%20right%20to%20return%20to.aspx.

change the system in ways that would lead to political equality between the two peoples. [49]

D   Counter-arguments

Several arguments can be and have been made to deny that the Apartheid Convention is even applicable to the case of Israel-Palestine. Some of them, such as the contention that Jews and Palestinians are not "races" and that, because Palestinian citizens of Israel enjoy the right to vote, the treatment of them by the Israeli State cannot constitute apartheid, are addressed and rejected above. Other arguments include:

1. *Consistency with international practice*: The Israeli doctrine of maintaining a Jewish majority, enabling the Jewish people to have its own nation-State, is consistent with the behaviour of States around the world, such as France, which express the self-determination of their respective ethnic nations. It is therefore unfair and exceptional treatment – and implicitly anti-Semitic – to target Israel as an apartheid State when it is only doing the same.

This common argument derives from miscasting how national identities function in modern nation States. In France, for example, anyone holding French citizenship, regardless of whether they are indigenous or of immigrant origin, are equal members of the French nation and enjoy equal rights. According to the Supreme Court, Israel is not the State of the "Israeli nation" but of the "Jewish nation".[85] Collective rights in Israeli law are explicitly conferred on Jews as a people and on no other collective identity: national rights for Jews, embedded in such laws as the Law of Return and the Citizenship Law (discussed above) do not extend to any other group under Israeli rule. Hence, racial-nationalist privileges are embedded in the legal and doctrinal foundations of the State. That is exceptional and would meet with opprobrium in any other country (as it did in apartheid South Africa).

2. *The standing of Palestinians as foreigners*: Palestinian residents of the occupied Palestinian territory are not citizens of the State and so the State does not owe them rights and treatment equal to that accorded to Israeli Jewish citizens and settlers.

The similarities between the legal situation in Palestinian territory under Israeli occupation and in Namibia under South African occupation have already been noted. Israel has denied Palestinians in the occupied Palestinian territory

---

85   George Rafael Tamarin v. State of Israel (1972) C.A.630/70.

Israeli citizenship because they are not Jews. As the "in-gathering" of Jews is a central mission of Israeli State institutions and the State promotes naturalisation of Jews from other [50] parts of the world, it is fair to assume that the Palestinians, born in territory under the State's exclusive control, would have been granted Israeli citizenship had they been Jewish (and had they wanted it). In its General Recommendation No. 30 on discrimination against non-citizens, the Committee on the Elimination of Racial Discrimination recommends that States parties to the International Convention on the Elimination of All Forms of Racial Discrimination should:

> Recognize that deprivation of citizenship on the basis of race, colour, descent, or national or ethnic origin is a breach of States parties' obligations to ensure non-discriminatory enjoyment of the right to nationality.[86]

The Apartheid Convention cites as crimes of apartheid "measures calculated to deny members of a racial group or groups" basic human rights, including "the right to a nationality" (article II (c)). Thus, the argument that Israel cannot be responsible for Palestinians who are non-citizens reinforces a finding of apartheid when one asks why they are not citizens. At the heart of the Israeli-Palestinian conflict is indeed the exclusion of the Palestinians, as non-Jews, from citizenship in the State that governs their country. (The liminal condition of living in a "State of Palestine" recently recognized by the General Assembly yet lacking all attributes of sovereignty has not provided Palestinians with a "citizenship" that has concrete application.)

3. *The purpose clause.* Israeli policies that oppress Palestinians are motivated by security concerns, and not the intention or desire to impose racial domination.

The Apartheid Convention and the Rome Statute define crimes of apartheid as acts committed for the purpose of establishing and maintaining domination by one racial group over another. It could be argued that Israeli practices are only temporary measures, the purpose of which is not racial domination, but only to maintain order until a peace agreement removes the need for such measures. However, the security issues related to Israeli measures relevant to this study are usually cited only in relation to the occupied Palestinian territory, while the apartheid regime is applied to the Palestinian people as a whole. Moreover, apartheid is prohibited under international law irrespective of its

---

86   CERD/C/64/Misc.11/rev.3, para. 14.

duration.[87] The [51] Apartheid Convention makes no distinction in terms of the period of time apartheid is carried out or the State's ultimate vision for the future.[88] [52]

3 Conclusions and Recommendations

A *Conclusions*

This report establishes, on the basis of scholarly inquiry and overwhelming evidence, that Israel is guilty of the crime of apartheid. However, only a ruling by an international tribunal in that sense would make such an assessment truly authoritative. The authors therefore urge the United Nations to implement this finding by fulfilling its international responsibilities in relation to international law and the rights of the Palestinian people as a matter of urgency, for two reasons. First, the situation addressed in the report is ongoing. Many investigations of crimes against humanity have concerned past behaviour or events, such as civil wars involving genocides, which have formally concluded. In such cases, the international community faces no particular pressure to act in a timely way to terminate an ongoing crime prior to investigating the legal facts of culpability. In the case of Israel-Palestine, any delay compounds the crime by prolonging the subjugation of Palestinians to the active practice of apartheid by Israel. Prompt action is accordingly imperative to avert further human suffering and end a crime against humanity that is being committed now.

Secondly, the extreme gravity of the charge requires prompt action. Since the 1970s, when the international campaign to oppose apartheid in southern Africa gathered momentum, apartheid has been considered in the annals of the United Nations and world public opinion to be second only to genocide in the hierarchy of criminality.[89] This report accordingly recommends that the international community act immediately, without waiting for a more formal

---

87   The uniquely extended character of the Israeli occupation has generated a new body of literature on the legal implications of "prolonged occupation". For more on this, see Tilley (ed.), *Beyond Occupation*, chap. 2.

88   The Government of apartheid South Africa also argued that racial domination was not a goal in itself but a defensive measure designed to preserve the way of life of the white population. Apartheid was presented as merely a stage on the path to a mutually beneficial end, in which all "peoples" of South Africa would enjoy self-determination and peaceful coexistence. In practice, the "homelands" system was geared towards stabilizing the low-cost workforce and white land tenure.

89   Genocide and apartheid are the only two international crimes, the commission of which States have a duty to prevent.

pronouncement regarding the culpability of the State of Israel, its Government and its officials for the commission of the crime of apartheid.

While urging swift action to oppose and end this apartheid regime, the authors of this report urge as a matter of highest priority that authoritative bodies be requested to review its findings. Opinions of the General Assembly, ICJ and ICC are especially crucial, although assessments by national courts would also be [53] relevant to interpreting international criminal law and appraising its implementation by Member States. On the basis of such findings, States and United Nations bodies could deliberate on a firm foundation of international law how best to discharge their responsibility to address and bring to an end the crime of apartheid and domination of the Palestinian people. In any event, pending that longer deliberative process, the authors of this report conclude that the weight of the evidence supports beyond a reasonable doubt the contention that Israel is guilty of imposing an apartheid regime on the Palestinian people.

The prohibition of apartheid is considered *jus cogens* in international customary law. States have a separate and collective duty (a) not to recognize an apartheid regime as lawful; (b) not to aid or assist a State in maintaining an apartheid regime; and (c) to cooperate with the United Nations and other States in bringing apartheid regimes to an end. A State that fails to fulfil those duties could itself be held legally responsible for engaging in wrongful acts involving complicity with maintaining an apartheid regime. The United Nations and its agencies, and all Member States, have a legal obligation to act within their capabilities to prevent and punish instances of apartheid that are responsibly brought to their attention.

Civil society institutions and individuals also have a moral duty to use the instruments at their disposal to raise awareness of this ongoing criminal enterprise, and to exert pressure on Israel to dismantle apartheid structures and negotiate in good faith for a lasting peace that acknowledges the rights of Palestinians under international law and makes it possible for the two peoples to live together on the basis of real equality.

Apartheid in southern Africa was brought to an end, in part, by the cumulative impact of a variety of measures, including economic sanctions and sports boycotts, undertaken with the blessing of United Nations bodies and many Member States, and with grassroots support in States with strong strategic and economic ties with South Africa. The effectiveness of the anti-apartheid campaign was in large part due to the transnational activism of civil society, which reinforced the intergovernmental consensus that took shape in the United Nations.

B Recommendations

The following recommendations cover general responsibilities and those of specific institutional actors. Their purpose is, first of all, to focus attention on the principal finding of this report, that Israel has imposed a regime of apartheid on the Palestinian people as a whole, thereby challenging the United Nations and other [54] international, national and civil society actors (including private citizens) to act in response. They are also designed to encourage the implementation of practical measures in accordance with international law to exert pressure on Israel to dismantle its apartheid regime and end the unlawful status quo by engaging in a peace process that seeks a just solution.

General Recommendations

1. United Nations bodies, national Governments and civil society actors, including religious organizations, should formally endorse the principal finding of this report that the treatment by Israel of the Palestinians is consistent with the crime of apartheid.
2. On that basis, those actors should examine what measures can be taken in accordance with their legal obligations, as set forth under the Apartheid Convention. As the crime of apartheid qualifies as a peremptory or *jus cogens* norm of international law, States are bound by the Convention even if they are not parties to it, and would have similar legal obligations even in the absence of the convention, because the crime of apartheid is prohibited under customary international law.

Recommendations for the United Nations

1. Each United Nations body should promptly consider what action to take in view of the finding that Israel maintains a racist regime of apartheid in its exercise of control over the Palestinian people, taking due account of the fragmentation of that people by Israel, which is itself an aspect of the control arrangements that rely on "inhuman acts" for the purpose of systematic racial domination.
2. ESCWA should take a central role in advocating international cooperation to end the apartheid regime. Its special role in this respect derives not only from the Commission's geographic position but also its mandate.
3. United Nations entities should cooperate with one another, and in particular with ESCWA, to discuss and disseminate this report. They should consider, possibly in cooperation with the Palestinian Government and other Palestinian institutions, convening a special meeting to assess how to follow up on and implement the recommendations of the report.
4. The General Assembly should, taking inspiration from resolution 1761(XVII) of 6 November 1962, revive the Special Committee against

Apartheid, and the United Nations Centre against Apartheid (1976–1991), which would report authoritatively on Israeli practices and policies relating to the crime of apartheid, including the legal and administrative instrumentalities used to [55] carry out the underlying criminal enterprise. Those bodies gathered and disseminated vital legal analysis and information with respect to South African apartheid. Those resources benefited not only jurists and scholars, but also civil society activists around the world, helping them to shape media presentations and public opinion, legitimating calls for boycotts, divestments and sanctions, and contributing overall to the formation of a transnational movement against apartheid in South Africa.

5. The Human Rights Council should be vested with particular responsibility for examining the findings of this report and reinforcing its recommendations. The Special Rapporteur on the situation of human rights in the Palestinian Territory occupied since 1967 should be instructed to report annually to the Council and the Third Committee of the General Assembly on steps taken to comply with the terms of the Apartheid Convention and to encourage member States of the Council to take appropriate action.

6. The competent bodies of the United Nations should consider seeking an advisory opinion from the ICJ as to whether the means used by Israel to maintain control over the Palestinian people amount to the crime of apartheid and, if so, what steps should be taken to end that situation promptly.

7. Pursuant to article 7 (1) (j) of the Rome Statute, the ICC should be formally encouraged to investigate, as a matter of urgency, whether the State of Israel, its Governments and individuals, in implementing policies and practices with respect to the Palestinian people, are guilty of the crime of apartheid and, if so, to act accordingly.

8. On the basis of this report, the Secretary-General should be respectfully urged to recommend to the General Assembly and the Security Council that a global conference be convened at an early date in order to consider what action should be taken by the United Nations and what might be recommended to civil society and private sector actors.

Recommendations for National Governments of Member States

1. National Governments should be reminded of their legal duty under international law to take appropriate action to prevent the crime of apartheid and punish its perpetrators, taking cognizance of the findings of this report and any parallel findings by competent bodies.

2. National Governments should, within the limits of their legislative, executive and judicial institutions, take appropriate action, including allowing criminal prosecutions of Israeli officials demonstrably connected with the practices of apartheid against the Palestinian people. [56]
3. National Governments, especially of member States of ECSWA, should explore ways of cooperating in the discharge of their duty to oppose and overcome the regime of apartheid.
4. National Governments should support boycott, divestment and sanctions activities and respond positively to calls for such initiatives.

Recommendations for Civil Society and Private Sector Actors

1. Civil society actors should be invited to submit to the Human Rights Council reactions to this report. A special meeting should be convened to consider those reactions and to plan appropriate next steps, including recommendations to the Human Rights Council and to the Office of the United Nations High Commissioner for Human Rights (OHCHR).
2. Efforts should be made to broaden support for boycott, divestment and sanctions initiatives among civil society actors.
3. Private sector actors should be made aware of the findings of this report and requested to act accordingly, including by informing the public about the criminality of the apartheid regime, and urging Governments to fulfil their obligations under the Apartheid Convention and to propose initiatives that could be undertaken by civil society. Private sector actors should also be reminded of their legal, moral and political responsibility to sever ties with commercial ventures and projects that directly or indirectly aid and abet the apartheid regime imposed. [57–58]

Annex I: Findings of the 2009 HSRC Report

Legal analysis cited here from *Beyond Occupation* draws from work by contributors to a study conducted between 2007 and 2009, under the auspices of the Human Sciences Research Council of South Africa (HSRC) and at the request of the South African Ministry of Foreign Affairs. Coordinated, co-authored and edited by Virginia Tilley, that study was issued in 2009 under the title *Occupation, Colonialism, Apartheid? A Reassessment of Israel's Practices in the Occupied Palestinian Territories under International Law*. Principal contributors included Iain Scobbie, Professor and Chair of International Law, University of Manchester (Great Britain); Max du Plessis, Associate Professor of Law, University of KwaZulu-Natal (Durban) and Senior Research Associate,

Institute for Security Studies; Rina Rosenberg, Esq., International Advocacy Director of Adalah/Legal Centre for Arab Minority Rights in Israel (Haifa); John Reynolds, formerly researcher at Al-Haq (Ramallah) and now lecturer in international law and critical legal studies, National University of Ireland-Maynooth; Victor Kattan, Senior Research Fellow at the Middle East Institute and an Associate Fellow at the Faculty of Law at the National University of Singapore; and Michael Kearney, now Senior Lecturer in Law at Sussex University (Great Britain).

The method was to review Israeli practices in accordance with the list of "inhuman acts" described in the Apartheid Convention. The team determined that Israel was practicing every act listed in the Convention except genocide and the ban on mixed marriages. Subsequently, Israel passed a law banning mixed marriages by people registered as having different religious identities. The revised version of the report published in 2012 was amended accordingly.

The list provided here is a summary of findings regarding those acts. Detailed empirical evidence, data and citations on each category are available in *Beyond Occupation* (chapter 4). [59]

Apartheid Convention, article II

(a) denial to a member or members of a racial group or groups of the right to life and liberty of person:
   (i) by murder of members of a racial group or groups;
   (ii) by the infliction upon the members of a racial group or groups of serious bodily or mental harm, by the infringement of their freedom or dignity, or by subjecting them to torture or to cruel, inhuman or degrading treatment or punishment;
   (iii) by arbitrary arrest and illegal imprisonment of the members of a racial group or groups;

Article II (a) is satisfied by Israeli measures serving to repress Palestinian dissent against the occupation and its system of domination. Israeli policies and practices include murder, in the form of targeted extrajudicial killings; torture and other cruel, inhuman or degrading treatment or punishment of detainees; a military court system that falls far short of international standards of due process, including fair trial; and arbitrary arrest and detention of Palestinians, including administrative detention imposed, often for extended periods, without charge or trial and lacking adequate judicial review. All of those practices are discriminatory, in that Palestinians are subject to different legal systems and different courts, which apply different standards of evidence and procedure that result in far more severe penalties than those applied to Jewish Israelis.

(b) deliberate imposition on a racial group or groups of living conditions calculated to cause its or their physical destruction in whole or in part;

Article II (b) takes its language from the Convention on the Prevention and Punishment of Crime of Genocide and is interpreted here as signifying a policy of genocide. Israeli policies and practices in the occupied Palestinian territory are not found to have the intent of causing the physical destruction of the Palestinian people in this sense. Israel pursues policies that are inimical to human health and life and so are serious violations of international humanitarian and human rights law: they include policies that cause human suffering, such as closures imposed on the Gaza Strip, thereby depriving Palestinians of access to essential health care, medicine, fuel and adequate nutrition. However, those policies do not meet the threshold of a deliberate policy of mass physical extermination. [60]

(c) any legislative measures and other measures calculated to prevent a racial group or groups from participation in the political, social, economic and cultural life of the country and the deliberate creation of conditions preventing the full development of such a group or groups, in particular by denying to members of a racial group or groups basic human rights and freedoms, including the right to work, the right to form recognized trade unions, the right to education, the right to leave and to return to their country, the right to a nationality, the right to freedom of movement and residence, the right to freedom of opinion and expression, and the right to freedom of peaceful assembly and association;

Article II (c) is satisfied on all counts:
(i) Restrictions on the Palestinians' right to freedom of movement are endemic, stemming from Israeli control of the occupied Palestinian territory border crossings, the wall in the West Bank, a matrix of checkpoints and separate roads, and obstructive and all-encompassing permit and ID systems.
(ii) The right of Palestinians to choose their own place of residence within their territory is severely curtailed by systematic administrative restrictions on residency and building in East Jerusalem, by discriminatory legislation that operates to prevent Palestinian spouses from living together on the basis of which part of the occupied Palestinian territory they originate from, and by the strictures of the permit and ID systems.
(iii) Palestinians are denied the right to leave and return to their country. Palestinian refugees living in the occupied Palestinian territory are not allowed to return to their homes inside Israel, while Palestinian refugees and involuntary exiles outside Israel and the territory are not allowed to

return to their homes in either the territory or Israel. Similarly, hundreds of thousands of Palestinians displaced from the West Bank and Gaza Strip in 1967 have been prevented from returning. Many Palestinian residents of the occupied territory must obtain Israeli permission (often denied) to leave it; political activists and human rights defenders are often subject to arbitrary and undefined "travel bans", and many Palestinians who travelled abroad for business or personal reasons have had their residence IDs revoked and been prohibited from returning.

(iv) Israel denies Palestinian refugees living in the occupied Palestinian territory the right to a nationality, denying them citizenship of the State (Israel) that governs the land of their birth, and also obstructing the exercise by the Palestinians of the right to self-determination and [61] preventing the formation of a Palestinian State in the West Bank (including East Jerusalem) and Gaza Strip.

(v) Palestinians are denied the right to freedom and residence through the cantonization of the West Bank, which confines them to designated areas on the basis of race; through bans on their returning to homes in the occupied Palestinian territory from which they were displaced by fighting and terror; and through restrictions on building permits that prevent them from establishing homes where they wish to live.

(vi) Palestinians are restricted in their right to work through Israeli policies that severely curtail Palestinian agriculture and industry in the occupied Palestinian territory, restrict exports and imports, and impose pervasive obstacles to internal movement that impair access to agricultural land and travel for employment and business. Since the second intifada, access for Palestinians to work inside Israel, once significant, has been dramatically curtailed and is now negligible. The unemployment rate in the occupied Palestinian territory as a whole has reached almost 50 per cent.

(vii) Palestinian trade unions exist but are not recognized by the Israeli Government or by the Histadrut (the largest Israeli trade union) and cannot effectively represent Palestinians working for Israeli employers and businesses in the occupied Palestinian territory. Palestinian unions are not permitted to function at all in Israeli settlements. Although they are required to pay dues to the Histadrut, the interests and concerns of Palestinian workers are not represented by the Histadrut; nor do they have a voice in its policies.

(viii) Israel does not operate the school system in the occupied Palestinian territory, but severely impedes Palestinian access to education on a routine basis through extensive school closures; direct attacks on schools; severe restrictions on movement, including travel to schools; and the arrest and detention of teachers and students. The denial by Israel of exit permits, particularly for Palestinians from the Gaza Strip, has prevented thousands of students from pursuing higher education abroad. Discrimination in education is further underlined by the parallel and greatly superior Jewish Israeli school system in Jewish settlements throughout the West Bank, to which Palestinians have no access.

(ix) Palestinians in the occupied Palestinian territory are denied the right to freedom of opinion and expression through censorship laws enforced by the military authorities and endorsed by the Supreme Court. Palestinian newspapers must have a military permit and articles must be pre-approved by the military censor. Since 2001, the Israeli Government Press Office has drastically limited press accreditation for Palestinian journalists, who are also subjected to systematic harassment, detention and confiscation of [62] materials, and in some cases assassination. The accreditation of foreign journalists working in the occupied territory may be revoked at the discretion of the Government Press Office Director on security grounds, which include writing stories that are deemed to "delegitimize" the State.[90] Foreign journalists are regularly barred from entering the Gaza Strip.

(x) The right to freedom of peaceful assembly and association is impeded through military orders. Military legislation bans public gatherings of 10 or more persons without a permit from the Israeli military commander. Non-violent demonstrations are regularly suppressed by the Israeli army with live ammunition, tear gas and arrests. Most Palestinian political parties have been declared illegal and institutions associated with those parties, such as charities and cultural organisations, are regularly subjected to closure and attack.

(xi) The prevention of full development in the occupied Palestinian territory and participation of Palestinians in political, economic, social and cultural life is most starkly demonstrated by the effects of the ongoing Israeli blockade of the Gaza Strip.

(d) any measures, including legislative measures, designed to divide the population along racial lines by the creation of separate reserves and ghettos for

---

90 "Cards will not be given under these rules to any applicant if the Director is of the opinion, after consultation with security authorities, that providing the Cards may endanger the State security", article 3 (f), Rules regarding cards for foreign media journalists, press technicians and media assistants. Available from http://gpoeng.gov.il/media/54705/gpo-rules.pdf.

the members of a racial group or groups, the prohibition of mixed marriages among members of various racial groups, the expropriation of landed property belonging to a racial group or groups or to members thereof;

Article II (d) is satisfied in the following ways:

(i) Israeli policies have divided the occupied Palestinian territory into a series of non-contiguous enclaves (Areas A and B in the West Bank, as a whole separated from the Gaza Strip) in which Palestinians are allowed to live and maintain a degree of local autonomy. Land between those enclaves is reserved exclusively for Jewish and State use: the Jewish settlement grid, nature reserves, agro-industry, military zones and so forth. Land not already used is considered "State land" and administered by State institutions for the benefit of the Jewish people. Segregation of the populations is ensured by pass laws that restrict Palestinians from visiting Jewish areas without a permit and ban Jewish-Israeli travel into [63] Palestinian zones. The wall and its infrastructure of gates and permanent and "floating" checkpoints enforce those restrictions.

(ii) Inter-faith marriages between Muslims or Christians with Jews are prohibited by law.[91] No civil marriage exists in Israel except for the tiny minority whose faith is not declared. Mixed-faith couples must leave the State to marry. Mixed marriages conducted outside of Israel are recognized by the State, provided that marriages among Jews accord with Orthodox Jewish law.

(iii) Israel has extensively appropriated Palestinian land in the occupied Palestinian territory for exclusively Jewish use. Private Palestinian land comprises about 30 per cent of the land unlawfully appropriated for Jewish settlement in the West Bank. Approximately 40 per cent of the West Bank is completely closed to use by the Palestinians, and significant restrictions are placed on access by them to much of the rest.

(e) Exploitation of the labour of the members of a racial group or groups, in particular by submitting them to forced labour;

Article II (e) is today not significantly satisfied, as Israel has raised barriers to Palestinian employment inside Israel since the 1990s and Palestinian

---

91 The Israeli prohibition of mixed marriages is mainly concerned with marriages involving Jews. This is effected by requiring that all marriages be conducted by religious authorities. Since Muslim law permits mixed marriages, marriage between Muslims and Christians is not prohibited. The aim of this arrangement is clear: to avoid blurring the social divisions between Jews and non-Jews. Similarly, under apartheid in South Africa, the Prohibition of Mixed Marriages Act of 1949 banned marriages between "Europeans and non-Europeans" but not between non-Europeans and other non-Europeans.

labour is now used extensively only in the construction and services sectors of Jewish-Israeli settlements in the occupied Palestinian territory. Otherwise, exploitation of labour has been replaced by practices that fall under article II (c), regarding the denial of the right to work.

(f) Persecution of organizations and persons, by depriving them of fundamental rights and freedoms, because they oppose apartheid.

Arrest, imprisonment, travel bans and the targeting of Palestinian parliamentarians, national political leaders and human rights defenders, as well as the closing down of related organisations by Israel, represent persecution for opposition to the system of Israeli domination in the occupied Palestinian territory, within the meaning of article II (f). Article II (f) is especially important in the occupied Palestinian territory, where "security" measures are focused on resistance to occupation. [64]

Annex II: Which Country?

Israeli policies confuse the issue in relation to the categorization under the Apartheid Convention of all acts fitting the purpose clause and preventing "participation in the political, social, economic and cultural life of the country" (article II (c)) as crimes of apartheid. The question is, from which "country" are Palestinians being denied equal rights and full participation? This question engages larger questions about the nature of the Israeli-Palestinian conflict itself.

1. The "country" from which Palestinians in the occupied Palestinian territory are excluded could arguably be Mandate Palestine as established by the League of Nations. The League's intention was for it to gain independence as a State representing the shared patrimony of the entire multi-sectarian population of Palestine. That model, overtaken by events, was confused from the start by language about a "Jewish national home" and in any case was rendered moot by war, expulsion and other events on the ground. However, exclusive Israeli control since 1967 over all of Mandate Palestine has preserved the original geographical unit of Palestine. Hence the "country" in which Palestinians are being deprived of rights could be the Palestine that was never allowed to form, and arguably should form. The remedy in that case is to restore the standing of the original Mandate, which holds that the region is properly one country that has wrongfully been divided by racial agendas.
2. The country from which Palestinians are excluded could be the "Arab State" recommended by resolution 181(II), which also never formed. This view accepts as authoritative the findings of the Special Committee on

Palestine in 1947 and as irreversible the events of the 1948 war, in which a "Jewish State" was formed in part of Mandate territory. What in more recent times has been declared the State of Palestine and sought recognition by the United Nations is a much reduced version of that "Arab State". Israeli policies remain aimed at depriving such a State of the essential attributes of sovereignty; those policies would have to be reversed for this approach to generate a true State. Since Israel shows no indication of changing its position, the alternative is that a Palestinian State be granted some political rights as "reserves" enjoying local autonomy, comparable to the Bantustans of southern Africa or Native American reservations in the United States. Such an arrangement is unlikely to [65] satisfy Palestinian aspirations for self-determination, however. It is more likely to lead ultimately to violence and insurrection by a terminally frustrated Palestinian population.

3. The "country" from which Palestinians are wrongfully deprived of equal rights may be the State of Israel. Accepting as irreversible the annexation measures of Israel in East Jerusalem and the West Bank, this approach would see Israel incorporating the occupied Palestinian territory fully into its governing institutions but dismantling the policies of racial oppression and domination that make Israel an apartheid State. Jews and Palestinians may, however, fear the consequences: enduring security perils for the former and enduring discrimination against the latter. [Back Cover]

This report examines, based on key instruments of international law, whether Israel has established an apartheid regime that oppresses and dominates the Palestinian people as a whole. Having established that the crime of apartheid has universal application, that the question of the status of the Palestinians as a people is settled in law, and that the crime of apartheid should be considered at the level of the State, the report sets out to demonstrate how Israel has imposed such a system on the Palestinians in order to maintain the domination of one racial group over others.

A history of war, annexation and expulsions, as well as a series of practices, has left the Palestinian people fragmented into four distinct population groups, three of them (citizens of Israel, residents of East Jerusalem and the populace under occupation in the West Bank and Gaza) living under direct Israeli rule and the remainder, refugees and involuntary exiles, living beyond. This fragmentation, coupled with the application of discrete bodies of law to those groups, lie at the heart of the apartheid regime. They serve to enfeeble opposition to it and to veil its very existence.This report concludes, on the basis of overwhelming evidence, that Israel is guilty of the crime of apartheid, and urges swift action to oppose and end it.

Report of the Special Rapporteur on the Situation of Human Rights in the Palestinian Territories Occupied Since 1967 (Oct. 23, 2017)

United Nations
General Assembly
A/72/556
Distr.: General
23 October 2017
Original: English

Seventy-second session
Agenda item 72 (c)
Promotion and protection of human rights: human rights situations and reports of special rapporteurs and representatives

Situation of human rights in the Palestinian territories occupied since 1967*

Note by the Secretary-General

The Secretary-General has the honour to transmit to the General Assembly the report of the Special Rapporteur on the situation of human rights in the Palestinian territories occupied since 1967, Michael Lynk, submitted in accordance with Human Rights Council resolution 5/1. [2]

Report of the Special Rapporteur on the situation of human rights in the Palestinian territories occupied since 1967

---

* The present report was submitted after the deadline in order to reflect the most recent developments.

Summary

The Special Rapporteur on the situation of human rights in the Palestinian territories occupied since 1967, Michael Lynk, hereby submits his second report to the General Assembly. The report is based primarily on information provided by victims, witnesses, civil society representatives, United Nations representatives and Palestinian officials in Amman, in connection with the mission of the Special Rapporteur to the region in May 2017. The report addresses a number of concerns pertaining to the situation of human rights in the West Bank, including East Jerusalem, and in Gaza. [3]

I Introduction

1. The present report provides a brief overview of the most pressing human rights concerns in the Occupied Palestinian Territory at the time of its submission, as identified by the Special Rapporteur on the situation of human rights in the Palestinian territories occupied since 1967 in conversations and meetings with civil society. The report then presents a detailed analysis of the international legal framework of the occupation as it continues past its fiftieth year.

2. The Special Rapporteur would like to draw attention to the fact that, while he stands ready to conduct a mission to the Occupied Palestinian Territory, permission to do so has not been granted by the Israeli authorities. The Special Rapporteur has regularly requested access to the Occupied Palestinian Territory from Israel, most recently on 24 March 2017. As at the writing of the present report, no reply had been received. The Special Rapporteur notes that his two immediate predecessors in this position were similarly not given access to the Occupied Palestinian Territory. The Special Rapporteur further notes that an open dialogue among all parties is essential for the protection and promotion of human rights and emphasizes that he is ready and willing to engage with all parties. In addition, he emphasizes that access to the territory is an important component in the development of a comprehensive understanding of the situation. This pattern of non-cooperation with the mandate is a serious concern. A full and comprehensive understanding of the situation based on first-hand observation is extremely beneficial to the work of Special Rapporteurs.

3. The report is based primarily on written submissions as well as consultations with civil society representatives, victims, witnesses, Palestinian

government officials and United Nations representatives held in Amman during the Special Rapporteur's annual mission to the region in May 2017.
4. In the present report, the Special Rapporteur focuses on the human rights and humanitarian law violations committed by Israel, as set out in the mandate of the Rapporteur.[1] The Rapporteur notes that human rights violations by any State party or non-State actor are deplorable and will only hinder the prospects for peace.
5. The Special Rapporteur wishes to express his appreciation for the full cooperation with his mandate extended by the Government of the State of Palestine. The Special Rapporteur also wishes to extend his thanks to all those who travelled to Amman to meet with him and to those who were unable to travel but made written or oral submissions. The Special Rapporteur acknowledges the essential work done by human rights defenders and civil society and expresses his commitment to supporting this work as much as possible.
6. The Special Rapporteur would like to note that several groups were unable to travel to Amman to meet with him owing to travel restrictions imposed by the Israeli authorities. This was particularly the case with individuals coming from Gaza; as a result, all individuals and organizations based in Gaza were consulted by videoconference.

II Current Human Rights Situation

7. In the fiftieth year of the occupation, the human rights situation in the Occupied Palestinian Territory is in a state of severe deterioration. The human rights and humanitarian law violations associated with the occupation have an impact on [4] every aspect of life for Palestinians living in the West Bank, including East Jerusalem, and Gaza. The present report does not provide a comprehensive overview of all issues of concern, but instead seeks only to highlight some of the most urgent concerns at this moment.

A *Gaza*
8. Since April 2017, Gaza has been facing a severe electricity crisis, which deteriorated even further over the course of June. As at the time of writing of the present report, no durable solution has been found and the

---

1 As specified in the mandate of the Special Rapporteur set out in Commission on Human Rights resolution 1993/2.

people of Gaza are living with often as little as four hours of electricity per day.[2] Gaza continued to experience electricity outages of 18–20 hours per day, undermining the provision of basic services.[3] The right to health for Palestinians is of particular concern as a result of this crisis, as hospitals and medical facilities are severely affected by the lack of electricity. Hospitals are postponing elective surgeries and are forced to discharge patients prematurely. In addition, water supplies are at risk, with most homes receiving water through the piped network for only a few hours every three to five days, while the desalination plants are functioning at only 15 per cent of their capacity. More than 108 million litres of untreated sewage were reportedly being discharged into the Mediterranean Sea every day.[4] The World Health Organization (WHO) noted that targeted humanitarian interventions were preventing "the complete collapse of the health sector" during the crisis.[5]

9. It must be noted that the humanitarian crisis in Gaza, both the recent sharp decline in the situation as well as the long-term challenges faced in Gaza over the past 10 years, is entirely human made. The current electricity crisis (the result of Israel's reduction in its supply of electricity to Gaza stemming from a decision of the Palestinian Authority prompted by the internal political divide between Hamas and Fatah) was entirely preventable. In addition, Israel, as the occupying power (A/HRC/34/38, paras. 10–12), is obligated to ensure that adequate hygiene and public health standards are maintained in the occupied territory, as well as to ensure the provision of food and medical care to the population under occupation.[6] The Special Rapporteur calls upon all parties to respect their obligations to the people of Gaza under international human rights and international humanitarian law.

10. Compounding the health concerns raised by the electricity crisis are the increasing difficulties faced by patients seeking to travel through the

---

[2] See www.haaretz.com/middle-east-news/palestinians/1.800735.

[3] Office for the Coordination of Humanitarian Affairs, "Humanitarian bulletin: Occupied Palestinian Territory" (August 2017). Available from www.ochaopt.org/sites/default/files/hummonitor_august_2017_2.pdf.

[4] Office for the Coordination of Humanitarian Affairs, "Gaza crisis: urgent funding appeal" (July 2017). Available from www.ochaopt.org/sites/default/files/gaza_urgent_humanitarian_funding_v5_3july2017_10am_1.pdf.

[5] World Health Organization (WHO), "WHO situation report: Gaza, Occupied Palestinian Territory – July to August 2017". Available from www.emro.who.int/images/stories/palestine/WHO-Special-Situation-Report-on-_Gaza_July_-_August._.pdf?ua=1.

[6] Geneva Convention relative to the Protection of Civilian Persons in Time of War, of 12 August 1949 (Fourth Geneva Convention), arts. 55 and 56.

Erez crossing point out of Gaza for medical treatment. The rate of Israel's denial or delay of permit requests rose in the second half of 2016 (A/HRC/34/70, para. 21). In July 2017, the situation remained concerning. Of permit applications in the month of July, 42.6 per cent were denied or delayed (787 applications).[7] Delayed response [5] times can lead to patients missing appointments and delaying critical care. In August 2017, five cancer patients died while awaiting permits to travel for needed care.[8]

B West Bank

11. The previous report of the Special Rapporteur highlighted the sharp rise in announcements of new settlement construction seen at the start of 2016 (A/HRC/34/70, paras. 9–12). According to Peace Now, there have been tenders for construction of 2,858 housing units since the start of 2017, a significant increase over 2016 (42 housing units) and more than have been recorded in the past 10 years at least.[9] In addition, for the first time in 25 years, the Prime Minister of Israel, Benjamin Netanyahu, announced a new settlement, on which ground was broken for construction in June.[10]

12. Accompanying the announcements above, there have been a number of statements from political leaders calling for continued settlement expansion and in many cases annexation.[11] At the beginning of the year, Mr. Netanyahu reportedly said, in a meeting with members of the inner security cabinet, that he had lifted all restrictions on construction in East Jerusalem and that he would also advance construction in West Bank settlements.[12]

---

7   WHO, "Health access for referral patients from the Gaza Strip", monthly report (July 2017). Available from http://www.emro.who.int/images/stories/palestine/documents/WHO_monthly_Gaza_access_report_July_2017.pdf?ua=1.

8   Ibid., (August 2017). Available from www.emro.who.int/images/stories/palestine/documents/WHO_monthly_Gaza_access_report_Aug_2017_Final.pdf?ua=1.

9   See http://peacenow.org.il/en/settlements-watch/settlements-data/construction.

10 Peter Beaumont, "Israel begins work in first settlement in 25 years as Jared Kushner flies in", *The Guardian*, 20 June 2017. Available from www.theguardian.com/world/2017/jun/20/israel-new-settlement-benjamin-netanyahu-jared-kushner-amichai-amona; and Maayan Lubell, "Israel cabinet approves first West Bank settlement in 20 years", Reuters, 30 March 2017. Available from www.reuters.com/article/us-israel-palestinians-settlement/israeli-cabinet-approves-first-west-bank-settlement-in-20-years-idUSKBN1711K6.

11 Amnesty International, "Israel/Occupied Palestinian Territory: a call to States to stop sustaining illegal settlements", public statement, 7 June 2017. Available from www.amnesty.nl/content/uploads/2017/06/Public-Rationale-English.pdf?x41591, p.2.

12 Barak Ravid, "Netanyahu pledges unrestricted construction in East Jerusalem, settlement blocs", *Haaretz*, 22 January 2017. Available from www.haaretz.com/israel-news/.premium-1.766796.

13. These statements, combined with the reality of the expansion of settlements and extensive announcements of new construction, put the two-state solution on life support, with a fading pulse, and ensure the continuation of human rights violations associated with settlements, including limitations on freedom of movement affecting the rights to education and health, heightened risk of arrest and arbitrary detention, use of land and natural resources thus hindering Palestinians' right to development, and many others. In addition, as emphasized in the Special Rapporteur's report to the Human Rights Council in 2017, Palestinians and Israelis seeking to draw attention to these human rights violations are increasingly targeted – in the West Bank with arrest and arbitrary detention and in Israel with campaigns and legislation seeking to delegitimize the work of human rights organizations (see A/HRC/34/70).

C   *East Jerusalem*

14. In East Jerusalem, as in the rest of the West Bank, settlements, as well as the demolition of homes and the displacement of Palestinians, are of deep concern. On 2 October 2017, Mr. Netanyahu announced his support for the Greater Jerusalem Bill – legislation that would reportedly extend the municipal boundaries of Jerusalem to include a number of settlements.[13] Accompanying moves such as this, demolitions and evictions of Palestinian residents of East Jerusalem continue at a high rate, with 116 total demolitions recorded from the start of the year through mid-September 2017, displacing 202 people.[14] Demolitions in East Jerusalem are justified by the occupying power on either an administrative basis (when buildings are built without proper permits, although permits are nearly impossible for Palestinians to obtain) (A/HRC/34/38, para. 26), or as a punitive measure against families of attackers or alleged attackers (A/HRC/34/36, para. 31, and A/HRC/34/38, paras. 30–33).

---

13 Peter Beaumont, "Netanyahu backs annexation of 19 West Bank settlements", *The Guardian*, 3 October 2017. Available from www.theguardian.com/world/2017/oct/03/netanyahu-backs-annexation-of-west-bank-settlements.

14 Office for the Coordination of Humanitarian Affairs, Occupied Palestinian Territory, "Protection of civilians, reporting period: 12–25 September 2017". Available from www.ochaopt.org/content/protection-civilians-report-12-25-september-2017.

III   Legal Framework of Occupation

15. In June 2017, Israel's occupation of the Palestinian territory (the West Bank, including East Jerusalem, and Gaza) marked its fiftieth anniversary. This is the longest-running military occupation in the modern world.[15] Notwithstanding insistent calls by the international community, most recently in 2016, that the Israeli occupation must come to a complete end,[16] that many of its features are in profound breach of international law,[17] and that its perpetuation both violates the fundamental right of the Palestinian people to self-determination[18] and undermines the possibility of a two-state solution,[19] it has become more entrenched and harsher than ever. Indeed, the Israeli occupation has become a legal and humanitarian oxymoron: an occupation without end.[20]

16. These resolutions adopted by the Security Council and the General Assembly in 2016 are far from the first time that the international community has spoken with urgency about ending Israel's occupation. Thirty-seven years ago, in June 1980, the Council, sufficiently alarmed by the duration and severity of the occupation and Israel's defiance of prior resolutions, adopted resolution 476 (1980). At the time, the Israeli occupation was already 13 years old. In resolution 476 (1980), the Council reaffirmed the overriding necessity to end the prolonged occupation of Arab territories occupied by Israel" and strongly deplored the continuing refusal of Israel to comply with the relevant resolutions of the Security Council and the General Assembly.

17. The inability to end the Israeli occupation has been an abject failure of international diplomacy, a darkening stain on the efficacy of international law and the source of multiple broken promises to the Palestinian people. Nor does the prolongation of this occupation serve the people of Israel, for it corrodes their society and their public institutions by entangling them in their Government's drive [7] to foreclose a viable and just

---

15   International Committee of the Red Cross (ICRC), "Fifty years of occupation: where do we go from here?", 2 June 2017. Available from www.icrc.org/en/document/fifty-years-occupation-where-do-we-go-here.
16   *See* General Assembly resolution 71/23.
17   Ibid. *See also* resolution 71/97.
18   *See* General Assembly resolution 71/184.
19   *See* Security Council resolution 2334 (2016).
20   John Kerry, Secretary of State of the United States of America, in his "Remarks on Middle East peace" on 28 December 2016, warned against Israel's "permanent occupation", "perpetual occupation" and "seemingly endless occupation" of the Palestinian territory; *see* https://2009-2017.state.gov/secretary/remarks/2016/12/266119.htm.

18. If Israel's occupation of the Palestinian territory by 1980 was already prolonged and if it was already a matter of overwhelming necessity to end it, and Israel had already demonstrated by 1980 its unwillingness to comply with the explicit directions of the international community, how are we, in 2017, to characterize the occupation? The prevailing approach of the international community has been to treat Israel as the lawful occupant of the Palestinian territory, albeit an occupant that has committed a number of grave breaches of international law in its conduct of the occupation, including the settlement enterprise,[21] the construction of the wall,[22] the annexation of East Jerusalem[23] and the systemic violations of Palestinian human rights.[24] In the view of the Special Rapporteur, while the lawful occupant approach may have been the appropriate diplomatic and legal portrayal of the occupation in its early years, it has since become wholly inadequate both as an accurate legal characterization of what the occupation has become and as a viable political, diplomatic and legal catalyst to compel Israel to completely and finally terminate the occupation in accordance with its international legal obligations.

19. In the present report, the Special Rapporteur considers whether Israel's role as an entrenched and defiant occupant of the Palestinian territory has now reached the point of illegality under international law. To make this determination, the core principles that govern the lawful conduct of an occupation under the relevant principles of international law are identified and employed to examine Israel's administration of the Occupied Palestinian Territory and assess whether Israel's role as the occupying power remains lawful or not.

A *General Principles of International Law and Occupation*

20. Two decades into the twenty-first century, the norm that guides our global community is that people are citizens, not subjects, of the State that rules them. Accordingly, they are entitled to express their legal identity and their inalienable rights through their sovereign State. Colonialism,

---

21 *See* Security Council resolution 2334 (2016).
22 Legal Consequences of the Construction of a Wall in the Occupied Palestinian Territory, Advisory Opinion, I.C.J. Reports 2004, p. 136, para. 142.
23 *See* Security Council resolution 478 (1980). *See also* General Assembly resolution 71/25.
24 *See* General Assembly resolution 71/98.

occupation and other forms of alien rule are very much the exception to this norm, and they can only be justified in law and international practice as a short-term and abnormal condition that is leading unhesitatingly towards self-determination and/or sovereignty. Most other forms of alien rule would be, ipso facto, unlawful.

21. In our modern world, fundamental rights and protections (including protections under international humanitarian law, civil and political rights such as the right to self-determination, and economic, social and cultural rights) are to be given a purposive and broad interpretation and a liberal application. This is because they embody the rights and freedoms that go to the core of our humanity and are meant to be universally available to, and actionable by, all of us.[25] Conversely, exceptions to these fundamental rights (such as military necessity, significant threats to national security or public emergencies) are to be interpreted and applied in a [8] measured and narrow fashion, so as not to unduly impair the breadth, accessibility and enjoyment of these fundamental rights by all peoples.[26]

22. Created in the aftermath of the bitter experiences of total war and extreme civilian suffering in the nineteenth and twentieth centuries, international humanitarian law is embodied in the Regulations annexed to the Convention respecting the Laws and Customs of War on Land of 1907 (the Hague Regulations), the Geneva Convention relative to the Protection of Civilians in Time of War of 12 August 1949 (the Fourth Geneva Convention) and the Protocol Additional to the Geneva Conventions of 12 August 1949 and relating to the protection of victims of international armed conflicts of 1977 (Protocol I), among other instruments, as well as in the practices of the modern world. Three of the core purposes of modern international humanitarian law as related to foreign military occupation are: (a) to closely regulate an occupation to ensure that the territory achieves, or is restored to, a state of sovereignty; (b) to prevent the territory from becoming a fruit of conquest; and (c) to safeguard the protected people under occupation. As with other areas of international law, international humanitarian law is constantly evolving – within the natural scope of its foundational instruments, principles and purposes – to address new challenges in humanitarian

---

25   International Covenant on Civil and Political Rights and International Covenant on Economic, Social and Cultural Rights.

26   International Covenant on Civil and Political Rights, art. 4 ("… may take measures derogating from their obligations under the present Covenant to the extent strictly required by the exigencies of the situation …"); and International Covenant on Economic, Social and Cultural Rights, art. 4.

protection in situations where the answers are not always expressly laid out in these primary documents.[27]

23. Two of the most significant developments in international law in recent years have been the acceptance that international human rights law, including the overarching right to self-determination, is integral to the application of the laws of occupation. The International Court of Justice has affirmed that international human rights law continues to apply in times of conflict and throughout an occupation.[28] In practice, this means that humanitarian law and human rights law are intended to be complementary, not mutually exclusive, in their application to an occupation,[29] and the protected people under occupation are to enjoy the full panoply of human rights, subject only to any legitimate derogations that are scrupulously justified either by emergencies or the requirements of military rule under occupation.[30]

24. As well, the right of peoples to self-determination, recognized as a right *erga omnes* in international law,[31] applies to all peoples under occupation and other forms of alien rule.[32] The Declaration on Principles of International Law concerning Friendly Relations and Cooperation among States in accordance with the Charter of the United Nations provides that: "Every State has the duty to refrain from any forcible action which deprives peoples ... of their right to self-determination and [9] freedom and independence".[33] In its advisory opinion on the *Legal Consequences of the Construction of a Wall in the Occupied Palestinian Territory*, the International Court of Justice expressly affirmed the right of the Palestinian people to self-determination, that Israel has a duty to

---

27 Eyal Benvenisti, *The International Law of Occupation* (Princeton, New Jersey, Princeton University Press, 2004) ("... it [is] not simply a task of looking up the relevant articles in The Hague Regulations or the Fourth Geneva Convention. International law has evolved significantly since the time these two instruments were drafted.").

28 Legal Consequences of the Construction of a Wall, Advisory Opinion, paras. 106–113; and Armed Activities in the Territory of the Congo (Democratic Republic of the Congo v. Uganda), Judgment, I.C.J. Reports 2005, p. 168, paras. 178 and 179.

29 Vaios Koutroulis, "The application of international humanitarian law and international human rights law in situations of prolonged occupation: only a matter of time?", *International Review of the Red Cross*, vol. 94, No. 885 (Spring 2012).

30 Noam Lubell, "Human rights obligations in military occupation", *International Review of the Red Cross*, vol. 94, No. 885 (Spring 2012).

31 *Legal Consequences of the Construction of a Wall, Advisory Opinion*, para. 88. This means that all States are required to do all that they can to secure self-determination for the people under alien rule.

32 Legal Consequences of the Construction of a Wall, Advisory Opinion, para. 88.

33 General Assembly resolution 2625 (XXV).

respect this right, and that a number of the features of the Israeli occupation had "severely impede[d]" the exercise of this right.[34] Furthermore, the evolution of the laws of occupation, and the application of the right to self-determination to these laws, has meant that sovereignty now lies with the people that live in the occupied territory and not in its government, and the occupying power is required to respect the political interests of this popular sovereignty, the people.[35]

25. Israel has occupied the Palestinian territory (the West Bank, including East Jerusalem, and Gaza) since June 1967. As such, the Fourth Geneva Convention applies in full. This legal determination has been affirmed by the Security Council on a consistent and regular basis, starting at the very beginning of the occupation in June 1967[36] and restated most recently in December 2016.[37] This is also the position stated at a 2014 Conference of High Contracting Parties to the Fourth Geneva Convention (A/69/711-S/2015/1, annex, para. 4). As such, the Palestinians in the occupied territory are "protected persons" under international humanitarian law, and are entitled to all of the protections of the Fourth Geneva Convention.[38] Israel has denied the application of the Fourth Geneva Convention and does not recognize the Palestinian territory as being occupied,[39] a position that the international community has widely rejected.[40]

26. With these principles and observations in mind, a four-part test is proposed to determine whether an occupier is administering the occupation in a manner consistent with international law and the laws of occupation, or whether it has exceeded its legal capacity and its rule is illegal.

---

34 Legal Consequences of the Construction of a Wall, Advisory Opinion, para. 122.
35 Benvenisti, The International Law of Occupation.
36 *See* Security Council resolution 237 (1967).
37 *See* Security Council resolution 2334 (2016).
38 Fourth Geneva Convention, art. 4.
39 Israel, Ministry of Foreign Affairs, "Israel settlements and international law", 30 November 2015 ("In legal terms, the West Bank is best regarded as territory over which there are competing claims which should be resolved in peace process negotiations"). Available from http://www.mfa.gov.il/mfa/foreignpolicy/peace/guide/pages/israeli%20settlements%20and%20international%20law.aspx. *See also Legal Consequences of the Construction of a Wall, Advisory Opinion,* paras. 90 and 93.
40 *See* resolution 71/96, affirming the applicability of the Fourth Geneva Convention to the Occupied Palestinian Territory, adopted by a vote of 168 to 6 with 6 abstentions. *See also* Aeyal Gross, *The Writing on the Wall: Rethinking the International Law of Occupation* (Cambridge, Cambridge University Press, 2017).

B   *Test as to Whether a Belligerent Occupier Remains a Lawful Occupant*

27. As the Israeli occupation of the Palestinian territory has lengthened in time, and with many of its features found to be in flagrant violation of international law, some international legal scholars have raised the issue of whether an occupation that was once regarded as lawful can cross a tipping point and become illegal. Professor Eyal Benvenisti has written that: "... it would seem that an occupant that in bad faith stalls efforts for a peaceful ending to its rule would be considered an aggressor and its rule would be tainted with illegality." Professors Ben-Naftali, Gross and Michaeli take a broader view, arguing that violation of any of the fundamental legal [10] principles of occupation (listed below) "renders an occupation illegal per se".[41] Professor Gross has extended this argument more recently to emphasize the importance of analysing whether an indefinite or permanent occupation has become illegal, so as to counter "... the risk of occupation becoming conquest or a new form of colonialism while hiding behind an imagined temporality".[42] They have provided the intellectual foundation for the following test.

28. The four elements of the lawful occupant test are as set out below.

(a) The belligerent occupier cannot annex any of the occupied territory

29. A belligerent occupier cannot, under any circumstances, acquire the right to conquer, annex or gain any legal or sovereign title over any part of the territory under its occupation. This is one of the most well-established principles of modern international law and it enjoys universal endorsement. This is the corollary of Article 2, paragraph 4, of the Charter of the United Nations, which forbids its members from: "... the threat or use of force against the territorial integrity or political independence of any state ...". Leading public international law scholars have endorsed the "no annexation" principle as a binding legal doctrine.[43] The General

---

41 Orna Ben-Naftali, Aeyal Gross and Keren Michaeli, "Illegal occupation: framing the Occupied Palestinian Territory", *Berkeley Journal of International Law*, vol. 23, No. 3 (2005).

42 Gross, *The Writing on the Wall*. *See also* Ardi Imseis, "Prolonged occupation of Palestine: the case for a second advisory opinion of the International Court of Justice", lecture, 7 October 2015. Available from www.youtube.com/watch?v=X2ijqm1m2Ak.

43 Malcolm N. Shaw, *International Law*, 8th ed. (Cambridge, Cambridge University Press, 2017) ("It is, however, clear today that the acquisition of territory by force alone is illegal under international law"); and Antonio Cassese, *International Law*, 2nd ed. (Oxford, Oxford University Press, 2005) ("... conquest does not transfer a legal title of sovereignty, even if it is followed by *de facto* occupation, and assertion of authority over the territory.").

30. The occupying power cannot impose conditions or create facts on the ground that are designed to establish a claim for title. This principle is anchored in the well-established prohibition in international humanitarian law against the transfer of civilians from the occupying power into the occupied territory, embedded in the Fourth Geneva Convention (art. 49) and its Protocol I (art. 85). Furthermore, the Rome Statute of the International Criminal Court of 1998 (A/CONF.183/9) defined such an act as a war crime (art. 8, para. 2 (b) (viii)). This strict prohibition is intended to forestall an occupier from demographically transforming the territory in order to advance its claim for sovereignty and, simultaneously, undermine the right of the protected population to self-determination.[44]

31. With specific reference to Israel's occupation of the Arab, including Palestinian, territories captured in June 1967, the Security Council endorsed the principle of "the inadmissibility of the acquisition of territory by war" in resolution 242 (1967) in November 1967. The Council has since reaffirmed this principle on at least seven subsequent occasions dealing with Israel's annexations of Arab territory.[45] This principle has also been the longstanding position of the General [11] Assembly.[46] The International Court of Justice held that the "... illegality of territorial acquisition resulting from the threat or use of force" has acquired the status of customary international law.[47] This absolute rule against the acquisition of territory by force makes no distinction as to whether the territory was occupied through a war of self-defence or a war of aggression; annexation is prohibited in both circumstances.[48]

---

44 Report to the Commission on Human Rights Subcommission on Prevention of Discrimination and Protection of Minorities (E/CN.4/Sub.2/1993/17), para. 17 ("Population transfer has been conducted with the effect or purpose of altering the demographic composition of a territory in accordance with policy objectives or prevailing ideology, particularly when that ideology or policy asserts the dominance of a certain group over another.").

45 *See* Security Council resolutions 2334 (2016), 497 (1981), 478 (1980), 476 (1980), 298 (1971), 267 (1969) and 252 (1968).

46 *See*, generally, General Assembly resolution 71/23.

47 Legal Consequences of the Construction of a Wall, Advisory Opinion.

48 Sharon Korman, *The Right of Conquest: The Acquisition of Territory by Force in International Law and Practice* (Oxford, Clarendon Press, 1996) ("... there has been widespread support for the view that Israel's incorporation of East Jerusalem is illegal on the grounds that ... the acquisition of territory by war, whether defensive or aggressive, is inadmissible ...").

(b) The belligerent occupation must be temporary and cannot be either permanent or indefinite; and the occupant must seek to end the occupation and return the territory to the sovereign as soon as reasonably possible

32. Belligerent occupation is inherently a temporary and exceptional situation where the occupying power assumes the role of a de facto administrator of the territory until conditions allow for the return of the territory to the sovereign,[49] which is the people of the territory. Because of the absolute prohibition against the acquisition of territory by force, the occupying power is prohibited from ruling, or attempting to rule, the territory on a permanent or even an indefinite basis.[50] As Professor Aeyal Gross has stated: "Temporality, together with the principles of self-determination and non-acquisition of territory by force, is what distinguishes occupation from conquest, and this distinction would be thwarted were occupation construed as indefinite."[51]

33. The laws of occupation do not set a specific length of time for the lawful duration of an occupation. However, the guiding principle that occupation is a form of alien rule which is a temporary exception to the norms of self-determination and sovereignty means that the occupying power is required to return the territory to the sovereign power in as reasonable and expeditious a time period as possible,[52] subject only to ensuring: (a) public safety and the security of the territory; (b) the resumption, or creation, of governing institutions and a functioning economy; and (c) the security of the occupying military. The occupying power, being obliged to work in good faith to achieve these goals consistent with the principles of the laws of occupation, would have no legitimate purpose to remain in the occupied territory beyond the time when conditions have allowed for the territory to be returned in toto to the sovereign power.[53] Indeed, the longer the occupation, the greater the justification that the

---

[49] Jean S. Pictet, ed., *Commentary IV: Geneva Convention Relative to the Protection of Civilian Persons in Time of War* (Geneva, ICRC, 1958) ("The occupation of territory in wartime is essentially a temporary, de facto situation, which deprives the occupied power of neither its statehood nor its sovereignty; it merely interferes with its power to exercise its rights.").

[50] Ben-Naftali, Gross and Michaeli, "Illegal occupation" ("Occupation is temporary. It may be neither permanent nor indefinite.").

[51] Gross, The Writing on the Wall.

[52] In resolution 1483 (2003), dealing with the occupation of Iraq in 2003, the Security Council noted the commitment of the occupying powers to return the governance of Iraq to its people "as soon as possible".

[53] Ben-Naftali, Gross and Michaeli, "Illegal occupation" ("The temporary, as distinct from the indefinite, nature of occupation is thus the most necessary element of the normative

occupying power must satisfy to defend its continuing presence in the occupied territory. [12]

(c) During the occupation, the belligerent occupier is to act in the best interests of the people under occupation

34. The occupying power, throughout the duration of the occupation, is to govern in the best interests of the people under occupation, subject only to the legitimate security requirements of the occupying military authority. This principle has been likened to a trust or fiduciary relationship in domestic or international law, where the dominant authority is required to act in the interests of the protected person or entity above all else.[54] Accordingly, the authority in power is prohibited from administering the trust in a self-serving or avaricious manner. It is also consistent with the strict requirement on the occupying power to observe, to the fullest extent possible, the human rights of the people under occupation.

35. This best interests principle is anchored in the underlying norms of the laws of occupation, specifically those provisions of the Hague Regulations and the Fourth Geneva Convention that preserve the rights of the protected people and strictly regulate the actions of the occupying power. This is consistent with the shifting of the law on occupation from its early focus on rights of States and political elites to its more contemporary focus on the protections provided for the people under occupation.[55] Article 43 of the Hague Regulations requires the occupying power to "restore, and ensure, as far as possible, public order and safety, while respecting, unless absolutely prevented, the laws in force in the country". The Fourth Geneva Convention expanded these obligations by requiring the occupying power to ensure a wide spectrum of protections, including the positive duties to protect children, maintain hospitals, preserve natural resources and provide for medical supplies and food. As well, it prohibits the occupant from inflicting collective punishment, pillage, corporal punishment and engaging in individual or mass forcible

---

regime of occupation, as it gives meaning and effect – both factual and legal – to the concepts of liberty, freedom, and the right to self-determination.").

54 Gross, The Writing on the Wall.

55 Benvenisti, *The International Law of Occupation* ("When the Security Council announced the applicability of the law of occupation to 2003 Iraq, it had to adapt a law that initially reflected the premise that kings were sovereigns and that international law should protect their possessions during wartime, to a new philosophy – the philosophy of international *humanitarian* law – which posited that peoples were the true sovereigns and that human rights had to be respected").

transfers or deportations.[56] These protections and prohibitions, together with the application of international human rights law, underscore the centrality of the best interests principle and the trustee character of the occupying power's responsibility.

(d) The belligerent occupier must administer the occupied territory in good faith, including acting in full compliance with its duties and obligations under international law and as a member of the United Nations

36. The principle of good faith is a cornerstone principle of the international legal system and has become an integral part of virtually all legal relationships in modern international law.[57] It has been described as the "cardinal rule of treaty interpretation", which dominates and underlies the entire interpretive process.[58] The principle requires a State to carry out its duties and obligations in an honest, loyal, reasonable, diligent and fair manner and with the aim of fulfilling the purposes of the legal responsibility, including an agreement or treaty.[59] Conversely, the good [13] faith principle prohibits States from participating in acts that would defeat the object and purpose of the obligation, or engaging in any abuse of rights that would mask an illegal act or the evasion of an obligation.[60]

37. The duty to act in good faith is found in many of the foundational instruments of international law, including the Charter (art. 2, para. 2), the Vienna Convention on the Law of Treaties (art. 26) and the Declaration on Principles of International Law concerning Friendly Relations and Cooperation among States. The International Court of Justice, in the 1974 nuclear tests case, recognized the primacy of good faith in international law, stating that: "One of the basic principles governing the creation and performance of legal obligations, whatever their source, is the principle of good faith."[61]

---

56 These rights and prohibitions under the Fourth Geneva Convention are summarized in Gross, *The Writing on the Wall*.
57 Andreas R. Ziegler and Jorun Baumgartner, "Good faith as a general principle of (international) law", in Andrew D. Mitchell, M. Sornarajah and Tania Voon, eds., *Good Faith and International Economic Law* (Oxford, Oxford University Press, 2015).
58 Eirik Bjorge, *The Evolutionary Interpretation of Treaties* (Oxford, Oxford University Press, 2014).
59 Markus Kotzur, "Good faith (bona fide)", in Rüdiger Wolfrum, ed., *Max Planck Encyclopedia of Public International Law* (Oxford, Oxford University Press, 2009).
60 Steven Reinhold, "Good faith in international law", *UCL Journal of Law and Jurisprudence*, vol. 2 (2013).
61 Nuclear Tests (Australia v. France), Judgment, I.C.J. Reports 1974, p. 253, para. 46.

38. Thus, under international law, a belligerent occupier is required to govern an occupied territory in good faith. This can be measured by whether the occupying power fulfils each of the three core principles governing an occupation stated above: (a) it does not annex any of the occupied territory; (b) it rules on a temporary basis only; and (c) it governs in the best interests of the protected people. As well, a belligerent occupier governing in good faith would also be required to: (d) comply with any specific directions issued by the United Nations or other authoritative bodies pertaining to the occupation,[62] and (e) comply with the specific precepts of international humanitarian law and international human rights law applicable to an occupation.

C   *Applicability of the 1971 Advisory Opinion of the International Court of Justice on Namibia (South West Africa)*[63]

39. In June 1971, the International Court of Justice issued an advisory opinion on Namibia, at the request of the Security Council, on the legal consequences of the continued presence of South Africa in Namibia. The Court determined that South Africa's administration of the mandate for Namibia had breached several fundamental obligations under international law, that it had been validly terminated by the United Nations and that South Africa's continued presence in the territory was thenceforth illegal. The Court's advisory opinion on the *Legal Consequences for States of the Continued Presence of South Africa in Namibia* contains a number of applicable precedents that support both the proposed four-part legality test and the analysis as to whether Israel's continuing role as occupant remains lawful. [14]

---

62   Article 25 of the Charter of the United Nations stipulates that: "The Members of the United Nations agree to accept and carry out the decisions of the Security Council in accordance with the present Charter."

63   Legal Consequences for States of the Continued Presence of South Africa in Namibia (South West Africa) notwithstanding Security Council resolution 276 (1970), Advisory Opinion, I.C.J. Reports 1971, p. 16. The Special Rapporteur owes an intellectual debt for his reading of the Namibia decision to: John Dugard, "A tale of two sacred trusts: Namibia and Palestine", in Tiyanjana Maluwa, ed., Law, Politics and Rights: Essays in Memory of Kader Asmal (Leiden, The Netherlands, Martinus Nijhoff Publishers, 2014); Norman Finkelstein, Gaza: An Inquest into its Martyrdom (Oakland, University of California Press, 2018) (forthcoming); and Stephanie Koury, "Legal strategies at the United Nations: a comparative look at Namibia, Western Sahara and Palestine", in Susan Akram and others, eds., International Law and the Israeli-Palestinian Conflict: A Rights-Based Approach to Middle East Peace (Abingdon, United Kingdom of Great Britain and Northern Ireland, Routledge, 2011).

40. After the First World War, the League of Nations, through article 22 of the Covenant of the League, directed that South Africa was to serve as the mandatory over South West Africa. Pursuant to paragraph 1 of article 22, South Africa's mandate was to administer South West Africa as a "sacred trust of civilization" until the territory was ready for independence. As the mandatory, South Africa was obliged to administer South West Africa as a trustee acting in the best interests of the territory and its peoples. The mandatory was accountable to the League of Nations for its administration.

41. After the Second World War, the United Nations assumed responsibility for the mandate system, now known as the international trusteeship system. South Africa refused to place South West Africa under the trusteeship supervision of the United Nations and it proceeded to introduce forms of apartheid into the territory, as well as engage in the de facto annexation of the territory. In 1966, the General Assembly revoked South Africa's mandate over South West Africa and declared that South Africa had no other right to administer the territory.[64] In January 1970, the Security Council declared that South Africa's continued presence in Namibia was "illegal", and stated that South Africa's "defiant attitude" towards the decisions of the Security Council "undermine[d] the authority of the United Nations".[65] Subsequently, in July 1970, the Council requested an advisory opinion from the International Court of Justice.[66]

42. The 1971 advisory opinion on Namibia by the International Court of Justice is a sturdy and germane precedent for the assessment of Israel's continuing occupation of the Palestinian territory. Although Namibia was a mandate territory under the trusteeship system, governed by the terms of article 22 of the Covenant, and the Palestinian territory is required to be governed by the laws of occupation, they are different branches of the same tree. Both South Africa (as the mandatory power) and Israel (as the occupying power) are prime examples of alien rule, the governing power in both cases is responsible for respecting the right to self-determination of the protected people, annexation in both cases was/is strictly prohibited, both powers were/are required to govern in the best interests of the protected people and to abstain from any self-serving practices, and the international community was/is responsible in both cases for the close

---

64 *See* General Assembly resolution 2145 (XXI).
65 *See* Security Council resolution 276 (1970).
66 *See* Security Council resolution 284 (1970).

supervision of the alien rule and for bringing this rule to a successful conclusion.

43. In its advisory opinion, the International Court of Justice articulated the following seven legal findings and principles with respect to the mandate territory of Namibia. The Special Rapporteur submits that these legal findings and principles are directly applicable to the question of the continued legality of Israel's occupation:

(a) Annexation is forbidden, the mandatory must act as a trustee for the benefit of the peoples of the territory, and the end result of the mandate must be the exercise of self-determination and independence;[67]

(b) All mandatory powers must fulfil their obligations in good faith. Acting contrary to any of the fundamental obligations of a mandate would all be evidence of a failure to satisfy the good faith obligation;[68] [15]

(c) The strict safeguards imposed by the international community on the mandatory are to ensure that mandate territories cannot become "the objects of disguised cessions". The mandatory cannot invoke any of its assigned rights as grounds for delaying or postponing the conclusion of the trusteeship relationship. Nor does a long occupation improve the claim of the mandatory power to annexing any of the territory of the mandate;[69]

(d) International law is not static but evolutionary, and its interpretation is influenced by subsequent developments in the law through the Charter of the United Nations and customary international law. Where the right exists as the general principle of law, it can be implied to be an integral part of the treaty or agreement;[70]

(e) The deliberate and persistent violation of a party's obligations destroys the very object and purpose of the relationship or vested power, and the party cannot thereby claim any of the rights which derive from that relationship;[71]

(f) The breach of the mandatory's fundamental obligations under international law can render its continuing presence in the mandate territory illegal. An illegal situation must be brought to an end, and

---

67 Legal Consequences for States of the Continued Presence of South Africa in Namibia, Advisory Opinion, paras. 45–47, 50, 53 and 83.
68 Ibid., paras. 53, 84, 90, 115, 116 and 128.
69 Ibid., paras. 54, 55, 66, 82 and 83.
70 Ibid, paras. 52, 53, 96–98, 100 and 133.
71 Ibid., paras. 84, 91, 95, 96, 98, 100 and 102.

Member States must recognize the illegality and invalidity of the situation, including the duty of non-recognition;[72]

(g) The determination that a mandatory power is in fundamental breach of its international obligations, that the mandate is revoked and that its continued presence in the mandate territory is illegal does not affect the ongoing application of the governing legal framework protecting the peoples of the mandate. As such, the mandatory continues to remain accountable for any violations of its international obligations and it must honour its duty to protect the rights of the peoples of the mandate.[73]

44. The 1971 advisory opinion on Namibia retains its relevance and its force of reasoning today. In 2004, the International Court of Justice, in the advisory opinion on the *Construction of a Wall*, relied upon the advisory opinion on Namibia with respect to its findings on the applicability of the right to self-determination to non-self-governing territories, including the Occupied Palestinian Territory.[74] The overriding similarities between the two situations (an alien power using the mask of an international supervisory regime to assert permanent control in a trust relationship) means that the legal principles pertaining to the illegal continuation by a mandatory of a mandate apply, mutatis mutandis, to the determination of whether an occupying power's ongoing occupation has become illegal.

D   *Application of the Legality Test to Israel's Occupation*
    Prohibition Against Annexation

45. Israel's formal annexation of East Jerusalem in 1967 and 1980, and its de facto annexation of significant parts of the West Bank, are intended to solidify its claim for sovereignty. This constitutes a flagrant breach of the absolute prohibition against annexation and violates Israel's obligations under international law. [16]

46. After capturing the Palestinian territory (the West Bank, including East Jerusalem, and Gaza) in the June 1967 war, Israel annexed East Jerusalem and parts of the West Bank in late June 1967 by a Cabinet decision. In July 1967, the General Assembly unanimously denounced the annexation and called upon Israel to rescind the measures that would alter the status of Jerusalem.[75] Subsequently, in July 1980, the Israeli Knesset adopted

---

72   Ibid., paras. 108, 109, 111, 115, 117, 122 and 123.
73   Ibid., paras. 118 and 125.
74   Legal Consequences of the Construction of a Wall, Advisory Opinion, para. 88.
75   *See* General Assembly resolutions 2253 (ES-V) and 2254 (ES-V).

the Basic Law on Jerusalem, declaring Jerusalem to be the "complete and united" capital of Israel. The Security Council in August 1980 censured Israel "in the strongest terms" for its enactment of the Basic Law, affirmed that the Law was in breach of international law, and determined that Israel's annexation was "null and void" and "must be rescinded forthwith."[76] Israel remains non-compliant with all United Nations resolutions on Jerusalem, there are presently about 210,000 Israeli settlers living in occupied East Jerusalem, and Israel has stated that it will not leave East Jerusalem.[77]

47. Beyond Jerusalem, Israel is actively establishing the de facto annexation of parts of the occupied West Bank. The International Court of Justice, in the advisory opinion on the *Construction of a Wall*, warned that the reality of the wall and the settlements regime was constituting a fait accompli and de facto annexation.[78] The Association for Civil Rights in Israel has characterized Israel's regime in the West Bank as an "occunexation."[79] Professor Omar Dajani has observed that, given the absolute prohibition today in international law against conquest, acquisitive States have an incentive to obfuscate the reality of annexation.[80] In the West Bank, Israel exercises complete control over Area C (making up 60 per cent of the West Bank), where its 400,000 settlers live in approximately 225 settlements. The settlers live under Israeli law in Israeli-only settlements, drive on an Israeli-only road system, and benefit greatly from the enormous sums of public money spent by Israel on entrenching, defending and expanding the settlements. Few of these benefits, except incidentally, flow to the Palestinians in Area C. Only 1 per cent of Area C is designated for Palestinian use, notwithstanding the approximately 300,000 Palestinians who live there.[81] What country would invest so heavily over so many

---

76 *See* Security Council resolution 478 (1980). *See also* Council resolution 476 (1980).
77 Prime Minister of Israel, Benjamin Netanyahu, in 2015: "Forty-eight years ago, the division of Jerusalem was ended and we returned to be united … We will keep Jerusalem united under Israeli authority." Available from www.cnn.com/2015/05/17/middleeast/israel-netanyahu-united-jerusalem/.
78 Legal Consequences of the Construction of a Wall, Advisory Opinion, para. 121.
79 Association for Civil Rights in Israel, "49 years of control without rights: human rights of the Palestinians in the West Bank and East Jerusalem – what has changed?", available from www.acri.org.il/en/wp-content/uploads/2016/06/49years2016-en.pdf.
80 Omar M. Dajani, "Israel's creeping annexation", *American Journal of International Law Unbound*, vol. 111 (2017).
81 Orhan Niksic, Nur Nasser Eddin and Massimiliano Cali, *Area C and the Future of the Palestinian Economy* (Washington, D.C., World Bank, 2014); and Diakonia International

years to establish so many immutable facts on the ground in an occupied territory if it did not intend to remain permanently?[82] [17]

Occupations Must be Temporary, and Not Indefinite or Permanent

48. Israel's occupation is 50 years old, and counting. The duration of this occupation is without precedent or parallel in today's world.[83] Professor Adam Roberts has stated that an occupation becomes prolonged if it lasts longer than five years into a period, closely resembling peacetime, when hostility is reduced.[84] Modern occupations that have broadly adhered to the strict principles concerning temporariness, non-annexation, trusteeship and good faith have not exceeded 10 years, including the American occupation of Japan, the Allied occupation of western Germany and the American-led coalition's occupation of Iraq.[85]

49. Employing the precept that the longer the occupation, the greater the onus on the occupying power to justify its continuation, Israel lacks any persuasive reason to remain as the occupant after 50 years. Israel has signed peace treaties with Egypt (1981) and Jordan (1994) that have stood the test of time, and the absence of peace agreements with its other two neighbours (the Syrian Arab Republic and Lebanon) cannot be invoked to justify its continuing occupation of the Palestinian territory. Contrary to the repeated declarations by many Israeli leaders, the Palestinian Authority is accepted by the international community as a legitimate negotiating partner for peace. The primary engine of Israel's ongoing occupation – the settlement enterprise – detracts from, rather than enhances, Israel's security.[86] Professor Gershon Shafir has written

---

Humanitarian Law Resource Centre, "Planning to fail: the planning regime in Area C of the West Bank – an international law perspective" (2013).

82 Benjamin Netanyahu, Prime Minister, Israel, in August 2017: ("We are here to stay forever. There will be no further uprooting of settlements in the Land of Israel ... This is our land.") Available from www.latimes.com/world/middleeast/la-fg-israel-netanyahu-settlements-20170828-story.html.

83 Yoram Dinstein, *The International Law of Belligerent Occupation* (Cambridge, Cambridge University Press, 2009).

84 Adam Roberts, "Prolonged military occupation: the Israeli Occupied Territories since 1967", *American Journal of International Law*, vol. 84, No. 1 (January 1990).

85 These three occupations are sometimes cited as examples of "transformative" occupations, which raise separate legal questions that are not addressed in the present report. *See*, generally, Gregory H. Fox, "Transformative occupation and the unilateralist impulse", *International Review of the Red Cross*, vol. 94, No. 885 (Spring 2012).

86 Israeli Council for Peace and Security (June 2012), quoted in Gershon Shafir, *A Half Century of Occupation: Israel, Palestine, and the World's Most Intractable Conflict* (Oakland, University of California Press, 2017), para. 98.

that: "A circular logic is in play here: Israel is able to use the stipulation of the temporary character of occupation to make long-term changes in the name of extended security risks, many of which are the result of the violations of the law of occupation."[87]

50. The only credible explanation for Israel's continuation of the occupation and its thickening of the settlement regime is to enshrine its sovereign claim over part or all of the Palestinian territory, a colonial ambition par excellence. Every Israeli Government since 1967 has pursued the continuous growth of the settlements, and the significant financial, military and political resources committed to the enterprise belies any intention on its part to make the occupation temporary.[88] Every Israeli Government since 1967 has left office with more settlers living in the occupied territory than when it assumed office. (Certainly, in various peace negotiation rounds in the 1990s and the 2000s, Israeli leaders had proposed to withdraw from some of the West Bank, but even in the most advanced of these negotiations – under Prime Minister Ehud Olmert between 2006 and 2008 – Israel insisted on keeping many of its settlements in East Jerusalem and the West Bank in any final agreement.)[89] The current Israeli Government is strongly committed to deepening [18] the settlement enterprise.[90] Professor Shafir observes that "temporariness remains an Israeli subterfuge for creating permanent facts on the ground", with Israel able to employ the seemingly indeterminate nature of the occupation's end-point to create a "permanent temporariness" that intentionally forestalls any meaningful exercise of self-determination and independence by the Palestinians.[91]

51. The Israeli occupation has long exceeded the temporariness principle under international law. It has not acted in a manner consistent with the requirement that it take all necessary steps to bring the occupation to a successful close in as reasonable and expeditious a time period as possible. Indeed, far from it. Whether the occupation is said to be indefinite

---

87   Shafir, A Half Century of Occupation.
88   Idith Zertal and Akiva Eldar, Lords of the Land: the War Over Israel's Settlements in the Occupied Territories, 1967–2007 (New York, Nation Books, 2007).
89   Dajani, "Israel's creeping annexation".
90   Samantha Power, Permanent Representative of the United States of America to the United Nations, "Speech after abstention on anti-settlement vote", New York, 23 December 2016. ("The Israeli Prime Minister recently described his government as 'more committed to settlements than any in Israel's history' …"). Available from www.timesofisrael.com/full-text-of-us-envoy-samantha-powers-speech-after-abstention-on-anti-settlement-vote/.
91   Shafir, A Half Century of Occupation.

or permanent, the lack of a persuasive justification for its extraordinary duration places Israel, as the occupying power, in violation of international law.

Best Interests/Trust Principle

52. Under international law, Israel is required to administer the Occupied Palestinian Territory in the best interests of the Palestinian people, the protected people under occupation, subject only to justified security concerns. It is prohibited from governing the occupied territory in an acquisitive or self-interested manner. Contrary to these requirements, Israel has acted in its own expansionary interests unaccompanied by most of the responsibilities attached to a belligerent occupier.

53. The social and economic impact of the occupation on the Palestinians in the occupied territory, which had always been disadvantageous, has become increasingly dire in recent years. According to recent reports by the World Bank[92] and the United Nations,[93] the expanding Israeli settlement enterprise and the supporting apparatus of occupation has deepened the already separate and distinctly inferior civil and economic conditions imposed upon Palestinians in the West Bank. There, the Palestinians are subject to a harsh and arbitrary legal system quite unequal to that enjoyed by the Israeli settlers.[94] Much of the West Bank is off-limits to Palestinians, and they regularly endure significant restrictions on their freedom of movement through closures, roadblocks, and the need for hard-to-obtain travel permits.[95]

54. Access to the natural resources of the occupied territory, especially to water, is disproportionately allocated to Israel and the settlers.[96] Similarly, the planning system administered by the occupying power for housing and commercial development throughout the West Bank, including East Jerusalem, is deeply discriminatory in favour of settlement construction,

---

[92] World Bank, "West Bank and Gaza: Area C and the future of the Palestinian economy", report No. AUS2922 (2013).

[93] Office for the Coordination of Humanitarian Affairs, Occupied Palestinian Territory, "Fragmented lives: humanitarian overview 2016" (2017).

[94] Limor Yehuda and others, "One rule, two legal systems: Israel's regime of laws in the West Bank" (Association for Civil Rights in Israel, 2014).

[95] See Human Rights Watch, World Report 2017: Events of 2016. Available from www.hrw.org/world-report/2017/country-chapters/israel/palestine.

[96] Amnesty International, "Troubled waters: Palestinians denied fair access to water" (London, 2009).

while imposing significant barriers on Palestinians,[97] including ongoing land confiscation,[98] home demolitions [19] and the denial of building permits.[99] Israel employs practices that in some cases may amount to the forcible transfer of Palestinians, primarily those living in rural areas, as a means of confiscating land for settlements, military weapons training areas and other uses exclusive to the occupying power that have little or nothing to do with its legitimate security requirements.[100]

55. As for East Jerusalem, the occupation has increasingly detached it from its traditional national, economic, cultural and family connections with the West Bank because of the wall, the growing ring of settlements and related checkpoints, and the discriminatory permit regime. It is neglected by the municipality in terms of services and infrastructure,[101] the occupation has depleted its economy and the Palestinians have only a small land area on which to build housing.[102]

56. In Gaza, Israel vacated its formal presence in 2005, but its effective control over the Strip – through its dominance over Gaza's land and sea frontiers and its air space – means that it retains its responsibilities as an occupier. As Tamir Pardo, former head of Israel's Mossad, stated recently: "Israel is responsible for the humanitarian situation [in Gaza], and this is the place with the biggest problem in the world today."[103] Since 2007, Israel has maintained a suffocating economic and travel blockade that has driven Gaza back to the dark ages. More than 60 per cent of the population of Gaza is reliant upon humanitarian aid, it is unable to secure more than one third of the electrical power that it requires, it will soon exhaust its

---

97 Human Rights Watch, "Separate and unequal: Israel's discriminatory treatment of Palestinians in the Occupied Palestinian Territories", 19 December 2010. Available from www.hrw.org/report/2010/12/19/separate-and-unequal/israels-discriminatory-treatment-palestinians-occupied.

98 Adam Aloni, Expel and Exploit: The Israeli Practice of Taking Over Rural Palestinian Land (B'Tselem, 2016).

99 Office for the Coordination of Humanitarian Affairs, "Fragmented lives".

100 Simon Reynolds, *Coercive Environments: Israel's Forcible Transfer of Palestinians in the Occupied Territory* (Badil Resource Centre for Palestinian Residency and Refugee Rights, 2017).

101 Association for Civil Rights in Israel, "East Jerusalem: facts and figures 2017", 21 May 2017. Available from http://www.acri.org.il/en/wp-content/uploads/2017/05/Facts-and-Figures-2017-1.pdf.

102 United Nations Conference on Trade and Development (UNCTAD), "The Palestinian economy in East Jerusalem: enduring annexation, isolation and disintegration", document UNCTAD/GDS/APP/2012/1.

103 Gili Cohen, "Ex-Mossad chief says occupation is Israel's only existential threat", *Haaretz*, 22 March 2017. Available from www.haaretz.com/israel-news/1.778650.

sources of safe drinking water and, virtually unique in the world, its gross domestic product is actually lower than it was in 2006.[104]

57. All these restrictions in the civil and commercial life of the Palestinians have created a shattered economic space which has resulted in a highly dependent and strangled economy, mounting impoverishment, daily impositions and indignities, and receding hope for a reversal of fortune in the foreseeable future.[105]

58. On the probative evidence, Israel, the occupying power, has ruled the Palestinian Territory as an internal colony, deeply committed to exploiting its land and resources for Israel's own benefit, and profoundly indifferent, at very best, to the rights and best interests of the protected people.[106] As such, Israel is in breach of [20] its obligations to administer the occupation as a trustee for the well-being of the protected people under occupation.

Good Faith

59. For an occupying power to govern an occupied territory in good faith, it must not only comply with the three principles stated above, but it must also be fully compliant with any specific directions issued by the United Nations or other authoritative bodies pertaining to the occupation. Further, it must comply with the specific precepts of international law, including humanitarian law and human rights law, applicable to an occupation.

60. Since 1967, the Security Council has adopted, in clear and direct language, more than 40 resolutions pertaining to Israel's occupation of the Palestinian Territory. On the settlements, the Council has variously stated that they "have no legal validity", they must be "dismantled" and they constitute a "flagrant violation under international law", and that settlement

---

104 United Nations country team in the Occupied Palestinian Territory, "Gaza ten years later", July 2017. Available from https://unsco.unmissions.org/sites/default/files/gaza_10_years_later_-_11_july_2017.pdf.

105 UNCTAD, "Report on UNCTAD assistance to the Palestinian people: developments in the economy of the Occupied Palestinian Territory", document UNCTAD/APP/2016/1. In this report, UNCTAD estimated that the Palestinian economy would be twice its present size in the absence of the Israeli occupation.

106 David Kretzmer, *The Occupation of Justice: The Supreme Court of Israel and the Occupied Palestinian Territories* (Albany, State University of New York Press, 2002) ("On the political level, the government relates to the Occupied Territories as colonies, with all that this entails: exploitation of their resources and markets for the benefit of the home country and its citizens and a clear distinction between the status of the "natives" and those of the settlers.").

activities must "immediately and completely cease" and they "are dangerously imperilling the viability of a two-state solution".[107] Similarly, the Council has affirmed, with specific reference to the Israeli occupation, that the acquisition of territory by war or by force is inadmissible.[108] The Council has censured "in the strongest terms" Israel's annexation of East Jerusalem, it has "deplored" Israel's "persistence in changing the physical character, demographic composition ... and status of the Holy City of Jerusalem", it has called these changes a "flagrant violation" of the Fourth Geneva Convention, and it has stated that these changes "must be rescinded."[109] Repeatedly, the Security Council has affirmed that the Fourth Geneva Convention applies to the Occupied Palestinian Territory and has called upon Israel to "scrupulously" abide by it.[110]

61. In the face of the persistent Israeli refusal to accept and apply any of these resolutions, the Security Council has "strongly deplored the continued refusal of Israel, the occupying power, to comply with the relevant resolutions of the Council and the General Assembly."[111] Immediately following the adoption of resolution 2334 (2016) by the Council in December 2016 condemning the settlement enterprise and Israel's failure to apply the Fourth Geneva Convention, Mr. Netanyahu sharply criticized the resolution and announced that Israel would not submit to it.[112] In October 2017, the United Nations Special Coordinator for the Middle East Peace Process reported to the Council that Israel was not complying with the resolution and that indeed its settlement activity was continuing at a high rate.[113]

62. Israel has been deemed to be in breach of many of the leading precepts of international humanitarian and human rights law. Its settlement

---

107 *See* Security Council resolutions 2334 (2016), 465 (1980), 452 (1979) and 446 (1979).
108 *See* Security Council resolutions 2334 (2016), 497 (1981), 478 (1980), 476 (1980), 298 (1971), 267 (1969), 252 (1968) and 242 (1967).
109 *See* Security Council resolutions 2334 (2016), 478 (1980) and 476 (1980).
110 *See* Security Council resolutions 2334 (2016), 478 (1980), 476 (1980), 471 (1980), 465 (1980), 452 (1979) and 446 (1979).
111 *See* Security Council resolutions 478 (1980), 476 (1980) and 446 (1979).
112 Isabel Kershner, "Netanyahu promises retribution for 'biased' U.N. resolution", *New York Times*, 24 December 2016. Available from www.nytimes.com/2016/12/24/world/middle east/israel-benjamin-netanyahu-united-nations.html.
113 Nickolay Mladenov, Special Coordinator for the Middle East Peace Process, "Briefing to the Security Council on the situation in the Middle East: report on Council resolution 2334 (2016)", 25 September 2017. Available from https://reliefweb.int/report/occupied-palestinian-territory/nickolay-mladenov-special-coordinator-middle-east-peace-3.

enterprise has been characterized as illegal by the Security Council.[114] The prohibited use of collective [21] punishment has been regularly employed by Israel through the demolition of Palestinian homes of families that are related to those suspected of terrorism or security breaches and by extended closures of Palestinian communities (which resumed in 2014, after a moratorium lasting since 2006).[115] Bedouin communities in the West Bank and East Jerusalem are the latest Palestinian communities to be at risk of forcible transfer instigated by the occupying power.[116] The right to liberty, with its accompanying right not to be subjected to arbitrary arrest, are violated by the high rates of arbitrary detention, including administrative detention, and the revocation of the residency rights of many thousands of Palestinians.[117] Freedom of movement is impaired through a complex system of administrative, bureaucratic and physical constraints that affects virtually every aspect of daily life for the Palestinians.[118] And above all, the entrenched and unaccountable occupation – through its denial of territorial integrity, genuine self-governance, a sustainable economy and a viable path to independence – substantively violates, and undermines, the right of the Palestinians to self-determination, the platform right that enables the realization of many other rights.

63. Whether measured by the criteria of substantive compliance with United Nations resolutions or by the satisfaction of its obligations as occupier under the framework of international law, Israel has not governed the Occupied Palestinian Territory in good faith. As a United Nations Member State with obligations, it has repeatedly defied the international community's supervisory authority over the occupation. As the occupant, it has consciously breached many of the leading precepts of international

---

114 *See* Security Council resolutions 2334 (2016), 478 (1980), 476 (1980), 471 (1980), 465 (1980), 452 (1979) and 446 (1979).
115 *See* www.btselem.org/topic/punitive_demolitions.
116 Office for the Coordination of Humanitarian Affairs, "Demolition and seizure of service infrastructure in Palestinian communities in Area C exacerbates risk of forcible transfer", 11 October 2017. Available from www.ochaopt.org/content/demolition-and-seizure-service-infrastructure-palestinian-communities-area-c-exacerbates.
117 Human Rights Watch, "Israel: 50 years of occupation abuses", 4 June 2017. Available from www.hrw.org/news/2017/06/04/israel-50-years-occupation-abuses.
118 Office of the United Nations High Commissioner for Human Rights, "Freedom of movement: human rights situation in the Occupied Palestinian Territory, including East Jerusalem" (February 2016). Available from www.ohchr.org/Documents/Countries/PS/SG_Report_FoM_Feb2016.pdf.

humanitarian law and international human rights law that govern an occupation.

IV Conclusion

64. International law is the promise that States make to one another, and to their people, that rights will be respected, protections will be honoured, agreements and obligations will be satisfied, and peace with justice will be pursued. It is a tribute to the international community that it has sustained this vision of international law throughout its supervision of Israel's occupation of the Palestinian territory. But it is no tribute that – as the occupation deepened, as the occupier's intentions became crystal clear, and as its defiance grew – the international community recoiled from answering Israel's splintering of the Palestinian territory and disfiguring of the laws of occupation with the robust tools that international law and diplomacy provide. International law, along with the peoples of Palestine and Israel, have all suffered in the process.

65. States who administer another territory under international supervision – whether as an occupier or a mandatory power – will cross the red line into illegality if they breach their fundamental obligations as alien rulers. The International Court of Justice in its advisory opinion on Namibia supports this conclusion. The Special Rapporteur submits that Israel's role as occupant has crossed this red line. The challenge now facing the international community is to [22] assess this analysis and, if accepted, to devise and employ the appropriate diplomatic and legal steps that, measure by measure, would completely and finally end the occupation. As Amos Schocken, the publisher of *Haaretz*, has written about his own country's leadership: "... international pressure is precisely the force that will drive them to do the right thing."[119]

66. A determination that Israel's role as occupant is now illegal would serve several significant purposes. First, it would encourage Member States to take all reasonable steps to prevent or discourage national institutions, organizations and corporations within their jurisdiction from engaging in activities that would invest in, or sustain, the occupation. Second, it would encourage national and international courts to apply the appropriate laws within their jurisdiction that would prevent or discourage

---

119 Amos Schocken, "Only international pressure will end Israeli apartheid", *Haaretz*, 22 January 2016. Available from www.haaretz.com/opinion/.premium-1.698874.

cooperation with entities that invest in, or sustain, the occupation. Third, it would invite the international community to review its various forms of cooperation with the occupying power as long as it continues to administer the occupation unlawfully. Fourth, it would provide a solid precedent for the international community when judging other occupations of long duration. Most of all, such a determination would confirm the moral importance of upholding the international rule of law when aiding the besieged and the vulnerable.

V   Recommendations

67. The Special Rapporteur recommends that the Government of Israel bring a complete end to the 50 years of occupation of the Palestinian territories in as expeditious a time period as possible, under international supervision.
68. The Special Rapporteur also recommends that the General Assembly:
    (a) Commission a United Nations study on the legality of Israel's continued occupation of the Palestinian territory;
    (b) Consider the advantages of seeking an advisory opinion from the International Court of Justice on the question of the legality of the occupation;
    (c) Consider commissioning a legal study on the ways and means that Member States can and must fulfil their obligations and duties to ensure respect for international law, including the duty of non-recognition, the duty to cooperate to bring to an end a wrongful situation and the duty to investigate and prosecute grave breaches of the Geneva Conventions;
    (d) Consider the adoption, in accordance with General Assembly resolution 377 (V), entitled "Uniting for peace", of a resolution with respect to the question of Palestine, in the event that there is a determination that Israel's role as occupier is no longer lawful. [23]

Report of the Special Rapporteur on the Situation of Human Rights in the Palestinian Territories Occupied Since 1967 (Apr. 13, 2017)

United Nations
General Assembly
A/HRC/34/70
Distr.: General
13 April 2017
Original: English

Human Rights Council
Thirty-fourth session
27 February-24 March 2017
Agenda item 7

Human rights situation in Palestine and other occupied Arab territories

Report of the Special Rapporteur on the situation of human rights in the Palestinian territories occupied since 1967*

Note by the Secretariat

The Secretariat has the honour to transmit to the Human Rights Council the report of the Special Rapporteur on the situation of human rights in the Palestinian territories occupied since 1967, submitted pursuant to Commission on Human Rights resolution 1993/2 A and Human Rights Council resolution 5/1. In it, the Special Rapporteur examines the current human rights situation in the Occupied Palestinian Territory, with a particular emphasis on the role and challenges faced by human rights defenders. [2]

---

* The present report was submitted after the deadline in order to reflect the most recent developments.

Report of the Special Rapporteur on the situation of human rights in the Palestinian territories occupied since 1967

I Introduction

1. The present report is the first submitted by the current Special Rapporteur to the Human Rights Council pursuant to Commission on Human Rights resolution 1993/2 A and Human Rights Council resolution 5/1, having assumed his mandate on 1 May 2016.[1] He is the seventh Special Rapporteur on the situation of human rights in the Palestinian territories occupied since 1967.
2. The Special Rapporteur would like to draw attention once again to the fact that he has not been granted access to the Occupied Palestinian Territory, nor have his requests to meet with the Permanent Representative of Israel to the United Nations been accepted. The Special Rapporteur notes that an open dialogue among all parties is essential for the protection and promotion of human rights. In addition, he emphasizes that access to the territory is an important component that helps in the development of a comprehensive understanding of the situation. While he notes that reliance on the exemplary work of a number of experienced and extremely competent civil society groups provides an excellent basis for his work, he laments being unable to meet many of those carrying out this work, due to his exclusion from the territory and the difficulties those individuals often face when seeking to obtain exit permits from the Israeli authorities, particularly from Gaza.
3. The present report is based primarily on written submissions and consultations with civil society representatives, victims, witnesses and United Nations representatives. The Special Rapporteur undertook his first mission to the region, to Amman, from 10 to 15 July 2016. In addition, throughout December 2016 he held consultations with civil society by videoconference and received a number of written submissions, in particular related to the work of human rights defenders.
4. In the present report, the Special Rapporteur focuses on the human rights and humanitarian law violations committed by Israel.[2] As the occupying Power, Israel has the legal obligation to ensure respect for and

---

[1] In October 2016, he also submitted a report to the General Assembly (A/71/554).
[2] As specified in the mandate of the Special Rapporteur set out in resolution 1993/2.

protection of the rights of Palestinians within its control.³ The mandate of the Special Rapporteur thus focuses on the responsibilities of the occupying Power, although he notes that human rights violations by any State party or non-State actors are deplorable and will only hinder the prospects for peace.

5. The Special Rapporteur wishes to express his appreciation for the full cooperation with his mandate extended by the Government of the State of Palestine. The Special Rapporteur also wishes to extend his thanks once again to all those who travelled to Amman in July 2016 to meet with him and to those who were unable to travel but made written or oral submissions. The Special Rapporteur acknowledges the essential work being done and efforts undertaken by such groups to create an environment in which human rights are respected and violations of human rights and international humanitarian law are not committed with impunity and without witnesses. The Special Rapporteur will support that work as much as possible.

6. The present report is set out in two parts. First, it provides an overview of the current human rights situation in the Occupied Palestinian Territory. This discussion, while not exhaustive, aims to highlight those human rights concerns the Special Rapporteur has identified as particularly pressing.

7. In the second part of the report, the Special Rapporteur examines the work of human rights defenders in the Occupied Palestinian Territory, both the growing challenges they [3] face and the critical work they do in attempting to bring justice to an environment in which human rights are increasingly subverted by a prolonged occupation soon to reach half a century.

II Current Human Rights Situation

8. Reports of recurring, persistent human rights violations, including excessive use of force, collective punishment, forced displacement and restrictions on the freedom of movement, have been reported throughout 2016 (see A/71/554). The backdrop against which all of this has occurred is one of what appears to be increasingly extreme rhetoric from Israeli political and government leaders. Legislation related to the legalization of

---

3 See Geneva Convention relative to the Protection of Civilian Persons in Time of War (Fourth Geneva Convention), art. 47.

outposts suggests an ever-shrinking opportunity for Palestinians to realize their right to self-determination. The international community, while seeking to spur the peace process, continues to fail to place human rights at the centre of its efforts.

A   Settlements

9. On 23 December 2016 in resolution 2334 (2016), the Security Council reaffirmed that the establishment of settlements in the West Bank was a flagrant violation under international law and a major obstacle to the achievement of the two-State solution and a just, lasting and comprehensive peace. Less than a month after the passage of that resolution, the Government of Israel announced plans for roughly 6,000 new settlement units in the West Bank, including East Jerusalem. It was proposed that several of those units would be built outside the current settlement blocs.[4] Approvals of settlement units in 2016 were limited in size to the hundreds, not thousands as in the most recent announcements. France noted in its condemnation of the announcement of the new units that the amount announced in the space of a week in 2017 was double the total number of units approved in 2016.[5] In addition, the second half of 2016 saw a year-end uptick in new construction over the previous two years.[6]

10. Along with the announcement of new settlement construction have come reports of increasing incidents of demolitions of Palestinian homes in the West Bank, including East Jerusalem. As of late January 2017, a total of 105 demolitions had been recorded in Area C and 14 in East Jerusalem since the start of the year.[7] Demolitions in 2016 in the entirety of the West Bank, including East Jerusalem, totalled 1,093,[8] which is the highest number recorded since the Office for the Coordination of Humanitarian Affairs began collecting the data in 2009.[9] The demolitions in 2016 displaced 1,593 Palestinians and negatively affected the livelihoods of 7,101

---

4 Gili Cohen, "Israel approves thousands of new settler homes ahead of West Bank outpost's evacuation," *Haaretz*, 21 March 2017; statement by the Special Rapporteur, available from www.ohchr.org/EN/NewsEvents/Pages/DisplayNews.aspx?NewsID=21141&LangID=E.
5 Statement by the spokesperson for the Ministry of Foreign Affairs and International Development, available from http://franceintheus.org/IMG/html/briefing/2017/DDB-2017-02-01.html.
6 *See*: http://peacenow.org.il/en/40-increase-construction-starts-west-bank-settlements-2016.
7 *See* www.ochaopt.org/content/protection-civilians-weekly-report-10-23-january-2017.
8 Ibid.
9 *See* www.ochaopt.org/content/record-number-demolitions-2016-casualty-toll-declines.

others.[10] Demolitions, threats of demolition and lack of protection from demolition all contribute to the creation of a coercive environment, in which people might feel that they have no choice but to leave their land and their homes (see A/HRC/31/43, para. 46). The risk of forcible transfer resulting from the coercive environment is particularly high among Bedouin communities in Area C (see A/71/355, para. 22).

11. February 2017 saw the passage of controversial legislation in the Knesset that legalized the confiscation of private Palestinian land. The so-called regularization bill legalizes roughly 3,000 housing units built on private Palestinian land in the West Bank, [4] which were previously considered illegal even under Israeli law. In 16 of the outposts affected, Palestinian landowners have successfully challenged the settlers' presence on the land in Israeli courts, which have issued demolition orders against the settlers' homes. However, those orders have yet to be implemented and under the new law implementation of the orders will be frozen for a year.[11]

12. The new legislation has triggered condemnation from the international community, with a spokesperson for the Federal Foreign Office in Germany stating that its confidence in the "Israeli Government's commitment to the two-state solution has been profoundly shaken" and the High Representative of the European Union noting that the law "would further entrench a one-state reality of unequal rights, perpetual occupation and conflict".[12] The spokesperson for the Secretary-General noted deep regret at the passage of the law, warning of far-reaching legal consequences for Israel and insisting on the need to avoid any actions that would derail the two-State solution.

East Jerusalem

13. Of the several thousand settlement homes announced in January 2017, 566 are to be built in East Jerusalem. At the same time that approval of the construction was announced, the Deputy Mayor of Jerusalem announced plans for the approval of 11,000 additional units, although it is

---

10 Ibid.
11 Allison Kaplan Sommer, "Explained: Israel's new land-grab law and why it matters," *Haaretz*, 7 February 2017.
12 *See* www.auswaertiges-amt.de/sid_C4BF59984EE3B4886B4BA626F47DA791/EN/Infoservice/Presse/Meldungen/2017/170207-ISR_Gesetz_Legalisierung_Aussenposten.html; and eeas.europa.eu/headquarters/headquarters-homepage_en/20104/Statement%20by%20High%20Representative/Vice-President%20Federica%20Mogherini%20on%20the%20%22Regularisation%20Law%22%20adopted%20by%20the%20Israeli%20Knesset.

not clear when these might move forward.[13] Of the home demolitions that took place in 2016, 88 occurred in East Jerusalem.[14]

14. Following the 1967 war, Israel unilaterally declared the annexation of East Jerusalem, in contravention of international law. The annexation has not been recognized by the international community and Palestinians, see East Jerusalem as the future capital of a Palestinian State. Palestinians living in the city in 1967 were given permanent resident status, which civil society has suggested is akin to treating them as persons who have voluntarily chosen to immigrate to Israel.[15] The permanent resident status can be revoked on a number of grounds[16] and since 1967 as many as 14,000 Palestinians have lost their status and been unable to continue living in, or return to, their homes in East Jerusalem.[17]

15. In addition to home demolitions, Palestinian residents of East Jerusalem are vulnerable to being forcibly evicted from their homes. According to the Office for the Coordination of Humanitarian Affairs, Israeli settler organizations seeking control of parts of East Jerusalem, particularly the Muslim and Christian areas of the old city, have launched eviction proceedings against Palestinian families. As of November 2016, that had affected 180 households (818 individuals, including 372 children).[18] At the same time, the [5] majority of the individuals affected by demolitions in 2016 were children (160 out of 295).[19]

16. As noted in the previous report of the Special Rapporteur, Palestinian communities in the West Bank, including East Jerusalem, are often subject to closures of streets that effectively seal off entire neighbourhoods, checkpoints and a heightened police presence, often as a form of collective punishment (see A/71/554, paras. 25–32). Defense for Children

---

13   Bethan McKennan, "Israel announces plans for a further 11,000 settler homes in East Jerusalem", *Independent*, 27 January 2017; "Israel approves 566 new homes in east Jerusalem settlements", *Deutsche Welle*, 22 January 2017.

14   B'Tselem, "Statistics on demolition of houses built without permits in East Jerusalem", 20 March 2017, available from www.btselem.org/planning_and_building/east_jerusalem_statistics.

15   B'Tselem, "Background on East Jerusalem", 11 May 2015, available from www.btselem.org/jerusalem.

16   Palestinians living in East Jerusalem must be able to prove the centre of their life is in East Jerusalem and may not live abroad for more than seven years if they wish to maintain their residency rights.

17   *See* www.ochaopt.org/location/east-jerusalem.

18   *See* www.btselem.org/planning_and_building/east_jerusalem_statistics and www.ochaopt.org/sites/default/files/evictions_community_sum_ej_2016_final_1_11_2016.pdf.

19   *See* www.btselem.org/planning_and_building/east_jerusalem_statistics.

International-Palestine has called 2016 the deadliest year in a decade for Palestinian children in the West Bank, including East Jerusalem, with 32 children killed by Israeli forces. Proximity to large numbers of police officers in a tense environment, the near daily need to pass through checkpoints and the risk of eviction and demolition not only put children at risk of arrest, detention and abuse, but they also significantly limit access to basic services, including education.

17. Education in Jerusalem has become a political tool for some members of the Government of Israel, with the Education Minister, Naftali Bennet, declaring the 2016 school year "United Jerusalem" year, noting that it marks the fiftieth year since Israel unilaterally annexed East Jerusalem. Schools in East Jerusalem already receive significantly less funding than those in West Jerusalem, despite the existence of laws and High Court rulings that aim to prevent such discriminatory practices.[20] A 2011 High Court ruling held that the shortage of classrooms in East Jerusalem in the official educational system constituted a violation of the students' right to education, and mandated the construction of thousands of additional classrooms.[21] As of 2016, the classroom shortage stood at 2,672, having only worsened since 2011.[22] Adalah, a legal centre for minority rights in Israel, noted that the High Court ruling made no mention of funding being conditional on the adoption of a particular curriculum and added that an unequal budgetary allocation that only had an impact on Arab schools would amount to discrimination.[23] The right to education is guaranteed by article 13 of the International Covenant on Economic, Social and Cultural Rights, to which Israel is a party. It therefore has an obligation to respect, protect and fulfil, with the obligation to fulfil incorporating the obligation to both facilitate and provide. The Committee on Economic, Social and Cultural Rights has further noted that education is both a human right in itself and an indispensable means of realizing

---

20 See Adalah, "Conditioning budgets for repairing East Jerusalem schools on adoption of Israeli curriculum is illegal", 17 August 2016 and Nir Hasson, "Arab students in Jerusalem get less than half the funding of Jewish counterparts", *Haaretz*, 23 August 2016.
21 Association for Civil Rights in Israel, "HCJ: authorities have 5 years to provide public education in East Jerusalem", 6 February 2011.
22 Ir Amim, "Between the hammer and the anvil: persistent neglect and attempted coercion in the East Jerusalem education system" (September 2016).
23 Adalah, "Conditioning budgets".

other human rights, and that it must be accessible to everyone, without discrimination.[24]

B   *Gaza*

18. In 2017, the Israeli blockade of Gaza enters its tenth year. As previously stated by the Special Rapporteur (A/71/554, para. 31) and the Secretary-General (A/HRC/24/30, paras. 21–23),[25] the closure of Gaza amounts to collective punishment, which is prohibited under international law.[26] Despite repeated calls to end the blockade from the international community, the situation on the ground is growing worse.[27] The movement of people in and [6] out of Gaza has in the past year become increasingly difficult as the number of permits revoked or denied has steadily increased. In addition, the infrastructure is under increasing strain and while some import restrictions have been lifted, that has not been enough to allow for the adequate maintenance and development of the public utilities needed to serve a densely populated area of nearly 2 million.

Permit Denials

19. Movement restrictions have been a permanent fixture of the blockade, with exit permits granted only to a small fraction of the population, usually patients seeking medical treatment, business people and the staff of humanitarian agencies. Even among those groups, permits have often been arbitrarily denied.

20. Indeed, a large majority of residents face the prospect of never being permitted to leave. Movement restrictions undermine the rights to health care, work, education and family life, and negatively affect the right of Palestinians to self-determination (see A/HRC/31/44, para. 11).

21. With the near-continuous closure of the Rafah crossing into Egypt since mid-2013, the Erez crossing has become the main entry and exit point for Palestinians in Gaza.[28] While travel out of Gaza through Erez has not

---

24 Committee on Economic, Social and Cultural Rights, general comment No. 13 (1999) on the right to education.

25 *See also* www.unrwa.org/newsroom/official-statements/remarks-un-secretary-general-ban-ki-moon-press-encounter-gaza.

26 Fourth Geneva Convention, art. 33. The Human Rights Committee has further noted that the prohibition on collective punishment is non-derogable: *see* general comment No. 29 (2001) on derogations from provisions of the Covenant during a state of emergency.

27 The previous report of the Special Rapporteur (A/71/554) addressed the economic and development impact of the blockade in depth.

28 Between October 2014 and the end of 2016, the Rafah crossing was open for a total of 83 days, *see* www.ochaopt.org/sites/default/files/crossing_december_2016.pdf.

been an impossibility since the imposition of the blockade and in fact the number of permits granted has seen a relative increase since 2013,[29] the second half of 2016 saw a high rate of permit denials and revocations for all classes of Gaza residents (merchants, patients and others).[30] According to figures provided to the Gisha Legal Center for Freedom of Movement by the Coordinator of Government Activities in the Territories (the Israeli agency that regulates movement of goods and people into and out of Gaza), in 2016 only 46 per cent of exit permit requests were granted, compared to 80 per cent in 2013.

22. The World Health Organization reported that as of October 2016, the approval rate for health permit applications had dropped to 44 per cent. In 2012 it had been as high as 92 per cent. Since then, there has been a steady decline in the approval rate, with the most dramatic drop seen between 2015 (77.5 per cent) and 2016 (44 per cent).[31] Physicians for Human Rights – Israel receives a steady stream of requests from patients seeking support in the event of their being denied a permit. In 2015, in 61.7 per cent of such cases the denials were successfully revoked.[32] In the first half of 2016, that rate was only 25 per cent.

23. Those seeking permits to accompany family members traveling for medical treatment have also been subject to greater rates of denial and increasing scrutiny. According to Physicians for Human Rights – Israel, after seeing an increase in denials of permit requests for medical escorts they inquired with the Israeli authorities as to whether the process had changed. At that time, the Coordinator of Government Activities in the Territories confirmed that it had implemented increased restrictions on those under the age of 55 seeking escort permits. In one case, a breastfeeding mother was prohibited from escorting her infant daughter for follow-up treatment to lifesaving surgery. The baby had to be escorted instead by her 74-year-old grandfather. This was a long and difficult journey for the grandfather, as well as for mother and daughter, owing to the age of the child and her dependence on breast milk.[33] [7]

---

29   See www.gisha.org/UserFiles/File/publications/Inside_look_at_gaza/Gaza_in_no.en.pdf.
30   See Gisha factsheet "Security blocks restricting travel through Erez Crossing", September 2016, available from www.gisha.org/publication/5551.
31   WHO, "Right to health: crossing barriers to access health in the occupied Palestinian territory, 2014–2015" (2016).
32   Physicians for Human Rights – Israel, submission to the Special Rapporteur, 7 November 2016. Note: these figures represent cases from both the West Bank and Gaza, with a majority of the cases coming from Gaza.
33   Ibid.

24. In December 2016, the Office for the Coordination of Humanitarian Affairs noted a serious deterioration in the access to Gaza and the ability to leave it for humanitarian staff, having documented an increase in permit denials from 4 per cent in 2015 to 40 per cent in the third quarter of 2016.[34] In addition, at that time, the Office reported that 60 United Nations national staff had not only been denied exit permits, but were prohibited from reapplying for a period of 12 months.[35] An increase in the revocation of permits for national staff of international organizations at the Erez crossing was also documented in 2016 as compared to 2015.[36]

25. Preventing humanitarian staff from entering and leaving Gaza may amount to a violation of the duty of the occupying Power to facilitate and allow the delivery of humanitarian aid, as provided for in article 23 of the Fourth Geneva Convention.[37] Furthermore, two humanitarian workers in Gaza were arrested by the Israeli authorities in 2016, allegedly for connections to Hamas. Restrictions on humanitarian work and human rights work only serve to further isolate the already vulnerable residents of Gaza. These events echo the harassment and challenges faced by human rights defenders working in the West Bank and Gaza, which are discussed in more detail below.

26. In 2016, exit permits were also increasingly denied, allegedly on security grounds and often without any further information given for the reason, making it practically impossible for decisions to be challenged.[38] There is a constant tension in all nations between balancing individual rights and freedoms with the security of the State, but that balance must constantly be sought. Any derogation from human rights law must be undertaken without discrimination, must be prescribed by law, must be narrowly tailored to a specific, legitimate purpose and must be both necessary and proportional to any threat.[39]

Infrastructure

27. While the residents of Gaza face increasing challenges in their attempts to move freely to other parts of the world, or even to the West Bank, the

---

[34] See www.ochaopt.org/content/serious-deterioration-access-humanitarian-staff-and-gaza.
[35] Ibid.
[36] Gisha, "Security blocks restricting travel through Erez Crossing".
[37] *See also* customary international humanitarian law rule 55.
[38] Gisha, "Security blocks restricting travel through Erez Crossing".
[39] *See*, for example, Office of the United Nations High Commissioner for Human Rights (OHCHR) fact sheet No. 32, "Human rights, terrorism and counter-terrorism" (2008), p. 24.

infrastructure of the densely populated area continues to crumble. That was demonstrated most starkly during an electricity crisis at the beginning of 2017. During that crisis, residents had access to as little as three hours of electricity per day, in the midst of a cold winter.[40] Even when not in crisis, residents of Gaza have access to electricity only in eight-hour cycles. In January 2017, they took to the streets to protest against the electricity shortage, calling on the authorities to find a solution to the ongoing problem.

28. Electricity shortages have been a regular occurrence since 2007 and have a significant impact on the provision of basic services, including access to health care, while also undermining livelihoods in an already precarious economic climate.[41] Electricity in Gaza is provided by Israel, Egypt and a power plant opened in Gaza in 2002. Israel controls its own sale of electricity to Gaza and the import of fuel. In 2007, Israel decided to reduce the amount of fuel and electricity to Gaza to an amount that, according to Gisha, fell short of meeting essential needs.[42] Owing to damage to the power plant caused by Israeli airstrikes, it does not operate at full capacity. Comprehensive repairs have not been conducted, in large part due to restrictions on the import of items the Israeli authorities consider to be "dual use". Israel also controls the entry and exit of individuals with the [8] necessary expertise to repair, maintain and upgrade the plant, as well as the exit of Palestinians from Gaza, who might seek to obtain the training they need.[43]

29. While the Israeli authorities claim that Hamas was to blame for the crisis, that ignores the fact that the crumbling infrastructure is in large part a result of the 10-year-long blockade of Gaza. While the political divide between Gaza and the West Bank plays a role in the difficulties faced by the residents of Gaza,[44] the biggest challenge comes from the illegal blockade and the fact that people and goods cannot move freely into and out of the territory.

---

40 Jack Khoury, "With only 3 hours of electricity a day, Gaza is 'on verge of explosion'," *Haaretz*, 7 January 2017.
41 *See* gaza.ochaopt.org/2015/07/the-humanitarian-impact-of-gazas-electricity-and-fuel-crisis/.
42 Gisha, "Hand on the switch: who's responsible for Gaza's infrastructure crisis?" (January 2017), p. 6.
43 Ibid.
44 *See* www.ochaopt.org/content/impact-internal-divide-municipal-services-gaza-strip and Gisha, "Hand on the switch".

III   Human Rights Defenders

30. Human rights defenders in Palestine and Israel who investigate the grave human rights situation in the Occupied Palestinian Territory are facing a steadily shrinking space for their indispensable work. In recent years, human rights organizations and individuals have engaged in highly effective local, regional and international advocacy and litigation, and have acted as witnesses and ambassadors of conscience in reminding the world that the occupation is becoming ever more immutable. As a result of their effectiveness, human rights defenders have been subjected to a range of physical attacks, incarceration and threats to their lives and safety. They have experienced sophisticated interference and toxic denunciations aimed at silencing their voices and discouraging their supporters, and engendering an increasingly hostile public atmosphere in Israel and in particular among the settlement movement, stoked by the political leadership and the media of the occupying Power and obstructive legislation enacted or being considered by the Knesset.

31. Human rights defenders have faced repeated violations of their fundamental freedoms of assembly, expression, movement and association. That disquieting trend has accompanied the deepening entrenchment of the occupation, as the political forces in favour of permanent rule by Israel over some or all of the Occupied Palestinian Territory have targeted Palestinian and Israeli human rights defenders as among the primary obstacles to the achievement of that goal.[45]

A   *Protection of Human Rights Defenders in International Law*

32. Through the instruments of international law and formal declarations, the international community has created a legal framework to protect the vital work of human rights defenders in advancing the cause of human rights globally and locally. Those legal protections are essential for a number of reasons. First, the work of human rights defenders is often the best, and sometimes the only, protection available to vulnerable and marginalized peoples. Second, the activities of human rights defenders are critical to ensuring that Governments and private actors can be held accountable for their behaviour, both to the citizenry and to the conscience of the world. Third, the actions of human rights defenders often place them in situations of danger and vulnerability with respect to

---

[45] For a comprehensive review of the situation of human rights defenders in the Occupied Palestinian Territory and Israel from 2006, see E/CN.4/2006/95/Add.3.

their own rights and safety. And fourth, the condition of human rights in any country or conflict situation can often be effectively measured by the respect accorded in practice to human rights defenders.

33. While the commitment of public authorities to enacting effective human rights legislation, to creating an independent and impartial judiciary, to maintaining the rule of law, to ensuring that its military and police uphold human rights norms and to encouraging a positive public climate for human rights is vital to the promotion of those fundamental rights, the civil society work of human rights defenders is equally indispensable. They are the canaries in the social mineshaft, offering early warning alerts about rights that are in [9] danger. They provide invaluable advocacy, independent and reliable analysis, effective protection, the courage to protest and oppose and both a progressive interpretation of existing rights and a vision of new rights in embryo. The work of human rights defenders animates and enlarges the enjoyment of human rights for the rest of us. They are commonly our first voices for human rights and, too often, our last line of defence. If their work is in jeopardy anywhere, we are all more precarious and less secure.

34. The rights and responsibilities that protect the work of human rights defenders are well-entrenched in international law. Among other primary human rights instruments, the Universal Declaration of Human Rights[46] and the International Covenant on Civil and Political Rights[47] both proclaim the inalienable freedoms of opinion and expression, movement and peaceful assembly and association. These fundamental instruments champion not only the human rights of all peoples, but also the activities of human rights defenders.

35. By its resolution 53/144, the General Assembly adopted by consensus the Declaration on the Right and Responsibility of Individuals, Groups and Organs of Society to Promote and Protect Universally Recognized Human Rights and Fundamental Freedoms (Declaration on Human Rights Defenders). The purpose of the Declaration is to secure and entrench the right of groups and individuals to defend human rights without fear or interference.[48] While not a binding legal instrument itself, the

---

46 While the Universal Declaration of Human Rights is not a legally binding instrument per se, virtually all of the rights therein are embedded in international law through subsequent legally binding treaties and conventions.
47 Israel is a party to the Covenant, having ratified it on 3 October 1991.
48 For a valuable overview of the Declaration, see Special Rapporteur on the situation of human rights defenders, Commentary to the Declaration on the Right and Responsibility of Individuals, Groups and Organs of Society to Promote and Protect Universally

Declaration enshrines many of the principles and rights that have been already grounded in international law through other conventions and covenants. In its preamble, the Declaration provides for, among other things, the following:

(a) The effective elimination of all violations of human rights and fundamental freedoms of peoples and individuals, including in relation to foreign domination or occupation;

(b) That the prime responsibility and duty to promote and protect human rights and fundamental freedoms lie with the State;

(c) The right and responsibility of individuals, groups and associations to promote respect for and foster knowledge of human rights and fundamental freedoms at the national and international levels.

36. The Declaration sets out a broad range of rights and protections for human rights defenders, including primarily to seek the protection and realization of human rights and fundamental freedoms at the national and international levels (art. 1). It reaffirms essential human rights in the context of this critical work, such as freedom of association and assembly and freedom of opinion and expression. It highlights particularly important rights and protections for human rights defenders, including the freedom to raise issues with and criticize governmental bodies (art. 8), the right to an effective remedy (art. 9) and the right to solicit, receive and utilize resources for the express purpose of peacefully promoting and protecting human rights (art. 13), among others.

37. The Declaration further imposes specific responsibilities and duties on States, including primarily the promotion, protection, and implementation of all human rights (art. 2). Specifically, States are called upon to provide effective remedy to those whose rights have been violated, to promptly and impartially investigate alleged violations (art. 9) and to promote public understanding of all human rights (art. 14). It need not be re-emphasized that these protections and obligations apply equally to human rights defenders, even if they [10] are openly critical of government entities, policies or actions in the name of promoting and protecting human rights (art. 12).

B   *Shrinking Space for Human Rights Defenders*

38. In compiling the evidence for the present report, the Special Rapporteur has been in direct communication with human rights organizations in

---

Recognized Human Rights and Fundamental Freedoms (July 2011) and OHCHR fact sheet No. 29.

Palestine and Israel. Their common observation was that the protections and respect accorded to them, which were already precarious by the end of 2008, had declined precipitously after operation Cast Lead in Gaza in December 2008 and January 2009. This hostile atmosphere for human rights defenders has since become even more overtly toxic and harsh since 2015, in the aftermath of operation Protective Edge in Gaza in 2014 and the subsequent initiation by the International Criminal Court of a preliminary investigation, with the cooperation of a number of Palestinian human rights defenders, into possible war crimes and crimes against humanity committed during the most recent Gaza conflict and by the Israeli settlement project. In the words of one leading human rights group: "We are seeing a general assault by the government and right-wing groups on those parts of Israeli society that are still standing up for democratic values. The aim is to silence us."[49]

Threats and Assaults

39. Palestinian human rights organizations report that they have endured a repressive working environment in recent years, with their day-to-day operations stymied by concerted efforts from the Government of Israel, the Israeli military, private Israeli organizations and unknown individuals or groups to discredit and sabotage their work.[50] The escalation in threats and physical assaults, cyberattacks, arrests and incarceration under military and administrative orders and bans and restrictions on movement is exacerbated by the absence of any effective means for remedies or protection. A report by the Human Rights Defenders Fund in 2015 found that the Israeli military and the occupation authorities had employed a promiscuous range of criminal, security and legal tools to harass and constrain the entirely legitimate and peaceful activities of human rights defenders in the Occupied Palestinian Territory. As the author observed: "In addition to draconian legislative attempts and ongoing efforts to depict them as public enemies, many human rights defenders, particularly activists, are the target of systematic criminalization efforts. Protesters are arrested and detained even when they do not break the law, they are

---

49 Sarit Michaeli, spokeswoman for B'Tselem, quoted in David Shulman, "Israel: the broken silence", *The New York Review of Books*, 7 April 2016.

50 The Special Rapporteur's mandate, as defined in resolution 1993/2, is focused on violations of the law committed by Israel as the occupying Power and thus the present analysis is limited to that discussion. There are undoubtedly other groups, such as the Government of the State of Palestine, who similarly have an obligation to respect and protect human rights, including those of human rights defenders.

subjected to strict conditions of release and are often indicted simply for their efforts to promote human rights."[51]

40. Al-Haq, a leading Palestinian non-governmental human rights organization, has endured a grievous pattern of threats and cyberattacks and a campaign of attempted interference with its work by persons unknown. Beginning in the autumn of 2015 and continuing into 2016, a series of detailed letters from either anonymous individuals or individuals impersonating someone else were sent to donors and partners of Al-Haq, purporting to raise serious concerns about fraud, corruption, financial disarray, lack of transparency and organizational disunity at the organization. Al-Haq was obliged to expend considerable resources refuting the unfounded allegations, including having its auditors, Ernst and Young, assure the partners and donors that there had been no financial or [11] institutional malfeasance. Other messages contained explicit threats to the lives or well-being of various Al-Haq employees, including its General Director, Shawan Jabarin.

41. The Al-Mezan Center for Human Rights, based in Gaza, received a series of anonymous e-mail messages, Facebook posts and calls in 2015 and 2016, sent to staff, donors and partners in which institutional corruption and mismanagement were alleged and explicit threats to the lives and safety of its employees were made. Like Al-Haq, Al-Mezan has been active since 2015 in advocating accountability before the International Criminal Court for possible war crimes.

42. Youth against Settlements, a Hebron-based human rights organization, has had its centre raided several times by Israeli soldiers and it has been effectively closed on occasions after the Israeli military declared the neighbourhood surrounding it to be a closed military zone.[52] In November 2016, the Israeli military conducted a night raid on the Health Development Information and Policy Institute, a Palestinian health advocacy organization based in Ramallah. They seized computers, servers and security camera footage, and left the offices in a shambles. In accordance with the Oslo Accords, the Palestinian Authority is supposed to have complete political and security control in Ramallah and other parts

---

[51] See www.alhaq.org/publications/papers/PHROC.Submission.to.UN.SR.on.the.OPT.Re.HRDs.Nov2016.pdf; Human Rights Defenders Fund, "Disturbing the peace: the use of criminal law to limit the actions of human rights defenders in Israel and the Occupied Palestinian Territories" (2015), p. 63.

[52] Submissions from human rights organizations to the Special Rapporteur.

of Area A of the West Bank, but the Israeli military routinely tramples over this nominal Palestinian sovereignty.[53]

43. A number of individual Palestinian human rights defenders have encountered death threats, arrest and imprisonment, property damage and substantive interference with their right to peacefully protest. A short list of some of them, who all engage in non-violent activity, includes:

Abdallah Abu Rahma, who was active in protests against the separation wall through the village of Bil'in, was arrested several times in 2016 and 2017 for his participation in non-violent events protesting against the occupation. In May 2016, he was arrested by Israeli soldiers for his involvement in the Alwada cycling marathon and held for 10 days. Most recently, he was arrested at an Israeli military court hearing, which he was attending to support six Palestinians who had been arrested for participating in a peaceful protest against the proposed annexation of occupied Palestinian lands in late January 2017. Additionally, Israeli soldiers have conducted night raids on his home and confiscated his laptop.[54]

Imad Abu Shamsiyeh filmed the extrajudicial execution of a gravely wounded Palestinian by an Israeli soldier, Elor Azaria, in March 2016 in Hebron. The film was subsequently released publicly by the Israeli human rights organization B'Tselem and the soldier was later convicted of manslaughter by an Israeli military court. Mr. Abu Shamsiyeh has since received multiple death threats from Israeli settlers living in the vicinity, anonymous death threats delivered by e-mail or posted on Facebook, travel restrictions, the stoning of his home by settlers, harassment of his family and a raid on his home by Israeli soldiers, with no accountability for these attacks and threats.[55]

Farid al-Atrash, a Palestinian lawyer with the Independent Commission for Human Rights in Bethlehem, was arrested by Israeli soldiers during a peaceful demonstration in Hebron in February 2016. He was charged with participating in an illegal demonstration and attacking soldiers, and remained in prison for four days before being released on bail. Video evidence appears to support his

---

53 Marsad, "Israeli forces invade Ramallah offices of healthwork NGO", 16 November 2016, available from www.marsad.ps/en/2016/11/16/israeli-forces-invade-ramallah-offices-healthwork-ngo/.

54 Communication to a group of Special Rapporteurs from Scales of Justice and others, 27 January 2017; Human Rights Defenders Fund, communiqué, 5 December 2016.

55 See https://www.frontlinedefenders.org/en/case/ongoing-threats-and-harassment-against-imad-abu-shamsiyya and Amnesty International, "Israeli government must cease intimidation of human rights defenders, protect them from attacks", 12 April 2016.

version that he [12] was peacefully holding a poster during the demonstration in front of Israeli soldiers when he was aggressively arrested.[56]

Issa Amro, founder of the Hebron-based Youth Against Settlements, a community organization advocating non-violent action, has recently been charged by the Israeli military on 18 counts, including insulting an Israeli officer and incitement in connection with his work organizing peaceful protests calling for the re-opening of Shuhada Street in Hebron. Some of the charges are stale, dating back to 2010. During two of his recent arrests, he states that he was beaten by Israeli police while in custody. Amnesty International has called the charges against Mr. Amro baseless and an attempt to silence him.[57]

Salah Khawaja, a member of the secretariat of the Boycott, Divestment, Sanctions national committee, was arrested during a night raid by the Israeli military on 26 October 2016 at his home in Ramallah (within Area A). His computer and phone were confiscated during the raid. He was subsequently detained and interrogated at the Israeli military facilities in Petah Tikvah. Reports suggest that he has been subject to harsh conditions during his incarceration, including strenuous interrogations, sleep deprivation and physical violence, with no charges laid against him and little or no access to a lawyer.[58]

Hasan Safadi, the media coordinator for Addameer, a Palestinian prisoner support and human rights organization, was arrested by Israeli forces on 1 May 2016 at the al-Karameh bridge crossing with Jordan when returning home from a conference on Arab youth in Tunisia. He has been held in administrative detention since then at Ktziot prison in Israel, with the administrative detention order extended for an additional six months from 8 December 2016.[59] The Special Rapporteur notes that Israel's administrative detention system probably violates the exceptional nature of the measure permitted under international law, as does the incarceration of protected persons outside the occupied territory or country, in line with articles 76 and 78 of the Fourth Geneva Convention.

44. One highly illustrative and disturbing example of the current climate is the series of sophisticated death threats and menacing accusations issued to Nada Kiswanson, a human rights lawyer in The Hague, where she represents Al-Haq and other human rights defenders in Europe and before the International Criminal Court. Beginning in February 2016 and

---

56   Amnesty International, "Israeli government must cease intimidation".
57   Ibid.
58   *See* European External Action Service, letter from the Managing Director for Middle East and North Africa concerning the arrest of Salah al Khawaja, 28 November 2016, and joint submission by 13 human rights defenders to the Special Rapporteur, 7 November 2016.
59   *See* www.frontlinedefenders.org/en/case/detention-hasan-safadi.

intensifying over the following months, Ms. Kiswanson received multiple phone and e-mail messages to private numbers and encrypted message services – some of them anonymous, others from individuals impersonating governmental, intergovernmental and international organizations – stating variously that she would be "eliminated", that she was "not safe at all and hopefully this would remain" and "Honey, you are in grave danger. You have to stop what you are doing". Thousands of fabricated leaflets with the Al-Haq logo were distributed to homes in the neighbourhood where she lives, describing Al-Haq as an organization "working to strengthen the Islamic base in the country", and asking for financial donations to be delivered to her home address. Funeral flowers were also left in front of her house. Amnesty International stated that it had to temporarily close its office in The Hague, after one of its employee's e-mail accounts had been hacked as a means of sending threats to Ms. Kiswanson. The Observatory for the Protection of Human Rights Defenders noted that these attacks demonstrated a high level of technological sophistication and financial backing. To date, police in the Netherlands have investigated the threats and have provided protection for Ms. Kiswanson, but they have been unable to locate their [13] source. This is the first known attack on Dutch soil against a human rights defender working on issues relating to the International Criminal Court.[60]

45. In June 2016, the Israeli military arrested Mohammed El-Halabi, the director of operations in Gaza for World Vision, on charges that he had diverted large amounts of aid money to the military wing of Hamas. World Vision is an international Christian humanitarian charity with global operations working on behalf of children and communities, and it has worked in Gaza for several decades. Mr. El-Halabi has been incarcerated by Israel since his arrest, with little access to legal counsel. World Vision stated in early February 2017 that it had not seen any credible evidence supporting the charges against Mr. El-Halabi and in fact the amount he was accused of diverting is much larger than the World Vision annual budget for Gaza. After conducting a thorough audit of its Gaza operations, World Vision stated that its review, to date, had not generated any concerns about the purported diversion of its resources. It has supported

---

60   Peter Cluskey, "No boundaries in threats to International Criminal Court", *Irish Times*, 16 August 2016, and Observatory for the Protection of Human Rights Defenders, "Attacks against Al-Haq's representative in Europe, Ms. Nada Kiswanson", 11 August 2016, and Amjad Iraqi, "Who's sending death threats to Palestinian advocates in The Hague", +972, 17 August 2016.

Mr. El-Halabi's presumption of innocence and his right to a fair trial. Mr. El-Halabi pleaded not guilty to the charges in early February 2017. His trial is continuing.[61]

46. Human rights organizations working in Gaza face a unique array of obstacles to the conduct of their work. Among the biggest is their non-existent freedom of movement, as described in detail above. For human rights defenders in Gaza this means that they are rarely allowed to journey to Israel, the West Bank or abroad. They cannot travel to regional or international human rights meetings and forums; they cannot attend external training programmes; their ability to participate by videoconferencing is restricted by the sporadic electricity supply in Gaza and the limitations of the medium; and their ability to interact, inform and work with the rest of the world is likewise diminished. This enforced isolation substantially impairs the protection and advancement of human rights in Gaza.[62]

47. Israeli human rights defenders who work on the many issues related to the Occupied Palestinian Territory are also experiencing an increasingly virulent environment. A moment that exemplifies this turning of the screw was in October 2016, when Hagai El-Ad, the Director-General of B'Tselem, together with Lara Friedman, the Director for Policy and Government Relations at Americans for Peace Now, delivered a presentation to the Security Council in New York. He warned of the expanding settlement enterprise and the deteriorating human rights situation for the Palestinians in the Occupied Palestinian Territory, and cited the need for effective international intervention to bring the Israeli occupation to an end.[63] In response, many in the Israeli political leadership stridently denounced B'Tselem, casting it as unpatriotic, traitorous and a political outcast. Prime Minister Benjamin Netanyahu condemned Mr. El-Ad for joining the "chorus of slander" against Israel, stating: "What these organizations cannot achieve through democratic elections in Israel, they try to achieve by international coercion."[64] The Likud Member of the Knesset and whip for the governing coalition, David Bitan, demanded

---

[61] *See also* Gili Cohen, "Top official in Christian aid group charged with funnelling funds to Hamas", *Haaretz*, 4 August 2016.

[62] Communications with leaders of the Palestine Center for Human Rights and the Al-Mezan Center for Human Rights; and Gisha, "Split apart. Palestinian civil society in its own words on the impact of the separation policy and the potential should the policy be reversed", March 2016.

[63] *See* www.btselem.org/settlements/20161014_security_council_address and peacenow.org/page.php?name=lara-addresses-the-unsc#.WNJ9UG_ytpg.

[64] *See* www.haaretz.com/israel-news/1.748737.

that Mr. El-Ad be stripped of his Israeli citizenship.[65] Danny Danon, Permanent Representative of Israel to the United Nations, said: "It is a shame that Israeli groups have been drafted into the diplomatic terror war that the Palestinians are waging against us."[66] [14]

48. Notwithstanding these toxic attacks and the failure of the Government to provide the protections and space for civil society to operate, several prominent Israeli intellectuals and advocates publicly defended B'Tselem and American Friends of Peace Now for their presentations at the Security Council. Zeev Sternhell stated that: "The one who forced the civil society groups to turn to international public opinion and international institutions is the government of Israel itself", while Michael Sfard, a human rights lawyer, wrote that "the occupation is not an internal Israeli matter. And even if it were, human rights are always a matter for the entire international community".[67]

49. Earlier, in December 2015, Im Tirtzu, an ultranationalist Israeli organization hostile to the country's human rights movement, released a short inflammatory video accusing four notable Israeli human rights leaders of abetting murder and terrorism and acting as hostile foreign agents and moles (*shtulim* in Hebrew).[68] The video, which has been viewed several hundred thousand times since its release, opens with a young Arab in a staged urban setting raising his arm to attack the viewer of the video with a knife. The frame freezes, and the narrator then intones:

> Before the next terrorist stabs you, he already knows that Yishai Menuhin, a planted agent belonging to Holland, will make sure to protect him from a Shin Bet interrogation. The terrorist also knows that Avner Gvaryahu, a planted agent belonging to Germany, will call the soldier who tries to prevent the attack a "war criminal". He also knows that Sigi Ben-Ari, a planted agent belonging to Norway, will protect him in court. Before the next terrorist stabs you, he already knows that Hagai El-Ad, a planted

---

65   *See* www.haaretz.com/israel-news/1.748609.
66   *See* hamodia.com/2016/10/16/netanyahu-leftist-groups-that-testified-at-u-n-security-council-beyond-the-pale/.
67   Zeev Sternhell, "Yes, Israelis, we must air our dirty laundry in public", *Haaretz*, 21 October 2016; Michael Sfard, "It's every Israeli's right, and duty, to speak up – including at the UN", *Haaretz*, 24 October 2016. Because of his human rights advocacy, Michael Sfard became the target of political espionage by Regavim, an ultranationalist and partly State-funded organization with close ties to the Israeli settlement movement: *see* Uri Blau, "Did Israeli settler group use government funds to spy on human rights NGOs?" *Haaretz*, 19 January 2016.
68   *See* www.youtube.com/watch?v=o2u_J2C-Lso.

agent belonging to the European Union, will call Israel a "war criminal". Hagai, Yishai, Avner and Sigi are Israelis. They live here with us, and are implants. While we fight terror, they fight us.

50. Dr. Yishai Menuhin is the Executive Director of the Public Committee against Torture, which campaigns against the harsh treatment by Israeli security organizations. Avner Gvaryahu is outreach director with Breaking the Silence, an organization of Israeli military veterans who publicize testimonies by Israeli soldiers in the Occupied Palestinian Territory, including accounts of human rights violations. Sigi Ben-Ari is a lawyer who works with Hamoked – Centre for the Defence of the Individual, which focuses on Israeli human rights violations in the Occupied Palestinian Territory through legal advocacy. And Hagai El-Ad is the Executive Director of B'Tselem. The video displays pictures of the four individuals. Im Tirtzu, while a private organization, has close ties to current and recent Israeli cabinet ministers and has a history of vehemently attacking Israeli civil liberties organizations and successfully lobbying the current Government to enact restrictive legislation against human rights defenders. Following the release of the video (along with an accompanying report by Im Tirtzu denouncing a wider number of Israeli human rights groups),[69] a number of staff in the targeted groups received death threats and the names, addresses and pictures of some of their staff were published on the Internet.[70] Among the commentaries in the Israeli press denouncing the Im Tirtzu video, Mira Sucharov wrote that it equated human rights and civil liberties with treason. She added that only a distinctly anti-democratic element of society would consider the upholding of basic democratic norms [15] and practices, including adhering to the rule of law and upholding the rights of the individual, as cause for inciting against the citizens engaged in those democratic practices.[71]

51. Breaking the Silence has faced an exceptionally harsh campaign of vilification by Israeli political leaders in recent months. Described by its Executive Director, Yuli Novak, as a "liberal and moderate" organization

---

69   See www.docdroid.net/9vaiR15/foreign-agents-report.pdf.html.
70   Ofra Edelman, "Left-wing Israeli activists facing violence, death threats", *Haaretz*, 29 July 2016; Human Rights Defenders Fund, communiqué to the Special Rapporteur; Chemi Shalev, "Im Tirtzu and the proto-fascist plot to destroy Israeli democracy", *Haaretz*, 16 December 2015; and Robert Mackey, "Group calls Israelis 'foreign agents' for work on behalf of Palestinians" *New York Times*, 15 December 2015.
71   "Im Tirtzu's pernicious video equates human rights with treason", *Haaretz*, 16 December 2015.

of Israeli combat soldiers who oppose the occupation "because to rule over millions of people without rights is immoral and bad for Israel", Breaking the Silence has been the target of repeated denunciations by the Ministers of Defence and Education, who have instructed the Israeli army and schools not to invite its members to speak at military and school events. When a non-profit art gallery in Jerusalem planned to host an event for Breaking the Silence in February 2017, the Jerusalem Municipality, following a directive from the Minister of Culture, ordered the gallery to be shut down.

52. In 2016, the President of Ben-Gurion University in Beersheva cancelled a decision by the heads of the Middle East Department to bestow an award on Breaking the Silence for Jewish-Arab understanding. In explaining her decision, the President stated that the organization was outside the national consensus. Lecturers at the university subsequently awarded an alternative prize to the organization as recompense. In February 2017, Prime Minister Netanyahu ordered the Ministry of Foreign Affairs to reprimand the Belgian ambassador to Israel after Belgian Prime Minister Charles Michel met with leaders from Breaking the Silence and B'Tselem during a State visit. Prime Minister Netanyahu had earlier called upon the Belgian and British Prime Ministers to stop any funding of Breaking the Silence by their Governments. In response to these attacks, *Haaretz*, in a recent editorial, criticized the political denunciations of Israeli human rights defenders, stating that "B'Tselem and Breaking the Silence are not only legitimate organizations, they should be a source of pride for Israel".[72]

53. This intensifying chill has been extended to international human rights organizations that investigate human rights concerns in the Occupied Palestinian Territory. In late February 2017, the Government of Israel rejected a work permit application submitted by Human Rights Watch for its recently appointed Director for Israel and Palestine. In its letter of rejection dated 20 February 2017, the Israeli Population and Immigration Authority stated that Human Rights Watch "public activities and reports have engaged in politics in the service of Palestinian propaganda, while falsely raising the banner of 'human rights'". The organization, which has

---

72 "Why Breaking the Silence?", *Haaretz*; "Way to go, silence-breakers", *Haaretz*; "Open season of regime opponents", *Haaretz*; "Netanyahu summons ambassador for rebuke over Belgium PM's meeting with left-wing NGOs", *Haaretz*; "Education Minister: Breaking the Silence poisons our children", *Arutz Sheva*; "Protesters chant in anger as 'Breaking the Silence' wins alternative university prize", *Haaretz*; "Court to decide if Israel can force Breaking the Silence to reveal its sources", *Haaretz*.

worked in Israel for almost three decades, has assiduously advocated for human rights in the Occupied Palestinian Territory. Over the years, it has issued a number of reports critical of Israel, but has also cited the Palestinian Authority and Hamas for human rights violations. Its research and advocacy for global human rights are well respected internationally.[73]

Restrictive legislation

54. Accompanying the mounting climate of threats and assaults on Palestinian and Israeli human rights defenders has been an assertive campaign by the Government of Israel to enact a series of restrictive statutes designed to circumscribe and publicly shame the work of human rights organizations in Israel who advocate for an end to the occupation. The most prominent of these statutes is the law requiring disclosure of support by foreign governmental entities (known as the NGO Disclosure Law), which was adopted by the Knesset in July 2016. The law requires that any Israeli non-governmental organization (NGO) that receives the majority of its funding from foreign State sources must declare that information in all communications with Israeli public officials, as well as in any media and [16] Internet communications and any advocacy literature and research reports. A breach of the law could trigger fines of NIS 29,000 (approximately $7,500). News reports have estimated that of the 27 Israeli NGOs believed to be affected by the law, 25 are human rights groups, such as B'Tselem, the Association for Civil Rights in Israel, Breaking the Silence and Ir Amin. The law was crafted so that it does not apply to Israeli NGOs that receive funding from foreign private sources, a number of which have a nationalist orientation and support many of the features of the occupation. Besides being opposed by many Israeli human rights defenders, the legislation was criticized by the United States of America Department of State, four major party coalitions in the European Parliament, United Nations human rights experts and the Office of the United Nations High Commissioner for Human Rights. The European Union stated that the NGO disclosure law undermined the values of democracy and freedom of speech in Israel and went beyond the legitimate need for transparency.[74]

---

73 See www.hrw.org/news/2017/02/24/israel-human-rights-watch-denied-work-permit.
74 "After contentious debate, Knesset passes NGO law", *The Times of Israel*, 12 July 2016; Barak Ravid, "European Union: 'NGO Law' risks undermining Israeli democratic values", *Haaretz*, 12 July 2016; "US voices concern for free speech over Israeli NGO bill", *Times of Israel*, 12 July 2016. See also www.ohchr.org/EN/NewsEvents/Pages/DisplayNews.aspx?NewsID=20177&LangID=E; and a letter to the President of Israel from 22 human

55. The Knesset has recently been considering several proposed bills, described below, that aim to further restrict the social and political space for Israeli human rights organizations working on issues dealing with the occupation.

56. One bill, proposed by members of the governing coalition, would eliminate the tax benefits for those Israeli residents who donate to any Israeli NGO that releases statements accusing the State of Israel of committing war crimes and any institution that takes part in calls for a boycott of the State of Israel. The Israel Democracy Institute has criticized the proposed legislation, stating that it contains a vague definition with a clear political element and that the question remains whether a non-profit that exposes war crimes carried out by Israel is harming the State or safeguarding its moral character.[75]

57. The Knesset is also deliberating on a bill that would impose fees on Israeli NGOs that receive more than 50 per cent of their funding from foreign government sources, when such organizations apply for State documents under the Freedom of Information Act. Currently, all NGOs are exempt from paying fees for information obtained under the Act. The proposed statute would not only require the targeted NGOs, a large number of whom are human rights defenders working on human rights issues related to the occupation, to pay the application fee, but would require them to pay double the normal fee.[76]

58. In January, the Knesset approved the preliminary reading of a bill that would empower the Minister of Education to forbid individuals or organizations from entering schools if their human rights or political activities outside school could, in the opinion of the Minister, "lead to Israeli soldiers' prosecution in international courts or foreign countries for actions carried out as part of their military duty". The bill would criminalize any individual or organization disobeying the Minister's direction and appears to be specifically aimed at Breaking the Silence. In speaking on behalf of the bill, the Minister stated: "Breaking the Silence doesn't only

---

rights organizations, 19 June 2016, available from www.acri.org.il/en/2016/06/19/dear-mr-president-from-22-human-rights-organizations/.

75 Jonathan Lis, "Ministers okay bill revoking tax exemptions for NGOs that accuse Israel of war crimes," *Haaretz*, 1 March 2017.

76 Jonathan Lis, "New Israeli bill would have left-wing NGOs pay for info from State", *Haaretz*, 26 February 2017.

want to poison the world against us, but to poison our children with their lying reports."[77]

59. In December 2016, a bill that would ban national service volunteers from working on a temporary basis with Israeli organizations that receive the majority of their funding from abroad passed its preliminary reading in the Knesset. The national service volunteer programme enables young Israelis to work at designated institutions and organizations as [17] an alternative to mandatory military service. Prime Minister Netanyahu promised to remove such organizations from the eligibility list following the criticism by B'Tselem of the country's settlement policy at the United Nations in October. Gisha, which would be adversely impacted by the proposed legislation, stated that the bill "is about labelling and excluding – as a first step towards delegitimizing – civil society organizations. To put it more bluntly – this is political persecution".[78]

60. In early March 2017, the Knesset enacted legislation that would deny an entry visa or residency permit to any non-citizen if that person had worked for an organization that had issued a public call to boycott the State of Israel or had agreed to participate in such a boycott. That would include anyone who focused their call for a boycott only on the Israeli settlements in the Occupied Palestinian Territory. The legislation appears to be the formalization of an earlier policy announced in August 2016 by the Minister of Public Security to deport international human rights defenders who support the Boycott, Divestment, Sanctions movement and to prevent others from entering the country. In December 2016, Isabel Apawo Phiri, a Malawian citizen who serves as Associate General Secretary of the World Council of Churches, was denied entry and then deported after arriving at Ben Gurion International Airport. The Israeli authorities asserted that the denial of entry was due to the alleged support of her organization for and involvement with the Boycott, Divestment, Sanctions movement.[79] Adalah, an Israeli human rights organization, criticized the legislation, stating: "Freedom of expression is not just the right to express oneself, but also the right to be exposed to

---

[77] Raoul Wootliff, "Bill banning Breaking the Silence from schools clears initial hurdle", *Times of Israel*, 11 January 2017.

[78] Gisha, "The battle is not for national service spots, it is for the very foundation of democracy in Israel", 10 November 2016.

[79] Ilan Lior, "In first, Israel denies entry to religious official citing support of BDS movement", *Haaretz*, 6 December 2016.

perspectives ... considered outrageous and infuriating by the majority of [Jewish] Israelis."[80]

61. Palestinian human rights organizations have stated that the Knesset statutes and proposed bills adversely affect them as well. Palestinian human rights defenders working in occupied East Jerusalem invariably possess an Israeli residency permit, which they fear may be revoked by the Ministry of the Interior on the grounds that they have breached their loyalty to the State of Israel by advocating human rights issues, supporting boycotts or encouraging the acknowledgment of the Palestinian exodus between 1947 and 1949 (the *Nakba*). Palestinian human rights organizations also state that these legislative offences intensify the atmosphere of fear and repression for human rights defenders. The impact is also being felt by Palestinian human rights defenders living in Israel on residency permits, such as Omar Barghouti, a co-founder of the Boycott, Divestment, Sanctions movement. Restrictions on his international travel were temporarily imposed in April 2016, just after the Intelligence and Transportation Minister had called for the "targeted civil elimination" of the leaders of the movement with the help of Israeli intelligence.[81]

C   *Conclusions*

62. The 50-year occupation of the Palestinian territories, which becomes more pervasive by the day with no end even remotely in sight, has been profoundly corrosive of human rights and democratic values. How could it be otherwise? To perpetuate an alien rule over almost 5 million people, against their fervent wishes, inevitably requires the repression of rights, erosion of the rule of law, the abrogation of international commitments, the imposition of deeply discriminatory practices, the hollowing-out of well-accepted standards of military behaviour, subjugation of the humanity of the "other", denial of trends that are plainly evident, the embrace of illiberal politics and – the focus of the present report – the scorning of those civil [18] society organizations that raise uncomfortable truths about the disfigured state of human rights under occupation.

63. A Government that honours human rights and democratic values, and takes seriously its obligations under the Declaration on Human Rights

---

80   *See* www.adalah.org/en/content/view/9043.
81   *See* communication sent to Special Rapporteurs by 12 Palestinian human rights organizations, "Urgent appeal concerning human rights defenders working on OPT and Israel," 13 June 2016, available from alhaq.org/images/stories/PDF/2012/Letter_on_HRDs_pdf.pdf; and Amnesty International, "Israeli government must cease intimidation".

Defenders would protect and encourage the work of human rights defenders, not ostracize and isolate them. It would publicly denounce any incitement against human rights defenders and would certainly not engage in inflaming the public against them. It would recognize the fundamental status in law of the freedoms of association, assembly, expression and opinion, and of movement, and would do all that it could to enable human rights defenders to enjoy them. Such a Government would respect the critical scrutiny of their work, even if their reports and allegations excoriated the conduct of that Government. It would treat all NGOs equitably. It would enact legislation to enlarge the freedoms of human rights defenders and it would never impose discriminatory statutes or programmes that impaired their work. If it was to criticize human rights defenders, its comments would be measured and constructive. If and when threats or acts of violence were directed towards human rights defenders, its military and police services would act promptly to impartially investigate and prosecute. It would strive to build collaborative relationships with human rights defenders and take advantage of their experience and expertise to deepen the respect of the public for human rights and their defenders. And such a Government – even one conducting a long-term occupation – would accept that human rights can be infringed only as a last measure and then only in a minimally impairing manner that is subject to meaningful judicial review.

64. In all these respects, the Government of Israel has been significantly deficient in honouring its obligations under the Declaration on Human Rights Defenders. On the evidence gathered for the present report, its treatment of human rights defenders, be they Palestinian, Israeli or international, who work on the vital issues arising from the occupation has been contrary to the basic guarantees of international human rights law. Nor is the situation improving. As the occupation becomes further entrenched[82] and as human rights defenders persist with their intrepid activism to investigate and oppose the regime of human rights violations that is integral to the occupation, all indications are that they will continue to be among the prime targets of those who are intolerant of their criticisms, yet alarmed by their effectiveness.

---

82 *See* Ian Fisher, "Israel passes provocative law to retroactively legalize settlements", *New York Times*, 6 February 2017, and Isabel Kershner, "Emboldened by Trump, Israel approves a wave of West Bank settlement expansion", *New York Times*, 24 January 2017.

IV Recommendations

65. The Special Rapporteur recommends that the Government of Israel comply with international law and bring a complete end to its 50 years of occupation of the Palestinian territories occupied since 1967. The Special Rapporteur further recommends that the Government of Israel take the following immediate measures:
    (a) Repeal its recent legislation confiscating private Palestinian lands;
    (b) Comply fully with Security Council resolution 2334 (2016) concerning the settlements;
    (c) End the practice of demolition of Palestinian homes and enable the creation of a fair and transparent building permit system that would comply with the right to housing;
    (d) Ensure the equitable funding of Palestinian education in East Jerusalem;
    (e) End the blockade of Gaza, lift all restrictions on imports and exports, and facilitate the rebuilding of its housing and infrastructure, with due consideration given to justifiable security considerations; [19]
    (f) Ensure freedom of movement and the establishment of an equitable permit system for the residents of the Occupied Palestinian Territory.

66. With respect to human rights defenders, the Special Rapporteur recommends that the Government of Israel immediately take the following measures:
    (a) Fully honour and implement the rights and obligations contained in the Declaration on Human Rights Defenders;
    (b) End the use of criminal, legal and security tools to obstruct the legitimate work of human rights defenders, including the use of arbitrary arrests and detentions, and ensure fair and speedy trials for any human rights defenders charged with an offence;
    (c) Fully respect the fundamental freedoms of assembly, association, expression and movement in the Occupied Palestinian Territory;
    (d) Actively combat incitement against the work of human rights defenders;
    (e) Repeal all restrictive legislation targeting human rights defenders;
    (f) Take all reasonable steps to demonstrate respect for the work of human rights defenders in the Occupied Palestinian Territory until the end of the occupation.

SECTION B

United Nations Resolutions

Draft United Nations Security Council Resolution S/2017/1060 (Dec. 17, 2017)

United Nations
Security Council
S/2017/1060
Provisional
17 December 2017
Original: English

Egypt: draft resolution

The Security Council,
   Reaffirming its relevant resolutions, including resolutions 242 (1967), 252 (1968), 267 (1969), 298 (1971), 338 (1973), 446 (1979), 465 (1980), 476 (1980), 478 (1980), and 2334 (2016),
   Guided by the purpose and principles of the Charter of the United Nations, and reaffirming inter alia, the inadmissibility of the acquisition of territory by force,
   Bearing in mind the specific status of the Holy City of Jerusalem and, in particular, the need for protection and preservation of the unique spiritual, religious and cultural dimensions of the City, as foreseen in the relevant United Nations resolutions,
   Stressing that Jerusalem is a final status issue to be resolved through negotiations in line with relevant United Nations resolutions,
   Expressing in this regard its deep regret at recent decisions concerning the status of Jerusalem

1. *Affirms* that any decisions and actions which purport to have altered, the character, status or demographic composition of the Holy City of Jerusalem have no legal effect, are null and void and must be rescinded in compliance with relevant resolutions of the Security Council, and in this regard, calls *upon* all States to refrain from the establishment of diplomatic missions in the Holy City of Jerusalem, pursuant to resolution 478 (1980) of the Security Council;

2. *Demands* that all States comply with Security Council resolutions regarding the Holy City of Jerusalem, and not to recognize any actions or measures contrary to those resolutions;
3. *Reiterates* its call for the reversal of the negative trends on the ground that are imperiling the two-State solution and for the intensification and acceleration of international and regional efforts and support aimed at achieving, without delay, a comprehensive, just and lasting peace in the Middle East on the basis of the relevant United Nations resolutions, the Madrid terms of reference, including the principle of land for peace, the Arab Peace Initiative and the Quartet Roadmap and an end to the Israeli occupation that began in 1967;
4. *Decides* to remain seized of the matter.

17-22683 (E)

United Nations General Assembly Resolution A/RES/ES-10/19 (Dec. 21, 2017)

A/RES/ES-10/19
Tenth emergency special session
Agenda item 5
Resolution adopted by the General Assembly on 21 December 2017
[without reference to a Main Committee (A/ES-10/L.22 and A/ES-10/L.22/Add.1)]

ES-10/19. Status of Jerusalem

The General Assembly,

Reaffirming its relevant resolutions, including resolution 72/15 of 30 November 2017 on Jerusalem,

Reaffirming also the relevant resolutions of the Security Council, including resolutions 242 (1967) of 22 November 1967, 252 (1968) of 21 May 1968, 267 (1969) of 3 July 1969, 298 (1971) of 25 September 1971, 338 (1973) of 22 October 1973, 446 (1979) of 22 March 1979, 465 (1980) of 1 March 1980, 476 (1980) of 30 June 1980, 478 (1980) of 20 August 1980 and 2334 (2016) of 23 December 2016,

Guided by the purposes and principles of the Charter of the United Nations, and reaffirming, inter alia, the inadmissibility of the acquisition of territory by force,

Bearing in mind the specific status of the Holy City of Jerusalem and, in particular, the need for the protection and preservation of the unique spiritual, religious and cultural dimensions of the city, as foreseen in relevant United Nations resolutions,

Stressing that Jerusalem is a final status issue to be resolved through negotiations in line with relevant United Nations resolutions,

Expressing, in this regard, its deep regret at recent decisions concerning the status of Jerusalem,

1. *Affirms* that any decisions and actions which purport to have altered the character, status or demographic composition of the Holy City of Jerusalem have no legal effect, are null and void and must be rescinded in compliance with relevant resolutions of the Security Council, and in this

regard calls upon all States to refrain from the establishment of diplomatic missions in the Holy City of Jerusalem, pursuant to Council resolution 478 (1980);

2. *Demands* that all States comply with Security Council resolutions regarding the Holy City of Jerusalem, and not recognize any actions or measures contrary to those resolutions;
3. *Reiterates its call for* the reversal of the negative trends on the ground that are imperilling the two-State solution and for the intensification and acceleration of international and regional efforts and support aimed at achieving, without delay, a comprehensive, just and lasting peace in the Middle East on the basis of the relevant United Nations resolutions, the Madrid terms of reference, including the principle of land for peace, the Arab Peace Initiative[1] and the Quartet road map,[2] and an end to the Israeli occupation that began in 1967;
4. *Decides* to adjourn the tenth emergency special session temporarily and to authorize the President of the General Assembly at its most recent session to resume its meeting upon request from Member States.

37th plenary meeting
21 December 2017

---

1 A/56/1026-S/2002/932, annex II, resolution 14/221.
2 S/2003/529, annex.

United Nations General Assembly Resolution A/RES/72/11 (Dec. 5, 2017)

United Nations
General Assembly
A/RES/72/11
Distr.: General
5 December 2017

Seventy-second session
Agenda item 38
Resolution adopted by the General Assembly on 30 November 2017
[without reference to a Main Committee (*A/72/L.13* and *A/72/L.13/Add.1*)]

72/11. Division for Palestinian Rights of the Secretariat

The General Assembly,

Having considered the report of the Committee on the Exercise of the Inalienable Rights of the Palestinian People,[1]

Taking note, in particular, of the action taken by the Committee and the Division for Palestinian Rights of the Secretariat in accordance with their mandates,

Recalling its resolution 32/40 B of 2 December 1977 and all its subsequent relevant resolutions, including its resolution 71/21 of 30 November 2016,

1. *Notes with appreciation* the action taken by the Secretary-General in compliance with its resolution 71/21;
2. *Considers* that, by providing substantive support to the Committee on the Exercise of the Inalienable Rights of the Palestinian People in the implementation of its mandate, the Division for Palestinian Rights of the Secretariat continues to make a constructive and positive contribution to raising international awareness of the question of Palestine and of the urgency of a peaceful settlement of the question of Palestine in all its

---

[1] Official Records of the General Assembly, Seventy-second Session, Supplement No. 35 (A/72/35).

aspects on the basis of international law and United Nations resolutions and the efforts being exerted in this regard and to generating international support for the rights of the Palestinian people;

3. *Requests* the Secretary-General to continue to provide the Division with the necessary resources and to ensure that it continues to effectively carry out its programme of work as detailed in relevant earlier resolutions, in consultation with the Committee and under its guidance;

4. *Requests* the Division, in particular, to continue to monitor developments relevant to the question of Palestine, to organize international meetings and activities in support of the Committee's mandate with the participation of all sectors of the international community and to ensure, within existing resources, the continued participation of eminent persons and international renowned experts in these meetings and activities, to be invited on a par with the members of the Committee, to liaise and cooperate with civil society and parliamentarians, including through the Working Group of the Committee and its associated "UN Platform for Palestine", to develop and expand the "Question of Palestine" website and the documents collection of the United Nations Information System on the Question of Palestine, to prepare and widely disseminate the publications listed in paragraph 87 of the report of the Committee, in the relevant official languages of the United Nations, and information materials on various aspects of the question of Palestine and to develop and enhance the annual training programme for staff of the Palestinian Government in contribution to Palestinian capacity-building efforts;

5. *Also requests* the Division, as part of the observance of the International Day of Solidarity with the Palestinian People on 29 November, to continue to organize, under the guidance of the Committee, an annual exhibit on Palestinian rights or a cultural event in cooperation with the Permanent Observer Mission of the State of Palestine to the United Nations, and encourages Member States to continue to give the widest support and publicity to the observance of the Day of Solidarity;

6. *Requests* the Secretary-General to ensure the continued cooperation with the Division of the United Nations system entities with programme components addressing various aspects of the question of Palestine and the situation in the Occupied Palestinian Territory, including East Jerusalem;

7. *Invites* all Governments and organizations to extend their cooperation to the Division in the performance of its tasks.

60th plenary meeting
30 November 2017

United Nations General Assembly Resolution A/RES/72/12 (Dec. 6, 2017)

United Nations
General Assembly
A/RES/72/12
Distr.: General
6 December 2017

Seventy-second session
Agenda item 38
Resolution adopted by the General Assembly on 30 November 2017 [without reference to a Main Committee (*A/72/L.14* and *A/72/L.14/Add.1*)]

72/12. Special information programme on the question of Palestine of the Department of Public Information of the Secretariat

The General Assembly,

Having considered the report of the Committee on the Exercise of the Inalienable Rights of the Palestinian People,[1]

Taking note, in particular, of the information contained in chapter VI of that report,

Recalling its resolution 71/22 of 30 November 2016,

Convinced that the worldwide dissemination of accurate and comprehensive information and the role of civil society organizations and institutions remain of vital importance in heightening awareness of and support for the inalienable rights of the Palestinian people, including the right to self-determination and independence, and for the efforts to achieve a just, lasting and peaceful settlement of the question of Palestine,

Recalling the mutual recognition between the Government of the State of Israel and the Palestine Liberation Organization, the representative of the Palestinian people, as well as the existing agreements between the two sides,

---

1 Official Records of the General Assembly, Seventy-second Session, Supplement No. 35 (A/72/35).

Affirming its support for a comprehensive, just, lasting and peaceful settlement to the Israeli-Palestinian conflict on the basis of the relevant United Nations resolutions, the terms of reference of the Madrid Conference, including the principle of land for peace, the Arab Peace Initiative adopted by the Council of the League of Arab States at its fourteenth session,[2] and the Quartet road map to a permanent two-State solution to the Israeli-Palestinian conflict, endorsed by the Security Council in resolution 1515 (2003) of 19 November 2003,[3]

Recalling the advisory opinion rendered on 9 July 2004 by the International Court of Justice on the legal consequences of the construction of a wall in the Occupied Palestinian Territory,[4]

Taking note of its resolution 67/19 of 29 November 2012,

Reaffirming that the United Nations has a permanent responsibility towards the question of Palestine until the question is resolved in all its aspects in a satisfactory manner in accordance with international legitimacy,

1. *Notes with appreciation* the action taken by the Department of Public Information of the Secretariat in compliance with resolution 71/22;
2. *Considers* that the special information programme on the question of Palestine of the Department is very useful in raising the awareness of the international community concerning the question of Palestine and the situation in the Middle East and that the programme is contributing effectively to an atmosphere conducive to dialogue and supportive of peace efforts and should receive the necessary support for the fulfilment of its tasks;
3. *Requests* the Department, in full cooperation and coordination with the Committee on the Exercise of the Inalienable Rights of the Palestinian People, to continue, with the necessary flexibility as may be required by developments affecting the question of Palestine, its special information programme for 2018–2019, in particular, inter alia:
    (a) To disseminate information on all the activities of the United Nations system relating to the question of Palestine and peace efforts, including reports on the work carried out by the relevant United Nations organizations, as well as on the efforts of the Secretary-General and his Special Envoy vis-à-vis the objective of peace;

---

[2] A/56/1026-S/2002/932, annex II, resolution 14/221.
[3] S/2003/529, annex.
[4] See A/ES-10/273 and A/ES-10/273/Corr.1.

(b) To continue to issue, update and modernize publications and audio-visual and online materials on the various aspects of the question of Palestine in all fields, including materials concerning relevant recent developments, in particular the efforts to achieve a peaceful settlement of the question of Palestine;

(c) To expand its collection of audiovisual material on the question of Palestine, to continue the production and preservation of such material and to update, on a periodic basis, the public exhibit on the question of Palestine displayed in the General Assembly Building as well as at United Nations headquarters in Geneva and Vienna;

(d) To organize and promote fact-finding news missions for journalists to the Occupied Palestinian Territory, including East Jerusalem, and Israel;

(e) To organize international, regional and national seminars or encounters for journalists aimed in particular at sensitizing public opinion to the question of Palestine and peace efforts and at enhancing dialogue and understanding between Palestinians and Israelis for the promotion of a peaceful settlement to the Israeli-Palestinian conflict, including by fostering and encouraging the contribution of the media in support of peace between the two sides;

(f) To continue to provide assistance to the Palestinian people in the field of media development, in particular through its annual training programme for Palestinian broadcasters and journalists;

4. *Encourages* the Department to continue organizing encounters for the media and representatives of civil society to engage in open and positive discussions to explore means for encouraging people-to-people dialogue and promoting peace and mutual understanding in the region.

60th plenary meeting
30 November 2017

United Nations General Assembly Resolution A/RES/72/13 (Dec. 6, 2017)

United Nations
General Assembly
A/RES/72/13
Distr.: General
6 December 2017

Seventy-second session
Agenda item 38 [without reference to a Main Committee (*A/72/L.15* and *A/72/L.15/Add.1*)]

72/13. Committee on the Exercise of the Inalienable Rights of the Palestinian People

The General Assembly,

Recalling its resolutions 181 (II) of 29 November 1947, 194 (III) of 11 December 1948, 3236 (XXIX) of 22 November 1974, 3375 (XXX) and 3376 (XXX) of 10 November 1975, 31/20 of 24 November 1976 and all its subsequent relevant resolutions, including those adopted at its emergency special sessions and its resolution 71/20 of 30 November 2016,

Recalling also its resolution 58/292 of 6 May 2004,

Having considered the report of the Committee on the Exercise of the Inalienable Rights of the Palestinian People,[1]

Recalling the mutual recognition between the Government of the State of Israel and the Palestine Liberation Organization, the representative of the Palestinian people, as well as the existing agreements between the two sides and the need for full compliance with those agreements,

Affirming its support for a comprehensive, just, lasting and peaceful settlement to the Israeli-Palestinian conflict on the basis of the relevant United Nations resolutions, the terms of reference of the Madrid Conference, including

---

1 Official Records of the General Assembly, Seventy-second Session, Supplement No. 35 (A/72/35).

the principle of land for peace, the Arab Peace Initiative adopted by the Council of the League of Arab States at its fourteenth session[2] and the Quartet road map to a permanent two-State solution to the Israeli-Palestinian conflict, endorsed by the Security Council in resolution 1515 (2003) of 19 November 2003,[3]

Recalling the relevant Security Council resolutions, including resolution 2334 (2016) of 23 December 2016, and underscoring in this regard, inter alia, the call upon all parties to continue, in the interest of the promotion of peace and security, to exert collective efforts to launch credible negotiations on all final status issues in the Middle East peace process and within the time frame specified by the Quartet in its statement of 21 September 2010,

Recalling also the advisory opinion rendered on 9 July 2004 by the International Court of Justice on the legal consequences of the construction of a wall in the Occupied Palestinian Territory,[4] and recalling further its resolutions ES-10/15 of 20 July 2004 and ES-10/17 of 15 December 2006,

Taking note of the application of Palestine for admission to membership in the United Nations, submitted on 23 September 2011,[5]

Recalling its resolution 67/19 of 29 November 2012, by which, inter alia, Palestine was accorded non-member observer State status in the United Nations, and taking note of the follow-up report of the Secretary-General,[6]

Taking note of the accession by Palestine to several human rights treaties and the core humanitarian law conventions, as well as other international treaties,

Noting with deep regret the passage of 50 years since the onset of the Israeli occupation and 70 years since the adoption of resolution 181 (II) on 29 November 1947 and the Nakba without tangible progress towards a peaceful solution, and stressing the urgent need for efforts to reverse the negative trends on the ground and to restore a political horizon for advancing and accelerating meaningful negotiations aimed at the achievement of a peace agreement that will bring a complete end to the Israeli occupation that began in 1967 and the resolution of all core final status issues, without exception, leading to a peaceful, just, lasting and comprehensive solution of the question of Palestine,

Reaffirming that the United Nations has a permanent responsibility towards the question of Palestine until the question is resolved in all its aspects in a satisfactory manner in accordance with international legitimacy,

---

2 A/56/1026-S/2002/932, annex II, resolution 14/221.
3 S/2003/529, annex.
4 *See* A/ES-10/273 and A/ES-10/273/Corr.1.
5 A/66/371-S/2011/592, annex I.
6 A/67/738.

1. *Expresses its appreciation* to the Committee on the Exercise of the Inalienable Rights of the Palestinian People for its efforts in performing the tasks assigned to it by the General Assembly, and takes note of its annual report, including the conclusions and valuable recommendations contained in chapter VII thereof, inter alia the recommendations for the redoubling of international efforts aimed at achieving a peaceful settlement of the question of Palestine, for an expanded multilateral framework for the revitalization of peace efforts, and for efforts to ensure fullest accountability and implementation of the long-standing parameters for peace in accordance with the relevant United Nations resolutions;

2. *Requests* the Committee to continue to exert all efforts to promote the realization of the inalienable rights of the Palestinian people, including their right to self-determination, to support the achievement without delay of an end to the Israeli occupation that began in 1967 and of the two-State solution on the basis of the pre-1967 borders and the just resolution of all final status issues and to mobilize international support for and assistance to the Palestinian people, and in this regard authorizes the Committee to make such adjustments in its approved programme of work as it may consider appropriate and necessary in the light of developments and to report thereon to the General Assembly at its seventy-third session and thereafter;

3. *Also requests* the Committee to continue to keep under review the situation relating to the question of Palestine and to report and make suggestions to the General Assembly, the Security Council or the Secretary-General, as appropriate;

4. *Further requests* the Committee to continue to extend its cooperation and support to Palestinian and other civil society organizations and to continue to involve additional civil society organizations and parliamentarians in its work in order to mobilize international solidarity and support for the Palestinian people, particularly during this critical period of political instability, humanitarian hardship and financial crisis, with the overall aim of promoting the achievement by the Palestinian people of its inalienable rights and a just, lasting and peaceful settlement of the question of Palestine, the core of the Arab-Israeli conflict, on the basis of the relevant United Nations resolutions, the terms of reference of the Madrid Conference, including the principle of land for peace, the Arab Peace Initiative and the Quartet road map;

5. *Commends* the efforts and activities of the Committee in upholding its mandate, including through cooperative initiatives with Governments,

relevant organizations of the United Nations system, intergovernmental organizations and civil society organizations;

6. *Also commends* the efforts of the Working Group of the Committee in coordinating the efforts of international and regional civil society organizations regarding the question of Palestine;

7. *Requests* the United Nations Conciliation Commission for Palestine, established under General Assembly resolution 194 (III), and other United Nations bodies associated with the question of Palestine to continue to cooperate fully with the Committee and to make available to it, at its request, the relevant information and documentation that they have at their disposal;

8. *Invites* all Governments and organizations to extend their cooperation and support to the Committee in the performance of its tasks, recalling its repeated call for all States and the specialized agencies and organizations of the United Nations system to continue to support and assist the Palestinian people in the early realization of their right to self-determination, including the right to their independent State of Palestine;

9. *Notes with appreciation* the efforts of the United Nations Conference on Trade and Development to compile a report to the General Assembly, pursuant to resolution 69/20 of 25 November 2014, on the economic costs of the Israeli occupation for the Palestinian people, and, while drawing attention to the alarming findings, as reflected in the recent report on United Nations Conference on Trade and Development assistance to the Palestinian people: developments in the economy of the Occupied Palestinian Territory,[7] calls for the exertion of all efforts for the provision of necessary resources to expedite completion and publication of the report, including the facilitation and coordination of pertinent inputs from the relevant organs, bodies and agencies of the United Nations system;

10. *Requests* the Secretary-General to circulate the report of the Committee to all the competent bodies of the United Nations, and urges them to take the necessary action, as appropriate;

11. *Requests* the Committee, bearing in mind the solemn anniversaries being observed in 2017 and the absence of tangible progress towards a peaceful solution, to continue to focus its activities throughout 2018 on efforts and initiatives to end the Israeli occupation that began in 1967 and to organize activities in this regard, within existing resources and in cooperation with Governments, relevant organizations of the United Nations

---

7 TD/B/63/3 and TD/B/63/3/Corr.1.

system, intergovernmental organizations and civil society organizations, aimed at raising international awareness and mobilizing diplomatic efforts to launch credible negotiations aimed at achieving without delay a just, lasting, comprehensive and peaceful solution to the question of Palestine in all its aspects;

12. *Requests* the Secretary-General to continue to provide the Committee with all the facilities necessary for the performance of its tasks.

60th plenary meeting
30 November 2017

United Nations General Assembly Resolution A/RES/72/14 (Dec. 7, 2017)

United Nations
General Assembly
A/RES/72/14
Distr.: General
7 December 2017

Seventy-second session
Agenda item 38
Resolution adopted by the General Assembly on 30 November 2017
[without reference to a Main Committee (*A/72/L.16* and *A/72/L.16/Add.1*)]

72/14. Peaceful settlement of the question of Palestine

The General Assembly,
 Recalling its relevant resolutions, including those adopted at its tenth emergency special session,
 Recalling also its resolution 58/292 of 6 May 2004,
 Recalling further relevant Security Council resolutions, including resolutions 242 (1967) of 22 November 1967, 338 (1973) of 22 October 1973, 1397 (2002) of 12 March 2002, 1515 (2003) of 19 November 2003, 1544 (2004) of 19 May 2004, 1850 (2008) of 16 December 2008 and 2334 (2016) of 23 December 2016,
 Recalling the affirmation by the Security Council of the vision of a region where two States, Israel and Palestine, live side by side within secure and recognized borders,
 Expressing its deep concern that it has been 70 years since the adoption of its resolution 181 (II) of 29 November 1947 and 50 years since the occupation of Palestinian territory, including East Jerusalem, in 1967, and that a just, lasting and comprehensive solution to the question of Palestine has yet to be achieved,
 Having considered the report of the Secretary-General submitted pursuant to the request made in its resolution 71/23 of 30 November 2016,[1]

---

[1] A/72/368-S/2017/741.

Reaffirming the permanent responsibility of the United Nations with regard to the question of Palestine until the question is resolved in all its aspects in accordance with international law and relevant resolutions,

Recalling the advisory opinion rendered on 9 July 2004 by the International Court of Justice on the legal consequences of the construction of a wall in the Occupied Palestinian Territory,[2] and recalling also its resolutions ES-10/15 of 20 July 2004 and ES-10/17 of 15 December 2006,

Convinced that achieving a just, lasting and comprehensive settlement of the question of Palestine, the core of the Arab-Israeli conflict, is imperative for the attainment of comprehensive and lasting peace and stability in the Middle East,

Stressing that the principle of equal rights and self-determination of peoples is among the purposes and principles enshrined in the Charter of the United Nations,

Reaffirming the principle of the inadmissibility of the acquisition of territory by war,

Reaffirming also the applicability of the Geneva Convention relative to the Protection of Civilian Persons in Time of War, of 12 August 1949,[3] to the Occupied Palestinian Territory, including East Jerusalem,

Recalling its resolution 2625 (XXV) of 24 October 1970, and reiterating the importance of maintaining and strengthening international peace founded upon freedom, equality, justice and respect for fundamental human rights and of developing friendly relations among nations irrespective of their political, economic and social systems or the level of their development,

Bearing in mind its resolution 70/1 of 25 September 2015, entitled "Transforming our world: the 2030 Agenda for Sustainable Development", in particular Sustainable Development Goal 16,

Stressing the urgent need for efforts to reverse the negative trends on the ground and to restore a political horizon for advancing and accelerating meaningful negotiations aimed at the achievement of a peace agreement that will bring a complete end to the Israeli occupation that began in 1967 and the resolution of all core final status issues, without exception, leading to a peaceful, just, lasting and comprehensive solution of the question of Palestine,

Reaffirming the illegality of the Israeli settlements in the Palestinian territory occupied since 1967, including East Jerusalem,

Expressing grave concern about the extremely detrimental impact of Israeli settlement policies, decisions and activities in the Occupied Palestinian

---

2 See A/ES-10/273 and A/ES-10/273/Corr.1.
3 United Nations, *Treaty Series*, vol. 75, No. 973.

Territory, including East Jerusalem, including on the contiguity, integrity and viability of the Territory, the viability of the two-State solution based on the pre-1967 borders and the efforts to advance a peaceful settlement in the Middle East,

Expressing grave concern also about all acts of violence, intimidation and provocation by Israeli settlers against Palestinian civilians, including children, and properties, including homes, mosques, churches and agricultural lands, condemning acts of terror by several extremist Israeli settlers, and calling for accountability for the illegal actions perpetrated in this regard,

Reaffirming the illegality of Israeli actions aimed at changing the status of Jerusalem, including settlement construction and expansion, home demolitions, evictions of Palestinian residents, excavations in and around religious and historic sites, and all other unilateral measures aimed at altering the character, status and demographic composition of the city and of the Territory as a whole, and demanding their immediate cessation,

Expressing its grave concern about tensions, provocations and incitement regarding the holy places of Jerusalem, including the Haram al-Sharif, and urging restraint and respect for the sanctity of the holy sites by all sides,

Reaffirming that the construction by Israel, the occupying Power, of a wall in the Occupied Palestinian Territory, including in and around East Jerusalem, and its associated regime are contrary to international law,

Encouraging all States and international organizations to continue to actively pursue policies to ensure respect for their obligations under international law with regard to all illegal Israeli practices and measures in the Occupied Palestinian Territory, including East Jerusalem, particularly Israeli settlements,

Expressing deep concern about the continuing Israeli policies of closures and severe restrictions on the movement of persons and goods, including medical and humanitarian and economic, via the imposition of prolonged closures and severe economic and movement restrictions that in effect amount to a blockade, as well as of checkpoints and a permit regime throughout the Occupied Palestinian Territory, including East Jerusalem,

Expressing deep concern also about the consequent negative impact of such policies on the contiguity of the Territory and the critical socioeconomic and humanitarian situation of the Palestinian people, which remains a disastrous humanitarian crisis in the Gaza Strip, as well as on the efforts aimed at rehabilitating and developing the damaged Palestinian economy, including reviving the agricultural and productive sectors, while taking note of developments regarding the situation of access there based on the trilateral agreement facilitated by the United Nations in this regard and on the resumption of some trade from Gaza to the West Bank for the first time since 2007, and, while recalling

Security Council resolution 1860 (2009) of 8 January 2009, calling for the full lifting of restrictions on the movement and access of persons and goods, taking into account the Agreement on Movement and Access of November 2005, including exports, which are crucial for social and economic recovery,

Recalling the mutual recognition 24 years ago between the Government of the State of Israel and the Palestine Liberation Organization, the representative of the Palestinian people,[4] and stressing the urgent need for efforts to ensure full compliance with the agreements concluded between the two sides,

Recalling also the endorsement by the Security Council, in its resolution 1515 (2003), of the Quartet road map to a permanent two-State solution to the Israeli-Palestinian conflict[5] and the call in Council resolution 1850 (2008) for the parties to fulfil their obligations under the road map and to refrain from any steps that could undermine confidence or prejudice the outcome of negotiations on a final peace settlement,

Stressing the road map obligation upon Israel to freeze settlement activity, including so-called "natural growth", and to dismantle all settlement outposts erected since March 2001,

Underscoring the demand by the Security Council, most recently in its resolution 2334 (2016), that Israel immediately and completely cease all settlement activities in the Occupied Palestinian Territory, including East Jerusalem, and that it fully respect all of its legal obligations in this regard,

Recalling the Arab Peace Initiative, adopted by the Council of the League of Arab States at its fourteenth session, held in Beirut on 27 and 28 March 2002,[6] and stressing its importance in the efforts to achieve a just, lasting and comprehensive peace,

Urging renewed and coordinated efforts by the international community aimed at restoring a political horizon and advancing and accelerating the conclusion of a peace treaty to attain without delay an end to the Israeli occupation that began in 1967 by resolving all outstanding issues, including all core issues, without exception, for a just, lasting and peaceful settlement of the Israeli-Palestinian conflict, in accordance with the internationally recognized basis of the two-State solution, and ultimately of the Arab-Israeli conflict as a whole for the realization of a comprehensive peace in the Middle East,

Welcoming, in this regard, the initiative launched by France, and taking note of the joint communiqué of 3 June 2016, aimed at mobilizing international support for Palestinian-Israeli peace and convening an international peace

---

4   *See* A/48/486-S/26560, annex.
5   S/2003/529, annex.
6   A/56/1026-S/2002/932, annex II, resolution 14/221.

conference, the ongoing efforts of the Quartet in the recent period to address the unsustainable situation on the ground and to promote meaningful negotiations and the ongoing regional efforts to advance the Arab Peace Initiative, as well as the respective efforts by China, Egypt, the Russian Federation and the United States of America,

Taking note of the report of the Quartet of 1 July 2016,[7] and stressing its recommendations as well as its recent statements, including those of 30 September 2015, 23 October 2015, 12 February 2016 and 23 September 2016, in which, inter alia, grave concerns were expressed that current trends on the ground are steadily eroding the two-State solution and entrenching a one-State reality and in which recommendations were made to reverse those trends in order to advance the two-State solution on the ground and create the conditions for successful final status negotiations,

Reiterating support for the convening of an international conference in Moscow, as envisioned by the Security Council in its resolution 1850 (2008) and the Quartet statement of 23 September 2011, and stressing the importance of multilateral support and engagement for the advancement and acceleration of peace efforts towards the fulfilment of a just, lasting and comprehensive solution to the question of Palestine,

Noting the important contribution to peace efforts of the United Nations Special Coordinator for the Middle East Peace Process and Personal Representative of the Secretary-General to the Palestine Liberation Organization and the Palestinian Authority, including within the framework of the activities of the Quartet and with regard to the trilateral agreement and recent developments regarding the Gaza Strip,

Welcoming the ongoing efforts of the Ad Hoc Liaison Committee for the Coordination of the International Assistance to Palestinians, under the chairmanship of Norway, and noting its recent meeting at United Nations Headquarters, on 18 September 2017, and the ongoing efforts to generate sufficient donor support in this critical period for urgently addressing the immense humanitarian, reconstruction and recovery needs in the Gaza Strip, bearing in mind the detailed needs assessment and recovery framework for Gaza developed with the support of the United Nations, the World Bank and the European Union, and furthering Palestinian economic recovery and development,

Recognizing the efforts being undertaken by the Palestinian Government, with international support, to reform, develop and strengthen its institutions and infrastructure, emphasizing the need to preserve and further develop Palestinian institutions and infrastructure, despite the obstacles presented by

---

[7] S/2016/595, annex.

the ongoing Israeli occupation, and commending in this regard the ongoing efforts to develop the institutions of an independent Palestinian State, including through the implementation of the Palestinian National Policy Agenda: National Priorities, Policies and Policy Interventions (2017–2022),

Expressing concern about the risks posed to the significant achievements made, as confirmed by the positive assessments made by international institutions regarding readiness for statehood, including by the World Bank, the International Monetary Fund, the United Nations and the Ad Hoc Liaison Committee, owing to the negative impact of the current instability and financial crisis being faced by the Palestinian Government and the continued absence of a credible political horizon,

Recognizing the positive contribution of the United Nations Development Assistance Framework, which is aimed, inter alia, at enhancing development support and assistance to the Palestinian people and strengthening institutional capacity in line with Palestinian national priorities,

Urging the full disbursement of pledges made at the Cairo International Conference on Palestine: Reconstructing Gaza, on 12 October 2014, for expediting the provision of humanitarian assistance and the reconstruction process,

Recalling the ministerial meetings of the Conference on Cooperation among East Asian Countries for Palestinian Development convened in Tokyo in February 2013 and Jakarta in March 2014 as a forum for the mobilization of political and economic assistance, including via exchanges of expertise and lessons learned, in support of Palestinian development, and encouraging the expansion of such efforts and support in the light of worsening socioeconomic indicators,

Recognizing the continued efforts and tangible progress made in the Palestinian security sector, noting the continued cooperation that benefits both Palestinians and Israelis, in particular by promoting security and building confidence, and expressing the hope that such progress will be extended to all major population centres,

Recognizing also that security measures alone cannot remedy the tensions, instability and violence, and calling for full respect for international law, including for the protection of civilian life, as well as for the promotion of human security, the de-escalation of the situation, the exercise of restraint, including from provocative actions and rhetoric, and the establishment of a stable environment conducive to the pursuit of peace,

Gravely concerned over the negative developments that have continued to occur in the Occupied Palestinian Territory, including East Jerusalem, including the escalation of violence and excessive use of force, resulting in a large number of deaths and injuries, mostly among Palestinian civilians, including children and women, as well as the continued construction and expansion of settlements and the wall, the arbitrary arrest and detention of more Palestinian civilians, the acts of violence, vandalism and brutality committed against Palestinian civilians by Israeli settlers in the West Bank, the widespread destruction of public and private Palestinian property, including religious sites, and infrastructure and the demolition of homes, including if carried out as a means of collective punishment, the internal forced displacement of civilians, especially among the Bedouin community, and the consequent deterioration of the socioeconomic and humanitarian conditions of the Palestinian people,

Deploring the continuing, negative repercussions of the conflicts in and around the Gaza Strip, the most recent in July and August 2014, which caused thousands of civilian casualties, the widespread destruction of thousands of homes and vital civilian infrastructure and the internal displacement of hundreds of thousands of civilians, as well as any violations of international law, including humanitarian and human rights law, in this regard, and continued delays in reconstruction and recovery,

Taking note of the report and findings of the independent commission of inquiry established pursuant to Human Rights Council resolution S-21/1,[8] and stressing the need to ensure accountability for all violations of international humanitarian law and international human rights law in order to end impunity, ensure justice, deter further violations, protect civilians and promote peace,

Expressing grave concern over the persisting disastrous humanitarian situation and socioeconomic conditions in the Gaza Strip as a result of the prolonged Israeli closures and severe economic and movement restrictions that in effect amount to a blockade,

Expressing grave concern also about the lasting consequences of such conflicts and measures on the civilian population and the living conditions in the Gaza Strip, as reflected in numerous reports, including the report of 26 August 2016 of the United Nations country team, entitled "Gaza: two years after", and the report of 11 July 2017, entitled "Gaza ten years later", and stressing that the situation is unsustainable and that urgent efforts are required to reverse the de-development trajectory in Gaza and respond adequately and immediately to the immense humanitarian needs of the civilian population,

Recalling the statement of the President of the Security Council of 28 July 2014,[9]

---

8 A/HRC/29/52.
9 S/PRST/2014/13; *see Resolutions and Decisions of the Security Council, 1 August 2013–31 July 2014* (S/INF/69).

Stressing the need for calm and restraint by the parties, including by consolidating the ceasefire agreement of 26 August 2014, achieved under the auspices of Egypt, to avert the deterioration of the situation,

Reiterating the need for the full implementation by all parties of Security Council resolution 1860 (2009) and General Assembly resolution ES-10/18 of 16 January 2009,

Stressing that a durable ceasefire agreement must lead to a fundamental improvement in the living conditions of the Palestinian people in the Gaza Strip, including through the sustained and regular opening of crossing points, and ensure the safety and well-being of civilians on both sides,

Expressing grave concern about the imprisonment and detention by Israel of thousands of Palestinians, including children, under harsh conditions, and all violations of international humanitarian law and human rights law which have occurred in this regard,

Emphasizing the importance of the safety, protection and well-being of all civilians in the whole Middle East region, and condemning all acts of violence and terror against civilians on both sides, including the firing of rockets,

Stressing the need for measures to be taken to guarantee the safety and protection of the Palestinian civilian population throughout the Occupied Palestinian Territory, consistent with the provisions and obligations of international humanitarian law,

Stressing also the need to respect the right of peaceful assembly,

Welcoming the formation of the Palestinian Government of national consensus under the leadership of the President, Mahmoud Abbas, consistent with Palestine Liberation Organization commitments and the Quartet principles, and emphasizing the need for respect for and the preservation of the territorial integrity and unity of the Occupied Palestinian Territory, including East Jerusalem,

Affirming the need to support the Palestinian Government of national consensus in its assumption of full government responsibilities in both the West Bank and the Gaza Strip, in all fields, as well as through its presence at Gaza's crossing points, welcoming in this regard the efforts of Egypt to facilitate and support Palestinian unity, and taking note of the Quartet statement of 28 September 2017,

Stressing the urgent need for sustained and active international involvement and for concerted initiatives to support the parties in building a climate for peace, to assist the parties in advancing and accelerating direct peace process negotiations for the achievement of a just, lasting and comprehensive peace settlement that ends the occupation which began in 1967 and results in the independence of a democratic, contiguous and viable State of Palestine living side by side in peace and security with Israel and its other neighbours, on the basis of relevant United Nations resolutions, the terms of reference of the Madrid Conference, the Quartet road map and the Arab Peace Initiative,

Taking note of the application of Palestine for admission to membership in the United Nations, submitted on 23 September 2011,[10]

Taking note also of its resolution 67/19 of 29 November 2012, by which, inter alia, Palestine was accorded non-member observer State status in the United Nations, and taking note of the follow-up report of the Secretary-General,[11]

Noting the accession by Palestine to several human rights treaties and the core humanitarian law conventions,

Acknowledging the efforts being undertaken by civil society to promote a peaceful settlement of the question of Palestine,

Recalling the findings by the International Court of Justice, in its advisory opinion, including on the urgent necessity for the United Nations as a whole to redouble its efforts to bring the Israeli-Palestinian conflict, which continues to pose a threat to international peace and security, to a speedy conclusion, thereby establishing a just and lasting peace in the region,[12]

Stressing the urgency of achieving without delay an end to the Israeli occupation that began in 1967,

Affirming once again the right of all States in the region to live in peace within secure and internationally recognized borders,

1. *Reaffirms* the necessity of achieving a peaceful settlement of the question of Palestine, the core of the Arab-Israeli conflict, in all its aspects, and of intensifying all efforts towards that end, and stresses in this regard the urgency of salvaging the prospects for realizing the two-State solution of Israel and Palestine, living side by side in peace and security within recognized borders, based on the pre-1967 borders, and making tangible progress towards implementing that solution and justly resolving all final status issues;

2. *Recalls* Security Council resolution 2334 (2016) and, inter alia, the call upon all parties to continue, in the interest of the promotion of peace and security, to exert collective efforts to launch credible negotiations on all final status issues in the Middle East peace process and within the time frame specified by the Quartet in its statement of 21 September 2010, and calls for its full implementation;

---

10   A/66/371-S/2011/592, annex I.
11   A/67/738.
12   A/ES-10/273 and A/ES-10/273/Corr.1, advisory opinion, para. 161.

3. *Calls once more for* the intensification of efforts by the parties, including through negotiations, with the support of the international community, towards the conclusion of a final peace settlement;
4. *Urges* the undertaking of renewed international efforts to achieve a comprehensive, just and lasting peace, based on the relevant United Nations resolutions, the terms of reference of the Madrid Conference, including the principle of land for peace, the Arab Peace Initiative adopted by the Council of the League of Arab States at its fourteenth session, the Quartet road map to a permanent two-State solution to the Israeli-Palestinian conflict, and the existing agreements between the Israeli and Palestinian sides;
5. *Stresses* the need for a resumption of negotiations based on the long-standing terms of reference and clear parameters and within a defined time frame aimed at expediting the realization of a just, lasting and comprehensive settlement, and in this regard encourages serious efforts by all concerned international and regional partners, including by the United States of America, the European Union, the Russian Federation and the United Nations, as members of the Quartet, and by the League of Arab States;
6. *Commends and encourages* continued serious regional and international efforts to follow up and promote the Arab Peace Initiative, including by the Ministerial Committee formed at the Riyadh summit in March 2007;
7. *Welcomes* the initiative launched by France aimed at mobilizing international support for Palestinian-Israeli peace, including the efforts to organize an international peace conference in Paris in January 2017, and the ongoing efforts of the Quartet to address the unsustainable situation on the ground and to promote meaningful negotiations, while stressing its recommendations, and the respective efforts by China, Egypt, the Russian Federation and the United States to promote dialogue and negotiations between the two parties;
8. *Calls for* the timely convening of an international conference in Moscow, as envisioned by the Security Council in its resolution 1850 (2008), for the advancement and acceleration of the achievement of a just, lasting and comprehensive peace settlement;
9. *Calls upon* both parties to act responsibly on the basis of international law and their previous agreements and obligations, in both their policies and actions, in order to urgently reverse negative trends on the ground and create the conditions necessary for the launching of a credible political horizon and the advancement of peace efforts;

10. *Calls upon* the parties themselves, with the support of the Quartet and other interested parties, to exert all efforts necessary to halt the deterioration of the situation, to reverse all unilateral and unlawful measures taken on the ground since 28 September 2000 and to refrain from actions that undermine trust or prejudge final status issues;
11. *Calls upon* the parties to observe calm and restraint and to refrain from provocative actions, incitement and inflammatory rhetoric, especially in areas of religious and cultural sensitivity, including in East Jerusalem, and calls for respect for the historic status quo at the holy places of Jerusalem, including the Haram al-Sharif, in word and in practice, and for immediate and serious efforts to defuse tensions;
12. *Underscores* the need for the parties to take confidence-building measures aimed at improving the situation on the ground, promoting stability, building trust and fostering the peace process, and stresses the need, in particular, for an immediate halt to all settlement activities and home demolitions, ending violence and incitement and undertaking measures to address settler violence and ensure accountability, and for the further release of prisoners and an end to arbitrary arrests and detentions;
13. *Stresses* the need for the removal of checkpoints and other obstructions to the movement of persons and goods throughout the Occupied Palestinian Territory, including East Jerusalem, and the need for respect and preservation of the territorial unity, contiguity and integrity of all of the Occupied Palestinian Territory, including East Jerusalem;
14. *Also stresses* the need for an immediate and complete cessation of all acts of violence, including military attacks, destruction and acts of terror;
15. *Reiterates its demand* for the full implementation of Security Council resolution 1860 (2009);
16. *Reiterates* the need for the full implementation by both parties of the Agreement on Movement and Access and of the Agreed Principles for the Rafah Crossing, of 15 November 2005, and the need, specifically, to allow for the sustained opening of all crossings into and out of the Gaza Strip for humanitarian supplies, movement and access of persons and goods, as well as for commercial flows, including exports, and all necessary construction materials, and stresses the urgent need to accelerate comprehensive reconstruction and to address the alarming unemployment rate, including among youth, including through the implementation of United Nations-led projects, civilian reconstruction activities and job-creation programmes, all of which are essential for alleviating the disastrous humanitarian situation, including the impact of the large-scale

displacement of civilians in July and August 2014, improving the living conditions of the Palestinian people and promoting the recovery of the Palestinian economy;

17. *Calls upon* Israel, the occupying Power, to comply strictly with its obligations under international law, including international humanitarian law, and to cease all of its measures that are contrary to international law and all unilateral actions in the Occupied Palestinian Territory, including East Jerusalem, that are aimed at altering the character, status and demographic composition of the Territory, including the confiscation and de facto annexation of land, and thus at prejudging the final outcome of peace negotiations, with a view to achieving without delay an end to the Israeli occupation that began in 1967;

18. *Reiterates its demand* for the complete cessation of all Israeli settlement activities in the Occupied Palestinian Territory, including East Jerusalem, and in the occupied Syrian Golan, and calls for the full implementation of the relevant Security Council resolutions, including resolution 2334 (2016), and for the consideration of measures of accountability, in accordance with international law, including without limitation in relation to the continued non-compliance with the demands for a complete and immediate cessation of all settlement activities and stressing that compliance with and respect for international humanitarian law and international human rights law is a cornerstone for peace and security in the region;

19. *Underscores* in this regard the affirmation by the Security Council in its resolution 2334 (2016) that it will not recognize any changes to the 4 June 1967 lines, including with regard to Jerusalem, other than those agreed by the parties through negotiations, and its call upon States to distinguish in their relevant dealings between the territory of the State of Israel and the territories occupied since 1967, as well as its determination to examine practical ways and means to secure the full implementation of its relevant resolutions;

20. *Reiterates* the need for Israel forthwith to abide by its road map obligation to freeze all settlement activity, including so-called "natural growth", and to dismantle settlement outposts erected since March 2001;

21. *Calls for* the cessation of all provocations, including by Israeli settlers, in East Jerusalem, including in and around religious sites;

22. *Demands* that Israel, the occupying Power, comply with its legal obligations under international law, as mentioned in the advisory opinion rendered on 9 July 2004 by the International Court of Justice and as

demanded in General Assembly resolutions ES-10/13 of 21 October 2003 and ES-10/15, and, inter alia, that it immediately cease its construction of the wall in the Occupied Palestinian Territory, including East Jerusalem, and calls upon all States Members of the United Nations to comply with their legal obligations, as mentioned in the advisory opinion;

23. *Reaffirms its commitment*, in accordance with international law, to the two-State solution of Israel and Palestine, living side by side in peace and security within recognized borders, based on the pre-1967 borders;

24. Calls for:
    (a) The withdrawal of Israel from the Palestinian territory occupied since 1967, including East Jerusalem;
    (b) The realization of the inalienable rights of the Palestinian people, primarily the right to self-determination and the right to their independent State;

25. *Stresses* the need for a just resolution of the problem of Palestine refugees in conformity with its resolution 194 (III) of 11 December 1948;

26. *Urges* Member States to expedite the provision of economic, humanitarian and technical assistance to the Palestinian people and the Palestinian Government during this critical period in order to help to alleviate the serious humanitarian situation in the Occupied Palestinian Territory, including East Jerusalem, which is dire in the Gaza Strip, to rehabilitate the Palestinian economy and infrastructure and to support the development and strengthening of Palestinian institutions and Palestinian State-building efforts in preparation for independence;

27. *Requests* the Secretary-General to continue his efforts with the parties concerned, and in consultation with the Security Council, including with regard to the reporting required pursuant to resolution 2334 (2016), towards the attainment of a peaceful settlement of the question of Palestine and the promotion of peace in the region and to submit to the General Assembly at its seventy-third session a report on these efforts and on developments on this matter.

60th plenary meeting
30 November 2017

United Nations General Assembly Resolution A/RES/72/15 (Dec. 7, 2017)

United Nations
General Assembly
A/RES/72/15
Distr.: General
7 December 2017

Seventy-second session
Agenda item 37
Resolution adopted by the General Assembly on 30 November 2017 [without reference to a Main Committee (*A/72/L.11* and *A/72/L.11/Add.1*)]

72/15. Jerusalem

The General Assembly,

Recalling its resolution 181 (II) of 29 November 1947, in particular its provisions regarding the City of Jerusalem,

Recalling also its resolution 36/120 E of 10 December 1981 and all its subsequent relevant resolutions, including resolution 56/31 of 3 December 2001, in which it, inter alia, determined that all legislative and administrative measures and actions taken by Israel, the occupying Power, which have altered or purported to alter the character and status of the Holy City of Jerusalem, in particular the so-called "Basic Law" on Jerusalem and the proclamation of Jerusalem as the capital of Israel, were null and void and must be rescinded forthwith,

Recalling further the Security Council resolutions relevant to Jerusalem, including resolution 478 (1980) of 20 August 1980, in which the Council, inter alia, decided not to recognize the "Basic Law" on Jerusalem,

Recalling Security Council resolution 2334 (2016) of 23 December 2016, in which the Council affirmed that it would not recognize any changes to the 4 June 1967 lines, including with regard to Jerusalem, other than those agreed by the parties through negotiations,

Recalling also the advisory opinion rendered on 9 July 2004 by the International Court of Justice on the legal consequences of the construction of a wall in the Occupied Palestinian Territory,[1] and recalling further its resolution ES-10/15 of 20 July 2004,

Expressing its grave concern about any action taken by any body, governmental or non-governmental, in violation of the above-mentioned resolutions,

Expressing its grave concern also, in particular, about the continuation by Israel, the occupying Power, of illegal settlement activities, including measures regarding the so-called E-1 plan, its construction of the wall in and around East Jerusalem, its restrictions on Palestinian access to and residence in East Jerusalem and the further isolation of the city from the rest of the Occupied Palestinian Territory, which are having a detrimental effect on the lives of Palestinians and could prejudge a final status agreement on Jerusalem,

Expressing its grave concern further about the continuing Israeli demolition of Palestinian homes and other civilian infrastructure in and around East Jerusalem, the revocation of residency rights, and the eviction and displacement of numerous Palestinian families from East Jerusalem neighbourhoods, including Bedouin families, as well as other acts of provocation and incitement, including by Israeli settlers, in the city, including desecration of mosques and churches,

Expressing its concern about the Israeli excavations undertaken in the Old City of Jerusalem, including in and around religious sites,

Expressing its grave concern, in particular, about tensions, provocations and incitement regarding the holy places of Jerusalem, including the Haram al-Sharif, and urging restraint and respect for the sanctity of the holy sites by all sides,

Reaffirming that the international community, through the United Nations, has a legitimate interest in the question of the City of Jerusalem and in the protection of the unique spiritual, religious and cultural dimensions of the city, as foreseen in relevant United Nations resolutions on this matter,

Having considered the report of the Secretary-General on the situation in the Middle East,[2]

1. *Reiterates its determination* that any actions taken by Israel, the occupying Power, to impose its laws, jurisdiction and administration on the Holy City of Jerusalem are illegal and therefore null and void and have no validity whatsoever, and calls upon Israel to immediately cease all such illegal and unilateral measures;
2. *Stresses* that a comprehensive, just and lasting solution to the question of the City of Jerusalem should take into account the legitimate concerns

---
1 See A/ES-10/273 and A/ES-10/273/Corr.1.
2 A/72/333.

of both the Palestinian and Israeli sides and should include internationally guaranteed provisions to ensure the freedom of religion and of conscience of its inhabitants, as well as permanent, free and unhindered access to the holy places by people of all religions and nationalities;

3. *Also stresses* the need for the parties to observe calm and restraint and to refrain from provocative actions, incitement and inflammatory rhetoric, especially in areas of religious and cultural sensitivity, and expresses its grave concern in particular about the recent series of negative incidents in East Jerusalem;

4. *Calls for* respect for the historic status quo at the holy places of Jerusalem, including the Haram al-Sharif, in word and practice, and urges all sides to work immediately and cooperatively to defuse tensions and halt all provocations, incitement and violence at the holy sites in the City;

5. *Requests* the Secretary-General to report to the General Assembly at its seventy-third session on the implementation of the present resolution.

60th plenary meeting
30 November 2017

United Nations General Assembly Resolution A/RES/72/80 (Dec. 14, 2017)

United Nations
General Assembly
A/RES/72/80
Distr.: General
14 December 2017

Seventy-second session
Agenda item 53
Resolution adopted by the General Assembly on 7 December 2017 [on the report of the Special Political and Decolonization Committee (Fourth Committee) (A/72/447)]

72/80. Assistance to Palestine refugees

The General Assembly,

Recalling its resolution 194 (III) of 11 December 1948 and all its subsequent resolutions on the question, including resolution 71/91 of 6 December 2016,

Recalling also its resolution 302 (IV) of 8 December 1949, by which, inter alia, it established the United Nations Relief and Works Agency for Palestine Refugees in the Near East,

Recalling further the relevant resolutions of the Security Council,

Aware of the fact that, for more than six decades, the Palestine refugees have suffered from the loss of their homes, lands and means of livelihood,

Affirming the imperative of resolving the problem of the Palestine refugees for the achievement of justice and for the achievement of lasting peace in the region,

Acknowledging the essential role that the Agency has played for over 65 years since its establishment in ameliorating the plight of the Palestine refugees through the provision of education, health, relief and social services and on-going work in the areas of camp infrastructure, microfinance, protection and emergency assistance,

Taking note of the report of the Commissioner-General of the Agency covering the period from 1 January to 31 December 2016,[1]

Taking note also of the report of the Commissioner-General of 30 June 2017, submitted pursuant to paragraph 57 of the report of the Secretary-General[2] and in follow-up to the update to the special report of 3 August 2015 of the Commissioner-General submitted pursuant to paragraph 21 of General Assembly resolution 302 (IV),[3] and expressing concern regarding the severe financial crisis of the Agency and the negative implications for the continued delivery of core programmes to the Palestine refugees in all fields of operation,

Aware of the growing needs of the Palestine refugees throughout all the fields of operation, namely, Jordan, Lebanon, the Syrian Arab Republic and the Occupied Palestinian Territory,

Expressing grave concern at the especially difficult situation of the Palestine refugees under occupation, including with regard to their safety, well-being and socioeconomic living conditions,

Expressing grave concern in particular at the grave humanitarian situation and socioeconomic conditions of the Palestine refugees in the Gaza Strip, and underlining the importance of emergency and humanitarian assistance and urgent reconstruction efforts,

Noting the signing of the Declaration of Principles on Interim Self-Government Arrangements on 13 September 1993 by the Government of Israel and the Palestine Liberation Organization[4] and the subsequent implementation agreements,

1. *Notes with regret* that repatriation or compensation of the refugees, as provided for in paragraph 11 of General Assembly resolution 194 (III), has not yet been effected, and that, therefore, the situation of the Palestine refugees continues to be a matter of grave concern and the Palestine refugees continue to require assistance to meet basic health, education and living needs;

2. *Also notes with regret* that the United Nations Conciliation Commission for Palestine has been unable to find a means of achieving progress in the implementation of paragraph 11 of General Assembly resolution 194 (III), and reiterates its request to the Conciliation Commission to continue exerting efforts towards the implementation of that paragraph and

---

1 Official Records of the General Assembly, Seventy-second Session, Supplement No. 13 (A/72/13/Rev.1).
2 A/71/849.
3 A/70/272, annex.
4 A/48/486-S/26560, annex.

to report to the Assembly on the efforts being exerted in this regard as appropriate, but no later than 1 September 2018;

3. *Affirms* the necessity for the continuation of the work of the United Nations Relief and Works Agency for Palestine Refugees in the Near East and the importance of its unimpeded operation and its provision of services, including emergency assistance, for the well-being, protection and human development of the Palestine refugees and for the stability of the region, pending the just resolution of the question of the Palestine refugees;

4. *Calls upon* all donors to continue to strengthen their efforts to meet the anticipated needs of the Agency, including with regard to increased expenditures and needs arising from conflicts and instability in the region and the serious socioeconomic and humanitarian situation, particularly in the Occupied Palestinian Territory, and those needs mentioned in recent emergency, recovery and reconstruction appeals and plans for the Gaza Strip and in the regional crisis response plans to address the situation of Palestine refugees in the Syrian Arab Republic and those Palestine refugees who have fled to countries in the region;

5. *Commends* the Agency for its provision of vital assistance to the Palestine refugees and its role as a stabilizing factor in the region and the tireless efforts of the staff of the Agency in carrying out its mandate.

66th plenary meeting
7 December 2017

United Nations General Assembly Resolution A/RES/72/81 (Dec. 14, 2017)

United Nations
General Assembly
A/RES/72/81
Distr.: General
14 December 2017

Seventy-second session
Agenda item 53
Resolution adopted by the General Assembly on 7 December 2017 [on the report of the Special Political and Decolonization Committee (Fourth Committee) (A/72/447)]

72/81. Persons displaced as a result of the June 1967 and subsequent hostilities

The General Assembly,

Recalling its resolutions 2252 (ES-V) of 4 July 1967, 2341 B (XXII) of 19 December 1967 and all subsequent related resolutions,

Recalling also Security Council resolutions 237 (1967) of 14 June 1967 and 259 (1968) of 27 September 1968,

Taking note of the report of the Secretary-General submitted in pursuance of its resolution 71/92 of 6 December 2016,[1]

Taking note also of the report of the Commissioner-General of the United Nations Relief and Works Agency for Palestine Refugees in the Near East covering the period from 1 January to 31 December 2016,[2]

Concerned about the continuing human suffering resulting from the June 1967 and subsequent hostilities,

---

1 A/72/313.
2 Official Records of the General Assembly, Seventy-second Session, Supplement No. 13 (A/72/13/Rev.1).

Taking note of the relevant provisions of the Declaration of Principles on Interim Self-Government Arrangements of 13 September 1993[3] with regard to the modalities for the admission of persons displaced in 1967, and concerned that the process agreed upon has not yet been effected,

Taking note also of its resolution 67/19 of 29 November 2012,

1. *Reaffirms* the right of all persons displaced as a result of the June 1967 and subsequent hostilities to return to their homes or former places of residence in the territories occupied by Israel since 1967;
2. *Stresses* the necessity for an accelerated return of displaced persons, and calls for compliance with the mechanism agreed upon by the parties in article XII of the Declaration of Principles on Interim Self-Government Arrangements of 13 September 1993 on the return of displaced persons;
3. *Endorses*, in the meantime, the efforts of the Commissioner-General of the United Nations Relief and Works Agency for Palestine Refugees in the Near East to continue to provide humanitarian assistance, as far as practicable, on an emergency basis, and as a temporary measure, to persons in the area who are currently displaced and in serious need of continued assistance as a result of the June 1967 and subsequent hostilities;
4. *Strongly appeals* to all Governments and to organizations and individuals to contribute generously to the Agency and to the other intergovernmental and non-governmental organizations concerned for the above-mentioned purposes;
5. *Requests* the Secretary-General, after consulting with the Commissioner-General, to report to the General Assembly before its seventy-third session on the progress made with regard to the implementation of the present resolution.

66th plenary meeting
7 December 2017

---

3 A/48/486-S/26560, annex.

United Nations General Assembly Resolution A/RES/72/82 (Dec. 14, 2017)

United Nations
General Assembly
A/RES/72/82
Distr.: General
14 December 2017

Seventy-second session
Agenda item 53
Resolution adopted by the General Assembly on 7 December 2017 [on the report of the Special Political and Decolonization Committee (Fourth Committee) (A/72/447)]

72/82. Operations of the United Nations Relief and Works Agency for Palestine Refugees in the Near East

The General Assembly,

Recalling its resolutions 194 (III) of 11 December 1948, 212 (III) of 19 November 1948, 302 (IV) of 8 December 1949 and all subsequent related resolutions, including its resolution 71/93 of 6 December 2016,

Recalling also the relevant resolutions of the Security Council,

Having considered the report of the Commissioner-General of the United Nations Relief and Works Agency for Palestine Refugees in the Near East covering the period from 1 January to 31 December 2016,[1]

Taking note of the letter dated 25 May 2017 from the Chair of the Advisory Commission of the Agency addressed to the Commissioner-General,[2] and noting the extraordinary meeting of the Commission held on 8 September 2016,

Underlining that, at a time of heightened conflict and instability in the Middle East, the Agency continues to play a vital role in ameliorating the plight

---

1 Official Records of the General Assembly, Seventy-second Session, Supplement No. 13 (A/72/13/Rev.1).
2 Ibid., pp. 7–9.

of the Palestine refugees through the provision of, inter alia, essential education, health, relief and social services programmes and emergency assistance to a registered population of more than 5.3 million refugees whose situation has become extremely precarious, in mitigating the consequences of alarming trends, including increasing violence, marginalization and poverty, in the areas of operation, and in providing a crucial measure of stability in the region,

Deeply concerned about the extremely critical financial situation of the Agency, caused by the structural underfunding of the Agency, as well as by rising needs and expenditures resulting from the deterioration of the socioeconomic and humanitarian conditions and the conflicts and rising instability in the region and their significant negative impact on the ability of the Agency to deliver essential services to the Palestine refugees, including its emergency, recovery, reconstruction and development programmes in all fields of operation,

Taking note of the report of the Secretary-General on the operations of the United Nations Relief and Works Agency for Palestine Refugees in the Near East,[3] submitted pursuant to resolution 71/93, and the request contained therein for broad consultations to explore all ways and means, including through voluntary and assessed contributions, to ensure that the Agency's funding is sufficient, predictable and sustained for the duration of its mandate, and considering the recommendations contained in the report,

Taking note also of the report of 30 June 2017 of the Commissioner-General, submitted pursuant to paragraph 57 of the report of the Secretary-General and in follow-up to the update to the special report of 3 August 2015 of the Commissioner-General,[4] submitted pursuant to paragraph 21 of General Assembly resolution 302 (IV), regarding the severe financial crisis of the Agency and the negative implications for the continued delivery of core Agency programmes to the Palestine refugees in all fields of operation,

Expressing appreciation for the efforts of donors and host countries to respond to the Agency's financial crisis, including through continued and, where possible, increased voluntary contributions, while acknowledging the steadfast support of all other donors to the Agency,

Noting that contributions have not been predictable enough or sufficient to meet growing needs and remedy the persistent shortfalls that are undermining the Agency's operations and efforts to promote human development and meet Palestine refugees' basic needs, and stressing the need for further efforts to comprehensively address the recurrent funding shortfalls affecting the Agency's operations,

---

3   A/71/849.
4   A/70/272, annex.

Recognizing the Agency's efforts to develop innovative and diversified means to mobilize resources, including through partnerships with international financial institutions, the private sector and civil society,

Commending the Agency for the measures taken to address the financial crisis, despite difficult operational circumstances, including through the implementation of the medium-term strategy for 2016–2021 and various internal measures to contain expenditures, reduce operational and administrative costs, maximize the use of resources and reduce the funding shortfalls, and expressing profound concern that, despite such measures, the Agency's programme budget, which is funded primarily by voluntary contributions from Member States and intergovernmental organizations, faces persistent shortfalls that are increasingly threatening the delivery of the Agency's core programmes of assistance to the Palestine refugees,

Encouraging the Agency to sustain those reform efforts, while also taking all possible measures to protect and improve the quality of access to and the delivery of core programmes of assistance,

Recalling its resolution 65/272 of 18 April 2011, in which it requested the Secretary-General to continue to support the institutional strengthening of the Agency,

Stressing the need to support the Agency's capacity to uphold its mandate and to avert the serious humanitarian, political and security risks that would result from any interruption or suspension of its vital work,

Recognizing that the recurring and growing financial shortfalls directly affecting the sustainability of the Agency's operations need to be remedied by examining new funding modalities designed to put the Agency on a stable financial footing to enable it to effectively carry out its core programmes in accordance with its mandate and commensurate with humanitarian needs,

Welcoming the affirmation in the New York Declaration for Refugees and Migrants, adopted by the General Assembly on 19 September 2016,[5] that, inter alia, the Agency, along with other relevant organizations, requires sufficient funding to be able to carry out its activities effectively and in a predictable manner,

Bearing in mind the 2030 Agenda for Sustainable Development,[6] including the pledge that no one will be left behind, emphasizing that the Sustainable Development Goals apply to all, including refugees, and commending the efforts of the Agency's programmes to promote 10 of the 17 Goals, as indicated in the report of the Secretary-General,

---

5 Resolution 71/1.
6 Resolution 70/1.

Welcoming the joint efforts of host countries and donors to mobilize support for the Agency, including the ministerial meetings convened on 26 September 2015 and 4 May 2016, at the high-level conference convened on 2 June 2015 in New York to commemorate the sixty-fifth anniversary of the commencement of the Agency's operations and at other high-level meetings,

Welcoming also the support for the Agency affirmed at the high-level meeting convened by the Organization of Islamic Cooperation, and co-sponsored by Jordan and Sweden, on 22 September 2017, aimed at urgently addressing the Agency's funding shortfall and contributing towards the expansion of donor support for the Agency,

Recalling Articles 100, 104 and 105 of the Charter of the United Nations and the Convention on the Privileges and Immunities of the United Nations,[7]

Recalling also the Convention on the Safety of United Nations and Associated Personnel,[8]

Recalling further its resolutions 71/129 of 8 December 2016 on the safety and security of humanitarian personnel and protection of United Nations personnel and 71/127 of 8 December 2016 on the strengthening of the coordination of emergency humanitarian assistance of the United Nations, calling upon, inter alia, all States to ensure respect for and the protection of all humanitarian personnel and United Nations and associated personnel, to respect the principles of humanity, neutrality, impartiality and independence for the provision of humanitarian assistance and to respect and ensure respect for the inviolability of United Nations premises,

Affirming the applicability of the Geneva Convention relative to the Protection of Civilian Persons in Time of War, of 12 August 1949,[9] to the Palestinian territory occupied since 1967, including East Jerusalem,

Aware of the continuing needs of the Palestine refugees in all fields of operation, namely Jordan, Lebanon, the Syrian Arab Republic and the Occupied Palestinian Territory,

Gravely concerned about the extremely difficult socioeconomic conditions being faced by the Palestine refugees in the Occupied Palestinian Territory, including East Jerusalem, particularly in the refugee camps in the Gaza Strip, as a result of the recurrent military operations, continuing prolonged Israeli closures, the construction of settlements and the wall, evictions, the demolition of homes and livelihood properties causing forced transfers of civilians, and the severe economic and movement restrictions that in effect amount to a

---

7   Resolution 22 A (I).
8   United Nations, *Treaty Series*, vol. 2051, No. 35457.
9   Ibid., vol. 75, No. 973.

blockade, which have deepened unemployment and poverty rates among the refugees, with potentially lasting, long-term negative effects, while taking note of developments with regard to the situation of access there,

Deploring the continuing and negative repercussions of the conflicts in and around the Gaza Strip, the most recent in July and August 2014, and the thousands of civilian casualties caused, as well as the widespread destruction of or damage to thousands of homes and vital civilian infrastructure, the internal displacement of hundreds of thousands of civilians and any violations of international law, including humanitarian and human rights law, in this regard,

Expressing grave concern, in this regard, about the lasting impact on the humanitarian and socioeconomic situation of the Palestine refugees in the Gaza Strip, including high rates of food insecurity, poverty, displacement and the depletion of coping capacities, and taking note in this regard of the United Nations country team reports of 26 August 2016, entitled "Gaza: two years after" and of July 2017, entitled "Gaza ten years later" and the alarming conditions and figures documented therein,

Deploring attacks affecting United Nations installations, including Agency schools sheltering displaced civilians, and all other breaches of the inviolability of United Nations premises during the conflict in the Gaza Strip in July and August 2014, as reported in the summary by the Secretary-General of the report of the Board of Inquiry[10] and by the independent commission of inquiry established pursuant to Human Rights Council resolution S-21/1,[11] and stressing the imperative of ensuring accountability,

Commending the Agency for its extraordinary efforts to provide shelter, emergency relief, medical, food, protection and other humanitarian assistance during the military operations of July and August 2014,

Recalling the temporary tripartite agreement facilitated by the United Nations in September 2014, and stressing the urgent need for the lifting of all Israeli closures and restrictions on the Gaza Strip and for the reconstruction of destroyed homes and infrastructure,

Recalling also its resolution ES-10/18 of 16 January 2009 and Security Council resolution 1860 (2009) of 8 January 2009, as well as the Agreement on Movement and Access of 15 November 2005,

Calling upon Israel to ensure the expedited and unimpeded import of all necessary construction materials into the Gaza Strip and to reduce the burdensome cost of importation of Agency supplies, while taking note of recent

---

10   S/2015/286, annex.
11   See A/HRC/29/52.

developments with regard to the tripartite agreement facilitated by the United Nations,

Expressing concern about the continuing classroom shortage in the Gaza Strip and the consequent negative impact on the right to education of refugee children,

Stressing the urgent need for the advancement of reconstruction in the Gaza Strip, including by ensuring the timely facilitation of construction projects, including extensive shelter repair, and the need for the accelerated implementation of other urgent United Nations-led civilian reconstruction activities,

Welcoming contributions made to the Agency's emergency appeals for the Gaza Strip, and calling urgently upon the international community for continued support in accordance with the Agency's strategic response plan,

Urging the full disbursement of pledges made at the Cairo International Conference on Palestine: Reconstructing Gaza, held on 12 October 2014, for ensuring the provision of the necessary humanitarian assistance and accelerating the reconstruction process,

Stressing that the situation in the Gaza Strip is unsustainable and that a durable ceasefire agreement must lead to a fundamental improvement in the living conditions of the Palestinian people in the Gaza Strip, including through the sustained and regular opening of crossing points, and must ensure the safety and well-being of civilians on both sides,

Affirming the need to support the Palestinian national consensus Government in its assumption of full government responsibilities in both the West Bank and the Gaza Strip, in all fields, as well as through its presence at Gaza's crossing points,

Noting with appreciation the progress made towards rebuilding the Nahr el-Bared refugee camp, commending the Government of Lebanon, donors, the Agency and other parties concerned for the continuing efforts to assist affected and displaced refugees, and emphasizing the need for the funding required to complete the reconstruction of the camp and end without delay the displacement from the camp of thousands of residents whose shelters have not been rebuilt,

Expressing deep concern at the critical situation of Palestine refugees in the Syrian Arab Republic and at the impact of the crisis on the Agency's installations and its ability to deliver its services, and regretting profoundly the loss of life and widespread displacement among refugees and the killing of 19 staff members of the Agency in the crisis since 2012,

Emphasizing the continuing need for assistance to Palestine refugees in the Syrian Arab Republic as well as those who have fled to neighbouring countries, and emphasizing the necessity of ensuring open borders for Palestine refugees fleeing the crisis in the Syrian Arab Republic, consistent with the principles of non-discrimination and non-refoulement under international law, and recalling in this regard the statement by the President of the Security Council of 2 October 2013[12] and the New York Declaration for Refugees and Migrants,

Aware of the valuable work done by the Agency in providing protection to the Palestinian people, in particular Palestine refugees, and recalling the need for the protection of all civilians in situations of armed conflict,

Deploring the endangerment of the safety of the Agency's staff and the damage and destruction caused to the facilities and properties of the Agency during the period covered by the report of the Commissioner-General, and stressing the need to maintain the neutrality and safeguard the inviolability of United Nations premises, installations and equipment at all times,

Deploring also the breaches of the inviolability of United Nations premises, the failure to accord the property and assets of the Organization immunity from any form of interference and the failure to protect United Nations personnel, premises and property,

Deploring further the killing and injury of Agency staff members by the Israeli occupying forces in the Occupied Palestinian Territory since September 2000, including the 11 Agency personnel killed during the military operations in the Gaza Strip in July and August 2014,

Deploring the killing and wounding of refugee children and women sheltering in the Agency schools by the Israeli occupying forces during the military operations of July and August 2014,

Affirming the need for accountability and compensation to victims of violations of international law in accordance with international standards by all sides,

Deeply concerned about the continuing imposition of restrictions on the freedom of movement and access of the Agency's staff, vehicles and goods, and the injury, harassment and intimidation of the Agency's staff, which undermine and obstruct the work of the Agency, including its ability to provide essential basic and emergency services,

Recalling the statement of 15 July 1999 and the declarations adopted on 5 December 2001 and on 17 December 2014[13] by the Conference of High Contracting Parties to the Fourth Geneva Convention, including the call upon parties to facilitate the activities of the Agency, to guarantee its protection and to refrain from levying taxes and imposing undue financial burdens,

---

12 S/PRST/2013/15; see *Resolutions and Decisions of the Security Council, 1 August 2013–31 July 2014* (S/INF/69).
13 A/69/711-S/2015/1, annex.

Aware of the agreement between the Agency and the Government of Israel,

Taking note of the agreement reached on 24 June 1994, embodied in an exchange of letters between the Agency and the Palestine Liberation Organization,[14]

1. *Reaffirms* that the effective functioning of the United Nations Relief and Works Agency for Palestine Refugees in the Near East remains essential in all fields of operation;

2. *Expresses its appreciation* to the Commissioner-General of the Agency, as well as to all the staff of the Agency, for their tireless efforts and valuable work, particularly in the light of the difficult conditions, instability and crises faced during the past year;

3. *Expresses special commendation* to the Agency for the essential role that it has played for more than 65 years since its establishment in providing vital services for the well-being, human development and protection of the Palestine refugees and the amelioration of their plight and for the stability of the region, and affirms the necessity for continuing the work of the Agency and its unimpeded operation and provision of services, pending the just resolution of the question of the Palestine refugees;

4. *Commends* the Agency for its extraordinary efforts, in cooperation with other United Nations agencies on the ground, to provide emergency humanitarian assistance, including shelter, food and medical aid, to refugees and affected civilians during and since the military operations in the Gaza Strip in July and August 2014, and recognizes its exemplary capacity to mobilize in emergency situations while continuously carrying out its core human development programmes;

5. *Expresses its appreciation* for the important support and cooperation provided by the host Governments to the Agency in the discharge of its duties;

6. *Also expresses its appreciation* to the Advisory Commission of the Agency, and requests it to continue its efforts and to keep the General Assembly informed of its activities;

7. *Takes note* of the report of the Working Group on the Financing of the United Nations Relief and Works Agency for Palestine Refugees in the Near East[15] and the efforts to assist in ensuring the financial security of the Agency, and requests the Secretary-General to provide the necessary services and assistance to the Working Group for the conduct of its work;

---

14 Official Records of the General Assembly, Forty-ninth Session, Supplement No. 13 (A/49/13), annex I.

15 A/72/326.

8. *Commends* the Agency for its six-year medium-term strategy for 2016–2021 and the Commissioner-General for his continuing efforts to increase the budgetary transparency and efficiency of the Agency, as reflected in the Agency's programme budget for the biennium 2018–2019;[16]
9. *Also commends* the Agency for sustaining its robust internal reform efforts, despite difficult operational circumstances, and recognizes its implementation of maximum efficiency procedures to contain expenditures, reduce operational and administrative costs, reduce its funding shortfalls and maximize the use of resources;
10. *Takes note* of the report of the Secretary-General on the operations of the United Nations Relief and Works Agency for Palestine Refugees in the Near East and the conclusions and recommendations contained therein;
11. *Appeals* to States and organizations for the maintenance of their voluntary contributions to the Agency, as well as an increase in contributions where possible, in particular to the Agency's programme budget, including in the consideration of their allocation of resources for international human rights, peace and stability, development and humanitarian efforts, to support the Agency's mandate and its ability to meet the rising needs of the Palestine refugees and essential associated costs of operations;
12. *Appeals* to States and organizations not currently contributing to the Agency to urgently consider making voluntary contributions in response to the calls of the Secretary-General for expansion of the Agency's donor base, in order to stabilize funding and ensure greater sharing of the financial burden of supporting the Agency's operations, in accordance with the continuing responsibility of the international community as a whole to assist the Palestine refugees;
13. *Calls for* the provision by donors of early annual voluntary contributions, less earmarking, and multi-year funding, in line with the Grand Bargain on humanitarian financing announced at the World Humanitarian Summit, held in Istanbul, Turkey, in May 2016, in order to enhance the Agency's ability to plan and implement its operations with a greater degree of assurance regarding resource flows;
14. *Also calls for* the full and timely funding by donors of the Agency's emergency, recovery and reconstruction programmes as set out in its appeals and response plans;
15. *Requests* the Commissioner-General to continue efforts to maintain and increase traditional donor support and to enhance income from

---

16 Official Records of the General Assembly, Seventy-second Session, Supplement No. 13A (A/72/13/Add.1).

non-traditional donors, including through partnerships with public and private entities;

16. *Encourages* the Agency to explore financing avenues in relation to the implementation of the Sustainable Development Goals;

17. *Urges* States and organizations to actively pursue partnerships with and innovative support for the Agency, including as recommended in paragraphs 47, 48 and 50 of the report of the Secretary-General, including through the establishment of endowments, trust funds or revolving fund mechanisms and assistance to the Agency to access humanitarian, development and peace and security trust funds and grants;

18. *Welcomes* pledges by States and organizations to provide diplomatic and technical support to the Agency, including engagement with international and financial development institutions, including the World Bank and the Islamic Development Bank, and, where appropriate, to facilitate support for the establishment of financing mechanisms that can provide assistance to refugees and in fragile contexts, including to meet the needs of the Palestine refugees, and calls for serious follow-up efforts;

19. *Requests* the Agency to continue to implement efficiency measures through its medium-term strategy and the development of a five-year proposal for stabilizing the Agency's finances, including specific and time-bound measures, and to continue to improve its cost efficiency and resource mobilization efforts;

20. *Calls upon* the members of the Advisory Commission and the Working Group on the Financing of the United Nations Relief and Works Agency for Palestine Refugees in the Near East to consider the relevant recommendations in the report of the Secretary-General, including to help the Agency to address resource mobilization challenges and to actively assist the Commissioner-General in the efforts to create sustainable, sufficient and predictable support for the Agency's operations;

21. *Takes note* of the recommendations of the Secretary-General regarding the support provided to the Agency from the regular budget of the United Nations;

22. *Endorses* the efforts of the Commissioner-General to continue to provide humanitarian assistance, as far as is practicable, on an emergency basis and as a temporary measure, to persons in the area who are internally displaced and in serious need of continuing assistance as a result of recent crises in the Agency's fields of operation;

23. *Encourages* the Agency to provide increased assistance, in accordance with its mandate, to affected Palestine refugees in the Syrian Arab Republic as well as to those who have fled to neighbouring countries, as

detailed in the Syrian regional crisis response plans, and calls upon donors to urgently ensure sustained support to the Agency in this regard in the light of the continuing grave deterioration of the situation and the growing needs of the refugees;

24. *Welcomes* the progress made thus far by the Agency in rebuilding the Nahr el-Bared refugee camp in northern Lebanon, and calls for donor funding to enable the expeditious completion of its reconstruction, for the continued provision of relief assistance to those displaced following its destruction in 2007 and for the alleviation of their ongoing suffering through the provision of the necessary support and financial assistance until the reconstruction of the camp is complete;

25. *Encourages* the Agency, in close cooperation with other relevant United Nations entities, to continue to make progress in addressing the needs, rights and protection of children, women and persons with disabilities in its operations, including through the provision of necessary psychosocial and humanitarian support, in accordance with the Convention on the Rights of the Child,[17] the Convention on the Elimination of All Forms of Discrimination against Women[18] and the Convention on the Rights of Persons with Disabilities;[19]

26. *Also encourages* the Agency to continue to reduce the vulnerability and improve the self-reliance and resilience of Palestine refugees through its programmes;

27. *Recognizes* the acute protection needs of Palestine refugees across the region, and encourages the Agency's efforts to contribute to a coordinated and sustained response in accordance with international law, including the Agency's development of its protection framework and function in all field offices, including for child protection;

28. *Commends* the Agency for its provision of humanitarian and psychosocial support and other initiatives that provide recreational, cultural and educational activities for children in all fields, including in the Gaza Strip, and, recognizing their positive contribution, calls for full support for such initiatives by donor and host countries and encourages the building and strengthening of partnerships to facilitate and enhance the provision of these services;

---

17 United Nations, *Treaty Series*, vol. 1577, No. 27531.
18 Ibid., vol. 1249, No. 20378.
19 Ibid., vol. 2515, No. 44910.

29. *Calls upon* Israel, the occupying Power, to comply fully with the provisions of the Geneva Convention relative to the Protection of Civilian Persons in Time of War, of 12 August 1949;
30. *Also calls upon* Israel to abide by Articles 100, 104 and 105 of the Charter of the United Nations and the Convention on the Privileges and Immunities of the United Nations in order to ensure the safety of the personnel of the Agency, the protection of its institutions and the safeguarding of the security of its facilities in the Occupied Palestinian Territory, including East Jerusalem, at all times;
31. *Takes note* of the investigations into the incidents affecting the Agency's facilities during the conflict in the Gaza Strip in July and August 2014, and calls for ensuring accountability for all violations of international law;
32. *Urges* the Government of Israel to expeditiously reimburse the Agency for all transit charges incurred and other financial losses sustained as a result of the delays and restrictions on movement and access imposed by Israel;
33. *Calls upon* Israel particularly to cease obstructing the movement and access of the staff, vehicles and supplies of the Agency and to cease levying taxes, extra fees and charges, which affect the Agency's operations detrimentally;
34. *Reiterates its call upon* Israel to fully lift the restrictions impeding or delaying the import of necessary construction materials and supplies for the reconstruction and repair of thousands of damaged or destroyed refugee shelters, and for the implementation of suspended and urgently needed civilian infrastructure projects in refugee camps in the Gaza Strip, noting the alarming figures reflected in the United Nations country team reports of 26 August 2016, entitled "Gaza: two years after" and of July 2017, entitled "Gaza ten years later";
35. *Requests* the Commissioner-General to proceed with the issuance of identification cards for Palestine refugees and their descendants in the Occupied Palestinian Territory;
36. *Notes with appreciation* the positive contribution of the Agency's microfinance and job creation programmes, encourages efforts to enhance the sustainability and benefits of microfinance services to a greater number of Palestine refugees, especially in view of the high unemployment rates affecting them, and youth in particular, welcomes the Agency's efforts to streamline costs and increase microfinance services through internal reform efforts, and calls upon the Agency, in close cooperation with the relevant agencies, to continue to contribute to the development of the

economic and social stability of the Palestine refugees in all fields of operation;

37. *Reiterates its appeals* to all States, the specialized agencies and non-governmental organizations to continue and to augment their contributions to the programme budget of the Agency, to increase their special allocations for grants and scholarships for higher education to Palestine refugees and to contribute to the establishment of vocational training centres for Palestine refugees, and requests the Agency to act as the recipient and trustee for the special allocations for grants and scholarships;

38. *Calls upon* the Commissioner-General to include, in the annual reporting to the General Assembly, assessments on the progress made to remedy the recurrent funding shortfalls of the Agency and ensure sustained, sufficient and predictable support for the Agency's operations, including through the implementation of the relevant provisions of the present resolution.

66th plenary meeting
7 December 2017

United Nations General Assembly Resolution A/RES/72/83 (Dec. 14, 2017)

United Nations
General Assembly
A/RES/72/83
Distr.: General
14 December 2017

Seventy-second session
Agenda item 53
Resolution adopted by the General Assembly on 7 December 2017 [on the report of the Special Political and Decolonization Committee (Fourth Committee) (*A/72/447*)]

72/83. Palestine refugees' properties and their revenues

The General Assembly,

Recalling its resolutions 194 (III) of 11 December 1948 and 36/146 C of 16 December 1981 and all its subsequent resolutions on the question,

Taking note of the report of the Secretary-General submitted pursuant to its resolution 71/94 of 6 December 2016,[1] as well as that of the United Nations Conciliation Commission for Palestine for the period from 1 September 2016 to 31 August 2017,[2]

Recalling that the Universal Declaration of Human Rights[3] and the principles of international law uphold the principle that no one shall be arbitrarily deprived of his or her property,

Recalling in particular its resolution 394 (V) of 14 December 1950, in which it directed the Conciliation Commission, in consultation with the parties concerned, to prescribe measures for the protection of the rights, property and interests of the Palestine refugees,

---

1 A/72/334.
2 A/72/332.
3 Resolution 217 A (III).

Noting the completion of the programme of identification and evaluation of Arab property, as announced by the Conciliation Commission in its twenty-second progress report,[4] and the fact that the Land Office had a schedule of Arab owners and a file of documents defining the location, area and other particulars of Arab property,

Expressing its appreciation for the preservation and modernization of the existing records, including the land records, of the Conciliation Commission, and stressing the importance of such records for a just resolution of the plight of the Palestine refugees in conformity with resolution 194 (III),

Recalling that, in the framework of the Middle East peace process, the Palestine Liberation Organization and the Government of Israel agreed, in the Declaration of Principles on Interim Self-Government Arrangements of 13 September 1993,[5] to commence negotiations on permanent status issues, including the important issue of the refugees,

1. *Reaffirms* that the Palestine refugees are entitled to their property and to the income derived therefrom, in conformity with the principles of equity and justice;
2. *Requests* the Secretary-General to take all appropriate steps, in consultation with the United Nations Conciliation Commission for Palestine, for the protection of Arab property, assets and property rights in Israel;
3. *Calls once again upon* Israel to render all facilities and assistance to the Secretary-General in the implementation of the present resolution;
4. *Calls upon* all the parties concerned to provide the Secretary-General with any pertinent information in their possession concerning Arab property, assets and property rights in Israel that would assist him in the implementation of the present resolution;
5. *Urges* the Palestinian and Israeli sides, as agreed between them, to deal with the important issue of Palestine refugees' properties and their revenues within the framework of the final status peace negotiations;
6. *Requests* the Secretary-General to report to the General Assembly at its seventy-third session on the implementation of the present resolution.

66th plenary meeting
7 December 2017

---

4 Official Records of the General Assembly, Nineteenth Session, Annexes, Annex No. 11, document A/5700.
5 A/48/486-S/26560, annex.

United Nations General Assembly Resolution A/RES/72/84 (Dec. 14, 2017)

United Nations
General Assembly
A/RES/72/84
Distr.: General
14 December 2017

Seventy-second session
Agenda item 54
Resolution adopted by the General Assembly on 7 December 2017 [on the report of the Special Political and Decolonization Committee (Fourth Committee) (*A/72/448*)]

72/84. Work of the Special Committee to Investigate Israeli Practices Affecting the Human Rights of the Palestinian People and Other Arabs of the Occupied Territories

The General Assembly,
 Guided by the purposes and principles of the Charter of the United Nations,
 Guided also by international humanitarian law, in particular the Geneva Convention relative to the Protection of Civilian Persons in Time of War, of 12 August 1949,[1] as well as international standards of human rights, in particular the Universal Declaration of Human Rights[2] and the International Covenants on Human Rights,[3]
 Recalling its relevant resolutions, including resolutions 2443 (XXIII) of 19 December 1968 and 71/95 of 6 December 2016, and the relevant resolutions

---

1 United Nations, *Treaty Series*, vol. 75, No. 973.
2 Resolution 217 A (III).
3 Resolution 2200 A (XXI), annex.

of the Human Rights Council, including resolutions S-12/1 of 16 October 2009,[4] S-21/1 of 23 July 2014[5] and 29/25 of 3 July 2015,[6]

Recalling also the relevant resolutions of the Security Council, including resolution 2334 (2016) of 23 December 2016,

Taking into account the advisory opinion rendered on 9 July 2004 by the International Court of Justice on the legal consequences of the construction of a wall in the Occupied Palestinian Territory,[7] and recalling in this regard its resolution ES-10/15 of 20 July 2004,

Recalling the statement of 15 July 1999 and the declarations adopted on 5 December 2001 and on 17 December 2014[8] by the Conference of High Contracting Parties to the Fourth Geneva Convention, and welcoming initiatives by States parties, both individually and collectively, according to article 1 of the Convention and aimed at ensuring respect for the Convention in the Occupied Palestinian Territory, including East Jerusalem,

Recalling also its resolution 58/292 of 6 May 2004,

Taking note of the report of the independent international fact-finding mission to investigate the implications of the Israeli settlements on the civil, political, economic, social and cultural rights of the Palestinian people throughout the Occupied Palestinian Territory, including East Jerusalem,[9]

Taking note also of Human Rights Council resolution 31/36 of 24 March 2016,[10]

Convinced that occupation itself represents a gross and grave violation of human rights,

Noting with deep regret that 50 years have passed since the onset of the Israeli occupation, and stressing the urgent need for efforts to reverse the negative trends on the ground and to restore a political horizon for advancing and accelerating meaningful negotiations aimed at the achievement of a peace agreement that will bring a complete end to the Israeli occupation that began in 1967 and the resolution of all core final status issues, without exception, leading to a peaceful, just, lasting and comprehensive solution for the question of Palestine,

---

4   See *Official Records of the General Assembly, Sixty-fourth Session, Supplement No. 53A* (A/64/53/Add.1), chap. I.
5   Ibid., *Sixty-ninth Session, Supplement No. 53* (A/69/53), chap. VI.
6   Ibid., *Seventieth Session, Supplement No. 53* (A/70/53), chap. II.
7   See A/ES-10/273 and A/ES-10/273/Corr.1.
8   A/69/711-S/2015/1, annex.
9   A/HRC/22/63.
10 See Official Records of the General Assembly, Seventy-first Session, Supplement No. 53 (A/71/53), chap. IV, sect. A.

Recognizing that the occupation and ensuing persistent and systematic violations of international law by Israel, including international humanitarian and human rights law, are considered to be the main sources of other Israeli violations and discriminatory policies against the Palestinian civilian population in the Occupied Palestinian Territory, including East Jerusalem,

Gravely concerned about the continuing detrimental impact of ongoing unlawful Israeli practices and measures in the Occupied Palestinian Territory, including East Jerusalem, including the excessive use of force by the Israeli occupying forces against Palestinian civilians, resulting in the death and injury of civilians and the widespread destruction of property and vital infrastructure, including during the Israeli military operations in the Gaza Strip in July and August 2014, as well as ongoing settlement activities and construction of the wall, the internal forced displacement of civilians, the imposition of collective punishment measures, particularly against the civilian population in the Gaza Strip, where continuing severe restrictions on movement amount to a blockade, and the detention and imprisonment of thousands of Palestinians,

Expressing grave concern about tensions, instability and violence in the Occupied Palestinian Territory, including East Jerusalem, due to the illegal policies and practices of Israel, the occupying Power, including, in particular, provocations and incitements regarding the holy places of Jerusalem, including the Haram al-Sharif,

Gravely concerned about all acts of violence, intimidation and provocation by Israeli settlers against Palestinian civilians and properties, including homes, mosques, churches and agricultural lands,

Gravely concerned also by reports regarding serious human rights violations and grave breaches of international humanitarian law committed during the military operations in the Gaza Strip between December 2008 and January 2009 and in July and August 2014, including the findings in the summary by the Secretary-General of the report of the Board of Inquiry[11] and in the report of the United Nations Fact-Finding Mission on the Gaza Conflict,[12]

Recalling the report of the independent commission of inquiry established pursuant to Human Rights Council resolution S-21/1,[13] and stressing the imperative of ensuring accountability for all violations of international humanitarian law and international human rights law in order to end impunity, ensure justice, deter further violations, protect civilians and promote peace,

---

11 See A/63/855-S/2009/250.
12 A/HRC/12/48.
13 A/HRC/29/52.

Having considered the report of the Special Committee to Investigate Israeli Practices Affecting the Human Rights of the Palestinian People and Other Arabs of the Occupied Territories[14] and the relevant reports of the Secretary-General,[15]

Recalling the Declaration of Principles on Interim Self-Government Arrangements of 13 September 1993[16] and the subsequent implementation agreements between the Palestinian and Israeli sides,

Stressing the urgency of bringing a complete end to the Israeli occupation that began in 1967 and thus an end to the violation of the human rights of the Palestinian people, and of allowing for the realization of their inalienable human rights, including their right to self-determination and their independent State,

Taking note of the application of Palestine for admission to membership in the United Nations, submitted on 23 September 2011,[17]

Recalling its resolution 67/19 of 29 November 2012, by which, inter alia, Palestine was accorded non-member observer State status in the United Nations, and taking note of the follow-up report of the Secretary-General,[18]

Noting the accession by Palestine to several human rights treaties and the core humanitarian law conventions, as well as other international treaties,

1. *Commends* the Special Committee to Investigate Israeli Practices Affecting the Human Rights of the Palestinian People and Other Arabs of the Occupied Territories for its impartiality and efforts in performing the tasks assigned to it by the General Assembly in spite of the obstruction of its mandate;

2. *Reiterates its demand* that Israel, the occupying Power, cooperate, in accordance with its obligations as a State Member of the United Nations, with the Special Committee in implementing its mandate, and deplores the continued lack of cooperation in this regard;

3. *Deplores* those policies and practices of Israel that violate the human rights of the Palestinian people and other Arabs of the occupied territories, as reflected in the report of the Special Committee covering the reporting period;

4. *Expresses grave concern* about the critical situation in the Occupied Palestinian Territory, including East Jerusalem, particularly in the Gaza

---

14 A/72/539.
15 A/72/296, A/72/314, A/72/538, A/72/564 and A/72/565.
16 A/48/486-S/26560, annex.
17 A/66/371-S/2011/592.
18 A/67/738.

Strip, as a result of unlawful Israeli practices and measures, and especially condemns and calls for the immediate cessation of all illegal Israeli settlement activities and the construction of the wall, the lifting of the blockade of the Gaza Strip, as well as a complete cessation of the excessive and indiscriminate use of force and military operations against the civilian population, settler violence, the destruction and confiscation of properties, including home demolitions as a measure of reprisal, the forced displacement of civilians, all measures of collective punishment, and the detention and imprisonment of thousands of civilians;

5. *Requests* the Special Committee, pending complete termination of the Israeli occupation, to continue to investigate Israeli policies and practices in the Occupied Palestinian Territory, including East Jerusalem, and other Arab territories occupied by Israel since 1967, especially Israeli violations of the Geneva Convention relative to the Protection of Civilian Persons in Time of War, of 12 August 1949, and to consult, as appropriate, with the International Committee of the Red Cross according to its regulations in order to ensure that the welfare and human rights of the peoples of the occupied territories, including prisoners and detainees, are safeguarded and to report to the Secretary-General as soon as possible and whenever the need arises thereafter;

6. *Also requests* the Special Committee to submit regularly to the Secretary-General periodic reports on the current situation in the Occupied Palestinian Territory, including East Jerusalem;

7. *Further requests* the Special Committee to continue to investigate the treatment and status of the thousands of prisoners and detainees, including children, women and elected representatives, in Israeli prisons and detention centres in the Occupied Palestinian Territory, including East Jerusalem, and other Arab territories occupied by Israel since 1967, and expresses grave concern about harsh conditions and ill-treatment of prisoners and recent hunger strikes, stressing the need for respect for all applicable rules of international law, including the Fourth Geneva Convention, the United Nations Standard Minimum Rules for the Treatment of Prisoners (the Nelson Mandela Rules)[19] and the United Nations Rules for the Treatment of Women Prisoners and Non-custodial Measures for Women Offenders (the Bangkok Rules);[20]

---

19   Resolution 70/175, annex.
20   Resolution 65/229, annex.

8. *Requests* the Secretary-General:
   (a) To provide the Special Committee with all necessary facilities, including those required for its visits to the occupied territories, so that it may investigate the Israeli policies and practices referred to in the present resolution;
   (b) To utilize his good offices to facilitate and support the Special Committee in carrying out its mandate;
   (c) To continue to make available such staff as may be necessary to assist the Special Committee in the performance of its tasks;
   (d) To circulate regularly to Member States the periodic reports mentioned in paragraph 6 above;
   (e) To ensure the widest circulation of the reports of the Special Committee and of information regarding its activities and findings, by all means available, through the Department of Public Information of the Secretariat and, where necessary, to reprint those reports of the Special Committee that are no longer available;
9. *Decides* to include in the provisional agenda of its seventy-third session the item entitled "Report of the Special Committee to Investigate Israeli Practices Affecting the Human Rights of the Palestinian People and Other Arabs of the Occupied Territories".

66th plenary meeting
7 December 2017

United Nations General Assembly Resolution A/RES/72/85 (Dec. 14, 2017)

United Nations
General Assembly
A/RES/72/85
Distr.: General
14 December 2017

Seventy-second session
Agenda item 54
Resolution adopted by the General Assembly on 7 December 2017
[on the report of the Special Political and Decolonization Committee (Fourth Committee) (*A/72/448*)]

72/85. Applicability of the Geneva Convention relative to the Protection of Civilian Persons in Time of War, of 12 August 1949, to the Occupied Palestinian Territory, including East Jerusalem, and the other occupied Arab territories

The General Assembly,

Recalling its relevant resolutions, including resolution 71/96 of 6 December 2016,

Bearing in mind the relevant resolutions of the Security Council,

Recalling the Regulations annexed to the Hague Convention IV of 1907, the Geneva Convention relative to the Protection of Civilian Persons in Time of War, of 12 August 1949,[1] and relevant provisions of customary law, including those codified in Additional Protocol I[2] to the four Geneva Conventions,[3]

Having considered the report of the Special Committee to Investigate Israeli Practices Affecting the Human Rights of the Palestinian People and Other Arabs of the Occupied Territories[4] and the relevant reports of the Secretary-General,[5]

---

1 United Nations, *Treaty Series*, vol. 75, No. 973.
2 Ibid., vol. 1125, No. 17512.
3 Ibid., vol. 75, Nos. 970–973.
4 A/72/539.
5 A/72/296, A/72/314, A/72/538, A/72/564 and A/72/565.

Considering that the promotion of respect for the obligations arising from the Charter of the United Nations and other instruments and rules of international law is among the basic purposes and principles of the United Nations,

Recalling the advisory opinion rendered on 9 July 2004 by the International Court of Justice,[6] and also recalling General Assembly resolution ES-10/15 of 20 July 2004,

Noting in particular the Court's reply, including that the Fourth Geneva Convention is applicable in the Occupied Palestinian Territory, including East Jerusalem, and that Israel is in breach of several of the provisions of the Convention,

Recalling the Conference of High Contracting Parties to the Fourth Geneva Convention on measures to enforce the Convention in the Occupied Palestinian Territory, including East Jerusalem, held on 15 July 1999, as well as the declarations adopted by the reconvened Conference on 5 December 2001 and on 17 December 2014,[7] and the urgent need for the parties to follow up the implementation of those declarations,

Welcoming and encouraging the initiatives by States parties to the Convention, both individually and collectively, according to article 1 common to the four Geneva Conventions, aimed at ensuring respect for the Convention, as well as the continuing efforts of the depositary State of the Geneva Conventions in this regard,

Noting the accession by Palestine on 1 April 2014 to the Geneva Conventions and Additional Protocol I,

Stressing that Israel, the occupying Power, should comply strictly with its obligations under international law, including international humanitarian law,

1. *Reaffirms* that the Geneva Convention relative to the Protection of Civilian Persons in Time of War, of 12 August 1949, is applicable to the Occupied Palestinian Territory, including East Jerusalem, and other Arab territories occupied by Israel since 1967;
2. *Demands* that Israel accept the de jure applicability of the Convention in the Occupied Palestinian Territory, including East Jerusalem, and other Arab territories occupied by Israel since 1967, and that it comply scrupulously with the provisions of the Convention;
3. *Calls upon* all High Contracting Parties to the Convention, in accordance with article 1 common to the four Geneva Conventions and as mentioned in the advisory opinion of the International Court of Justice of 9 July 2004, to continue to exert all efforts to ensure respect for its provisions by

---

6 See A/ES-10/273 and A/ES-10/273/Corr.1.
7 A/69/711-S/2015/1, annex.

Israel, the occupying Power, in the Occupied Palestinian Territory, including East Jerusalem, and other Arab territories occupied by Israel since 1967;

4. *Notes* the reconvening by Switzerland, the depositary State, of the Conference of High Contracting Parties to the Fourth Geneva Convention on 17 December 2014, and calls for efforts to uphold the obligations reaffirmed in the declarations adopted on 5 December 2001 and 17 December 2014;
5. *Welcomes* initiatives by States parties, in accordance with article 1 of the Convention, aimed at ensuring respect for the Convention;
6. *Reiterates* the need for speedy implementation of the relevant recommendations contained in the resolutions adopted by the General Assembly, including at its tenth emergency special session and including resolution ES-10/15, with regard to ensuring respect by Israel, the occupying Power, for the provisions of the Convention;
7. *Requests* the Secretary-General to report to the General Assembly at its seventy-third session on the implementation of the present resolution.

66th plenary meeting
7 December 2017

United Nations General Assembly Resolution A/RES/72/86 (Dec. 14, 2017)

United Nations
General Assembly
A/RES/72/86
Distr.: General
14 December 2017

Seventy-second session
Agenda item 54
Resolution adopted by the General Assembly on 7 December 2017 [on the report of the Special Political and Decolonization Committee (Fourth Committee) (*A/72/448*)]

72/86. Israeli settlements in the Occupied Palestinian Territory, including East Jerusalem, and the occupied Syrian Golan

The General Assembly,

Guided by the principles of the Charter of the United Nations, and affirming the inadmissibility of the acquisition of territory by force,

Recalling its relevant resolutions, including resolution 71/97 of 6 December 2016, as well as those resolutions adopted at its tenth emergency special session,

Recalling also the relevant resolutions of the Security Council, including resolutions 242 (1967) of 22 November 1967, 446 (1979) of 22 March 1979, 465 (1980) of 1 March 1980, 476 (1980) of 30 June 1980, 478 (1980) of 20 August 1980, 497 (1981) of 17 December 1981, 904 (1994) of 18 March 1994 and 2334 (2016) of 23 December 2016,

Reaffirming the applicability of the Geneva Convention relative to the Protection of Civilian Persons in Time of War, of 12 August 1949,[1] to the Occupied Palestinian Territory, including East Jerusalem, and to the occupied Syrian Golan,

---

1 United Nations, *Treaty Series*, vol. 75, No. 973.

Affirming that the transfer by the occupying Power of parts of its own civilian population into the territory it occupies constitutes a breach of the Fourth Geneva Convention and relevant provisions of customary law, including those codified in Additional Protocol I[2] to the four Geneva Conventions,[3]

Recalling the advisory opinion rendered on 9 July 2004 by the International Court of Justice on the legal consequences of the construction of a wall in the Occupied Palestinian Territory,[4] and recalling also General Assembly resolutions ES-10/15 of 20 July 2004 and ES-10/17 of 15 December 2006,

Noting that the International Court of Justice concluded that "the Israeli settlements in the Occupied Palestinian Territory (including East Jerusalem) have been established in breach of international law",[5]

Taking note of the recent reports of the Special Rapporteur of the Human Rights Council on the situation of human rights in the Palestinian territories occupied since 1967,[6]

Recalling the report of the independent international fact-finding mission to investigate the implications of the Israeli settlements on the civil, political, economic, social and cultural rights of the Palestinian people throughout the Occupied Palestinian Territory, including East Jerusalem,[7]

Recalling also the statement of 15 July 1999 and the declarations adopted on 5 December 2001 and on 17 December 2014[8] by the Conference of High Contracting Parties to the Fourth Geneva Convention on measures to enforce the Convention in the Occupied Palestinian Territory, including East Jerusalem, aimed at ensuring respect for the Convention in the Occupied Palestinian Territory, including East Jerusalem,

Recalling further the Declaration of Principles on Interim Self-Government Arrangements of 13 September 1993[9] and the subsequent implementation agreements between the Palestinian and Israeli sides,

Recalling the Quartet road map to a permanent two-State solution to the Israeli-Palestinian conflict,[10] and emphasizing specifically its call for a freeze on all settlement activity, including so-called natural growth, and the

---

2   Ibid., vol. 1125, No. 17512.
3   Ibid., vol. 75, Nos. 970–973.
4   See A/ES-10/273 and A/ES-10/273/Corr.1.
5   Ibid., advisory opinion, para. 120.
6   A/HRC/34/70; see also A/72/556.
7   A/HRC/22/63.
8   A/69/711-S/2015/1, annex.
9   A/48/486-S/26560, annex.
10 S/2003/529, annex.

dismantlement of all settlement outposts erected since March 2001, and the need for Israel to uphold its obligations and commitments in this regard,

Recalling also its resolution 67/19 of 29 November 2012,

Noting the accession by Palestine to several human rights treaties and the core humanitarian law conventions, as well as other international treaties,

Aware that Israeli settlement activities involve, inter alia, the transfer of nationals of the occupying Power into the occupied territories, the confiscation of land, the forced transfer of Palestinian civilians, including Bedouin families, the exploitation of natural resources, the fragmentation of territory and other actions against the Palestinian civilian population and the civilian population in the occupied Syrian Golan that are contrary to international law,

Bearing in mind the extremely detrimental impact of Israeli settlement policies, decisions and activities on the ongoing regional and international efforts to resume and advance the peace process, on the prospects for the achievement of peace in the Middle East in accordance with the two-State solution of Israel and Palestine, living side by side in peace and security within recognized borders, on the basis of the pre-1967 borders, and on the viability and credibility of that solution,

Expressing grave concern about the continuation by Israel, the occupying Power, of settlement activities in the Occupied Palestinian Territory, including East Jerusalem, and condemning those activities as violations of international humanitarian law, relevant United Nations resolutions, the agreements reached between the parties and obligations under the Quartet road map and as actions in defiance of the calls by the international community to cease all settlement activities,

Deploring in particular Israel's construction and expansion of settlements in and around occupied East Jerusalem, including its so-called E-1 plan that aims to connect its illegal settlements around and further isolate occupied East Jerusalem, the continuing demolition of Palestinian homes and eviction of Palestinian families from the city, the revocation of Palestinian residency rights in the city, and ongoing settlement activities in the Jordan Valley, all of which further fragment and undermine the contiguity of the Occupied Palestinian Territory,

Taking note of the Quartet report of 1 July 2016,[11] and stressing its recommendations, as well as its recent statements, including of 30 September 2015, 23 October 2015, 12 February 2016 and 23 September 2016, in which the Quartet members concluded that, inter alia, the continuing policy of settlement con-

---

11 S/2016/595, annex.

struction and expansion, designation of land for exclusive Israeli use and denial of Palestinian development, including the recent high rate of demolitions, are steadily eroding the two-State solution,

Deploring the continuing unlawful construction by Israel of the wall inside the Occupied Palestinian Territory, including in and around East Jerusalem, and expressing its concern, in particular, about the route of the wall in departure from the Armistice Line of 1949, which is causing humanitarian hardship and a serious decline of socioeconomic conditions for the Palestinian people, is fragmenting the territorial contiguity of the Territory and undermining its viability, and could prejudge future negotiations and make the two-State solution physically impossible to implement,

Deeply concerned that the wall's route has been traced in such a way as to include the great majority of the Israeli settlements in the Occupied Palestinian Territory, including East Jerusalem,

Condemning acts of violence and terror against civilians on both sides, and recalling the need to end all acts of violence, including acts of terror, provocation, incitement and destruction,

Condemning also all acts of violence, destruction, harassment, provocation and incitement by Israeli settlers in the Occupied Palestinian Territory, including East Jerusalem, against Palestinian civilians, including children, and their properties, including historic and religious sites, and agricultural lands, as well as acts of terror by several extremist Israeli settlers, and calling for accountability for the illegal actions perpetrated in this regard,

Taking note of the relevant reports of the Secretary-General, including pursuant to Security Council resolution 2334 (2016),[12]

Noting the special meeting of the Security Council convened on 26 September 2008, as well as the meeting of the Council of 18 February 2011,

1. *Reaffirms* that the Israeli settlements in the Occupied Palestinian Territory, including East Jerusalem, and in the occupied Syrian Golan are illegal and an obstacle to peace and economic and social development;
2. *Calls upon* Israel to accept the de jure applicability of the Geneva Convention relative to the Protection of Civilian Persons in Time of War, of 12 August 1949, to the Occupied Palestinian Territory, including East Jerusalem, and to the occupied Syrian Golan and to abide scrupulously by the provisions of the Convention, in particular article 49, and to comply with all of its obligations under international law and cease immediately all actions causing the alteration of the character, status and

---

12   A/72/296, A/72/314, A/72/538, A/72/539, A/72/564 and A/72/565.

demographic composition of the Occupied Palestinian Territory, including East Jerusalem, and of the occupied Syrian Golan;

3. *Reiterates its demand* for the immediate and complete cessation of all Israeli settlement activities in all of the Occupied Palestinian Territory, including East Jerusalem, and in the occupied Syrian Golan, and calls in this regard for the full implementation of all the relevant resolutions of the Security Council, including, inter alia, resolutions 446 (1979), 452 (1979) of 20 July 1979, 465 (1980), 476 (1980), 1515 (2003) of 19 November 2003 and 2334 (2016);

4. *Recalls* the affirmation by the Security Council, in its resolution 2334 (2016), that it will not recognize any changes to the 4 June 1967 lines, including with regard to Jerusalem, other than those agreed by the parties through negotiations;

5. *Condemns* settlement activities in the Occupied Palestinian Territory, including East Jerusalem, and in the occupied Syrian Golan and any activities involving the confiscation of land, the disruption of the livelihood of protected persons, the forced transfer of civilians and the de facto annexation of land;

6. *Calls for* the consideration of measures of accountability, in accordance with international law, in the light of continued non-compliance with the demands for a complete and immediate cessation of all settlement activities, stressing that compliance with and respect for international humanitarian law and international human rights law is a cornerstone for peace and security in the region;

7. *Stresses* that a complete cessation of all Israeli settlement activities is essential for salvaging the two-State solution on the basis of the pre-1967 borders, and calls for affirmative steps to be taken immediately to reverse the negative trends on the ground that are imperilling the viability of the two-State solution;

8. *Demands* that Israel, the occupying Power, comply with its legal obligations, as mentioned in the advisory opinion rendered on 9 July 2004 by the International Court of Justice;

9. *Reiterates its call* for the prevention of all acts of violence, destruction, harassment and provocation by Israeli settlers, especially against Palestinian civilians and their properties, including historic and religious sites and including in Occupied East Jerusalem, and their agricultural lands;

10. *Calls for* accountability for the illegal actions perpetrated by Israeli settlers in the Occupied Palestinian Territory, and stresses in this regard the

need for the implementation of Security Council resolution 904 (1994), in which the Council called upon Israel, the occupying Power, to continue to take and implement measures, including the confiscation of arms, aimed at preventing illegal acts of violence by Israeli settlers, and called for measures to be taken to guarantee the safety and protection of the Palestinian civilians in the occupied territory;

11. *Stresses* the responsibility of Israel, the occupying Power, to investigate all acts of settler violence against Palestinian civilians and their properties and to ensure accountability for these acts;

12. *Calls upon* all States and international organizations to continue to actively pursue policies that ensure respect for their obligations under international law with regard to all illegal Israeli practices and measures in the Occupied Palestinian Territory, including East Jerusalem, particularly Israeli settlement activities;

13. *Recalls*, in this regard, the statement of 15 July 1999 and the declarations adopted on 5 December 2001 and on 17 December 2014 by the Conference of High Contracting Parties to the Fourth Geneva Convention on measures to enforce the Convention in the Occupied Palestinian Territory, including East Jerusalem, and welcomes in this regard initiatives by States parties, both individually and collectively, in accordance with article 1 of the Convention, aimed at ensuring respect for the Convention;

14. *Also recalls* that the Security Council, in its resolution 2334 (2016), called upon all States to distinguish, in their relevant dealings, between the territory of the State of Israel and the territories occupied since 1967;

15. *Calls upon* all States, consistent with their obligations under international law and the relevant resolutions, and bearing in mind the advisory opinion of the International Court of Justice of 9 July 2004, not to render aid or assistance in maintaining the situation created by illegal settlement activities;

16. *Calls upon* the relevant United Nations bodies to take all necessary measures and actions within their mandates to ensure full respect for and compliance with Human Rights Council resolution 17/4 of 16 June 2011,[13] concerning the Guiding Principles on Business and Human Rights[14] and other relevant international laws and standards, and to ensure the implementation of the United Nations "Protect, Respect and

---

13 *See Official Records of the General Assembly, Sixty-sixth Session, Supplement No. 53* (A/66/53), chap. III, sect. A.
14 A/HRC/17/31, annex.

Remedy" Framework, which provides a global standard for upholding human rights in relation to business activities that are connected with Israeli settlements in the Occupied Palestinian Territory, including East Jerusalem;

17. *Requests* the Secretary-General to report to the General Assembly at its seventy-third session on the implementation of the present resolution.

66th plenary meeting
7 December 2017

United Nations General Assembly Resolution A/RES/72/87

United Nations
General Assembly
A/RES/72/87
Distr.: General
14 December 2017

Seventy-second session
Agenda item 54

Resolution adopted by the General Assembly on 7 December 2017 [on the report of the Special Political and Decolonization Committee (Fourth Committee) (*A/72/448*)]

72/87. Israeli practices affecting the human rights of the Palestinian people in the Occupied Palestinian Territory, including East Jerusalem

The General Assembly,
 Recalling the Universal Declaration of Human Rights,[1]
 Recalling also the International Covenant on Civil and Political Rights,[2] the International Covenant on Economic, Social and Cultural Rights and the Convention on the Rights of the Child,[3] and affirming that these human rights instruments must be respected in the Occupied Palestinian Territory, including East Jerusalem,
 Reaffirming its relevant resolutions, including resolution 71/98 of 6 December 2016, as well as those adopted at its tenth emergency special session,
 Recalling the relevant resolutions of the Human Rights Council,
 Recalling also the relevant resolutions of the Security Council, and stressing the need for their implementation,

---

1 Resolution 217 A (III).
2 *See* resolution 2200 A (XXI), annex.
3 United Nations, *Treaty Series*, vol. 1577, No. 27531.

Having considered the report of the Special Committee to Investigate Israeli Practices Affecting the Human Rights of the Palestinian People and Other Arabs of the Occupied Territories[4] and the report of the Secretary-General on the work of the Special Committee,[5]

Taking note of the recent reports of the Special Rapporteur of the Human Rights Council on the situation of human rights in the Palestinian territories occupied since 1967,[6] as well as of other relevant recent reports of the Human Rights Council,

Taking note also of the recent report by the Economic and Social Commission for Western Asia on the economic and social repercussions of the Israeli occupation on the living conditions of the Palestinian people in the Occupied Palestinian Territory, including East Jerusalem, and the Arab population in the occupied Syrian Golan,[7]

Deeply regretting that 50 years have passed since the onset of the Israeli occupation, and stressing the urgent need for efforts to reverse the negative trends on the ground and to restore a political horizon for advancing and accelerating meaningful negotiations aimed at the achievement of a peace agreement that will bring a complete end to the Israeli occupation that began in 1967 and the resolution of all core final status issues, without exception, leading to a peaceful, just, lasting and comprehensive solution of the question of Palestine,

Aware of the responsibility of the international community to promote human rights and ensure respect for international law, and recalling in this regard its resolution 2625 (XXV) of 24 October 1970,

Recalling the advisory opinion rendered on 9 July 2004 by the International Court of Justice on the legal consequences of the construction of a wall in the Occupied Palestinian Territory,[8] and recalling also General Assembly resolutions ES-10/15 of 20 July 2004 and ES-10/17 of 15 December 2006,

Noting in particular the Court's reply, including that the construction of the wall being built by Israel, the occupying Power, in the Occupied Palestinian Territory, including in and around East Jerusalem, and its associated regime are contrary to international law,

Taking note of its resolution 67/19 of 29 November 2012,

---

4   A/72/539.
5   A/72/296.
6   A/HRC/34/70; see also A/72/556.
7   A/72/90-E/2017/71.
8   *See* A/ES-10/273 and A/ES-10/273/Corr.1.

Noting the accession by Palestine to several human rights treaties and the core humanitarian law conventions, as well as other international treaties,

Reaffirming the principle of the inadmissibility of the acquisition of territory by force,

Reaffirming also the applicability of the Geneva Convention relative to the Protection of Civilian Persons in Time of War, of 12 August 1949,[9] to the Occupied Palestinian Territory, including East Jerusalem, and other Arab territories occupied by Israel since 1967,

Reaffirming further the obligation of the States parties to the Fourth Geneva Convention under articles 146, 147 and 148 with regard to penal sanctions, grave breaches and responsibilities of the High Contracting Parties,

Recalling the statement of 15 July 1999 and the declarations adopted on 5 December 2001 and on 17 December 2014[10] by the Conference of High Contracting Parties to the Fourth Geneva Convention on measures to enforce the Convention in the Occupied Palestinian Territory, including East Jerusalem, aimed at ensuring respect for the Convention in the Occupied Palestinian Territory, including East Jerusalem,

Reaffirming that all States have the right and the duty to take actions in conformity with international law and international humanitarian law to counter deadly acts of violence against their civilian population in order to protect the lives of their citizens,

Stressing the need for full compliance with the Israeli-Palestinian agreements reached within the context of the Middle East peace process, including the Sharm el-Sheikh understandings, and the implementation of the Quartet road map to a permanent two-State solution to the Israeli-Palestinian conflict,[11]

Stressing also the need for the full implementation of the Agreement on Movement and Access and the Agreed Principles for the Rafah Crossing, both of 15 November 2005, to allow for the freedom of movement of the Palestinian civilian population within and into and out of the Gaza Strip,

Gravely concerned by the tensions and violence in the recent period throughout the Occupied Palestinian Territory, including East Jerusalem and including with regard to the holy places of Jerusalem, including the Haram al-Sharif, and deploring the loss of innocent civilian life,

Recognizing that security measures alone cannot remedy the escalating tensions, instability and violence, and calling for full respect for international law,

---

9   United Nations, *Treaty Series*, vol. 75, No. 973.
10 A/69/711-S/2015/1, annex.
11 S/2003/529, annex.

including humanitarian and human rights law, including for the protection of civilian life, as well as for the promotion of human security, the de-escalation of the situation, the exercise of restraint, including from provocative actions and rhetoric, and the establishment of a stable environment conducive to the pursuit of peace,

Expressing grave concern about the continuing systematic violation of the human rights of the Palestinian people by Israel, the occupying Power, including that arising from the excessive use of force and military operations causing death and injury to Palestinian civilians, including children, women and non-violent, peaceful demonstrators; the arbitrary imprisonment and detention of Palestinians, some of whom have been imprisoned for decades; the use of collective punishment; the closure of areas; the confiscation of land; the establishment and expansion of settlements; the construction of a wall in the Occupied Palestinian Territory in departure from the Armistice Line of 1949; the destruction of property and infrastructure; the forced displacement of civilians, including attempts at forced transfers of Bedouin communities; and all other actions by it designed to change the legal status, geographical nature and demographic composition of the Occupied Palestinian Territory, including East Jerusalem,

Gravely concerned by the ongoing demolition by Israel, the occupying Power, of Palestinian homes, as well as of structures, including schools, provided as international humanitarian aid, in particular in and around Occupied East Jerusalem, including if carried out as an act of collective punishment in violation of international humanitarian law, which has escalated at unprecedented rates, and by the revocation of residence permits and eviction of Palestinian residents of the City of Jerusalem,

Deploring the continuing and negative consequences of the conflicts in and around the Gaza Strip, most recently in July and August 2014, and the thousands of civilian casualties caused, along with the widespread destruction of thousands of homes and vital civilian infrastructure, the internal displacement of hundreds of thousands of civilians, and any violations of international law, including humanitarian and human rights law, in this regard,

Gravely concerned about the disastrous humanitarian situation and the critical socioeconomic and security situation in the Gaza Strip, including that resulting from the prolonged closures and severe economic and movement restrictions that in effect amount to a blockade and deepen poverty and despair among the Palestinian civilian population,

Expressing grave concern about the alarming conditions and figures reflected in the United Nations country team reports of 26 August 2016, entitled "Gaza: two years after", and of July 2017, entitled "Gaza ten years later",

Recalling the statement by the President of the Security Council of 28 July 2014,[12]

Stressing the need for the full implementation by all parties of Security Council resolution 1860 (2009) of 8 January 2009 and General Assembly resolution ES-10/18 of 16 January 2009,

Stressing also that the situation in the Gaza Strip is unsustainable and that a durable ceasefire agreement must lead to a fundamental improvement in the living conditions of the Palestinian people in the Gaza Strip, including through the sustained and regular opening of crossing points, and ensure the safety and well-being of civilians on both sides, and regretting the lack of progress made in this regard,

Gravely concerned by reports regarding serious human rights violations and grave breaches of international humanitarian law committed during the military operations in the Gaza Strip between December 2008 and January 2009, including the findings in the summary by the Secretary-General of the report of the Board of Inquiry[13] and in the report of the United Nations Fact-finding Mission on the Gaza Conflict,[14] and the findings of the United Nations Headquarters Board of Inquiry into certain incidents that occurred in the Gaza Strip between 8 July and 26 August 2014[15] and of the independent commission of inquiry established pursuant to Human Rights Council resolution S-21/1,[16] and reiterating the necessity for serious follow-up by all parties of the recommendations addressed to them towards ensuring accountability and justice,

Stressing the need for protection of human rights defenders engaged in the promotion of human rights issues in the Occupied Palestinian Territory, including East Jerusalem, to allow them to carry out their work freely and without fear of attacks and harassment,

Expressing deep concern about the short- and long-term detrimental impact of widespread destruction and the continued impeding of the reconstruction process by Israel, the occupying Power, on the human rights situation and on the socioeconomic and humanitarian conditions of the Palestinian civilian population,

Expressing deep concern also about the Israeli policy of closures and the imposition of severe restrictions, including through hundreds of obstacles to movement, checkpoints and a permit regime, all of which obstruct the

---

12 S/PRST/2014/13; see *Resolutions and Decisions of the Security Council, 1 August 2013–31 July 2014* (S/INF/69).
13 *See* A/63/855-S/2009/250.
14 A/HRC/12/48.
15 *See* S/2015/286, annex.
16 A/HRC/29/52.

freedom of movement of persons and goods, including medical and humanitarian goods, and the follow-up and access to donor-funded projects of development cooperation and humanitarian assistance, throughout the Occupied Palestinian Territory, including East Jerusalem, and impair the Territory's contiguity, consequently violating the human rights of the Palestinian people and negatively impacting their socioeconomic and humanitarian situation, which remains dire in the Gaza Strip, and the efforts aimed at rehabilitating and developing the Palestinian economy, while taking note of developments with regard to the situation of access there and the resumption of some trade from Gaza to the West Bank for the first time since 2007, and calling for the full lifting of restrictions,

Expressing grave concern that thousands of Palestinians, including many children and women, as well as elected representatives, continue to be held in Israeli prisons or detention centres under harsh conditions, including unhygienic conditions, solitary confinement, the extensive use of administrative detention of excessive duration without charge and denial of due process, lack of proper medical care and widespread medical neglect, including for prisoners who are ill, with the risk of fatal consequences, and denial of family visits, that impair their well-being, and expressing grave concern also about the ill-treatment and harassment and all reports of torture of any Palestinian prisoners,

Expressing deep concern about the recent hunger strikes by numerous Palestinian prisoners in protest of the harsh conditions of their imprisonment and detention by the occupying Power, while taking note of agreements reached on conditions of detention in Israeli prisons and calling for their full and immediate implementation,

Recalling the United Nations Standard Minimum Rules for the Treatment of Prisoners (the Nelson Mandela Rules)[17] and the United Nations Rules for the Treatment of Women Prisoners and Non-custodial Measures for Women Offenders (the Bangkok Rules),[18] and calling for respect for those Rules,

Recalling also the prohibition under international humanitarian law of the deportation of civilians from occupied territories,

Deploring the practice of withholding the bodies of those killed, and calling for the release of the bodies that have not yet been returned to their relatives, in line with international humanitarian law and human rights law, in order to ensure dignified closure in accordance with their religious beliefs and traditions,

---

17   Resolution 70/175, annex.
18   Resolution 65/229, annex.

Stressing the need for the prevention of all acts of violence, harassment, provocation and incitement by extremist Israeli settlers and groups of armed settlers, especially against Palestinian civilians, including children, and their properties, including homes, agricultural lands and historic and religious sites, including in Occupied East Jerusalem, and deploring the violation of the human rights of Palestinians in this regard, including acts of violence leading to death and injury among civilians,

Convinced of the need for an international presence to monitor the situation, to contribute to ending the violence and protecting the Palestinian civilian population and to help the parties to implement the agreements reached, and in this regard recalling the positive contribution of the Temporary International Presence in Hebron,

Noting the continued efforts and tangible progress made in the Palestinian security sector, and noting also the continued cooperation that benefits both Palestinians and Israelis, in particular by promoting security and building confidence, and expressing the hope that such progress will be extended to all major population centres,

Urging the parties to observe calm and restraint and to refrain from provocative actions, incitement and inflammatory rhetoric, especially in areas of religious and cultural sensitivity, including in East Jerusalem, and to take every possible step to defuse tensions and promote conditions conducive to the credibility and success of the peace negotiations,

Emphasizing the right of all people in the region to the enjoyment of human rights as enshrined in the international human rights covenants,

1. *Reiterates* that all measures and actions taken by Israel, the occupying Power, in the Occupied Palestinian Territory, including East Jerusalem, in violation of the relevant provisions of the Geneva Convention relative to the Protection of Civilian Persons in Time of War, of 12 August 1949, and contrary to the relevant resolutions of the Security Council, are illegal and have no validity;

2. *Demands* that Israel, the occupying Power, cease all practices and actions that violate the human rights of the Palestinian people, including the killing and injury of civilians, the arbitrary detention and imprisonment of civilians, the forced displacement of civilians, including attempts at forced transfers of Bedouin communities, the destruction and confiscation of civilian property, including home demolitions, including if carried out as collective punishment in violation of international humanitarian law, and any obstruction of humanitarian assistance, and that it fully respect human rights law and comply with its legal obligations in this regard, including in accordance with relevant United Nations resolutions;

3. *Also demands* that Israel, the occupying Power, comply fully with the provisions of the Fourth Geneva Convention of 1949 and cease immediately all measures and actions taken in violation and in breach of the Convention;

4. *Calls for* urgent measures to ensure the safety and protection of the Palestinian civilian population in the Occupied Palestinian Territory, including East Jerusalem, in accordance with the relevant provisions of international humanitarian law and as called for by the Security Council in its resolution 904 (1994) of 18 March 1994;

5. *Also calls for* full cooperation by Israel with the relevant special rapporteurs and other relevant mechanisms and inquiries of the Human Rights Council, including the facilitation of entry to the Occupied Palestinian Territory, including East Jerusalem, for monitoring and reporting on the human rights situation therein according to their respective mandates;

6. *Demands* that Israel, the occupying Power, cease all of its settlement activities, the construction of the wall and any other measures aimed at altering the character, status and demographic composition of the Occupied Palestinian Territory, including in and around East Jerusalem, all of which, inter alia, gravely and detrimentally impact the human rights of the Palestinian people, and the prospects for achieving without delay an end to the Israeli occupation that began in 1967 and a just, lasting and comprehensive peace settlement between the Palestinian and Israeli sides, and calls for the full respect and implementation of all relevant General Assembly and Security Council resolutions in this regard, including Security Council resolution 2334 (2016) of 23 December 2016;

7. *Calls for* urgent attention to the plight and the rights, in accordance with international law, of Palestinian prisoners and detainees in Israeli jails, including those on hunger strike, calls for efforts between the two sides for the further release of prisoners and detainees, and also calls for respect for the United Nations Standard Minimum Rules for the Treatment of Prisoners (the Nelson Mandela Rules) and the United Nations Rules for the Treatment of Women Prisoners and Non-custodial Measures for Women Offenders (the Bangkok Rules);

8. *Condemns* all acts of violence, including all acts of terror, provocation, incitement and destruction, especially the excessive use of force by the Israeli occupying forces against Palestinian civilians, particularly in the Gaza Strip, which have caused extensive loss of life and vast numbers of injuries, including among thousands of children and women, massive damage and destruction to homes, economic, industrial and agricultural properties, vital infrastructure, including water, sanitation and electricity

networks, religious sites and public institutions, including hospitals and schools, and United Nations facilities, and agricultural lands, and large-scale internal displacement of civilians;

9. *Expresses grave concern* at the firing of rockets against Israeli civilian areas, resulting in loss of life and injury;

10. *Reiterates its demand* for the full implementation of Security Council resolution 1860 (2009);

11. *Demands* that Israel, the occupying Power, comply with its legal obligations under international law, as mentioned in the advisory opinion rendered on 9 July 2004 by the International Court of Justice and as demanded in General Assembly resolutions ES-10/15 and ES-10/13 of 21 October 2003, and that it immediately cease the construction of the wall in the Occupied Palestinian Territory, including in and around East Jerusalem, dismantle forthwith the structure situated therein, repeal or render ineffective all legislative and regulatory acts relating thereto, and make reparations for all damage caused by the construction of the wall, which has gravely impacted the human rights and the socioeconomic living conditions of the Palestinian people;

12. *Reiterates* the need for respect for the territorial unity, contiguity and integrity of all of the Occupied Palestinian Territory and for guarantees of the freedom of movement of persons and goods within the Palestinian territory, including movement into and from East Jerusalem, into and from the Gaza Strip, between the West Bank and the Gaza Strip, and to and from the outside world;

13. *Calls upon* Israel, the occupying Power, to cease its imposition of prolonged closures and economic and movement restrictions, including those amounting to a blockade on the Gaza Strip, and in this regard to fully implement the Agreement on Movement and Access and the Agreed Principles for the Rafah Crossing, both of 15 November 2005, in order to allow for the sustained and regular movement of persons and goods and for the acceleration of long overdue and massive reconstruction needs and economic recovery in the Gaza Strip, while noting the tripartite agreement facilitated by the United Nations in this regard;

14. *Urges* Member States to continue to provide emergency assistance to the Palestinian people to alleviate the financial crisis and the dire socioeconomic and humanitarian situation, particularly in the Gaza Strip;

15. *Emphasizes* the need to preserve and develop the Palestinian institutions and infrastructure for the provision of vital public services to the Palestinian civilian population and the promotion of human rights, including civil, political, economic, social and cultural rights, and welcomes

in this regard the agreement signed in Cairo on 12 October 2017,[19] the implementation of which would be an important step towards achieving Palestinian unity and lead to the effective functioning of the Palestinian national consensus government, including in the Gaza Strip, under the leadership of President Mahmoud Abbas, consistent with the Palestine Liberation Organization commitments and the Quartet principles;

16. *Urges* all States and the specialized agencies and organizations of the United Nations system to continue to support and assist the Palestinian people in the early realization of their inalienable human rights, including their right to self-determination, as a matter of urgency, in the light of the fiftieth year of the Israeli occupation and the continued denial and violation of the human rights of the Palestinian people;

17. *Requests* the Secretary-General to report to the General Assembly at its seventy-third session on the implementation of the present resolution.

66th plenary meeting
7 December 2017

---

19   S/2017/899, annex.

United Nations General Assembly Resolution A/RES/72/134 (Jan. 15, 2018)

United Nations
General Assembly
A/RES/72/134
Distr.: General
15 January 2018

Seventy-second session
Agenda item 73 (b)
Resolution adopted by the General Assembly on 11 December 2017 [without reference to a Main Committee (*A/72/L.25* and *A/72/L.25/Add.1*)]

72/134. Assistance to the Palestinian people

The General Assembly,

Recalling its resolution 71/126 of 8 December 2016, as well as its previous resolutions on the question,

Recalling also the signing of the Declaration of Principles on Interim Self-Government Arrangements in Washington, D.C., on 13 September 1993, by the Government of the State of Israel and the Palestine Liberation Organization, the representative of the Palestinian people,[1] and the subsequent implementation agreements concluded by the two sides,

Recalling further all relevant international law, including humanitarian and human rights law, and, in particular, the International Covenant on Civil and Political Rights,[2] the International Covenant on Economic, Social and Cultural Rights, the Convention on the Rights of the Child[3] and the Convention on the Elimination of All Forms of Discrimination against Women,[4]

---

1   A/48/486-S/26560, annex.
2   *See* resolution 2200 A (XXI), annex.
3   United Nations, *Treaty Series*, vol. 1577, No. 27531.
4   Ibid., vol. 1249, No. 20378.

Gravely concerned at the difficult living conditions and humanitarian situation affecting the Palestinian people, in particular women and children, throughout the occupied Palestinian territory, particularly in the Gaza Strip where economic recovery and vast infrastructure repair, rehabilitation and development are urgently needed, especially in the aftermath of the conflict of July and August 2014,

Conscious of the urgent need for improvement in the economic and social infrastructure of the occupied territory,

Welcoming, in this context, the development of projects, notably on infrastructure, to revive the Palestinian economy and improve the living conditions of the Palestinian people, stressing the need to create the appropriate conditions to facilitate the implementation of these projects, and noting the contribution of partners in the region and of the international community,

Aware that development is difficult under occupation and is best promoted in circumstances of peace and stability,

Noting the great economic and social challenges facing the Palestinian people and their leadership,

Emphasizing the importance of the safety and well-being of all people, in particular women and children, in the whole Middle East region, the promotion of which is facilitated, inter alia, in a stable and secure environment,

Deeply concerned about the negative impact, including the health and psychological consequences, of violence on the present and future well-being of children in the region,

Conscious of the urgent necessity for international assistance to the Palestinian people, taking into account the Palestinian priorities, and recalling in this regard the National Early Recovery and Reconstruction Plan for Gaza,

Expressing grave concern about the grave humanitarian situation in the Gaza Strip, and underlining the importance of emergency and humanitarian assistance and the need for the advancement of reconstruction in the Gaza Strip,

Welcoming the results of the Conference to Support Middle East Peace, convened in Washington, D.C., on 1 October 1993, the establishment of the Ad Hoc Liaison Committee for the Coordination of the International Assistance to Palestinians and the work being done by the World Bank as its secretariat and the establishment of the Consultative Group, as well as all follow-up meetings and international mechanisms established to provide assistance to the Palestinian people,

Underlining the importance of the Cairo International Conference on Palestine: Reconstructing Gaza, held on 12 October 2014, and urging the timely and full disbursement of pledges for expediting the provision of humanitarian assistance and the reconstruction process,

Recalling the International Donors' Conference for the Palestinian State, held in Paris on 17 December 2007, the Berlin Conference in Support of Palestinian Civil Security and the Rule of Law, held on 24 June 2008, and the Palestine Investment Conferences, held in Bethlehem from 21 to 23 May 2008 and on 2 and 3 June 2010, and the International Conference in Support of the Palestinian Economy for the Reconstruction of Gaza, held in Sharm el-Sheikh, Egypt, on 2 March 2009,

Welcoming the ministerial meetings of the Conference on Cooperation among East Asian Countries for Palestinian Development, convened in Tokyo in February 2013 and in Jakarta in March 2014, as a forum to mobilize political and economic assistance, including through exchanges of expertise and lessons learned, in support of Palestinian development,

Welcoming also the latest meetings of the Ad Hoc Liaison Committee for the Coordination of the International Assistance to Palestinians, held in Brussels on 27 May 2015 and in New York on 25 September 2013, 22 September 2014, 30 September 2015, 19 September 2016 and 18 September 2017,

Welcoming further the activities of the Joint Liaison Committee, which provides a forum in which economic policy and practical matters related to donor assistance are discussed with the Palestinian Authority,

Welcoming the implementation of the Palestinian National Development Plan 2011–2013 on governance, economy, social development and infrastructure and the adoption of the Palestinian National Development Plan 2014–2016: State-building to Sovereignty, and stressing the need for continued international support for the Palestinian State-building process, as outlined in the summary by the Chair of the meeting of the Ad Hoc Liaison Committee held on 22 September 2014,

Stressing the need for the full engagement of the United Nations in the process of building Palestinian institutions and in providing broad assistance to the Palestinian people,

Recognizing, in this regard, the positive contribution of the United Nations Development Assistance Framework 2014–2016, which is aimed, inter alia, at enhancing developmental support and assistance to the Palestinian people and strengthening institutional capacity in line with Palestinian national priorities,

Welcoming steps to ease the restrictions on movement and access in the West Bank, while stressing the need for further steps to be taken in this regard, and recognizing that such steps would improve living conditions and the situation on the ground and could promote further Palestinian economic development,

Welcoming also the tripartite agreement facilitated by the United Nations regarding access to the Gaza Strip, and calling for its full implementation and complementary measures that address the need for a fundamental change in policy that allows for the sustained and regular opening of the border crossings for the movement of persons and goods, including for humanitarian and commercial flows and for the reconstruction and economic recovery of Gaza,

Stressing that the situation in the Gaza Strip is unsustainable and that a durable ceasefire agreement must lead to a fundamental improvement in the living conditions of the Palestinian people in the Gaza Strip and ensure the safety and well-being of civilians on both sides,

Stressing also the urgency of reaching a durable solution to the crisis in Gaza through the full implementation of Security Council resolution 1860 (2009) of 8 January 2009, including by preventing the illicit trafficking in arms and ammunition and by ensuring the sustained reopening of the crossing points on the basis of existing agreements, including the 2005 Agreement on Movement and Access between the Palestinian Authority and Israel,

Stressing, in this regard, the importance of the effective exercise by the Palestinian Authority of its full government responsibilities in the Gaza Strip in all fields, including through its presence at the Gaza crossing points,

Noting the active participation of the United Nations Special Coordinator for the Middle East Peace Process and Personal Representative of the Secretary-General to the Palestine Liberation Organization and the Palestinian Authority in the activities of the Special Envoys of the Quartet,

Reaffirming the necessity of achieving a comprehensive resolution of the Arab-Israeli conflict in all its aspects, on the basis of relevant Security Council resolutions, including resolutions 242 (1967) of 22 November 1967, 338 (1973) of 22 October 1973, 1397 (2002) of 12 March 2002, 1515 (2003) of 19 November 2003, 1850 (2008) of 16 December 2008 and 1860 (2009), as well as the terms of reference of the Madrid Conference and the principle of land for peace, in order to ensure a political solution, with two States – Israel and an independent, democratic, contiguous, sovereign and viable Palestinian State – living side by side in peace and security and mutual recognition,

Having considered the report of the Secretary-General,[5]

---

5   A/72/87-E/2017/67.

Expressing grave concern about continuing violence against civilians,

1. *Takes note* of the report of the Secretary-General;
2. *Expresses its appreciation* to the Secretary-General for his rapid response and ongoing efforts regarding assistance to the Palestinian people, including with regard to the emergency humanitarian needs in the Gaza Strip;
3. *Also expresses its appreciation* to the Member States, United Nations bodies and intergovernmental, regional and non-governmental organizations that have provided and continue to provide assistance to the Palestinian people;
4. *Stresses* the importance of the work of the United Nations Special Coordinator for the Middle East Peace Process and Personal Representative of the Secretary-General to the Palestine Liberation Organization and the Palestinian Authority and of the steps taken under the auspices of the Secretary-General to ensure the achievement of a coordinated mechanism for United Nations activities throughout the occupied territories;
5. *Urges* Member States, international financial institutions of the United Nations system, intergovernmental and non-governmental organizations and regional and interregional organizations to extend, as rapidly and as generously as possible, economic and social assistance to the Palestinian people, in close cooperation with the Palestine Liberation Organization and through official Palestinian institutions;
6. *Welcomes* the meetings of the Ad Hoc Liaison Committee for the Coordination of the International Assistance to Palestinians of 25 September 2013, 22 September 2014, 27 May and 30 September 2015, 19 September 2016 and 18 September 2017, the outcome of the Cairo International Conference on Palestine: Reconstructing Gaza, held on 12 October 2014, and the generous donor response to support the needs of the Palestinian people, and urges the rapid disbursement of donor pledges;
7. *Stresses* the importance of following up on the results of the Cairo International Conference on Palestine: Reconstructing Gaza to effectively promote economic recovery and reconstruction in a timely and sustainable manner;
8. *Calls upon* donors that have not yet converted their budget support pledges into disbursements to transfer funds as soon as possible, encourages all donors to increase their direct assistance to the Palestinian Authority in accordance with its government programme in order to enable it to build a viable and prosperous Palestinian State, underlines the need for

equitable burden sharing by donors in this effort, and encourages donors to consider aligning funding cycles with the Palestinian Authority's national budget cycle;

9. *Calls upon* relevant organizations and agencies of the United Nations system to intensify their assistance in response to the urgent needs of the Palestinian people in accordance with priorities set forth by the Palestinian side;

10. *Expresses its appreciation* for the work of the United Nations Relief and Works Agency for Palestine Refugees in the Near East, and recognizes the vital role of the Agency in providing humanitarian assistance to the Palestinian people, particularly in the Gaza Strip;

11. *Calls upon* the international community to provide urgently needed assistance and services in an effort to alleviate the difficult humanitarian situation being faced by Palestinian women, children and their families and to help in the reconstruction and development of relevant Palestinian institutions;

12. *Stresses* the role that all funding instruments, including the European Commission's Palestinian-European Mechanism for the Management of Socioeconomic Aid and the World Bank trust fund, have been playing in directly assisting the Palestinian people;

13. *Urges* Member States to open their markets to exports of Palestinian products on the most favourable terms, consistent with appropriate trading rules, and to implement fully existing trade and cooperation agreements;

14. *Calls upon* the international donor community to expedite the delivery of pledged assistance to the Palestinian people to meet their urgent needs;

15. *Stresses*, in this context, the importance of ensuring free humanitarian access to the Palestinian people and the free movement of persons and goods;

16. *Also stresses* the need for the full implementation by both parties of existing agreements, including the Agreement on Movement and Access and the Agreed Principles for the Rafah Crossing, of 15 November 2005, to allow for the freedom of movement of the Palestinian civilian population, as well as for imports and exports, within and into and out of the Gaza Strip;

17. *Further stresses* the need to ensure the safety and security of humanitarian personnel, premises, facilities, equipment, vehicles and supplies, as well as the need to ensure safe and unhindered access by humanitarian personnel and delivery of supplies and equipment, in order to allow such personnel to efficiently perform their task of assisting affected civilian populations;

18. *Urges* the international donor community, United Nations agencies and organizations and non-governmental organizations to extend to the Palestinian people, as rapidly as possible, emergency economic assistance and humanitarian assistance, particularly in the Gaza Strip, to counter the impact of the current crisis;
19. *Stresses* the need for the continued implementation of the Paris Protocol on Economic Relations of 29 April 1994, fifth annex to the Israeli-Palestinian Interim Agreement on the West Bank and the Gaza Strip, signed in Washington, D.C., on 28 September 1995,[6] including with regard to the full, prompt and regular transfer of Palestinian indirect tax revenues;
20. *Requests* the Secretary-General to submit a report to the General Assembly at its seventy-third session, through the Economic and Social Council, on the implementation of the present resolution, containing:
    (a) An assessment of the assistance actually received by the Palestinian people;
    (b) An assessment of the needs still unmet and specific proposals for responding effectively to them;
21. *Decides* to include in the provisional agenda of its seventy-third session, under the item entitled "Strengthening of the coordination of humanitarian and disaster relief assistance of the United Nations, including special economic assistance", the sub-item entitled "Assistance to the Palestinian people".

70th plenary meeting
11 December 2017

---

6 A/51/889-S/1997/357, annex.

United Nations General Assembly Resolution A/RES/72/160 (Jan. 23, 2018)

United Nations
General Assembly
A/RES/72/160
Distr.: General
23 January 2018

Seventy-second session
Agenda item 71
Resolution adopted by the General Assembly on 19 December 2017
[on the report of the Third Committee (A/72/438)]

72/160. The right of the Palestinian people to self-determination

The General Assembly,

Aware that the development of friendly relations among nations, based on respect for the principle of equal rights and self-determination of peoples, is among the purposes and principles of the United Nations, as defined in the Charter,

Recalling, in this regard, its resolution 2625 (XXV) of 24 October 1970, entitled "Declaration on Principles of International Law concerning Friendly Relations and Cooperation among States in accordance with the Charter of the United Nations",

Bearing in mind the International Covenants on Human Rights,[1] the Universal Declaration of Human Rights,[2] the Declaration on the Granting of Independence to Colonial Countries and Peoples[3] and the Vienna Declaration and Programme of Action adopted at the World Conference on Human Rights on 25 June 1993,[4]

---

1 Resolution 2200 A (XXI), annex.
2 Resolution 217 A (III).
3 Resolution 1514 (XV).
4 A/CONF.157/24 (Part I), chap. III.

Recalling the Declaration on the Occasion of the Fiftieth Anniversary of the United Nations,[5]

Recalling also the United Nations Millennium Declaration,[6]

Recalling further the advisory opinion rendered on 9 July 2004 by the International Court of Justice on the legal consequences of the construction of a wall in the Occupied Palestinian Territory,[7] and noting in particular the reply of the Court, including on the right of peoples to self-determination, which is a right *erga omnes*,[8]

Recalling the conclusion of the Court, in its advisory opinion of 9 July 2004, that the construction of the wall by Israel, the occupying Power, in the Occupied Palestinian Territory, including East Jerusalem, along with measures previously taken, severely impedes the right of the Palestinian people to self-determination,[9]

Stressing the urgency of achieving without delay an end to the Israeli occupation that began in 1967 and a just, lasting and comprehensive peace settlement between the Palestinian and Israeli sides, based on the relevant resolutions of the United Nations, the Madrid terms of reference, including the principle of land for peace, the Arab Peace Initiative[10] and the Quartet road map to a permanent two-State solution to the Israeli-Palestinian conflict,[11]

Stressing also the need for respect for and preservation of the territorial unity, contiguity and integrity of all of the Occupied Palestinian Territory, including East Jerusalem, and recalling in this regard its resolution 58/292 of 6 May 2004,

Recalling its resolution 71/184 of 19 December 2016,

Recalling also its resolution 67/19 of 29 November 2012,

Affirming the right of all States in the region to live in peace within secure and internationally recognized borders,

1. *Reaffirms* the right of the Palestinian people to self-determination, including the right to their independent State of Palestine;
2. *Urges* all States and the specialized agencies and organizations of the United Nations system to continue to support and assist the Palestinian people in the early realization of their right to self-determination.

73rd plenary meeting
19 December 2017

---

5   Resolution 50/6.
6   Resolution 55/2.
7   *See* A/ES-10/273 and A/ES-10/273/Corr.1.
8   Ibid., advisory opinion, para. 88.
9   Ibid., para. 122.
10 A/56/1026-S/2002/932, annex II, resolution 14/221.
11 S/2003/529, annex.

United Nations General Assembly Resolution A/RES/72/240 (Jan. 18, 2018)

United Nations
General Assembly
A/RES/72/240
Distr.: General
18 January 2018

Seventy-second session
Agenda item 63
Resolution adopted by the General Assembly on 20 December 2017 [on the report of the Second Committee (*A/72/428*)]

72/240. Permanent sovereignty of the Palestinian people in the Occupied Palestinian Territory, including East Jerusalem, and of the Arab population in the occupied Syrian Golan over their natural resources

The General Assembly,

Recalling its resolution 71/247 of 21 December 2016, and taking note of Economic and Social Council resolution 2017/30 of 25 July 2017,

Recalling also its resolutions 58/292 of 6 May 2004 and 59/251 of 22 December 2004,

Reaffirming the principle of the permanent sovereignty of peoples under foreign occupation over their natural resources,

Guided by the principles of the Charter of the United Nations, affirming the inadmissibility of the acquisition of territory by force, and recalling relevant Security Council resolutions, including resolutions 242 (1967) of 22 November 1967, 465 (1980) of 1 March 1980, 497 (1981) of 17 December 1981 and 2334 (2016) of 23 December 2016,

Recalling its resolution 2625 (XXV) of 24 October 1970,

Bearing in mind its resolution 70/1 of 25 September 2015, entitled "Transforming our world: the 2030 Agenda for Sustainable Development",

Reaffirming the applicability of the Geneva Convention relative to the Protection of Civilian Persons in Time of War, of 12 August 1949,[1] to the Occupied Palestinian Territory, including East Jerusalem, and other Arab territories occupied by Israel since 1967,

Recalling, in this regard, the International Covenant on Civil and Political Rights[2] and the International Covenant on Economic, Social and Cultural Rights, and affirming that these human rights instruments must be respected in the Occupied Palestinian Territory, including East Jerusalem, as well as in the occupied Syrian Golan,

Recalling also the advisory opinion rendered on 9 July 2004 by the International Court of Justice on the legal consequences of the construction of a wall in the Occupied Palestinian Territory,[3] and recalling further its resolutions ES-10/15 of 20 July 2004 and ES-10/17 of 15 December 2006,

Recalling further its resolution 67/19 of 29 November 2012,

Taking note of the accession by Palestine to several human rights treaties and the core humanitarian law treaties, as well as to other international treaties,

Expressing its concern about the exploitation by Israel, the occupying Power, of the natural resources of the Occupied Palestinian Territory, including East Jerusalem, and other Arab territories occupied by Israel since 1967,

Expressing its grave concern about the extensive destruction by Israel, the occupying Power, of agricultural land and orchards in the Occupied Palestinian Territory, including the uprooting of a vast number of fruit-bearing trees and the destruction of farms and greenhouses, and the grave environmental and economic impact in this regard,

Expressing its grave concern also about the widespread destruction caused by Israel, the occupying Power, to vital infrastructure, including water pipelines, sewage networks and electricity networks, in the Occupied Palestinian Territory, in particular in the Gaza Strip during the military operations of July and August 2014, which, inter alia, has polluted the environment and which negatively affects the functioning of water and sanitation systems and the water supply and other natural resources of the Palestinian people, and stressing the urgency of the reconstruction and development of water and other vital civilian infrastructure, including the project for the desalination facility for the Gaza Strip,

---

1 United Nations, *Treaty Series*, vol. 75, No. 973.
2 *See* resolution 2200 A (XXI), annex.
3 *See* A/ES-10/273 and A/ES-10/273/Corr.1.

Expressing its grave concern further about the negative impact on the environment and on reconstruction and development efforts of unexploded ordnance that remains in the Gaza Strip as a result of the conflict in July and August 2014, and commending the efforts of the Mine Action Service of the United Nations for the safe removal of such ordnance,

Expressing its grave concern about the chronic energy shortage in the Gaza Strip and its detrimental impact on the operation of water and sanitation facilities, which threaten to further erode groundwater resources, of which only 5 percent remains potable,

Recalling the 2009 report by the United Nations Environment Programme regarding the grave environmental situation in the Gaza Strip, and relevant reports by the United Nations country team, including "Gaza in 2020: a liveable place?", "Gaza: two years after" and "Gaza ten years later", and stressing the need for follow-up to the recommendations contained therein,

Deploring the detrimental impact of the Israeli settlements on Palestinian and other Arab natural resources, especially as a result of the confiscation of land and the forced diversion of water resources, including the destruction of orchards and crops and the seizure of water wells by Israeli settlers, and of the dire socioeconomic consequences in this regard,

Recalling the report of the independent international fact-finding mission to investigate the implications of the Israeli settlements on the civil, political, economic, social and cultural rights of the Palestinian people throughout the Occupied Palestinian Territory, including East Jerusalem,[4]

Aware of the detrimental impact on Palestinian natural resources being caused by the unlawful construction of the wall by Israel, the occupying Power, in the Occupied Palestinian Territory, including in and around East Jerusalem, and of its grave effect as well on the economic and social conditions of the Palestinian people,

Stressing the urgency of achieving without delay an end to the Israeli occupation that began in 1967 and a just, lasting and comprehensive peace settlement on all tracks, on the basis of Security Council resolutions 242 (1967), 338 (1973) of 22 October 1973, 425 (1978) of 19 March 1978, 1397 (2002) of 12 March 2002 and 2334 (2016), the principle of land for peace, the Arab Peace Initiative[5] and the Quartet performance-based road map to a permanent two-State solution to the Israeli-Palestinian conflict,[6] as endorsed by the Council in its

---

4 A/HRC/22/63.
5 A/56/1026-S/2002/932, annex II, resolution 14/221.
6 S/2003/529, annex.

resolution 1515 (2003) of 19 November 2003 and supported by the Council in its resolution 1850 (2008) of 16 December 2008,

Stressing also, in this regard, the need for respect for the obligation upon Israel under the road map to freeze settlement activity, including so-called "natural growth", and to dismantle all settlement outposts erected since March 2001,

Stressing further the need for respect and preservation of the territorial unity, contiguity and integrity of all of the Occupied Palestinian Territory, including East Jerusalem,

Recalling that the Security Council, in its resolution 2334 (2016), underlined that it would not recognize any changes to the 4 June 1967 lines, including with regard to Jerusalem, other than those agreed by the parties through negotiations,

Recalling also the need to end all acts of violence, including acts of terror, provocation, incitement and destruction,

Taking note of the report prepared by the Economic and Social Commission for Western Asia on the economic and social repercussions of the Israeli occupation on the living conditions of the Palestinian people in the Occupied Palestinian Territory, including East Jerusalem, and of the Arab population in the occupied Syrian Golan, as transmitted by the Secretary-General,[7]

1. *Reaffirms* the inalienable rights of the Palestinian people and of the population of the occupied Syrian Golan over their natural resources, including land, water and energy resources;
2. *Demands* that Israel, the occupying Power, cease the exploitation, damage, cause of loss or depletion and endangerment of the natural resources in the Occupied Palestinian Territory, including East Jerusalem, and in the occupied Syrian Golan;
3. *Recognizes* the right of the Palestinian people to claim restitution as a result of any exploitation, damage, loss or depletion or endangerment of their natural resources resulting from illegal measures taken by Israel, the occupying Power, and Israeli settlers in the Occupied Palestinian Territory, including East Jerusalem, and expresses the hope that this issue will be dealt with within the framework of the final status negotiations between the Palestinian and Israeli sides;
4. *Stresses* that the wall and settlements being constructed by Israel in the Occupied Palestinian Territory, including in and around East Jerusalem, are contrary to international law and are seriously depriving the Palestinian people of their natural resources, and calls in this regard for

---
[7] A/71/86-E/2016/13.

full compliance with the legal obligations affirmed in the 9 July 2004 advisory opinion of the International Court of Justice and in relevant United Nations resolutions, including General Assembly resolution ES-10/15;

5. *Calls upon* Israel, the occupying Power, to comply strictly with its obligations under international law, including international humanitarian law, and to cease immediately and completely all policies and measures aimed at the alteration of the character and status of the Occupied Palestinian Territory, including East Jerusalem;

6. *Also calls upon* Israel, the occupying Power, to bring a halt to all actions, including those perpetrated by Israeli settlers, harming the environment, including the dumping of all kinds of waste materials, in the Occupied Palestinian Territory, including East Jerusalem, and in the occupied Syrian Golan, which gravely threaten their natural resources, namely water and land resources, and which pose an environmental, sanitation and health threat to the civilian populations;

7. *Further calls upon* Israel to cease its destruction of vital infrastructure, including water pipelines, sewage networks and electricity networks, and to cease its demolition and confiscation of Palestinian homes and civilian infrastructure, agricultural lands and water wells, which, inter alia, have a negative impact on the natural resources of the Palestinian people, stresses the urgent need to advance reconstruction and development projects in this regard, including in the Gaza Strip, and calls for support for the necessary efforts in this regard, in line with the commitments made at, inter alia, the Cairo International Conference on Palestine: Reconstructing Gaza, held on 12 October 2014;

8. *Calls upon* Israel, the occupying Power, to remove all obstacles to the implementation of critical environmental projects, including sewage treatment plants in the Gaza Strip and the reconstruction and development of water infrastructure, including the project for the desalination facility for the Gaza Strip;

9. *Also calls upon* Israel not to impede Palestinian development and export of discovered oil and natural gas reserves;

10. *Calls for* the immediate and safe removal of all unexploded ordnance in the Gaza Strip and for support for the efforts of the Mine Action Service of the United Nations in this regard, and welcomes the extensive efforts exerted by the Mine Action Service to date;

11. *Encourages* all States and international organizations to continue to actively pursue policies to ensure respect for their obligations under international law with regard to all illegal Israeli practices and measures in

the Occupied Palestinian Territory, including East Jerusalem, particularly Israeli settlement activities and the exploitation of natural resources;

12. *Underscores*, in this regard, the call by the Security Council, in its resolution 2334 (2016), upon all States to distinguish, in their relevant dealings, between the territory of the State of Israel and the territories occupied since 1967;

13. *Requests* the Secretary-General to report to the General Assembly at its seventy-third session on the implementation of the present resolution, including with regard to the cumulative impact of the exploitation, damage and depletion by Israel of natural resources in the Occupied Palestinian Territory, including East Jerusalem, and in the occupied Syrian Golan, and with regard to the impact of such practices on the promotion of the Sustainable Development Goals,[8] and decides to include in the provisional agenda of its seventy-third session the item entitled "Permanent sovereignty of the Palestinian people in the Occupied Palestinian Territory, including East Jerusalem, and of the Arab population in the occupied Syrian Golan over their natural resources".

74th plenary meeting
20 December 2017

---

8 *See* resolution 70/1.

United Nations Human Rights Council Resolution A/HRC/RES/34/28 (Apr. 11, 2017)

United Nations
General Assembly
A/HRC/RES/34/28
Distr.: General
11 April 2017

Original: English
Human Rights Council
Thirty-fourth session
27 February–24 March 2017
Agenda item 7

Resolution adopted by the Human Rights Council on 24 March 2017

34/28. Ensuring accountability and justice for all violations of international law in the Occupied Palestinian Territory, including East Jerusalem

The Human Rights Council,

Guided by the purposes and principles of the Charter of the United Nations,

Recalling the relevant rules and principles of international law, including international humanitarian law and human rights law, in particular the Geneva Convention relative to the Protection of Civilian Persons in Time of War, of 12 August 1949, which is applicable to the Occupied Palestinian Territory, including East Jerusalem,

Recalling also the Universal Declaration of Human Rights and the other human rights covenants, including the International Covenant on Civil and Political Rights, the International Covenant on Economic, Social and Cultural Rights and the Convention on the Rights of the Child,

Recalling further the statement of 15 July 1999 and the declarations adopted on 5 December 2001 and on 17 December 2014 by the Conference of High Contracting Parties to the Fourth Geneva Convention on measures to enforce the Convention in the Occupied Palestinian Territory, including East

Jerusalem, at which the High Contracting Parties reaffirmed, inter alia, their commitment to uphold their obligation to ensure respect for the Convention in the Occupied Palestinian Territory, including East Jerusalem,

Recalling its relevant resolutions, including resolutions S-9/1 of 12 January 2009, 19/17 of 22 March 2012 and S-21/1 of 23 July 2014,

Recalling also the advisory opinion rendered on 9 July 2004 by the International Court of Justice on the legal consequences of the construction of a wall in the Occupied Palestinian Territory,

Expressing its appreciation to the independent commission of inquiry on the 2014 Gaza conflict, and all other relevant United Nations mechanisms, as well as the treaty bodies and other United Nations bodies, for their reports,

Recognizing the work of Palestinian, Israeli and international civil society actors and human rights defenders in documenting and countering violations of international law in the Occupied Palestinian Territory, including East Jerusalem,

Affirming the obligation of all parties to respect international humanitarian law and international human rights law,

Emphasizing the importance of the safety and well-being of all civilians, and reaffirming the obligation to ensure the protection of civilians in armed conflict,

Gravely concerned by reports regarding serious human rights violations and grave breaches of international humanitarian law, including possible war crimes, including the findings of the United Nations Fact-Finding Mission on the Gaza Conflict, of the United Nations independent international fact-finding mission to investigate the implications of Israeli settlements on the civil, political, economic, social and cultural rights of the Palestinian people throughout the Occupied Palestinian Territory, including East Jerusalem, of the independent commission of inquiry on the 2014 Gaza conflict, and of the boards of inquiry convened by the Secretary-General,

Condemning all violations of human rights and of international humanitarian law, and appalled at the widespread and unprecedented levels of destruction, death and human suffering caused in the Occupied Palestinian Territory, including East Jerusalem,

Stressing the urgency of achieving without delay an end to the Israeli occupation that began in 1967, and affirming that this is necessary in order to uphold human rights and international law,

Deploring the non-cooperation by Israel with all Human Rights Council fact-finding missions and the independent commission of inquiry on the 2014 Gaza conflict and the refusal to grant access to, and cooperate with, international human rights bodies and a number of United Nations special procedures seeking to investigate alleged violations of international law in the Occupied Palestinian Territory, including East Jerusalem,

Regretting the lack of implementation of the recommendations contained in the report of the independent commission of inquiry on the 2014 Gaza conflict,[1] the United Nations independent international fact-finding mission to investigate the implications of Israeli settlements on the civil, political, economic, social and cultural rights of the Palestinian people throughout the Occupied Palestinian Territory, including East Jerusalem, and the United Nations Fact-Finding Mission on the Gaza Conflict, which follows a pattern of lack of implementation of recommendations made by United Nations mechanisms and bodies,

Alarmed that long-standing systemic impunity for international law violations has allowed for the recurrence of grave violations without consequence, and stressing the need to ensure accountability for all violations of international humanitarian law and international human rights law in order to end impunity, ensure justice, deter further violations, protect civilians and promote peace,

Regretting the lack of progress in the conduct of domestic investigations in accordance with international law standards, and aware of the existence of numerous legal, procedural and practical obstacles in the Israeli civil and criminal legal system contributing to the denial of access to justice for Palestinian victims and of their right to an effective judicial remedy,

Emphasizing the need for States to investigate and prosecute grave breaches of the Geneva Conventions of 1949 and other serious violations of international humanitarian law, to end impunity, to uphold their obligations to ensure respect, and to promote international accountability,

Noting the accession by the State of Palestine on 2 January 2015 to the Rome Statute of the International Criminal Court,

1. *Welcomes* the report of the independent commission of inquiry on the 2014 Gaza conflict;[1]
2. *Calls upon* all duty bearers and United Nations bodies to pursue the implementation of the recommendations contained in the reports of the independent commission of inquiry on the 2014 Gaza conflict, the United Nations independent international fact-finding mission to investigate the implications of Israeli settlements on the civil, political, economic, social and cultural rights of the Palestinian people throughout the Occupied Palestinian Territory, including East Jerusalem,[2] and the United Nations

---

1 A/HRC/29/52.
2 A/HRC/22/63.

Fact-Finding Mission on the Gaza Conflict,[3] in accordance with their respective mandates;

3. *Notes* the importance of the work of the independent commission of inquiry on the 2014 Gaza conflict, the United Nations independent international fact-finding mission to investigate the implications of Israeli settlements on the civil, political, economic, social and cultural rights of the Palestinian people throughout the Occupied Palestinian Territory, including East Jerusalem, and the United Nations Fact-Finding Mission on the Gaza Conflict, and the information collected regarding grave violations in support of future accountability efforts, in particular information on alleged perpetrators of violations of international law;

4. *Emphasizes* the need to ensure that all those responsible for violations of international humanitarian law and international human rights law are held to account, through appropriate, fair and independent national or international criminal justice mechanisms, and to ensure the provision of effective remedy to all victims, including full reparations, and stresses the need to pursue practical steps towards these goals to ensure justice for all victims and to contribute to the prevention of future violations;

5. *Stresses* that all efforts to end the Israeli-Palestinian conflict should be grounded in respect for international humanitarian law and international human rights law, and should ensure credible and comprehensive accountability for all violations of international law in order to bring about sustainable peace;

6. *Calls upon* the parties concerned to cooperate fully with the preliminary examination of the International Criminal Court and with any subsequent investigation that may be opened;

7. *Denounces* all acts of intimidation and threats directed at civil society actors and human rights defenders involved in documenting and countering violations of international law and impunity in the Occupied Palestinian Territory, including East Jerusalem, and calls upon all States to ensure their protection;

8. *Calls upon* all States to promote compliance with international law, and all High Contracting Parties to the Fourth Geneva Convention to respect, and to ensure respect for, international humanitarian law in the Occupied Palestinian Territory, including East Jerusalem, in accordance with article 1 common to the Geneva Conventions, and to fulfil their obligations under articles 146, 147 and 148 of the said Convention with regard to penal sanctions, grave breaches and the responsibilities of the High

---

3   A/HRC/12/48.

Contracting Parties, including by ensuring that they do not become involved in internationally unlawful conduct;

9. *Recommends* that the General Assembly remain apprised of the matter until it is satisfied that appropriate action with regard to implementing the recommendations made by the United Nations Fact-Finding Mission on the Gaza Conflict in its report[3] has been or is being taken appropriately at the national or international levels to ensure justice for victims and accountability for perpetrators;
10. *Requests* the United Nations High Commissioner for Human Rights to report on the implementation of the present resolution to the Human Rights Council at its thirty-seventh session;
11. *Decides* to remain seized of the matter.

58th meeting

24 March 2017

[Adopted by a recorded vote of 30 to 2, with 15 abstentions. The voting was as follows:

In favour:

Bangladesh, Belgium, Bolivia (Plurinational State of), Botswana, Brazil, Burundi, China, Congo, Côte d'Ivoire, Cuba, Ecuador, Egypt, El Salvador, Ghana, Indonesia, Iraq, Kyrgyzstan, Mongolia, Nigeria, Philippines, Portugal, Qatar, Republic of Korea, Saudi Arabia, Slovenia, South Africa, Switzerland, Tunisia, United Arab Emirates, Venezuela (Bolivarian Republic of)

Against:

Togo, United States of America

Abstaining:

Albania, Croatia, Ethiopia, Georgia, Germany, Hungary, India, Japan, Kenya, Latvia, Netherlands, Panama, Paraguay, Rwanda, United Kingdom of Great Britain and Northern Ireland]

United Nations Human Rights Council Resolution A/HRC/RES/34/29 (Apr. 12, 2017)

United Nations
General Assembly
A/HRC/RES/34/29
Distr.: General
12 April 2017

Original: English
Human Rights Council
Thirty-fourth session
27 February–24 March 2017
Agenda item 7

Resolution adopted by the Human Rights Council on 24 March 2017

34/29. Right of the Palestinian people to self-determination

The Human Rights Council,

Guided by the purposes and principles of the Charter of the United Nations, in particular the provisions of Articles 1 and 55 thereof, which affirm the right of peoples to self-determination, and reaffirming the need for the scrupulous respect of the principle of refraining in international relations from the threat or use of force, as specified in the Declaration on Principles of International Law concerning Friendly Relations and Cooperation among States in accordance with the Charter of the United Nations, adopted by the General Assembly in its resolution 2625 (XXV) of 24 October 1970, and affirming the inadmissibility of acquisition of territory resulting from the threat or use of force,

Guided also by the provisions of common article 1 of the International Covenant on Economic, Social and Cultural Rights and the International Covenant on Civil and Political Rights, which affirms that all peoples have the right to self-determination,

Guided further by the International Covenants on Human Rights, the Universal Declaration of Human Rights and the Declaration on the Granting of

Independence to Colonial Countries and Peoples, in particular article 1 thereof, and by the provisions of the Vienna Declaration and Programme of Action, adopted on 25 June 1993 by the World Conference on Human Rights,[1] and in particular Part I, paragraphs 2 and 3, relating to the right of self-determination of all peoples and especially those subject to foreign occupation,

Recalling General Assembly resolutions 181 A and B (II) of 29 November 1947 and 194 (III) of 11 December 1948, and all other relevant United Nations resolutions, including those adopted by the General Assembly, the Commission on Human Rights and the Human Rights Council, that confirm and define the inalienable rights of the Palestinian people, particularly their right to self-determination,

Recalling also Security Council resolutions 242 (1967) of 22 November 1967, 338 (1973) of 22 October 1973, 1397 (2002) of 12 March 2002 and 1402 (2002) of 30 March 2002,

Taking note of General Assembly resolution 67/19 of 29 November 2012,

Reaffirming the right of the Palestinian people to self-determination in accordance with the provisions of the Charter, relevant United Nations resolutions and declarations, and the provisions of international covenants and instruments relating to the right to self- determination as an international principle and as a right of all peoples in the world, and emphasizing that this *jus cogens* norm of international law is a basic prerequisite for achieving a just, lasting and comprehensive peace in the Middle East,

Deploring the plight of millions of Palestine refugees and displaced persons who have been uprooted from their homes, and expressing deep regret about the fact that more than half of the Palestinian people continue to live in exile in refugee camps throughout the region and in the diaspora,

Affirming the applicability of the principle of permanent sovereignty over natural resources to the Palestinian situation as an integral component of the right to self- determination,

Recalling the conclusion of the International Court of Justice, in its advisory opinion of 9 July 2004, that the right to self-determination of the Palestinian people, which is a right *erga omnes*, is severely impeded by Israel, the occupying Power, through the construction of the wall in the Occupied Palestinian Territory, including East Jerusalem, which, together with the Israeli settlement enterprise and measures previously taken, results in serious violations of international humanitarian and human rights law, including the forcible transfer of Palestinians and Israeli acquisition of Palestinian land,

---

[1] A/CONF.157/23.

Considering that the right to self-determination of the Palestinian people is being violated further by Israel through the existence and ongoing expansion of settlements in the Occupied Palestinian Territory, including East Jerusalem,

Noting that the failure to bring the occupation to an end after 50 years heightens the international responsibility to uphold the human rights of the Palestinian people, and expressing its deep regret that the question of Palestine remains unresolved 70 years since the resolution on partition,

Reaffirming that the United Nations will continue to be engaged on the question of Palestine until the question is resolved in all its aspects in accordance with international law,

1. *Reaffirms* the inalienable, permanent and unqualified right of the Palestinian people to self-determination, including their right to live in freedom, justice and dignity and the right to their independent State of Palestine;
2. *Deeply regrets* the onset of the fiftieth year of the Israeli occupation, calls upon Israel, the occupying Power, to immediately end its occupation of the Occupied Palestinian Territory, including East Jerusalem, and reaffirms its support for the solution of two States, Palestine and Israel, living side by side in peace and security;
3. *Expresses grave concern* at the fragmentation and the changes in the demographic composition of the Occupied Palestinian Territory, including East Jerusalem, which are resulting from Israel's continuing construction and expansion of settlements, forcible transfer of Palestinians and construction of the wall, stresses that this fragmentation, which undermines the possibility of the Palestinian people realizing their right to self-determination, is incompatible with the purposes and principles of the Charter of the United Nations, and emphasizes in this regard the need for respect for and preservation of the territorial unity, contiguity and integrity of all of the Occupied Palestinian Territory, including East Jerusalem;
4. *Confirms* that the right of the Palestinian people to permanent sovereignty over their natural wealth and resources must be used in the interest of their national development, the well-being of the Palestinian people and as part of the realization of their right to self-determination;
5. *Calls upon* all States to ensure their obligations of non-recognition, non-aid or assistance with regard to the serious breaches of peremptory norms of international law by Israel, and also calls upon them to cooperate further to bring, through lawful means, an end to these serious breaches and a reversal of Israel's illegal policies and practices;
6. *Urges* all States to adopt measures as required to promote the realization of the right to self-determination of the Palestinian people, and to render

assistance to the United Nations in carrying out the responsibilities entrusted to it by the Charter regarding the implementation of this right;

7. *Decides* to remain seized of the matter.

58th meeting

24 March 2017

[Adopted by a recorded vote of 43 to 2, with 2 abstentions. The voting was as follows:

In favour:

Albania, Bangladesh, Belgium, Bolivia (Plurinational State of), Botswana, Brazil, Burundi, China, Congo, Côte d'Ivoire, Croatia, Cuba, Ecuador, Egypt, El Salvador, Ethiopia, Georgia, Germany, Ghana, Hungary, India, Indonesia, Iraq, Japan, Kenya, Kyrgyzstan, Latvia, Mongolia, Netherlands, Nigeria, Philippines, Portugal, Qatar, Republic of Korea, Rwanda, Saudi Arabia, Slovenia, South Africa, Switzerland, Tunisia, United Arab Emirates, United Kingdom of Great Britain and Northern Ireland, Venezuela (Bolivarian Republic of)

Against:

Togo, United States of America

Abstaining:

Panama, Paraguay]

United Nations Human Rights Council Resolution A/HRC/RES/34/30 (Apr. 11, 2017)

United Nations
General Assembly
A/HRC/RES/34/30
Distr.: General
11 April 2017

Original: English
Human Rights Council
Thirty-fourth session
27 February–24 March 2017
Agenda item 7

Resolution adopted by the Human Rights Council on 24 March 2017

34/30. Human rights situation in the Occupied Palestinian Territory, including East Jerusalem

The Human Rights Council,

Recalling the Universal Declaration of Human Rights, the International Covenant on Civil and Political Rights, the International Covenant on Economic, Social and Cultural Rights, the Convention on the Rights of the Child and the Optional Protocol thereto on the involvement of children in armed conflict, the Convention on the Elimination of All Forms of Discrimination against Women, the Convention against Torture and Other Cruel, Inhuman or Degrading Treatment or Punishment and the International Convention on the Elimination of All Forms of Racial Discrimination, and affirming that these human rights instruments, among others, are applicable to and must be respected in the Occupied Palestinian Territory, including East Jerusalem,

Recalling also relevant resolutions of the Human Rights Council,

Taking note of the recent reports of the Special Rapporteur on the situation of human rights in the Palestinian territories occupied since 1967,[1] and other relevant recent reports of the Human Rights Council,

Deeply regretting the onset of the fiftieth year of the Israeli occupation, and stressing the urgent need for efforts to reverse the negative trends on the ground and to restore a political horizon for advancing and accelerating meaningful negotiations aimed at the achievement of a peace agreement that will bring a complete end to the Israeli occupation that began in 1967 and the resolution of all core final status issues, without exception, leading to a peaceful, just, lasting and comprehensive solution of the question of Palestine,

Noting the accession by Palestine to several human rights treaties and the core humanitarian law conventions, and its accession on 2 January 2015 to the Rome Statute of the International Criminal Court,

Deploring Israel's recurrent practice of withholding Palestinian tax revenues,

Aware of the responsibility of the international community to promote human rights and ensure respect for international law,

Recalling the advisory opinion rendered on 9 July 2004 by the International Court of Justice, and recalling also General Assembly resolutions ES-10/15 of 20 July 2004 and ES-10/17 of 15 December 2006,

Noting in particular the Court's reply, including that the construction of the wall being built by Israel, the occupying Power, in the Occupied Palestinian Territory, including in and around East Jerusalem, and its associated regime are contrary to international law,

Reaffirming the principle of the inadmissibility of the acquisition of territory by force, and deeply concerned at the fragmentation of the Occupied Palestinian Territory, including East Jerusalem, through the construction of settlements, settler roads and the wall, and other measures that are tantamount to de facto annexation of Palestinian land,

Emphasizing the applicability of the Geneva Convention relative to the Protection of Civilian Persons in Time of War, of 12 August 1949, to the Occupied Palestinian Territory, including East Jerusalem, and reaffirming the obligation of the States parties to the Fourth Geneva Convention under articles 146, 147 and 148 with regard to penal sanctions, grave breaches and responsibilities of the High Contracting Parties,

Reaffirming that all States have the right and the duty to take actions in conformity with international human rights law and international humanitarian law to counter deadly acts of violence against their civilian population in order to protect the lives of their citizens,

---

1 A/71/554 and A/HRC/34/70.

Stressing the need for full compliance with the Israeli-Palestinian agreements reached within the context of the Middle East peace process, including the Sharm el-Sheikh understandings, and the implementation of the Quartet road map to a permanent two-State solution to the Israeli-Palestinian conflict,

Stressing also the importance of accountability in preventing future conflicts and ensuring that there is no impunity for violations and abuses, thereby contributing to peace efforts and avoiding the recurrence of violations of international law, including international humanitarian law and international human rights law,

Expressing grave concern at the continuing systematic violation of the human rights of the Palestinian people by Israel, the occupying Power, including that arising from the excessive use of force and military operations causing death and injury to Palestinian civilians, including children and women, and to non-violent, peaceful demonstrators and to journalists, including through the use of live ammunition; the arbitrary detention of Palestinians, some of whom have been detained for decades; the use of collective punishment; the closure of areas; the confiscation of land; the establishment and expansion of settlements; the construction of a wall in the Occupied Palestinian Territory in departure from the Armistice Line of 1949; the forcible displacement of civilians, including of Bedouin communities; the policies and practices that discriminate against and disproportionately affect the Palestinian population in the Occupied Palestinian Territory, including East Jerusalem; the discriminatory allocation of water resources between Israeli settlers, who reside illegally in the Occupied Palestinian Territory, and the Palestinian population of the said Territory; the violation of the basic right to adequate housing, which is a component of the right to an adequate standard of living; the destruction of property and infrastructure; and all other actions by it designed to change the legal status, geographical nature and demographic composition of the Occupied Palestinian Territory, including East Jerusalem,

Gravely concerned by the ongoing demolition by Israel, the occupying Power, of Palestinian homes and of structures provided as humanitarian aid, in particular in occupied East Jerusalem, including when carried out as an act of collective punishment in violation of international humanitarian law, the occurrence of which has escalated at unprecedented rates, and by the revocation of residence permits and the eviction of Palestinian residents of the City,

Deploring the conflict in and around the Gaza Strip in July and August 2014 and the civilian casualties caused, including the killing and injury of thousands of Palestinian civilians, including children, women and elderly persons, the widespread destruction of thousands of homes and of civilian infrastructure, including schools, hospitals, water sanitation and electricity networks, economic, industrial and agricultural properties, public institutions, religious sites and United Nations schools and facilities, the internal displacement of hundreds of thousands of civilians, and any violations of international law, including humanitarian and human rights law, in this regard,

Gravely concerned in particular about the disastrous humanitarian situation and the critical socioeconomic and security situations in the Gaza Strip, including that resulting from the prolonged continuous closures and severe economic and movement restrictions that in effect amount to a blockade, and from the continuing and vastly negative repercussions of the military operations between December 2008 and January 2009, in November 2012 and in July and August 2014, and about the firing of rockets into Israel,

Stressing that the situation in the Gaza Strip is unsustainable and that a durable ceasefire agreement must lead to a fundamental improvement in the living conditions of the Palestinian people in the Gaza Strip, including through the sustained and regular opening of crossing points, and ensure the safety and well-being of civilians on both sides,

Affirming the need to support the Palestinian national consensus Government in its assumption of full government responsibilities in both the West Bank and the Gaza Strip, in all fields, and through its presence at Gaza crossing points,

Expressing deep concern at the short- and long-term detrimental impact of such widespread destruction and the continued impediments to the reconstruction process on the human rights situation and on the socioeconomic and humanitarian conditions of the Palestinian civilian population, and calling upon the international community to step up its efforts in order to provide the Gaza Strip with the assistance that it requires,

Stressing the need to end immediately the closure of the Gaza Strip and for the full implementation of the Agreement on Movement and Access and the Agreed Principles for the Rafah Crossing, both of 15 November 2005, to allow for the freedom of movement of the Palestinian civilian population within and into and out of the Gaza Strip, while taking into account Israeli concerns,

Stressing also the need for all parties, in conformity with the relevant provisions of international humanitarian law, to cooperate fully with the United Nations and other humanitarian agencies and organizations and to ensure the safe and unhindered access of humanitarian personnel, and the delivery of supplies and equipment, in order to allow such personnel to perform efficiently their task of assisting affected civilian populations, including refugees and internally displaced persons,

Expressing deep concern at the Israeli policy of closures and the imposition of severe restrictions and checkpoints, several of which have been transformed into structures akin to permanent border crossings, other physical obstacles and a permit regime, which are applied in a discriminatory manner affecting the Palestinian population only and all of which obstruct the freedom of movement of persons and goods, including medical and humanitarian goods, throughout the Occupied Palestinian Territory, including East Jerusalem, and impair the Territory's contiguity, consequently violating the human rights of the Palestinian people and negatively affecting their socioeconomic and humanitarian situation, which remains dire in the Gaza Strip, and the efforts aimed at rehabilitating and developing the Palestinian economy,

Convinced that the Israeli occupation has gravely impeded the efforts to achieve sustainable development and a sound economic environment in the Occupied Palestinian Territory, including East Jerusalem, and expressing grave concern at the consequent deterioration of economic and living conditions,

Deploring all policies and practices whereby Israeli settlers, who reside illegally in the Occupied Palestinian Territory, including East Jerusalem, are accorded preferential treatment over the Palestinian population in terms of access to roads, infrastructure, land, property, housing, natural resources and judicial mechanisms, resulting in widespread human rights violations of Palestinians,

Emphasizing that the destruction of property and the forced displacement of Palestinian communities in the Occupied Palestinian Territory, including East Jerusalem, constitute, in all but the most limited cases as specified under international law, violations of the prohibitions on the destruction of property and on forcible transfers, respectively, under articles 53 and 49 of the Fourth Geneva Convention,

Deeply concerned at reports of the hampering and destruction of humanitarian assistance by Israel, contributing to a coercive environment that can lead to the forcible transfer of Palestinian civilians in the Occupied Palestinian Territory,

Expressing deep concern that thousands of Palestinians, including many children and women and elected members of the Palestinian Legislative Council, continue to be detained and held in Israeli prisons or detention centres under harsh conditions, including unhygienic conditions, solitary confinement, lack of proper medical care, denial of family visits and denial of due process, that impair their well-being, and expressing deep concern also at the ill-treatment and harassment of any Palestinian prisoner and all reports of torture,

Expressing deep concern also at the recent hunger strikes by numerous Palestinian prisoners in protest at the harsh conditions of their imprisonment and detention by the occupying Power, while taking note of the agreement reached in May 2012 on conditions of detention in Israeli prisons and calling for its full and immediate implementation,

Recalling the United Nations Standard Minimum Rules for the Treatment of Prisoners (the Nelson Mandela Rules) and the United Nations Rules for the Treatment of Women Prisoners and Non-custodial Measures for Women Offenders (the Bangkok Rules), and calling for respect for those rules,

Recalling also the prohibition under international humanitarian law of the deportation of civilians from occupied territories,

Deploring the practice of withholding the bodies of those killed, and calling for the release of the bodies that have not yet been returned to their relatives, in accordance with international humanitarian law and human rights law,

Expressing concern at the possible consequences of the enactment by Israel, the occupying Power, of military orders regarding the detention, imprisonment and deportation of Palestinian civilians from the Occupied Palestinian Territory, including East Jerusalem, and recalling in this regard the prohibition under international humanitarian law of the deportation of civilians from occupied territories,

Stressing the need for the protection of human rights defenders engaged in the promotion of human rights issues in the Occupied Palestinian Territory, including East Jerusalem, to allow them to carry out their work freely and without fear of attacks, harassment, arbitrary detention or criminal prosecution,

Convinced of the need for an international presence to monitor the situation, to contribute to ending the violence and protecting the Palestinian civilian population and to help the parties to implement the agreements reached, and in this regard recalling the positive contribution of the Temporary International Presence in Hebron,

Recognizing the continued efforts and tangible progress made in the Palestinian security sector, noting the continued cooperation that benefits both Palestinians and Israelis, in particular by promoting security and building confidence, and expressing the hope that such progress will be extended to all major population centres,

Emphasizing the right of all people in the region to the enjoyment of human rights as enshrined in the international human rights covenants,

1. *Stresses* the need for Israel, the occupying Power, to withdraw from the Palestinian territory occupied since 1967, including East Jerusalem, so as to enable the Palestinian people to exercise its universally recognized right to self-determination;
2. *Reiterates* that all measures and actions taken by Israel, the occupying Power, in the Occupied Palestinian Territory, including East Jerusalem, in

violation of the relevant provisions of the Geneva Convention relative to the Protection of Civilian Persons in Time of War, of 12 August 1949, and contrary to the relevant resolutions of the Security Council are illegal and have no validity;

3. *Demands* that Israel, the occupying Power, comply fully with the provisions of the Fourth Geneva Convention of 1949 and cease immediately all measures and actions taken in violation and in breach of the Convention;

4. *Calls for* urgent measures to ensure the safety and protection of the Palestinian civilian population in the Occupied Palestinian Territory, including East Jerusalem, in accordance with the relevant provisions of international humanitarian law and as called for by the Security Council in its resolution 904 (1994) of 18 March 1994;

5. *Demands* that Israel, the occupying Power, cease all practices and actions that violate the human rights of the Palestinian people, and that it fully respect human rights law and comply with its legal obligations in this regard, including in accordance with relevant United Nations resolutions;

6. *Reiterates* the need for respect for the territorial unity, contiguity and integrity of all of the Occupied Palestinian Territory and for guarantees of the freedom of movement of persons and goods within the Palestinian territory, including movement into and from East Jerusalem, into and from the Gaza Strip, between the West Bank and the Gaza Strip, and to and from the outside world;

7. *Also reiterates* the responsibility of Israel, the occupying Power, to respect the right to health of all persons within the Occupied Palestinian Territory and to facilitate the immediate, sustained and unfettered passage of humanitarian relief, including the access of medical personnel, their equipment, transport and supplies to all areas under occupation, including the Gaza Strip, and stresses the need for the unhindered passage of ambulances at checkpoints, especially in times of conflict;

8. *Demands* that Israel, the occupying Power, cease immediately its imposition of prolonged closures and economic and movement restrictions, including those amounting to a blockade on the Gaza Strip, which severely restricts the freedom of movement of Palestinians within, into and out of Gaza and their access to basic utilities, housing, education, work, health and an adequate standard of living via various measures, including import and export restrictions, that have a direct impact on livelihoods, economic sustainability and development throughout Gaza, aggravating the state of de-development in Gaza, and in this regard calls upon Israel to implement fully the Agreement on Movement and Access

and the Agreed Principles for the Rafah Crossing, in order to allow for the sustained and regular movement of persons and goods and for the acceleration of long overdue reconstruction in the Gaza Strip;

9. *Expresses grave concern* at the confiscation and damage by Israel of fishing nets in the Gaza Strip for which there is no discernible security justification;
10. *Condemns* all acts of violence, including all acts of terror, provocation, incitement and destruction, especially the excessive use of force by the Israeli occupying forces against Palestinian civilians, particularly in the Gaza Strip, where bombardment of populated areas has caused extensive loss of life and a vast number of injuries, including among thousands of children and women, massive damage and destruction to homes, economic, industrial and agricultural properties, vital infrastructure, including water, sanitation and electricity networks, religious sites and public institutions, including hospitals and schools, and United Nations facilities, and agricultural lands, and large-scale internal displacement of civilians, and the excessive use of force by the Israeli occupying forces against Palestinian civilians in the context of peaceful protests in the West Bank;
11. *Also condemns* the firing of rockets against Israeli civilian areas resulting in loss of life and injury;
12. *Calls upon* Israel to cease all violations of the right to education of Palestinians, including those stemming from restrictions on movement and incidents of harassment and attacks on school children and educational facilities by Israeli settlers and as a result of Israeli military action;
13. *Also calls upon* Israel to end all harassment, threats, intimidation and reprisals against human rights defenders and civil society actors who peacefully advocate for the rights of Palestinians in the Occupied Palestinian Territory, including by cooperating with United Nations human rights bodies, and underscores the need to investigate all such acts, to ensure accountability and effective remedies, and to take steps to prevent any further such threats, attacks, reprisals or acts of intimidation;
14. *Expresses deep concern* at the conditions of the Palestinian prisoners and detainees, including minors, in Israeli jails and detention centres, demands that Israel, the occupying Power, fully respect and abide by its international law obligations towards all Palestinian prisoners and detainees in its custody, and also expresses its concern at the continued extensive use of administrative detention, calls for the full implementation of the agreement reached in May 2012 for a prompt and independent

investigation into all cases of death custody, and also calls upon Israel to release immediately all Palestinian prisoners, including Palestinian legislators, detained in violation of international law;

15. *Calls for* urgent attention to the plight and the rights, in accordance with international law, of Palestinian prisoners and detainees in Israeli jails, including those on hunger strikes, and calls for respect for the United Nations Standard Minimum Rules for the Treatment of Prisoners (the Nelson Mandela Rules) and the United Nations Rules for the Treatment of Women Prisoners and Non-custodial Measures for Women Offenders (the Bangkok Rules);

16. *Calls upon* Israel to explicitly prohibit torture, including psychological torture and other cruel, inhuman or degrading treatment or punishment;

17. *Demands* that Israel cease its policy of transferring prisoners from the Occupied Palestinian Territory into the territory of Israel, and respect fully its obligations under article 76 of the Fourth Geneva Convention;

18. *Urges* Israel to ensure that any arrest, detention and/or trial of Palestinian children is in line with the Convention on the Rights of the Child, including by refraining from holding criminal proceedings against them in military courts that, by definition, fall short of providing the necessary guarantees to ensure respect for their rights and that infringe upon their right to non-discrimination;

19. *Deplores* the resumption by Israel of the policy of punitive home demolitions and the ongoing policy of revoking the residency permits of Palestinians living in East Jerusalem through various discriminatory laws, and the demolition of residential structures and the forced eviction of Palestinian families, in violation of their basic right to adequate housing and in violation of international humanitarian law;

20. *Expresses concern* at the Citizenship and Entry into Israel Law adopted by the Knesset, which suspends the possibility, with certain rare exceptions, of family reunification between Israeli citizens and persons residing in the Occupied Palestinian Territory, including East Jerusalem, thus adversely affecting the lives of many families;

21. *Demands* that Israel, the occupying Power, cease all of its settlement activities, the construction of the wall and any other measures aimed at altering the character, status and demographic composition of the Occupied Palestinian Territory, including in and around East Jerusalem, all of which have, inter alia, a grave and detrimental impact on the human rights of the Palestinian people and the prospects for a peaceful settlement;

22. *Also demands* that Israel, the occupying Power, comply with its legal obligations under international law, as mentioned in the advisory opinion rendered on 9 July 2004 by the International Court of Justice and as demanded by the General Assembly in its resolutions ES-10/15 of 20 July 2004 and ES-10/13 of 21 October 2003, and that it immediately cease the construction of the wall in the Occupied Palestinian Territory, including in and around East Jerusalem, dismantle forthwith the structure situated therein, repeal or render ineffective all legislative and regulatory acts relating thereto, and make reparation for all damage caused by the construction of the wall, which has had a grave impact on the human rights and the socioeconomic living conditions of the Palestinian people;
23. *Calls upon* Israel to immediately cease any demolitions or plans for demolitions that would result in the forcible transfer or forced eviction of Palestinians, particularly in the vulnerable areas of the Jordan Valley, the periphery of Jerusalem and the South Hebron Hills, to facilitate the return of those Palestinian communities already subjected to forcible transfer or eviction to their original dwellings and to ensure adequate housing and legal security of tenure;
24. *Urges* Israel to ensure that water resource allocation in the Occupied Palestinian Territory is not discriminatory and does not result in water shortages disproportionately affecting the Palestinian population of the West Bank, and to take urgent steps to facilitate the restoration of the water infrastructure of the West Bank, including in the Jordan Valley, affected by the destruction of the wells of local civilians, roof water tanks and other water and irrigation facilities under military and settler operation since 1967;
25. *Deplores* the illegal Israeli actions in occupied East Jerusalem, including home demolitions, evictions of Palestinian residents, excavations in and around religious and historic sites, and all other unilateral measures aimed at altering the character, status and demographic composition of the city and of the territory as a whole;
26. Expresses grave concern at:
    (*a*) The restrictions imposed by Israel that impede access of Christian and Muslim worshippers to holy sites in the Occupied Palestinian Territory, including East Jerusalem, and calls upon Israel to include guarantees for non-discrimination on grounds of religion or belief as well as for the preservation and peaceful access to all religious sites;

(b) The increasing tensions in occupied East Jerusalem and the wider region, including those stemming from attempts aimed at illegally changing the status quo of holy sites;

27. *Urges* Member States to continue to provide emergency assistance to the Palestinian people to alleviate the financial crisis and the dire socioeconomic and humanitarian situation, particularly in the Gaza Strip;
28. *Emphasizes* the need to preserve and develop the Palestinian institutions and infrastructure for the provision of vital public services to the Palestinian civilian population and the promotion of human rights, including civil, political, economic, social and cultural rights;
29. *Urges* all States and the specialized agencies and organizations of the United Nations system to continue to support and assist the Palestinian people in the early realization of their inalienable human rights, including their right to self-determination, as a matter of urgency, in the light of the onset of the fiftieth year of the Israeli occupation and the continued denial and violation of the human rights of the Palestinian people;
30. *Deplores* the persistent non-cooperation of Israel with special procedure mandate holders and other United Nations mechanisms, and stresses the need for Israel to abide by all relevant United Nations resolutions and to cooperate with the Human Rights Council, all special procedures and the Office of the United Nations High Commissioner for Human Rights;
31. *Requests* the High Commissioner to report on the implementation of the present resolution to the Human Rights Council, with a particular focus on the factors perpetuating the arbitrary detention of Palestinian prisoners and detainees in Israeli jails in consultation with the Working Group on Arbitrary Detention, at its thirty-seventh session;
32. *Decides* to remain seized of the matter.

58th meeting

24 March 2017

[Adopted by a recorded vote of 41 to 2, with 4 abstentions. The voting was as follows:

In favour:
Albania, Bangladesh, Belgium, Bolivia (Plurinational State of), Botswana, Brazil, Burundi, China, Côte d'Ivoire, Croatia, Cuba, Ecuador, Egypt, El

Salvador, Ethiopia, Georgia, Germany, Ghana, Hungary, India, Indonesia, Iraq, Japan, Kenya, Kyrgyzstan, Latvia, Mongolia, Netherlands, Nigeria, Philippines, Portugal, Qatar, Republic of Korea, Saudi Arabia, Slovenia, South Africa, Switzerland, Tunisia, United Arab Emirates, United Kingdom of Great Britain and Northern Ireland, Venezuela (Bolivarian Republic of)

Against:

Togo, United States of America

Abstaining:

Congo, Panama, Paraguay, Rwanda]

United Nations Human Rights Council Resolution A/HRC/RES/34/31 (Apr. 3, 2017)

United Nations
General Assembly
A/HRC/RES/34/31
Distr.: General
3 April 2017

Original: English
Human Rights Council
Thirty-fourth session
27 February–24 March 2017
Agenda item 7

Resolution adopted by the Human Rights Council on 24 March 2017

34/31. Israeli settlements in the Occupied Palestinian Territory, including East Jerusalem, and in the occupied Syrian Golan

The Human Rights Council,

Guided by the principles of the Charter of the United Nations, and affirming the inadmissibility of the acquisition of territory by force,

Reaffirming that all States have an obligation to promote and protect human rights and fundamental freedoms, as stated in the Charter and elaborated in the Universal Declaration of Human Rights, the International Covenants on Human Rights and other applicable instruments,

Recalling the relevant resolutions of the Commission on Human Rights, the Human Rights Council, the Security Council and the General Assembly reaffirming, inter alia, the illegality of the Israeli settlements in the occupied territories, including in East Jerusalem,

Recalling also Human Rights Council resolution 19/17 of 22 March 2012, in which the Council decided to establish an independent international fact-finding mission to investigate the implications of the Israeli settlements on the human rights of the Palestinian people throughout the Occupied Palestinian Territory, including East Jerusalem,

Reaffirming the applicability of the Geneva Convention relative to the Protection of Civilian Persons in Time of War, of 12 August 1949, to the Occupied Palestinian Territory, including East Jerusalem, and to the occupied Syrian Golan, and recalling the declarations adopted at the Conferences of High Contracting Parties to the Fourth Geneva Convention, held in Geneva on 5 December 2001 and 17 December 2014,

Noting the accession by Palestine to several human rights treaties and the core humanitarian law conventions, and its accession on 2 January 2015 to the Rome Statute of the International Criminal Court,

Affirming that the transfer by the occupying Power of parts of its own civilian population to the territory it occupies constitutes a breach of the Fourth Geneva Convention and relevant provisions of customary law, including those codified in Additional Protocol I to the four Geneva Conventions,

Recalling the advisory opinion rendered on 9 July 2004 by the International Court of Justice on the legal consequences of the construction of a wall in the Occupied Palestinian Territory, and recalling also General Assembly resolutions ES-10/15 of 20 July 2004 and ES-10/17 of 15 December 2006,

Noting that the International Court of Justice concluded, inter alia, that the Israeli settlements in the Occupied Palestinian Territory, including East Jerusalem, had been established in breach of international law,

Taking note of the recent relevant reports of the Secretary-General, the Office of the United Nations High Commissioner for Human Rights, the Special Committee to Investigate Israeli Practices Affecting the Human Rights of the Palestinian People and Other Arabs of the Occupied Territories and the treaty bodies monitoring compliance with the human rights treaties to which Israel is a party, and the recent reports of the Special Rapporteur on the situation of human rights in the Palestinian territories occupied since 1967,

Recalling the report of the independent international fact-finding mission to investigate the implications of the Israeli settlements on the civil, political, economic, social and cultural rights of the Palestinian people throughout the Occupied Palestinian Territory, including East Jerusalem,[1]

Expressing its grave concern at any action taken by any body, governmental or non-governmental, in violation of the Security Council and General Assembly resolutions relevant to Jerusalem,

Noting that Israel has been planning, implementing, supporting and encouraging the establishment and expansion of settlements in the Occupied

---

1 A/HRC/22/63.

Palestinian Territory, including East Jerusalem, since 1967, through, inter alia, the granting of benefits and incentives to settlements and settlers,

Recalling the Quartet road map to a permanent two-State solution to the Israeli-Palestinian conflict, and emphasizing specifically its call for a freeze on all settlement activity, including so-called natural growth, and the dismantlement of all settlement outposts erected since March 2001, and the need for Israel to uphold its obligations and commitments in this regard,

Taking note of General Assembly resolution 67/19 of 29 November 2012, by which, inter alia, Palestine was accorded the status of non-member observer State in the United Nations, and also of the follow-up report thereon of the Secretary-General,[2]

Aware that Israeli settlement activities involve, inter alia, the transfer of nationals of the occupying Power into the occupied territories, the confiscation of land, the destruction of property, including homes and projects funded by the international community, the forcible displacement of Palestinian civilians, including Bedouin families, the exploitation of natural resources, the conduct of economic activity for the benefit of the occupying Power, the disruption of the livelihood of protected persons and the de facto annexation of land, and other actions against the Palestinian civilian population and the civilian population in the occupied Syrian Golan that are contrary to international law,

Affirming that the Israeli settlement activities in the Occupied Palestinian Territory, including East Jerusalem, undermine regional and international efforts aimed at the realization of the two-State solution of Israel and Palestine, living side by side in peace and security within recognized borders, on the basis of the pre-1967 borders, and stressing that the continuation of these policies seriously endangers the viability of the two-State solution, undermining the physical possibility of its realization, and entrenching a one-State reality of unequal rights,

Noting in this regard that the Israeli settlements fragment the West Bank, including East Jerusalem, into isolated geographical units, severely limiting the possibility of a contiguous territory and the ability to dispose freely of natural resources, both of which are required for the meaningful exercise of Palestinian self-determination,

Noting that the settlement enterprise and the impunity associated with its persistence, expansion and related violence continue to be a root cause of many violations of the Palestinians' human rights, and constitute the main factors perpetuating Israel's belligerent occupation of the Palestinian Territory, including East Jerusalem, since 1967,

---

[2] A/67/738.

Condemning the continuation by Israel, the occupying Power, of settlement activities in the Occupied Palestinian Territory, including in East Jerusalem, in violation of international humanitarian law, relevant United Nations resolutions, the agreements reached between the parties and obligations under the Quartet road map, and in defiance of the calls by the international community to cease all settlement activities,

Deploring in particular the construction and expansion of settlements by Israel in and around occupied East Jerusalem, including its so-called E-1 plan, which aims to connect its illegal settlements around and further isolate occupied East Jerusalem, the continuing demolition of Palestinian homes and eviction of Palestinian families from the city, the revocation of Palestinian residency rights in the city and ongoing settlement activities in the Jordan Valley, all of which further fragment and undermine the contiguity of the Occupied Palestinian Territory,

Expressing grave concern at the continuing construction by Israel of the wall inside the Occupied Palestinian Territory, including in and around East Jerusalem, in violation of international law, and expressing its concern in particular at the route of the wall in departure from the Armistice Line of 1949, which is causing humanitarian hardship and a serious decline in socioeconomic conditions for the Palestinian people, is fragmenting the territorial contiguity of the Territory and undermining its viability, and could prejudge future negotiations by creating a fait accompli on the ground that could be tantamount to de facto annexation in departure from the Armistice Line of 1949, and make the two-State solution physically impossible to implement,

Deeply concerned that the wall's route has been traced in such a way to include the great majority of the Israeli settlements in the Occupied Palestinian Territory, including East Jerusalem,

Gravely concerned at all acts of violence, destruction, harassment, provocation and incitement by extremist Israeli settlers and groups of armed settlers in the Occupied Palestinian Territory, including East Jerusalem, against Palestinian civilians, including children, and their properties, including homes, agricultural lands and historic and religious sites, and the acts of terror carried out by several extremist Israeli settlers, which are a long-standing phenomenon aimed at, inter alia, displacing the occupied population and facilitating the expansion of settlements,

Expressing concern at ongoing impunity for acts of settler violence against Palestinian civilians and their properties, and stressing the need for Israel to investigate and to ensure accountability for all of these acts,

Aware of the detrimental impact of the Israeli settlements on Palestinian and other Arab natural resources, especially as a result of the confiscation of land and the forced diversion of water resources, including the destruction of orchards and crops and the seizure of water wells by Israeli settlers, and of the dire socioeconomic consequences in this regard, which precludes the Palestinian people from being able to exercise permanent sovereignty over their natural resources,

Noting that the agricultural sector, considered the cornerstone of Palestinian economic development, has not been able to play its strategic role because of the dispossession of land and the denial of access for farmers to agricultural areas, water resources and domestic and external markets owing to the construction, consolidation and expansion of Israeli settlements,

Aware that numerous Israeli policies and practices related to settlement activity in the Occupied Palestinian Territory, including East Jerusalem, create a system that privileges Israeli settlements and settlers, against the Palestinian people and in violation of their human rights,

Recalling Human Rights Council resolution 22/29 of 22 March 2013, in follow-up to the report of the independent international fact-finding mission to investigate the implications of Israeli settlements on the civil, political, economic, social and cultural rights of the Palestinian people throughout the Occupied Palestinian Territory, including East Jerusalem,

Recalling also the Guiding Principles on Business and Human Rights, which place responsibilities on all business enterprises to respect human rights by, inter alia, refraining from contributing to human rights abuses arising from conflict, and call upon States to provide adequate assistance to business enterprises to assess and address the heightened risks of abuses in conflict-affected areas, including by ensuring that their current policies, legislation, regulations and enforcement measures are effective in addressing the risk of business involvement in gross human rights abuses,

Noting that, in situations of armed conflict, business enterprises should respect the standards of international humanitarian law, and concerned that some business enterprises have, directly and indirectly, enabled, facilitated and profited from the construction and growth of the Israeli settlements in the Occupied Palestinian Territory,

Reaffirming the fact that the High Contracting Parties to the Geneva Convention relative to the Protection of Civilian Persons in Time of War, of 12 August 1949, undertook to respect and to ensure respect for the Convention in all circumstances, and that States should not recognize an unlawful situation arising from breaches of peremptory norms of international law,

Emphasizing the importance for States to act in accordance with their own national legislation on promoting compliance with international humanitarian law with regard to business activities that result in human rights abuses,

Concerned that economic activities facilitate the expansion and entrenchment of settlements, aware that the conditions of harvesting and production of products made in settlements involve, inter alia, the exploitation of the natural resources of the Occupied Palestinian Territory, including East Jerusalem, and calling upon all States to respect their legal obligations in this regard,

Aware that products wholly or partially produced in settlements have been labelled as originating from Israel, and concerned about the significant role that the production and trade of such products plays in helping to support and maintain the settlements,

Aware also of the role of private individuals, associations and charities in third States that are involved in providing funding to Israeli settlements and settlement-based entities, contributing to the maintenance and expansion of settlements,

Noting that a number of business enterprises have decided to disengage from relationships or activities associated with the Israeli settlements owing to the risks involved,

Expressing its concern at the failure of Israel, the occupying Power, to cooperate fully with the relevant United Nations mechanisms, in particular the Special Rapporteur on the situation of human rights in the Palestinian territories occupied since 1967,

1. *Reaffirms* that the Israeli settlements established since 1967 in the Occupied Palestinian Territory, including East Jerusalem, and in the occupied Syrian Golan are illegal under international law, and constitute a major obstacle to the achievement of the two-State solution and a just, lasting and comprehensive peace, and to economic and social development;

2. *Calls upon* Israel to accept the de jure applicability of the Geneva Convention relative to the Protection of Civilian Persons in Time of War, of 12 August 1949, to the Occupied Palestinian Territory, including East Jerusalem, and to the occupied Syrian Golan, to abide scrupulously by the provisions of the Convention, in particular article 49 thereof, and to comply with all its obligations under international law and cease immediately all actions causing the alteration of the character, status and demographic composition of the Occupied Palestinian Territory, including East Jerusalem, and the occupied Syrian Golan;

3. *Demands* that Israel, the occupying Power, immediately cease all settlement activities in all the Occupied Palestinian Territory, including East Jerusalem, and in the occupied Syrian Golan, and calls in this regard for the full implementation of all relevant resolutions of the Security Council, including, inter alia, resolutions 446 (1979) of 22 March 1979, 452

(1979) of 20 July 1979, 465 (1980) of 1 March 1980, 476 (1980) of 30 June 1980, 1515 (2003) of 19 November 2003 and 2334 (2016) of 23 December 2016;

4. *Also demands* that Israel, the occupying Power, comply fully with its legal obligations, as mentioned in the advisory opinion rendered on 9 July 2004 by the International Court of Justice, including to cease forthwith the works of construction of the wall being built in the Occupied Palestinian Territory, including in and around East Jerusalem, to dismantle forthwith the structure therein situated, to repeal or render ineffective forthwith all legislative and regulatory acts relating thereto, and to make reparation for the damage caused to all natural or legal persons affected by the construction of the wall;

5. *Condemns* the continuing settlement and related activities by Israel, including the expansion of settlements, the expropriation of land, the demolition of houses, the confiscation and destruction of property, the forcible transfer of Palestinians, including entire communities, and the construction of bypass roads, which change the physical character and demographic composition of the occupied territories, including East Jerusalem and the Syrian Golan, and constitute a violation of the Geneva Convention relative to the Protection of Civilian Persons in Time of War, of 12 August 1949, and in particular article 49 thereof;

6. *Also condemns* the construction of new housing units for Israeli settlers in the West Bank and around occupied East Jerusalem, as they seriously undermine the peace process and jeopardize the ongoing efforts by the international community to reach a final and just peace solution compliant with international law and legitimacy, including relevant United Nations resolutions, and constitute a threat to the two-State solution;

7. *Expresses its grave concern* at declarations by Israeli officials calling for the annexation of Palestinian land, and reaffirms the prohibition of the acquisition of territory resulting from the use of force;

8. *Also expresses its grave concern* at, and calls for the cessation of:
    (a) The operation by Israel of a tramway linking the settlements with West Jerusalem, which is in clear violation of international law and relevant United Nations resolutions;
    (b) The expropriation of Palestinian land, the demolition of Palestinian homes, demolition orders, forced evictions and "relocation" plans, the obstruction and destruction of humanitarian assistance and the creation of a coercive environment and unbearable living conditions by Israel in areas identified for the expansion and construction of settlements, and other practices aimed at the forcible

transfer of the Palestinian civilian population, including Bedouin communities and herders, and further settlement activities, including the denial of access to water and other basic services by Israel to Palestinians in the Occupied Palestinian Territory, including East Jerusalem, particularly in areas slated for settlement expansion, and including the appropriation of Palestinian property through, inter alia, the declaration of so-called "State lands", closed "military zones", "national parks" and "archaeological" sites to facilitate and advance the expansion or construction of settlements and related infrastructure, in violation of Israel's obligations under international humanitarian law and international human rights law;

(c) Israeli measures in the form of policies, laws and practices that have the effect of preventing Palestinians from full participation in the political, social, economic and cultural life of the Occupied Palestinian Territory, including East Jerusalem, and prevent their full development in both the West Bank and the Gaza Strip;

9. *Calls upon* Israel, the occupying Power:

(a) To end without delay its occupation of the territories occupied since 1967, to reverse the settlement policy in the occupied territories, including East Jerusalem and the Syrian Golan, and, as a first step towards the dismantlement of the settlement enterprise, to stop immediately the expansion of existing settlements, including so-called natural growth and related activities, to prevent any new installation of settlers in the occupied territories, including in East Jerusalem, and to discard its E-1 plan;

(b) To put an end to all of the human rights violations linked to the presence of settlements, especially of the right to self-determination, and to fulfil its international obligations to provide effective remedy for victims;

(c) To take immediate measures to prohibit and eradicate all policies and practices that discriminate against and disproportionately affect the Palestinian population in the Occupied Palestinian Territory, including East Jerusalem, by, inter alia, putting an end to the system of separate roads for the exclusive use of Israeli settlers, who reside illegally in the said territory, to the complex combination of movement restrictions consisting of the wall, roadblocks and a permit regime that only affects the Palestinian population, the application of a two-tier legal system that has facilitated the establishment and consolidation of the settlements, and other violations and forms of institutionalized discrimination;

(d) To cease the requisition and all other forms of unlawful appropriation of Palestinian land, including so-called "State land", and its allocation for the establishment and expansion of settlements, and to halt the granting of benefits and incentives to settlements and settlers;

(e) To put an end to all measures and policies resulting in the territorial fragmentation of the Occupied Palestinian Territory, including East Jerusalem, and which are isolating Palestinian communities into separate enclaves, and deliberately changing the demographic composition of the Occupied Palestinian Territory;

(f) To take and implement serious measures, including confiscation of arms and enforcement of criminal sanctions, with the aim of ensuring full accountability for, and preventing, all acts of violence by Israeli settlers, and to take other measures to guarantee the safety and protection of Palestinian civilians and Palestinian properties in the Occupied Palestinian Territory, including East Jerusalem;

(g) To bring to a halt all actions, including those perpetrated by Israeli settlers, harming the environment, including the dumping of all kinds of waste materials in the Occupied Palestinian Territory, including East Jerusalem, and in the occupied Syrian Golan, which gravely threaten their natural resources, namely water and land resources, and which pose an environmental, sanitation and health threat to the civilian population;

(h) To cease the exploitation, damage, cause of loss or depletion and endangerment of the natural resources of the Occupied Palestinian Territory, including East Jerusalem, and of the occupied Syrian Golan;

10. *Welcomes* the adoption of the European Union Guidelines on the eligibility of Israeli entities and their activities in the territories occupied by Israel since June 1967 for grants, prizes and financial instruments funded by the European Union since 2014;

11. *Urges* all States and international organizations to ensure that they are not taking actions that either recognize, aid or assist the expansion of settlements or the construction of the wall in the Occupied Palestinian Territory, including East Jerusalem, and to continue to actively pursue policies that ensure respect of their obligations under international law with regard to these and all other illegal Israeli practices and measures in the Occupied Palestinian Territory, including East Jerusalem;

12. *Reminds* all States of their legal obligations as mentioned in the advisory opinion of the International Court of Justice of 9 July 2004 on the legal

consequences of the construction of a wall in the Occupied Palestinian Territory, including not to recognize the illegal situation resulting from the construction of the wall, not to render aid or assistance in maintaining the situation created by such construction, and to ensure compliance by Israel with international humanitarian law as embodied in the Geneva Convention relative to the Protection of Civilian Persons in Time of War of 12 August 1949;

13. *Calls upon* all States:
    (a) To distinguish, in their relevant dealings, between the territory of the State of Israel and the territories occupied since 1967, including not to provide Israel with any assistance to be used specifically in connection with settlements in these territories with regard to, inter alia, the issue of trade, consistent with their obligations under international law;
    (b) To implement the Guiding Principles on Business and Human Rights in relation to the Occupied Palestinian Territory, including East Jerusalem, and to take appropriate measures to help to ensure that businesses domiciled in their territory and/or under their jurisdiction, including those owned or controlled by them, refrain from committing, contributing to, enabling or benefiting from the human rights abuses of Palestinians, in accordance with the expected standard of conduct in the Guiding Principles and relevant international laws and standards, by taking appropriate steps in view of the immitigable nature of the adverse impact of their activities on human rights;
    (c) To provide guidance to individuals and businesses on the financial, reputational and legal risks, including the possibility of liability for corporate involvement in gross human rights abuses and the abuses of the rights of individuals, of becoming involved in settlement-related activities, including through financial transactions, investments, purchases, procurements, loans, the provision of services, and other economic and financial activities in or benefiting Israeli settlements, to inform businesses of these risks in the formulation of their national action plans for the implementation of the Guiding Principles on Business and Human Rights, and to ensure that their policies, legislation, regulations and enforcement measures effectively address the heightened risks of operating a business in the Occupied Palestinian Territory, including East Jerusalem;
    (d) To increase monitoring of settler violence, with a view to promoting accountability;

14. *Calls upon* business enterprises to take all measures necessary to comply with their responsibilities under the Guiding Principles on Business and Human Rights and other relevant international laws and standards with respect to their activities in or in relation to the Israeli settlements and the wall in the Occupied Palestinian Territory, including East Jerusalem, and to avoid contributing to the establishment, maintenance, development or consolidation of Israeli settlements or the exploitation of the natural resources of the Occupied Palestinian Territory;
15. *Requests* that all parties concerned, including United Nations bodies, implement and ensure the implementation of the recommendations contained in the report of the independent international fact-finding mission to investigate the implications of Israeli settlements on the civil, political, economic, social and cultural rights of the Palestinian people throughout the Occupied Palestinian Territory, including East Jerusalem, and endorsed by the Human Rights Council through its resolution 22/29, in accordance with their respective mandates;
16. *Calls upon* the relevant United Nations bodies to take all necessary measures and actions within their mandates to ensure full respect for and compliance with Human Rights Council resolution 17/4 of 16 June 2011, on the Guiding Principles on Business and Human Rights and other relevant international laws and standards, and to ensure the implementation of the United Nations "Protect, Respect and Remedy" Framework, which provides a global standard for upholding human rights in relation to business activities that are connected with Israeli settlements in the Occupied Palestinian Territory, including East Jerusalem;
17. *Takes note* of the statement of the Working Group on the issue of human rights and transnational corporations and other business enterprises in follow-up to Human Rights Council resolution 22/29;
18. *Requests* the United Nations High Commissioner for Human Rights to report on the implementation of the provisions of the present resolution to the Human Rights Council at its thirty-seventh session;
19. *Decides* to remain seized of the matter.

58th meeting

24 March 2017

[Adopted by a recorded vote of 36 to 2, with 9 abstentions. The voting was as follows:

In favour:

Bangladesh, Belgium, Bolivia (Plurinational State of), Botswana, Brazil, Burundi, China, Congo, Côte d'Ivoire, Cuba, Ecuador, Egypt, El Salvador, Ethiopia, Germany, Ghana, India, Indonesia, Iraq, Japan, Kenya, Kyrgyzstan, Mongolia, Netherlands, Nigeria, Philippines, Portugal, Qatar, Republic of Korea, Saudi Arabia, Slovenia, South Africa, Switzerland, Tunisia, United Arab Emirates, Venezuela (Bolivarian Republic of)

Against:

Togo, United States of America

Abstaining:

Albania, Croatia, Georgia, Hungary, Latvia, Panama, Paraguay, Rwanda, United Kingdom of Great Britain and Northern Ireland]

SECTION C

Cases

Amicus Curaie, Submitted by Susan Akram (Redacted) (Sweden) (Jan. 20, 2017)

Legal Opinion in the Case
XX

A   Interest of Amicus Curiae

1. This brief *amicus curiae* is submitted by Susan M. Akram, Clinical Professor at Boston University School of Law (BUSL), and Director of the International Human Rights clinic at BUSL. Professor Akram has extensively researched, written, published and taught on the rights of Palestinian refugees under international law. Since 1993, she has taught International Refugee Law, International Human Rights Law, United States Immigration Law, and has supervised students representing immigrants and refugees in the United States and in international fora in the immigration and international human rights clinical programs. Prior to joining the faculty at BUSL, she was the director of two immigration and refugee programs, the Immigration Project of Public Counsel, a public interest law firm in Los Angeles, California, and the Political Asylum/Immigration Representation Project in Boston, Massachusetts. She was the interim director of the United States Refugee Resettlement Program after the first Gulf War, responsible for resettling thousands of refugees from the camps in Saudi Arabia during 1992–1993. She is a past recipient of a Fulbright Senior Scholarship, teaching and researching on Palestinian refugee rights at Al-Quds University in the West Bank; she has also taught international refugee law at the American University in Cairo as a distinguished visiting professor; and regularly teaches a course on Palestinian Refugees under International Law at Oxford University's Refugee Studies Centre.

2. Among her publications relating to the Palestinian-Israeli conflict and Palestinian refugees and international law are: Still Waiting for Tomorrow:

The Law and Politics of Unresolved Refugee Crises;[1] International Law and the Israeli-Palestinian Conflict;[2] The Arab-Israeli Conflict, entry in the Max Planck Encyclopedia of Public International Law;[3] Refugees and the Right of Return;[4] Temporary Protection as an Instrument for Implementing the Right of Return for Palestinian Refugees;[5] UNRWA and Palestinian Refugees;[6] and Reinterpreting Palestinian Refugee Rights under International Law.[7]

3. Professor Akram has provided expert opinion in many cases, including a detailed amicus curiae brief with Prof. Guy Goodwin-Gill in the first U.S. appeal in Palestinian cases on Article 1D at the Board of Immigration Appeals, a brief which has been widely cited and was published in the Journal of Palestine Studies.[8]

4. Among the publications produced by Professor Akram and her clinical students at the Boston University International Human Rights clinic are: Closing Protection Gaps: Handbook on Protection of Palestinian Refugees in States Signatories to the 1951 Refugee Convention;[9] Protecting Syrian Refugees: Laws, Policies and Global Responsibility-Sharing;[10] Tibet's Stateless Nationals III: The Status and conditions of Tibetan Refugees in India.[11]

---

1   Still Waiting for Tomorrow: The Law and Politics of Unresolved Refugee Crises (Susan M. Akram & Tom Syring, eds., 2014).
2   International Law and the Israeli-Palestinian Conflict (Susan M. Akram et al., eds., 2011).
3   Susan M. Akram & Michael Lynk, The Arab-Israeli Conflict, in Max Planck Encyclopedia of Public International Law (Rudiger Wolfrum ed., 2012).
4   Susan M. Akram, Refugees and the Right of Return, in Encyclopedia of the Israeli-Palestinian Conflict (Cheryl Rubenberg ed., 2010).
5   Susan M. Akram & Terry Rempel, Temporary Protection as an Instrument for Implementing the Right of Return for Palestinian Refugees, 22 B.U. Int'l L.J. 1 (2004).
6   Susan M. Akram, UNRWA and Palestinian Refugees, in The Oxford Handbook of Refugee & Forced Migration Studies (Elena Fiddian-Qasmiyeh et al., eds., 2014).
7   Susan M. Akram, Reinterpreting Palestinian Refugee Rights under International Law, in Palestinian Refugees and the Right of Return (Naseer Aruri, ed., 2001).
8   Susan M. Akram & Guy Goodwin-Gill, Brief Amicus Curiae on the Status of Palestinian Refugees under International Law, 11 Palestine Y.B. of Int'l L. (2000–1).
9   Closing Protection Gaps: Handbook on Protection of Palestinian Refugees in States Signatories to the 1951 Refugee Convention (Susan M. Akram & Nidal al-Azza, eds., 2d ed., 2015).
10 Susan M. Akram et al., *Protecting Syrian Refugees: Laws, Policies and Global Responsibility-Sharing* (2015), http://www.bu.edu/law/files/2015/09/SyriaReport.pdf.
11 Tibet Justice Center et al., *Tibet's Stateless Nationals III: The Status and conditions of Tibetan Refugees in India* (2016), http://www.tibetjustice.org/wp-content/uploads/2016/09/TJCIndiaReport2016.pdf.

5. This brief was written with the assistance of Boston University Human Rights Clinic Supervising Attorney Yoana Kuzmova and Boston University Law Students Arwa al-Ali, Dalia Fuleihan, Rima Mahmoud, Ryan Corbett, Noah Potash and Tessa Stillings.
6. The interest of amicus is in the proper application of international refugee and human rights law to Palestinian refugees, and in the development of a correct understanding of the international instruments that affect the rights and status of Palestinian refugees worldwide. Neither Professor Akram nor her students have received compensation or remuneration for this or any other interventions she has made in Palestinian refugee and asylum cases anywhere in the world.

B Summary of Argument

7. Palestinian refugees fall under a legal regime that is distinct from all other refugees in the world.[12] As such, they are covered by a series of special provisions that apply only to them and no other refugees. Their special status resulted from the decisions of the drafters of key international treaties to exclude Palestinian refugees from the mandate of the United Nations High Commissioner for Refugees (UNHCR) and the 1954 Convention on the Status of Stateless Persons, and to conditionally exclude them from the benefits of the 1951 Convention on the Status of Refugees.[13]
8. Three main reasons were behind the decision of United Nations (UN) delegates who drafted the special regime for Palestinian refugees to create a special regime for them. First, in 1948 and 1949, prior to the drafting of the Conventions on the status of Refugees and Stateless People, the UN had already established two agencies specifically for the Palestinian refugees, the United Nations Conciliation Commission on Palestine (UNCCP) and the United Nations Relief and Works Agency for Palestine Refugees (UNRWA), authorized to provide international protection and assistance to the refugees respectively.[14] Because two specialized agencies had already been established with exclusive mandates towards this

---

12 *See* Akram & Goodwin-Gill, *supra* note 8, at 190.
13 *See* Lex Takkenberg, The Status of Palestinian Refugees in International Law, 54–65 (1998).
14 *See* G.A. Res. 194 (III), ¶ 11, U.N. Doc. A/RES/48/194 (Dec. 11, 1948) [hereinafter G.A. Res. 194]; G.A. Res. 302 (IV), U.N. Doc. A/RES/49/302 (Dec. 8, 1949) [hereinafter G.A. Res. 302]; *see also* Akram & Guy-Goodwin, *supra* note 8, at 192–201; Takkenberg, *supra* note 13, at 21–32.

9. refugee population, the UN delegates deemed it duplicative and unnecessary for UNHCR to also have responsibility for the Palestinian refugees.¹⁵

9. Second, the UN delegates recognized that, unlike all other refugees who were under consideration at the time of drafting the UNHCR Statute, the Refugee and Stateless Persons Conventions, the Palestinians had become refugees because of action taken by the UN – the decision to partition Palestine through UNGA Res. 181, which led to the creation of Israel and the resulting flight of hundreds of thousands of Palestinian refugees.¹⁶ Hence, the UN had special responsibility to ensure a particular protection regime was in place to implement the durable solutions that the UN had already incorporated in the first resolutions it had passed concerning the Palestinian refugees. As the delegates recorded in the *travaux preparatoires* of the Refugee Convention, the Palestinian refugees should not be subsumed in a regime designed for all other refugees, as the UN had particular responsibility for them.¹⁷

10. Third, the UN Resolutions that established the UNCCP and UNRWA had set up a specific formulation required to reach a durable solution for these refugees – return to their homes and lands, restitution of their properties, and compensation for their losses – and it was the UN that was responsible for ensuring implementation of this formula for the entire population of Palestinians.¹⁸ Until that durable solution formula was implemented, Palestinians as an entire category were to remain the responsibility of the UN as a special category of 'refugees.'

11. It is only with this historical context in mind that the 'Palestinian clauses' of Article 1D in the Refugee Convention, Article 1 in the Convention on Stateless Persons, and Paragraph 7(c) of the UNHCR Statute can be understood. This context also clarifies the bifurcated mandate of UNRWA/UNCCP (and today, UNHCR), and its consequences for the Palestinian refugee at issue in this case.¹⁹

12. It is the opinion of this amicus that the European Court of Justice (ECJ), in El Kott v. B.A.H, has articulated an incorrect interpretation of Article 1D.

---

15   See Takkenberg, *supra* note 13, at 61.
16   *Id.* at 62.
17   *Id.*
18   See G.A. Res. 194, *supra* note 14; G.A. Res. 302, *supra* note 14.
19   See 1951 Convention Relating to the Status of Refugees, art. 1D, July 28, 1951, 189 U.N.T.S. 150 [hereinafter 1951 Refugee Convention]; 1954 Convention relating to the Status of Stateless Persons, art. 1, Sept. 28, 1954, 360 U.N.T.S. 117 [hereinafter 1954 Stateless Convention]; Statute of the Office of the United Nations High Commissioner for Refugees, G.A. 428 (V), ¶ 7(c), U.N. Doc. A/RES/428(V) (Dec. 14, 1950).

A historically accurate analysis of the drafting of Art. 1D that takes into account treaty interpretive rules compels a finding that is a Palestinian refugee who cannot be returned to Gaza or to any of the countries of his previous residence without violation of Sweden's obligations under international law.

C Statement of Facts

The relevant facts, are as follows.

13. XX is a Palestinian refugee born to parents who are Palestinian refugees originally registered as such in Gaza. XX's family originated from what is now Israel but fled to Gaza in 1948, where they registered with the United Nations Relief and Works Agency for Palestine Refugee (UNRWA). Before 1967, the family left for Kuwait because of the instability and conflict in Gaza. After the Israeli invasion of Gaza in 1967, the family could not return.
14. XX was born in Kuwait in __, but as a Palestinian refugee he and his family were not entitled to permanent residence or citizenship in Kuwait, under Kuwaiti law. During the first Gulf War, in 1992, along with several thousand other Palestinians, XX and his family were expelled to Iraq.
15. As a result of the second Gulf War and the U.S. invasion of Iraq, Palestinians in Iraq were targeted for persecution and extreme violence, and thousands of Palestinians fled Iraq, primarily to Syria and Jordan. XX fled from Iraq to Syria in 2009, but was neither registered with, nor received any assistance from UNRWA in Syria. He arrived in Sweden that same year.
16. XX has never been to Gaza, and he cannot go to Gaza because of entry restrictions. He does not have any valid documents entitling him to enter Gaza, but his family remains registered as 'Palestine refugees' with UNRWA in Gaza.

D The Legal Status of Palestinian Refugees under International Law

17. *Amicus curiae* submits below a brief review of the historical background, legal framework and treaty interpretation of the international refugee status of Palestinians under the 1951 Refugee Convention and 1967 Protocol, and EU Council Directive 2004/83 purporting to incorporate Article 1D into EU law.

Brief Historical Background of the Palestinian Refugee Problem

18. The origins of the Palestinian refugee problem – relevant to understanding the status of Palestinians as refugees and stateless persons today – are in the international recognition of Palestinians as a people attached to a territory whose right to self-determination was legally recognized by the end of World War I. This recognition was derived from the British government's commitment to the Sherif of Mecca that if the Arab provinces of the Ottoman Empire in the Levant joined the Allied forces in the war against the Ottomans, the Allies would secure the independence of the Arab states, including Palestine. The Arabs joined the Allied cause against the Ottomans based on this commitment, memorialized in the Hussein-McMahon letters.[20]

19. In June 1919, following World War I, the Covenant of the League of Nations, Article 22, recognized the "people" of Palestine, comprising at the time approximately 670,000 Arabs and approximately 56,000 Jews (approximately 90% and 9% of the population respectively), as entitled to independence after a period of League supervision under the trusteeship of Great Britain. Britain was to administer this trusteeship as a 'Class A' Mandate, pending full independence once the process for independent administration was complete. The Palestine Mandate was formalized by the League Council in July 1922.[21]

20. Palestinians were recognized as a distinct nationality in the Treaty of Lausanne of August 6, 1924. Under the Treaty, all Ottoman nationals who were habitual residents of Palestine as of that date were automatically recognized as nationals of the Palestinian state. The British Mandate government passed the Palestinian Citizenship Order (1925), implementing the Treaty and giving precise definitions of the 'nationals' of Palestine.[22] It issued thousands of Palestinian passports under 'Article 1 or 3 of the Palestinian Citizenship Order, 1925–41,' which were recognized around the world. British and other foreign courts – including those of Israel – recognized 'Palestinian' as a distinct nationality up until 1950, when Israel revoked the British nationality legislation.[23]

21. Palestinian nationality legislation recognized both Arabs and Jews who were Ottoman Nationals and habitual residents in Palestine as of the date

---

20 Akram & Lynk, *supra* note 3, at ¶ 12.
21 *Id.* at ¶ 16.
22 Mutaz Qafisheh, The International Law Foundations of Palestinian Nationality: A Legal Examination of Palestinian Nationality under the British Rule 97–109 (2007).
23 *R. v. Ketter* [1940] 1 K.B. 787.

of the Lausanne Treaty (August 6, 1924) as Palestine Nationals, without discrimination as to race, religion or language. This definition was incorporated and expanded as the basis for who was a 'Palestine/Palestinian refugee' for purposes of all subsequent UN resolutions, the UN agencies responsible for Palestinian refugees, and the treaties and instruments governing their status. It remains the internationally-recognized definition of Palestinian national status until today, despite subsequent developments.[24]

22. Jewish immigration to Palestine was facilitated by the British Mandate government as a response to the rise of Hitler and persecution of Jews across Europe, and to the commitment of the British Cabinet to a 'national home for the Jewish people' in Palestine. This commitment was a British cabinet endorsement of a letter submitted to it by Lord Balfour in 1917, seeking the government's support for a Jewish claim in Palestine. The letter, though endorsed by the British cabinet, was defeated in both houses of Parliament when put to a vote the same year. Nevertheless, influential Zionists succeeded in pressuring the British cabinet to incorporate the substance of the Declaration into the Mandate administration in order to allow unrestricted Jewish immigration, and pressure the Mandatory government to protect Jewish immigrants' interests over those of the native Palestinians in the territory.[25]

23. British policies that favored Jewish immigration; massive fraudulent land transfers from Palestinian landholders to Zionist organizations; and Zionist terrorism to force recognition of a Jewish homeland, resulted in armed conflict throughout Palestine by 1945. Under the Balfour commitment, Jewish immigration to Palestine increased dramatically against the wishes of the native Palestinians, and by 1947 Jews numbered 600,000 while Palestinians were 1,200,000. The vast majority of Jews were recent immigrants during the Mandate.[26]

24. Following the bombings of British personnel and institutions by Zionist terrorist gangs, the British announced the early termination of their Mandate responsibilities and in early April 1947, turned the problem over to the newly-established United Nations.[27] The UN debated several

---

24 Qafisheh, *supra* note 22, at 5.
25 Akram, *Refugees and the Right of Return*, *supra* note 4, at 1233–34.
26 United Nations Special Committee on Palestine, *Report to the General Assembly*, U.N. Doc. A/364, Ch. II, para. 12 (Sept. 3 1947) [hereinafter UNSCOP Report].
27 Akram & Lynk, *supra* note 3, at ¶ 24.

proposals submitted to the General Assembly, and voted by a narrow margin to divide the territory of historic Palestine into two states.[28]

25. UN General Assembly Resolution 181(II) of 29 November 1947 proposed to divide Palestine into a 'Jewish' and an 'Arab' state with economic union between them. Based on the Report of the UN Special Committee on Palestine (UNSCOP), the territorial division would give the 'Arab' state a population of 725,000 Palestinians and 10,000 Jews, while the 'Jewish' state would comprise 498,000 Jews and 407,000 Palestinians as well as 90,000 Arab Bedouins. Jerusalem was to be internationalized under UN auspices, and would have a population of 100,000 Jews and 105,000 Arabs.[29]

26. Although Jews constituted only 1/3 of the population and owned no more than 7% of the land, Resolution 181 proposed allocating 55% of Mandate Palestine to the bare majority of Jews in the 'Jewish' state, while 44% of Palestine was allocated to the overwhelming majority of Palestinians in the 'Arab' state. The UN sought to reconcile the massive land theft this would precipitate by incorporating a series of pre-conditions to recognizing the two states into Resolution 181 and requiring a one-year period of UN supervision to ensure these prerequisites were met.[30]

27. Resolution 181 required each of the two states to enact a Constitution guaranteeing equal rights, including minority religious and political rights, prior to statehood recognition. Individuals from either state would be free to choose in which state they would be citizens. No provision permitted forcible transfer of anyone from one to another state. Jerusalem was to be a *corpus separatum* under international trusteeship, and freedom of movement and economic union was to be established between the two entities. When these requirements were met, independence was to be granted by 1 August 1948.[31]

28. None of these preconditions were met, and the Zionist militias expelled or forced hundreds of thousands of Palestinians to flee from areas allocated to the 'Jewish' state and areas allocated to the Arab state through a campaign of fear, terror and massacres. Approximately 730,000 Palestinians became refugees in neighboring states by the time Israel declared its

---

28 *See* G.A. Res. 181 (II), U.N. Doc. A/RES/181 (II) (Nov. 29, 1947) [hereinafter G.A. Res. 181].
29 Akram & Lynk, *supra* note 3, at ¶ 26.
30 G.A. Res. 181, *supra* note 28.
31 Akram & Lynk, *supra* note 3, at ¶ 26.

state, in a territory comprising 78% of historic Palestine (well beyond the 55% allocated in Res. 181) on 15 May 1948.[32]

29. Immediately after declaring its state, Israel implemented policies and interim legislation to prevent Palestinian refugees from returning, and to lay claim to Palestinian land. The series of plans included "Retroactive Transfer: A Scheme for the Solution of the Arab Question in the State of Israel," implementing measures to destroy Palestinian population centers; settle Jews in Arab areas; and pass legislation prohibiting refugees from returning to their homes and lands.[33]

30. Another series of regulations and laws known as 'Absentee Property' laws were also passed, which defined Palestinians who had left for even short periods to flee the fighting as 'absentees.' Once defined as such, their homes and lands were declared 'absentee property' and confiscated by the state. Another set of laws declared Palestinians remaining on their lands as 'present absentees,' and also subject to land confiscation. Various laws subsequently converted these absentee properties into 'Israel lands,' which could only be held in perpetuity for the benefit of Jews.[34]

31. In 1952, Israel passed its Citizenship/Nationality Law, which retroactively repealed Palestinian citizenship as incorporated in the Palestine British Citizenship law of 1925. The Israeli Nationality Law recognized all Jewish immigrants to Palestine as entitled to Israeli nationality, but placed such stringent conditions on the eligibility of Palestinians that few could qualify. The law also recognized any Jew from anywhere in the world as automatically eligible for Israeli nationality. Moreover, only Jewish nationals were entitled to the use and benefit of confiscated Palestinian properties that became 'Israel lands.'[35]

32. Thus, "through its laws of nationality, citizenship, and land regulation, Israel denationalized the majority of Palestinian Arabs from the nationality of their homeland; permanently expropriated Arab lands, homes, and collective properties; and created an entire population of stateless persons."[36]

33. As the massive Palestinian refugee population flooded into Lebanon, Jordan, Syria, Egypt and the West Bank (held by Jordan) and Gaza (held by Egypt), the UN took on direct responsibility for them. In Resolution

---

32 *Id.* at ¶ 27.
33 Susan M. Akram, Reframing the Right of Return, in International Law and the Israeli-Palestinian Conflict 17 (Susan M. Akram et al., eds., 2011).
34 Akram, *Refugees and the Right of Return, supra* note 4, at 1239.
35 *Id.*
36 *Id.*

194 of 11 December 1948, the General Assembly established the United Nations Conciliation Commission on Palestine (UNCCP), which took over the mandate of the first UN Mediator on Palestine, Count Folke Bernadotte, who had just been assassinated by the Zionist terrorist group, the Stern Gang.[37]

34. The UNCCP had a multi-pronged mandate concerning Palestine and the Palestinians. It was entrusted with mediating and resolving all 'outstanding issues between the parties.' It was also entrusted with the mandate of 'international legal protection' towards the refugees according to the precise durable solution spelled out in Paragraph 11 of the Resolution itself.[38]

35. Res. 194 does not include a definition of the Palestinian refugees for whom the UNCCP was responsible. However, the UNCCP was instructed on the definition of 'Palestine refugee' through a series of Working Papers authored by the UN Secretariat during the drafting of Res. 194, and incorporated in the UNCCP's *Analysis of paragraph 11 of the General Assembly's Resolution of 11 December 1948*, authored by its Legal Advisor.[39]

36. The *Analysis* states that the terms of Resolution 194 cover categories of persons collectively called 'Palestinian refugees' including: 1. 'persons of Arab origin who, after 29 November 1947, left territory at present under the control of the Israel authorities and who were Palestinian citizens at that date'; 2. 'stateless persons of Arab origin who after 29 November 1947 left the aforementioned territory where they had been settled up to that date'; 3. 'Persons of Arab origin who left the said territory after 6 August 1924 and before 29 November 1947 and who were Palestinian citizens at that time'; and 4. 'persons of Arab origin who left the territory in question before 6 August 1924 and who, having opted for Palestinian citizenship, retained that citizenship up to 29 November 1947.'[40]

37. In sum, the definition included the entire population of Arab Palestinians whose Palestinian nationality dated back to the 1924 Treaty of Lausanne and their progeny, as well as habitual residents of Palestine at the time of the Partition Resolution who left the area that became Israel after 29 November 1947 and subsequently became stateless; and anyone whose citizenship derived from the Lausanne Treaty but had left Palestine

---

37 Akram, *Reframing the Right of Return, supra* note 33, at 29.
38 G.A. Res. 194, *supra* note 14.
39 Analysis of paragraph 11 of the General Assembly's Resolution of 11 December 1948, U.N. Doc. A/AC/25/W/45 (May 15, 1950).
40 Akram, *UNRWA and Palestinian Refugees, supra* note 6, at 231–32.

before 29 November 1947. The definition also included internally displaced persons – not relevant for the purposes of this brief.[41]

38. The UNCCP was required to facilitate the durable solution incorporated in Res. 194, para. 11, to the entire category of 'Palestinian refugees' as defined above. Paragraph 11 instructs that the Palestinian refugees are to be permitted to return to their homes at the 'earliest practicable date,' compensation for lost property should be paid to those not choosing to return, and for other property loss or damage under international legal principles. The paragraph instructs the UNCCP to achieve these obligations.[42] The drafting history of this paragraph indicates that each clause was carefully crafted to be consistent with existing international law principles regarding the rights of refugees to return to their homes, to obtain restitution for confiscated property, and to obtain compensation for all losses.[43]

39. On December 8, 1949, one year after establishing the UNCCP and giving it a specific mandate of *refugee protection*, the UN General Assembly passed Resolution 302(IV) establishing the United Nations Relief and Works Agency for Palestine Refugees (UNRWA), with a complementary mandate of *refugee assistance*. Taking over from a series of *ad hoc* agencies that had been providing humanitarian assistance to the massive Palestinian refugee populations, UNRWA was initially established for a three-year period to provide relief to almost one million needy refugees in the five main host areas.[44]

40. UNRWA inherited the rolls of needy refugees from predecessor agencies, and consolidated its criteria for who would be eligible for its services in its Eligibility Regulations. UNRWA's initial working definition for a Palestine refugee was "a needy person who, as a result of the war in Palestine, has lost his home and his means of livelihood."[45] This category was later expanded to include 'Displaced Persons' who were forced to leave their homes in the 1967 conflict.[46]

---

41 *See* Terry M. Rempel, *The United Nations Conciliation Commission for Palestine, Protection, and a Durable Solution for Palestinian Refugees*, Badil Information & Discussion Brief (June 2000), http://www.badil.org/phocadownload/Badil_docs/bulletins-and-briefs/Brief-No.5.pdf.
42 *See* Akram, Reinterpreting Palestinian Refugee Rights under International Law, *supra* note 7.
43 Akram & Lynk, *supra* note 3, at ¶ 98 & ff.
44 G.A. Res. 302, *supra* note 14.
45 Don Peretz, *Who is a Refugee?*, 2 Palestine-Israel J. (1995).
46 *Id.*

41. UNRWA's current Consolidated Eligibility and Registration Instructions (CERI) define Palestine refugees as 'persons whose normal place of residence was Palestine during the period 1 June 1946 to 15 May 1948, and who lost both home and means of livelihood as a result of the 1948 conflict.' 'Palestine refugees' are the largest group registered with UNRWA, but not the only category eligible for UNRWA services.[47] UNRWA only operates in five designated host territories: Jordan, Lebanon, Syria, the West Bank and Gaza.[48]

42. UNRWA's refugee definition was initially a subcategory of the UNCCP-defined group of Palestine refugees who were 'in need.' However, UNRWA's refugee definition is not connected to legal protection, but covers groups and categories of vulnerable Palestinian refugees who are registered on the basis of need for humanitarian aid. This humanitarian assistance today includes food assistance, but also education, health provision, social services, microfinance and microenterprise development. It does not, however, have a mandate to provide legal protection, nor does it claim to or have any authority to provide access to durable solutions for the Palestinian refugees to whom it provides services.[49]

The Drafting History of the 'Palestinian Clauses' in the 1951 Refugee Convention and Related Instruments

43. While the Palestinian refugee tragedy was unfolding with the direct engagement of the UN, the General Assembly was also engaged in drafting the first comprehensive international treaty governing the rights of refugees and obligations of states towards them. The drafting history of this treaty, the 1951 Refugee Convention, along with the Statute of the UNHCR – the Agency to be entrusted with protection of refugees defined under the Convention[50] – is critical to understanding the status of Palestinians as refugees today.

44. The General Assembly's designates drafted the Refugee Convention in three stages between January 1950–July 1951. Initially, the UN considered the problem of refugees together with stateless and displaced persons, and contemplated a single treaty that would govern the rights of all three categories of post-World-War vulnerable populations, and define states' obligations towards them. The proposal for a single treaty dissolved during the debates, as states could not reach consensus on key issues,

---

47 Akram, *UNRWA and Palestinian Refugees*, supra note 6, at 232.
48 Id.
49 Id.
50 1951 Refugee Convention, supra note 19, at preamble.

and the decision was made to draft a separate treaty for each group. Nevertheless, the initial draft proposed to the General Assembly was for all three categories.[51]

45. The Ad Hoc Committee on Statelessness and Related Problems prepared the first Draft Convention Relating to the Status of Refugees in January of 1950, incorporating a consensus definition of refugee which included prior groups and categories of refugees from earlier instruments and a new, individualized definition based on the well-founded fear of persecution criteria.[52]

46. The individualized definition, which became the international definition of refugee incorporated in Article 1A(2) of the Refugee Convention, defines a refugee as any individual unable or unwilling to return to his country due to a well-founded fear of persecution for reasons of race, religion, nationality, membership of a particular social group or political opinion. The Refugee Convention restricted this definition to post-World War II refugees from Europe, who were the main refugees of concern to the UN.[53]

47. When the Draft Convention was debated in the Third Committee of the General Assembly in December, 1950 along with the draft Statute of the UNHCR, the refugee definitions were heavily debated. The *travaux preparatoires* indicate that the Palestinian refugee problem consumed much of the delegates' discussions. During this phase, the Arab delegates submitted an amendment to the Draft UNHCR Statute stating that: "The mandate of the High Commissioner's Office shall not extend to categories of refugees at present placed under the competence of other organs or agencies of the United Nations."[54]

48. Although not included in the draft amendment, the drafting history is clear that this clause referred only to Palestinian refugees. The reasons for the amendment were also made clear in the discussion. The concern was that if the definition of refugee was to be broadened to others than the European World War refugees, then Palestinians had to be excluded, as they had already been provided for through two previously-established UN organs, UNCCP and UNRWA.[55]

---

51 Paul Weis, The Refugee Convention 1951: The Traveux Preparatories Analyzed with a Commentary 17, http://www.unhcr.org/4ca34be29.pdf.
52 *Id.* at 32.
53 *See* 1951 Refugee Convention, *supra* note 19, at art. 1(A)(2).
54 Takkenberg, *supra* note 13, at 61.
55 Weis, *supra* note 51, at 108–09.

49. As the Lebanese delegate stated, the UN had special responsibility towards the Palestinians as they were the only refugees who had become refugees as a "direct result of a decision taken by the United Nations itself ... The Palestine refugees were therefore a direct responsibility on the part of the United Nations and could not be placed in the general category of refugees ... Furthermore, the obstacle to their repatriation was not dissatisfaction with their homeland, but the fact that a Member of the United Nations was preventing their return."[56]

50. The delegate from Saudi Arabia confirmed the relationship of the refugee definition in the Refugee Convention with the durable solution already incorporated for Palestinian refugees in Res. 194, para. 11. He stated: "The Arab States desired that [Palestine] refugees should be aided pending their repatriation, repatriation being the only real solution of their problem ... Pending a proper settlement [of the Arab-Israeli conflict], the Palestine refugees should continue to be granted a separate and special status."[57]

51. The UNHCR Statute was adopted by UNGA Res. 428(V) on 14 December 1950, and included the slightly amended clause as proposed by the Arab states. Paragraph 7(c) of the Statute states that the Agency's competence shall not extend to persons 'who continue to receive from other organs or agencies of the United Nations protection or assistance.'[58]

52. This 'exclusion clause' was also incorporated into the Refugee Convention as the first sentence of Article 1D. The first sentence of Article 1D states: "This Convention shall not apply to persons who are at present receiving from organs or agencies of the United Nations other than the United Nations High Commissioner for Refugees protection or assistance."[59]

53. The exclusion clause was further incorporated into the Draft Protocol on Stateless Persons, discussed by the General Assembly during the December 1950 debates. At the same time, the General Assembly decided to convene a Conference of Plenipotentiaries to complete both the Convention Relating to the Status of Refugees and the Protocol on Stateless Persons.[60]

54. The *travaux* reveal that during the last phase of the drafting of the Convention at the Conference of Plenipotentiaries on the Status of

---

56 *Id.* at 257; Takkenberg, *supra* note 13, at 62.
57 Takkenberg, at 62; Akram, *UNRWA and Palestinian Refugees, supra* note 6.
58 1951 Refugee Convention, *supra* note 19, at art. 1(D).
59 *Id.*
60 Takkenberg, *supra* note 13, at 185.

Refugees and Stateless Persons in Geneva from 2–25 July 1951, the Palestinian refugee issue was again debated. The Arab delegates realized that their exclusion clause was problematic and risked defeating the very purpose of the 'separate and special' regime that had been established. The Egyptian delegate proposed a second amendment in order, as he stated "to make sure that Arab refugees from Palestine, who were still refugees when the organs or agencies of the United Nations at present providing them with protection or assistance ceased to function, would automatically come within the scope of the Convention."[61]

55. The second amendment passed at the very end of the drafting process, and the final language incorporated as Article 1D of the Refugee Convention appears as:

> This Convention shall not apply to persons who are at present receiving from organs or agencies of the United Nations other than the United Nations High Commissioner for Refugees protection or assistance.
>
> When such protection or assistance has ceased for any reason, without the position of such persons being definitively settled in accordance with the relevant resolutions adopted by the General Assembly of the United Nations, these persons shall *ipso facto* be entitled to the benefits of this Convention.[62]

56. While the Conference adopted the 1951 Refugee Convention in July of that year, it decided to table the draft Protocol on Stateless Persons for later consideration. However, the final Convention on the Status of Stateless Persons, which was adopted three years later, retained the first (exclusion) sentence regarding Palestinians. The provision appears in Art. 1 of that treaty as: "This Convention shall not apply: (i) To persons who are at present receiving from organs or agencies of the United Nations other than the United Nations High Commissioner for Refugees protection or assistance so long as they are receiving such protection or assistance."[63] The second sentence was not included in the 1954 Stateless Persons Convention.

57. The second sentence was also not included in the UNHCR Statute, which the General Assembly had already passed six months prior to the adoption

---

61 *Id.* at 64.
62 For the assertion that the second clause of Art. 1D was added very late in the drafting process, *see* Takkenberg, *supra* note 13, at 67.
63 1954 Stateless Convention, *supra* note 19.

of the Refugee Convention. Paragraph 7(c) of the Statute has only the clause which excludes Palestinians from the mandate of the UNHCR. Para. 7(c) states: "... the competence of the High Commissioner.... shall not extend to a person: ... (c) Who continues to receive from other organs or agencies of the United Nations protection or assistance."[64]

58. Unfortunately, because the second sentence was drafted so late, there was no time to correct the inconsistencies between the first and second sentences. Hence, the ambiguities left in the meaning of the various clauses of the Article can only be understood with reference to the drafting history itself.

The Meaning of the Two Clauses of Article 1D under Treaty Interpretive Rules in Light of the Drafting History

59. The ambiguities in Article 1D are: a) Who are the 'persons' referred to who are excluded by the first sentence and included by the second? b) What is the time period indicated by the term 'at present receiving'? c) Which are the 'organs or agencies of the United Nations' referred to in the first sentence? d) What is the meaning of the terms 'protection' and 'assistance' in both sentences? e) What is the meaning of the terms in the second sentence: 'ceased for any reason,' 'position ... being definitively settled in accordance with relevant UNGA resolutions', *ipso facto,* and 'the benefits of this Convention'?

60. The key inconsistency in Article 1D is the discrepancy between the reference to 'protection or assistance' in the first sentence and 'protection or assistance' in the second sentence.

61. Correctly interpreting Article 1D requires application of the Vienna Convention on the Law of Treaties (VCLT), which governs these treaty provisions. Article 31 of the VCLT provides, in relevant part:

   1. A treaty shall be interpreted in good faith in accordance with the ordinary meaning to be given to the terms of the treaty in their context and in the light of its object and purpose ...

   4. A special meaning shall be given to a term if it is established that the parties so intended....[65]

62. Article 32 of the VCLT provides:

Recourse may be had to supplementary means of interpretation, including the preparatory work of the treaty and the circumstances of its conclusion, in order to confirm the meaning resulting from the application

---

64 Statute of the Office of the United Nations High Commissioner for Refugees, *supra* note 19, at. ¶ 7.
65 Vienna Convention on the Law of Treaties, art. 31, May 23, 1969, 1155 U.N.T.S. 331.

of article 31, or to determine the meaning when the interpretation according to article 31: (a) leaves the meaning ambiguous or obscure; or (b) leads to a result which is manifestly absurd or unreasonable.[66]

63. The VCLT requires reference to the *travaux preparatoires* of Article 1D and its related provisions to clarify the ambiguities and inconsistencies, as well as the 'special meaning' of terms used by the drafters by reference to historical and prior legal documents that define and interpret those terms.

The Convention Shall Not Apply to 'Persons' ...

64. Article 1D's reference to 'persons'[67] rather than 'refugees' indicates that the refugee definition in Art. 1A was not the criterion to be applied to determine the status of Palestinian refugees. The balance of the Refugee Convention refers to 'refugees,' meaning those defined as such under Art. 1A.[68] The drafting history, described above, clarifies that only Palestinian refugees, defined by reference to the categories of Palestinians covered by Res. 194 and the mandate of the UNCCP, are the 'persons' referred to in Art. 1D.[69] Thus, the 'persons' for purposes of Art. 1D are all those Palestinians meeting the group or category definition under Res. 194, and not the individualized definition of refugee found in Art. 1A(2).

... at present receiving from organs or agencies of the UN other than the UNHCR ...

65. The time to which the 'at present' language refers is the time of application of the provision to a particular refugee; in other words, the time of adjudication of each Palestinian claim to refugee status. The *travaux*, the drafting papers of UNGA Res. 194 and its companion UN Legal Counsel opinions and the UN Secretariat interpretive papers make clear that the purpose of establishing the UNCCP, UNRWA and the 'special' regime for Palestinian refugees was to ensure that Palestinians received protection and assistance at all times.[70] Hence, as long as they were receiving *both* aspects of international attention from the UN, they were not covered by the Refugee Convention, nor would they need the protection or assistance of the third international refugee agency, the UNHCR. Any past time would be irrelevant to this obvious purpose. The European Court of

---

66 *Id.* at art. 32.
67 *See* 1951 Refugee Convention, *supra* note 19, at art. 1D.
68 *Id.* at art. 1A.
69 Takkenberg, *supra* note 13, at 60–62, 90.
70 *Id.* at 64–65.

Justice has confirmed this conclusion in both *Bolbol* and *El Kott*,[71] reversing the opposite conclusion reached in the UK case of *Ibrahim Said v. The Secretary of State for the Home Department* (Oct. 26, 2012).[72]

66. The only organs or agencies 'other than the UNHCR' referenced in the *travaux* with regard to this provision were UNRWA and UNCCP. The point of establishing UNCCP and UNRWA was to ensure that Palestinians would receive international protection and humanitarian assistance through two agencies with complementary but distinct competencies towards this refugee population.[73]

'... protection or assistance'... in the first and second sentences

67. Although the terms 'protection' and 'assistance' were used interchangeably with regard to the two agencies, UNCCP and UNRWA, it is clear from the *travaux* that the drafters understood the distinct mandates of each one. UNCCP, the first UN agency established exclusively for Palestinians, was given a mandate of international protection, and charged with carrying out a specified durable solution incorporated into its founding Resolution 194 in Para. 11.[74] UNCCP's mandate covered all 'Palestinian refugees' defined in specified categories in the working papers and notes of the UNCCP Secretariat and the Legal Advisor, discussed above.[75] The General Assembly gave the UNCCP an indefinite mandate, anticipating that it would continue functioning until it was able to implement the durable solution required in Res. 194, para. 11 – return to their homes, restitution of their properties, and compensation for their losses.[76]

68. UNRWA, in contrast, established a year later, was given a mandate of only humanitarian assistance, to be provided to a subset of the Palestinian population defined for Res. 194 who were 'in need.'[77] The UN gave UNRWA a short-term, three-year mandate, anticipating that the UNCCP would accomplish its task and the refugees would return home in the near future.[78]

---

71 C-31/09, Bolbol v. Bevándorlási és Állampolgársági Hivatal, 2010 E.C.R. I-05539; C-364/11[hereinafter Bolbol]; El Kott v. Bevándorlási és Állampolgársági Hivatal,, C-364/11 (CJEU 2012). (CJEU 2012) [hereinafter El Kott].
72 Ibrahim Said v. The Secretary of State for the Home Department, [2012] UKUT 00413(IAC).
73 Badil, 'Closing Protection Gaps: Handbook on Protection of Palestinian Refugees in States Signatories to the 1951 Refugee Convention' (BADIL Resource Center for Palestinian Residency and Refugee Rights, 2005), at 28–35.
74 G.A. Res. 194, *supra* note 14.
75 *Id.*
76 *Id.*
77 G.A. Res. 302, *supra* note 14.
78 *Id.* at ¶ 6.

69. Thus, the drafters referred to the term 'protection' as shorthand for what the UNCCP was providing, while the term 'assistance' referred to what UNRWA was offering the Palestinian refugees. Both were necessary to fully provide for the legal and quotidian needs of the refugees; together they formed the 'special' regime referred to in the *travaux*.

70. The disjunctive 'or' in this clause is more ambiguous in light of the clear purpose set out in the drafting history outlined above. The 'or' in the first sentence is inconsistent with the disjunctive 'or' in the first clause of the second sentence, but the inconsistency is explained by a drafting error occurring because of the two sentences being proposed as amendments at different times during the drafting process.[79] The separate timing of the amendments, and the purpose for each of them, is explained above.[80]

71. The inconsistency between the language of the first sentence ('at present receiving ... protection or assistance') and the language of the second sentence ('when such protection or assistance has ceased') was noted, but not corrected in time for the vote on the adoption of the Convention.[81] Thus, a literal reading of the disjunctive (under Article 31 of VCLT)[82] in the first sentence would mean that Palestinian refugees are to be excluded from the 1951 Convention regime as long as they are receiving *either* protection *or* assistance, while the second sentence would mean they are to be re-included in the Convention regime if either protection *or* assistance has failed.[83]

72. However, such a reading violates Art. 32 of the VCLT,[84] as it leads to an absurd result, and one which would defeat the object and purpose of Art. 1D. Reading the two clauses as above would make them mutually exclusive: Palestinian refugees cannot both be excluded if they receive either protection or assistance and included if they receive either protection or assistance. In other words, the second sentence would simply have the effect of duplicating the first.

73. The only way to reconcile these two sentences, in light of the provision's object and purpose, is by understanding what was meant by the 'special' regime for Palestinian refugees. The special regime established through two UN agencies was intended to provide both international legal protection and humanitarian assistance until the specified durable solution

---

79   See Takkenberg, *supra* note 13, at 63–67.
80   See *infra* ¶¶ 43–58.
81   Takkenberg, *supra* note 13, at 67.
82   See Vienna Convention on the Law of Treaties, *supra* note 65, at art. 31.
83   1951 Refugee Convention, *supra* note 19.
84   See Vienna Convention on the Law of Treaties, *supra* note 65, at art. 32.

of Para. 11 was achieved.⁸⁵ Thus, the second sentence as a whole is best understood as a contingent inclusion clause – Palestinian refugees were to be re-included in the Refugee Convention regime if *either prong* of this special regime were to fail.

74. Reading the 'protection or assistance' clauses with the rest of Art. 1D in drafting context reveals that Palestinians were to be automatically re-included under the Refugee Convention *if* the protection provided by UNCCP *or* the humanitarian assistance provided by UNRWA were to fail for any reason whatsoever AND the required durable solution set down by the UN had not been achieved for them. That is, such persons are to continue to receive the status of 'Palestinian refugees' if either protection or assistance ceased for whatever reason, and their status as an entire group was unresolved according to the provisions under UNGA 194, para. 11.

75. In short, the context clarifies that the drafters meant 'This Convention shall not apply to persons at present receiving ... protection *and* assistance' in the first sentence, and "When such protection or assistance has ceased ...' in the second sentence. Another way of understanding the drafters' intent is to attach the disjunctive in the first sentence to the reference to 'organs or agencies ... providing protection [or] assistance,' rather than attaching the disjunctive to 'at present receiving ...' Both of these are correct interpretations in light of the object and purpose and the interpretive rules of the VCLT.

When such protection or assistance has ceased for any reason ...

76. This clause reinforces the interpretation above that Palestinian refugees were to be re-included into the Refugee Convention regime if *either* assistance *or* protection had ceased from one or other of the agencies established for them without achieving the required durable solution.

77. This contingency was met by the mid-1950s with the cessation of UNCCP protection activities towards the Palestinian refugees. The UNCCP ceased most of its protection activities between the mid-1950's and early 1960's, both due to its inability to accomplish what it was entrusted to do to bring about the durable solution for the refugees – implement return, restitution and compensation – and its inability to achieve the other aspect of its mandate – resolve the outstanding issues between the parties to the Arab-Israeli conflict.⁸⁶

---

85 *See* United Nations Secretariat, *UNCCP Memorandum on Relations Between UNRWA and UNCCP*, (Mar. 30, 1950) U.N. Doc. A/AC.25/W/42.
86 Badil, *supra* note 73, at 28–33.

78. Recognizing that the UNCCP was unable to achieve the main purpose for its establishment, the UNGA passed a series of measures that reduced its funding, and for all intents and purposes the Agency became defunct. However, the UNCCP continues to exist *de jure*, comprising three UN States Parties (Turkey, France and the United States) with an office in the UN in New York, which issues yearly Progress Reports that indicate its inability to achieve its mission.[87]

79. The UNCCP's inability to provide any meaningful protection for Palestinians, despite its continued legal existence, satisfies the 'for any reason' clause, and should have triggered the re-inclusion of Palestinian refugees into the Convention regime fifty years ago. From that time on, Palestinian refugees as a group or category have had no UN agency mandated to implement the key aspect of international protection – durable solutions – that the UNCCP was established to ensure, and hence, one of the two prongs of their special regime long since ceased to function.[88]

… without the position of such persons being definitively settled in accordance with the relevant resolutions adopted by the General Assembly of the United Nations …

80. The meaning of this clause is completely clear from the discussions in the *travaux* reviewed above. The definition of Palestinian/Palestine refugee, the agencies comprising the 'special' regime for them, and the terms of the durable solution prescribed by the UN had been established under Resolutions 194 and 302(IV), passed in 1948 and 1949 respectively.[89] These were clearly the frame of reference for the Convention drafters.[90]

81. Specifically, the 'definitive settlement' referred to Para. 11 of Res. 194, which incorporated the UN's consensus of the durable solution that had to be implemented for Palestinian refugees. That only 'return, restitution and compensation,' as described in Para. 11 would satisfy the rights of the refugees and obligation of the UN towards them is also clarified in the remarks of the delegates who drafted Art. 1D.[91]

… these persons shall ipso facto be entitled to the benefits of this Convention.…

82. The final *ipso facto* clause reinforces the interpretation that Palestinian refugees falling under the group definition of UNGA Res. 194, for whom either protection or assistance has ceased for any reason whatsoever, and

---

[87] *Id.* at 31.
[88] *Id.* at 28–33.
[89] *See* G.A. Res. 194, *supra* note 14; G.A. Res. 302, *supra* note 14.
[90] Takkenberg, *supra* note 13, at 64–65.
[91] *See* G.A. Res. 194, *supra* note 14.

whose durable solution of return, restitution and compensation has not been achieved, are to *automatically* be covered by the provisions of the Refugee Convention.

83. Since the meaning of *ipso facto* is 'by that fact alone,' it would be absurd to interpret the clause to mean that Palestinians who satisfy the pre-conditions for inclusion in the Convention as an entire group or category would then only qualify to have their status assessed under the individual criteria of Art. 1A(2).

84. Interpreting the phrase, the 'benefits of [the] Convention' requires a close reading of the Refugee Convention itself. The Convention establishes certain standards of treatment and benefits to be granted to refugees, which increase over time and as the refugee's legal status becomes more permanent in the host country.[92]

85. The core non-derogable obligation is *non-refoulement*, enshrined in Art. 33 of the Convention.[93] The *non-refoulement* principle applies from the recognition of a refugee's status until such time as she is granted asylum or more permanent status under the adjudicating state's domestic law. The Refugee Convention places no greater obligation on states than to grant a refugee *non-refoulement* for as long as the risk to her life or freedom continues – or *non-refoulement through time*.[94]

86. There is no indication in either Art. 1D or its drafting history that the phrase 'the benefits of this Convention' was intended to provide Palestinian refugees any different treatment from other Convention refugees once they qualify for re-inclusion in the Convention regime. Hence, the only obligation on host states under this clause is to provide, at minimum, *non-refoulement through time*. States are free to grant any additional status and rights beyond *non-refoulement* according to the Convention scheme of greater rights over time, and consistent with their domestic law.

87. However, the second sentence of Art. 1D changes the conditions which trigger when a Palestinian refugee can no longer be considered a refugee; in other words, the application of the cessation clauses in the Refugee Convention differs with regard to Palestinian refugees.

The Refugee Convention Cessation and Exclusion Clauses

88. A person otherwise meeting the refugee definition is not entitled to the benefits of the 1951 Convention if she falls under one of the exclusion or cessation clauses in Articles 1C, 1E and 1F.

---

92 Badil, *supra* note 73, at 44.
93 *See* 1951 Refugee Convention, *supra* note 19, at art. 33.
94 Badil, *supra* note 73, at 45.

89. Before examining these provisions, it is important to understand that even if some of the cessation or exclusion clauses apply to Palestinian refugees, they remain refugees with regard to the rights and obligations concerning the durable solution of return, housing and property restitution, and compensation under the terms of Res. 194, Para. 11.[95]

90. Article 1C, the cessation clause that applies to all other refugees under the terms of the Convention, states: "This Convention shall cease to apply to any person *falling under the terms of Section A* ..."[96] Palestinian refugees do not fall under Section A of the Convention, but under Section D; hence, the normal cessation clauses of Art. 1C (1)-(6) do not apply to them.

91. Article 1E states: "This Convention shall not apply to a person who is recognized by the competent authorities of the country in which he has taken residence as having the rights and obligations which are attached to the possession of the nationality of that country."[97] Although Palestinians would be covered by this provision, its application must be assessed in each individual case, taking into account the lack of permanent status available to Palestinians in Arab host states, their status as stateless persons, and the lack of a UN Agency or mechanism to provide protection or durable solutions to them.

92. Article 1F excludes from the benefits of the Refugee Convention persons who have committed war crimes, crimes against humanity and other serious crimes.[98] Palestinians who are also covered by this provision would be undeserving of the protections of the Convention. Amicus knows of no facts that would indicate Art. 1F applies to XX.

E The European Court of Justice's Interpretation of Article 1D in *El Kott* is Inconsistent with the Plain Language, Drafting History and Object and Purpose of the Provision

93. Article 12 of Directive 2004/83 incorporates Article 1D into binding European Union law.[99] The ECJ has interpreted the EU Directive incorporating Article 1D in two recent cases. In the first case, *Bolbol v.*

---

95 *Id.* at 53.
96 1951 Refugee Convention, *supra* note 19, at art. 1C.
97 *Id.* at art. 1E.
98 *Id.* at art. 1F.
99 Council Directive 2004/83, art. 12(1)(a), 2004 O.J. (L 304) (EC).

Bevandorlasi es Allampolgarsagi Hivatal (*Bolbol I*) decided on June 17, 2010, the ECJ addressed several of the ambiguities in Article 1D. It found that the phrase 'at present' meant the time of adjudication of the claim to refugee status – in other words, the present time. It then interpreted the phrase 'receiving ... protection or assistance' as meaning that "a person receives protection or assistance from an agency of the United Nations other than UNHCR, when that person has actually availed himself of that protection or assistance." Since the applicant, Mrs. Bolbol, a Palestinian from Gaza, was not registered with UNRWA, she had not "availed herself of the protection or assistance from UNRWA."[100]

94. Two years later, the ECJ heard the second case, *El Kott v. Bevándorlási és Állampolgársági Hivatal*, in which it addressed the two questions left open by the Court in *Bolbol*: when 'protection or assistance' is deemed to have ceased, and what are the 'benefits of the Convention' under the second sentence of 1D.

95. This case involved a group of stateless Palestinian refugees from Lebanon who were denied refugee status in Hungary.[101] The Palestinian refugees were registered with UNRWA in Lebanon prior to arriving in Hungary. Their reasons for leaving the UNRWA area included threats and arson to El Kott's home, among other things. In this case, the court made the following ruling:

> [C]essation of protection or assistance from organs or agencies of the United Nations other than the High Commission for Refugees (HCR) 'for any reason' includes the situation in which a person who, after actually availing himself of such protection or assistance, ceases to receive it for a reason beyond his control and independent of his volition.... The second sentence of Article 12(1)(a) of Directive 2004/83 must be interpreted as meaning that ... the fact that someone is *ipso facto* 'entitled to the benefits of [the] directive' means that that Member State must recognize him as a refugee within the meaning of Article 2(c) of the directive and that person must automatically be granted refugee status, provided always that he is not caught by Article 12(1)(b) or (2) and (3) of the directive.[102]

96. In *El Kott*, the ECJ found that UNRWA was unable to meaningfully provide protection to the Palestinian refugees in Lebanon, and that Hungary

---

100 *Bolbol, supra* note 71, at ¶ 55.
101 *El Kott, supra* note 71.
102 *Id.*

was therefore required to grant them refugee status.[103] The ECJ's interpretation in *El Kott* and in the earlier case of *Bolbol* both determined that actual UNRWA registration or eligibility for UNRWA registration was definitive proof of 'Palestinian refugee' status.[104]

97. The Migration Court of Appeal in Sweden issued a decision in accordance with *El Kott* when it interpreted the application of Article 1D to a Palestinian refugee from Syria.[105] In this case, a Palestinian refugee ("A") was initially denied refugee status by the Migration Court because it did not find she had demonstrated that she was a refugee as there was no well-founded fear of persecution. Additionally, the Court claimed that A's temporary residence status in Sweden is the reason UNRWA's aid has ceased. A's appeal to the Migration Court of Appeal claimed she was entitled to refugee status because she was registered with UNRWA and had been receiving aid from them ever since she was a child. She fled a refugee camp in Syria which was administered by UNRWA and claimed she was unable to return due to individual and general danger. Since she was unable to return to Syria, she was unable to avail herself of UNRWA's assistance, therefore entitling her to refugee status under Article 1D.[106]

98. The Migration Court of Appeal, relying on *El Kott*, granted A refugee status. It stated that, in terms of analyzing UNRWA assistance, the circumstances surrounding the cessation of its assistance needed to be considered, such as whether the person in question was forced to leave due to a serious threat to personal safety and whether UNRWA did not have the "ability to guarantee living conditions its duties demand."[107] The Migration Court of Appeal concluded that A was entitled to refugee status because UNRWA assistance ceased when she left Syria and, considering the prevailing armed conflict in Syria, A was unable to return.[108]

99. These interpretations of the questions raised under Article 1D are inconsistent with the plain language, drafting history and object and purpose of the provision with regard to the status of Palestinians as refugees and stateless persons under international law.

100. First, all three cases discussed above conflate 'protection' with 'assistance,' and fail to make the critical distinction between the mandates of the agencies established for Palestinian refugees. The cases, although

---

103 *Id.*
104 *Id.*; *Bolbol*, *supra* note 71.
105 Migration Court of Appeal of Sweden, Case UM 1590-13 (Nov. 26, 2013).
106 *Id.*
107 *Id.*
108 *Id.*

mentioning the UNCCP, fail to recognize that it was the *only* UN Agency with a mandate of international protection for Palestinians, and that UNRWA does not have, and never had, that mandate, particularly with regard to the most critical component of protection, the ability to implement a durable solution to their refugee condition.

101. Advocate-General Sharpston, in her Opinion to the *El Kott* Court, in a footnote, stated: "It is common ground that the phrase 'organs or agencies of the United Nations other than the United Nations High Commissioner for Refugees' has referred in fact solely to UNRWA since 1958... Except where otherwise specified, therefore, I shall treat 'organs or agencies of the United Nations other than the United Nations High Commissioner for Refugees' and 'UNRWA' as equivalents. It is also common ground that UNRWA was not set up to provide, nor has it ever provided, 'protection' to Palestinian refugees. It is not in a position to provide anything other than 'assistance.' I shall therefore refer to 'UNRWA assistance' rather than 'UNRWA protection or assistance.'"[109] The Court in *El Kott* refers to this footnote by claiming that "UNRWA is the only United Nations organ or agency ... referred to in the first sentence of Art. 12(1)(a) of the Directive ... and the first sentence of Article 1D."[110]

102. The first part of the Advocate-General's statement is simply incorrect, and made without reference to the historical record and *travaux* of Article 1D, which makes abundantly clear that 'organs or agencies' referred to both UNCCP and UNRWA.[111] The second part of the statement is correct, but the Advocate-General and the *El Kott* Court failed to understand the significance of it for correctly interpreting the references to 'protection or assistance.'

103. By failing to understand the UNCCP as the protection agency for Palestinian refugees, the ECJ does not address the significance of the 'cessation' of protection by that agency. Thus, the ECJ wrongly focuses only on whether UNRWA's assistance has ceased, whereas an accurate interpretation of this phrase requires applying the cessation of

---

109 Court of Justice of the European Union, "Opinion of Advocate General Sharpston," Case C-364/11, *Mostafa Abed El Karem El Kott and Others v. Bevándorlási És Állampolgársági Hivatal* (Sept. 13, 2012), n. 6 http://curia.europa.eu/juris/document/document.jsf?text=&docid=126801&pageIndex=0&doclang=EN&mode=lst&dir=&occ=first&part=1&cid=886362 [hereinafter Opinion of Advocate General Sharpston].

110 *El Kott, supra* note 71, at ¶ 44.

111 Akram & Rempel, *supra* note 5, at 81.

UNCCP's protection to Palestinian refugees as the trigger for re-including Palestinians in the 'benefits of the Convention' under the second sentence of 1D.[112]

104. Second, the cases erroneously reinvent the phrase 'when protection or assistance has ceased for any reason' into 'when protection or assistance has ceased *for a reason beyond his control and independent of his volition.*'[113] The italicized quote was substituted for the phrase 'for any reason,' but has no textual or drafting history support whatsoever.

105. Regardless of whether it is correct to focus only on the cessation of UNRWA's assistance as the trigger for re-inclusion of a Palestinian into the Convention regime, the inquiry must focus on cessation for any reason, and not whether the reason relates to a volitional act of the individual or otherwise. The text does not support the narrowing of the 'reasons' in any way.

106. By replacing 'for any reason,' with 'beyond his control and independent of his volition,' the ECJ has subverted the plain language of the text and defeated the object and purpose of the provision. *For any reason* can include all manner of reasons, including, but not limited to, reasons beyond the individual's control or independent of his volition, but the latter cannot be understood as narrowing the scope of the phrase itself.[114]

107. Third, the cases fail to recognize the purpose and components of the 'special' regime established for Palestinian refugees,[115] and the protection gap that has resulted from the collapse of that regime with the demise of the UNCCP.

108. As described in detail above, the special regime was established to ensure that Palestinians were defined as refugees as an entire group or category based primarily on their internationally-recognized nationality from 1924, and their expulsion and dispossession from their homes and lands as a result of the creation of Israel.

109. This entire group was guaranteed both international protection and assistance through the establishment of two agencies, UNCCP and UNRWA, which were given those separate mandates respectively by the UN. Because Palestinians' protection and assistance needs were already guaranteed by two separate agencies, the UN delegates drafted Article 1D

---

112   Badil, *supra* note 73, at 92.
113   1951 Refugee Convention, *supra* note 19, at art. 1D.
114   Badil Resource Center for Palestinian Residency & Refugee Rights, Closing Protection Gaps: Handbook on Protection of Palestinian Refugees in States Signatories to the 1951 Refugee Convention, 57 (Susan Akram & Nidal al-Azza eds. 2nd ed. 2015).
115   *Id.* at 25.

of the Refugee Convention, Article 1 of the Stateless Persons Convention and Paragraphs 7(c) of the UNHCR Statute to exclude Palestinians from the Refugee and Stateless convention regimes and the mandate of UNHCR so their situation would not be 'submerged' with that of all other refugees.[116] Both protection and assistance were to be guaranteed until the durable solution established by Res. 194 was implemented. If either prong of the regime failed in the absence of achieving the required durable solution, the second sentence of Article 1D was to be triggered to bring the entire category of Palestinian refugees into the fallback regime of the Refugee Convention.

110. Because the Arab states were the proponents of the 'special' regime and the drafters of the legal provisions establishing it, they have refused to become parties to the Refugee Convention.[117] As persistent objectors to the Refugee Convention, Jordan, Lebanon and Syria – the main host states for Palestinian refugees – are non-parties to the Refugee Convention or Protocol, and have not implemented legislation granting residence or nationality to the vast majority of Palestinian refugees residing in their territories.[118] Nor have they passed domestic legislation to recognize Palestinians in their territories as 'refugees.' The same is true of the Gulf Arab states; they are not parties to the Refugee Convention, nor offer refugee, residence or national status to Palestinians.[119]

111. Thus, given the cessation of the UNCCP's actual protection towards them, and the lack of any refugee recognition or residence status in the Arab states, a minority of the over 6 million Palestinian refugees falling under the definition for Res. 194 has any access whatsoever to legal protection. Approximately 5 million Palestinians are registered with UNRWA, but registration provides no legal protection and, in particular, no access to any durable solution whatsoever in the Arab world.[120]

112. By failing to understand that the 'special' status of Palestinians was contingent on their continuing to receive protection *and* assistance from the two Agencies responsible for them, the ECJ has construed the two uses of 'protection or assistance' in 1D in an absurd manner contrary to treaty interpretive rules: it considers provision of either protection or assistance sufficient to both exclude from and include Palestinian refugees into the

---

116 *See* U.N. GAOR, 5th Sess., 328th mtg. at ¶ 52, U.N. Doc. A/C.3/SR.328 (Nov. 27, 1950).
117 Badil, *supra* note 73, at 76 n. 381.
118 *Id.* at xiii.
119 *Id.* at 17–19.
120 *Id.* at 14.

Convention regime. This interpretation allows a regime that was to ensure enhanced protection (both protection and assistance at all times from two separate Agencies) from the UN[121] to dissolve into one that provides no protection for Palestinians whatsoever.

113. The ECJ Court and Attorney-General Sharpston make a series of assumptions that are clearly erroneous in light of this history and the interpretive rules. Attorney-General Sharpston sets out, in paragraph 23, a series of 'guiding principles' to her interpretation of the questions arising under Article 1D, in which she states, *inter alia*:
    - all genuine refugees deserve protection and assistance;
    - displaced Palestinians are to be given special treatment and consideration ...
    - the condition that assistance must have ceased cannot be construed so as to trap such persons in the UNRWA zone, unable to claim refugee status elsewhere until the Palestine problem is resolved and UNRWA wound up'...
    - nor can it entitle every displaced Palestinian to leave the UNRWA zone voluntarily and claim automatic refugee status elsewhere ...[122]

114. In para. 24, Attorney-General Sharpston draws a set of conclusions from these principles, including that the interpretation must result in 'universal protection' ... and 'no overlap between UNRWA and UNHCR.'[123]

115. These guiding principles and conclusions have no basis in the drafting history or VCLT interpretive rules. Moreover, applying the principles results in an absurd outcome, and one that is inconsistent with the principles themselves. Although she acknowledges the difference between protection and assistance, and that UNRWA has no protection mandate (see para. 101), she fails to recognize that all of the millions of Palestinians in the five UNRWA territories have *no* access to durable solutions – whether they are registered with UNRWA or not.[124]

116. Under Attorney-General Sharpston's interpretation – and that of the *El Kott* Court – Palestinians are not given the protection and assistance she claims are due all refugees, much less the 'special treatment and consideration' she recognizes to which they are entitled.[125] First, there is no overlap between UNRWA and UNHCR, either in the UNRWA fields or

---

121 *See* United Nations Secretariat, UNCCP Memorandum on Relations Between UNRWA and UNCCP, U.N. Doc. A/AC.25/W/42 (Mar. 30, 1950).
122 Opinion of Advocate General Sharpston, *supra* note 109.
123 *Id.*
124 Akram, UNRWA and Palestinian Refugees, *supra* note 6.
125 Opinion of Advocate General Sharpston, *supra* note 109.

outside of them. UNHCR has no protection mandate towards Palestinian refugees in any of the UNRWA areas. Paragraph 7(c) of its Statute has only an exclusion clause, while the Arab states have, as a whole, refused to ratify the Refugee Convention/Protocol, and have restricted UNHCR's services to only non-Palestinian refugees through their agreements with the Agency.[126] Nor does UNHCR have a protection mandate towards Palestinians as stateless persons for parallel reasons.[127] The Arab states are not signatories to either the 1954 Convention on Stateless Persons or the 1961 Convention on Statelessness and do not recognize Palestinians as 'stateless.'[128] Article 1 of the Stateless Persons Convention excludes Palestinians, and UNHCR has not extended its protection role under the 1961 Convention on the Reduction of Statelessness towards Palestinians.[129]

117. Because the states in which they reside do not provide them with protection, recognition as refugees or legal status, Palestinian refugees have remained for over sixty years in limbo: refugees in fact but not law, stateless persons in fact but not law,[130] and with access to durable solutions through no UN Agency when they were to be guaranteed protection and assistance through two.[131]

118. Attorney-General Sharpston's principle that a Palestinian should not be entitled to leave the UNRWA areas and automatically claim refugee status elsewhere also has no historical, drafting or interpretive support. All Palestinians defined as refugees under Res. 194 should be entitled to claim automatic refugee status under Article 1D if they are outside of UNRWA territories, just like any other refugee.[132] The Convention does not require any state to grant them asylum, residence or any other status besides *non-refoulement through time.*

119. This interpretation is textually and legally correct, and simply places Palestinian refugees on a similar plane as all other refugees in the world, with UNRWA providing assistance in five areas (as any other humanitarian assistance agencies that operate for particular refugees in different

---

126 Akram, UNRWA and Palestinian Refugees, *supra* note 6.
127 Id.
128 Id.
129 Id.
130 Badil, *Closing Protection Gaps, supra* note 114, at 6.
131 Susan M. Akram & Terry Rempel, Recommendations for Durable Solutions for Palestinian Refugees: A Challenge to the Oslo Framework, 11 Pal. Y.B. Int'l L. 1, 66 (2000).
132 U.N. High Commissioner for Refugees, Revised Note on the Applicability of Article 1D of the 1951 Convention relating to the Status of Refugees to Palestinian Refugees, at 2 (Oct. 2009).

countries of the world) and UNHCR providing protection and access to durable solutions for those refugees able to access its services outside their country of origin or, for stateless persons, their state of last habitual residence.[133]

120. It is with these inconsistencies and the consequences of erroneous interpretations of Article 1D that the Swedish court must examine XX's application for refugee status.

F XX is a Palestinian Refugee under the meaning of Article 1D, as well as a stateless person, and entitled to the benefits of the 1951 Convention as applied by Sweden

121. XX is a stateless Palestinian refugee. His status as Palestinian refugee registered with UNRWA in Gaza has never ceased, despite his birth in Kuwait and his subsequent displacement to Iraq and Syria. He was neither eligible for citizenship in Kuwait, nor entitled to return there after his family was expelled in 1992. He was not eligible for naturalization nor any other permanent status in Iraq prior to his family's forced displacement from Iraq in 2009. He was not entitled to refugee status in Syria nor any other permanent status until he was forced to flee Syria, and he cannot be returned there. He was not registered with UNRWA, nor did he receive UNRWA assistance or protection – such as was available to Palestinian refugees – in any of the countries in which he stayed until he arrived in Sweden.

122. The 1951 Convention and the 1967 Protocol govern this case.[134] Sweden has signed and ratified the 1951 Convention and acceded to its 1967 Protocol.

123. XX's family was registered with UNRWA in Gaza. Under Sweden's own application of Article 1D and Article 12(1)(a) of the Directive 2004/83, as a registered UNRWA Palestine refugee, XX qualifies as such under Sweden's interpretation of Article 1D under *El Kott v. BAH*.[135]

124. XX remains a Palestinian refugee, though born outside of Gaza in 1984, by virtue of the application of Article 1D to subsequent generations of

---

133 Akram & Rempel, *supra* note 133, at 67.
134 *See* 1951 Refugee Convention, *supra* note 19, at art. 1D; Protocol Relating to the Status of Refugees, Jan. 31, 1967, 606 U.N.T.S. 167.
135 *El Kott*, *supra* note 71.

refugees;[136] the ECJ opinions of *Bolbol*[137] and *El Kott*;[138] UNHCR's interpretations in its most recent *Note on the Applicability of Article 1D*;[139] and UNRWA's Consolidated Instructions incorporating the UN Resolutions to include subsequent generations of 1948 Palestine refugees and 1967 displaced Palestinians even if they have never been in an UNRWA area.[140]

125. Under the interpretation offered by *amicus*, the fact that XX is a Palestinian refugee within the meaning of the first sentence of Article 1D, and that protection has 'ceased' within the second sentence of Article 1D, qualify him for the benefits of the Refugee Convention, however Sweden interprets those benefits through its domestic law.

126. Alternatively, under Sweden's current application of Article 1D, XX should be considered to have left an UNRWA area due to a reason beyond his control.[141] The only UNRWA area where XX is registered is based on his family's registration in Gaza. XX was not born in Gaza, and his family is ineligible to go to Gaza. XX has no status, identity or other documents entitling him to return or to be admitted to any of the countries in which he has lived prior to entering Sweden.

127. UNHCR has amended its interpretation of Article 1D in two *Notes on the Applicability of Article 1D of the 1951 Convention Relating to the Status of Refugees to Palestinian Refugees* (2009 and 2013). UNHCR's 2013 *Note* states: "The phrase 'ceased for any reason'... should not be construed restrictively. The phrase would include the following: (i) the termination of UNRWA as an agency; (ii) the discontinuation of UNRWA's activities; or (iii) any objective reason outside the control of the person concerned such that the person is unable to (re-) avail themselves of the protection or assistance of UNRWA. Both protection-related as well as practical, legal or safety barriers to return are relevant to this assessment."[142]

128. The *Note* then lists objective reasons for inability to return, and practical, legal and safety barriers to return. Legal barriers include "absence of

---

136   G.A. Res. 37/120 (Dec. 16, 1982).
137   *Bolbol, supra* note 71.
138   *El Kott, supra* note 71.
139   U.N. High Commissioner for Refugees, Note on UNHCR's Interpretation of Article 1D of the 1951 Convention relating to the Status of Refugees and Article 12(1)(a) of the EU Qualification Directive in the context of Palestinian refugees seeking international protection (May 2013) [hereinafter Note on UNHCR's Interpretation of Article 1D of the 1951 Convention].
140   U.N.R.W.A., Consolidated Eligibility and Registration Instructions (CERI) (Oct. 2009), https://www.unrwa.org/sites/default/files/2010011995652.pdf.
141   Badil, *Closing Protection Gaps, supra* note 114, at 200.
142   Note on UNHCR's Interpretation of Article 1D of the 1951 Convention, *supra* note 141, at 4.

documentation to travel to, or transit, or to re-enter and reside, or where the authorities in the receiving country refuse his or her re-admission or the renewal of his or her travel documents."[143]

129. XX is registered with UNRWA in Gaza. He is unable to return to Gaza, as all entry to Gaza is controlled by the Israeli occupation authorities. Only Palestinians who were residing in Gaza and the West Bank when Israel invaded and occupied the Palestinian territories in 1967 were registered on the Israeli population registry. Only those Palestinians so registered, and their descendants born in and residing in the West Bank and Gaza are entitled to remain or to enter there. Since XX has never been to Gaza, he will not be permitted to enter there as a matter of Israeli occupation law.

130. XX is not entitled to return to the place of last temporary residence in an UNRWA area, as he was not registered with UNRWA in Syria; even if he were eligible for UNRWA registration there, the agency can neither protect him nor provide him assistance in Syria. The situation in Syria is continuously deteriorating to dangerous levels, making the risk to personal safety high.[144] The conflict is making it even more difficult to deliver humanitarian aid since roads used to transfer supplies are often closed, and it has been reported that humanitarian aid accessibility is decreasing.[145] UNRWA's mandate focuses on providing food, education, health, and welfare.[146] Although UNRWA has mischaracterized some of it activities as "protection" they do not meet the definition of international protection for refugees, as acknowledged by Attorney-General Sharpston (see para. 101 above). Currently, UNRWA cannot guarantee the provision of basic necessities such as food, shelter, and healthcare – in other words, it cannot guarantee the living conditions its duties demand – let alone ensure XX's personal safety in Syria.

131. Under Sweden's interpretation of Article 1D, if XX is a Palestinian refugee and UNRWA assistance has 'ceased,' then the next issue is whether he falls under one of the cessation or exclusion clauses of the Refugee Convention.[147]

---

143 *Id.* at 5.
144 *See* European Commission, Humanitarian Aid and Civil Protection, Syria Fact Sheet, (Sept. 2016), https://coi.easo.europa.eu/administration/euinstitutions/PLib/syria_en_916.pdf.
145 Note on UNHCR's Interpretation of Article 1D of the 1951 Convention, *supra* note 141, at 2.
146 Akram, *UNRWA and Palestinian Refugees, supra* note 6, at 4.
147 *See* Badil, *Closing Protection Gaps, supra* note 114, at 280.

132. There is no evidence that XX has committed any crimes that would exclude him from refugee status under Article 1F.
133. As discussed above, Palestinian refugees are not covered by the cessation clause of Article 1C.
134. Article 1E does not preclude XX from the benefits of the Convention because he 'is not recognized by competent authorities in either of the countries in which he previously resided as having the rights and obligations attached to nationality.'[148]

i   *Status in Kuwait*

135. XX was born in Kuwait in __. Kuwait is not an UNRWA field of operation, and the Agency has no mandate to deliver services to Palestinian refugees anywhere in the Gulf.[149]
136. Kuwait does not offer naturalization to Palestinians or, indeed, to most foreigners, even children born on its territory. Palestinians, like other foreigners, are only entitled to remain in Kuwait as long as they are sponsored by an employer, and their employment contracts remain valid.[150]
137. Before the first Gulf war, Palestinians were able to obtain employment, but were not entitled to status or permanent residence. Palestinians formed a large segment of the population of Kuwait from the 1960s to 1990. In fact, Palestinians numbered approximately 400,000–450,000 by 1989, while Kuwaitis numbered 550,000.[151] Palestinians also formed a key part of the economic and cultural development of Kuwait.[152] Despite the vital role Palestinians played in Kuwaiti society, they were not entitled to permanent residence in Kuwait, but could only remain in Kuwait as long as they had valid employment and were sponsored by their employers.[153] In the 1980s, the Kuwaiti government began a process of Kuwaitization to reduce the presence of non-Kuwaitis in the economy and civil service.[154] This led to increased pressure to reduce the number of Palestinians employed and reduce their benefits.[155]

---

148 Convention Relating to the the Status of Refugees, *supra* note 113, at art. 1E.
149 Akram, *UNRWA and Palestinian Refugees*, *supra* note 6, at 7.
150 Badil, *supra* note 73, at 18.
151 Toufic Haddad, Palestinian Forced Displacement from Kuwait: The Overdue Accounting, Badil Resource Center for Palestinian Residency and Refugee Rights (2010), http://www.badil.org/en/component/k2/item/1514-art07.html.
152 *Id.*
153 Anne M. Lesch, *Palestinians in Kuwait*, 20 J. Palestine Stud. 42 (1991).
154 Haddad, *supra* note 153.
155 *Id.*

138. After the invasion of Iraq into Kuwait in 1990, Palestinians were considered security threats and then 'traitors' because of Palestinian leader Yasser Arafat's position allying the PLO with Iraq.[156] When Iraq was defeated, Kuwait expelled Palestinians from the country *en masse*.[157]

139. XX was expelled from Kuwait after the first Gulf War and does not have identity or travel documents that provide him the right to return there. After Kuwait gained its independence from Iraq in 1992, most Palestinians residing in Kuwait were forcibly expelled. Many techniques were used to accomplish this goal, including firing Palestinian employees and not rehiring them, expelling Palestinian students from schools, ending education subsidies to Palestinians, and creating economic disincentives to remain such as health fees.[158] In addition, other mechanisms such as arbitrary arrest and torture were employed to force Palestinians out of Kuwait.[159]

140. Most Palestinians expelled from Kuwait went to Iraq or Jordan.[160] Because Palestinians were never granted citizenship or any other status in Kuwait, none of the Palestinians expelled in the 1990s have the right to return to Kuwait.[161]

ii   *Status in Iraq*

141. Following the family's expulsion from Kuwait, the XX family lived in Iraq from 1992–2009. Before the Iraq war in 2003, Palestinians in Iraq enjoyed many of the same rights as Iraqi citizens. Like citizens, Palestinians were given five-year travel documents, but since the 1990s these documents have not been widely recognized by other governments.[162] Prior to 2003, XX may have been considered to have 'the rights and obligations attached to nationality' for purposes of Article 1E.

142. However, after the US invasion of Iraq in 2003 and the defeat of Saddam Hussein, Palestinians were targeted for persecution. XX was forced to leave Iraq due to increasing hostility towards and persecution of Palestinians in Iraq. Palestinians faced not only generalized violence but

---

156   Takkenberg, *supra* note 13, at 18.
157   *Id.*
158   Haddad, *supra* note 153.
159   *Id.*
160   Badil Resource Center for Palestinian Residency & Refugee Rights, Survey of Palestinian Refugees and Internally Displaced Persons 2008–2009, 31 (2009).
161   Badil, *supra* note 73, at 18.
162   Badil, Survey of Palestinian Refugees and Internally Displaced Persons, *supra* note 162, at 112.

persecution on the basis of nationality.[163] Palestinians were the victims of eviction, arbitrary detention, kidnapping, torture, rape, and extra-judicial killings.[164]

143. Furthermore, after 2003, residency permits needed to be renewed every two months through a complicated and humiliating process, and the Iraqi government passed laws to prevent Palestinians from obtaining citizenship.[165] Many Palestinians were forced to leave Iraq after 2003 as a direct result of this persecution.

144. Palestinians who left Iraq do not have the right to return.[166] While some Palestinians carry travel documents issued by the Iraqi government, the Iraqi embassy in Sweden has stated that it will enforce a no-return policy for Palestinians because many Palestinians have been outside the country for more than six months.[167]

iii   *Status in Syria*

145. XX was forced to leave Iraq in 2009 due to persecution, and went to Syria where Palestinians from Iraq also faced persecution. Many Palestinians fleeing Iraq after the American occupation were either denied entry at the border or placed in the al-Hol refugee camp just inside the Syrian border.[168] Many Palestinians from Iraq also resided in Damascus without documentation.[169]

146. Sweden now accepts asylum seekers from Syria regardless of whether they have been individually persecuted. Before 2013, Sweden accepted Syrian asylum seekers and stateless Palestinians from Syria, but only gave them three-year residence permits.[170] After 2013, Swedish policy has been that "[a]ll of those seeking asylum from Syria will now be granted permanent residence in Sweden, even those who have not been threatened individually."[171] XX arrived in Sweden prior to 2013, but cannot be

---

163 *Id.* at 32; U.S. Department of State: Bureau of Democracy Human Rights, and Labor, Country Reports on Human Rights Practices: Iraq (2010).
164 Badil, Survey of Palestinian Refugees and Internally Displaced Persons, *supra* note 162, at 32.
165 *Id.* at 112.
166 Badil, *Closing Protection Gaps, supra* note 114, at 200.
167 *Id.*
168 *Id.* at 33.
169 *Id.*
170 *Id.* at 203.
171 Asylum in Sweden Advisory Service, *Seek Asylum in Sweden – Are you eligible?* http://www.seekasylumsweden.info/.

returned to Syria. Even ignoring the continuing civil war in the country, XX never obtained any permanent legal status in Syria.

147. XX cannot return to Syria under the *El Kott* standard. In *El Kott*, the European Court of Justice found that mere absence or voluntary departure from UNRWA's area of operations is not enough to indicate cessation of such protection or assistance.[172] However, the Court found that if a person was forced to leave UNRWA's area of operations, this may lead to a finding that assistance has ceased.[173] The Court left the determination of whether an individual's departure was voluntary or forced to the discretion of the national authorities and courts.[174] Nevertheless, the Court held that "a Palestinian refugee must be regarded as having been forced to leave UNRWA's area of operations if his personal safety is at serious risk and if it is impossible for that agency to guarantee that his living conditions in that area will be commensurate with the mission entrusted to that agency."[175]

148. UNHCR guidance suggests that states must "bear in mind the broad durable solutions context of refugee protection" when considering cessation for an individual case.[176] Therefore, cessation should not "result in persons residing in a host State with an uncertain status ... [or] result either in persons being compelled to return to a volatile situation."[177] Swedish courts have considered cases in which individuals apply for new passports from their country of origin to have availed themselves of state protection, and therefore subject to cessation of protection.

149. In the present case, XX has not been afforded status commensurate with that of a citizen in any country in which he has lived. Therefore, he does not fit within the criteria outlined in Article 1E and cannot be denied protection on that ground.[178] Because XX has not committed any serious crimes as outlined in Article 1F[179] and has not received protection equal to that of a citizen in any country, he should not be excluded from protection.

---

172   *El Kott*, *supra* note 71, at ¶ 41.
173   *Id.* ¶ 59.
174   *Id.* ¶ 61.
175   *Id.* ¶ 63.
176   U.N. High Commissioner for Refugees, Guidelines on International Protection: Cessation of Refugee Status under Article 1C(5) and (6) of the 1951 Convention relating to the Status of Refugees, HCR/GIP/03/03 (Feb. 10, 2003).
177   Id.
178   *See* 1951 Refugee Convention, *supra* note 19, at art. 1E.
179   *See id.* at art. 1F.

G Conclusion

150. XX has no legal right to return to Palestine, Iraq, or Kuwait. Given the ongoing conflict in Syria and the serious danger posed to XX's life and safety, he cannot be expected to return to Syria. Moreover, XX has not availed himself of the protection of Syria, Iraq, or Kuwait since fleeing each of these countries. Therefore, XX remains a Palestinian refugee entitled to and deserving of protection under international and Swedish law.

Dated: January 20, 2017
Boston, Massachusetts

/s/ Susan M. Akram
Amicus Curiae
Clinical Professor
Boston University School of Law
International Human Rights Clinic
765 Commonwealth Ave.
Boston, Massachusetts
02215
U.S.A.
(617) 353-3148

Council v Hamas, Judgement of the Court (Grand Chamber) (European Union) (July 26, 2017)

JUDGMENT OF THE COURT (Grand Chamber)

26 July 2017*

(Appeal – Common foreign and security policy – Fight against terrorism – Restrictive measures against certain persons and entities – Freezing of funds – Common Position 2001/931/CFSP – Article 1(4) and (6) – Regulation (EC) No 2580/2001 – Article 2(3) – Retention of an organisation on the list of persons, groups and entities involved in terrorist acts – Conditions – Factual basis of the decisions to freeze funds – Decision taken by a competent authority – Obligation to state reasons)

In Case C-79/15 P,

APPEAL under Article 56 of the Statute of the Court of Justice of the European Union, brought on 20 February 2015,

Council of the European Union, represented by B. Driessen, G. Étienne and M. Bishop, acting as Agents,

appellant,

supported by:

French Republic, represented by D. Colas, F. Fize and G. de Bergues, acting as Agents,

intervener in the appeal,

the other parties to the proceedings being:

---

* Language of the case: French.

Hamas, established in Doha (Qatar), represented by L. Glock, advocate,

applicant at first instance,

European Commission, represented by F. Castillo de la Torre, M. Konstantinidis and R. Tricot, acting as Agents,

intervener at first instance,

THE COURT (Grand Chamber),

composed of K. Lenaerts, President, A. Tizzano, Vice-President, L. Bay Larsen, T. von Danwitz (Rapporteur), J.L. da Cruz Vilaça and M. Vilaras, Presidents of Chambers, J. Malenovský, E. Levits, J.-C. Bonichot, A. Arabadjiev, C. Vajda, S. Rodin, F. Biltgen, K. Jürimäe and C. Lycourgos, Judges,

Advocate General: E. Sharpston,

Registrar: V. Giacobbo-Peyronnel, Administrator,

having regard to the written procedure and further to the hearing on 3 May 2016,

after hearing the Opinion of the Advocate General at the sitting on 22 September 2016,

gives the following

Judgment

1 By its appeal, the Council of the European Union asks the Court to set aside the judgment of the General Court of the European Union of 17 December 2014, *Hamas* v *Council* (T-400/10, 'the judgment under appeal', EU:T:2014:1095), by which the General Court annulled:
- Council Decisions 2010/386/CFSP of 12 July 2010 (OJ 2010 L 178, p. 28), 2011/70/CFSP of 31 January 2011 (OJ 2011 L 28, p. 57), 2011/430/CFSP of 18 July 2011 (OJ 2011 L 188, p. 47) updating the list of persons, groups and entities subject to Articles 2, 3 and 4 of Common Position 2001/931/CFSP on the application of specific measures to combat terrorism, Council Decisions 2011/872/CFSP of 22 December 2011 (OJ 2011 L 343, p. 54), 2012/333/CFSP of 25 June 2012 (OJ 2012 L 165, p. 72), 2012/765/

CFSP of 10 December 2012 (OJ 2012 L 337, p. 50), 2013/395/CFSP of 25 July 2013 (OJ 2013 L 201, p. 57), 2014/72/CFSP of 10 February 2014 (OJ 2014 L 40, p. 56) and 2014/483/CFSP of 22 July 2014 (OJ 2014 L 217, p. 35) updating and, where appropriate, amending, the list of persons, groups and entities subject to Articles 2, 3 and 4 of Common Position 2001/931/CFSP on the application of specific measures to combat terrorism, and repealing, respectively, Decisions 2011/430, 2011/872, 2012/333, 2012/765, 2013/395 and 2014/72; and

– Council Implementing Regulations (EU) No 610/2010 of 12 July 2010 (OJ 2010 L 178, p. 1), (EU) No 83/2011 of 31 January 2011 (OJ 2011 L 28, p. 14), (EU) No 687/2011 of 18 July 2011 (OJ 2011 L 188, p. 2), (EU) No 1375/2011 of 22 December 2011 (OJ 2011 L 343, p. 10), (EU) No 542/2012 of 25 June 2012 (OJ 2012 L 165, p. 12), (EU) No 1169/2012 of 10 December 2012 (OJ 2012 L 337, p. 2), (EU) No 714/2013 of 25 July 2013 (OJ 2013 L 201, p. 10), (EU) No 125/2014 of 10 February 2014 (OJ 2014 L 40, p. 9), and (EU) No 790/2014 of 22 July 2014 (OJ 2014 L 217, p. 1) implementing Article 2(3) of Regulation (EC) No 2580/2001 on specific restrictive measures directed against certain persons and entities with a view to combating terrorism, and repealing, respectively, Implementing Regulations (EU) No 1285/2009, No 610/2010, No 83/2011, No 687/2011, No 1375/2011, No 542/2012, No 1169/2012, No 714/2013 and No 125/2014;

(together 'the acts at issue'), in so far as those acts concern Hamas, including Hamas-Izz al-Din al-Qassem ('Hamas').

Legal context

United Nations Security Council Resolution 1373 (2001)

2 On 28 September 2001, the United Nations Security Council adopted Resolution 1373 (2001) laying out wide-ranging strategies to combat terrorism and in particular the financing of terrorism. Point 1(c) of that resolution provides, inter alia, that all States are to freeze without delay funds and other financial assets or economic resources of persons who commit, or attempt to commit, terrorist acts or participate in or facilitate the commission of terrorist acts; of entities owned or controlled by such persons; and of persons and entities acting on behalf of, or at the direction of such persons and entities.

3 The resolution does not provide a list of persons to whom those restrictive measures must be applied.

EU law

Common Position 2001/931/CFSP

4   In order to implement Resolution 1373 (2001), the Council adopted, on 27 December 2001, Common Position 2001/931/CFSP on the application of specific measures to combat terrorism (OJ 2001 L 344, p. 93).

5   Article 1 of Common Position 2001/931 provides:

> 1. This Common Position applies in accordance with the provisions of the following Articles to persons, groups and entities involved in terrorist acts and listed in the Annex.
> ...
> 4. The list in the Annex shall be drawn up on the basis of precise information or material in the relevant file which indicates that a decision has been taken by a competent authority in respect of the persons, groups and entities concerned, irrespective of whether it concerns the instigation of investigations or prosecution for a terrorist act, an attempt to perpetrate, participate in or facilitate such an act based on serious and credible evidence or clues, or condemnation for such deeds. Persons, groups and entities identified by the Security Council of the United Nations as being related to terrorism and against whom it has ordered sanctions may be included in the list.
>
> For the purposes of this paragraph "competent authority" shall mean a judicial authority, or, where judicial authorities have no competence in the area covered by this paragraph, an equivalent competent authority in that area.
> ...
> 6. The names of persons and entities on the list in the Annex shall be reviewed at regular intervals and at least once every six months to ensure that there are grounds for keeping them on the list.

Regulation (EC) No 2580/2001

6   The Council considered that a regulation was necessary to implement at Community level the measures set out in Common Position 2001/931, and adopted Regulation (EC) No 2580/2001 of 27 December 2001 on specific restrictive measures directed against certain persons and entities with a view to combating terrorism (OJ 2001 L 344, p. 70).

7   Article 2 of that regulation provides:

   1. Except as permitted under Articles 5 and 6:
   (a) all funds, other financial assets and economic resources belonging to, or owned or held by, a natural or legal person, group or entity included in the list referred to in paragraph 3 shall be frozen;
   (b) no funds, other financial assets and economic resources shall be made available, directly or indirectly, to, or for the benefit of, a natural or legal person, group or entity included in the list referred to in paragraph 3.
   2. Except as permitted under Articles 5 and 6, it shall be prohibited to provide financial services to, or for the benefit of, a natural or legal person, group or entity included in the list referred to in paragraph 3.
   3. The Council, acting by unanimity, shall establish, review and amend the list of persons, groups and entities to which this Regulation applies, in accordance with the provisions laid down in Article 1(4), (5) and (6) of Common Position 2001/931/CFSP; such list shall consist of:
   (i) natural persons committing, or attempting to commit, participating in or facilitating the commission of any act of terrorism;
   (ii) legal persons, groups or entities committing, or attempting to commit, participating in or facilitating the commission of any act of terrorism;
   (iii) legal persons, groups or entities owned or controlled by one or more natural or legal persons, groups or entities referred to in points (i) and (ii); or
   (iv) natural legal persons, groups or entities acting on behalf of or at the direction of one or more natural or legal persons, groups or entities referred to in points (i) and (ii).

Background to the dispute and the acts at issue

8   On 27 December 2001, the Council adopted Common Position 2001/931, Regulation No 2580/2001 and Decision 2001/927/EC establishing the list provided for in Article 2(3) of Regulation No 2580/2001 ('the list at issue') (OJ 2001 L 344, p. 83). Hamas appeared on the lists annexed to Common Position 2001/931 and Decision 2001/927.

9   That listing was maintained by subsequent acts of the Council, including by the acts at issue.

10   In the statements of reasons relating to those acts, the Council described Hamas as a terrorist group and referred to a number of terrorist acts

which Hamas is said to have carried out from 2005 onwards. In addition, the Council referred, in particular, to a decision adopted in 2001 by the United Kingdom of Great Britain and Northern Ireland and two decisions adopted in the same year by the authorities of the United States of America. The United Kingdom decision is a decision of the Secretary of State for the Home Department proscribing Hamas, which is considered to be an organisation involved in acts of terrorism. The decisions of the authorities of the United States consist in a government decision designating Hamas as a foreign terrorist organisation, pursuant to section 219 of the US Immigration and Nationality Act, and a decision designating Hamas as an entity expressly identified as an international terrorist entity, pursuant to Executive Order 13224 (together 'the decisions of the United States authorities'). Having found that the aforementioned decision of the United Kingdom was reviewed regularly by an internal government committee and that the decisions of the United States authorities were subject to both administrative and judicial review, the Council considered that those decisions had been adopted by competent authorities, for the purposes of Article 1(4) of Common Position 2001/931. Lastly, the Council noted that those decisions still remained in force and indicated that the reasons for including Hamas on the list at issue remained valid.

The procedure before the General Court and the judgment under appeal

11 By an application lodged at the General Court Registry on 12 September 2010, Hamas brought an action for annulment of Decision 2010/386 and Implementing Regulation No 610/2010. Those measures were repealed and replaced, successively, by the Council measures of January, July and December 2011, June and December 2012, July 2013 and February and July 2014 mentioned in paragraph 1 of the present judgment, and Hamas therefore successively modified the form of order initially sought, so as to ensure that its action covers the annulment of those measures also, in so far as they concern Hamas.

12 In support of its application for annulment of the Council measures of July 2010 and January 2011 mentioned in paragraph 1 of the present judgment, Hamas put forward four pleas in law, alleging, respectively, breach of its rights of defence; a manifest error of assessment; breach of the right to property; and breach of the obligation to state reasons. In support of its application for annulment of the measures adopted by the Council in the period from July 2011 to July 2014 and mentioned in paragraph 1 of the present judgment (together 'the measures adopted by the Council in the period from July 2011 to July 2014'), Hamas put forward eight pleas in law, alleging, respectively, infringement of Article 1(4) of Common Position

2001/931; errors as to the accuracy of the facts; an error of assessment as to the terrorist nature of that entity; failure to take sufficient account of the development of the situation 'owing to the passage of time'; breach of the principle of non-interference; breach of the obligation to state reasons; breach of its rights of defence and of the right to effective judicial protection; and breach of the right to property.

13 The General Court upheld the fourth and sixth pleas raised against the measures adopted by the Council in the period from July 2011 to July 2014 and, on that basis, annulled the acts at issue in so far as they concerned Hamas.

Forms of order sought

14 The Council claims that the Court should:
- set aside the judgment under appeal;
- give final judgment in the matters that are the subject of the appeal; and
- order Hamas to pay the costs incurred by the Council at first instance and in the appeal.

15 Hamas asks the Court to dismiss the appeal. In the alternative, should the Court be required to give final judgment in the matters that are the subject of the appeal, it maintains all the pleas in law put forward, and the form of order sought, in the proceedings before the General Court. Hamas also asks the Court to order the Council to pay the costs incurred by Hamas at first instance and in the appeal.

16 The European Commission has intervened in support of the form of order sought by the Council in its appeal.

17 The French Republic asks the Court to set aside the judgment under appeal, to give final judgment in the matters that are the subject of the appeal and to dismiss Hamas' action.

The appeal

The first ground of appeal

Arguments of the parties

18 By its first ground of appeal, which relates in particular to paragraphs 101, 103, 109 to 111, 121, 125 to 127 and 141 of the judgment under appeal, the Council submits, first, that that judgment is based on the mistaken premiss that the Council must regularly provide new reasons for retaining Hamas on the list at issue. In the absence of any annulment or withdrawal of the national decisions on which the initial entry of Hamas on that

list was based, and in the absence of other material that might support the withdrawal of Hamas from that list, the Council was, it claims, entitled to maintain Hamas on the list at issue solely on the basis of the national decisions that justified that entity's initial listing.

19 Second, the Council maintains that the General Court was wrong to reject the use of open source material for the purposes of periodic reviews. The Council contends that it must be able to rely to that end on material other than national decisions, since in many cases there are no national decisions taken after the initial entry of a person or entity on the list at issue. The General Court's reasoning is, it argues, contrary to the objective of combating terrorism to which Common Position 2001/931 refers.

20 The Commission and the French Republic intervening in support of the Council's arguments underline in particular the distinction which Common Position 2001/931 draws between, on the one hand, the initial entry of an entity on the list at issue, referred to in Article 1(4) of that common position, and, on the other hand, the subsequent reviews provided for in Article 1(6) thereof.

21 By contrast, according to Hamas, the Council is wrong to claim that it could have maintained Hamas on the list at issue solely on the basis of the national decisions that justified its initial entry on that list. The Council's assertion that the General Court wrongly ruled out the use of open source information falls foul of Article 1(4) of Common Position 2001/931, as interpreted by the Court in the judgment of 15 November 2012, *Al-Aqsa* v *Council* and *Netherlands* v *Al-Aqsa*(C-539/10 P and C-550/10 P, EU:C:2012:711), which requires, in order to guarantee the protection of the persons or entities concerned and in the absence of the European Union's own means of investigation, that the restrictive measures imposed by the Union be based on material actually examined and accepted in decisions of national competent authorities. Hamas argues that that requirement applies, given the seriousness of the impact of restrictive measures on the persons or entities concerned, also to the reviews prescribed in Article 1(6) of Common Position 2001/931.

22 The difficulty, encountered following Hamas' proscription in the United Kingdom and the freezing of its funds by the United States authorities, of obtaining new decisions of competent national authorities does not affect the Council's obligation to rely only on facts assessed by such authorities. That difficulty could, moreover, be resolved by seeking, if need be, the views of a competent national authority on a specific act capable of constituting a terrorist act.

Findings of the Court

23 The first ground of appeal concerns the conditions under which the Council may, when reviewing the entry of a person or entity on the list at issue, as it is required to do under Article 1(6) of Common Position 2001/931, retain that person or entity on that list. In order to determine those conditions, it is necessary to interpret Article 1(6) of Common Position 2001/931, taking into account in particular its relationship with Article 1(4), which governs the conditions for the initial listing of the person or entity concerned.

24 The Court has ruled, with regard to initial decisions on the freezing of funds, that the wording of Article 1(4) of Common Position 2001/931 refers to the decision taken by a national authority by requiring that precise information or evidence in the file exists which shows that such a decision has been taken. That requirement seeks to ensure that, in the absence of any means at the disposal of the Union to carry out its own investigations regarding the involvement of a person or entity in terrorist acts, the Council's decision on the initial listing is taken on a sufficient factual basis enabling the Council to conclude that there is a danger that, if preventive measures are not taken, the person or entity concerned may continue to be involved in terrorist activities (see, to that effect, judgment of 15 November 2012, *Al-Aqsa* v *Council* and *Netherlands* v *Al-Aqsa*, C-539/10 P and C-550/10 P, EU:C:2012:711, paragraphs 69, 79 and 81).

25 As regards, on the other hand, subsequent fund-freezing decisions, it is apparent from the case-law of the Court that the essential question when reviewing whether to continue to include a person or entity on the list at issue is whether, since the inclusion of that person or that entity on that list or since the last review, the factual situation has changed in such a way that it is no longer possible to draw the same conclusion in relation to the involvement of that person or entity in terrorist activities (judgment of 15 November 2012, *Al-Aqsa* v *Council* and *Netherlands* v *Al-Aqsa*, C-539/10 P and C-550/10 P, EU:C:2012:711, paragraph 82).

26 In the present case, the General Court held, in paragraphs 101 and 125 of the judgment under appeal, that the list of terrorist acts which Hamas was said to have committed since 2005, set out in the statements of reasons relating to the acts at issue, played a decisive role in the Council's decision to continue to freeze Hamas' funds. In paragraphs 110 and 127 of the judgment under appeal, the General Court held that the reference to any new terrorist act which the Council inserts in its statement of reasons during a review pursuant to Article 1(6) of Common Position 2001/931

must have been the subject of an examination and a national decision by a competent authority. Having found, notably in paragraphs 109 and 131 of the judgment under appeal, that the Council had based its allegations concerning terrorist acts which Hamas is said to have committed from 2005 onwards not on such decisions but on information which it obtained from the press and the internet, the General Court accordingly annulled the acts at issue.

– The first part of the first ground of appeal

27   By the first part of its first ground of appeal, the Council maintains that the General Court erred in law by finding that the Council was required regularly to provide new reasons justifying Hamas' retention on the list at issue and that it could not, in the absence of material supporting Hamas' removal from that list, retain Hamas on the list solely on the basis of the national decisions on which its initial listing was based.

28   As is apparent in particular from paragraph 119 of the judgment under appeal, the General Court, at least implicitly, considered that the United Kingdom's decision and/or the decisions of the United States authorities did not constitute in themselves a sufficient basis for maintaining Hamas on the list at issue.

29   It must be recalled, in that regard, that it is apparent from the case-law cited in paragraph 25 of the present judgment that, in the context of a review pursuant to Article 1(6) of Common Position 2001/931, the Council may maintain the person or entity concerned on the list at issue if it concludes that there is an ongoing risk of that person or entity being involved in the terrorist activities which justified their initial listing. The retention of a person or entity on the list at issue is, therefore, in essence, an extension of the original listing.

30   In the process of verifying whether the risk of the person or entity concerned being involved in terrorist activities is ongoing, the subsequent fate of the national decision that served as the basis for the original entry of that person or entity on the list at issue must be duly taken into consideration, in particular the repeal or withdrawal of that national decision as a result of new facts or material or any modification of the competent national authority's assessment.

31   That said, the question that arises in this case is whether the fact that the national decision that served as the basis for the original listing is still in force can, in itself, be considered sufficient for the purpose of maintaining the person or entity concerned on the list at issue.

32   In that regard, if, in view of the passage of time and in the light of changes in the circumstances of the case, the mere fact that the national decision

that served as the basis for the original listing remains in force no longer supports the conclusion that there is an ongoing risk of the person or entity concerned being involved in terrorist activities, the Council is obliged to base the retention of that person or entity on the list on an up-to-date assessment of the situation, and to take into account more recent facts which demonstrate that that risk still exists (see, by analogy, judgment of 18 July 2013, *Commission and Others* v *Kadi*, C-584/10 P, C-593/10 P and C-595/10 P, EU:C:2013:518, paragraph 156).

33   In the present case, a significant period of time elapsed between, on the one hand, the adoption of the national decisions which served as the basis for the original entry of Hamas on the list at issue and the original listing itself, in 2001, and, on the other, the adoption of the acts at issue, in the period from 2010 to 2014. The Council was therefore obliged to base Hamas' retention on that list on more recent material demonstrating that there was still a risk that Hamas was involved in terrorist activities. Consequently, contrary to what is claimed by the Council, the General Court did not err in law in considering, at least implicitly, that the decisions of the United States authorities and/or the decision of the United Kingdom did not in themselves constitute a sufficient basis for the acts at issue.

34   The first part of the first ground of appeal must therefore be rejected.

– The second part of the first ground of appeal

35   In the second part of the first ground of appeal, the Council submits that the General Court erred in law in ruling, notably in paragraphs 109, 110, 125 to 127 and 141 of the judgment under appeal, that the Council was required to rely exclusively on material contained in the national decisions of competent authorities in order to maintain a person or entity on the list at issue, and that the Council had infringed both Article 1 of Common Position 2001/931 and its obligation to state reasons by relying in this instance on information obtained from the press and the internet.

36   As regards, in the first place, Article 1 of Common Position 2001/931, it must be noted first of all that that article draws a distinction between the initial entry of a person or entity on the list at issue, referred to in paragraph 4 thereof, and the retention on that list of a person or entity already listed, referred to in paragraph 6 thereof.

37   Under Article 1(4) of Common Position 2001/931, the initial entry of a person or entity on the list at issue presupposes the existence of a national decision by a competent authority or of a decision of the United Nations Security Council imposing a sanction.

38 No such condition is laid down in Article 1(6) of Common Position 2001/931, however, according to which 'the names of persons and entities on the list in the Annex shall be reviewed at regular intervals and at least once every six months to ensure that there are grounds for keeping them on the list'.

39 That distinction is attributable to the fact that, as has been stated in paragraph 29 of the present judgment, the retention of a person or entity on the fund-freezing list is, in essence, an extension of the original listing and presupposes, therefore, that there is an ongoing risk of the person or entity concerned being involved in terrorist activities, as initially established by the Council on the basis of the national decision on which that original listing was based.

40 Thus, although Article 1(6) of Common Position 2001/931 requires the Council to carry out at least once every six months a 'review' to ensure that there continue to be grounds for 'keeping' on that list a person or entity already listed on the basis of a national decision taken by a competent authority, it does not require any new material on which the Council may rely in order to justify the retention of the person or entity concerned on the list at issue to have been the subject of a national decision taken by a competent authority after the decision on which the initial listing was based. By imposing such a requirement, the General Court transposed the condition concerning the existence of such a decision, which is laid down in Article 1(4) of Common Position 2001/931 solely in relation to the initial entry of a person or entity on that list, to the reviews which the Council is required to carry out under Article 1(6) of that common position. In so doing, the General Court failed to have regard to the distinction between the original decision placing a person or entity on the list at issue and the subsequent decision maintaining the person or entity concerned on that list.

41 Next, it must be noted that the General Court's interpretation of Article 1 of Common Position 2001/931 is based, at least implicitly, on the consideration that either the competent national authorities regularly adopt decisions on which the reviews the Council is required to carry out under Article 1(6) of Common Position 2001/931 may be based, or the Council has the option, if necessary, of asking those authorities to adopt such decisions.

42 However, that consideration has no basis in EU law.

43 It must be made clear in that regard that the fact that the Member States are to inform the Council of decisions adopted by their competent authorities and to transmit those decisions to it does not mean that those

44 Moreover, in the absence of any specific basis in the restrictive measures regime established by Common Position 2001/931, the principle of sincere cooperation enshrined in Article 4(3) TEU does not permit the Council to require the competent authorities of the Member States to adopt, if necessary, national decisions that may serve as the basis for the reviews the Council is required to carry out pursuant to Article 1(6) of that common position.

45 On the contrary, it must be noted that that regime does not provide any mechanism that would enable the Council to be provided, if necessary, with national decisions adopted after the initial listing of the person or entity concerned, in order to carry out the reviews it is required to carry out pursuant to Article 1(6) of that common position and in the context of which it is required to verify that there is still a risk that that person or entity is involved in terrorist activities. Without such a mechanism, it cannot be held that that regime requires the Council to carry out those reviews entirely on the basis of such national decisions, if the means that are to be available to the Council for that purpose are not to be restricted unduly.

46 Lastly, it should be noted that, contrary to what the General Court found, notably in paragraph 110 of the judgment under appeal, its interpretation of Article 1 of Common Position 2001/931 is also not justified by the need to protect the persons or entities concerned.

47 It must be stated that, as regards the initial listing, the person or entity concerned is protected, in particular by the possibility of challenging both the national decisions that served as the basis for that listing, before the national courts, and the listing itself, before the Courts of the European Union.

48 In the case of subsequent fund-freezing decisions, the person or entity concerned is protected, inter alia, by the possibility of bringing an action against such decisions before the Courts of the European Union. These are required to determine, in particular, first, whether the obligation to state reasons laid down in Article 296 TFEU has been complied with and, therefore, whether the reasons relied on are sufficiently detailed and specific, and, second, whether those reasons are substantiated (see, by analogy, judgments of 18 July 2013, *Commission and Others* v *Kadi*, C-584/10 P, C-593/10 P and C-595/10 P, EU:C:2013:518, paragraphs 118 and 119, and of 28 November 2013, *Council* v *Fulmen and Mahmoudian*, C-280/12 P, EU:C:2013:775, paragraph 64).

49 In that context, it must be made clear that the person or entity concerned may, in the action challenging their retention on the list at issue, dispute all the material relied on by the Council to demonstrate that the risk of their involvement in terrorist activities is ongoing, irrespective of whether that material is derived from a national decision adopted by a competent authority or from other sources. In the event of challenge, it is for the Council to establish that the facts alleged are well founded and for the Courts of the European Union to determine whether they are made out (see, by analogy, judgments of 18 July 2013, *Commission and Others* v *Kadi*, C-584/10 P, C-593/10 P and C-595/10 P, EU:C:2013:518, paragraphs 121 and 124, and of 28 November 2013, *Council* v *Fulmen and Mahmoudian*, C-280/12 P, EU:C:2013:775, paragraphs 66 and 69).

50 It follows that the General Court erred in law when it ruled that the Council had infringed Article 1 of Common Position 2001/931 by relying, in the statements of reasons relating to the acts at issue, on material from sources other than national decisions adopted by competent authorities.

51 As regards, in the second place, the infringement of the obligation to state reasons identified by the General Court, it must be borne in mind that the assessment by the General Court as to whether the statement of reasons is or is not sufficient is subject to review by the Court on an appeal (see judgment of 18 July 2013, *Commission and Others* v *Kadi*, C-584/10 P, C-593/10 P and C-595/10 P, EU:C:2013:518, paragraph 140 and the case-law cited).

52 In the present case, it is apparent in particular from paragraph 141 of the judgment under appeal that, in order to find that there had been an infringement of the obligation to state reasons, the General Court relied solely on the absence of any reference – as regards the list of terrorist acts allegedly committed by Hamas from 2005 – in the statements of reasons relating to the acts at issue to national decisions by competent authorities. The General Court's finding of an infringement of the obligation to state reasons is thus the direct consequence of the finding of an infringement of Article 1 of Common Position 2001/931, in respect of which it has been established that it is vitiated by an error of law.

53 Consequently, the General Court's error of law in connection with its interpretation of Article 1 has the effect that its finding of an infringement by the Council of the obligation to state reasons is also vitiated by an error of law.

54 Since the second part of the first ground of appeal must, therefore, be upheld, the judgment under appeal must on that basis be set aside in its

entirety, and there is no need to rule on the second and third grounds of appeal.

The action before the General Court

55   In accordance with the first paragraph of Article 61 of the Statute of the Court of Justice of the European Union, the Court may, where it has quashed the decision of the General Court, either itself give final judgment in the matter, where the state of the proceedings so permits, or refer the case back to the General Court for judgment.

56   Since the General Court has ruled only on the fourth and sixth pleas in law in the application made by Hamas for annulment of the measures adopted by the Council in the period from July 2011 to July 2014, and the other pleas in law relied on before the General Court raise in part questions relating to the assessment of facts, the Court considers that the state of the proceedings is not such as to permit final judgment to be given in the action, and that the case must be referred back to the General Court and the costs reserved.

On those grounds, the Court (Grand Chamber) hereby:

1. Sets aside the judgment of the General Court of the European Union of 17 December 2014, *Hamas v Council* (T-400/10, EU:T:2014:1095);
2. Refers the case back to the General Court of the European Union;
3. Reserves the costs.

[Signatures]

SECTION D
Legislation

∴

Law for the Regularization of Settlement in Judea and Samaria, 5777–2017 (Israel)

Law for the Regularization of Settlement in Judea and Samaria, 5777–2017[1]

Objective: 1. The objective of this law is to regularize settlement in Judea and Samaria, and to enable it to continue to strengthen and develop.

Definitions 2. In this law –

"Area" – as defined in the Emergency Regulations (Judea and Samaria – Adjudication of Offense and Legal Assistance), 5727–1967,[2] as extended and amended by law, from time to time;

"Holder of land rights" - someone who has proven that he is registered as the title holder of land or that he is entitled to be registered as the title holder of land;

"Planning processes" – including the granting of building permits based on plans that will be approved;

"The state's consent" – explicit or implicit, in advance or after the fact, including assistance in laying infrastructure, granting incentives, making plans, issuing publications aimed at encouraging construction or development or participation in cash or in kind;

"Settlement" – including a neighborhood or expansion of the settlement, all of the residences in it, the facilities, the agricultural land that serves its needs, public buildings that serve the residents, means of production, as well as access roads and infrastructure for water, communication, electricity and sewage;

"Objections Committee" – the committee established under section 10;

"Assessment Committee" – the committee established under section 9;

---

[1] Source: https://www.adalah.org/uploads/uploads/Settlement_Regularization_Law_English_FINAL_05032017.pdf. Approved by the Knesset on 10 Shevat 5777 (6 February 2017); bill and explanatory notes published in Knesset Proposed Laws – 672, from 7 Kislev 5777 (7 December 2016), p. 44.
Book of Laws 2604, 17 Shevat 5777 (13 February 2017).

[2] Collection of Regulations 5727, p. 2741; Book of Laws 5728, p. 20; 5772, p. 476.

"Jordanian Land Law" – Land Law (Acquisition for Public Needs) No. 2 of 1953, as amended in the Order Regarding the Land Law (Acquisition for Public Needs) (Order No. 321) (Judea and Samaria), 5729–1969;[3] [2]

"The state" – the government of Israel or one of the government ministries, the authorities in the area, a local authority or regional authority in Israel or in the area and a settlement institution;

"Settlement institution" – as defined in the Candidates for Agricultural Settlement Law, 5713–1953;[4]

"The officer in charge" – the officer in charge of government property in the Judea and Samaria area under the Order Regarding Government Property;

"Land requiring regularization" – land in the area for which the rights to use and hold it, or part of it, are not assigned to the authorities in the area or to the officer in charge;

"Order Regarding Government Property" – Order Regarding Government Property (Judea and Samaria) (No. 59), 5727–1967;[5]

"Authorities in the area" – whoever has assumed all of the government authorities under section 3 of the Proclamation Concerning Administrative and Judicial Procedures (Judea and Samaria) (No. 2), 5727–1967,[6] or under another legal directive that comes to replace it.

Registration of Land Requiring Regularization or Appropriating Rights to Use and Hold It

3. If the authorities in the area find that during the period preceding the publication of this law, settlement was constructed in good faith on lands that require regularization or received the state's consent for its construction, the following directives will apply to all of the land on which that settlement was built as of the eve of this law's publication:
   (1) Land where there is no holder of land rights – the officer in charge will register it as government property, under section 2C of the Order Regarding Government Property;
   (2) (A) Land where there is a holder of land rights – the authorities of the area will appropriate the rights to use and hold the land, and will transfer them to the officer in charge if the sum invested in building the settlement exceeded, at the time of

---

3 Collection of Proclamations, Orders and Appointments, 5729, p. 644.
4 Book of Laws, 5713, p. 126.
5 Collection of Proclamations, Orders and Appointments, 5727, p. 162.
6 Collection of Proclamations, Orders and Appointments, 5727, p. 3.

construction, the value of the land without the settlement at that time; [3]

(B) The appropriation of the rights to use and hold the land as stated in this section will be executed, to the extent possible, in accordance with the directives of the Jordanian Land Law, as long as they do not contradict the directives of this law, and it will remain in effect until there is a political resolution regarding the status of the area and settlement in it.

Date for Registering Land or Assuming Rights to Use and Hold Land

4. (A) The officer in charge will register the land as government property in accordance with section 3(1) within 12 months of the date of this law's publication.
(B) The authorities in the area will appropriate the rights to use and hold the land in accordance with section 3(2) within 6 months of the date of this law's publication.

Allocating Land Rights

5. Within 60 days of the registration or appropriation of rights as stated in section 4, as applicable, the officer in charge will allocate the rights to use and hold the land that was registered or had its rights appropriated as stated, for the purposes of the settlement that was constructed on that land, via a settlement institution.

Completing Planning Processes

6. (A) The state will endeavor to complete the planning processes for the land that was registered or had its rights appropriated under section 3, as swiftly as possible.
(B) The planning processes for the land as stated in subsection (A) will be executed, as much as possible, attentively toward the need to regularize existing construction.

Suspension and Expiration of Proceedings

7. (A) If the authorities in the area find that the conditions stipulated at the beginning of section 3 are met in the settlement, all existing enforcement proceedings and administrative orders concerning that settlement will be suspended until the completion of the planning processes under section 6, with the exception of proceedings and orders for which judicial orders or rulings have been issued in regard to their implementation.

(B) If the planning processes are completed according to section 6, all of the enforcement proceedings and administrative orders suspended under subsection (A) will expire. [4]
(C) The directives of this section will not apply to a structure whose demolition is necessary in order to prevent endangering human life.

Compensation

8. (A) If the authorities in the area appropriate the rights to use and hold land in accordance with the directives of section 3(2), the holder of land rights will be entitled to annual usage fees of 125% of the proper value of the usage fees as determined by the Assessment Committee under section 9(C) (hereinafter: proper value), to capitalized usage fees for a period of 20 years, each time at a rate of 125% of the proper value, or to alternative land to the extent possible in the circumstances of the cases, according to his choice.
(B) If the holder of land rights does not choose one of the compensation options under subsection (A) by the date of the allocation of land rights under section 5, he will be entitled to annual usage fees at a rate of 125% of the proper value.
(C) Payment of compensation under this section will be executed within 3 months of the date of determining the proper value of the usage fees under section 9(C)(2).
(D) If the officer in charge learns there is a holder of rights to land he has registered as government property under section 3(1), the directives of section 3(2) will apply, and the holder of the land rights will be entitled to compensation under the directives of this section.
(E) The directives of this section and of sections 9 and 10 will not delay the processes under sections 3 to 6.

Assessment Committee

9. (A) The justice minister, in consultation with the defense minister, will form an Assessment Committee to implement the directives of this law, and these are its members:
    (1) A representative to be appointed by the justice minister from among his ministry's employees – and he will be the chairperson;
    (2) A representative to be appointed by the finance minister among his ministry's employees;
    (3) A representative of the authorities in the area, to be appointed by the defense minister;

(B) The justice minister will determine the hearing procedures at the Assessment Committee. [5]
(C) (1) The Assessment Committee will determine the proper value of the usage fees or the alternative land to be offered to the holder of land rights, as applicable, after hearing the arguments of the holder of land rights – if he presented arguments, and after weighing all of the circumstances of the case.
(2) The decision of the Assessment Committee under section (1) will be made within 3 months of the day it finishes hearing the arguments of the holder of land rights or from the day the holder of land rights was slated to present his arguments according to the hearing procedures defined under subsection (B).

Objections Committee

10. (A) The justice minister, in consultation with the defense minister, will form an Objections Committee for the purpose of implementing the directives of this law, and these are its members:
    (1) A representative of the authorities in the area who is qualified to be a magistrate's court judge, to be appointed by the justice minister, with the consent of the defense minister – and he will be the chairperson;
    (2) A representative to be appointed by the chief government appraiser from among the employees of his office;
    (3) A land appraiser whose name is listed in the registry of certified appraisers under the directives of section 202C of the Planning and Building Law, 5725–1965,[7] to be appointed by the chairperson of the Council of Land Appraisers.
(B) A holder of land rights who believes he was harmed by the Assessment Committee's decision under section 9(C)(1), is entitled to submit an objection to the Objections Committee about the decision.
(C) Decisions by the Objections Committee will be made by majority opinion of the committee's members; if there is no single majority opinion, the chairperson's opinion will be the deciding opinion.
(D) The Objections Committee will not be bound by the legal proceedings and rules of evidence practiced in the courts, and will operate

---

7 Book of Laws 5725, p. 307.

in a way that it deems most helpful in making a just and rapid decision on the objection. [6]

(E) The Objections Committee is authorized to approve the decision made by the Assessment Committee, in its entirety or in part, to overturn or amend it, to return the matter to the Assessment Committee for re-discussion or to adopt any other decision in its place.

Transition Directive for Communities Listed in the Addendum

11. (A) (1) During the period of 12 months from the date of this law's publication, all of the existing enforcement proceedings and administrative orders regarding settlement in the communities listed in the Addendum will be suspended.
    (2) During the period defined in paragraph (1), the authorities in the area will determine whether the conditions stipulated at the beginning of section 3 exist in the communities listed in the Addendum.
    (3) If the authorities in the area determine that the conditions stipulated at the beginning of section 3 exist in the communities listed in the Addendum, the directives of this law will apply to them.
    (4) The directives of this subsection will not apply to –
(A) Enforcement proceedings and administrative orders regarding settlement in the communities listed in the Addendum for which judicial orders or rulings have been issued in regard to their implementation.
(B) A structure whose demolition is necessary in order to prevent endangering human life.
(B) The justice minister, with the approval of the Knesset's Constitution, Law and Justice Committee, is entitled to add, through an order, communities to the Addendum.

Addendum

(Section 11)
(1) Ofra
(2) Netiv Ha'avot
(3) Eli
(4) Kochav Hashachar
(5) Mitzpe Kramim [7]
(6) Elon Moreh

(7) Ma'ale Michmas
(8) Shavei Shomron
(9) Kedumim
(10) Psagot
(11) Beit El
(12) Yitzhar
(13) Har Bracha
(14) Modi'in Illit
(15) Nokdim
(16) Kochav Ya'akov

Benjamin Netanyahu
Prime Minister

Reuven Rivlin
President

Ayelet Shaked
Justice Minister

Yuli-Yoel Edelstein
Knesset Speaker

SECTION E

Other

Statement Issued by the Central Council of the Palestine Liberation Organization (PLO)

Unofficial translation of the statement:

Statement issued by the Central Council of the Palestine Liberation Organization (PLO)*

January 14, 2018

Ramallah, Palestine

The Palestine Liberation Organization's Central Council held its twenty-eighth ordinary session, under the name "Jerusalem the eternal capital of the State of Palestine", between January 14–15 2018 in the city of Ramallah, in the presence of President Mahmoud Abbas.

A total of 87 members out of 109 members attended the session, while a number of members were unable to attend because they were arrested or prevented by Israel.

President of the Central council Salim Al-Za'noun began the session by saying that "The time has come for our Palestinian Central Council, that is representing the Palestinian National Council, which took the decision to establish the Palestinian National Authority to be the core of the state, to decide its future and function and to reconsider the recognition of the State of Israel until it recognizes the State of Palestine with Jerusalem as its capital and accept the refugees' return based on resolution 194."

Al-Za'noun stressed that the Central Council rejects any ideas that are being circulated as part of the so-called "deal of the century", because they violate international law and resolutions of the international community and seek to impose a deficient solution that does not meet the minimum of Palestinians' legitimate rights.

---

* Source: *UPDATE: PLO Central Council decides to suspend Oslo agreement*, WAFA (Jan. 15, 2018), http://english.wafa.ps/page.aspx?id=zbyLEda96057575031azbyLEd.

He called for finding other international pathways under the auspices of the United Nations to sponsor solving the Palestinian cause.

He said, "Our success in facing these risks and challenges requires accelerating the steps of implementing reconciliation and ending the division, and developing a plan to strengthen national partnership within the framework of the PLO, as the supreme national political and legal reference for our people."

Al-Za'noun proposed to hold a session of the National Council, in which both Hamas and the Islamic Jihad will be invited with the task of reshaping, choosing or electing a new national council, as stipulated by the system of elections of the National Council.

"We respect and appreciate the position of Arabs and their support for the Palestinian cause. We demand the implementation of the decisions of the Arab summits on Jerusalem, especially the Amman summit of 1980, which called for severing all relations with any state that recognizes Jerusalem as the capital of Israel or transfers its embassy to it."

He stressed that the sacrifices and struggles of prisoners in Israeli jails obligate Palestinians to provide all forms of support and that the dignity of Palestinians remains above any consideration.

Meanwhile, President Abbas reiterated commitment to a two-state solution based on international resolutions, the Arab peace initiative on the 1967 borders, the cessation of settlements' expansion and unilateral actions. He affirmed that Palestinians will continue to seek the Security Council until full membership is achieved.

He stressed that Palestinians will not accept what the US attempts to impose, and that the PLO will reconsider its relations with Israel, yet engage in any serious peace negotiations under the auspices of the UN.

First: US recognition of Jerusalem

1. To condemn and reject the decision of US President Donald Trump, recognizing Jerusalem as the capital of Israel, and transferring his country's embassy from Tel Aviv to Jerusalem, and work to reverse this decision.
2. The Council considered that the US administration, by announcing this decision, has lost its eligibility to function as a mediator and sponsor of the peace process and will not be a partner in this process unless the decision is reversed.
3. The Council stressed its rejection of President Trump's policy that is aimed at presenting a project or ideas that contravene the resolutions of international community to resolve the conflict, which revealed its essence by declaring Jerusalem as the capital of Israel. The Council stressed the need to abolish the Congress's decision to consider the PLO

as a terrorist organization since 1987, and the State Department's decision to close the Office of the PLO general delegation in Washington on November 17, 2017.

Second: The relationship with Israel (the occupation):

> In light of the withdrawal of the occupying state from all agreements and revoking them by practice and imposing a fait accompli, and with the Central council stressing that the direct goal is the independence of the State of Palestine, which requires transition from self-governing to the stage of a state that is struggling for independence, with East Jerusalem as its capital and on the borders of 4 June 1967, in implementation of the resolutions of the National Council, including the Declaration of Independence in 1988, and relevant UN resolutions, including the General Assembly resolution 67/19 of 29/11/2012, as the political and legal basis for Palestinians reality, and the affirmation of adherence to the territorial unity of the State of Palestine, and the rejection of any divisions or facts imposed contrary to that;

The Central Council decided that the transitional period stipulated in the agreements signed in Oslo, Cairo and Washington, with its obligations no longer stand.

1. The Central Council calls upon the international community to assume its responsibilities on the basis of relevant UN resolutions to end the occupation and enable the State of Palestine to achieve its independence and to exercise its full sovereignty over its territory, including its capital, East Jerusalem, on the borders of 4 June 1967.
2. Assign the Executive Committee of the Palestine Liberation Organization to suspend recognition of Israel until it recognizes the State of Palestine on the 1967 borders and revokes the decision to annex East Jerusalem and expand and build settlements.
3. The Central Council reaffirms its decision to stop security coordination in all its forms and to break away from the relationship of economic dependence established by the Paris Economic Agreement, to achieve the independence of the national economy. It requests the Executive Committee of the PLO and the institutions of the State of Palestine to start implementing this.
4. Continue to work with world countries to boycott Israeli colonial settlements in all fields, to work on publishing the database for companies operating in Israeli settlements by the United Nations and to emphasize the illegality of Israeli colonial settlements since 1967.

5. Adopt the BDS movement and call on world countries to impose sanctions on Israel to put an end to its flagrant violations of international law and to end its continued aggression against the Palestinian people and the apartheid regime imposed on them.
6. Reject and condemn the Israeli occupation and apartheid that Israel is trying to enshrine as an alternative to the establishment of an independent Palestinian state, and affirm the determination of the Palestinian people to resist by all means.
7. Reject any proposals or ideas for transitional solutions or interim stages, including the so-called state with temporary borders.
8. Refuse to recognize Israel as a Jewish state.

Third: The internal Palestinian situation:

1. Adhere to the reconciliation Agreement signed in 2017 and its execution mechanisms, the latest of which is the Cairo agreement in 2017 and the provision of means of support for its implementation, and enable the Government of National unity to assume its responsibilities fully in the Gaza Strip in accordance with the Amended Basic Law, and then conduct general elections and hold the Palestinian National Council session no later than the end of 2018 in order to achieve political partnership within the framework of the PLO, the legitimate and sole representative of the Palestinian people, and work to form a government of national unity in order to strengthen the political partnership and the unity of the Palestinian political system.
2. Affirm the right of our people to exercise all forms of resistance against the occupation in accordance with the provisions of international law and to continue to activate, support and strengthen the peaceful popular resistance.
3. Affirm the need to support Palestinians and their steadfastness in the eternal capital of the State of Palestine, Jerusalem and affirm the need to support their struggle against the Israeli measures aimed at Judaizing the Holy City.
4. Take all measures to support our people in the Gaza Strip, who faced the Israeli aggression and the Israeli siege and provide the support they need, including freedom of movement, access to health, the reconstruction and the mobilization of the international community to break the siege.
5. The Central Council condemns the leaking of the property by the Greek Orthodox church to Israeli institutions and companies and calls for accountability of those responsible. It supports the struggle of the Palestinian people from the Orthodox community in order to preserve their rights and their role in administering the affairs of the Orthodox Church and preserving its property.

Fourth: The Security Council, the General Assembly and the International Criminal Court:
1. Continue to work to provide international protection to the Palestinian people in the territory of the occupied State of Palestine (West Bank, including East Jerusalem and the Gaza Strip) based on the Security Council resolution 605 for the year (1987), 672 (1967) and (1990), 904 of (1998), and the Fourth Geneva Convention of 1949 (Protection of Civilians in Time of War).
2. Continue to work to strengthen the status of the State of Palestine in international forums and activate the request for full membership of the State of Palestine in the United Nations.
3. Provide referral on various issues (settlement, prisoners, aggression on the Gaza Strip) to the International Criminal Court.
4. Continue to join to international institutions and organizations, including the specialized agencies of the United Nations.

Fifth: The Arab and Islamic levels:
1. Call for activating the resolution of the 1980 Amman Summit, which obliges the Arab states to sever all ties with any state that recognizes Jerusalem as the capital of Israel and transfers its embassy to it, which has been reaffirmed in a number of other Arab summits with the request of the Organization of Islamic Cooperation member states to do the same.
2. Adhere to the Arab peace initiative and reject any attempts to change or alter it and maintain its priorities.
3. Work with the Arab countries (The Arab League), the Islamic countries (OIC) and the Non-Aligned Movement to hold an international conference with full powers to launch the peace process and in coordination with the EU countries, Russia, China, Japan and other international groups on the basis of relevant international resolutions and benefit from the outcomes of the 2017 Paris conference in a way as to ensure the end of the Israeli occupation and the empowerment of the State of Palestine with East Jerusalem as its capital on the 1967 borders and exercise its independence and sovereignty and to resolve the refugee issue on the basis of UN Resolution 194 and other final status issues in accordance with the resolutions of the international community within a specific time frame.
4. The League of Arab States, the OIC, the Non-Aligned Movement and the African Union must stand firm in front of world countries that violated the resolutions of these collective frameworks on voting against the United Nations General Assembly resolution on Jerusalem 21/12/2017.
5. The Central council condemned US threats to cut aid to UNRWA, which is seen as a way for the US to abandon its responsibility over a refugee crisis that it has aided in creating and calls on the international

community to commit itself to securing the necessary funds for UNRWA, which would put an end to the continued decline in the Agency's services and instead improve its role in providing basic services to the victims of the Nakbah and ensure a decent life for refugees as a responsibility that the international community should fulfill in accordance with resolution 194.
6. The Central Council rejects foreign intervention in Arab countries and calls for a political solution and dialogue in order to end the crises and wars experienced by some Arab countries. It calls for maintaining the unity of these countries and defying attempts to divide and alleviating the suffering of Arabs.

Sixth: Develop mechanisms to implement the decisions of the previous Central Council to represent women by at least 30% in all institutions in the State of Palestine and to harmonize the laws in accordance with the Convention on the Elimination of all Forms of Discrimination Against Women (CEDAW).

Seventh: The Central Council salutes the masses of Palestinians in refugee camps and exile camps in Syria, Lebanon and the Diaspora who affirm their adherence to the right of return every day. The Executive Committee is mandated to continue and intensify work with the Palestinian communities in the world and to communicate with international parties to mobilize support in facing decisions that aim to liquidate the Palestinian cause.

Eighth: The Central Council salutes the struggle and steadfastness of the prisoners in the Israeli jails and calls for their support in their daily confrontation and calls on national and international institutions to bring up their cases in all forums until their release. The Council condemns the arrest and intimidation of children, including Ahed Tamimi, which has become a symbol of Palestinian pride in the face of occupation as well as dozens of other children.

It condemns the deliberate killings and field executions committed by Israel, as well as the killing of Ibrahim Abu Thuraya, and condemns the continued detention of the bodies of Palestinians in the numbers graves, and calls for their unconditional release.

Ninth: The Central Council salutes Palestinians for their response to President Trump's decision to recognize Jerusalem as the capital of Israel and transfer the US Embassy to it. It salutes the souls of Palestinians who rose for Palestine and al-Aqsa.

M.H.

Statement by (United States) President Trump on Jerusalem

Diplomatic Reception Room*

1:07 P.M. EST

THE PRESIDENT: Thank you. When I came into office, I promised to look at the world's challenges with open eyes and very fresh thinking. We cannot solve our problems by making the same failed assumptions and repeating the same failed strategies of the past. Old challenges demand new approaches.

My announcement today marks the beginning of a new approach to conflict between Israel and the Palestinians.

In 1995, Congress adopted the Jerusalem Embassy Act, urging the federal government to relocate the American embassy to Jerusalem and to recognize that that city – and so importantly – is Israel's capital. This act passed Congress by an overwhelming bipartisan majority and was reaffirmed by a unanimous vote of the Senate only six months ago.

Yet, for over 20 years, every previous American president has exercised the law's waiver, refusing to move the U.S. embassy to Jerusalem or to recognize Jerusalem as Israel's capital city.

Presidents issued these waivers under the belief that delaying the recognition of Jerusalem would advance the cause of peace. Some say they lacked courage, but they made their best judgments based on facts as they understood them at the time. Nevertheless, the record is in. After more than two decades of waivers, we are no closer to a lasting peace agreement between Israel and the Palestinians. It would be folly to assume that repeating the exact same formula would now produce a different or better result.

Therefore, I have determined that it is time to officially recognize Jerusalem as the capital of Israel.

---

* Source: Statement by President Trump on Jerusalem, White House (Dec. 6, 2017), https://www.whitehouse.gov/briefings-statements/statement-president-trump-jerusalem/.

While previous presidents have made this a major campaign promise, they failed to deliver. Today, I am delivering.

I've judged this course of action to be in the best interests of the United States of America and the pursuit of peace between Israel and the Palestinians. This is a long-overdue step to advance the peace process and to work towards a lasting agreement.

Israel is a sovereign nation with the right like every other sovereign nation to determine its own capital. Acknowledging this as a fact is a necessary condition for achieving peace.

It was 70 years ago that the United States, under President Truman, recognized the State of Israel. Ever since then, Israel has made its capital in the city of Jerusalem – the capital the Jewish people established in ancient times. Today, Jerusalem is the seat of the modern Israeli government. It is the home of the Israeli parliament, the Knesset, as well as the Israeli Supreme Court. It is the location of the official residence of the Prime Minister and the President. It is the headquarters of many government ministries.

For decades, visiting American presidents, secretaries of state, and military leaders have met their Israeli counterparts in Jerusalem, as I did on my trip to Israel earlier this year.

Jerusalem is not just the heart of three great religions, but it is now also the heart of one of the most successful democracies in the world. Over the past seven decades, the Israeli people have built a country where Jews, Muslims, and Christians, and people of all faiths are free to live and worship according to their conscience and according to their beliefs.

Jerusalem is today, and must remain, a place where Jews pray at the Western Wall, where Christians walk the Stations of the Cross, and where Muslims worship at Al-Aqsa Mosque.

However, through all of these years, presidents representing the United States have declined to officially recognize Jerusalem as Israel's capital. In fact, we have declined to acknowledge any Israeli capital at all.

But today, we finally acknowledge the obvious: that Jerusalem is Israel's capital. This is nothing more, or less, than a recognition of reality. It is also the right thing to do. It's something that has to be done.

That is why, consistent with the Jerusalem Embassy Act, I am also directing the State Department to begin preparation to move the American embassy from Tel Aviv to Jerusalem. This will immediately begin the process of hiring architects, engineers, and planners, so that a new embassy, when completed, will be a magnificent tribute to peace.

In making these announcements, I also want to make one point very clear: This decision is not intended, in any way, to reflect a departure from our strong commitment to facilitate a lasting peace agreement. We want an agreement that is a great deal for the Israelis and a great deal for the Palestinians. We are not taking a position of any final status issues, including the specific boundaries of the Israeli sovereignty in Jerusalem, or the resolution of contested borders. Those questions are up to the parties involved.

The United States remains deeply committed to helping facilitate a peace agreement that is acceptable to both sides. I intend to do everything in my power to help forge such an agreement. Without question, Jerusalem is one of the most sensitive issues in those talks. The United States would support a two-state solution if agreed to by both sides.

In the meantime, I call on all parties to maintain the status quo at Jerusalem's holy sites, including the Temple Mount, also known as Haram al-Sharif.

Above all, our greatest hope is for peace, the universal yearning in every human soul. With today's action, I reaffirm my administration's longstanding commitment to a future of peace and security for the region.

There will, of course, be disagreement and dissent regarding this announcement. But we are confident that ultimately, as we work through these disagreements, we will arrive at a peace and a place far greater in understanding and cooperation.

This sacred city should call forth the best in humanity, lifting our sights to what it is possible; not pulling us back and down to the old fights that have become so totally predictable. Peace is never beyond the grasp of those willing to reach.

So today, we call for calm, for moderation, and for the voices of tolerance to prevail over the purveyors of hate. Our children should inherit our love, not our conflicts.

I repeat the message I delivered at the historic and extraordinary summit in Saudi Arabia earlier this year: The Middle East is a region rich with culture, spirit, and history. Its people are brilliant, proud, and diverse, vibrant and strong. But the incredible future awaiting this region is held at bay by bloodshed, ignorance, and terror.

Vice President Pence will travel to the region in the coming days to reaffirm our commitment to work with partners throughout the Middle East to defeat radicalism that threatens the hopes and dreams of future generations.

It is time for the many who desire peace to expel the extremists from their midst. It is time for all civilized nations, and people, to respond to disagreement with reasoned debate – not violence.

And it is time for young and moderate voices all across the Middle East to claim for themselves a bright and beautiful future.

So today, let us rededicate ourselves to a path of mutual understanding and respect. Let us rethink old assumptions and open our hearts and minds to possible and possibilities. And finally, I ask the leaders of the region – political and religious; Israeli and Palestinian; Jewish and Christian and Muslim – to join us in the noble quest for lasting peace.

Thank you. God bless you. God bless Israel. God bless the Palestinians. And God bless the United States. Thank you very much. Thank you.

(The proclamation is signed.)

END

1:19 P.M. EST

Index

AALCO (Asian-African Legal Consultative Organization)   18n63
Abbas, Mahmoud   142, 192, 517, 518
abductions   50, 58, 60
Absentee Property laws   459
Abu Rahma, Abdallah   310
Abu Shamsiyeh, Imad   310
accountability
  gaps in   70, 75, 78, 82, 130
  for violations of international law   416–420
ACRI (Association for Civil Rights in Israel)   284, 317
acts of aggression   134–135
actus reus   42, 50, 59, 60, 66, 77
Adalah: Centre for Legal Rights of the Arab Minority in Israel   241n65, 300, 319
Addameer   311
Additional Protocol I (of GCIV)
  in general   272
  apartheid in   214
  Article 85   276
  Article 85(4)(a)   66–67, 70
Admissions Committee Law (2011)   241
African National Congress   217
Agreement on the Gaza Strip and the Jericho Area   120
Akram, Susan M.   451–488
Al-Aqsa v. Council case   496, 497
Albanese, Francesca   3–32
Albania   109–110
allocations, of land   6n7, 458–459, 507–512
Al-Mezan Center for Human Rights   309
Al-Za'noun, Salim   517–518
American Friends of Peace Now   313–314
Amicus Curaie   451–488
Amoroso, Daniele   84–116
Amro, Issa   311
anti-colonial movements   159
anti-Semitism
  and apartheid charges   203–205
  in Europe   157–158
  as form of racism   224
  new definition of   203
apartheid
  and anti-Semitism   203–205
  as crime against humanity   214
  definitions of   187, 206, 214, 217
  as discrete practice   219–221
  generated by anonymous structural conditions   221–222
  gravity of charge of   204, 252
  as international crime   213, 253
  and Israel's statehood   221
  precedents of   218
  as private behaviour   222
  prohibition of   213
  and purpose and intent clause   187, 207, 219–220, 231–232, 251–252
  and racial discrimination   222
  and racial groups   208, 223
  and South Africa's statehood   221
  used of term   217–218
  as war crime   214
  see also apartheid regimes
Apartheid Convention. *see* International Convention on the Suppression and Punishment of the Crime of Apartheid
apartheid regimes
  in general   88
  in Israel
    in general   170, 184–185, 186–187
    applicability of ICSPCA on   211, 251, 257–263
    compared to South Africa   216–219
    establishment of   206
    government policies. *see* Israeli government, apartheid policies of
  in South Africa
    compared to Israel   216–219
    end of   253
    fragmentation of black South Africans by   247
    international rejection of   213, 214
    public discourse about   152
    and security issues   252n88
    and statehood   221
    transition from   150, 155n7
  in South West Africa (Namibia)   216, 218–219, 280–283
  mention of   38
  see also apartheid; settler colonialism
Arab identity   225–226

Arab League 10, 521
Arab peoples, self-determination of 159
Arab State
  Palestine Mandate partition in Jewish and 164–166, 225, 229, 458
  Palestinian exclusion from 262–263
Arab-Israeli War (1948) 6, 229
Arab-Israeli War (1967) 229
Arafat, Yasser 212, 485
ARSIWA (Draft Articles on State Responsibility for Internationally Wrongful Acts) 39, 47
Asia
  refugees in 16
  rejection of international refugee laws in
    in general 16–17, 18–19
    reasons for 18n65
  see also South-East Asia
Asian-African Legal Consultative Organization (AALCO) 18n63
assistance
  to Palestinian refugees 355–359
  to Palestinians 401–407
  in Refugee Convention 466–471
Association for Civil Rights in Israel (ACRI) 284, 317
al-Atrash, Farid 310–311
Australia v. France (Nuclear Tests) case 279
aut dedere aut iudicare principle 131
authority, in NHS model 94–95, 96, 98
Aysev, Uzay Yasar 33–83
Azaria, Elor 310

BADIL Resource Center for Palestinian Residency and Refugee Rights 7n12
Balad (Arab-Israeli party) 241n63
Balfour Declaration 5n4, 155, 158–159, 160, 161, 169, 204
Bangkok Principles on the Status and Treatment of Refugees 18, 30, 31
Barnidge, Robert P., Jr. 191–196
bases of power, in NHS model 98, 99
Basic Law (Israeli Constitution)
  Article 7 (a) 234
  Freedom of Occupation 232, 240
  Human Dignity and Liberty 232, 239
  and illegality of discrimination or resistance to discrimination 223

Israel Lands 235
  Jewish-racial domination in 234
  land policies in 207
Bedouin communities 291, 298
Belgium 55–56, 316
Ben-Ari, Sigi 314–315
Ben-Gurion University (Beersheva) 316
Benjamin, Walter 172, 174, 175–176, 188
Ben-Naftali, Orna 275
Bennet, Naftali 300
Bensouda, Fatou 124, 125
Benvenisti, Eyal 275
Bernadotte, Folke 178
best interest/trust principle 278–279, 284–289
Beyond Occupation: Apartheid, Colonialism and International Law in the Occupied Palestinian Territories (ed. Tilley) 202, 256, 257
birth registration procedures 23
Bisharat, George 148–152
Bitan, David 313–314
Black's Law Dictionary 38, 144
Blake v. Guatemala case 60
Bolbol v. Bevándorlási és Állampolgársági Hivatal case 468, 473–474
Boycott, Divestment, Sanctions (BDS) movement 169, 193, 311, 319, 519–520
breaches, instantaneous 39–40
Breaking the Silence 315–316, 317
British Royal Commission of Inquiry 165–166
B'Tselem
  Haaretz on 316
  release of video by 310
  restrictive legislation against 317, 319
  threats and assaults on 310, 313–314, 315
Buttu, Diana 191–196

Cambodia 18
Capital (Marx) 174–175
Carter, Jimmy 245
Carty, Anthony 183
Casablanca Protocol (1965) 10
Cassese, Antonio 90–92
CAT (Convention against Torture and Other Cruel, Inhuman or Degrading Treatment or Punishment) 29

INDEX 529

Catalonia 105–106
catastrophe. *see* Nakba
CEDAW (Convention on the Elimination of All Forms of Discrimination Against Women) 522
Cheng, Judge Tien-Hsi 41n26
children, conscription of 37, 38, 45–46, 51–52, 74–75
citizenship
 in France 250
 in Israel 209, 231, 237, 241, 251
Citizenship Law/Nationality Law (1952) 7n9, 233, 237, 241, 459
civil rights movement 152
colonialism
 legitimacy of 159
 and self-determination 88–90
 see also settler colonialism
Commission and Others v. Kadi case 499, 501, 502
Committee on the Elimination of Racial Discrimination 251
Committee on the Exercise of the Inalienable Rights of the Palestinian People 334–338
commodity fetishism 174–175
Common Position 2001/931/CFS 492, 493, 496–502
community, in NHS model 95
complementarity, in Rome Statute 126, 129
composite crimes 39, 42n29, 43, 44
conscription
 of children 37, 38, 45–46, 51–52, 74–75
 meaning of word 74
Consolidated Eligibility and Registration Criteria (CERI) 8n17
conspiracy, as continuing crime 37, 55
continuing crimes
 Article 8(2)(b)(viii) as 71–76
 definitions of
  in general 36, 37–38, 144
  ECtHR on 41–42
  elements in 50–51
  gaps in approach to 37–39
  overview 46–52
 examples of 47, 50, 55
 Israeli settlements in West Bank as 76–81, 143–144
 and temporal jurisdiction 36, 58, 61, 143–144

continuous crimes
 Article 8(2)(b)(viii) as 69
 definitions of
  in general 36, 38
  ECtHR on 42–43
  overview 41–46
 ECtHR jurisprudence on 69–70
 and temporal jurisdiction 36, 58, 60–61
Convention against Torture and Other Cruel, Inhuman or Degrading Treatment or Punishment (CAT) 29
Convention on the Elimination of All Forms of Discrimination Against Women (CEDAW) 522
Convention on the Status of Stateless Persons (1954) 30, 453, 465
Convention Relating to the Status of Refugees. *see* Refugee Convention (1951)
Convention respecting the Laws and Customs of War on Land (1907) 235n53, 278
Coordinator of Government Activities in the Territories 302
Council v. Fulmen and Mahmoudian case 501, 502
Council v. Hamas case
 actions before General Court in 503
 arguments for appeal in 495–496
 background to dispute in 493–494
 findings of court in 497–503
 judgement in 490–491
 judgement under appeal in 494–495
 legal context of 491–493
Court of Justice of the European Union
 Council v. Hamas case. *see Council v. Hamas* case
Covenant of the League of Nations, Article 22 161, 166, 229n35, 456
Crawford, James 136, 137n93
CRC (Convention on the Rights of the Child) 29
Crimea 83n234, 88n13, 103n82, 105n89
crimes against humanity, apartheid as 214
Critique of Violence (Benjamin) 174, 175–176
Croatia, borders of 137
customary rules
 formation of 97
 and self-determination 89–90
Cyprus 109, 110–111

Dajani, Omar 284
Dannon, Danny 314
Davies, Sara E. 16n57, 17n58, 19, 19n66
De Becker case 55–56
decision-making process
  in NHS model
    in general 95–96, 97–98, 100
    and self-determination 106
Declaration of Principles of International Law Concerning Friendly Relations and Cooperation (UNGA) 164
Declaration of Principles on Interim Self-Government Arrangements (DOP) 191, 193, 356, 359, 374, 378, 401
Declaration of the Establishment of the State of Israel (1948) 163, 184, 227, 232
Declaration on Principles of International Law concerning Friendly Relations and Cooperation among States (1970) 273, 279
Declaration on the Granting of Independence to Colonial Countries and Peoples (1960) 87
Declaration on the Right and Responsibility of Individuals, Groups and Organs of Society to Promote and Protect Universally Recognized Human Rights and Fundamental Freedoms (Declaration on Human Rights Defenders) 306–307
Declaration on the Rights of Indigenous Peoples (2007) 86, 87
decolonization 109
demolition/destruction, of property 122, 127, 297–298, 299
destruction. *see* demolition/destruction
Development Authority 235
displacements, of Palestinian
  refugees 13–15, 26–27, 149, 358–359, 458–459
Division for Palestinian Rights of the Secretariat 329–330
domains
  in fragmentation. *see* fragmentation
  use of word 231n41
DOP (Declaration of Principles on Interim Self-Government Arrangements) 191, 193, 356, 359, 374, 378, 401

Draft Articles on State Responsibility for Internationally Wrongful Acts (ARSIWA) 39, 47
Dugard, John 217–218, 219n20, 246

East Jerusalem
  Bedouin communities in 291
  Israeli occupation/annexation of
    in general 283–285
    and best interest principle 284–289
    permanency of 284–287
    and security issues 285–286
    status of 230
  Israeli settlements in
    expansion of 192, 298–299
    resolutions on
      of UNGA 384–390
      of UNHRC 437–448
  Jordanian governance of 229
  Palestinians in
    children in 299–300
    demolition of property of 299
    and education 300–301
    evictions of 269, 299
    fragmentation of neighbourhoods of 243
    permanent residents status of 209–210, 230–231, 239, 242–244, 299
    punitive actions against 269, 299
    and street closures 299
  State lands in 235
  see also Jerusalem
Eban, Abba 177, 178, 182
ECCC (Extraordinary Chambers in the Courts of Cambodia) 37, 44, 57–58
economic apartheid 221
ECtHR (European Court of Human Rights). *see* European Court on Human Rights
effective control 136–137, 180
El Kott v. Bevándorlási és Állampolgársági Hivatal case
  Article 1D interpretation in 474–481
  description of 455
  and XX's status
    under Article 1D 481–484
    in Iraq 485–486
    in Kuwait 484–485

INDEX 531

as Palestinian refugee 488
  in Syria 486–487
  mention of 468
El-Ad, Hagai 313–314
electricity crisis, in Gaza Strip 266–268, 304
Elements of Crime (of ICC)
  Article 7(1)(g)(2) 59
  Article 7(1)(i-j) 58
  contextual element found in 45
  footnote 44 in 66–67, 70, 72, 143
  and instantaneous, continuous, and continuing crimes 38
  and temporal jurisdiction 58–59
  transfer of populations in 65–67, 72–74
El-Halabi, Mohammed 312–313
enforced disappearances 38, 47, 58, 59–60, 143
enforcement jurisdiction 129–130
enlistment
  meaning of word 74
  see also conscription
enslavement 37, 38
environmental justice 151
Erekat, Saeb 192
Eretz-Israel (Land of Israel) 105n88, 157, 162, 163, 227–228, 237
ethno-nationalist views, on self-determination 88–89, 109–110
European Commission (EC)
  Decision 2001/927/EC 493
  Regulation No 2580/2001 492–493
European Commission of Human Rights 48–49
European Court of Human Rights (ECtHR)
  cases of
    De Becker 55–56
    Loizidou v. Turkey 41, 48
  and temporal jurisdiction 55–56
  views of
    on composite crimes 43
    on continuing crimes 41–42
    on continuous crimes 42–43, 69–70
evictions 269, 299
exit permits 303
expropriations, *de facto* vs. *de jure* 48–49
Extraordinary Chambers in the Courts of Cambodia (ECCC) 37, 44, 57–58
Eysinga, Judge Willem van 41n26

ezrahut (citizenship), vs. nationality 209, 231, 237, 241

Falk, Richard 149, 152, 153–170, 184, 186, 188, 201–263, 219n20, 246
Fawzi, Mahmoud Bey 182–183
fetishism, commodity 174–175
The Fictions of the "Illegal" Occupation in the West Bank and Gaza (Sayed) 179–180
Fishman, Robert 220–221
Forces Patriotiques pour la Libération du Congo (FPLC) 45–46
Fourth Geneva Convention (GCIV)
  Additional Protocol I to
    in general 272
    apartheid in 214
    Article 85 276
    Article 85(4)(a) 66–67, 70
  applicability of, on Israeli occupation of Palestinian territory 274, 381–383
  Article 8 131–132
  Article 47 131–132
  Article 49 276
  Article 49(6) 66–67, 70, 71–72
  Article 146(2) 131
  best interest principle in 278
  creation of 272
  and jurisdiction of Palestine 131–133
  and Palestinians in oPt 230, 274
  protected persons in 132, 278
  transfer of populations in 67, 71–72
  travaux preparatoires of 67
Fourth Geneva Convention Relative to the Protection of Civilian Persons in Times of War (1949). *see* Fourth Geneva Convention (GCIV)
FPLC (Forces Patriotiques pour la Libération du Congo) 45–46
fragmentation
  of black South Africans 247
  of Palestinian neighbourhoods 243
  of Palestinians 238–250
    in general 166n28, 208–209
    four domains of 209, 211, 231, 239
    domain 1 209, 239, 240–242
    domain 2 209–210, 239, 242–244
    domain 3 210, 239, 244–248
    domain 4 210, 239, 248–250

France 250
Frankfurt School 175
fraud 43
Friedman, Lara 313
future trends, in NHS model 111–113

Gaza Flotilla raid (2010) 127–128
Gaza for World Vision 312
Gaza Strip
  Egyptian governance of 229
  electricity crisis in 266–268, 304
  environmental concerns 151
  Hamas' control of 121–122, 139–140, 239
  human rights defenders working in 312–313
  humanitarian staff in 303
  infrastructure in 303–304, 371
  Israeli control of
    in general 121–122, 229–230
    as apartheid regime 245
    and best interest 288
    dual governance regime of 180–181, 245–246
    illegality of 179–180
    as military occupation 244–245
  Operation Protective Edge in 121, 122, 126, 143
  Palestinian refugees in
    camps for 371
    numbers of 7
    and Six Day War 13–14
    temporary protection of 9–10
  Palestinians in
    human rights situation of 394–395, 428–429, 431–432
    humanitarian situation of 394–395, 396
    permit denials to 301–303
    status of 137
Gaza-Jericho Agreement (1994) 191n1
GCIV (Fourth Geneva Convention). see Fourth Geneva Convention
gender and sexual preference justice 151
genocide
  under Article 6(a) (Elements of Crime) 60–61
  as continuous crime 41, 44–45
  excluded from Israeli apartheid policies 210, 247, 257, 258
  and hierarchy in criminality 252
  see also Holocaust
Gisha Legal Center for Freedom of Movement 302, 319
global apartheid 221
Goldberg, David Theo 188
good faith, in international law 279–280, 289
Great Britain. see United Kingdom
Great War 5n4, 155, 160, 456
Greater Jerusalem Bill 269
Green Line 133, 137–138, 166, 230, 243
Gross, Aeyal 275
Gunneflo, Markus 171–188
Gurmendi, Judge de 38
Gvaryahu, Avner 314–315

Haaretz (newspaper) 316
Haganah 6n7
Hague Regulations (1907) 235n53, 278
Halachah (Jewish law) 227
Halpern, Jeff 156
Hamas
  and Gaza Strip 121–122, 139–140, 239
  retention on terrorist organization list. see Council v. Hamas case
  rift between PA and 139–142
  support for ICC 142
Hamas-Izz al-Din al-Qassem. see Council v. Hamas case
Hamoked – Centre for the Defence of the Individual 315
Al-Haq 309, 311–312
Health Development Information and Policy Institute 309
Hedrick, Todd 175
Henckaerts, Jean-Marie 131
Higgins, Rosalyn 92
Holocaust 156, 158
HSRC (Human Sciences Research Council of South Africa) 245, 247, 256–262
Human Rights Committee 56–57
human rights defenders
  and international law 305–307
  in Israel/Palestine
    restrictive legislation against 317–320
    threats and assaults on 308–317
    violation of rights of 305
Human Rights Defenders Fund 308

human rights situation
    of Palestinians
        in Gaza Strip   394–395, 428–429,
            431–432
        in oPt   391–400, 425–436
Human Rights Watch   316
Human Sciences Research Council of South
    Africa (HSRC)   245, 247, 256–262
humanitarian staff   303
hunger strikes   379, 396, 398, 429, 433
Hussein, Sherif of Mekka   225, 456
Hussein-McMahon letters   456

IACtHR (Inter-American Court of Human
    Rights)   56, 60
*Ibrahim Said v. The Secretary of State for the
    Home Department* case   468
ICC (International Criminal Court). *see*
    International Criminal Court
ICCPR (International Covenant on Civil and
    Political Rights)   29, 57, 306
ICERD (International Convention on the
    Elimination of All Forms of Racial
    Discrimination). *see* International
    Convention on the Elimination of All
    Forms of Racial Discrimination
ICESCR (International Covenant on
    Economic, Social and Cultural
    Rights)   29, 300
ICJ (International Court of Justice). *see*
    International Court of Justice
ICTR (International Criminal Tribunal for
    Rwanda). *see* International Criminal
    Tribunal for Rwanda
ICTY (International Criminal Tribunal for the
    former Yugoslavia)   37, 55
ILC (International Law Commission)   38
illegality
    of annexation of occupied
        territory   252n88
    of discrimination or resistance to
        discrimination   223
    of Israeli Settlements   78, 121, 138–139
    of occupation of West Bank and Gaza
        Strip   179–180
Im Tirtzu   314–315
immigration
    to Israel   236
    to Palestine Mandate   161, 163, 457

imprisonment, as continuing crime   38
inalienable rights, of Palestinians   334–338
Independent Commission for Human
    Rights   310
Indonesia
    and international human rights laws   29
    refugees/asylum-seekers in
        numbers of   21–22
        Palestinian   23
        status of   22
        and UNHCR   21–23
    visa policies of   4
infrastructure, in Gaza Strip   303–304, 371
inhuman acts
    in general   187, 220
    in Israeli scenario   247
    and purpose and intent clause   231–232
instantaneous breaches   39–40
instantaneous crimes
    Article 8(2)(b)(viii) as   68
    definitions of
        in general   36
        overview   39–41
    and temporal jurisdiction   36
Inter-American Court of Human Rights
    (IACtHR)   56, 60
Interim Agreement on the West Bank and the
    Gaza Strip. *see* Oslo Accords/Agreements
international community
    legal obligations to oppose apartheid
        in general   214–215
        in Israel   212, 258
        recommendations   254, 255–256
International Convention on the Elimination
    of All Forms of Racial Discrimination
    (1965; ICERD)
    apartheid in   204, 206, 217
    racial discrimination in   214, 224
    mention of   251
International Convention on the Protection
    of All Persons from Enforced
    Disappearance   29, 43n35
International Convention on the Suppression
    and Punishment of the Crime of
    Apartheid (ICSPCA; 1973)
    adoption of   152
    apartheid in
        as crime against humanity   214
        definition of   206, 217

International Convention (cont.)
    and inhuman acts   187, 220, 231–232
    and purpose and intent clause   187,
        207, 219–220, 231–232, 251–252
    and right to nationality   251
    applicability of
        in Israeli scenario
            in general   211
            Article II(a)   257
            Article II(b)   258
            Article II(c)   251, 258–261,
                262–263
            Article II(d)   261
            Article II(e)   261–262
            Article II(f)   262
    racial discrimination in   208
    racial groups in   223, 224
International Court of Justice (ICJ)
    advisory opinions of
        on construction of Israeli wall   137–138, 139, 208, 212, 273, 283, 284
        on Namibia   280
    and border determination   134, 136
    cases of
        Lubanga   38, 45–46, 51, 58
        Nuclear Tests (Australia v. France)   279
    and continuing, continuous and instantaneous crime   38
    core documents of. *see* Elements of Crime; Rome Statute
International Covenant on Civil and Political Rights (ICCPR)   29, 57, 306
International Covenant on Economic, Social and Cultural Rights (ICESCR)   29, 300
International Criminal Court (ICC)
    and acts of aggression   134–135
    findings of, in *Situation in Georgia*   135
    and Israeli West Bank settlement activities
        in general   34–35
        before June   2014 36
        and temporal jurisdiction   35–36
    judgements of, *Katanga*   64
    jurisdiction in oPt of
        in general   118–119, 127
        temporal   35–36, 142–146
        territorial   128–142
        and automatic jurisdiction   129
        and boundaries of oPt   135–139
        and domestic jurisdiction   128–129
        and Oslo Accords   128
        and PA-Hamas quarrel   140, 142
        and territorial uncertainty of oPt   134–135
    jurisdiction of, temporal   52–54
    Office of the Prosecutor of. *see* Office of the Prosecutor (of ICC; OTP)
    preliminary investigation of
        in Palestine   125–127
        Situation in the Republic of Korea   128
        Situation on Registered Vessels of the Union of the Comoros, the Hellenic Republic and the Kingdom of Cambodia   127–128
    Statute of Rome of. *see* Statute of Rome
    support for   142
International Criminal Tribunal for Rwanda (ICTR)
    and definition of continuing crime   37–38, 144
    Nahimana v. The Prosecutor   37–38, 41, 144
    and temporal jurisdiction   54, 58
International Criminal Tribunal for the former Yugoslavia (ICTY)   37, 54–55
international human rights laws
    and Indonesia   29
    and Malaysia   29
    and occupational laws   273
    and Thailand   29
    violations of, during Operation Protective Edge   122, 126
international humanitarian laws
    transfer of populations in   66, 73
    violations of, during Operation Protective Edge   122, 126
international law
    accountability for violations of   416–420
    and apartheid   187
    complicity in, Israel's settler colonialism   172, 186, 188
    good faith in   279–280, 289
    and human rights defenders   305–307
    on Israeli occupation of Palestinian territory   274
    and justice   152, 416–420
    NHS' views on

analytical model for 97–100
overview 94–97
on occupation 271–274
positivist views on 96
self-determination in 86–87
statehood in 182–183
see also international human rights laws; international humanitarian laws; international refugee laws
International Law Commission (ILC)
Draft Articles on State Responsibility for Internationally Wrongful Acts 39, 47
transfer of populations in 71
international refugee laws, Asian rejection of 16–17, 18–19
interpretations, rules on, of VCLT 62–63, 466–467, 469
Ir Amin 317
Iraq 14
Irgun 6n7
irredentist claims 109–110
Israel
apartheid regime in
in general 170, 184–185, 186–187
compared to South Africa 216–219
establishment of 206
see also Israeli government, apartheid policies of; Zionist movement
and East Jerusalem
in general 230, 283–285
and best interest principle 284–289
permanency of 284–287
and security issues 285–286
see also Israeli settlements
and Gaza Strip
in general 121–122, 229–230
as apartheid regime 245
and best interest 288
dual governance regime of 180–181, 245–246
illegality of control of 179–180
as military occupation 244–245
Operation Protective Edge in 121, 122, 126, 143
human rights defenders in
threats and assaults on 313–317
violation of rights of 305
Jewish immigration to 236

as Jewish State 155–156, 161, 232–238, 262–263
Jews, self-determination of 194
military prowess of 168
NGO's in 317–319
and oPt
applicability of
advisory opinion on Namibia 218–219, 280–283
Fourth Geneva Convention on 274, 381–383
lawful occupants test 283–292
dual governance regime of 180–181, 244–248
international law on 273–274
legal framework of 270–271
not complying to international law 289–292
and Palestine. *see* Israel/Palestine relationship
Palestinians in
under civil law with restrictions 209, 231, 239, 240–242
as racial group 225–226
voting rights of 211, 215, 218, 234
and PLO 519–520
as racial state 231–238
settler colonialism of
in general 149, 154, 165, 180–181, 185
international law's complicity in 172, 186, 188
statehood of
acceptance of 156, 193
and apartheid 221
declaration of independence 163, 184, 227, 232
establishment of 6, 229
recognition of 185
and two-state solution 157, 166, 247, 458, 518
war crimes, unwillingness to investigate 126
and West Bank
in general 229–230, 283–285
and best interest/trust principle 284–289
dual governance regime of 180–181, 246–248

Israel (cont.)
    illegality of control of   179–180
    permanency of   284–287
        and security issues   285–286
    and Zionist movement. *see* Zionist
        movement
Israel Defense Forces (IDF)   121–122
Israel Lands Authority (ILA)   207
Israeli Development Authority   207
Israeli government
    apartheid policies of
        and Apartheid Convention
            in general   211
            Article II(a)   257
            Article II(b)   258
            Article II(c)   251, 258–261,
                262–263
            Article II(d)   261
            Article II(e)   261–262
            Article II(f)   262
        bans on challenges to racial
            domination   234
        citizenship/nationality
            distinction   209, 231, 237, 241
        demographic engineering   207–208,
            233–234
        fragmentation of Palestinians
            238–250
            in general   208–209
            four domains of   209, 211, 231, 239
            domain 1   209, 239, 240–242
            domain 2   209–210, 239, 242–244
            domain 3   210, 239, 244–248
            domain 4   210, 239, 248–250
        genocide excluded   210, 247, 257, 258
    legislation
        Absentee Property laws   459
        Basic Law (Constitution). *see* Basic
            Law
        Citizenship Law/Nationality
            Law   7n9, 233, 237, 241, 459
        Law of Return   7n9, 227, 233, 237,
            240–241
        State Property Law   207
        World Zionist Organisation –
            Jewish Agency Status Law   232,
            235, 236
        national institutions   235–236

Retroactive Transfer: A Scheme for the
    Solution of the Arab Question in
    the State of Israel   459
    and security issues   251–252
    and creation of PA   120
    and Gaza Strip   121–122
    settlements policies of   286
Israeli Lands Authority (ILA)   235
Israeli law
    collective rights in   250
    see also under specific laws
Israeli-Palestinian Interim Agreement on the
    West Bank and the Gaza Strip (Oslo
    Accord II)   120, 230, 247
*Israeli Practices Towards the Palestinian People
    and the Question of Apartheid* (Falk &
    Tilley)   184, 186, 201–263
Israeli settlements
    in East Jerusalem
        expansion of   192, 298–299
        resolutions on
            of UNGA   384–390
            of UNHRC   437–448
    in oPt
        resolutions on
            of UNGA   384–390
            of UNHRC   437–448
    in Syrian Golan   384–390, 437–448
    in West Bank
        as continuing crime   76–81, 143–144
        expansion of   192, 268–269, 297–298
        and ICC   34–36
        illegality of   78, 121, 138–139
        before June   2014 36, 143
        and Law for the Regularization of
            Settlement in Judea and
            Samaria   507–513
        numbers of   120
        policies regarding   76–77, 144–145
        settler population of   192
        State involvement in   246–247, 286
        status of   120–121
        and temporal jurisdiction   35–36,
            143–144
        territory of   138–139
Israeli-Palestinian Interim Agreement on the
    West Bank and Gaza Strip (1995)   212
Israel/Palestine relationship
    as asymmetric conflict   154

INDEX   537

and decolonizing struggles   153–154
dissemination of information
  on   331–333
influences on
  of Balfour Declaration   155, 158–159,
    160, 169
  of both World Wars   155
  of British Mandate over
    Palestine   5n4, 159
  of partition   164–165
  of Zionist movement   156–158,
    160–161, 163–165, 167–168
overview of   5 n4
peaceful solution to conflict in   339–351
in PLO Central Council statement   2018
  519–520
and two-state solution   157, 166, 247, 458,
  518
UNSC deliberations on UK proposal
  (1967)
  of Eban, Abba   182
  of Fawzi, Mahmoud Bey   183
  ignoring of Palestinian rights
    in   177–178
  and status of Palestine   182
  of Tomeh, George   177–179

Jabotinsky, Vladimir   226
JCE (joint criminal enterprise)   37, 43, 57
Jennings, Ivor   88n9
Jerusalem
  in Resolution 181(II) (UNGA)   458
  in Resolution 7215 (UNGA)   352–354
  US recognition of   518–519, 523–526
  see also East Jerusalem
Jerusalem Embassy Act (1995)   523
Jerusalem Programme (of JA-WZO)   233
Jewish Agency   207
Jewish Agency – World Zionist Organisation
  (JA-WZO)   233, 236
Jewish identity   226
Jewish immigration   161, 163, 236, 457
Jewish National Fund (JNF)   207, 227, 235,
  236
Jewish State
  and international community   161
  Palestine Mandate partition in Arab
    and   164–166, 225, 229, 458

Palestinian exclusion from   155–156,
  262–263
and racial discrimination   232–238
Jews
  in Israel   150
  as racial group   208, 226–228
joint criminal enterprise (JCE)   37, 43, 57
Jordan
  governance of West Bank   229
  Palestinian refugees in
    expulsion of   14, 27
    numbers of   7, 248
    status of   10, 248–249
Judea   507–513
jurisdiction
  of ICC, temporal   52–54
  of ICC in oPt
    in general   118–119, 127
    temporal   35–36, 142–146
    territorial   128–142
      and automatic jurisdiction   129
      and boundaries of oPt   135–139
      and domestic jurisdiction   128–131
      and Oslo Accords   128, 130–131
      and PA-Hamas quarrel   140, 142
      and territorial uncertainty of
        oPt   134–135
  of PA in oPt
    delegation to ICC
      in general   128–130
      and Oslo Accords   128, 130–131
    and Fourth Geneva
      Convention   131–133
    and PA-Hamas quarrel   139–140
justice
  facets of   149–151
  fetishizing of   175
  and historical injustices   176
  and international law   152, 416–420
  of natural law   176
  of positive law   174, 176
  re-centering of   148–152
  for violations of international
    law   416–420

Kampala amendments   134
Katanga judgement   64
Kattan, Victor   257

Kearny, Michael   257
Keren Hayesod (United Jewish Appeal)   236
Keren Kayemet Le-Israel (Jewish National Fund; JNF)   207, 227, 235, 236
Kerry, John   166, 245
Kfar Etzion settlement   76–77, 79
Khawaja, Salah   311
al-Khudayri, Yassir   117–147
kidnappings. *see* abductions
Kiswanson, Nada   311–312
Kontorovich, Eugene   128
Kosovo   88n13, 109–110
Kuwait   14

land allocations   6n7, 458–459, 507–512
Land of Israel (Eretz-Israel)   105n88, 157, 162, 163, 227–228, 237
landownership   48, 136, 298
Lasswell, Harold D.   87, 94n42
Lauterpacht, Hersch   85
Law and Politics: Options and Strategies of International Law for the Palestinian People Conference (2013)   171–172
Law for the Regularization of Settlement in Judea and Samaria   507–513
Law of Return (1950)   227, 237, 240
lawful occupants test
  applicability in Israeli scenario   283–292
  overview   275–280
League of Arab States   10, 521
League of Nations. *see* Covenant of the League of Nations
Lebanon
  Palestinian refugees in
    camps for   370
    and civil war   14
    numbers of   7
    temporary protection of   9–10
Legal Consequences for States of the Continued Presence of South Africa in Namibia (Advisory Opinion of ICJ)   280
Legal Consequences of the Construction of a Wall in the Occupied Palestinian Territory (Advisory Opinion of ICJ)   137–138, 139, 208, 212, 273, 283, 284
legality principle   53, 63–64
Lehi   6n7
Lenin, Vladimir   159

le'um (nationality), vs. citizenship   209, 231, 237, 241
Li, Darryl   181
liberal-democratic views, on self-determination   88–89
Libya   14
Life is Negotiations (Erekat)   192
list of persons/groups involved in terrorist acts, retention of Hamas on   489–503
Loizidou v. Turkey case   41, 48
London-Zurich Agreements (1959)   109
Lubanga case   38, 45–46, 51, 58
Lukács, Georg   175
Lynk, Michael
  report UN Doc A/72/556   264–293
    conclusion of   292–293
    on East Jerusalem   269
    on Gaza Strip   266–268
    introduction in   265–266
    on Israeli occupation of Palestinian territory
      applicability of advisory opinion on Namibia   280–283
      applicability of lawful occupants test   283–292
      international law on   274
      Israeli's refusal to comply to international law   289–292
      legal framework of   270–271
    on occupation
      international law on   271–274
      lawful occupants test   275–280
    recommendations in   293
    on West Bank   268–269
  report UN Doc A/HRC/34/70   294–322
    conclusion of   320–321
    on East Jerusalem   298–301
    on Gaza Strip
      humanitarian staff, restriction on movement of   303
      infrastructure in   303–304
      permit denials   301–303
    on human rights defenders
      and international law   305–307
      restrictive legislation against   317–320
      threats and assaults on   308–317
      violation of rights of   305

INDEX 539

    introduction in   295–296
    recommendations in   322
    on West Bank   297–298
    mention of   178

Maale Adumim settlement   81
Malaysia
    and international human rights laws   29
    refugees/asylum-seekers in
        numbers of   23
        Palestinian   20n72, 23–25
        Rohingya   25
        status of   24–25
        and UNHCR   23–25
    visa policies of   24
Mandate Agreement for Palestine   161, 166
Mandate System   161, 166
Marx, Karl   174–175
Marxism   173, 174
Masad Complex   165
Masri, Mazen   185
May, Teresa   159n18
McDougal, Myres S.   87, 94n42
medical treatment   302
Meindersma, Christa   71
Memorandum of Association of the Jewish National Fund   227
mens rea   40, 42, 45, 54, 60–61
Menuhin, Yishai   314–315
Michaeli, Keren   275
Michel, Charles   316
Migration Court of Appeal (Sweden)   475
minorities, trapped   104, 110, 113
Mizrahi Jews   150, 151
Moreno Ocampo, Luis   123
murder, as instantaneous crime   40

Nahimana v. The Prosecutor case   37–38, 41, 144
Nahr el-Bared refugee camp   370
Nakba (catastrophe)   6, 149, 155–156, 320
Namibia (South West Africa)   216, 218–219
Nasser, Gamal Abdul   225
national service volunteers   319
Nationalis Party (South Africa)   217
nationality (*le'um*), vs. citizenship   209, 231, 237, 241

Nationality Law. *see* Citizenship Law/Nationality Law
native populations, in settler-colonial states   161–162
negative exceptionalism   157
negotiations
    continuing   194–196
    periods of lack of   193
    seen as sacred   192–193
Netanyahu, Benjamin   159n18, 246n79, 269, 290, 313, 316, 319
Netherlands v. Al-Aqsa case   496, 497
New Haven School of international law (NHS)
    criticism of   93–94
    policy-oriented jurisprudence of   87
    views on international law of analytical model for. *see* NHS model
Newton, Michael   128
NGO Disclosure Law (2016)   317
NHS model
    authority in   94–95, 96, 98
    bases of power in   98, 99
    community in   95
    decision-making process in
        in general   95–96, 97–98, 100
        and self-determination   106
    future trends in   111–113
    participants in
        in general   94, 97–98, 99–100
        and self-determination   101–102, 106–107
    past trends in   95–96, 108–111
    people in   101–102
    perspectives in   97–98, 99
    and self-determination   102–106
    policy recommendations in   113–114
    principle of procedure in   99
    situations/arenas in   99
    strategies in   98–99
    values in   94
Non-Alignment Movement   521
Non-custodial Measures for Women Offenders (the Bangkok Rules)   379, 396, 398, 430, 433
Non-Governmental Organizations (NGO's)   317–319

non-refoulement principle   17, 29–30, 472
  see also refoulement
non-retroactivity ratione personae
  principle   53
Non-Self-Governing Territories   109
Nordau, Max   226
Notes for a Critique of Hegel's Philosophy of Right (Marx)   175
Novak, Yuli   315–316
Nsengiyumva case   55
Nuclear Tests (Australia v. France) case   279
nullum crimen sine lege principle   53, 63–64
Nuremberg indictment   72n190, 73–74n201

Obama, Barack   166
Observatory for the Protection of Human
  Rights Defenders   312
occupation
  administering of territory
    under   279–280
  and annexation of occupied
    territory   275–276
  and best interest/trust
    principle   278–279
  temporary nature of   277–278
  see also East Jerusalem; Gaza Strip;
    Occupied Palestinian Territories; West
    Bank
Occupation, Colonialism, Apartheid? A Reassessment of Israel's Practices in the Occupied Palestinian Territories under International Law (ed. Tiley)   257
occupational laws
  in general   179–181, 187, 271–274
  and international human rights laws   273
  and right to self-determination   273
Occupied Palestinian Territories (oPt)
  human rights defenders in
    threats and assaults on   308–313
    violation of rights of   305
  and ICC jurisdiction
    in general   118–119, 127
    temporal   35–36, 142–146
    territorial   128–142
      and automatic jurisdiction   129
      and boundaries of oPt   135–139
      and domestic jurisdiction   128–129
      and Oslo Accords   128, 130
      and PA-Hamas quarrel   140, 142
      and territorial uncertainty of
        oPt   134–135
  infrastructure in   414
  Israeli control of
    applicability of
      advisory opinion on
        Namibia   218–219, 280–283
      Fourth Geneva Convention   274,
        381–383
      lawful occupants test   283–292
    dual governance regime of   180–181,
      244–248
    international law on   273–274
    legal framework of   270–271
    not complying to international
      law   289–292
  Israeli settlements in
    resolutions on
      of UNGA   384–390
      of UNHRC   437–448
  jurisdiction of PA in
    delegation to ICC
      in general   128–130, 133
      and Oslo Accords   128, 130–131
    and Fourth Geneva
      Convention   131–133
    Oslo II Accord (1995) on
      in general   120, 128
      and jurisdiction of ICC   128, 130
      and jurisdiction of PA   133
  Palestinians in
    demolition of property of   429
    evictions of   429
    human rights situation of   391–400,
      425–436
    under military law   210, 239, 244–248
    sovereignty of   410–415
    status as foreigner of   250–251
  territorial boundaries of
    determining of   135–139
    uncertainty of   133–136
  and UNGA   133–134, 410–415
  violation of international law
    in   416–420
  see also East Jerusalem; Gaza Strip;
    Palestine; West Bank
occupied territories

INDEX

annexation of   275–276
transfer of populations into   71–74
Office for the Coordination of Humanitarian Affairs   302
Office of the Prosecutor (of ICC; OTP)
   and PA
      in general   122, 123–124
   preliminary investigation of
      in general   125–126
      and complementarity   126–127
      and gravity of alleged crimes   127
Olmert, Ehud   245, 286
On Self-Determination, Statehood, and the Law of Negotiation: The Case of Palestine (Barnidge, Jr.)   191–196
Operation Cast Lead (2008–2009)   121
Operation Pillar of Defense (2012)   121
Operation Protective Edge (2014)   121, 122, 126, 143
opinio necessitatis   97
Organisation of Islamic Cooperation (OIC)   521
original justice   150
Oslo Accords/Agreements
   and acceptance of Israel   193
   and ICC jurisdiction   128, 130–131, 146
   language use in   192
   main principles of   191–192
   on oPt
      in general   120, 128
      and jurisdiction of PA   128, 130–131
   overview of   191–192n1
   side effects of   192
   mention of   230
Oslo II Accord (1995). *see* Oslo Accords/Agreements
OTP (Office of the Prosecutor of ICC). *see* Office of the Prosecutor (of ICC; OTP)
Ottoman Empire   5n4, 456

Palestine
   governance of   140–141
   influences on, of both World Wars   155
   and Israel. *see* Israel/Palestine relationship
   and political independence   156
   and two-state solution   157, 166, 247, 458, 518
   and UNGA

      observer state status of   123–124
   statehood of   138
   and UNSC Resolution 242   166, 176–177
   see also Occupied Palestinian Territories; Palestine Mandate; Palestinian National Authority
Palestine Liberation Organization (PLO)
   Central Council statement   2018 517–522
      on Arabic cooperation   521–522
      on future and function of PA   517–518
      on internal Palestinian situation   520–521
      on international protection of Palestinians   521
      on relationship with Israel   519–520
      on US recognition of Jerusalem   518–519
   Charter of   225–226
   and creation of PA   120, 140
   goals of   149
   and Israel   519–520
   representative mandate of   140–142
   and two-state solution   166, 518
Palestine Mandate
   in general   5n4, 157
   British withdrawal from   164, 229
   establishment of   228–229
   Jewish immigration to   161, 163, 457
   Jewish opposition to British   160–161, 163–164
   Palestinian self-determinations during   161
   partition in Arab and Jewish State   164–166, 225, 229, 458
Palestine Yearbook of International Law (Vol. XV)   185
Palestinian Authority (PA) passports   21, 23, 24, 25
Palestinian Interim Self-Governing Authority (PA). *see* Palestinian National Authority
Palestinian National Authority (PA)
   creation of   120, 140
   future and function of   517–518
   jurisdiction in oPt of
      delegation to ICC
         in general   128–130, 133
         and Oslo Accords   128, 130–131

Palestinian National Authority (PA) (cont.)
    and Fourth Geneva
        Convention 131–133
    and PA-Hamas quarrel 139–140
    and Office of the Prosecutor (of ICC; OTP)
        in general 122, 123–124
        preliminary investigation of
            in general 125–126
            and complementarity 126–127
            and gravity of alleged crimes 127
    rift between Hamas and 139–142
    and Rome Statute
        Article 12(3) 123, 124, 143
        ratification of 118–119, 124, 140, 141
    sovereignty of 194
    support for ICC 142
    and West Bank 139–140
Palestinian National Council 517
Palestinian refugees
    compensation of 9, 178–179
    definitions of
        in Refugee Convention 11n30
        in UNCCP 460–461
        in UNRWA 7–8, 8n20, 461–462
    destinations of 7, 27
    displacements of 13–15, 26–27, 149, 233, 358–359, 458–459
    distribution of 248
    in Gaza Strip
        camps for 371
        numbers of 7
        and Six Day War 13–14
        temporary protection of 9–10
    historical background to 456–457
    in Jordan
        expulsion of 14, 27
        numbers of 7, 248
        status of 10, 248–249
    in Kuwait 14
    in Lebanon
        camps for 370
        and civil war 14
        numbers of 7
        temporary protection of 9–10
    in Libya 14
    non-registered 8n20
    numbers of 7, 13–15
    properties and revenues of 373–374
    and 'protection gap' 11–13, 32
    and *refoulement* 26–27
    registered with UNRWA 7, 8n20, 248
    right to return of, refusal of 9, 178–179, 208, 210, 233, 249, 459
    in South-East Asia
        in general 4, 15–16, 20–21
        increase of 26, 27, 31
        Indonesia 23
        legal framework available to 28–29, 31–32
        in Malaysia 20n72, 23–25
        registration of 28
        Thailand 25–26
        and UNHCR 29
        visa policies for 21
    status of
        in general 9–10, 231
        under international law 455–473
        reasons for exceptional 453–454, 463–464
        and Refugee Convention 466–472
    in Syrian Arab Republic
        fleeing from country 14, 26–27, 365–366
        numbers of 7, 248
        temporary protection of 9–10
    and UN 459
    and UNGA
        endorsement of UNRWA definition for 8
        resolutions on 355–359
        return of 9
    and UNHCR 8n20, 9, 12
    in West Bank
        numbers of 7
        and Six Day War 13–14
        temporary protection of 9–10
    see also Palestinians; refugees/asylum-seekers
Palestinians
    assistance to, resolutions on 401–407
    in East Jerusalem
        children in 299–300
        demolition of property of 299
        and education 300–301

INDEX 543

evictions of   269, 299
fragmentation of neighbourhoods
    of   243
permanent residents status of   209–
    210, 230–231, 239, 242–244, 299
punitive actions against   269, 299
and street closures   299
exclusion of, from which
    country   262–263
forcible displacement of   233
fragmentation of   238–250
    in general   166n28, 208–209
    four domains of   209, 211, 231, 239
    domain 1   209, 239, 240–242
    domain 2   209–210, 239, 242–244
    domain 3   210, 239, 244–248
    domain 4   210, 239, 248–250
in Gaza Strip
    human rights situation of   394–395,
        428–429, 431–432
    humanitarian situation of   394–395,
        396
    permit denials to   301–303
inalienable rights of   334–338
in Israel
    under civil law with restrictions   209,
        231, 239, 240–242
    as racial group   225–226
    voting rights of   211, 215, 218, 234
nationality of, by Treaty of
    Lausanne   456–457, 460
nationality/citizenship of   209, 231, 237,
    241, 251
opposition to Zionism of   161
in oPt
    evictions of   429
    human rights situation of   391–400,
        425–436
    under military law   210, 239, 244–248
    sovereignty of, UNGA resolutions
        on   410–415
    status as foreigner of   250–251
as racial group   208
rejection of partition by   164, 165–166
right to self-determination of
    in general   137–138, 169
    Barnidge on   194

and Covenant of League of
    Nations   166
denial of   194
legal status of   208, 212, 273–274
during mandate period   161
resolutions on
    of UNGA   408–409
    of UNHRC   421–424
and UNSC deliberations   179
self-determination of
    in general   137, 169
    Barnidge on   194
    and Covenant of League of
        Nations   166
    during mandate period   161
    and UNSC   179
in West Bank
    children's plight   299–300
    demolition of property of   297–298
    fragmentation of   247
    punitive actions against   299
    and street closures   299
see also Palestinian refugees
Pan-African Congress   217
Pappé, Ilan   6n7
Pardo, Tamir   288
participants, in NHS model
    in general   94, 97–98, 99–100
    and self-determination   101–102, 106–107
Partition Plan   6n6, 164–166
Pashukanis, Evgeny   175
past trends, in NHS model
    in general   95–96
    and self-determination   108–111
PCIJ (Permanent Court of International
    Justice). see Permanent Court of
    International Justice
Peel Commission   165–166
people
    definitions of   88
    in NHS model   101–102
Permanent Court of International Justice
    (PCIJ)   40–41, 136
permits
    denials of
        in general   301–303
        to human rights organizations   316
        to humanitarian staff   303

persecution 38
perspectives, in NHS model
    in general 97–98, 99
    and self-determination 102–106
Philippines 18
Phiri, Isabel Apawo 319
Phosphates in Morocco case 40–41
Physicians for Human Rights-Israel 302
Plan Dalet (Plan 'D') 6n7
Plessies, Max du 256
policy-oriented approach, to
    self-determination 100–115
positivist, views of international law 96
prescriptive jurisdiction 129–130
principles of procedures, in NHS model 99
prisoners/detainees 257, 379, 396, 398, 429–430
property, demolition/destruction of 122, 127, 297–298, 299
prostitution, enforced 38
protected persons 132, 278
protection, in Refugee Convention 466–471
'protection gap,' of Palestinian refugees 11–13, 32
protective justice 150
Protocol on the Treatment of Palestinian Refugees (1965). *see* Casablanca Protocol (1965)
Public Committee against Torture, 315
punitive actions, against Palestinians 269, 291, 299
purpose and intent clause 187, 207, 219–220, 231–232, 251–252

Quebec 107n95

Rabin, Yitzhak 212
racial discrimination
    anti-Semitism as form of 224
    and apartheid 222
    definitions of 208, 214, 224
    and Jewish State 232–238
    prohibition of 206, 213
    and territorial separation 104
racial groups
    and apartheid 208, 223
    and identity 224–225
    Jews as 208
    Palestinians as 208
racism, social 222
    see also racial discrimination
Radstan, Rod 129
Ramat Shlomo settlement 81
Reference re Secession of Quebec 107n95
refoulement 26–27
    see also non-refoulement principle
refugee camps 370, 371
Refugee Convention (1951)
    applicability of 12–13
    Article 1A 17, 472
    Article 1A2 of 11n30, 20
    Article 1C 473
    Article 1D
        in general 11–13, 20, 454, 464–465
        and *Bolbol v. Bevándorlási és Állampolgársági Hivatal* case 473–474
        and *El Kott v. Bevándorlási és Állampolgársági Hivatal* case
            interpretation of 474–481
            XX's status under 481–484
        interpretation of, in general 466–472
    Article 1E 473
    Article 1F 473
    Article 31 19
    Article 33 472
    Asian states signing of 17n58, 18
    as benchmark 17
    cessations and exclusion clauses
        in 472–473
    definition in
        of Palestinian refugee 11n30
        of refugee 463
    drafting history of 462–466
    obligations in 471–472
    Palestinian refugees under mandate of
        protection 11–12
        recognition of 8n20
        status of 8–9n21, 9, 11
    principle of non-refoulement in 17
    travaux preparatoires of 454, 463, 464–465, 467, 468–469, 471, 476
Refugee Status Determination (RSD) 20
refugees/asylum-seekers

INDEX 545

definitions of 463
in Indonesia
    numbers of 21–22
    status of 22
    and UNHCR 21–23
in Malaysia
    numbers of 23
    Rohingya 25
    status of 24–25
    and UNHCR 23–25
in South-East Asia
    living conditions of 30
    status of 19
    UNHCR registration of 20
in Thailand
    status of 25–26
    and UNHCR 26
see also Palestinian refugees
regime, definition of 220–221
regional justice 151
Regularization Bill 298
Regulation No 2580/2001 (EC) 492–493
Report of the Special Rapporteur on the Situation of Human Rights in the Palestinian Territories Occupied Since 1967, UN Doc A/72/556. *see* Lynk, Michael
Report of the Special Rapporteur on the Situation of Human Rights in the Palestinian Territories Occupied Since 1967, UN Doc A/HRC/34/70. *see* Lynk, Michael
Resolution 34/28 (UNHCR) 416–420
Resolution 34/29 (UNHCR) 421–424
Resolution 34/30 (UNHCR) 425–436
Resolution 34/31 (UNHCR) 437–448
Resolution 53/144 (UNGA) 306
Resolution 67/19 (UNGA) 138
Resolution 70/1 (UNGA) 340, 362, 410
Resolution 72/11 (UNGA) 329–330
Resolution 72/12 (UNGA) 331–333
Resolution 72/13 (UNGA) 334–338
Resolution 72/14 (UNGA) 339–351
Resolution 72/15 (UNGA) 352–354
Resolution 72/80 (UNGA) 355–357
Resolution 72/81 (UNGA) 358–359
Resolution 72/82 (UNGA) 360–372
Resolution 72/83 (UNGA) 373–374
Resolution 72/84 (UNGA) 375–380
Resolution 72/85 (UNGA) 381–383
Resolution 72/86 (UNGA) 384–390
Resolution 72/87 (UNGA) 391–400
Resolution 72/134 (UNGA) 401–407
Resolution 72/160 (UNGA) 408–409
Resolution 72/240 (UNGA) 410–415
Resolution 181(II) (UNGA) 164, 225, 229, 339, 458
Resolution 194 (UNGA) 9, 249, 460–461, 468, 471–472
Resolution 242 (UNSC) 166, 176–177, 252n88
Resolution 302(IV) (UNGA) 461
Resolution 395(V) (UNGA) 214
Resolution 428(V) (UNGA) 464
Resolution 1373 (UNSC) 491
Resolution 2334 (UNSC) 290, 297
Resolution 2625 (UNGA) 166
Reynolds, John 257
Ribeiro, Laura 185–186
right to return, of Palestinian refugees, refusal of 9, 178–179, 208, 210, 233, 249, 459
right to self-determination
    and occupational laws 273
    of Palestinians
        in general 137–138, 169
        Barnidge on 194
        and Covenant of League of Nations 166
        denial of 194
        legal status of 208, 212, 273–274
        during mandate period 161
        resolutions on
            of UNGA 408–409
            of UNHRC 421–424
        and UNSC deliberations 179
Rohingya refugees 25
Rome Statute (of ICC)
    apartheid in
        as crime against humanity 214
        definition of 206
        and purpose and intent clause 187, 207, 220, 251–252
    Article 8(2)(b)(viii) 51–52, 75
        as continuing crime 71–76
        as continuous crime 69
        and GCIV 66–67

Rome Statute (of ICC) (cont.)
  as instantaneous crime   68
  interpretations of crimes in
    in general   61–62
    at ICC   62–65
  transfer of populations in   36, 66, 67–71, 276
  and West Bank settlement activities   35–36, 76–81
  in 'Zutphen Draft'   68
  Article 8(2)(b)(xxvi)   51–52
  Article 8(2)(e)(vii)   74–75
  Article 12(3), Palestine and   123, 124, 143
  Article 17   78, 129
  Article 17 (2)   126
  Article 21   72
  Article 21(3)   63
  Article 22(1)   53
  Article 22(2)   63, 64, 70, 74
  Article 24(1)   53–54
  Article 53   125
  Article 53(1)   34–35
  complementarity in   126, 129
  and definition of continuing, continous and instantaneous crime   38
  interpretation of   63
  Kampala amendments to   134
  Palestinian ratification of   118–119, 124, 140, 141
  purpose of   63
  racial groups in   223
  and temporal jurisdiction of ICC   52–53
  territorial integrity in   135
  and territorial jurisdiction of ICC   130–131
  travaux preparatoires of   36, 38, 61, 68
Ronen, Yael   138
Rosenberg, Rina   257
Russia   83n234, 88n13, 103n82, 105n89
Russian Revolution (1917)   159
Rustin, Bayard   152

Safadi, Hasan   311
Samaria   507–513
Sampson, Nikos   110
Sayed, Hani   179–181, 187
SCC (Supreme Court Chamber of ECCC)   57

Scobbie, Iain   256
SCSL (Special Court for Sierra Leone)   37
security
  and apartheid policies   251–252
  and occupation   285–286
self-determination
  of Arab peoples   159
  Cassese on   90–92
  and customary rules   89–90
  definitions of   85–86, 87–88
  and disidentification with dominant group   114
  functions of   91
  and inclusiveness/exclusiveness   104–105
  internal/external   102–103
  in international law   86–87
  intrusive responses to   108
  of Israeli Jews   194
  as legal right   167
  and NHS model
    in general   100–101
    decision-making process in   106
    future trends in   111–113
    participants in   101–102, 106–107
    past trends in   108–111
    perspectives in   102–106
    policy recommendations in   113–114
  of Palestinians
    in general   137, 169
    Barnidge on   194
    and Covenant of League of Nations   166
    during mandate period   161
    and UNSC   179
  and reallocation of wealth   113–114
  recognition/non-recognition   107
  in United Nations Charter   166–167
  visions of
    anti-colonial   88, 89, 112
    ethno-nationalist vision   88–89, 113
    liberal-democratic   88, 89, 112
settler colonialism
  of Israel
    in general   149, 154, 165, 180–181, 185
    international law's complicity in   172, 186, 188
    native populations in   161–162
    see also apartheid regimes

INDEX

sexual slavery   37, 38, 59
Sfard, Michael   235, 314
Sha'ath, Nabil   192
Shafir, Gershon   285–286
Shahabuddeen, Judge   41
Situation in Georgia   135
Situation in the Republic of Korea   128
Situation on Registered Vessels of the Union of the Comoros, the Hellenic Republic and the Kingdom of Cambodia   127–128
situations/arenas, in NHS model   99
Six Day War   13–14
Snyder, Timothy   168n33
social justice   150–151
South Africa
    apartheid regime in
        compared to Israel   216–219
        end of   253
        fragmentation of black South Africans by   247
        international rejection of   213, 214
        public discourse about   152
        and security issues   252n88
        and South West Africa   216, 218–219, 280–283
        and statehood   221
        transition from   150, 155n7
South Africa's Freedom Charter   150
South West Africa (Namibia)   216, 218–219, 280–283
South-East Asia
    Palestinian refugees in
        in general   4, 15–16, 20–21
        increase of   26, 27, 31
        Indonesia   23
        legal framework available to   28–29, 31–32
        Malaysia   20n72, 23–25
        registration of   28
        Thailand   25–26
        and UNHCR   29
        visa policies for   21
    and Refugee Convention (1951)   18
    refugees/asylum-seekers in
        living conditions of   30
        status of   19
        UNHCR registration of   20

    and rejection of international refugee laws   18, 28, 31
    and UNHCR   32
    visa policies of   4, 21, 24
    see also Asia
sovereignty
    over territory
        and effective control   136–137
        and right to self-determination   137–138
Soviet Union   237
Special Committee to Investigate Israeli Practices Affecting the Human Rights of the Palestinian People and Other Arabs of the Occupied Territories   375–380
Special Court for Sierra Leone (SCSL)   37
Special Statistical Bulletin on the 67th Anniversary of the Palestinian Nakba (Palestinian Central Bureau of Statistics)   7n12
SPRIL questionnaires   4 n2
Stahn, Carsten   129
state illegitimacy   152
State of Terror: How Terrorism Created Modern Israel (Suarez)   164
State Property Law (1951)   207
statehood
    and apartheid   221
    in international law   182–183
    of Israel
        acceptance of   156, 193
        and apartheid   221
        declaration of independence   163, 184, 227, 232
        establishment of   6, 229
        recognition of   185
    Montevideo criteria for   135, 185–186
    of Palestine   138
Statute of Autonomy of Catalonia (2006)   105–106
Statute of Rome. *see* Rome Statute (of ICC)
Sternhell, Zeev   314
strategies, in NHS model   98–99
Suarez, Thomas   164
Sucharov, Mira   315
Suez canal   160
Supreme Court Chamber (of ECCC)   57

Sykes-Picot Agreement 159–160, 228–229n35
symmetry, between domestic and ICC's jurisdiction 126
Syrian Arab Republic
  Palestinian refugees in
    fleeing from country 14, 26–27, 365–366
    numbers of 7, 248
    temporary protection of 9–10
Syrian Golan 384–390, 410–415, 437–448

temporal jurisdiction
  and continuing crimes 36, 58, 61, 143–144
  and continuous crimes 36, 58, 60–61
  and Elements of Crime (of ICC) 58–59
  and European Court of Human Rights (ECtHR) 55–56
  and Extraordinary Chambers in the Courts of Cambodia (ECCC) 57–58
  and instantaneous crimes 36
  and Inter-American Court of Human Rights (IACtHR) 56, 60
  and International Criminal Court (ICC) 35–36, 52–54
  and International Criminal Tribunal for Rwanda (ICTR) 54, 58
  and International Criminal Tribunal for the former Yugoslavia (ICTY) 54–55
  and Rome Statute (of ICC) 52–53
territorial integrity, in Rome Statute 135
territory
  sovereignty over
    and effective control 136–137
    and right to self-determination 137–138
terrorist acts 489–503
Thailand
  and international human rights laws 29
  refugees/asylum-seekers in
    Palestinian 25–26
    status of 25–26
    and UNHCR 26
Tilley, Virginia 152, 184, 186, 188, 201–263, 256
Timor Leste 18
Tomeh, George 177
transfer of populations
  in Article 8(2)(b)(viii) 61–62
  in Elements of Crime (of ICC) 65–66, 72–74
  in Fourth Geneva Convention 67, 71–72
  in international humanitarian law 66, 73
  International Law Commission on 71
  Meindersma on 71
  into occupied territories 71–74
  in Rome Statute 36, 66, 67–71, 276
  into West Bank. *see* West Bank, Israeli settlements
transitional justice 150
trapped minorities 104, 110, 113
travaux preparatoires
  of Fourth Geneva Convention (GCIV) 67
  of Refugee Convention 454, 463, 464–465, 467, 468–469, 471, 476
  of Rome Statute (of ICC) 36, 38, 61, 68
Treat of Lausanne (1924) 456–457, 460
Trotsky, Leon 159
Trump, Donald 518–519, 523–526
trust/best interest principle 278–279, 284–289
Turkel Commission 126
two-state solution 157, 166, 247, 458, 518

Ukraine 83n234, 103n82, 106n93
UN Commission of Inquiry, on Operative Protective Edge 121
UNCCP (United Nations Conciliation Commission for Palestine) 9, 11–12
UNESCO (United Nations Educational, Scientific and Cultural Organization) 141
United Democratic Front 217
United Jewish Appeal (Keren Hayesod) 236
United Kingdom (UK)
  Balfour Declaration 5n4, 155, 158–159, 160, 161, 169, 204
  presence in Palestine
    in general 5n4, 157
    Zionist opposition to 160–161, 163–164, 457
  Sykes-Picot Agreement 159–160, 228–229n35
United Nations Centre against Apartheid 255
United Nations Charter

INDEX 549

apartheid in 206
Article 1(2) 166–167
Article 55 213
racial discrimination in 213
self-determination in 166–167
United Nations Conciliation Commission for Palestine (UNCCP)
   in general 9, 11–12
   definition of Palestinian refugee in 460–461
   establishment of 453–454, 460
   mandate of 460–461, 468–469
United Nations Educational, Scientific and Cultural Organization (UNESCO) 141
United Nations General Assembly (UNGA)
   and oPt, territorial boundaries of 133–134
   and apartheid 214, 281
   conventions of, International Convention on the Suppression and Punishment of the Crime of Apartheid 152
   and Palestine
      observer state status of 123–124
      statehood of 138
   and Palestinian refugees
      endorsement of UNRWA definition for 8
      return of 9
   and partition plan for Palestine 164
   resolutions of
      indefinite language in 177
      on Israel/Palestine 177
      Resolution 53/144 306
      Resolution 67/19 138
      Resolution 70/1 340, 362, 410
      Resolution 72/11 329–330
      Resolution 72/12 331–333
      Resolution 72/13 334–338
      Resolution 72/14 339–351
      Resolution 72/15 352–354
      Resolution 72/80 355–357
      Resolution 72/81 358–359
      Resolution 72/82 360–372
      Resolution 72/83 373–374
      Resolution 72/84 375–380
      Resolution 72/85 381–383
      Resolution 72/86 384–390
      Resolution 72/87 391–400
      Resolution 72/134 401–407
      Resolution 72/160 408–409
      Resolution 72/240 410–415
      Resolution 181(II) 164, 225, 229, 339, 458
      Resolution 194 9, 249, 460–461, 468, 471–472
      Resolution 302(IV) 461
      Resolution 395(V) 214
      Resolution 428(V) 464
      Resolution 1761(XVII) 214
      Resolution 2625 166
United Nations High Commissioner for Human Rights (UNHCHR) 256
United Nations High Commissioner for Refugees (UNHCR)
   history of 20n71
   and Palestinian refugees 8n20, 9, 12
   and refugees in South-East Asian countries
      birth registration procedures of 23
      in Indonesia 21–23
      in Malaysia 23–25
      registration and RSD of 20, 28
      in Thailand 26
United Nations Human Rights Council (UNHRC)
   in general 255, 256
   resolutions of
      Resolution 34/28 416–420
      Resolution 34/29 421–424
      Resolution 34/30 425–436
      Resolution 34/31 437–448
   Statute of 454
United Nations Relief and Works Agency for Palestine Refugees in the Near East (UNRWA)
   definition of Palestinian refugee in 7–8, 8n20, 461–462
   establishment of 10, 453–454, 461
   financing of 356, 361–362, 367–369
   mandate of 461, 468–469
   on number of refugees 7
   Palestinian refugees under mandate of 11–12, 248, 249
   UNGA resolution on 360–372
United Nations Rules for the Treatment of Women Prisoners 379, 396, 398, 430, 433

United Nations Secretary General (UNSG)
  and acts of aggression   134–135
  and Palestine, status of   123–124
United Nations Security Council (UNSC)
  and apartheid   281
  Common Position 2001/931/CFS   492, 493, 496–502
  deliberations on Israel/Palestine of
    of Eban, Abba   182
    of Fawzi, Mahmoud Bey   183
    ignoring of Palestinian rights in   177–178
    of Lynk, Michael   178
    on status of Palestine   182
    of Tomeh, George   177–179
  resolutions of
    on Israeli occupation of Palestinian territory   289–290
    Resolution 242   166, 176–177, 252n88
    Resolution 1373   491
    Resolution 2334   290, 297
United Nations Special Committee against Apartheid   214, 217, 254–255
United Nations Special Coordinator for the Middle East Peace Process   290
United Nations Standard Minimum Rules for the Treatment of Prisoners (the Nelson Mandela Rules)   379, 396, 398, 430, 433
United Nations (UN)
  and apartheid   254–255
  Palestinian application for admission to   195
  and Palestinian refugees   459
  PLO representative at   141
  see also under specific UN bodies
United States, recognition of Jerusalem   518–519, 523–526
United States Institute of Peace   86
United States National Civil Rights Museum   152
Universal Declaration of Human Rights (1948)
  apartheid in   206
  Article 2   213–214
  racial discrimination in   213–214
  mention of   306

UNRWA. *see* United Nations Relief and Works Agency for Palestine Refugees in the Near East

values
  in NHS model   94
  taxonomy of   94n42
VCLT (Vienna Convention on the Law of Treaties). *see* Vienna Convention on the Law of Treaties
video
  by Abu Shamsiyeh, Imad   310
  by Im Tirtzu   314–315
Vienna Convention on the Law of Treaties (VCLT)   62–63, 279, 466–467, 469
visa policies   4, 21, 24
voting rights   211, 215, 218, 234

wall/barrier   137–138, 139, 208, 212, 273, 283, 284
West Bank
  Bedouin communities in   291
  Israeli control of, illegality of   179–180
  Israeli occupation of
    in general   229–230, 283–285
    and best interest/trust principle   284–289
    dual governance regime of   180–181, 246–248
    permanency of   284–287
    and security issues   285–286
  Israeli settlements in
    as continuing crime   76–81, 143–144
    expansion of   192, 268–269, 297–298
    and ICC   34–36
    illegality of   78, 121, 138–139
    before June 2014   36, 143
    and Law for the Regularization of Settlement in Judea and Samaria   507–513
    numbers of   120
    policies regarding   76–77, 144–145
    settler population of   192
    State involvement in   246–247, 286
    status of   120–121
    and temporal jurisdiction   35–36, 143–144

territory of   138–139
Jordanian governance of   229
Palestinian refugees in
   numbers of   7
   and Six Day War   13–14
   temporary protection of   9–10
Palestinians in
   children's plight   299–300
   demolition of property of   297–298
   fragmentation of   247
   punitive actions against   299
   and street closures   299
PA's control of   139–140
State lands in   235
status of   137
West Bank barrier   137–138, 139, 208, 212, 273, 283, 284
Wilson, Woodrow   159
World Health Organization (WHO)
   on electricity crisis in Gaza Strip   266–268
   on health permit applications   302
world power process   94
World War I   5n4, 155, 160, 456
World War II   155, 168

World Zionist Organisation – Jewish Agency Status Law (1952)   232, 235, 236
World Zionist Organization   207

X v. United Kingdom case   48–49

Youth Against Settlements   309, 311

Zionist movement
   in general   5n4
   acceptance of partition by   164, 166
   and Balfour Declaration   155, 158–159, 160, 169
   commitment to Palestine   154–155, 157–158, 163
   foundations of   149, 156–157, 164–166, 167–168, 237–238
   military forces of   165
   and Mizrahi Jews   150
   opposition to Great Britain   160–161, 163–164, 457
   success of   162, 168
   support for   158
   and two-state solution   157, 166
   see also settler colonialism

Printed in the United States
By Bookmasters